EARLY NEW ENGLAND

To Professor John Murrin

with ~~deepest~~ thanks

for your help

[signature]

August, 2006

EMORY UNIVERSITY STUDIES IN LAW AND RELIGION

John Witte Jr., General Editor

BOOKS IN THE SERIES

Faith and Order: The Reconciliation of Law and Religion
Harold J. Berman

The Ten Commandments in History:
Mosaic Paradigms for a Well-Ordered Society
Paul Grimley Kuntz

Theology of Law and Authority in the English Reformation
Joan Lockwood O'Donovan

Political Order and the Plural Structure of Society
James W. Skillen and Rockne M. McCarthy

The Idea of Natural Rights:
Studies on Natural Rights, Natural Law, and Church Law, 1150-1625
Brian Tierney

The Fabric of Hope: An Essay
Glenn Tinder

Religious Human Rights in Global Perspective: Legal Perspectives
Johan D. van der Vyver and John D. Witte

Early New England: A Covenanted Society
David A. Weir

Religious Human Rights in Global Perspective: Religious Perspectives
John D. Witte and Johan D. van der Vyver

EARLY NEW ENGLAND

A Covenanted Society

David A. Weir

William B. Eerdmans Publishing Company
Grand Rapids, Michigan / Cambridge, U.K.

Wm. B. Eerdmans Publishing Co.
255 Jefferson Ave. S.E., Grand Rapids, Michigan 49503 /
P.O. Box 163, Cambridge CB3 9PU U.K.

Printed in the United States of America

10 09 08 07 06 05   7 6 5 4 3 2 1

Library of Congress Cataloging-in-Publication Data

Weir, David A.
Early New England: a covenanted society / David A. Weir.
p.   cm. — (Emory University studies in law and religion)
Includes bibliographical references (p.) and index.
ISBN 0-8028-1352-6 (pbk.: alk. paper)
1. Church and state — New England — History.
2. New England — Church history.
I. Title.   II. Series.
BR530.W45   2005

322′.1′097409032 — dc22

2004047243

www.eerdmans.com

Dedicated to the memory of my paternal grandparents:

William Wilbur Weir
1893-1990

and

Elizabeth Vesta Ewing Weir
1894-1988

"Now to him who is able to do immeasurably more than all we ask or imagine, according to his power that is at work within us, to him be glory in the church and in Christ Jesus throughout all generations, for ever and ever! Amen."

Ephesians 3:20-21

Contents

Acknowledgments

It would be impossible to extend my thanks to every person who has helped in an undertaking that has lasted for twenty years, but certain people and organizations did have a crucial role in allowing me to start, encouraging me to persevere, and spurring me on to finish. The Department of Religion of Princeton University admitted me to the History of Christianity program in 1980, and the seed of this volume appeared in 1992 as a dissertation devoted to the process of church formation in early New England. I would like to thank them for their forbearance and assistance over the years. Princeton University was a wonderful place to work and provided me with extraordinary resources for graduate study. Dean John F. Wilson, Agate Brown and George L. Collord Professor of Religion, Emeritus and formerly Dean of the Graduate School of Princeton University, gave unsparingly of his time and energy over the years, and his wise counsel was unmatched by any other dissertation committee chairman that I know of. The other members of my graduate committee each contributed in his own way to the project when it took the form of a dissertation. I would like to extend my thanks to Professor Albert J. Raboteau, Henry W. Putnam Professor of Religion, Professor Horton M. Davies, Henry W. Putnam Professor of Religion, Emeritus, and Professor John M. Murrin of the Department of History for their extensive assistance. Professor R. Paul Ramsey, while no longer with us, fostered my work in many important ways. Finally, it was Professor Michael McGiffert of the College of William and Mary, Williamsburg, Virginia, who encouraged me to go beyond my initial end point of 1680 and finish out the seventeenth century. Finally, I would like to extend my thanks to Professor John Witte of Emory University Law School, along with Dr. Charles Van Hof, Jennifer Hoffman, and the editors at the William

B. Eerdmans Publishing Company; their patience and help during the last several years has been extraordinary.

My parents, Richard B. and Jean C. Weir, gave a tremendous amount of help in encouragement, finance, and proofreading. My wife Bonnie joined me in the middle of this project and has encouraged and helped me through to the end; I could not have done it without her. Janelle, Elise, Timothy and Isaiah Weir have joined us in the final stretch and have provided their parents with a whole new perspective on the blessings of the covenant.

The research for this manuscript began at the American Antiquarian Society in Worcester, Massachusetts, during the summer of 1984, where I was the Frances Hiatt Fellow for that year. During the year 1984-85 I was awarded a Charlotte W. Newcombe Dissertation Fellowship by the Woodrow Wilson National Fellowship Foundation; I am glad that I can finally report to them that I am finished. Centenary College granted me two leaves of absence, one during the fall of 1991 and a second during the fall of 1995, and the Centenary College Alumni Association graciously provided me with some grants for computer time on the Research Libraries Information Network (RLIN).

Pilgrimages to various libraries over the years have been made pleasant and rewarding by the staffs. My "second home" was the Firestone Library of Princeton University, and the Speer Library of Princeton Theological Seminary was my next reference point when Firestone did not have an item. I extend my thanks to the interlibrary loan divisions of the Firestone and Centenary College libraries for their help over the years. My thanks also should be extended to the staff of the American Antiquarian Society; I was told in 1984 that I had the record for "the most systematic use" of the collection; perhaps someone has taken my place by now. Their collection of New England local history is unparalleled. The Local History and Genealogy Collection of the New York Public Library was also helpful when I could not locate an item in Princeton or in Worcester. I also visited the following libraries in search of information: the Boston Public Library; the British Library; the Ann Mary Brown Library, Brown University, Providence, Rhode Island; the Columbia University Library System; the Concordia College Library, Bronxville, New York; the Congregational Library, Boston; the Connecticut State Library, Hartford; the Family History Library of the Church of Jesus Christ of Latter-day Saints, Scarsdale, New York; the Harvard University Library System, Cambridge, Massachusetts; the Haverford College Library, Magill Library and the Quaker Collection of

Haverford College, Haverford, Pennsylvania; the Library of Congress, Washington, D.C.; the Massachusetts Archives, Boston; the Massachusetts Historical Society, Boston; the Mount Vernon, New York, Public Library; the New England Historic Genealogical Society, Boston; the New Hampshire Historical Society, Concord; the New York Genealogical and Biographical Society, New York; the New York Historical Society, New York; the Bobst Library, New York University, New York; the New Jersey Historical Society, Newark; the Rhode Island Historical Society, Providence; the Rutgers University Library System; the Sarah Lawrence College Library, Bronxville, New York; the Schomburg Center for Research in Black Culture (a division of the New York Public Library), New York; the Union Theological Seminary Library, New York; Dr. Williams's Library, London; and the Yale University Library System, New Haven, Connecticut.

Over a two-year period I corresponded with hundreds of town and church clerks in New England as I tried to ascertain the status and location of the original covenant documents of the towns and churches they served. While I cannot name each of them here, I am grateful for their efforts on my behalf.

D.A.W.
Nyack College
Nyack, New York

List of Tables and Figures

Abbreviations

AASP	American Antiquarian Society, *Proceedings*
AASTC	American Antiquarian Society, *Transactions and Collections*
AHR	*American Historical Review*
AQ	*American Quarterly*
ARG	*Archive für Reformationsgeschichte*
ARPMB	*Acts and Resolves of the Massachusetts Bay Province*
ASCH, *Papers*	American Society of Church History, *Papers*
AV	Authorized Version of the Bible (1611)
BCL	American Congregational Association Library (Boston), *Bulletin*
BCP	Church of England, *Book of Common Prayer*
BHH	*Baptist History and Heritage*
BSRK	*Die Bekenntnisschriften der reformierten Kirche*
CBJ	*Connecticut Bar Journal*
CH	*Church History*
CM	*Connecticut Magazine*
CNEB	Committee for a New England Bibliography
Colls.	*Collections*
CQ	*Congregational Quarterly*
CRevAS	*Canadian Review of American Studies*
CSLB	Connecticut State Library, *Bulletin*
CSMP	Colonial Society of Massachusetts, *Publications*
CTC	Connecticut Colony
DARB	*Dictionary of American Religious Biography*, 2nd edn.
DECH	*A Dictionary of English Church History*
DNE	Dominion of New England
EAL	*Early American Literature*

EIHC	Essex Institute, *Historical Collections*
ELJ	*Emory Law Journal*
FHLC™M #	Family History Library Catalog™ Microfilm Number
F+H	*Fides et Historia*
HMPEC	*Historical Magazine of the Protestant Episcopal Church*
HNH	*Historical New Hampshire*
HThR	*Harvard Theological Review*
IND	Independent Colony
ISBE	*International Standard Bible Encyclopedia*
JAS	*Journal of American Studies*
JBS	*Journal of British Studies*
JCR	*Journal of Christian Reconstruction*
JCS	*Journal of Church and State*
JEH	*Journal of Ecclesiastical History*
JFHS	Friends' Historical Society, *Journal*
JHI	*Journal of the History of Ideas*
JHUSHPS	Johns Hopkins University, Studies in Historical and Political Science
JLR	*Journal of Law and Religion*
JR	*Journal of Religion*
JRH	*Journal of Religious History*
JURCHS	United Reformed Church History Society, *Journal*
MBC	Massachusetts Bay Colony
MBP	Massachusetts Bay Province
MeHSC	Maine Historical Society, *Collections*
MeP	Maine Province
MHSC	Massachusetts Historical Society, *Collections*
MHSP	Massachusetts Historical Society, *Proceedings*
NEHGR	*New England Historical and Genealogical Register*
NHC	New Haven Colony
NHCHSJ	New Haven Colony Historical Society, *Journal*
NHCHSP	New Haven Colony Historical Society, *Papers*
NHHSC	New Hampshire Historical Society, *Collections*
NHHSP	New Hampshire Historical Society, *Proceedings*
NHP	New Hampshire Province
NHSP	New Hampshire. *State Papers*
NJHSC	New Jersey Historical Society, *Collections*
NJHSP	New Jersey Historical Society, *Proceedings*
NNC	New Netherland Colony
NPC	New Plymouth Colony
NSHE	*The New Schaff-Herzog Encyclopedia of Religious Knowledge*

NYSHAP	New York State Historical Association, *Proceedings*
NYSHC	New York State Historical Society, *Collections*
NYHSQ	New York State Historical Society, *Quarterly*
OED	*Oxford English Dictionary*
PCRM	Maine, Province, *Province and Court Records of Maine*
P+P	*Past and Present*
PRCC	*Public Records of the Colony of Connecticut*
QH	*Quaker History*
RCAMBC	*Records of the Court of Assistants of the Massachusetts Bay Colony*
RCJNH	*Records of the Colony or Jurisdiction of New Haven, . . . 1653 [-1665].*
RCNP	*Records of the Colony of New Plymouth in New England*
RCPNH	*Records of the Colony and Plantation of New Haven, . . . 1638 . . . [-] 1649*
RCRI	*Records of the Colony of Rhode Island*
RIC	Rhode Island Colony
RIH	*Rhode Island History*
RIHS	Rhode Island Historical Society
RIHSC	Rhode Island Historical Society, *Collections*
RM	*Records of the Governor and Company of the Massachusetts Bay*
SCH	Studies in Church History (ASCH, Chicago)
SCH(L)	Studies in Church History (London)
SCJ	*Sixteenth Century Journal*
SPG	Society for the Propagation of the Gospel
TCHS	Congregational Historical Society, *Transactions*
Thorpe, *Federal and State Constitutions*	Francis N. Thorpe, *The Federal and State Constitutions, Colonial Charters, and Other Organic Laws of the States*
UHSP	Unitarian Historical Society (Boston), *Proceedings*
Walker, *Creeds and Platforms*	Williston Walker, *The Creeds and Platforms of Congregationalism*
WCF	*Westminster Confession of Faith*
WMQ	*William and Mary Quarterly*
Worthley, *Inventory*	H. F. Worthley, *An Inventory of the Records of the Particular (Congregational) Churches of Massachusetts*
WPA	Works Progress Administration

For bibliographical details concerning the works that are not serials, see the Bibliographical Essay.

Explanation of Quotation Style and Terminology

For the quotations in this book, I have attempted to recreate as much as possible the exact wording and layout of each source cited in the footnotes. In some cases the printed sources cited modernize or modify the original manuscript sources that they are trying to recreate faithfully. This is especially the case for legislative and ecclesiastical records. Furthermore, even with all of the fonts available to modern computer users, it is often impossible to recreate seventeenth-century orthography. I have therefore modified the nonmodern orthography and used the roman lettering that the orthographic figures stand for. I have often elided paragraph indentations; they may be there in the original manuscript source and also in the published version, but they do not add to the content of the quotation and are simply there as a habit of the record-keeper's style and as a way to call attention to the various motions and decisions of the governing body. I also have not included the italicizations of words and phrases. The stars * * * are used by several modern editors to indicate that the material there is unavailable. In the case of the Westfield, Massachusetts, First Church *Records,* for example, a well-meaning bookbinder sliced off the edges of the original manuscript as he rebound it. The square brackets [ ] are the interpolations of the various modern editors and are published in the cited sources; my own interpolations are included in brackets that take the following form: { }. Standard guidelines for the transcription of manuscripts can be found in "Report on Editing Historical Documents," Institute of Historical Research, *Bulletin,* 1-2 (1923-25), 6-25.

For titles of published works, especially those published before 1800, I have retained the exact spelling of words, but have used my own judgment whether the first and following letters of a word should be uppercase or lowercase, since early modern printers, editors, and authors did not follow any consistent rules with respect to titles of books. Individuals referred to in the titles are spelled exactly as they are found *on the title page,* but individuals cited as authors are spelled according to the standards found in the standard modern bibliographies and the *DNB* and *DAB.* At times the titles of early modern books consist of "essays" of dozens, even hundreds, of words. I have used ellipses when I cite the short title of a work, but I have not used ellipses in the initial citation of a work when I feel that the essential title of the work has been communicated even though the title continues on. Punctuation of titles was usually altered to fit modern standards.

All dates are given in the Julian, or Old Style (O.S.) calendar. Further information about calendrics can be found in the Explanatory Note to Appendix I, Columns 7-10.

Unless otherwise noted, biblical quotations are from the Authorized Version of 1611 (AV). While a more modern translation might be helpful in understanding the original biblical text, we want to understand the scriptural passages as the early New Englanders comprehended them, and therefore a contemporaneous translation was used in the discussion of passages that the early New Englanders were citing or commenting on.

Introduction

Good and upright God is, therefore
will sinners teach the way.
The meek he'le guide in judgement:&
will teach the meek his way.
Iehovahs paths they mercy are,
all of them truth also;
to them that keep his covenant,
and testimonies do.
For thy names sake O Iehovah,
freely doe thou remitt
mine owne perverse iniquitie:
because that great is it.
Who fears the Lord, him hee will teach
the way that he shall chuse.
his soule shall dwell at ease, his seed
as heirs the earth shall vse.
The secret of God is with those
that doe him reverence:
and of his covenant he them
will give intelligence.

(Psalm 25:8-14; Bay Psalm Book)[1]

This volume is a critical monograph dealing with the covenant texts that emerged from the formation of civil and religious institutions on a local and colonial level in early New England. Those texts instituted and reflect a series of changes that occurred during the period 1620 to 1708 with respect to the relationship between religion, religious institutions, and the civil magistracy. These changes differed from colony to colony, but they do reflect large-scale trends that are important and need to be pursued and explicated. As I have uncovered and analyzed these covenant documents and the rituals surrounding their signing, I have been asking in particular two critical questions about the nature of the fundamental commitments that New Englanders made during the seventeenth century: (1) Were the early New England civil covenants primarily theocentric, christocentric, or secular? (2) How do the covenants, both church and civil, relate to the account of Puritan covenant theology articulated most famously by Perry Miller but revised extensively by his successors?[2]

The terms "civil covenant" and "church covenant" refer to written documents that were relatively brief and that spell out the initial vision for a New England community or religious body. They are often found at the beginning of official record books for both churches and towns. This initial vision more often than not articulated a communal relationship vertically with God and horizontally between the residents of the community. In the church covenants, the documents always spoke of the divine-human relationship. In the civil covenants, the vertical divine-human relationship could sometimes be obscured in favor of horizontal economic and political relationships, leading us to surmise that one of the roots of modern and postmodern secularism can be found in the Protestantism of the early modern world. When the civil covenants were more secularized and concerned with this world, however, the implicit assumption was that the residents of each community were working within the framework of values articulated by the world of Protestant Christianity — a point that we will elaborate as we examine these documents. The only religious institution in seventeenth-century New England that was explicitly non-Christian during the seventeenth century was the Touro Synagogue of Newport, Rhode Island. Yet the Jews of that community shared a common ethical stance with the Christians of New England, since both shared the Old Testament heritage of "the law, the prophets and the writings."

An examination of the town and church records from seventeenth-century New England reveals that, while the church covenants were standard and easily identifiable in the church record books, a variety of documents were entered into the town books and put forth as civil covenants. In addition, town historians, in their search for the earliest charter, often proffered documents in their local histories as the original town or civil covenant. For our purposes, however, we will accept as a civil covenant only those written documents that actually transferred or awarded the power of governance and the sword to a local town, plantation, or colony. The charters and patents issued by the Crown and in certain cases the Parliament of Old England to the larger New England colonies fit into this category, as do the local town combinations signed by the settlers. Included also are the charters and patents issued by central colonial governments to the local towns.

The study is comprehensive in scope, in that I have systematically examined the formation of every civil and religious institution founded in New England before 1708 for which evidence is extant, including those communities found beyond the current state borders of New England (for example, Westchester County and Long Island, New York, along with the New Jersey communities that originated in early New England). In the process, I have developed an unpublished collection of copies of the surviving covenant documents — both civil and ecclesiastical — of seventeenth-century New England. Begun in 1984 at the American Antiquarian Society in Worcester, Massachusetts, this collection of covenant documents represents a substantial effort to make an exhaustive search of all of the relevant sources for the initial civil and ecclesiastical covenantal commitments that the early New Englanders made. My explorations led me to thousands of town and church histories, to the published and unpublished records of the towns and the churches, to the published legislative minutes and unpublished legislative records of the central governments, to the serial publications of the state — and in some cases county — historical societies, and to the unpublished town and church records. For the ecclesiastical covenants, the only collection that is in any way analogous to what I have done is the one by William E. Barton, *Congregational Creeds and Covenants*.[3] But that collection encompasses over three hundred years of congregational history in North America, and it includes only a few of the seventeenth-century New England church covenants. For the civil covenants, more has been done, but again, the existing collections were not methodical and comprehensive in scope. The extant collections covered the entire colonial period up to 1783 rather than seventeenth-century New England only, focused on the charters at the colonial level rather than at the local level, were often limited to published civil covenants, and frequently published the civil covenants in abridged form.[4]

The thesis of the book is that the content of the early New England church and civil covenants reflected a counterpoint of unity and diversity over the seventeenth century. During the period before and during the English Revolution, the civil covenants were diverse documents because they were generated by an array of different individual communities. Because the new world was a "*tabula rasa*," and because civil institutions were well-established in the old world, there were few patterns for civil covenanting found in Europe, especially England. Therefore, each town in early New England drew up its combination or compact as it saw best. The civil authority adapted the well-known practice of church covenanting to legitimize itself. During the same period of time, on the other hand, the church covenants were fairly standard, following what I call a formulary or template that I define in Chapter 4: The Church Covenants of Early New England I: The Standing Order. This was because church covenanting had been practiced in Old England by both Separatists and non-separating Puritans, and because the practice had been a matter of discussion and debate.

After the Restoration (1660), however, the civil covenants more and more became standardized documents handed down from a superior authority. Usually these later civil covenants were charters or patents drawn up by the central government of the colony. The practice of combination became rare as a means of establishing the local civil magistracy in the post-Restoration period. The church documents, on the other hand, started to reflect diverse content and forms. There are several reasons for this. The Congregational Way opened the door for diversification of doctrine and practice, while the Quakers and Anabaptists started to infiltrate the New England world. In order to shore up doctrinal unity in the churches of New England, many New England churches that were gathering themselves began to write a confession of faith that they attached to their covenant, usually as a preamble. Ironically, that confessional practice led to even greater diversification of religious commitment within the New England world, because each congregation started to set its own doctrinal standards. For seventeenth-century New England, this confessional process culminated in the Manifesto of Boston's Brattle Street Church. While politically the New England colonies became more unified from the top down during the seventeenth century, the seeds of religious, cultural, and intellectual diversification in New England were sown at the grassroots level in the middle of the seventeenth century by the followers of the Congregational Way in the church. This process can be traced in the church and town records of early New England.

The genesis of this project began in 1981, when I was in Scotland studying the history of the covenant idea as a theological motif, a study that resulted in a work on the emergence of the theological concept of the Edenic covenant in early modern Reformed theology.[5] Since that time I have continued my exploration of the covenant idea, focusing on early New England. Along with my engagement with the covenant concept I became particularly interested in the vision that colonial Americans developed of how the interplay between the church and the civil order (or perhaps religion and the civil order) should function on a local level. Furthermore, I have begun to examine how that vision (and consequent practice) changed over the years, until the United States emerged and the early national period of American history began. It seems to me that up until now the focus has been on a colonial/state level and, after 1789, also on a federal level. However, little attention has been paid by scholars to this question on the local level.[6]

My reading of various seventeenth-century New England authors, along with the magisterial research of Perry Miller and his successors, led me to the realization that several distinct genres of covenantal literature emerged from the welter of Puritan writing in both Old and New England. Furthermore, that collection of covenantal literature emerged from a much larger tradition found in biblical studies, ancient Middle Eastern history, and general human history.[7] The *covenant idea* is actually a cluster of ideas that can be found in many cultures, but most particularly in the cultures of the ancient Middle East and the biblical tradition that emanated from that world. Both Jews and Christians have utilized the theme extensively, thereby developing the covenant idea into the *covenant theology*, whereby God reveals himself in a series of biblical covenants found in the canonical text of the Old Testament.[8] The early modern and colonial American literature of covenant theology is vast, and was produced not only by Anglo-American Puritans but also by European Continental theologians, as my first publication on the covenant theme illustrated. This literature treats the covenant as a formal theological principle that is used as the organizing motif for confessional theology and for Christian evangelism. The *federal theology* is a subdivision of covenant theology. The federal theology postulates a prelapsarian Edenic covenant that was broken by the first Adam and fulfilled by the second Adam, Jesus Christ. The covenant relationship, therefore, between God and humanity was not only salvific but institutional, binding all people everywhere to the stipulations that God had ordained in Scripture. The body of literature devoted to *covenant ecclesiology* is smaller. These works deal with the doctrine of the church — its marks, its function, and its covenantal position before God. Then there is the literature of *covenant polity,* both ecclesiastical and civil. Here we run into the theme of the organization of church and civil society built around covenant documents. Finally, there are *the covenant documents themselves,* documents that emerged out of the theological ideas of covenant. I had seen several examples of civil and church covenants from New England, but I was fairly certain that there were more, and that the common documents published — the Mayflower Compact and the church covenants of Salem and Dedham, Massachusetts Bay Colony, for example — were only the tip of the iceberg of a much larger body of material. One of the fundamental premises of this study is that these covenant documents are of tremendous importance to the history of the colonial New England world, and that they are one of the axiomatic templates for not only the development of the British colonial world of North America but the early national period of United States history as well.

We should also point out that covenants, at least those within the Christian church, were not creeds. Creeds are brief statements of belief, organized and codified so that the faithful can recite them easily. Both the Apostles' Creed and Nicene Creed, therefore, are organized around the theme of (1) God the Father, the Creator; (2) God the Son, the Redeemer; (3) God the Holy Spirit, the one who applies the work of redemption to the created beings whom God the Son redeemed; (4) the universal church; (5) the afterlife; and (6) the conclusion of the temporal, fallen world and the beginning of the eternal, redeemed, world.[9] Furthermore, covenants are not confessions of faith. In the history of Christianity, confessions of faith expound the doctrinal commitments (dogma) of a particular branch of the church. A confession of faith differentiates one branch of Christianity from another. A creed, on the other hand, differentiates the tree (Christianity) from other trees (religions other than Christianity).[10]

In contrast to both creeds and confessions of faith, covenants within the Christian tradition focus on the relationship of the community or the individual or both with God and with Jesus Christ. At times the civil magistracy, under the influence of the church, also covenanted with God, and, more rarely, with Jesus Christ. Furthermore, in a secondary way, the covenants of the church served as models for relationships within the broader world, including the civil magistracy. Thus, while a particular state within Christendom might not have expressed official allegiance to Jesus Christ or to God, the commitments that the state made and supervised (contracts, last wills and testaments, and so forth) could reflect the influence of both the biblical idea of covenant and the specific covenants of Christian history.

In the biblical record, the covenant is seldom divorced from law, and in the Mosaic epoch the conditions of the covenant were expressed in terms of law. Thus the Decalogue and the civil and ceremonial laws uttered by God at Sinai are often termed "the Sinaitic covenant."[11] The New England Puritans, with their affinity for the Old Testament, were of course aware of this relationship between covenant and law. In the initial stages of the codification of law in seventeenth-century New England, the lawmakers drew upon Old Testament statutes for some of their legal codes. The use of biblical laws and penalties by the early New England legal codes — particularly by the central governments — reflected the covenantal thought to which the majority of New Englanders had committed themselves in the documents we are examining. This monograph deals only with the covenant documents themselves, but the formulation of law was linked to covenanting. While we will not explore the legal codes, we need to remember that in most of the colonies the codes were closely related to the covenants.[12]

As I pursued my research I kept coming across descriptions of the founding of these covenanted institutions of church and civil order and the covenants by which they were generated, approved, and signed. I soon began to recognize a social dynamic in the ceremonies and rituals surrounding their signing. I focused my earlier explorations on the process by which early New England society founded its most cherished institution — the church — and on how the civil authority interacted with and sometimes even supervised that process. I also explored the social patterns that emerged in the formation of the gathered church.[13]

The year 1680 became my original end point because in that year the Reforming Synod in the Massachusetts Bay Colony, held in 1679, sent out its call for covenant renewal by the churches. Several conversations with some helpful scholars convinced me, however, that I should not stop in 1680 but should continue my investigations at least until 1692, when the fallout from the rule of King James II and the Glorious Revolution had filtered down to New England. To draw a full picture of the covenant in early New England, moreover, this study would have to include the period of crisis between 1686 and 1692. Between 1686 and 1689 the New England colonies were merged into the Dominion of New England under the rule of Edmund Andros. From 1689 to 1692 the Massachusetts Bay Colony was without a charter and a sense of political crisis gripped the area, a plight that contributed to the hysteria characterizing the Salem witch trials of 1692. I finally chose 1708 as an end point because in that year the churches in the Connecticut Colony adopted the Saybrook Platform. Ending the study in 1708 allowed me a glimpse of things to come. I am therefore able to present a comprehensive picture of the civil and church covenant documents in seventeenth-century New England.

The study begins with a broad picture of Christianity in the European world, and then focuses on the religious upheaval in England during the sixteenth and seventeenth centuries. The focus further narrows to English Puritanism between 1560 and 1640. The critical point to grasp is that European Christendom had evolved a parochial system in which most residents of a parish were members in good standing of the local parish church if they avoided heresy and criminal activity. Protestant England inherited this system from the Roman Catholic tradition and continued to follow it during the Tudor and Stuart periods. As English Protestants read, studied, argued, and examined Scripture, however, an increasing number of them became dissatisfied with the ecclesiology of the parochial system and hoped to modify the system or abandon it altogether. They disagreed about what should take its place; many proposed a voluntary church, by means of which God would gather his true elect saints, as an alternative. The instrument by which the church was gathered was the church covenant.

When the separating and non-separating Puritans came to the shores of New England, they settled in a world where there were no established civil or ecclesiastical institutions. Some of the groups that came did have — or later acquired — charters from the English government, but to a large degree the New Englanders found that they had to inaugurate and institute their own procedures and institutions for the society they were building. But the leaders of the early New Englanders knew how to gather a church by church covenant, and for this reason they adapted the practice of church covenanting to the establishment of civil authority, thus generating a series of civil covenants that paralleled the church covenants. The goal of this volume, then, is to articulate the covenantal commitments that the early New Englanders made for both church and state. A variety of covenant texts will be examined as *exempla* of the larger covenantal themes and archetypes that were emerging in early New England. It is of course impossible to write up every covenant that was signed, but by looking critically at a variety of examples from various regions and periods of times we can explicate some of the foundational visions that the early New Englanders had. And this is especially the case when we can set them against the backdrop of all of the surviving covenant documents, both civil and ecclesiastical.

The process by which these civil and ecclesiastical covenants were subscribed to and signed is called "covenanting." There is a definite contrast between New England civil covenanting and New England church covenanting.[14] An examination of the narratives that surround these documents indicates that on the whole the early New Englanders took church covenanting much more seriously than they did civil covenanting. Sometimes it took years to gather a church, and when a church covenant was finally signed and the church was gathered, or founded, an entire day was spent in solemn worship and religious exercise. Certain patterns emerge in the church gatherings. They tended to be in the middle of the week when neighboring pastors could assist. More were held in late autumn than at other times of the year, because that is when farmers were less busy: the harvest was in. The average age of the charter members, or foundation members, of the newly gathered churches was about forty-two. In cases where we have contemporaneous economic evidence almost all of the foundation members could be found in the upper half of the tax list or land distribution list. Generally, a small group of people prepared for the church gathering with the local clergyman for as much as a year or more before the ceremony took place.

Civil covenanting, on the other hand, was a mundane affair around which there was very little ceremony. A methodical examination of the extant civil covenants indicates that, with a few exceptions, there was no formal covenant ceremony that was analogous to the church covenanting ritual. For the most part, the civil covenant documents simply appear at the beginning of the town records, sometimes simply as legislative minutes. They seemed to have been passed around for signatures over a period of many days. The anomalies are interesting, and we will allude to them later, but on the whole there is less to say concerning the process of establishing a civil magistracy within a particular area.

The one thing that we can say is that in the period before 1660, the majority of civil covenants were established by all of the male members of the community and appeared in the form of a combination or compact. The second generation of New England civic leaders moved away from communal compacts and allowed the committee system to articulate a covenantal vision for the civic sphere that was commonplace and conventional. The civil covenants of the second half of the seventeenth century more often assume an implicit Christian commitment rather than an explicit dedication to God or Christ. Such an implicit commitment emerged as New England began seeing itself as an extension of Old England. Old England was part of Christendom, with an established state religion and state church, and so, therefore, was New England. Interestingly enough, we shall see that both of the Native American civil covenants that survive have strong christological statements: John Eliot and Thomas Mayhew make explicit for the Native Americans what was implicit to them as Englishmen. Christological statements concerning the sovereignty of Christ do appear in the early New England covenants, but rarely if at all in the civil covenants; they occur, rather, in the ecclesiastical covenants.

The book proceeds with a chapter that examines the colonial charters granted to the New England colonies in the seventeenth century. The chapter argues that before c. 1650 the Crown and Parliament followed different political and religious policies in New England and Old England. Instead of centralizing power, they allowed each of the colonies to follow its own vision of the proper relationship between religion, church, and state. As the outlines of the First British Empire emerged, however, the authorities in England wanted the colonies to follow a consistent and unified policy — a desire reflected in the charters that they negotiated with the colonists.[15] The Massachusetts Bay Colony lost its charter in 1684, and the one issued in 1691 differed profoundly from the charter of 1629. For one thing, England required that each New England colony tolerate dissenters, allowing them to function at least as second-class citizens.

The study continues with an examination of the local civil covenants. These were documents from the grassroots, and they reflect a variety of visions for the early New England civil magistracy. Before 1660 most of the local civil covenants were combinations and reflect a wide variety of configurations of church, state, and religion. After the Restoration, however, the civil covenants became more standardized. Ultimately, patents and charters issued by the central colonial governments became the predominant form of civil covenant by the beginning of the eighteenth century. Fewer people signed the civil covenants that appeared as compacts, and the work of composing a grassroots compact was often left in the hands of a committee, who often served as the sole signers as well — "on behalf of the rest."

The book concludes with a discussion of the ecclesiastical covenants. Three chapters examine the ecclesiastical covenants of early New England. The first considers the covenants of the standing order of established New England congregational churches, arguing that while the church covenants lacked uniformity, they did follow a pattern that we will call the "covenant formulary." They were not contracts, but documents that reflected the grace of God. They permitted no opportunity for "bargaining" with God. And they changed little as the century progressed, though after 1647 congregations began to include confessions of faith with their covenants to prove their orthodoxy or to make manifest to the younger generation what they believed.

A second chapter on church covenants deals with the non-established and/or dissenting churches and religious bodies. Baptists covenanted, in their own way, and Quakers and Anglicans also bound themselves together, although their methods cannot be considered covenantal. The final chapter discusses the emergence of brief confessional statements as preludes or postludes to the church covenants themselves, a practice that emerged as the influence of the documents of the Westminster Assembly (1643-47), the Cambridge Platform (1648), the Savoy Declaration (1658), the Reforming Synod of 1679-80, and the Saybrook Platform (1708) established nonbinding but colony-wide norms for the Congregational standing order of New England. The dialectic between orthodoxy and dissent is illustrated in these confessional statements, for as the standing order tried to articulate a confessional stance that was similar to, yet different from, the Westminster Assembly, it allowed dissenters in New England (for example, Baptists) to assert their orthodoxy and yet their dissent from the standing order. With the Savoy Declaration urging the waning government of Cromwell to allow dissent within the bounds of trinitarian orthodoxy, New England began to fracture religiously even as it was moving in the direction of a cohesive political uniformity. By 1660, the separating and non-separating Puritan experiment in New England had failed, and New England began to reflect a chastened and changed Old England.

The evidence, rich and varied, has frustrating gaps, some bridgeable, others not. In some cases we have eyewitness accounts but no covenant documents. In others, we have covenant documents, but no account — and sometimes no idea — of who the original signers were. At times we can identify the founding members, but have neither covenant nor firsthand account. Nevertheless, the evidence is still overwhelming, and no attempt will be made to analyze all of it. We will focus on churches and towns that typify patterns of covenant activity, and try to weave them into a coherent picture of foundational covenanting.

The most accessible sources for this study were the vast number of local histories published by the towns and churches of New England. Exploring this huge lode of seventeenth-century local history brought excellent results. While some of these local chronicles left much to be desired in their analytical angle of vision, many are competent, and almost all richly document the foundation of a town or church or both. The local historians are eager to cite — often with liberal quotations — the original documents. What these histories lack in critical analysis they make up for in intimate knowledge of local detail and prosopographical information. Very often, especially during the nineteenth century, a classic *magnum opus* was produced upon which most of the other histories were based. This fact largely negated the need for consultation of multiple secondary sources for many towns and their churches. The Committee for a New England Bibliography has recently produced a bibliography of New England in nine quarto volumes. This invaluable resource enabled me to identify critical items for this study.[16]

When consulting the records of the towns and churches I ran into problems. Many civil and ecclesiastical institutions have lost their records, usually through fire (one church complained that their Puritan pastor had absconded with the records when he was dismissed in a church squabble!).[17] Some of the records have large gaps. Some local records were not kept until several decades after the founding, or overzealous clerks copied records into new books and "dispensed" with what they thought was "unimportant," or sometimes the original clerks were simply poor record keepers. On the whole, we have a better grasp of what church records are available than we do of available town records. Many of the church records for Massachusetts were published; the publication of records for Maine, New Hampshire, Rhode Island, Connecticut, and Long Island (New York) is spottier. Many of the unpublished Connecticut church records are deposited in the Connecticut State Library in Hartford. The work of genealogists has greatly advanced the publication of valuable records, particularly church records, and the *New England Historical and Genealogical Register,* the *Collections* of the Essex Institute, the Maine Historical Society, the Massachusetts Historical Society, the New Hampshire Historical Society, and the Old Colony Historical Society should be highlighted as particularly useful sources.

A larger number of the town records, on the other hand, remain unpublished.[18] The town records consist chiefly of land transactions, minutes of town meetings, vital statistics, and tax lists. They are often lengthy and complex, usually consisting of scattered pages sometimes bound together (and sometimes unbound). These annals disclose the nitty-gritty of town and church formation, and give valuable sociological evidence about the town financiers (usually called "proprietors"), the town founders, and the church founders — hardly ever identical groups. While full runs of many town records remain unpublished, extensive portions are often quoted in the "classic" local histories. The Family History Library System associated with The Church of Jesus Christ of Latter-day Saints makes available to its local branches the microfilms of many unpublished ecclesiastical and civil records. We are fortunate in having virtually all of the seventeenth-century records for each colony's legislature. These journals and law books give us evidence of how central governments regulated town and church foundings; they are listed chronologically for each colony in the Bibliographical Essay, and the codes under which references to them are made are found in the *Abbreviations* list.

The geographical range of New England stretched much further along the eastern North American seacoast than it does now. While certainly including the traditional New England states, this range involved much of Long Island (especially its north shore), now part of New York State. New Haven and Connecticut colonies both had towns on Long Island, and some of the English towns moved back and forth between independency, the Connecticut Colony, the New Haven Colony, the New Netherland Colony, and later the New York Colony. The towns of Newark, Woodbridge, Piscataway, and Elizabeth, New Jersey, were founded by New England Puritans. So was the town of Cohanzy, in southern New Jersey. For a period during the 1640s the New Haven Colony had a small outpost on the Delaware River at a place called Varkin's Kill; this outpost was eventually taken over by the Dutch and the Swedes, and in modern times it is known as Salem, New Jersey. And the leaders of the Massachusetts Bay Colony had extensive contact with a Puritan colony in Nansemond, now Nansemond County, Virginia; that colony ultimately resettled to form what is now Annapolis, Maryland. Between 1691 and 1713 Nova Scotia or Acadia was under the jurisdiction of the Massachusetts Bay Province. Finally, a gathered church was sent out as a missionary venture to Dorchester, South Carolina; by the 1750s the children of that group had abandoned Dorchester and migrated inland to form one of the first Presbyterian churches in Georgia, the Midway Presbyterian Church. Such geographical expansion involved us in explorations into the state records and histories of many states, colonies, and Canadian provinces: New York and its antecedent colony, New Netherland; New Jersey and its antecedent colonies of East New Jersey and West New Jersey; Maryland, Virginia, and South Carolina; and finally Nova Scotia, New Brunswick, and Newfoundland.

The study of the covenant idea in New England history is a long, intricate, and continuing discussion to which many individuals have contributed, the most notable of whom is Perry Miller.[19] Since the Miller synthesis of the 1940s and 1950s, intellectual historians of the later twentieth century have focused their attention on the intellectual themes that Miller put forth as being central to the New England mind-set while social historians have focused on individual towns and churches to see whether these ideas were being worked out. The result has been to cast doubt on the Miller thesis of a single "New England Mind" and to point out that many individual communities — and indeed the various colonies — were not as united as had once been thought.[20] There has been little if any analysis of the texts of the church covenants,[21] while the study of the civil covenants has been limited in scope or set against the backdrop of larger questions of the emergence of the modern American political tradition.[22]

This study attempts to delineate and typify important features of seventeenth-century New England society and its culture through the founding documents of its towns and churches. I hope that analysis of both the commonalities and the differences may increase our understanding of colonial American history and of America's place in world history.

✑ 1 ✑

The European Background

*All ends of th' earth remember shall
and turne unto the Lord:
and thee all heathen-families
to worship shall accord.
Because unto Iehovah doth
the kingdome appertaine:
and he among the nations
is ruler Soveraigne.*

(Psalm 22:27-28; Bay Psalm Book)

The framework of the ecclesiastical organization, and some of the civil organization, of early colonial New England had its origins in the parochial system of Europe and Old England. Since many who came to New England were unhappy with both the church and the state in Old England, they abandoned many of the ecclesiastical and civil institutions of the English world that they associated with the oppression of the Stuart regime. Nevertheless, at the most fundamental level most early New Englanders thought like the Europeans that they were, and when it came time to arrange the institutions of church and state, all of the colonies except Rhode Island unconsciously adopted the European arrangement of a state church. The manner in which that system functioned is foreign to many people of modern times.

Ever since the first century the Christian church has struggled over its organization, particularly when Christianity left the eastern Mediterranean and spread to the Roman Empire, eastern and western. The early church was a tiny minority in the empire, and its members joined voluntarily. Nevertheless, the Old Testament could not be forgotten. In the two millennia before Jesus Christ, the Israelites had conquered Canaan, divided it, and constructed a worship center in Jerusalem. Support for the temple in Jerusalem was not voluntary, but coercive; every obedient Israelite had to give a tenth, or tithe, of the produce of the land to the Lord.[1] Often through the centuries the Israelites failed to obey this law; but early Christians who studied the Old Testament could not forget it.

Because early Christianity had a voluntary, often persecuted membership, it did not have to face problems of compulsory support, though it did, however, develop an episcopal government, and located church centers in major cities where a bishop supervised surrounding smaller churches in other parts of the city, the suburbs, or the rural countryside. But after Emperor Constantine converted to Christianity and led many of his followers into the church, the status of Christianity as a minority religion changed, and the Roman civil regime started to support the church. Emperor Theodosius eventually made Christianity the official religion of the empire, the western side of the empire fell to the barbarians, and the barbarians adopted the Roman religion — now Christianity. In the same way that Romans followed Constantine into the church, the barbarian tribes followed their leaders. Mass baptisms were common, and by A.D. 500 the church had to train vast numbers of people — both barbarian and Roman — who knew little about Christianity, its canonical Scriptures, its worship, its doctrines, or its behavioral standards.[2]

To cope, the church adopted the governmental divisions of the empire, a system developed by Diocletian at the end of the third century. Each part of the empire was divided into tiny *paroikii*, or parishes, and the church adopted this division as it secured hegemony over the European and Mediterranean world. Each parish was linked to a bishop in a larger city, and the bishops were linked by patriarchs, who resided in five cities: Rome, Constantinople, Antioch, Jerusalem, and Alexandria. The church therefore moved from an organization based on voluntaristic principles to a compulsory organization including all the citizens of a geographical region, whether willing or unwilling. Unexpectedly, the church found itself repeating the experience of the Israelites who established dominance over Canaan. Although they had no divine command to extirpate all current inhabitants, dealt with a geographical area vastly larger, and had in the New Testament no explicit instructions as to how Christians were to conduct themselves in positions of power, they did discover in the Old Testament ideas about power, and they debated for the next 1,500 years how the Old Testament should be used in the Christian era. One facet of Israelite experience adopted by the European Christians was the financial practice of tithes, or tenths. The European church required that all citizens of a parish — including such minorities as Jews — remit 10 percent of their income to the local parish priest and church.[3]

For a millennium and a half after the conversion of Constantine, the church upheld the political regimes and they upheld the church. At times the two battled ferociously, but both ecclesiastical and civil control were exercised at national and local levels by officials usually committed to upholding the power of both ecclesiastical and civil regimes. Alternatives were available — monasteries took over huge expanses of land, town guilds often had their own chapels, and the elite nobility had private chapels — but every Christian in Europe was answerable to some form of ecclesiastical authority.

England was no exception. By 1086, the *Domesday Book* indicated that the realm was divided into about 8,000 parishes.[4] Each parish had as its nerve center one — and *only* one — church, which all the people in the parish were obligated to attend and support. The boundary lines between parishes were somewhat fluid, but every scrap of land in England was accounted for either parochially or monastically. Each parish reported to its bishop in its episcopal city: the bishop reported to the archbishop of Canterbury; and the archbishop reported to the pope in Rome and the Crown in London. The system of tithes was entrenched, and depending on the size of the parish the tithes could generate large or small amounts of income. To found a new church in England during the medieval and early modern periods required establishing a new parish, which entailed an act of parliament. To establish a church independent of parliamentary, episcopal, and royal authority was illegal, and an act of treason against Crown and church.[5]

The early modern period saw the beginning of the end of the parochial and diocesan system that had embodied "one, holy, catholic, and apostolic church" for 1,000 years. The European expansion into the Americas opened up vast tracts of land for settlement by Europeans unhappy with either their financial condition or the spiritual condition of their churches. The Spanish conquest of South America resulted in a flood of gold and silver into the European economic system, bringing long-term inflation. This economic change made it harder for peasants to stay on the land on the basis of the old medieval prices, for landlords to keep the old medieval rents and to refrain from enclosing the land for more efficient agriculture, and for the church to collect the medieval tithes.

Second, Martin Luther in 1517 launched the Reformation that split Western Christianity and led to the fierce wars between 1540 and 1648. Finally, while Henry VIII of England at first condemned the Protestant revolt he ended up joining it as a matter of convenience, to justify his divorce from Catherine of Aragon, who had failed to produce a male heir. Consequently, the Roman Catholic Church in England became the Protestant Church of England, and between 1529 and 1536 the king and parliament severed all ties with Rome.[6] England retained an episcopal polity and the parochial system for the new national church, but by 1546 the king had dissolved the monastic system. Its lands were given to royal favorites or sold off to the highest bidder, and were not used to form new parishes.[7] Apart from the brief reign of Mary Tudor (1553-58), England became a Protestant country with a national church that was episcopal in government and geographically and parochially structured. All English people were obligated to support a church that, by the decree of the king but not necessarily the desire of its members, was now Protestant.[8]

After the death of Henry VIII in 1546/7 three of his children, all different in religious conviction, came to the throne. Edward VI, the only son, set England moving in a Protestant direction during his brief reign, 1546/7-53. At his death, his half-sister Mary took the throne for an even briefer reign, 1553-58. The daughter of Catherine of Aragon, she was a staunch Roman Catholic determined to return England to the papal fold. Two decisions especially alienated Mary from her people: her decision to marry the Catholic king of Spain, Philip II, and her policy of publicly burning defiant Protestants at the stake.[9] With Mary's reign the population began to lean toward Protestantism, and when Elizabeth I came to the throne at Mary's death in 1558, Elizabeth adopted a mild form of Protestantism that was specifically vague in its doctrine and restrained in its program of reformation.[10]

It was disappointment in the Elizabethan reforms that started the fragmentation of English Protestantism and led to a Puritan movement that took on many forms over the next century. Historians still argue about its definition.[11] For this section of our study, we shall concern ourselves only with the Puritanism of Old England in the period 1560-1640, concentrating on the ideas and practices that influenced the Puritanism of New England.

English Puritanism after 1560 developed at a time when the practices and theologies of the Reformation churches were coming to maturity. Luther was now dead, and Calvin had just finished the final 1559 edition of his *Institutes*. The Catholic Council of Trent was concluding, and it allowed no concessions to the Protestants. Although the Treaty of Augsburg (1555) recognized Protestants within the Holy Roman Empire, the struggle between Protestants and Roman Catholics was being taken up by the magistrates as well as the theologians. Protestants, with their emphasis on the lay understanding of Scripture, quarreled among themselves over the Lord's Supper, providence, predestination and foreknowledge, the atonement, the church, baptism, the relationship between the church and the civil magistrate, ecclesiastical polity, apostolic succession, ordination, reason and rationality in theology, worship and its regulation, Christian experience and conversion, the Holy Spirit in the Christian life, and the millennium and what would happen at the end of the world.

In England, variations on these problems tried the Church of England between the reigns of Elizabeth I and Anne — the years 1558 to 1714. The Puritan movement began with an argument over vestments in worship.[12] It was transformed in the 1570s by disputes over church government: many who identified themselves as Puritans stood for a presbyterian form of church polity.[13] Others thought that the Church of England was beyond hope of reformation, and so, in scattered parts of England, but particularly around London and in the southeast, some withdrew from the parochial church and formed their own churches without episcopal, legislative, or monarchical approval.[14] For these Separatists, who now adopted congregational church government, the church depended not upon parochial geography but on a covenantal bond rooted in an intense religious experience and a commitment to Protestant doctrine.[15] Members came from several parishes; the criterion for admission to these voluntary groups was not geographical proximity but submission to a written covenant.

The Crown deemed such actions as treasonous against a divinely sanctioned Church of England. While Separatism attacked the national polity, it also tore at the fabric of the local social polity, both civil and ecclesiastical. It threatened the system of compulsory tithes,[16] and strained the local communal structure of early modern agricultural society.[17] To withdraw from the local parish was a bold step indeed. Sometimes it was done secretly, with Separatists supporting two churches financially. Others publicly took the step, or were exposed publicly, and died for it, condemned as traitors.[18] Still others fled to the European continent, particularly Holland.[19]

After the suppression of the Presbyterian movement in the early

1590s, Puritanism turned their attention in other directions. Inspired by the preaching of William Perkins, the minister of the Parish of Great St. Andrews in Cambridge,[20] a generation of Puritan clerics trained at Cambridge University became preoccupied with conversion. They concluded that many in England, perhaps the majority, considered themselves Christians when in fact they were not. These "experimental Puritans" thought that the problem was not simply church government but hypocrisy. Since the parochial system counted all but the most scandalous as Christians — and could be lax with discipline — hypocrites abounded within the Church.[21] The Puritan preachers remembered the Sermon on the Mount:

> Not euery one that saith vnto me, Lord, Lord, shall enter into the kingdome of heauen: but he that doth the will of my father which is in heauen. Many will say to me in that day, Lord, Lord, haue we not prophecied in thy name? and in thy name haue cast out deuils? and in thy name done many wonderfull works? And then wil I professe vnto them, I neuer knew you: Depart from me, ye that worke iniquity. (Matthew 7:21-23)

For the experimental preacher, therefore, it was incumbent upon the church to restrict admission to baptism and the Lord's Supper, excluding not only "open and notorious evil livers" but also everyone who gave only assent to Christian belief (a type of faith called "historical faith") but who gave no evidence of having "saving faith," or a living faith wherein a person experienced the presence and power of the living God, realized his wickedness, repented of sin, embraced Jesus Christ, claimed Christ's righteousness in order to stand before God, and sought to live a holy and godly life. According to experimental Puritanism, to admit unworthy members to the Lord's Supper and to baptize their children would simply allow them to "drink damnation unto themselves" and to bring God's judgment on the entire parish (1 Corinthians 11:27-32).

The zeal of the experimental Calvinists, however, led to dilemmas.[22] While such concern could protect the Lord's table validly and could drive home to the scandalous the danger of eternal damnation, it could also lead to pastoral problems. The first was the problem of assurance. Experimental preaching had the potential to keep worthy partakers from the sacraments and throw them into anxiety about their salvation. The sensitive conscience might ask: "Am I really saved? Have I deceived myself all of these years?" Second, if Jesus said that "faith as a mustard seed" could save some

(Matthew 17:20), how much was enough for justification before God and the gift of eternal life? How is such faith measured?[23]

Third was the problem of judgment. By whom should faith be measured? The penitent sinner could display his or her faith to four audiences. First was God, the one who knew all things, including a sinner's heart. Second was the self: sinners could know their hearts, but the psyche could also play tricks on the mind, granting a sense of assurance one day but doubt the next. Third was the church, particularly the elders, who held the keys to the kingdom of heaven and the sacraments.[24] Fourth was the unregenerate world in general. It was this set of problems that Max Weber tried to explain in *The Protestant Ethic and the Spirit of Capitalism.*[25] Weber maintained that the theology of the Calvinists affected their conduct in society. Weber's evidence was weak, but recent scholarship on Puritan theology and psychology suggests that he was not far off the mark; the dynamic that he tried to grasp, however, was far more complex and subtle than he imagined. Besides grappling with election, Puritan preaching proclaimed that, in gratefulness and obedience to God true Christians were obligated to commit themselves to ethical rigor and hard work for the glory and honor of God.[26]

The fourth quandary of experimental preaching was the danger of emphasizing works over grace.[27] In zeal for repentance, one could fall into the trap of emphasizing good works as the ground for justification and thus fall into the pit of legalism or Roman Catholicism. The believer who found himself thinking that justification came from works might experience intense anxiety. Or, he might unwittingly teach others to overemphasize works, thus fertilizing the field of legalistic piety. This problem had its mirror opposite, which created a fifth potential problem: overemphasizing grace. Some English Calvinists struggled with antinomianism and even with libertinism.[28]

Sixth was the problem of the apostate. What was the status of erstwhile saints who had lapsed into serious sin? Were they still justified before God? If yes, would others follow the same route and live a recklessly sinful life with the hope of eternal security? If no, would one suggest that good works were required for justification? What should the church do with the lapsed who desired restoration? At what point should ecclesiastical — and civil — discipline begin? Was "penance" required for restoration? How then could Protestant churches avoid the cycle of penance emphasized by the Catholics? After 1580, some Protestant theologians began to think it possible to fall from grace, an idea later affirmed by the followers of James Arminius (1560-1609).[29] But such thinking implied that works were bound up with justification.

A final unexpected problem that could emerge from experimental spirituality was pride. A person might begin with a tender conscience, convinced of being "a worm, and no man" (Psalm 22:6), hoping thereby to receive God's grace, or at least to be ready with a "prepared heart" if God sovereignly worked through the Holy Spirit.[30] But then one ran the subtle danger of pride in one's humility.

In the parochial system of England, with its 8,000 or so parishes, experimental Puritans were in the minority — albeit a significant minority. These pietistic Puritans refused to follow the Separatists out of the Church of England, but rather worked for reformation. But how did an experimental preacher find a parish, and what happened if it refused to accept his preaching once he was there? Or, what if parishioners searching for Puritan zeal felt it lacking in their parish minister? The parochial system rarely allowed members to choose a pastor. Rather, an elaborate patronage system meant that parish ministers were usually appointed by one of three authorities: a local aristocrat or gentryman, the local bishop, or the Crown itself. The average church member had little or no say.[31] Seekers for experimental preaching could go in two directions: they could cross parochial boundaries to a church in a neighboring parish that had Puritan preaching (an act that could bring the ire of the authorities) or they could go to Puritan "Lectures," or preaching services, which some parishes held on the weekday — often on Thursday afternoon, and generally in connection with a local market day.[32] On the other side of the coin, parishioners unhappy with experimental Puritan zeal might also flee to a neighboring parish. In either case, the tithe had to be paid to one's home parish.[33]

With the ascendancy of Archbishop William Laud and his Arminian supporters in the late 1620s and early 1630s,[34] a group of wealthy Puritan merchants and nobility tried to use the patronage system to place more Puritan preachers in parishes: the Crown, to raise money, sold off rights to appoint parish ministers, a right called the feoffee of impropriation. Puritans who had purchased these rights could appoint ministers even from another part of England, or against the will of the parishioners who did not want an experimental preacher. Such attempts to manipulate ecclesiastical patronage were short-lived, especially when Laud came to understand the Puritan scheme and put a stop to it around 1633.[35]

Two alternatives attracted separating and non-separating experimental Puritans: flight to the European continent or the new world. On the continent, the refugees would be strangers in a strange land. Furthermore, they might have to submit to a strange ecclesiastical system, and live with the threat that their ethnic and linguistic identity would eventually be lost. Permanent emigration to the Americas was something that the Spanish had done for a century, but the English, Dutch, and French were only beginning. Faced with a world without settled European — or more specifically, English — Christians, a world of relatively nomadic Native Americans, how would they organize the region civilly and ecclesiastically? Would it copy the English parochial and episcopal system, with its patronage system and the habitual danger of admitting the scandalous and the unconverted to the sacraments? How would the new hegemony be established, and who would establish it? Might not emigration to "Virginia" afford zealous Puritans a chance both to practice true Reformed Christianity and show England — and indeed the whole European world — how a true Christian society and church should function?[36] It was this challenge that faced the old Englanders as they attempted to establish a new England.

The Colonial Charters of Early New England

Why rage the Heathen furiously?
muse vaine things people do;
Kings of the earth doe set themselves,
Princes consult also:
with one consent against the Lord,
and his anoynted one.
Let us asunder break their bands,
their cords bee from us throwne.
Who sits in heav'n shall laugh; the lord
will mock them; then will he
Speak to them in his ire, and wrath:
and vex them suddenlie.
But I annoynted have my King
upon my holy hill
of Zion: The established
counsell declare I will.
God spake to me, thou art my Son;
this day I thee begot.
Aske thou of me, and I will give
the Heathen for thy lot:
and of the earth thou shalt possesse
the utmost coasts abroad.
thou shalt them break as Potters sherds
and crush with yron rod.
And now yee Kings be wise, be learn'd
yee Iudges of th'earth (Heare.)

Serve yee the lord with reverence,
rejoyce in him with feare.
Kisse yee the Sonne, lest he be wroth,
and yee fall in the way,
when his wrath quickly burnes, oh bleste
are all that on him stay.

(Psalm 2: Bay Psalm Book)

The vast majority of people coming to New England in the seventeenth century were often at odds with the central government and monarchy of Old England, more often than not because of religion. Nevertheless, as the New Englanders began to establish institutions in the New World that were patterned after the Old World, they were very conscious of the fact that, at least technically, they existed and functioned at the good pleasure of the government of Old England and more specifically, at the good pleasure of the crown of England.[1] In the first half of the century, the New Englanders took advantage of a remote location, a civil war and a revolution, and a general lack of interest on the part of the English government to function as they saw fit. In the second half of the century, however, circumstances changed. England survived its civil war and revolution, and the decline of Spain and the rise of France and Holland as major trading competitors compelled the English to become much more familiar with the route to North America and the Caribbean. By 1700 a trip to America, while fraught with danger from storm, shipwreck, and piracy, was a much more routine thing than it was in 1620.[2] The consequence for New England was that Old England became much better acquainted with New England and its activities, and by the 1680s Old England began to think in terms of an empire centered on the east coast of North America.[3]

All of the colonies of New England, therefore, worked assiduously at the delicate task of walking a fine line in their relationship to the English government.[4] That relationship was defined as one between superior (Old England) and inferior (each individual colony) and was demarcated in a series of covenants called charters and patents. While the charters and patents of all of the colonies of New England have been published, republished, and analyzed, much of the analysis is dated, and has not been done against the backdrop of modern studies of the covenant idea.[5] It is not possible nor necessary to analyze every aspect of the charters and patents in this inquiry; rather, we will limit our focus to the questions framed by the larger contours of this study, the question of the relationship between church, state, religion, God, and Jesus Christ. As we note new features and modifications of the preceding documents, we will get a sense of the general outline and shape of these documents, and also see them as the backdrop to the local civil covenants of seventeenth-century New England.

As stated in the Introduction, we will take as our definition of a civil covenant a document that legally established a civil government at either the local or colonial level. Charter and patent were the means by which the relationship between Old England and New England was articulated during the seventeenth century. A **charter** was a grant from a superior to an inferior that granted certain responsibilities, privileges, titles, offices, and rights to the inferior party.[6] Usually, these responsibilities and privileges involved the duties of governance; when boroughs and corporations were formed in Old England charters were issued by the Crown. At least technically, the inferior party functioned under the supervision and authority of the superior party. Biblical scholars would phrase this in terms of suzerain and vassal, the suzerain being the superior party (the "lord") and the vassal being the inferior party. A **patent** was similar, but usually involved the grant of one specific right, privilege, title, office, or piece of property.[7] Thus, a patent was a more focused and specific document than a charter. This is reflected in the modern usage of the word, where it is the protection of a specific invention or device.

There were six periods between 1606 and 1691 when New Englanders found themselves negotiating with the government of Old England in order to define the relationship of the government of the colonies to the government of the old world. Each period is marked by the issuance of new charters by the monarchy or by Parliament. The first period was that of early exploration (1607-20), when the New World of North America was a place of great risk and when no one was sure whether the English colonial enterprise in that region would survive. The second period was 1625-38, the span of time when Charles I was moving to centralize the English government and Archbishop Laud was attempting to transform the Church of England into the Anglo-Catholic institution that the king envisioned. The third period of time, 1639-49, was the period when Charles I found himself in trouble with Parliament, and when several New England colonies found themselves negotiating with Parliament rather than the Crown over details of a charter. The fourth period was 1660-65, at the beginning of Charles II's reign, when the monarchy was reasserting its authority over the realm of England both at home and abroad. The next critical period was the reign of James II (1685-88), when the English government was beginning to eye the North American colonies as crown jewels for its empire. Finally, the sixth period of time was 1688-91, when the English government that emerged from the Glorious Revolution made significant shifts in its policy toward New England and when it launched its imperial ambitions.[8]

When one looks at the charters issued from Whitehall in London,[9] especially in comparison to the civil covenants generated by the New Englanders themselves, several features immediately come to our attention. The charters and patents were legal instruments drafted — and crafted — by lawyers employed by the Crown and, during the disturbances of the 1640s, by the Parliament. They followed a model developed in the English common law tradition over a period of several centuries, and a careful reading of them indicates that for each point of the charter every possible legal ramification had been explored and addressed, leading to documents that were thorough and verbose. The fact that many of these documents involved the transfer of land as well as the transfer of governmental authority added to their bulk. Finally, it is plain that the lawyers who wrote them had access to the royal collection of all the New England charters, for many of them cite extensively from the preceding patents and charters in the historical prologues that are so often found at the beginning of these legal instruments. Furthermore, the wording of the charters and patents is repetitive, in that standard ways of establishing, for instance, a judicial system were perfected and simply lifted from one document and placed in another. What one really has to look for, therefore, are the deviations from the norm, the clauses of the documents that are unlike what has gone before and that set new precedents.

The First Charter of Virginia is our point of departure.[10] Issued on Thursday, April 10, 1606, by James I, the charter began by dividing up the merchants who had petitioned for a colony in America into two groups.[11] The first group was based in London and wished to settle along the coast of North America between 34° and 41° latitude — the region that roughly stretches from the southern corner of present-day North Carolina to Greenwich, Connecticut. This group ultimately settled Virginia and became known as the London or Merchant's Company.[12] The second group was based in the west country, in the towns of Bristol, Exeter, and Plymouth, and wished to settle between 38° and 45° latitude — the region that roughly stretches from the southern border of Delaware to the southern border of New Brunswick. This group was ultimately based in Plymouth,

Devonshire, and granted the Mayflower pilgrims permission to settle within their realm; it would be called the Plymouth Company.[13] The 1606 Virginia Charter commenced a theme that would be found in many of the future charters: one stated purpose of the whole project was the conversion of the Native American population to not only Christianity but a European way of life:

> We, greatly commending, and graciously accepting of, their desires for the furtherence of so noble a work, which may, by the providence of Almighty God, hereafter tend to the glory of his divine majesty, in propagating the Christian religion to such people, as yet live in darkness and miserable ignorance of the true knowledge and worship of God, and may in time bring the infidels and savages, living in those parts, to human civility, and to a settled and quiet government; do, by these our Letters-Patents, graciously accept of, and agree to, their humble and well-intended desires.[14]

Whether James I and his grantees truly intended this as a primary purpose for the American plantations is somewhat doubtful — James's grantees were more interested in the religious aspects of the project than the monarch was. Nevertheless, conversion of the native Americans became part of the rhetoric of the English colonial projects in America, and would ultimately inspire John Eliot, Roger Williams, Jonathan Edwards, and David Brainerd. Modern and postmodern historians, influenced by the social and behavioral sciences, tend to discount this type of language as rhetoric. Economic historians maintain that the New Englanders really came for economic gain,[15] while anthropologists, joined by political historians, tend to maintain that most New Englanders came because they had lost all hope of establishing hegemony in Old England. In order to vent their frustration, the New Englanders went somewhere else to establish dominance over a group of non-Europeans.[16]

While it is accurate to say that the charters spent a lot more words on economic and political subjects than on religious subjects, the various schools of thought concerning the migrational motives of the early New England colonists — indeed, of just about any group that came to colonial North America — forget two things. First, the complexity of the human psyche cannot simply be reduced to any one motivating force for migration: any individual could have numerous reasons for migrating to the new world. Not all of these reasons were publicly expressed, nor were they necessarily written down. In each individual motivating factors were given different weights. Economic, political, and religious factors were certainly often public and primary, but the fact that a person's parents, grandparents, or in-laws were deceased could weigh just as heavily in a decision to make the journey as any form of religious pressure or desire for economic advancement.

Second, we need to remember that virtually all English inviduals, Anglican, Puritan, Roman Catholic, Separatist, Baptist, Presbyterian, or Congregationalist, operated within a common worldview that was teleological. "He ascended into heaven, and sitteth on the right hand of God the Father Almighty, from thence he shall come to judge the quick and the dead" together with the affirmation of "the resurrection of the body; and the life everlasting," are phrases that could be found in the Roman Catholic mass, the Book of Common Prayer, and the Westminster Shorter Catechism.[17] The belief that Christ would come again to judge the living and the dead, rewarding his followers with eternal life in the new heavens and the new earth, and rewarding rebels and pagans with eternal wrath in hell, tended to override more modern impulses of "live and let live," at least in the area of religious belief. Anglican, Puritan, and Catholic believers all agreed that the best thing they could do for a Native American who grew up outside of Christendom would be the sharing of the Christian faith, in order to save his body and soul from perdition. The Bay Psalm Book put it aptly: "Kisse yee the Sonne, lest he be wroth, and yee fall in the way, when his wrath quickly burnes, oh bleste are all that on him stay."[18]

How do the charters and patents treat Christianity and the Christian God? Three approaches can be discerned. The first approach has as its focus the personal Christian God. In some cases, God is identified — and remotely addressed — as the sustainer of life and the foundation of the civil state. A sense of this way of thinking can be found in some of the phrases of the 1606 Virginia Charter: "James, by the Grace of God . . . ," and "We, greatly commending, and graciously accepting of, their desires for the furtherence of so noble a work, which may, by the providence of Almighty God, hereafter tend to the glory of his divine majesty. . . ." The second approach can also be found in the 1606 Virginia Charter: ". . . in propagating the Christian religion to such people, as yet live in darkness and miserable ignorance. . . ."[19] Here the author treats Christianity in a somewhat detached way, as a body of collected beliefs to be promulgated and circulated to those ignorant or dismissive of the faith. The third way is to focus on the institution that Christianity spawned — the church. Instead of the glory of

God or the multiplication and growth of the faith and the faithful, it is the establishment of the church — usually the *true* church — in a region where the church has not yet been established. While these might be subtle distinctions, whichever has first place — God, the faith, or the church — will affect attitudes, actions, and intentions on the part of those who granted the charters and patents and those who received the grants.

We can use the 1606 Virginia Charter as a baseline model for the other charters that were issued by the English Crown over the next eighty-five years. The 1606 charter went on to establish a government for the entire territory. A local council, on site in America, would have authority over the day-to-day operations of each colony. Those two councils, one for the north and one for the south, would report to a central council in England, to be named "our Council of Virginia." Because it was his council, the monarch, of course, would have veto power over any decision any council made. Bypassed in the governance arrangements, it seems, were the commercial corporations organized in Plymouth and London who were the sponsors of the colonies. The Crown saw the commercial corporations as private entities undertaking this activity for personal gain: if the colonies were a success, the Crown would then take them over and they would reap rewards for the private investors; if they were a failure, the Crown lost nothing and the investors lost everything.

The Virginia Charter went on to discuss various aspects of economic and political consequence for the two colonies.[20] Strikingly absent is any mention of an ecclesiastical establishment for the colony: while the Christian religion was to be the established religion, the charter made no provision for the Church of England to have dominance in either the first colony or the second colony. Ultimately, of course, the Anglicans would come to predominate in the first plantation, the southern plantation governed by the London corporation (Virginia), while the Puritans would dominate the second plantation (New Plymouth), on the northern land that was originally controlled by the Plymouth, Devonshire, corporation.[21]

Jamestown and the Colony of Virginia were founded in 1607, on the basis of the 1606 Charter of Virginia. Unlike the northern colony, we have no record that the residents of Jamestown signed a compact or combination to supplement the 1606 charter itself.[22] In 1619 the Mayflower Pilgrims secured permission from the London Company (renamed in 1609 as the South Virginia Company) to settle in the northern part of the southern colony of "Virginia," and from the Plymouth Company (separated from the South Virginia Company in 1619) to settle in the second northern colony.

However, the pilgrim Separatists supplemented the 1606 Charter with the Mayflower Compact.

One week and one day before the signing of the Mayflower Compact, on Friday, November 3, 1620, the Charter of New England was issued by James I. In so many ways, the Charter of New England had more far-reaching effects than the Mayflower Compact, in that it encompassed a much larger amount of territory and was the basis for many of the future charters issued by the Crown. This charter was later revoked by Charles I after he demanded that it be surrendered, an example of centralization of power in the middle of the 1630s.[23] Quoted often in the charters and land grants of 1620-35, citations of the 1620 charter disappeared from the charters issued after 1640 by Parliament, Charles II, and James II. Interestingly enough, it was cited once again in 1691, when William and Mary issued the new Massachusetts Bay Province Charter.

The 1620 Charter of New England is twice as long as the 1606 Virginia Charter and much more specific. It references the 1606 Virginia Charter, and thus derives its legal precedent from that initial charter. Purposely forgetting that the Dutch had settled New Amsterdam and established New Netherland, it stated that "there is noe other the Subjects of any Christian King of State, by any Authority from their Soveraignes, Lords, or Princes, actually in Possession of any of the said Lands or precincts, whereby any Right, Claim, Interest, or Title, may, might, or ought by that Meanes accrue, belong, or appertaine unto them, or any of them."[24] The English were very much aware of the epidemic of illness that had decimated the Native American population:

> And also for that We have been further given certainly to knowe, that within these late Yeares there hath by God's Visitation raigned a wonderfull Plague, together with many horrible Slaugthers, and Murthers, committed amongs the Sauages and brutish People there, heertofore inhabiting, in a Manner to the utter Destruction, Deuastacion, and Depopulacion of that whole Territorye, so that there is not left for many Leagues together in a Manner, any that doe claime or challenge any Kind of Interests therein, nor any Superious Lord or Souveraigne to make Claime thereunto, whereby We in our Judgement are persuaded and satisfied that the appointed Time is come in which Almighty God in his great Goodness and Bountie towards Us and our People, hath thought fitt and determined, that those large and goodly Territoryes, deserted as it were by their naturall Inhabitants, should be

possessed and enjoyed by such of our Subjects and People, as heertofore have and hereafter shall by his Mercie and Favour, and by his Powerfull Arme, be directed and conducted hither. In Contemplacioin and serious Consideration whereof, Wee have thougt it fitt according to our Kingly Duty, soe much as in Us lyeth, to second and followe God's sacred Will, rendering reverend Thanks to his Divine Majestie for his gracious favour in laying open and revealing the same unto us, before any other Christian Prince or State, by which Meanes without Offence, and as We trust to His Glory, Wee may with Boldness goe on to the settling of soe hopefull a Work, which tendeth to the reducing and Conversion of such Sauages as remaine wandering in Desolacion and Distress, to Civil Societie and Christian Religion, to the Inlargement of our own Dominions, and the Aduancement of the Fortunes of such of our good Subjects as shall willingly intresse themselves in the said Imployment, to who We cannot but give singular Commendations for their soe worthy Intention and Enterprize.[25]

While the English were probably not cognizant of the fact that it was they who brought the disease, they were certainly aware of the fact that the area was being depopulated. They also were aware of strife and division in the Native American world of northeast North America, strife that may have been due in part to a split among the Native Americans over how they should respond to the Europeans, whether they be French, English, or Dutch.[26] That the English monarch and his people were "seconding and following God's sacred will" fell in conveniently with the project of national expansion and fierce competition with the French, the Dutch, and the Spanish.

The 1620 charter also gives greater liberty of government to the newly established Council for New England, still based in Plymouth, Devonshire. While the 1606 First Charter of Virginia explicitly stated that the old Plymouth Company was charged with the enforcement of all royal "Laws, Ordinances, and instructions,"[27] the Council for New England now had the opportunity not only to shape the form of the government but also to formulate and enact laws of their own, provided they were not in conflict with the laws of England:

And further, of our especial Grace, certaine Knowledge, and mere Motion, for Us, our Heires and Successors, Wee do by these presents give and grant full Power and Authority to the said Councill and their Successors, that the said Councill for the Time being, or the greater Part of them, shall and may, from time to time, nominate, make, constitute, ordaine and confirme by such Name or Names, Style or Styles, as to them shall seeme Good; and likewise to revoke, discharge, change, and alter, as well all and singular, Governors, Officers, and Ministers, which hereafter shall be by them thought fitt and needful to be made or used, as well to attend the Business of the said Company here, as for the Government of the said Collony and Plantation, and also to make, ordaine, and establish all Manner of Orders, laws, Directions, instructions, Forms, and Ceremonies of Government and Magistracy fitt and necessary for an concerning the Government of the said Collony and Plantation, so always as the same be not contrary to the Laws and Statutes of this our Realme of England, and the same att all Times hereafter to abrogate, revoke, or change, not only within the Precincts of the said Collony, but also upon the Seas in going and coming to and from the said Collony, as they in their good Discretions shall thinke to be fittest for the good of the adventurers and Inhabitants there.[28]

The granting of freedom in government was reinforced by two other provisions of this charter: the Council for New England had the right to banish and expel any who attempted "Destruction, Invasion, Detriment, or Annoyance to the said Collony and Plantation."[29] While the Council for New England never authorized the banishment of Roger Williams, Anne Hutchinson, John Wheelwright, or the Quakers, this power would be utilized by some of the colonies during on-site conflicts. Finally, the Crown granted the right to the president of the Council for New England or his deputy, or any two members of the council, to administer the Oaths of Allegiance and Supremacy in matters concerning the northern colony or second colony. Furthermore, the right to compose *ad hoc* oaths was granted by the Crown to the same parties should the need arrive. What we are beginning to see is the delegation of tasks by the Crown to the people most interested in the colony: James and his Privy Council were beginning to realize that trying to accomplish tasks when such great distance separated the center of the government of England from the colonies in North America was not very realistic. Most of the royal officials had never been to America, and therefore had difficulty comprehending and overseeing details, and the time it took to transport orders prevented the efficient discharge of governmental functions and responsibilities.

There are two references to religion in this 1620 charter, and those two references embrace the three stances which were elucidated earlier.

The charter opens up with the stock phrase "James, by the Grace of God. . . ." But it goes on to speak of the Christian religion not only objectively but also subjectively, as it commits itself and the entire colonial project, at least in lip service, to God:

> We according to our princely Inclination, favouring much their worthy Disposition, in Hope thereby to advance the inlargement of Christian Religion, to the Glory of God Almighty, as also by that Meanes to stretch out the Bounds of our Dominions, and to replenish those Deserts with People governed by Lawes and Magistrates, for the peacable Commerce of all, that in time to come shall have occasion to traffique into those Territoryes. . . .[30]

The topic of religion is not pursued throughout the rest of the charter until we come to the end, at which point the Crown points out not what it wants to see, but what it does not want to see in the northern colony:

> And lastly, because the principall Effect which we can desire or expect of this Action, is the Conversion and Reduction of the People in those Parts unto the true Worship of God and Christian Religion, in which Respect, Wee would be loath that any Person should be permitted to pass that Wee suspected to affect the Superstition of the Chh of Rome, Wee do hereby declare that it is our Will and Pleasure that none be permitted to pass, in any Voyage from time to time to be made into the said Country, but such as shall first have taken the Oathe of Supremacy; for which Purpose, Wee do by these Presents give full Power and Authority to the President of the Said Councill, to tender and exhibit the said Oath to all such Persons as shall at any time be sent and imployed in the said Voyage.[31]

The Oath of Supremacy was the oath imposed on all clergymen and public officials recognizing that the monarch was "the only supreme governor of this realm, and of all other her highness's dominions and countries, as well in all spiritual or ecclesiastical things or causes as temporal."[32] This act, favored by Anglicans, allowed the monarch to interfere in church affairs. A Roman Catholic would never take such an oath, at least truthfully, because Roman Catholics affirmed that only the pope, as Christ's vicar on earth, had ultimate authority over the church. But there were others who could not take such an oath: Separatists, for instance, could never make such an acknowledgment, and Presbyterians, at least English Presbyterians, objected vehemently to the oath.[33] Ironically, the Pilgrim Separatists arrived on the shores of New England one week after the Charter of the Council for New England had passed the royal seals on Friday, November 3, 1620. They had permission from the old Plymouth Company in Devon to be there, but William Bradford, in *Of Plymouth Plantation, 1620-1647,* gives no evidence that they took the Oath of Supremacy.[34] In trying to prevent Roman Catholics from going to New England, the Crown implied via negative wording that it wanted to see the Church of England established in the region. But neither the Crown nor the established church made much of an effort to do anything about that goal. When the non-separating Puritans started to come in 1628 and 1629, the non-separating Puritans maintained that *they* were the true Church of England, reformed and cleansed of accretions and errors.[35]

During the next fifteen years the 1620 New England Charter was the foundation for all governmental actions in the region of the second, northern colony, now called New England (in contrast to the first, southern colony known as Virginia). The Council for New England in Devonshire used it as a basis to grant the region now known as Maine to Sir Ferdinando Gorges and John Mason, and Charles I used it as the basis for granting a charter to the Massachusetts Bay Colony in 1628/9. The same year, 1629, the Council for New England granted a charter to William Bradford as a representative of the New Plymouth Colony.

We will not look in detail at the 1622 Grant of the Province of Maine to Sir Ferdinando Gorges and Captain John Mason,[36] except to say that it is essentially a patent issued by the Council for New England for the territory between the Merrimack and Kennebec Rivers. The territory granted to Gorges included the coast of what is now New Hampshire, and Gorges wanted to essentially treat the region as his feudal estate.[37] There is no mention of things religious or ecclesiastical in the grant, but there is a subtle modification of the governance arrangement. Gorges was instructed to make laws that were as close as possible to the laws of England:

> And the said Sr. Ferdinando Gorges and Capt. John Mason doe further covenant for them, their heyres and assignes, that they will establish such government in the said porcons of lands and islands granted unto them, and the same will from time to time continue, as shall be agreeable, as neere as may be to the laws and customs of the realme of England; and if they shall be charged at any time to have neglected their duty therein, that thus they will conforme the same according to the di-

rections of the President and councill; or in default thereof it shall be lawful for any of the aggrieved inhabitants and planters, being tenn's upon ye said lands, to appeal to ye chief courts of justices of the President and councill.

This provision is in marked contrast to what was granted to the Council for New England itself, which had authority to do as it pleased in matters of government as long as it did not contradict the laws of England. Here the Council is forcing Gorges to enact and enforce laws that conform to the legal statutes of the realm of England.

In comparison to the Maine and New Hampshire provinces, and the Connecticut, New Plymouth, and Rhode Island colonies, the Massachusetts Bay Colony outweighed the other entities economically, politically, numerically, and in terms of influence. Massachusetts Bay had something of a false start in the region of what is now Salem, Massachusetts, in 1628,[38] but the phenomenal growth in the colony began in earnest in 1629, as it became evident that Charles I was embarking upon personal rule and had dismissed Parliament. Interestingly enough, it was Charles I who issued the charter of the Massachusetts Bay Colony on Wednesday, March 4, 1628/9. At this point, Puritans of whatever stripe were a definable group in the English world, and it could not have escaped Charles's attention that the original six individuals who purchased the Massachusetts Bay region from the Council for New England were staunch Puritans,[39] and that the addition of twenty more individuals were also of the Puritan party. Nevertheless, there was no requirement for religious conformity in the charter, nor for the establishment of the Church of England, and the governor and company of the Massachusetts Bay rejoiced at the possibility of filling that void with what turned out to be non-separating Puritanism. In a famous and shrewd move that same year, the principal leaders of the Massachusetts Bay concluded that the seat of government was where the charter was, and that the charter should be moved to America, where it would be remote from the long arm of the king.[40] Indeed, they were right: the Council for New England, the parent company of the Massachusetts Bay, had its charter recalled in 1635. The Massachusetts Bay charter remained in Massachusetts all during the English Civil War, the Cromwellian regime, and most of the reign of Charles II, until it was vacated in 1684.[41]

Based on the 1620 New England Charter, the 1629 Massachusetts Bay charter transferred the territory between the Charles and Merrimack Rivers, along with a three-mile-wide strip of land south of the Charles

River, to the Massachusetts Bay Colony. The three-mile boundary did not remain in force and was modified later.[42] Because of the prominence and influence of Massachusetts Bay upon New England, many have looked upon this charter as the model and most famous example of New England royal charters. However, the 1629 charter had what were by then becoming stock and standard paragraphs for a royal charter dealing with New England: it is not all that different from the New England Charter of 1620.

The major difference from the precedents set in previous charters was the fact that there were other new members of the company known as freemen. Up to this point in New England the only people who could be recipients of a charter, patent, or land grant were the leaders. For the first time the 1629 Massachusetts Bay charter anticipates not only leaders but also rank-and-file members, and these members were "to be free of the said Company and Body."[43] The charter states:

> And our Will and Pleasure is, and Wee doe hereby for Vs, our Heires and Successors, ordeyne and graunte, That from henceforth for ever, there shalbe one Governor, one Deputy Governor, and eighteene Assistants of the same Company, to be from tyme to tyme constituted, elected and chosen out of the Freemen of the saide Company, for the tyme being, in such Manner and Forme as hereafter in theis Presents is expressed, which said Officers shall applie themselves to take Care for the best disposeing and ordering of the generall buysines and Affiares of, for, and concerning the said Landes and Premisses hereby mencoed, to be graunted, and the Plantacion thereof, and the Government of the People there.[44]

The governing council (later called the General Court) and the freemen who assembled when the General Court met could set the standards for admission to the Company and could admit or deny to admit as they saw fit. Both powers were not lost on this group of Puritans:

> WEE DOE for Vs, our Heires and Successors, give and graunte to the said Governor and Company, and their Successors, That the Governor, or in his absence, the Deputie Governor of the saide Company for the tyme being, and such of the Assistants and Freeman of the saide Company as shalbe present, or the greater nomber of them so assembled, whereof the Governor or Deputie Governor and six of the Assistants at the least to be seaven, shall have full Power and authoritie to choose,

nominate, and appointe, such and soe many others as they shall thinke fitt, and that shall be willing to accept the same, to be free of the said Company and Body, and them into the same to admitt; and to elect and constitute such Officers as they shall thinke fitt and requisite, for the ordering, mannaging, and dispatching of the Affiares of the saide Govenor and Company, and their Successors; And to make Lawes and Ordinances for the Good and Welfare of the saide Company, and for the Government and ordering of the saide Landes and Plantac~on, and the People inhabiting and to inhabite the same, as to them from tyme to tyme shalbe thought meete, soe as such Lawes and Ordinances be not contrarie or repugnant to the Lawes and Statuts of this our Realme of England.[45]

Furthermore, unlike the requirements outlined in the earlier charters, the officers of the governor and company of the Massachusetts Bay in New England did not have to appear before a royal official to either swear allegiance to the Crown or to take their oaths of office: rather, Mathew Cradocke was to take his oath of allegience before the royal officials, and then he was empowered to hear the oaths of the other officers of the company, and the other officers of the company were empowered to hear the oaths of new, incoming officers.[46] The end result was something akin to apostolic succession: the privilege of government was transferred from one person to another without the originator being present. None other than Charles I signed a document giving a band of Puritans tremendous liberty in England's new colonies. Puritans therefore limited the status and privileges of a freeman to members of the gathered church until the issuance of the Massachusetts Bay Province Charter in 1691.

We have noted already that, while Christianity was the assumed and implied faith of both royalty and corporation, there was no establishment of the Church of England, nor was there a requirement for religious conformity or uniformity. What the charter does say, albeit as an addendum to a larger thought, is that the publicly stated purpose of the Massachusetts Bay Colony was to aid in the conversion of the remaining Native Americans to faith in Jesus Christ:

AND, Wee doe of our further Grace, certen Knowledg and meere Moc~on, give and graunte to the saide Governor and Company, and their Successors, That it shall and maie be lawful, to and for the Governor or Deputie Governor, and such of the Assistants and Freemen of

the said Company for the Tyme being as shalbe assembled in any of
their generall Courts aforesaid . . . from tyme to tyme, to make,
ordeine, and establishe all Manner of wholesome and reasonable Orders, Lawes, Statutes, and Ordin~nces . . . for the directing, ruling, and
disposeing of all other Matters and Thinges, whereby our said People,
Inhabitants there, may be soe religiously, peacablie, and civilly governed, as their good Life and orderlie Conversacon, maie wynn and in-
cite the Natives of {the} Country, to the Knowledg and Obedience of
the onlie true God and Sauior of Mankinde, and the Christian Fayth,
which is our Royall Intencon, and the Adventurers free Profession, is
the principall Ende of this Plantacion.[47]

While the sincerity of the commitment to the stated principal purpose of the
Massachusetts Bay Colony varied among those who were parties to the charter, such thinking is part of the very fabric of historic Christianity since apostolic times. The second half of the above paragraph is an echo of the scriptural statements and injunction found in 1 Peter, where the entire Christian
church is seen as a light to the Gentiles who were their neighbors:

But yee are a chosen generation, a royall Priesthood, an holy nation, a
peculiar people, that yee should shewe forth the praises of him, who
hath called you out of darknes into his marueilous light: Which in time
past were not a people, but are now the people of God: which had not
obteined mercie, but now haue obteined mercy. Dearely beloued, I be-
seech you as strangers and pilgrimes, abstaine from fleshly lusts, which
warre against the soule, Hauing your conuersation honest among the
Gentiles, that whereas they speake against you as euill doers, they may
by your good works which they shall behold, glorifie God in the day of
visitation. (1 Peter 2:9-12)

It would take John Eliot to point out to the Massachusetts Puritans that
they had done little to effect that primary purpose during the first two decades of the existence of the Massachusetts Bay Colony.[48] Perry Miller has
maintained that the Massachusetts Bay people saw the primary purpose of
their project not to be the conversion of the Native Americans. Rather, the
primary purpose was to show Old England, and the rest of Protestant
Christendom, how to be a truly Christian nation. Instead of reforming an
old church in an old social realm, the non-separating Puritans' "errand into
the wilderness" was to form a new social realm and transplant into that

realm a truly reformed church patterned after apostolic times.[49] Of course, such a vision would never be articulated in a charter controlled and issued by Charles I, but surely he could and did not overlook the fact that the movers and shakers behind the Massachusetts Bay plantation were poles apart from his vision for the Church of England. While William Laud and the program called Laudianism would not be instituted until after Laud was ordained as Archbishop of Canterbury in 1633, by 1629 the monarch was already married to the French Roman Catholic Henrietta Maria, and relations between Charles and the Puritans were already strained. That strain was accentuated by the difficult relations Charles was having with Parliament in general.[50] While both Parliament and the Massachusetts Bay agreed that Christianity was to be the established religion of the new colonial realm, Charles's decision not to define what variety of Christianity should be established in the Massachusetts Bay indicates that he was willing to marginalize a specific group of churchmen with whom he strongly disagreed but whom he was not willing to cut off completely from participation in the realm known as England.

This last point is of relevance to the next document we want to briefly reflect on: the charter issued to William Bradford for New Plymouth Colony by the Council for New England. While Charles was willing to give the non-separating Puritans of the Massachusetts Bay a royal charter, he was not willing to do the same for the Separatists of the New Plymouth Colony. Even though the Council for New England encouraged them to incorporate,[51] New Plymouth Colony had to settle for a charter issued by the Council for New England. Ultimately this situation would lead to the demise of the colony and its merger with the Massachusetts Bay Province in 1691-92. Issued on Wednesday, January 13, 1629/30, the charter itself had few if any novel provisions in it, and its mention of religious matters was minimal. At one point the charter pointed out that while New Plymouth might have been a marginal proposition at best in 1621 and 1622, by 1629 and 1630 the colony had stabilized to such a degree that its population now numbered almost 300 persons, and that this was due to the sovereignty of God.[52] A little further on in the document the matter of religion and piety is mentioned as a subsidiary matter to a larger point — the awarding of the Kennebec River Valley to New Plymouth, a valley that had been in the hands of Sir Ferdinando Gorges since 1622. The wording is as follows:

> And for as much as they have noe conveniente place either of tradinge or ffishinge within their own precincts whereby (after soe longe travell

and great paines,) so hopefull a plantac~on may subsiste, as alsoe that they may bee incouraged the better to proceed in soe pious a worke which may especially tend to the propagation of religion and the great increase of trade to his Ma^{ts} realmes, and the advancement of the publique plantac~on, the said councell have further given, graunted, bargained sold enfeoffed allotted assigned and sett over {the Kennebec River Valley}.[53]

Why is it that a nation so intensely religious as seventeenth-century England would not articulate that religious vision more explicitly within these charter documents? The answer can be found within the question. While England was intensely religious, that intensity led to bitter division, and any clearly articulated theocentric — or christocentric — vision could possibly fan the flames of controversy.[54] Becoming too specific in theology could lead to the jettisoning of the whole project, and it must be remembered that the Council for New England was issuing this patent to people who had fled royal displeasure in 1608 and who were categorized as Separatists in the English religious world. For the Council to call attention to the deviant ecclesiological stances of these separated brethren would only lead to controversy, and possibly an inquiry from the Crown itself. As the Council for New England well knew, it existed at the pleasure of the king, and six years later the king did indeed exercise his right to disorganize the company in 1635. But the Crown did not bother, or did not have time, to disorganize and reorganize the two colonies that had been formed under the auspices of the Council for New England and its revoked charter. Also, as we have pointed out earlier, the charters and patents were legal documents, written by lawyers to achieve a specific aim. The lawyers themselves knew that too much attention to religion would bring trouble. Furthermore, they were working within an established legal tradition of royal charters issued by the Crown to various boroughs and corporations in England: in their mind-set, precedent was more important than experiment and innovation.[55]

While the Massachusetts Bay and Plymouth colonies were receiving their charters in 1629, there was also some significant activity concerning the lands to the north of the Massachussetts Bay: the president and Council for New England transferred the area that we now know as the coast of New Hampshire to Captain John Mason.[56] According to the indenture of Saturday, November 7, 1629, the area between the Merrimack and Piscataqua Rivers was sold to Mason.[57] Since 1622 Sir Ferdinando Gorges and Mason had been

partners in holding title to the territory between the Merrimack and
Kennebec Rivers. From this point on, the region known as Maine was divided up into two sections, with the Piscataqua River as the border. To the
south was the Mason grant which became New Hampshire Province; to the
north was the Gorges grant which became Maine Province. The document
transferring the territory was a routine indenture that was similar to the earlier land transfers. Again, the Council for New England called for conformity
of the laws of the new Province of New Hampshire to the laws of England; the
council also appointed Captain Walter Neale to be its representative and to
make sure that the provisions of the transfer were being carried out.[58] In
1635, Mason confirmed his patent for New Hampshire Province with no
mention of ecclesiastical establishment or matters of religion.

Towards the end of Charles I's period of personal rule, the Crown
confirmed the grant of the area between the Piscataqua and Kennebec
Rivers to Sir Ferdinando Gorges. With the dissolution of the Plymouth
Company in 1619 and the revocation of the Charter of the Council for New
England in 1635, Gorges, like Mason before him, wanted to make sure that
he had full title to the land. Even though the king was now embattled in his
own realm, a royal grant was still a safer route to follow than simply holding the land on the basis of the old grant to the Council for New England.
This document, issued on Wednesday, April 3, 1639, supplemented the
documents from the Council for New England that granted the same land;
its contents, however, were quite different from the documents issued by
the Council for New England. Indeed, it was unlike any other document issued to establish European hegemony over New England, for it spelled out
an Anglican vision for at least part of the territory of New England.[59]

The Gorges Grant of 1639 began like most of the other charters, letters patents, and grants that had preceded it. The Crown confirmed to
Gorges the territory that had already been given to him in earlier years. But
as the document proceeds we begin to realize that there were differences
when we come to the property and rights of the church and the state's ownership thereof:

> And Wee Doe name, ordeyne and appoynt that the porcon of the
> Mayne Lande and Premises aforesaide shall forever hereafter bee called
> The Province or Countie of Mayne and not by any other name or
> names whatsoever with all and singular Soyle and Grounds thereof . . .
> and alsoe All Patronages and Advowsons Free Disposicons and
> Donacons of all and every such Churches and Chappells as shalbee

made and erected within the said Province and Premisses or any of them with full power lycense and authority to builde and erecte or cause to be builte and erected soe many Churches and Chappells there as to the said Sir Ferdinando Gorges his heires and assignes shall seeme meete and convenient, and to dedicate and consecrate the same or cause the same to bee dedicated and consecrated according to the Ecclesiasticall Lawes of this our Realme of England togeather with all and singular and as large and ample Rights Jurisdiccons Priviledges Prerogatives Royalties Liberties Immunityes Franchises Preheminences and Hereditaments as well by Sea as by Lande within the said Province and Premisses and the Precincts and Coasts of the same or any of them and within the Seas belonging or adjacent to them or any of them as the Bishopp or Durham within the Bishopricke or Countie Palatine of Duresme in our Kingdome of England now hath, useth or enjoyeth or of right hee ought to have, use or enjoye within the said Countie Palatine as if the same were herein particularly menconed and expressed.[60]

The type of community envisioned in the above paragraph is Anglican rather than Puritan. Puritans never spoke of "chapels," for the word "chapel" had several connotations with which they strenuously disagreed. In the seventeenth century the word "chapel" often meant a place where relics of the saints could be found, a notion that would be odious to the Puritan mind-set with its desire for purity of worship and disdain for Roman Catholic and Laudian High Anglican ceremonies. Second, "chapel" connoted a place where worship went on in private, out of the sight and out of the reach of the authority of the church. In 1639, the connotation was made even more offensive because Queen Henrietta Maria maintained a private Roman Catholic chapel in Whitehall, complete with a Catholic chaplain imported from France. Finally, the concept of chapel also included a consecrated altar, reflecting the Anglican priority of sacred space over and against the Puritan priority of sacred people.[61]

The churches and chapels were to be dedicated and consecrated using the rites and ceremonies of the Church of England, a very different procedure from the gathering of the Puritan churches of New England. Furthermore, their establishment, location, and number were firmly under the authority of the civil realm; Ferdinando Gorges controlled the church, an Erastian arrangement whereby the state dominated the church.[62] It was the responsibility of Gorges to set up courts of justice for both the church and the state:

> And Wee Doe further by these Presents for us our heires and successors
> give and graunte unto the said Sir Fardinando Gorges his heires and
> assignes full power and authoritie . . . to erect Courtes of Justice as well
> ecclesiastical as civill and temporall whatsoever and to appoynt and con-
> stitute from tyme to tyme Judges Justices Magistrates and Officers. . . .[63]

The structure of the court system was to reflect and be based upon the old parochial arrangements of England, arrangements adopted by the reformed and
Protestant Church of England during the Henrician and Edwardian reigns:

> And Wee doe further for us our heires and successors give and graunte
> unto the said Sir Fardinando Gorges his heires and assignes full power
> and authorities to divide all or anie parte of the Territories hereby
> graunted or menconed to bee graunted as aforesaid into Provinces
> Counties Citties Townes Hundreds and Parishes or such other partes or
> porcons as hee or they shall thinke fitt and in them every or any of
> them to appoynt and allott out such porcons of Lande for publique
> uses Ecclesiasticall and Temporall of what kinde soever. . . .[64]

The Puritan colonies also divided themselves up into counties, cities,
towns, and parishes (but not provinces or hundreds), but none of the
charters granted by the Crown explicitly award them that privilege. Probably the Crown thought the Puritans so unpredictable that not even the Puritans themselves could foresee how they would arrange themselves civilly
and ecclesiastically once they arrived. Gorges, on the other hand, was Anglican and predictable, and it was the Crown's desire that he replicate as
much as possible the system of Old England. Later on in the 1639 document the Crown enabled Gorges to perform this task by granting him the
right to incorporate political subdivisions:

> And Wee Doe for us our heires and successors further give and graunte
> unto the said Sir Fardinando Gorges his heires and assignes . . . leave
> lycense and power . . . to the said several Citties Borroughes and
> Townes to graunte Letters or Charters of Incorporacons with all
> Libertyes and thinges belonging to the same and in the said severall
> Cittyes Boroughes and Townes to constitute such. . . .[65]

The Crown further made it very clear that Gorges was to establish the
Church of England as the true church in the Province of Maine:

And for the better governement of such our Subjects and others as att any tyme shall happen to dwell or reside within the said Province and Premisses or passe to or from the same our will and pleasure is that the Religion nowe professed in the Church of England and Ecclesiasticall Governement nowe used in the same shalbee forever hereafter professed and with asmuch convenient speede as may bee settled and established in and throughout the said Province and Premisses, and every of them.[66]

The High Church, Laudian Anglicanism of Charles I was of a different stripe than Elizabethan or Jacobean Anglicanism, and left little if any room for Low Church Puritanism.

The arrangements for Gorges's civil authority also reflected a desire on the part of the Crown to replicate as much as possible the magistracy of Old England. This is a grant of territory to a particular individual; one person, therefore, had much more power, authority, and influence than a group of people. Indeed, Gorges was the only person who really could be deemed a baron of New England. The 1639 grant makes that fact clear in the following way:

And Wee Doe for us our heires and successors create ordeyne and constitute the said Fardinando Gorges his heires and assignes the true and absolue Lords and Proprietors of all and every the aforesaid Province of Mayne and Premisses aforesaid and all and every the Lymitts and Coasts thereof Saveing always the faith and allegiance and the Supreame Dominion due to us our heires and successors.[67]

Not only did Gorges have the right to set up the judicial system, he had the right to dismiss and remove judges, magistrates, and officers whom he deemed unfit for office. He himself was also a court of appeal and he had the right of pardon in criminal and civil cases.[68] In clauses that were reminiscent of the early and high medieval periods Gorges was even allowed to set up manors.[69]

The approach to the law and the statutes that Charles I adopted in Gorges's realm was different from that adopted for Gorges's Puritan neighbors to the south. Not only were the laws not to be contradictory to the laws of England, they were to conform as nearly as possible to the statutes of Old England. We pointed out earlier that it was the Council for New England, not the Crown, that had demanded that the laws passed in America

conform as nearly as possible to the laws of England. Now, probably as a result of the crisis with Parliament, the crisis in Scotland, and the reports
trickling back to Whitehall and Westminster about stringent Old Testament civil statutes being passed in the Puritan colonies further south, the
Crown stated that the legal foundation of the Gorges territory was to conform unto English common law:

> . . . And Wee Doe for us our heires and successors of theise Presents
> give and graunte unto the said Sir Fardinando Gorges his heires and
> assignes power and authority with the assent of the greater parte of the
> Freeholders of the said Province and Premisses for the tyme being
> (when there shalbee any) whoe are to bee called thereunto from tyme
> to tyme when and as often as it shalbee requisite to make ordeyne and
> publish Lawes Ordinances and Constitucons reasonable and not repug-
> nant or contrary but agreeable (as neere as conveniently may bee) to
> the Lawes of England for the publique good of the said Province and
> Premisses and of the Inhabitants thereof. . . .[70]

As one reads the Gorges grant, one gets the sense that Gorges himself
is being given a lot of power, but that there are no checks or balances set up
against him. A more careful look at the clauses of the charter, however, reveals that the Crown had placed some sort of rein on Gorges. The charter
reminded Gorges that while he may be the principal figure in the area we
now know as Maine, the Crown reserved for itself final authority and
power:

> And Wee Doe for us our heires and successors create ordeyne and con-
> stitute the said Fardinando Gorges his heires and assignes the true and
> absolue Lords and Proprietors of all and every the aforesaid province of
> Mayne and Premisses aforesaid and all and every the Lymitts and
> Coasts thereof Saveing always the faith and allegiance and the
> Supreame Dominion due to us our heires and successors.[71]

Not only did the Crown remind Gorges that it had veto power over his decrees and actions, it also mentioned but did not explicitly organize the inhabitants, called freeholders rather than freemen, into a body politic. Note
that in the above quotation concerning the laws of Maine the Crown
"assignes power and authority with the assent of the greater parte of the
Freeholders of the said Province and Premisses."[72] How the greater part of

the freeholders were to express their assent was not explicitly laid out, since the Crown doubted that anybody was presently over there "(when there shalbee any)."[73] As a temporary stopgap measure, Gorges was given the right to make and enforce his own laws "not contrary or repugnant to the laws of England," but he was *not* given extreme punitive authority:

> And because such Assemblies of Freehoulders for makeing of Lawes cannot alwayes bee soe suddenly called as there may bee occasion to require the same Wee Doe therefore for us our heires and successors give and graunte unto the said Sir Fardinando Gorges his heires and assigns full power and authoritie that hee the said Sir Fardinando Gorges his heires and assignes by him and themselves or by his or theire Deputies, Magiestrates or Officers in that behalfe lawfully constituted shall or maye from tyme to tyme make and ordeyne fitt and wholesome Ordinances within the said Province or Premisses aforesaid to bee kepte and established as well for the keepeing of the peace as for the better governement of the people there abideing or passing to or from the same and to publishe the same to all to whome itt maye appertain and concerne which Ordinances Wee Doe for us our heires and successors straightly comand to bee inviolably observed within the said Province and Premisses under the penaltie therein expressed soe as the same Ordinances bee reasonable and not repugnant or contrary but as neere as may bee agreeable to the Lawes and Statutes of our Kingdome of England and soe as the same Ordinances doe not extend to the bindeing chargeing or takeing away of the right or interest of any person or persons in their lives members Freehoulds Goodes or Chattells whatsoever.[74]

The final check on Gorges's authority and power was the explicit statement that he was subordinate to the Lords and Other Commissioners for Foreign Plantations, a body created by Laud in 1634.[75] While Gorges could hold sway in his territory, the Crown gave due notice that appeals against his conduct in both civil and ecclesiastical matters could be pursued to Whitehall. While it was certainly not convenient, those who objected did have a court of appeal:

> But Wee Doe nevertheles hereby signifie and declare our will and pleasure to bee the powers and authorities hereby given to the said Sir Fardinando Gorges his heires and assignes for and concerning the Government both Ecclesiastical and Civill within the said Province and

Premisses shalbee subordynate and subject to the power and reglement
of the Lords and other Comissioners here for forraigne Plantacons for
the tyme being. . . .[76]

The Gorges Grant is significant because no other charter issued for
New England by the Crown reflects as much as the Gorges document does
a vision for New England that is explicitly European, English, and Anglican. Even more specifically, no other New England civil charter of the seventeenth century specifically articulates a vision for the church and its government. The absence of that vision in the other charters issued to groups
who leaned more towards a Puritan vision of faith and life indicates that
the Crown was well aware of what it was doing: it was allowing the Puritans of Old England to travel to the margins of the English world to find
their own way, rather than supervising them in a heavy-handed fashion.
When the Crown, however, had opportunity to fashion a charter for a
gentryman who specifically wanted an Anglican configuration patterned
after the Old World, the Crown was most happy and willing to give its
thoughts on the matter. What the Crown had in mind as an ideal was uniformity and continuity with Old England. Ironically, the English did not
flock in droves to Gorges's colony — they were happy with the Anglican
and English world in which they were located, and had no desire to relo-
cate themselves to a foreign land that was trying to imitate the real thing.
The people who were unhappy in England, however, were quite willing to
plant new roots in a new land, and there was no lack of personnel to popu-
late the colonies to the south of Gorges's plantation.

The charter concludes by recognizing the four *loci* of authority in its
worldview: Scripture, the form of established Christianity taught in England in 1639, the statutes and laws of England, and allegiance to the
Crown. As far as Charles I and his lawyers were concerned, this was the
glue holding together the social fabric of England:

And further Wee Will and by these Presents for us our heires and successors Doe graunte to the said Sir Fardinando Gorges his heires and
assignes that these our Letters Patents . . . shalbee in all things and to
all intents and purposes firme good effectualll and sufficient in the lawe
. . . (noe interpretacon being made of any worde or sentence Whereby
Gods worde true Christian Religion now taught professed and
maynteyned the fundamentall Laws of this Realme or Alleagiance to us
our heirs or successors may suffer prejudice or diminucon). . . .[77]

The next four years, however, would strain this fabric incredibly, as the Crown and Parliament edged closer and closer to civil war. The war did begin in earnest in September 1642. By 1646 Charles I had lost the war, and for the next fourteen years Parliament and Cromwell in varying arrangements governed the nation. It was within the context of the First English Civil War (1642-46) that Roger Williams made the journey to England in 1643-44 to apply for a patent for the Rhode Island Colony.[78]

The Patent for Providence Plantations, issued by a Parliamentary commission on Thursday, March 14, 1643/4, "in the Nineteenth Year of the Reign of our Sovereign Lord King Charles, and in the year of our Lord God, 1643," is a much shorter document than the ponderous royal charters of the previous quarter century.[79] The document incorporates and unites into one colony what had been up to this point one independent colony, Providence, and two plantations, Portsmouth and Newport, that had formed the Rhode Island Colony in 1640/1.[80] The only entity that did not come under the charter was the Warwick Colony of Samuel Gorton. Gorton and his followers had had earlier conflicts with the Massachusetts Bay authorities, the Plymouth Colony authorities, the Newport authorities, and the Providence authorities. Gorton and his circle are sometimes referred to as anarchists who wanted no government; in actuality, they contended that while they believed in the institution of government they did not recognize the governments of Providence, Newport, or Portsmouth, because none of those governments were instituted by the home government of England. Neither did they recognize a formal government amongst themselves — again because they felt that they themselves had not been instituted and constituted by the government of England. Once Providence, Portsmouth, and Newport did get a charter, however, the settlers of Warwick constituted themselves a town and joined the Colony of Rhode Island and Providence Plantations.[81]

The 1643/4 patent began by pointing out the new locus of authority in the absence of Charles I: on Thursday, November 2, 1643, Sir Robert Dudley, Earl of Warwick, had been appointed by the House of Lords — but not the House of Commons — as Governor in Chief and Lord High Admiral of all of the colonies along the North American coast.[82] The Lords had also appointed a commission of five members of the House of Lords and thirteen members of the House of Commons to serve as "Commissioners, to Join in Aid and Assistance With the Said Earl." The governor and commissioners were granted all governing authority along the North American coast; they were also allowed to distribute that authority as they saw fit.[83]

Thus, instead of the Crown granting certain powers to a private company, Parliament, in the absence of the Crown, arrogated to itself authority over the territory and then granted that authority to its own commission. In effect, with Parliament at war with the Crown, the entire edifice of authority which the Crown had set up was removed from royal hands and placed in parliamentary hands.

Realizing the tenuous nature of the Providence Plantation's claim upon its land, and realizing that Newport and Portsmouth's claim was not that much better, Roger Williams and others decided that they should apply for some sort of legal document while the window of parliamentary opportunity lay open. Dealing with a parliamentary commission was more palatable to them than dealing with royal lawyers.

The resulting document is therefore not modeled after the royal charters and patents. It simply describes the territory, and speaks of the application of various people in the region:

> And whereas divers well affected and industrious English Inhabitants, of the Towns of Providence, Portsmouth, and Newport in the tract aforesaid, have adventured to make a nearer neighborhood and Society with the great Body of the Narragansets, which may in time by the blessing of God upon their Endeavours, lay a sure foundation of Happiness to all America.[84]

Like the Massachusetts Bay Colony to the north, this letter of incorporation also speaks of the conversion of the Native Americans to Christianity, if in an elliptical way: "Happiness to all America" is the goal of the plantation, and happiness in the Puritan worldview was the knowledge of God and his salvation. The charter went on to grant:

> . . . full Power and Authority to rule themselves, and such others as shall hereafter inhabit within any Part of the said Tract of land, but such a Form of Civil Government, as by voluntary consent of all, or the greater Part of them, they shall find most suitable to their Estate and Condition; and, for that End, to make and ordain such Civil Laws and Constitutions, and to inflict such punishments upon Transgressors, and for Execution thereof, so to place, and displace Officers of Justice, as they, or the greater Part of them, shall by free Consent agree unto. Provided nevertheless, that the said Laws, Constitutions, and Punishments, for the Civil Government of the said Plantations, be conform-

able to the laws of England, so far as the Nature and Constitution of the place will admit.[85]

In earlier sections of this chapter we have looked carefully at what the charters said concerning the legal structure of each colony, and this case is no exception, particularly because this is the only charter issued by the legislative body of England. In the case of Rhode Island, Parliament wanted the laws of Rhode Island to conform to the laws of England. Not passing laws "repugnant" or "contradictory" to the laws of England was not enough; rather, the laws should fall in line with the English legal tradition. While the nascent Rhode Island legal code was given a certain amount of restriction, the absence of boundaries for other aspects of Rhode Island colonial life in the rest of this document is significant. There are no elaborate descriptions of the land and all of the economic benefits that could be gleaned from it, nor is there, in technical terms, the direct granting or sale of land. Nothing is mentioned concerning the religious life of the populace, nor is there any mention of Christianity specifically or of the governance of the church or churches located in the region.[86]

If we were to strictly follow the chronological outline that we have thus far pursued in this chapter, we should next consider the Charter of Connecticut granted by Charles II in April 1662. However, one year and three months after the Connecticut Charter was issued the Crown also granted a Charter to "Rhode Island and Providence Plantations," and it is to that document that we will turn next, since we want to compare it to the Parliamentary Patent issued twenty years earlier in 1643/4. Signed by Charles II on Wednesday, July 8, 1663, and awarded to the General Assembly of Rhode Island, the 1663 Rhode Island Charter marks a significant turning point in the history of the royal charters issued to New England. The significant section for our purposes is found in the first two or three pages. The charter opens with a historical prologue, pointing out that the application for a charter emerged not from the Crown but from a group of twenty-four leading people in Rhode Island. Furthermore, it states that these individuals had come to the new world for religious purposes, their own religious purposes first and then the conversion of the Native Americans:

> . . . Whereas wee have been informed, by the humble petition of our trustie and well beloved subject, John Clarke, on the behalf of Benjamine Arnold {etc.} . . . that they, pursueing, with peacable and

loyall mindes, their sober, serious and religious intentions, of godlie
edifeing themselves, and one another, in the holie Christian ffaith and
worshipp as they were perswaded; together with the gaineing over and
conversione of the poore ignorant Indian natives, in those partes of
America, to the sincere professione and obedience of the same ffaith
and worship, did, not onlie by the consent and good encouragement of
our royall progenitors, transport themselves out of this kingdome of
England into America, but alsoe, since their arrivall there, after their
first settlement amongst other our subjects in those parts, ffor the
avoideing of discorde, and those manie evills which were likely to en-
sue upon some of those oure subjects not being able to beare, in these
remote parties, theire different apprehensions in religious concerne-
ments, and inn pursueance of the afforesayd ends, did once againe
leave theire desireable stationes and habitationes, and with excessive
labour and travell, hazard and charge, did transplant themselves into
the middest of the Indian natives. . . .[87]

There are several notable aspects of this paragraph, a paragraph written by
a royal administration and signed by a monarch that had been profoundly
shaken by the events of the previous quarter century. The first item to note
is that the hidden, or at least unstated, agenda of so many in the Great Migration was admitted by at least one colony and then by the Crown: many
(but not all) had come to the new world for religious reasons, specifically,
because of an argument with the Church of England, its bishops, and the
Crown over the nature of Christianity and the church in England. In this
document, missionary activities among the Native Americans followed, but
those activities came second, not first. Nobody, of course, had been fooled
the first time around, but now the ultimate and true purpose of the "Puritan" New England plantations had been publically articulated — in a royal
document, no less.

We note secondly that the 1663 charter matter-of-factly admits that
dissent existed not only in England but also in the remote parts of New England; ". . . as they were perswaded" is a phrase that refers to decisions and
thoughts about "the holy Christian faith and worship" as found in Old England. But then the charter continues on and notes that even in New England's Puritan Zion there were dissenters, and that conflict over matters
religious had led to Rhode Island's founding. That the new king acknowledged "different apprehensions in religious concernments" not only in the
Anglican world but also in the Puritan world without wholesale condem-

nation is evidence of a new line of reasoning on the part of the royal administration.

Finally, the 1663 Rhode Island charter explicitly made the assumption that within the geographical realm of New England there could be a place where dissenters could gather and form a colony or plantation that had a religious commitment different from the dominant royal commitment to the Church of England and the Anglican establishment. While such an assumption had been implicit in earlier royal charters, this is the first time that a legal document recognized an entity in the English realm that is not bound to follow the pattern of the established church. Both Crown and colony looked upon it as a "lively experiment":

> And whereas, in their humble addresse, they have ffreely declared, that it is much on their hearts (if they may be permitted), to hold forth a livlie experiment, that a most flourishing civil state may stand and best bee maintained, and that among our English subjects, with a full libertie in religious concernements; and that true pietye rightly grounded upon gospell principles, will give the best and greatest security to sovereignetye, and will lay in the hearts of men the strongest obligations to true loyaltye.[88]

This 1663 charter, along with the Providence Civil Covenant of 1637-39, is the first attempt in the Western world to legally separate the civil magistracy from civil religion and an established state church. We should note that civil religion is not the same thing as the established state church. The state church is an institution with records, buildings, financial dealings, and personnel; civil religion is something more amorphous, and can be described as a cluster of ideas that can be sustained by the state church (or by the state itself) and that form the often submerged foundations of societal life.

The "lively experiment" of the Rhode Islanders was not devoid of a civil religion; instead, its civil religion consisted of a commitment to privatization of religiosity with the hope that the virtues and values of private commitments would spill over into the public arena of civil discourse, a public arena that nevertheless was stripped of any outward religious commitment save for a vague and non-specific acknowledgment that 99 percent of the population could be characterized as at least nominally Christian.[89] According to the petitioners to the Crown, this new approach to religion and civic responsibility would ultimately lead to greater public righteousness and a higher degree of true patriotic fervor for the English world. While this is an important first step in the secularization process that has come to dominate the West in modern times, the Rhode Islanders were not secularists: note their commitment to "true piety rightly grounded upon gospel principles." Rather, they maintained that a commitment to Crown and Parliament that included public membership in a parish of the Church of England too often led to hypocrisy: people were saying and doing one thing outwardly while believing something else inwardly. This state of affairs was detrimental not only to the life of the church but to the life of the body politic. The Crown therefore made a new decree:

> Now know yee, that wee beinge willinge to encourage the true hopefull undertakeinge of oure sayd loyall and loveinge subjects, and to secure them in the free exercise and enjoyment of all theire civill and religious rights, appertaining to them, as our loveing subjects; and to preserve unto them that libertye, in the true Christian ffaith and worshipp of God, which they have sought with soe much travaill, and with peacable myndes, and loyall subjectione to our royall progenitors and ourselves, to enjoye; and because some of the people and inhabitants of the same colonie cannot, in theire private opinions, conform to the publique exercise of religion, according to the litturgy, formes and ceremonyes of the Church of England, or take or subscribe the oaths and articles made and established in that behalfe; and for that the same, by reason of the remote distances of thos places, will (as wee hope) bee noe breach of the unities and unifformitie established in this nation: Have therefore thought fitt, and doe hereby publish, graunt, ordeyne and declare, That our royall will and pleasure is, that noe person within the sayd colonye, at any tyme hereafter, shall bee any wise molested, punished, disquieted, or called in question, for any differences in opinione in matters of religion, and doe not acutally disturb the civill peace of our sayd colony; but that all and everye person and persons may, from tyme to tyme, and at all tymes hereafter, freelye and fully have and enjoye his and theire owne judgements and consciences in matters of religious concernments, throughout the tract of lande hereafter mentioned; they behaving themselves peacablie and quietlie, and not useing this libertie to lycentiousnesse and profanenesse, nor to the civill injurye or outward disturbeance of others. . . . And that they may bee in the better capacity to defend themselves, in theire just rights and libertyes against all the enemies of the Christian ffaith, and others, in all respects, wee

have further thought fit, and at the humble petition of the persons aforesayd are gratiously pleased to declare, That they shall have and enjoye the benefitt of our late act of indemnity and ffree pardon, as the rest of our subjects in other our dominions and territoryes have; and to create and make them a bodye politique or corporate, with the powers and priviledges hereinafter mentioned.[90]

It was now no longer treasonous to be a heretic. Or at least having a different interpretation of the faith "once delivered to the saints" was no longer heresy, and therefore not treasonous. The broader picture that this charter draws assumes and implies that the Christian faith would still be the established and dominant faith of the realm. But the door had been opened for competing versions of that faith to coexist side by side without the interference of the civil magistrate. In this arrangement, each local region (colony) would decide whether it wanted an established church and an articulated version of civil religion, but it would then allow dissenters to function, as long as they remained in the pale of orthodox Christianity. The fact that the Thirty-nine Articles of the Church of England were drawn up with enough ambiguity to encompass a broad spectrum of Anglicanism helped keep the pale wide and broad. In the unlikely event that the Crown had adopted the Westminster standards developed in the 1640s by the Westminster Assembly, the spectrum of what could be called Christianity would have been considerably narrower.

The fact that four Quakers had been executed by the Massachusetts Bay Colony in 1659-60, along with the excesses on both sides of the Atlantic during the 1640s, led to another critically important section of the new charter. Rhode Islanders, known for their unorthodox interpretations of the faith, were to be allowed freedom to travel throughout all of the New England colonies without hindrance. The Crown was not forcing plantations and colonies with a rigid interpretation of Christianity to accept them as new residents, but they were not to be bothered as they made their way throughout his majesty's realm of New England:

> And further, our will and pleasure is, that in all matters of publique controversy which may fall out betweene our Colony of Providence Plantations, and the rest of our Colonies in New-England, itt shall and may bee lawfull to and for the Governor and Company of the sayd Colony of Providence Plantations to make their appeales therein to vs, our heirs and successours, for redresse in such cases, within this our realme of En-

gland: and that itt shall bee lawfull to and for the inhabitants of the sayd
Colony of Providence Plantations, with out let or molestation, to passe
and repasse with freedome, into and thorough the rest of the English
Colonies, vpon their lawfull and civill occasions, and to converse, and
hold commerce and trade, with such of the inhabitants of our other English Collonies as shall bee willing to admitt them thereunto, they
behaveing themselves peaceably among them. . . .[91]

The new royal policy concerning religion in the colonies stands in
marked contrast to what was happening in Old England. In Old England, a
series of acts called the Clarendon Code were put into effect. The new laws
did not condemn dissenters to the category of heretics and therefore traitors, but they were designed to completely marginalize dissent to the fringes
of English society. One of the significant aspects of the Clarendon Code was
that it was passed by Parliament and did not emanate from the Crown. The
Crown had lost its power of church discipline with the dissolution of the
Court of High Commission, and that court was not restored to power in
1660-62. Parliament, therefore, and not the Crown, started to take on the
task of enforcing religious uniformity, or at least managing religious dissent.
The Corporation Act of 1661 stated that all town officials must swear an
oath of allegiance to the Crown and commune in the Church of England in
order to serve in their offices (mirroring, ironically, the New Haven Colony
ordinances of 1639 concerning service in civil government). In addition,
those who had sworn allegiance to the Solemn League and Covenant of
1643 in the heat of the English Revolution were to swear publicly and in
writing that they had renounced it.[92] The Act of Uniformity, passed in 1662,
ordered all clergy to give wholehearted assent and consent to the worship in
the *Book of Common Prayer.*[93] This statute led to the Great Ejection of 1662,
in which between 1,800 and 2,000 Puritan clergy were ejected from their parochial charges for refusing to conform to the rites and ceremonies of the
Church of England.[94] The next year the Crown issued the Rhode Island
Charter, with its much more liberal provision for dissent. But in Old England Parliament continued to harass dissent on into the next decade, and in
fact, decades. The Conventicle Act of 1664 labeled all meetings of five or
more persons for nonconformist worship seditious.[95] The modification of
1670 reduced the penalties, but increased the government's power of investigation.[96] The Five Mile Act of 1665 increased the pressure on noncon-
formists: no dissenting minister might live within five miles of a town, or
teach unless he had taken the Oath of Allegiance.[97]

The New England charters issued in the wake of the Restoration add considerably to the picture of religion in Restoration England, in that they reflect a more liberal policy on the part of the Crown toward religious dissent in New England. While that royal policy was more liberal than Laudian Anglicanism, it was also more uniform toward New England. In the reluctant toleration of religious dissent the New Englanders mirrored Old England in reverse: Congregationalist Puritans had hegemony in all colonies but Rhode Island, while Anglicans had hegemony in Old England.

During the early 1660s, two other colonies were also seeking royal charters. The Colony of New Haven and the Colony of Connecticut were neighbors, and both had formed themselves by self-generated compact rather than by any sort of royal authority.[98] On Wednesday, April 23, 1662, Charles II issued a charter to Connecticut, the stronger but more liberal of the two colonies.[99] There is nothing extraordinary about this charter; it deals with all of the usual political and economic topics, such as government, fishing, emigration, trade, and so forth. The only thing that is different about the 1662 Connecticut Charter is its silence concerning matters of religion. Charles II is acknowledged to be king "by the grace of God," but there is nothing more.[100] At a time when the Restoration Parliament was tightening up on religious dissent in Old England via the Clarendon Code, Charles II was pursuing a *laissez-faire* attitude toward religion, church, and state in his Connecticut Colony. Unlike the Rhode Islanders, the Connecticut people could not ask for privatization of religion, and asking for royal approval of a professedly Puritan colony would only stir up the waters of kingly displeasure. Both monarch and colonists therefore decided tacitly that no mention of religion would be the best route to follow: Connecticut could pursue its ecclesiastical policy as it saw best, and Charles II would not be forced to place his blessing on it.

The New Haven Colony, on the other hand, had to search its soul in the years after the Connecticut charter was granted. The strictest of the New England colonies, it was not granted a charter,[101] and ultimately the New Haven Colony lost its identity by reluctantly merging with the Connecticut Colony on Thursday, April 20, 1665.[102] The New Haven Colony, like the New Plymouth Colony, therefore never had any form of royal or parliamentary approval. The New Haven Colony set as its goal meticulous adherence to Puritan tenets that were more ideals than realities in other colonies: the gathered church, the civil government to be conducted only by church members on both a colonial and local level, rigorous standards for admittance to the church, the Old Testament civil law as the foundation for colonial and local statutes, and Puritan Christianity as the only established religion in the realm with no dissent allowed. The failure to sustain that vision for more than a quarter of a century (1639-65) was a great blow to its citizenry, and some even tried to start again by founding Newark, New Jersey.[103] The merger with Connecticut Colony kept them within the pale of orthodox Puritanism, but as far as the New Haven people were concerned, Connecticut was "soft" on inner godliness and external public virtue.

Connecticut and New Haven were not the only colonies where activity emerged in the wake of the Restoration. On Saturday, March 12, 1664, Charles II also granted land to his brother, James Stuart, Duke of York and the future James II of England.[104] The beginning of the area that was given lay between what is today Bristol, Maine, up to the St. Croix River, the border with New Brunswick. This land was located just to the north of the Gorges grant and had been granted to the now-defunct Council for New England. The Maine tract, however, was a small sliver of what the Crown had actually granted. The grant went on to include all of the land to the St. Lawrence River, along with the land between the Hudson River and the Connecticut River, Long Island, and New Jersey. Finally, to top it all off, the grant awarded Martha's Vineyard and Nantucket to James II. Essentially, the Crown was claiming all of the land belonging to the Netherlands, with which it was at war, and at the same time was surrounding the existing New England colonies with a royal band of authority.[105] Like the Connecticut Charter, the stated focus of the grant to the Duke of York was economic and political; there was no mention made of religion or its establishment. This is significant given the fact that the other grant of land in New England made to a faithful Anglican, Sir Ferdinando Gorges, had specific instructions about religion, church, and state. At this point James was a Protestant Anglican raised by a French Roman Catholic mother (Henrietta Maria); it would not be until 1668 or 1669 that he would convert to the Roman Catholic faith. But the mere fact that he was a son of Charles I and Henrietta Maria made him highly suspect in the eyes of the New Englanders. What New England Puritan could trust one who had been raised in the shadow of the Roman Catholic Chapel Royal in Whitehall and who had later spent eleven years in France, Spain, Flanders, and Belgium?[106] Ultimately, the New Englanders would be correct in their assessment that James wished to seize power in the entire region of northeast North America, but it would be twenty years before their anxieties took on flesh in the form of Sir Edmund Andros. The extent of the grant to James may have seemed excessive, but on Thursday, September 8, 1664, a fleet sent by James himself captured New Amsterdam at the mouth of the Hudson River. Except for a brief period in 1673-74, when the Dutch regained the southern part of the Hudson Valley and part of Long Island, the only other European rivals for the northeastern section of North America were the French.

That did not mean, however, that all was harmony and peace in England's governance of New England during the remainder of the seventeenth century. In 1680, the Crown decided that it had to take action concerning the New Hampshire towns of Portsmouth, Hampton, Dover, and Exeter. In the previous forty-two years, these towns had submitted themselves to the authority of the Massachusetts Bay Colony — Hampton in 1638-39, Portsmouth and Dover in 1641, and Exeter in 1643. Because of the Civil War, the Crown did nothing about this state of affairs, even though it knew that these towns were in the region granted to Captain John Mason. Mason had died in December 1635, at the age of forty-nine. Mason's family had abandoned hope of securing rulership of New Hampshire in the twenty-five years after his death. But with the Restoration, the descendants of John Mason spent 1660-80 reasserting their claim to New Hampshire, much to the horror of the residents of New Hampshire Province and the Massachusetts Bay Colony. The emergence of New Hampshire Province in 1680 was a compromise measure.[107] The Crown decided to challenge the claim of Massachusetts Bay to the four New Hampshire towns by setting up a president and council for the province of New Hampshire. It appointed John Cutt the first president:

> Whereas our colony of ye Massachusetts al^s Mattachusetts Bay in New-England in America, have taken upon themselves to exercise a Government & Jurisdiction, over ye Inhabitants & Planters in ye Towns of Portsmouth, Hampton, Dover Excester, & all other ye Towns & land in ye Province of New-Hampshire . . . not having any legall right or authority so to do: Which said Jurisdiction & all further exercise thereof, We have thought fit by the advice of Our Privy Council to inhibit & restrain for the future; And do hereby inhibit and restrain ye same. And whereas ye Government of y^t part of the said Province of New-Hampshire, so limited & bounded as aforesaid hath not yet bin granted unto any person or persons whatsoever but ye same still remains & is under Our im'ediate care & protection; To the end therefore, y^t Our loving Subjects, ye Planters and Inhabitants within ye limits aforesaid, may be protected and Defended in their respective rights, liberties &

properties, & y^t due & impartiall Justice may be duly administred in all
cases civill & criminall; & y^t all possible care may be taken for ye quiet
& orderly Government of ye same: Now know ye, that We by & with y^e
advice of our Privy Council, have thought fit to erect, & constitute, &
by these p^{r}sents for us o^r hrs & success^{rs} do erect, & constitute, & appoint a President & Councell, to take care of ye said Tract of land called
The Province of New-Hampshire, & of the Planters & Inhabitants
thereof; & to Order, rule & Govern ye same according to such methods
& regulations, as are herein after specified & declared.[108]

Cutt's 1680 commission was the first in a series of efforts of the Crown to
curtail the power of the Massachusetts Bay government, efforts that would
lead to the vacating of the 1629 charter in the High Court of Chancery at
Westminster on Wednesday, June 18, 1684. The decree was finalized on
Thursday, October 23, 1684.[109] The vacating of the charter was also a prelude to the autocratic rule accorded Sir Edmund Andros during the reign of
James II (1685-88).[110] In comparison to the governance system granted to
John Mason and Ferdinando Gorges in 1622[111] and to Mason alone in
1629[112] the 1680 document is marked by several innovations. The first was
the judicial policy that all capital crimes should be automatically appealed
to the Crown in Whitehall.[113] This is evidence that the monarchy felt that
the Massachusetts Bay was dispatching criminals into the next life too easily, too quickly, and for the wrong crimes. The second modification is one
in which we are especially interested. While the 1629 grant to Mason made
no mention whatsoever of religious policy, the 1680 commission decisively
awarded liberty of conscience in matters of religion to all Protestants and
extended "most favored church status" to the Church of England. The legal
dominance of the Congregational Way was thus neutralized and given
second-class rank. In the same breath we once again find the consistent
theme of the hoped-for conversion of the Native American, ostensibly from
the mouth of Charles II, a monarch whom the Massachusetts Bay elders
were privately classifying as a reprobate:

> And above all things we do by these p^{r}sents will, require & comand
> Our said Councell to take all possible care for ye discountenancing of
> vice, & incouraging of vertue & good living; that by such examples y^e
> infidel may be invited & desire to partake of ye Christian Religion, &
> for ye greater ease and satisfac'on of o^r s^d loving subjects in matters of
> Religion We do hereby will, require & com'and y^t liberty of conscience

shall be allowed unto all protestants: & y^t such especially as shall be conformable to ye rites of ye Church of Engl^d, shall be particularly countenanced & incouraged.[114]

No group in the four towns of New Hampshire took up the offer of Anglican favoritism. The next time there was any significant ecclesiastical activity that was initiatory in nature was when the Exeter-2 First Church regathered itself in September 1698.[115]

The third novelty is the fact that now the Crown was requiring that the newly established president and council of New Hampshire send back to England their governance documents for review and possible modification or veto on the part of either the king himself or the Privy Council:

> . . . and Lastly our will & pleasure is that the saide president & Counsill for ye time being doe prepare & send into England such *** & methods for theire one prosedings as maye best suite with the Constitution of the saide province of newhamshire — for ye better establishing of Our authority theire and the goverment thereof that wee and our privi Councill maye examin & allter or aprove the same. . . .[116]

The use of the phrase "ye better establishing of Our authority theire" indicates that the Crown was trying to control matters in regions that up until this time it had considered marginal.

Charles II, however, did not live to see the results of the charter revocation in the Massachusetts Bay. He died on Friday, February 6, 1684/5. Since he had no legitimate children, the throne passed to his brother, James II, the Duke of York and the second son of Charles I and Henrietta Maria. James had been raised an Anglican in a family with a Roman Catholic mother, and in 1668 or 1669 he was admitted to the communion of the Church of Rome. Charles II insisted that his brother continue to receive the Anglican sacraments until 1672, and James attended Anglican services until 1676. Despite his conversion to Roman Catholicism, both of his daughters were raised as Protestants, and both became reigning Queens of England: Mary II, from 1689 to 1694 and Anne, from 1702 to 1714.

We should recall that James had already been given control of a vast tract of territory that stretched from the southern tip of New Jersey up to the St. Lawrence River and included the islands bordering on New England (Long Island, Martha's Vineyard, Nantucket). Since 1664, James's holdings had essentially formed a ring of royal authority around New England. With his accession to the throne he proceeded to rule Old England in the style of his father, but unlike his progenitor he also sought to establish that form of rule not only at the center of English society but on the margins as well. The person who was to effect this new agenda on the margins — the colonies of northeast North America — was Sir Edmund Andros.[117] The outcome of these and similar policies in both Old and New England led to the abdication of James II in 1688 and to the "Glorious Revolution" of 1688-89.

It is not our purpose in this chapter to explore in detail the administration of Andros, which lasted from December 1686 until April 1689, a period of a little over two years. This period was, however, a time of tremendous crisis in New England. James issued a commission to Andros on Thursday, June 3, 1686, one and one-half years after James's accession to the throne.[118] This was renewed on Saturday, April 7, 1688.[119] An examination of the two documents reveals that James said nothing concerning religion, church, and state. He did, however, essentially sweep away the authority of all previous governance documents and place absolute authority in the hands of Andros as James's personal vice regent.[120] Accelerating a drive for absolute monarchical power at a far more rapid rate than his ill-fated father, James II made Andros "Captain Generall and Governor" of the Dominion of New England[121] and gave him "full power and authority to suspend any member of our Councill from sitting voting and assisting therein, as . . . {he should} find just cause for so doing."[122] Furthermore, Andros was authorized to establish laws that were then to be reported to England for royal approval:

> And Wee do hereby give and grant unto you full power and authority, by and with the advise and consent of our said Councill or the major part of them, to make constitute and ordain lawes statutes and ordinances for the public peace welfare and good governm[t] of our said territory & dominion and of the people and inhabitants thereof, and such others as shall resort thereto, and for the benefit of us, our heires and successors. Which said lawes statutes and ordinances, are to be, as near as conveniently may be, aggreeable to the lawes & statutes of this our kingdom of England: Provided that all such lawes statutes and ordinances of what nature or duration soever, be within three months, or sooner, after the making of the same, transmitted unto Us, under our Seal of New England, for our allowance or disapprobation of them, as also duplicates thereof by the next conveyance.[123]

Among other privileges Andros was given the power to tax and to establish tax rates — a feature of his commission that would add fuel to the fire of New England's indignation. All of the other rights and privileges that had been granted in the various charters over the previous seventy-eight years to groups of people, whether they were mercantile companies or colonial legislatures, were now transferred to one person, the personal representative of the king. Andros's commission, styled as "letters patents,"[124] ended with the reiteration of his appointment as "Captain Generall and Governor in Cheif," and the entire document paved the way for his autocratic blunders that have become legendary.[125]

During his brief time as Captain General and Governor in Chief Andros did not expend a lot of effort to limit the Congregational Way in New England. The Board of Trade intended that religious liberty be promulgated in the Dominion of New England and that the Church of England was to be "encouraged."[126] Andros's strategy in reclaiming the entire northeast region of North America was to establish a beachhead at Boston, the symbolic center of resistance, and then work at overcoming resistance in the rest of New England. He concluded that he could govern much more docile and submissive colonies like New York from a distance. Boston therefore became the capital of the new Dominion of New England. Therefore, while communities all over New England and their respective colonies had cause for concern regarding the Andros administration, they were not affected in the same way that Boston was.

Andros lost no time in establishing the Church of England in Boston. The afternoon of his inauguration day, Monday, December 20, 1686, Andros proposed that one of the Boston meeting houses be shared for both Puritan and Anglican worship. Andros met immediate resistance, and during the ensuing winter the Anglicans met in the Deputies Chamber of the Boston Town House, the building where the general court of the Massachusetts Bay Colony met and which was also the center of Boston's civil government. Finally, on Wednesday, March 23, 1686/7, the keys to the building of the Third or Old South Church of Boston were confiscated and the building was used for Anglican worship according to the rites found in the *Book of Common Prayer* until Andros was overthrown two years and one month later.[127] The congregation of Boston Third Church was allowed to use its building only when the Anglican services were not in progress. The arbitrary seizure of the building and the usurpation of authority over its use was offensive, but what sparked the anger of the entire colony even more than the control of the church's property was the knowl-

edge that worship repugnant to the Puritan conscience was being coer-
cively offered in space that had been reserved for Puritan worship. Judge
Sewall articulated the ire of New England well when he spoke with one of
Andros's assistants about land that Andros wanted to expropriate for an
Anglican church:

> Captain [Benjamin] Davis spake to me for Land to set a Church on. I
> told him could not, would not, put Mr. Cotton's Land to such an use,
> and besides, 'twas Entail'd. After, Mr. Randolph saw me, and had me to
> his House to see the Landscips of Oxford Colledges and Halls. Left me
> with Mr. Ratcliff, who spake to me for Land at Cotton-Hill for a Church
> which were going to build: I told him I could not, first because I would
> not set up that which the People of N.E. came over to avoid: 2d the
> Land was Entail'd. In after discourse I mentioned chiefly the Cross in
> Baptism and Holy Dayes.[128]

Instead of focusing in on the judicial rights of the congregation, something
a judge might be inclined to do, Sewall rather focused in on the question of
purity of worship, an issue at the very heart of the Puritan conscience and
raison d'etre. The perspective of Edward Randolph, a devoted Anglican and
royalist who supervised the vacating of the charter and paved the way for
the coming of Andros, also affirms that the central issue of conflict was
worship:

> Boston, New England, Augt 2nd, 1686.

> . . . Their ministry exclaim against ye common prayer, calling it man's in-
> vention, and that there is more hopes the whoremongers and adulterers
> will go to heaven than those of ye C. of Eng. By these wicked doctrines
> they poison the people, and their ministry carry it as high as ever.[129]

Mercifully for the New Englanders, the Andros regime came to an end on
Thursday and Friday, April 18 and 19, 1689; Andros had been in power for
only a little over two years. Led (significantly) by five clergy of Boston,
along with other prominent leaders of the town, a Committee of Public
Safety was formed and took control not only of Boston but also of the entire
Massachusetts Bay Colony. Andros was sent home to England. He was re-
leased without formal trial by the Lords of the Committee for Trade and
Plantations. From 1692 to 1698 he served as Governor of Virginia, during

which time he founded the College of William and Mary. After serving as the Governor of the Island of Jersey from 1704 to 1706, he died in London in 1713/14.[130]

Life returned to normal for much of New England during the spring and summer of 1689. Connecticut, Rhode Island, New Hampshire, and Maine had their governance restored under the authority of the patents and charters issued to them in the pre-Andros period. Such was not the case for the Massachusetts Bay and Plymouth colonies. New Plymouth Colony never had a royal charter,[131] and the Massachusetts Bay Colony had had its royal charter vacated and nullified even before the death of Charles II. Reverend Increase Mather was therefore commissioned by the Massachusetts Bay Colony to go to London and negotiate a new charter for the Massachusetts Bay.[132] It took two years to accomplish the task, but on Saturday, October 3, 1691, Westminster issued a charter that united the New Plymouth Colony and the Massachusetts Bay Colony into one corporate body called the Massachusetts Bay Province.[133] An examination of the charter reveals that in the historical prologue of the charter the advisers and lawyers of William and Mary resurrected the precedent of the 1620 Great Charter of New England issued to the Council for New England, made defunct by Mary's grandfather Charles I in the 1630s.[134]

The 1691 charter differs significantly from the 1629 charter in several ways. After a lengthy historical prologue, the charter immediately turns to the matter of geography and expands the geographical authority of the Massachusetts Bay Province — at least in theory. The Crown combined Maine, New Brunswick, and Nova Scotia (also known as Acadia) and made it the northern sector of the province.[135] Only New Hampshire stood in the way. Maine continued as a part of Massachusetts until the Missouri Compromise in 1820, when it was admitted as a free state of the Union and Missouri was admitted a slave state. Nova Scotia was released from the authority of the Massachusetts Bay in 1713, and New Brunswick came out of Nova Scotia in 1784.[136] During the period 1691 to 1714, Nova Scotia and what is now New Brunswick had only a few marginal communities that were devoted mainly to fishing and trading, and the Massachusetts authorities paid little attention to that sector of the province.[137] No Puritan congregational churches were established in any of the communities in New Brunswick or Nova Scotia during this interval.

The second significant difference from the earlier charter is the establishment of new criteria for admission to the franchise. Setting aside the requirement of the Massachusetts Bay Colony that only church members be allowed to participate in civil government,[138] the charter stipulated a property requirement:

> . . . noe Freeholder or other Person shall have a Vote in the Elecc~on of Members to serve in any Greate or Generall Courte or Assembly to be held as aforesaid who at the time of such Elecc~on shall not have an estate of Freehold in Land within Our said Province or Territory to the value of Forty Shillings per Annu at the least or other estate to the value of Forty pounds Sterl'.[139]

It should be noted that the term "Freeman," with its connotation of church membership, had been changed to "Freeholder," implying that property and financial status were the criteria by which eligibility for the franchise was to be determined.

The third major modification found in the 1691 charter was that the major executive officers — governor, lieutenant or deputy governor, and secretary — were now to be appointed by the Crown. Furthermore, the royal governor had veto power over any legislation that the General Court brought.[140] A further check on the legislation was that the Crown itself reserved veto power for a period of three years over legislation passed by the Massachusetts legislature.

In the matter of religion, church, and state, the Crown also exercised its prerogative decisively — this time in the direction of greater liberty, at least for Protestants in general. Specifically excluded from any legal standing in the colony were Roman Catholics:

> . . . and for the greater Ease and Encouragement of Our Loveing Subjects Inhabiting our said Province or Territory of the Massachusetts Bay and of such as shall come to inhabit there Wee doe by these presents for vs Our heires and Successors Grant Establish and Ordaine that for ever hereafter there shall be a liberty of Conscience allowed in the Worshipp of God to all Christians (Except Papists) Inhabiting or which shall Inhabit or be Resident within our said Province or Territory.[141]

We need to remember, however, that there was still an established religion in the Massachusetts Bay — trinitarian Christianity — and that there was still an established Christian church governed in a congregational manner. The only thing that the 1691 charter granted was liberty in the realm of worship. The Baptists, Anglicans, and Quakers could therefore establish their own religious institutions without interference from the civil magistrate, and if these dissenters did not appear for worship at the established Congregational church on Sunday morning they could not be prosecuted. The charter said nothing about the system of compulsory tithes for the established church, leaving that matter up to the colonial authorities. The net result in Massachusetts was that dissenters like Baptists and Quakers ended up paying two tithes: one to the local parochial Congregational church in the town where they were located, and the other to the congregation to which they had bound themselves for conscience' sake. Quakers especially resented this, and in unflagging exasperation kept detailed and lengthy records of "Meetings for Sufferings," a communal lament at which they listed the goods or money taken from them for the rates to support the local Congregational minister ("the priest's rate").[142] Dissenters, therefore, could be prosecuted for not paying their tithes or for disturbing the public worship of the established church or for breaking the sanctity of the Sabbath day, even if they had a different theological understanding of the Sabbath or its practice. In certain respects they were second-class citizens, and their religious institutions were relegated to the outer margins of society: they did not have the support of the civil establishment, they did not get the best piece of land at the center of town for their church buildings, nor were they invited to help govern Harvard College, let alone be instructors there. Nevertheless, the dissenters of the period after 1691 had a much easier life than the Antinomians of the 1630s and the Quakers and Baptists of the 1650s and 1660s. The provisions concerning church, state, and religion in the Massachusetts charter of 1691 are a mirror image of the Toleration Act of 1689, a statute that exempted persons who took the Oaths of Allegiance and Supremacy from the penalties of existing laws against conventicles and that also released dissenting ministers from religious impediments provided they signed the Thirty-nine Articles of the Church of England.[143] In that mirror image, however, those who would be dissenters in Old England had hegemony in New England, and their detractors in New England were either more radical dissenters (Baptists, Quakers) or displaced, expatriate Anglicans.

The charters issued to the various New England colonies by the government of Old England between 1606 and 1691 set parameters for religious activity and the role of the church and the state on both a colonial and a local level. They were legal documents, drafted by lawyers, and, while tedious, were precise and comprehensive. The Crown lawyers had access to the "files" of Whitehall and Westminster, and therefore could craft the documents utilizing precedent. The charters display standard legal phraseology, but the variations in terms indicate that they were not rubber stamps of royal authority but reflected a carefully thought-out agenda. While the documents were issued by superiors (Crown, Parliament, and groups of merchants) to subordinates (other merchants and, later, legislatures), the fact that there were variations in terms, particularly in the areas of religion, church, and state, indicates that the subordinate parties negotiated with the superior parties over these issues and the superior party allowed a certain amount of give and take in these critical areas. The leadership of each colony read these documents thoroughly and were conversant with them; they did not simply collect dust in a corner as ceremonial and symbolic texts.

The New Englanders had greater flexibility during the first part of the seventeenth century with respect to religious matters than their Puritan colleagues in Old England had; however, as the historical situation changed and the century progressed the Crown started to enter into the affairs of each colony more intimately and colonial policies concerning church, state, and religion more closely reflected what was going on in the old country. All through the century Old England was moving towards a fluid situation in which there was an established state religion with an official state church, along with (reluctant) allowance for dissent. The New England colonies followed that pattern as well.

New England missed the first attempt of the 1630s to centralize the English monarchy into a powerful, absolute entity — a major purpose of the Great Migration was to avoid "the Antichrist," and they did so. However, the second attempt in the 1680s truly was a frightening moment for all of New England: in one fell swoop James II essentially awarded personal rule like that of Charles I to Sir Edmund Andros — the only time a New England charter or patent granted unchecked absolute power concerning laws, taxes, religion, church, and state to one individual.[144] Besides the veiled intention of centralizing absolute power into the monarchy, there was a more public intention on the part of James II (and Charles II before him), of wanting to tighten the grasp around New England because of aggressive French encroachment on English colonies in all parts of the world. James II, however, became so offensive to so many people so quickly that he was pushed off the throne, and by that time Parliament had become so powerful that it could effectively neutralize the king's designs.

By 1692, the policies concerning church, state, and religion in the New England colonies more closely reflected the policies of Old England after the Glorious Revolution of 1688-89, with the exception that the variety of Christian church that had hegemony over a particular colony was a different "denomination" from the Church of England. Instead of forcing the colony to accept the Church of England as the only lawful state church, Parliament, Whitehall, and Canterbury allowed each colony to have its own state-supported church and its own version of Christianity as the official religion of the colony. The one proviso was that each colony had to allow freedom of worship for dissenting Protestant groups, whether they be Anglican, Baptist, Quaker, or Presbyterian. It should be noted, however, that freedom of worship did not entail disestablishment of religion and secularization of institutional life, nor did it prohibit each colony from making life difficult for dissenters to the established state church: Baptists, Quakers, and Anglicans still had to pay the compulsory tithes, and there were no laws protecting dissenting religious groups from bias. Harvard could therefore quietly refuse to admit Quakers and towns had every right to not elect Baptists to civil office on account of religious belief and conviction. Civil affairs functioned with the blessing and guidance of the state church, and dissenters had their houses of worship on the side streets of town and not on the town square.

A summary of the situation in each colony is now in order; we will move from north to south. By 1692, the experiment to make Maine an Anglican colony had failed. Congregationalists from the southern sector of New England certainly had not migrated there, and Anglicans in Old England had not felt the urge to migrate in the same way that Puritans had: even during the Interregnum Anglicans had no impetus to settle a region just north of an area where Puritans were dominant. The lack of a critical mass of committed Anglicans willing to come and settle Maine added to the premonition of governmental change in the region: in 1692, the Anglican colony of Gorgeana was dissolved and placed under the authority of the Massachusetts Bay Province.[145] This time, however, the charter under which Maine was now governed was the 1692 charter and not the 1629 charter. New Hampshire in 1692 had been a separate royal province since 1679, and it would continue as such until 1776. The Crown appointed its governor, and its laws and charters, along with capital criminal cases, were subject to the review of the authorities in London. The Church of England was legally the favored church, but no Anglican church was founded in New Hampshire during the period 1680 to 1708, and all other Protestants had "liberty of conscience" in matters of religion. What "liberty of conscience" entailed was not spelled out explicitly, but the Crown was aware that the four current towns of New Hampshire were dominated by Puritans and not Anglicans. Freedom of worship was therefore most certainly countenanced, but technically the Congregational churches of the four towns were no longer the established state churches. Nevertheless, if the Puritan conscience desired to influence the public and civic life of the colony, it had every right to do so, as long as it did so within the parameters developed by the Crown and by Parliament.

The Massachusetts Bay Colony and the New Plymouth Colony had undergone the most substantial change by the year 1692. The nerve center of dissent to Anglicanism, and certainly the most populous region of New England, the two colonies were perpetually resented by royal and ecclesiastical authorities in Old England. New Plymouth Colony never did receive a royal charter, and Massachusetts Bay Colony had its charter vacated in 1684. The death of Charles II prevented the consequences of the vacation of the charter to be developed immediately, but in 1686 James II sent over Edmund Andros to set up the Dominion of New England; the capital of the new entity was Boston. The revolution against Andros, along with the Glorious Revolution against James II, prevented an absolute vice-monarchy to be set up in New England and in the Massachusetts region. However, the accession of William and Mary and the many Parliamentary moves made during the period 1689-91 did not nullify the vacation of the charter for the Massachusetts Bay. When the dust had settled, the grandchildren of the New Plymouth Separatists had been merged with the grandchildren of the Massachusetts Bay non-separating Puritans to form the Massachusetts Bay Province. As in New Hampshire, London appointed the governor, and the Massachusetts Bay Province was required to allow liberty of conscience in matters of worship to other Protestants even though the established state church was the Congregational church and the established state religion was trinitarian Christianity. Furthermore, the Crown erased the limitation of the franchise and service in public office to church members only: a property requirement was substituted, and males who qualified were no longer "freemen" but were "freeholders."

Rhode Island returned to its 1663 charter as soon as Edmund Andros was deposed, and it continued with its policy of no established state church, a policy that had been established in Providence in 1637-39. Nevertheless, the "lively experiment" that it initiated was not an experiment in modern secularism. Rather, it was an early modern experiment in which the "enemies of the Christian faith" would be defeated by a government based on "true piety rightly grounded upon gospel principles." The Rhode Islanders hoped that the internalized principles of Christian faith would spill over into civic virtue, but not impede upon the right of private conscience and freedom of worship.

The strictest of the New England colonies, the New Haven Colony, had dissolved in the wake of the Restoration and was merged with the Connecticut Colony in 1665. It had lasted only a quarter of a century. Those who wished to continue the New Haven vision founded Newark and Elizabeth, New Jersey; ironically, by 1692, the First Congregational Churches of both settlements were moving in the direction of Presbyterianism, and in the next generation annexed themselves to the main body of Presbyterians.[146]

Like Rhode Island, Connecticut Colony returned to its 1662 charter, and in some sense the Connecticut situation changed least in the seventeenth century. The 1662 charter said nothing about religion, church, and state, and that state of affairs continued until 1818. Connecticut did not revise its charter during or after the American Revolution, nor did it tamper with it in the wake of the constitutional convention of 1789. The Congregational church was the *de facto* established church, and the formulation concerning church, state, and religion in Connecticut was that found in the Fundamental Orders of Connecticut articulated in 1639 by the towns of Hartford, Wethersfield, and Windsor. The Fundamental Orders, which we shall look at in the next chapter, were explicitly Christian and Congregational. Perhaps the reason the Crown said nothing concerning religion, church, and state in the Connecticut charter while it was saying much more concerning such matters in the 1663 Rhode Island charter is that Connecticut had not whipped Baptists out of their environs nor had they hung Quakers, as the Massachusetts Bay Colony had done during the Interregnum.

The relationship between religion, specifically Christianity, church, and state varied from colony to colony in New England. The New Englanders took advantage of a surprisingly *laissez-faire* policy on the part of James I and Charles I to formulate what each colony wanted with respect to these matters. As the century progressed and New England came to be seen as part of a larger first English empire, and then first British empire, Old England became increasingly interested in what was going on across the ocean. However, chastened by the upheavals of the middle decades of 1630 to 1662, Whitehall, Westminster, and Lambeth Palace did not impose a unified Anglican vision on the colonies during the second half of the century. Rather, each colony negotiated with the Crown separately for its legitimacy, and the give and take over the matter of religion, church, and state was one of the chief bargaining chips in each individual case. The Crown, along with the Anglicans of Old England, were increasingly interested in economic matters during the latter half of the century, while the Puritans of New England were anxious to preserve the freedom they had experienced in the earlier part of the century to make their own arrangements over religion, church, and state. The Crown did not put into effect the parliamentary Clarendon Codes in New England, and it continued to allow dissenters to develop their hegemony in New England, but together with the Crown the colonies forged a new covenant after the Revolution and the Interregnum, a covenant that gave each colony freedom in matters of religion but that allowed religious dissenters to exist undisturbed as second-class citizens. Indeed, that was the only policy concerning religion, church, and state that united all of the colonies after 1692.

Given these parameters of freedom, and seeing how they changed over time, we must now look at what the New Englanders themselves did on a colonial level as they worked within these boundaries. We will now move on to the civil covenants generated from the grass roots up, that is, covenants spawned in New England on site.

∾ 3 ∾

The Civil Covenants of Early New England

> God gracious be to us, & give
> his blessing us unto,
> let him upon us make to shine
> his countenance also. Selah.
> That there may be the knowledg of
> thy way the earth upon,
> and also of thy saving health
> in every nation.
> O God let thee the people prayse,
> let all people prayse thee.
> O let the nations rejoyce,
> and let them joyfull bee:
> For thou shalt give judgement unto
> the people righteously,
> also the nations upon earth
> thou shalt them lead safely. Selah.
> O God let thee the people prayse
> let all people prayse thee.
> Her fruitfull increase by the earth
> shall then forth yeilded bee:
> God ev'n our owne God shall us blesse.
> God I say blesse us shall,
> and of the earth the utmost coasts
> they shall him reverence all.

(Psalm 67; Bay Psalm Book)

We have seen that the colonial charters and patents were formal legal covenants that were comprehensive and precise in their legal terminology and
language. They extended formal legal privileges to civil and economic corporations, whether they be small plantations or large colonies. They also
carried with them the authority of Crown or Parliament, and were generated by a higher authority for a lesser authority. But that is only part of the
picture of the civil covenant in seventeenth-century New England. An examination of many "Town Books" and early town records reveal four types
of civil covenants that established local civil government: combination or
compact, charter, patent, and legislative action.

Appendix 1 lists the extant New England civil covenants for the period
1620 to 1708, while Table 1 summarizes that information by category: As we
look at the approximately 101 civil covenants that survive, we find that, unlike many of the church covenants, there is no uniform model that all of them
follow, save for the covenants that are charters and patents and were therefore
patterned on legal precedents. Nor is there a formulary that serves as a para-
digm for these documents, as is the case in the ecclesiastical covenants that
we will examine. As we consider various examples, however, we will see re-
current themes and concerns that are common to all of them. In particular, as
we have done for the early colonial charters, we will look for the configurations of church, state, and religion that are outlined in their clauses.

Table 1
Typology and Enumeration of Surviving New England
Local Civil Covenants, 1620-1708

	Combination/ Compact	Charter	Legislative Record	Patent
1620-1640	20	0	2	0
1641-1660	18	6	1	3
1661-1680	18	8	1	12
1681-1700	2	1	11	12
1700-1708	2	1	0	5
Totals	60	16	15	32

While the legal charters discussed in the previous chapter provided
the framework for the New England colonies, the colonists found that once

they arrived, there was no central governing authority or office of the Crown to which to turn. They were left to their own devices to formulate and develop a local civil government. As new towns were formed, the original local governments of the plantations founded from 1620 to 1650 soon realized that they could not supervise neighboring towns, and so central colonial governments emerged out of the original town governments, with the original plantation or town now tending to its own local affairs. In the absence of a strong central civil authority, the colonists established their own local governments by combination or compact. But gradually, the local towns began to rely upon that central government for legitimation of the town's existence. This chapter will therefore focus upon two groups of documents. The first group will be the combinations and compacts generated by the early New Englanders. The second group will be the patents and legislative statutes granted by the central colonial governments to the towns. Generally, the combinations and compacts appear during the earlier part of the seventeenth century; the patents and legislative statutes from the central government appear during the latter half of the century.[1]

While the Plymouth Plantation, the New Plymouth Colony, and the Mayflower Compact are subjects of prodigious study in American history, we cannot consider the topic of the civil covenant without exploring in some detail the document signed on Saturday, November 11, 1620.[2] We will therefore begin our discussion with an examination of the genesis of the New Plymouth Plantation and Colony.[3]

The original document of the Mayflower Compact does not survive. The earliest written text that we have of this document is found in *Mourt's Relation,* published in London in 1622, but in that recension no signers are listed.[4] Nathaniel Morton published the text and signers in his 1669 history of New Plymouth. The volume is entitled *New England's Memorial* and was also published in London. We must remember, however, that its publication came half a century after the events of 1620.[5] William Bradford records the text of the Mayflower Compact in his manuscript "Of Plymouth Plantation, 1620-1647"; that rendition records the list of passengers on the *Mayflower* but not the signers.[6] Thus, the earliest text of the Mayflower Compact that we have dates to 1622, while the earliest list of signers can be dated to a source forty-nine years after the fact.[7] But although Nathaniel Morton was not an eyewitness to the events (he came to New Plymouth at the age of eleven in 1623), he probably was working from the original manuscript of the compact. Morton's aunt, his mother's sister, married Governor William Bradford in 1623. Because Morton's father died in 1624, Morton was then

adopted into the William Bradford home, where he developed a close relationship with Bradford. In 1634, at age twenty-one, Morton became Bradford's clerk and amanuensis, a position he held until Bradford's death in
1657. From December 1647 to his death in 1685, Morton was Secretary and
Keeper of the Records for New Plymouth Colony. He held a similar position
in Plymouth First Church.[8] Because of his official status and his familial
connections, his listing of the signers has gone unchallenged.

It is well known that the Separatists of the New Plymouth Colony had
originated in Scrooby, England, and had settled in Leyden, Holland, during
the period following 1609. After nine years or so of living in Holland, a substantial number had decided that their future lay in the New World. The
Leyden Separatists had many discussions as they embarked upon their plan.
Bradford indicates that ultimately two regions were selected as possible sites
for a plantation. Some of the group wanted to go to Guyana; the problem
with that site, of course, was that the Spanish would push them out. The
other group wanted to go to Virginia. The objections raised about Virginia
centered around the free exercise of their religion. They feared that the Virginia authorities might treat them as if they were in England, or worse than
if they were in England. However, if they lived too far away from the protection of the English, they would enjoy neither economic sustenance or the
defense offered by their fellow countrymen.[9] They finally chose to live next
to their Anglican colleagues instead of the Roman Catholic Spaniards, but
determined to locate their plantation outside of the immediate gaze of the
Virginia Colony. Bradford describes the decision in this manner:

> But at length the conclusion was to live as a distinct body by them-
> selves under the general Government of Virginia; and by their friends
> to sue to His Majesty that he would be pleased to grant them freedom
> of religion. And that this might be obtained they were put in good hope
> by some great persons of good rank and quality that were made their
> friends. Whereupon two were chosen . . . and sent into England (at the
> charge of the rest) to solicit this matter, who found the Virginia Com-
> pany very desirable to have them go thither and willing to grant them a
> patent, with as ample privileges as they had or could grant to any; and
> to give them the best furtherance they could. And some of the chief of
> that Company doubted not to obtain their suit of the King for liberty in
> religion, and to have it confirmed under the King's broad seal, accord-
> ing to their desires. But it proved a harder piece of work than they took
> it for; for though many means were used to bring it about, yet it could

not be effected. For there were divers of good worth laboured with the King to obtain it, amongst whom was one of his chief secretaries, Sir Robert Naunton. And some others wrought with the Archbishop to give way thereunto, but it proved all in vain. Yet thus far they prevailed, in sounding His Majesty's mind, that he would connive at them and not molest them, provided they carried themselves peacably. But to allow or tolerate them by his public authority, under his seal, they found it would not be.[10]

The two men sent to England were John Carver and Robert Cushman.[11] They returned to Holland with the news of the Virginia Company's willingness to grant a patent but Westminster and Canterbury's unwillingness to grant a formal guarantee of freedom of religion to the Leyden group. Nevertheless, James I had indicated by word of mouth that he would informally tolerate the Separatists by ignoring them ("connive at them"). Without a written guarantee, however, the Leyden people knew that at the time of James's death that policy could immediately change. The term "freedom of religion" should be used with qualifications here: the Leyden group desired freedom of religion in the areas of worship, doctrine, and ecclesiastical governance for their own group exclusively. While they may not have had a state church in mind, they were fleeing the Netherlands, where they felt that freedom of religion for groups and for individuals had turned into moral license, chaos, and ecclesiastical disarray.

Since James I had not officially granted religious freedom, not all of the Leyden group wanted to accept the proposal from the Virginia Company. However, four possible scenarios were laid out that persuaded the protesters to accede to it. The first scenario was one that they did not follow, and that was to not petition the Crown for religious freedom. The possible consequence in that case was that Westminster could actively prosecute an attack upon the plantation both legally and militarily. The second scenario was to ask the monarchy for religious freedom, to be rejected, and to not go. The third possible scenario was to petition for religious freedom, to be rejected with some qualification, but to move forward anyway and hope for the best. The fourth possible alternative was to petition the Crown, have the petition for religious freedom granted, but then to have Westminster find some other excuse to assault the plantation and to go back on its word. While many in the Leyden company wanted a royal guarantee of freedom of religion, the fourth scenario was pointed out to them as a distinct possibility. Ultimately, the Leyden Pilgrims selected the third option.

The next step in the process was to secure a formal agreement with the Virginia Company and then to begin to raise capital from sympathetic friends who were wealthy. Messengers were again sent, "for which end they had instructions given them upon what conditions they should proceed with them, or else to conclude nothing without further advice."[12] Westminster and Canterbury evidently put immediate pressure on the Virginia Company to inquire of the Leyden Separatists about their views of religion, for Cushman and Carver returned from Leyden to England carrying a document signed by John Robinson and William Brewster that indicated the degree to which the Separatists were willing to conform to the polity and doctrine of the Church of England. These articles, dating to 1617, reveal that these Separatists were perhaps not as separated from the Church of England as might be imagined by some.[13] The first article acquiesces in recognizing the Thirty-nine Articles of the Church of England as a valid confession. Since the Westminster standards developed by Puritans and Presbyterians were not articulated until the 1640s, this affirmation is not that striking. It would not be until after the Westminster Assembly that Puritans, Presbyterians, Congregationalists, and Baptists would build an agenda shaped by the Westminster standards.

The second affirmation, however, indicates that the Separatists desired to keep "spirituall communion" with the Church of England; further, they resolved that they would "pracktis in our parts all lawfull thinges."[14] What these lawful things were was not indicated, but they should be read against the backdrop of the Puritan and Reformed agenda. At the heart of the Puritan platform was a concern for the worship of God and its purity. Within the Protestant world, two schools of thought had emerged over the issue of worship. The first school, represented by the Lutherans and Anglicans, concluded that what was not forbidden in the Scripture was permitted in the worship service. Thus, both Lutherans and Anglicans utilized a modified and simplified form of the mass in their worship service and permitted three-dimensional statues and two-dimensional pictures of Jesus, Mary, and various saints in church buildings. Furthermore, they followed a written liturgy and retained the outlines of the church calendar in their worship practices. The second school, represented by Puritans, Presbyterians, Congregationalists, and Baptists, concluded that what was not explicitly commanded (what was not "lawful") was forbidden in the worship of God. Following, therefore, what is termed the regulative principle of worship, their worship service did not in any way reflect the medieval mass. No statues or pictures were permitted in the worship building ("Thou shalt not make vnto thee any grauen Image, or any likenesse of anything that is in heauen aboue, or that is in the earth beneath, or that is in the water vnder the earth. Thou shalt not bow downe they selfe to them, nor serue them . . ." Exodus 20:4-5a). In place of a prayer book that outlined a liturgy and from which prayers were read, the Puritan worship service consisted of extemporaneous prayer, the reading of scripture, the singing of the Psalms of the Old Testament, a lengthy and detailed sermon, and the giving of tithes and offerings. No vestments were worn by the clergy, and there was no choir; instead, the congregation sang *a capella* as a united body from a psalter. While both Anglicans and Puritans had these "lawful" elements of worship in their weekly service — prayer, scripture reading, psalm singing, a sermon, the offering — the Puritans objected to the embellishments that were added to the worship service by the Anglicans, additions that the Puritans said were not commanded by God in scripture.[15]

The desire of the Leyden Separatists to have "spiritual communion" with the Church of England belies a desire on their part to be free of tangible, ecclesiastical communion with the state church. In some sense, their quarrel was more with the archbishop of Canterbury and the Convocation of Bishops than it was with the monarch: they did not want Canterbury sending authorities over to North America who would supervise their worship, doctrine, and church government. They were willing to accede somewhat, however, to the requirements of the monarch concerning their ecclesiastical life, and to continue to have a vague sort of "spiritual" communion with the established church. They therefore recognized the Thirty-nine Articles, emphasized that their separatistic church shared the elements of worship common to all Christian churches, and acknowledged begrudgingly that the Church of England could be considered a true church — otherwise they would not be able to have even "spiritual" communion. Furthermore, in the fourth and fifth articles they reluctantly acknowledged that the power of bishops was legal.[16]

While they kept the state church at arm's length, the Leyden Separatists took pains both in this 1617 document and in the 1620 Mayflower Compact itself to acknowledge the authority of the monarch and the civil magistrate. As Reformed Christians, they knew that the New Testament commanded them to obey the civil magistrate and all who were in authority (Romans 13). Thus, the fourth of the Seven Articles affirmed obedience to the king, and the seventh article promised that the members of the Leyden congregation would give "untto all Superiors dew honor."[17] The only exception would be if the monarch of the government commanded them to do something "against God's Word" — such as conform to the worship of the Church of England. At that point, they would feel duty-bound to disobey the government and resolve to follow the example of the apostles Peter and John who said to the Sanhedrin that they must obey God rather than men (Acts 4:19; 5:29).

The final affirmation that the Leyden Separatists had to make can be found in the sixth article. There, they further acknowledged the king's authority by agreeing to the principle that no synod or other body could have ecclesiastical jurisdiction except by the king's authority. The Separatists were already committed to the congregational form of church government, and therefore the ecclesiastical jurisdiction that they set up was limited to their congregation only — hardly a threat to the dominant hierarchy. Westminster and Canterbury were fearful, however, of the threat of the presbyterian governance structure threatening to take over the Church of England, and while congregationalism was in principle opposed to the interference of synods or other regional governing bodies, the authorities in London considered Separatists and Presbyterians to be of the same stripe. The 1617 articles were concessions made to the Virginia Company, not to the Crown or to Parliament. The articles did, however, depart from the stance that the Separatists had historically held and that continued to be held by many of the more dedicated members of the Leyden Separatist church.[18]

Cushman and Carver came to the conclusion that even though the Seven Articles satisfied the Virginia Company, they needed more time and more consultation, and so they returned to Leyden. Sir Edwin Sandys, a member of the Virginia Company, wrote a letter to Robinson and Brewster on Monday, November 17, 1617, that complimented the work of Cushman and Carver and encouraged the Leyden congregation in their endeavor.[19] Knowing that Sandys was wealthy, influential, and helpful to their cause, Robinson and Brewster responded with a letter outlining their determination to push ahead with the project and not to waste the good will that Sandys had extended toward them. At that point they described their project in covenantal terms, because they wanted to assure Sandys that they were utterly serious in this endeavor:

> 4. We Are knit together as a body in a most strict and sacred bond and covenant of the Lord, of the violation whereof we make great conscience, and by virtue whereof we do hold ourselves straitly tied to all care of each other's good and of the whole, by every one and so mutually.[20]

Little did Robinson and Brewster know how strained those covenantal ties would become in the next three years.

At some point in late 1617 or early 1618 a patent was granted by the Virginia Company to the Leyden Separatists. Regrettably, no copy of this document survives. However, because the Leyden group did not end up anywhere close to Jamestown, Virginia, the patent was never used. At about the same time in early 1618, the Leyden group held a day of prayer and fasting "to seek the Lord for His direction."[21] While the Virginia Company had given its consent, it also had made further inquiries concerning some of the points of the Seven Articles. The queries were made at the instigation of some of the members of the Privy Council, who were not totally satisfied concerning three points: church polity, the Oath of Supremacy, and the administration of baptism. On Tuesday, January 27, 1617/18, Robinson and Brewster therefore wrote a letter to Sir John Wolstonholme, a member of the Council for Virginia, which was the governing body for the Virginia Company. In the letter, Robinson and Brewster defended themselves against what they termed "unjust insinuations" and stated that they were in agreement with most of the polity of the French Reformed Church (an ally that might actually raise the eyebrows of the officials of England). Of far greater significance was the fact that they assured the Virginia Company that they would be willing to take the Oath of Supremacy in addition to the Oath of Allegiance if they were required to do so: "The oath of Supremacy we shall willingly take if it be required of us, and that convenient satisfaction be not given by our taking the oath of Allegiance."[22] In essence, therefore, they were willing to acknowledge the monarch as the supreme governor in matters ecclesiastical as well as temporal, and at least technically to admit that he had the final say in the matters of their separated church. Ultimately, in order to fulfill their desire for a plantation in the New World, where they could covenant with God and with one another, this particular group of Separatists was willing to enter into a covenant with authorities who had been deemed so evil that the Separatists had resolved to separate from them in earlier years.

Two weeks later, on Saturday, February 14, 1617/18, Sabine Staresmore, who was acting as a courier for Robinson and Brewster, wrote a letter to the two elders. Staresmore stated that John Wolstenholme had informed him upon the delivery of the letter from Robinson and Brewster that both the king and the bishops had consented to tolerating but not sanctioning the Separatist plantation.[23] It seemed the way was clear for the plantation to proceed. However, another delay managed to stall the project for over a year. Just at this point, 1618 and 1619, the Virginia Company found itself entangled in a major split over the election of officers, specifically their treasurer.

The business of the company came to a standstill during these months, and the Leyden group could do nothing until this dispute had been resolved.[24]

But after many setbacks, discouragements, divisions, and complaints, the New England project moved forward in July 1620 toward a departure date. The Leyden people departed Holland around July 22, embarking from Delftshaven to join other Separatist settlers from England. Before they left Leyden, Robinson led the entire congregation in a day of prayer and fasting. He took as his text Ezra 8:21: "And there at the river, by Ahava, I proclaimed a fast, that we might humble ourselves before our God, and seek of him a right way for us, and for our children, and for all our substance."[25] The biblical context of this verse is the trip that Ezra and the Israelites made from Babylon to Jerusalem after the Second Temple had been rebuilt. By August 5, 1620, the colonists were ready. The departing group of "Pilgrims" now consisted of three groups of people: the Separatists from Leyden and England (mainly London); the "Strangers," who had been added to provide a critical mass of settlers for the success of the colony; and the sailors, who had been hired to stay in New England for one year.[26] At the point of embarkation, they gathered together and a farewell letter from John Robinson was read to the entire group.[27] The letter had five points. In the first point, Robinson exhorted the company of voyagers to be at peace with God.[28] In the last four points, Robinson expounded upon the necessity that the voyagers get along with their neighbors. In the second and third points Robinson pointed out many things that any Christian pastor would bring up to his flock: that the group should endeavor to live at peace with all men, and that offense should not be taken or given easily, but that the voyagers should keep a watchful care over their dealings with their neighbors. Robinson also pointed out that many were strangers to one another, and did not know the quirks that would give offense to each other.

It is Robinson's fourth point that we want to focus our attention upon. Robinson addressed the particular situation that the voyagers found themselves in: they were starting a community that, for at least seven years, would require its members to work together for the common good for two-thirds of the time. For those seven years, the voyagers had to think communally and not individually: "A fourth thing there is carefully to be provided for, to wit, that with your common employments you join common affections truly bent upon the general good. . . ."[29]

The *Mayflower* departed Old England on September 6, 1620, and arrived at Cape Cod on November 9. The next six weeks were spent scouting out a place for settlement, and at the end of December they concluded that the area we know as Plymouth, Massachusetts, would be the place of settlement. On Saturday, November 11, however, before coming ashore, they signed the Mayflower Compact. Because of divisions that had emerged over the previous years in the planning and execution of the voyage, it is little wonder that when they arrived on the other side of the ocean quarrels would continue to surface. Bradford recounts the November 1620 scene in this way:

> I shall a little return back, and begin with a combination made by them before they came ashore; being the first foundation of their government in this place. Occasioned partly by the discontented and mutinous speeches that some of the strangers amongst them had let fall from them in the ship. . . . And partly that such an act by them done, this their condition considered, might be as firm as any patent, and in some respects more sure.[30]

The mutinous speeches by some of the "Strangers" revolved around a fact that the "Strangers" knew: the New Plymouth Plantation was not the same as the Virginia Company, and the land was technically claimed by the Virginia Company. Therefore, the "Strangers" reasoned that they should be under the more lenient and Anglican government of the Virginia Company rather than the more strict and Puritan government of the Council for New England. Some of the "Strangers" were therefore saying that "when they came ashore they would use their own liberty, for none had power to command them, the patent they had being for Virginia and not for New England, which belonged to another government, with which the Virginia company had nothing to do."[31]

The Mayflower Compact was therefore created out of great division and tension, and reflects the wishes of one group — the Separatists — over the wishes of two other groups — the "Strangers," who would have to live with it for a long time, and the sailors, who could legally sail away in December 1621. Its famous text is as follows:

IN THE NAME OF GOD, AMEN.

> We whose names are underwritten, the loyal subjects of our dread Sovereign Lord King James, by the Grace of God of Great Britain, France, and Ireland King, Defender of the Faith, etc.
>
> 　　Having undertaken, for the Glory of God and advancement of the Christian Faith and Honour of our King and Country, a Voyage to plant

the First Colony in the Northern Parts of Virginia, do by these presents solemnly and mutually in the presence of God and one of another, Covenant and Combine ourselves together into a Civil Body Politic, for our better ordering and preservation and furtherance of the ends aforesaid; and by virtue hereof to enact, constitute and frame such just and equal Laws, Ordinances, Acts, Constitutions and Offices, from time to time, as shall be thought most meet and convenient for the general good of the Colony, unto which we promise all due submission and obedience. In witness whereof we have hereunder subscribed our names at Cape Cod, the 11th of November, in the year of the reign of our Sovereign Lord King James, of England, France and Ireland, the eighteenth, and of Scotland the fifty-fourth. Anno Domini 1620.

This hastily conceived and terse document reveals some of the thought patterns of the Separatists as they confronted a major governance crisis. They had made it to New England, but they knew well that they could freeze to death in the approaching winter, that their food supply was limited, that they had no housing, and that they were divided into three groups of Separatists, "Strangers," and sailors. The Mayflower Compact, therefore, was a civil covenant designed for survival rather than a carefully conceived long-range plan for the future.

We should note several prominent features of this famous document. First, a major feature of its phrases is allegiance to the standing order of Old England and its king, James I. At the very beginning, all of the signers are identified as loyal subjects of the English monarchy. Besides the "advancement of the Christian Faith" — which we will address in a moment — the colony was undertaken for nationalistic purposes: the honor of king and country. The framework of the civil government echoes the political and civil structures of Old England — "such just and equal Laws, Ordinances, Acts, Constitutions and Offices" — and the compact concludes with regnal dating, not only for the throne of "England, France and Ireland" but also Scotland. The explicit allegiance to the Crown was purposely done in the face of those who questioned whether the Separatists had any authority from the Crown to set up a civil government. Indeed, the colony in 1629 procured an explicit charter from the Council for New England in Old England to confirm any legal doubts as to whether they had authority in the region.[32]

The quarrel of the Separatists who dominated the first days of the New Plymouth Colony was not so much with the English state as it was with the English church, even though those in the English state saw the Separatists as traitorous criminals. And even leaders of this group of Separatists signed documents modifying its ecclesiological stance to placate the Crown, Canterbury, and the Virginia Company. As time progressed, however, and as the English Civil War and Revolution drew near, other groups of Puritans, including those called non-separating Puritans, began silently to pass over references to the English Crown, indicating that their quarrel was with both church and Crown.[33]

The number of words devoted to the theological underpinnings of the civil government of the New Plymouth Colony were fewer. The compact did identify its source of authority as God, and assumed that Anglican and Puritan (and Separatist, "Stranger," and sailor) would identify this God as the biblical God. In the next paragraph three purposes were given for the plantation: the glory of God, the advancement of the Christian faith, and the honor of king and country. The order of the three purposes reflects the priorities that the Separatists had — God first, faith second, national identity third — but when all was said and done much more was said about the English nation in the compact than about God and faith. The need to assert the authority and power of England's Crown in the face of rebellion overshadowed the desire to establish the New Plymouth Colony as a Christian state, but did not completely eclipse it. Nevertheless, the purpose of the Mayflower Compact included not only a theocentric and christocentric commitment but an anthropocentric commitment to the "general good of the Colony." The fact that the Mayflower Compact was written to force a consensus that the emerging colony could pass "Laws, Ordinances, Acts, Constitutions and Offices, from time to time, as shall be thought most meet and convenient" indicates that no grand plan had been laid down for what the Separatist colony would look like. The fact that they had arrived safely after years of travail was enough.

The evidence presented by Bradford indicates that the founders of New Plymouth Colony did not have a grand blueprint of government formulated in their minds — a blueprint that was based upon a theological formulation that had been carefully thought out as a theoretical schema in Europe. Rather, the original New Plymouth Colony government was an institution that developed in response to a specific need and that then evolved organically over time. During the early years it was a government that was a "committee of the whole," the "whole" consisting of all the males who signed the document. That some of the men who signed the compact did so under pressure is obvious, and no doubt that duress continued on through the 1620s and was felt keenly by the "Strangers": while all the males might have been equal, some were more equal than others. Nevertheless, the New Plymouth colonists persevered through the first years of incredible hardship, and after one generation began to multiply. Beginning in 1636 the New Plymouth Colony spawned eight towns in the 1630s, two towns in the 1640s, one town in the 1650s, four towns in the 1660s, and five towns in the 1680s, along with a total of thirty-eight Native American Praying Towns whose foundation dates are undocumented.[34] While the New Plymouth Colony was always smaller in comparison to the colonies of Massachusetts Bay and Connecticut, it did not collapse after the first rugged decade, but prospered.[35]

Besides individual persons combining together to form a governmental structure, individual towns also combined to form unified and more powerful governmental structures. Such is the case with the Connecticut Colony, in which three towns — Hartford, Wethersfield, and Windsor — adopted the famous "Fundamental Orders of Connecticut" on Monday, January 14, 1638/9. All three of these towns were settled by individuals from parent towns in the Massachusetts Bay Colony in the period 1634-36: Hartford emanated from Cambridge, Windsor from Dorchester, and Wethersfield from Watertown. And before the Fundamental Orders were adopted, the governance of this area was sponsored by the authorities of the Massachusetts Bay Colony, who had appointed a temporary commission of eight men to govern the area. The purpose of this governance was not to extend the boundaries of the Bay Colony, but to provide a governance structure until a permanent structure could be set up.[36] Among the eight commissioners was Roger Ludlow, who had some legal training and who later wrote most of the Fundamental Orders.[37] The Connecticut Colony therefore technically derived its political authority from the Massachusetts Bay, and not from signing the Fundamental Orders. However, the Fundamental Orders fleshed out the early governance structure of the Connecticut Colony.

The Fundamental Orders consist of eleven points, and conclude with oaths for public officials.[38] The eleven points essentially deal with the nuts and bolts of the election and formation of the general court. While the Fundamental Orders call the new government a confederation,[39] that is actually a misnomer, because the tenth point explicitly places ultimate power in the general court and not in the towns: *"In w^c said Generall Courts shall consist the supreme power of the Comonwelth, and they only shal haue power to make laws or repeale thē. . . ."*[40] Of most relevance to our discussion is the introductory paragraph, all of which is explicitly Christian:

Forasmuch as it hath pleased the Allmighty God by the wise disposi-
tion of his diuyne p^{r}uidence so to Order and dispose of things that we
the Inhabitants and Residents of Windsor, Harteford and Wethersfield
are now cohabiting and dwelling in and vppon the River of
Conectecotte and the Lands thereunto adioyneing; And well knowing
where a people are gathered togather the word of God requires that to
mayntayne the peace and vnion of such a people there should be an orderly and decent Gouernment established according to God, to order
and dispose of the affayres of the people at all seasons as occation shall
require; doe therefore assotiate and conioyne our selues to be as one
Publike State or Comonwealth; and doe, for our selues and our Successors and such as shall be adioyned to vs att any tyme hereafter, enter
into Combination and Confederation togather, to mayntayne and
p^{r}searue the liberty and purity of the gospell of our Lord Jesus wch we
now p^{r}fesse, as also the disciplyne of the Churches, wch according to
the truth of the said gospell is now practised amongst vs; As also in o^r
Ciuell Affaires to be guided and gouerned according to such Lawes,
Rules, Orders and decrees as shall be made, ordered & decreed, as
followeth: . . .[41]

The rationale for the government is carefully laid out: scripture requires
that a government should be established for the peace and union of people
who are gathered together. The goals of the government are also stated: to
order civil affairs; to establish laws, rules, and orders for those civil affairs;
to preserve the liberty and purity of the gospel; and to preserve the congregational "discipline," or form of church government. The Connecticut government of the seventeenth century was explicitly Christian, but gave
broad latitude to the general court to discern how Christ and the scriptures
were to be worked out in public affairs.

A contrast to the makeshift measures of the Mayflower Compact and
the somewhat broad Christian vision of Connecticut Colony are the carefully thought-out covenantal commitments of the New Haven Plantation,
articulated in June 1639. The New Haven Plantation was a corporate body
that quickly evolved into the New Haven Colony.[42] The New Haven founders saw civil government as a holy and sacred institution that was as important as the church and that should be wholly dedicated to God. The account of the founding of New Haven can be found at the beginning of the
colony records.[43] The records begin with a listing of "The Names of All the
Freemen of the Courte of Newhaven."[44] On Tuesday, June 4, 1639, these

seventy freemen met to formulate the civil government of New Haven. According to tradition, this meeting was held in the "Great Barn" of Robert
Newman.[45] The meeting was moderated by Rev. John Davenport.[46] Davenport held degrees from three colleges in Oxford: Brazenose, Merton, and
Magdelen Hall. After serving a short chaplaincy in Durham, Davenport was
the curate of St. Lawrence Jewry, London, between 1619 and 1624 and then
moved to the position of vicar of St. Stephen's Coleman Street, London,
where he served from 1624 to 1633. In 1633 he was forced to flee Archbishop Laud and ended up in Amsterdam, where he served as co-vicar with
John Paget of the English Church. Davenport managed to get into a controversy over baptism with Paget and returned to England in 1635. He arrived
in Boston, Massachusetts Bay Colony, in 1637 at the height of the
antinomian controversy and proceeded to plan a colony for those who had
become his followers.[47] Both Massachusetts Bay and New Plymouth desired his presence, but Davenport ultimately decided that he should be in-
strumental in founding a plantation based on theological principles different from the colonies of Massachusetts Bay and Connecticut and the
plantations found in the area known today as Maine, New Hampshire, and
Rhode Island. Thus, unlike the New Plymouth Colony, the New Haven
Colony did have a blueprint for the organization of both church and state, a
schematic developed in the wake of the personal rule of Charles I and the
policies of Laudianism. The outline of Davenport's vision can be found in a
book published many years after the initial formation of the New Haven
Colony and wrongly attributed to John Cotton. *A Discourse About Civil
Government in a New Plantation Whose Design is Religion*[48] was published as
the New Haven Colony was preparing to merge with the Connecticut Colony. Davenport and others of the "old school" that had lost control of the
leadership of the colony felt that the New Haven Colony was selling out the
original vision, and so they published the *Discourse About Civil Government*
in an attempt to resurrect the initial covenant vision of 1639. Those unhappy with the merger with the Connecticut Colony prepared to start all
over again, this time in East New Jersey, where they founded Newark in the
1660s. Davenport felt that he was too old to pioneer, and so he remained in
New Haven. After members supportive of the half-way covenant left
Boston's First Church to form Boston's Third Church, the First Church of
Boston managed to lure Davenport away from New Haven, but Boston's
First Church enjoyed his ministry for only two years, 1668-70; Davenport
died in early 1670.

Davenport's *Discourse* claims that the central design of the New Haven Plantation and Colony was religion, but Charles Sorensen claims that of equal importance in the formation of New Haven was the development of English mercantile interests along the Long Island Sound in competition with the Dutch of the Hudson Valley.[49] Nevertheless, Thomas Fugill's narration of the events of June 4, 1639, reveals that Davenport was firmly in control of the proceedings, and the wealthy merchants of the founding group deferred to him. The June 4 meetings were called for two purposes: "to consult about settling ciuill Gouernmen^t according to God, and about the nomination of persons thatt might be founde by consent of all fittest in all respects for the foundacon worke of a church. . . ."[50] The proceedings began with "the solemne invocation of the name of God in prayer, [for] the presence and help of his speritt, and grace in those weighty businesses. . . ."[51] The group saw itself as attempting to discern the mind of God concerning the establishment of civil government, and the method by which this was done was for Davenport to propose a series of five queries concerning civil government and a sixth query concerning the gathering of a church. Davenport "earnestly pressed" the group to understand completely what they were doing:

> For the better inableing them to discerne the minde of God and to agree accordingly concerning the establishm^t of ciuill order, Mr. John Davenport propounded diuers quæres to them publiquely praying them to consider seriously in the presence and feare of God the weight of the busines they met about, and nott to be rash or sleight in giueing their votes to things they understoode nott, butt to digest fully and throughly whatt should be propounded to them, and without respect to men as they should be satisfied and p{er}swaded in their owne mindes to giue their answers in such sort as they would be willing they should stand upon recorde for posterity.[52]

The invocation of future generations added an even greater sense of gravity to the event, and Davenport showed himself to be an adept leader in the way he led the group to the consensus that he wanted. In order to accomplish a sense of unanimity and finality among the group Davenport skillfully arranged the procedure in such a way that the meeting voted twice on each query: once during the time that Davenport propounded and explained the question, and then a second time after Davenport's words had been written down by Mr. Robert Newman. It was Newman who read the query the second time from his handwritten manuscript, adding a second voice to the proceedings and therefore giving the sense that Davenport was not too domineering. ". . . Mr. Robt. Newman was intreated to write in carracters and to read distinctly and audibly in the hearing of all the people whatt was propounded and accorded on that itt might appeare thatt all consented to matters propounded according to words written by him."[53]

The five queries concerning civil government move from the theme of the sufficiency of scripture, to the theme of covenant, to the action of constituting the body of free planters, to the purpose of civil government, and finally to the proper personnel for civil government. Davenport began by inquiring of the assembled group whether they believed that the Bible provided an adequate foundation for both civil and church government:

> QUÆR. 1. Whether the Scripturs doe holde forth a perfect rule for the direction and gouernm^t of all men in all duet[ies] w^{c}h they are to performe to God and men as well in the gou^{r}m^t of famylyes and commonwealths as in matters of the chur. This was assented vnto by all, no man dissenting as was expressed by holding up of hands. Afterward itt was read ou^t to them thatt they might see in whatt words their vote was expressed: They againe expressed their consent thereto by holdeing up their hands, no man dissenting.[54]

While most, if not all, Puritans would assert that the Bible provided guidance for the regulation and governance of the church, the question of how the Bible should guide and direct the civil government under the administration of the new covenant was a more problematic issue. As noted earlier, the New Testament was written in a context in which Christians were a tiny minority in the vast Roman Empire, and it therefore did not give explicit instructions to Christians on how to conduct themselves in positions of civil power and authority. The Old Testament, on the other hand, was written in the historical context of the Israelites holding hegemony over the inhabitants of the geographical territory of Israel, and therefore there was a great deal of material concerning civil law, in addition to the legal injunctions concerning the cultic life of ancient Israel. Thus, in the post-Reformation world, one of the major issues of discussion in the early modern Protestant church was the degree to which the Old Testament Mosaic civil laws were valid for Christendom.[55] Traditionally, the Old Testament Mosaic law had been divided up into moral, ceremonial, and civil components. The moral law was summed up in the Decalogue given at Mount Sinai, while the ceremonial law and the civil law were outworkings of the Ten

Commandments in the life of the people of Israel. Orthodox, Roman Catholic, and Protestant Christians all affirmed the moral law as the foundation for civic life and virtue, but the New Testament book of Hebrews teaches that the ministry, death, and resurrection of Jesus Christ was the fulfillment of the ceremonial law. The ceremonial law was therefore a type — a prophetic picture — of the future work of Christ. Thus, in Christian thinking, while the moral law was still in effect, the ceremonial law had been fulfilled by Jesus Christ and was therefore null and void.

The question therefore remaining in Christian theology and practice concerns the civil law: what place does it have in the new covenant administration? Christians have affirmed various answers, with most saying that the Mosaic civil law also was no longer valid. Some Christians, however, particularly in the Protestant and Reformed camp, have affirmed that various individual statutes of the civil law were still valid and should be built into the criminal code of local jurisdictions and regions. This was particularly the case for offenses that carried the death penalty in the Old Testament: murder, blasphemy, adultery, witchcraft, sodomy, murder, and so on. The New Haven Puritans took the stance that some, but not all, of the Mosaic civil law was valid for all people, both Christian and non-Christian, in a Christian commonwealth ("a perfect rule for the direction and gouernmt of all men in all duet[ies]").[56] New Haven was not the only colony that took this stance, but they were the only ones to articulate this position in the inauguration of the civil government.[57] What the New Haven colonists did not explicate in their commitment to the law of God was the issue of interpretation and the hermeneutical framework for that interpretation, a problem that would arise in coming years as individual cases came before the magistracy. As we shall see, responsibility for both the principles of interpretation and the interpretation itself was vested in the civil officers, a group of people derived from the gathered church.

The second query that Davenport laid before the New Haven assembly concerned the civil covenant that had been entered into at an earlier time. Regrettably, this covenant document no longer exists, but from the query we can get a sense of its content:

> QUÆR. 2. Whereas there was a cou^t solemnly made by the whole assembly of freeplanters of this plantation the first day of extraordenary humiliation wch we had after wee came together, thatt as in matters thatt concerne the gathering and ordering of a chur. so likewise in all publique offices wch concerne ciuill order, as choyce of magistrates and

officers, makeing and repealing of lawes, devideing alottm^{ts} of inheritance and all things of like nature we would all of vs be ordered by those rules wch the scripture holds forth to vs. . . . Itt was demaunded whether all the free planters doe holde themselues bound by thatt couenant in all businesses of thatt nature wch are expressed in the couen^t to submitt themselves to be ordered by the rules held forth in the scripture.[58]

The leaders of the assembly — John Davenport, Robert Newman, and Thomas Fugill — were careful to point out in an aside that a church had not yet been gathered, and that therefore the covenant signed on that earlier day and ratified on June 4 was called a plantation covenant and not a church covenant:

> This couen^t was called a plantation couen^t to distinguish itt from [a] chur. couen^t wch coud nott att thatt time be made, a chur. nott being then gathered, butt was deferred till a chur. might be gathered according to God. Itt was demaunded whether all the free planters doe holde themselvues bound by thatt couenant in all businesses of thatt nature wch are expressed in the couen^t to submitt themselves to be ordered by the rules held forth in the scripture.[59]

At this point we can see the New Haven founders struggling with the question of which should come first, civil government or church fellowship. Davenport and the other New Haven leaders believed that only church members should have authority in civil government, but they also knew that they did not want to rush into the establishment of a church. The establishment of a church was often a painstaking process that was of tremendous importance to the New England Puritans. Nevertheless, there was the daily need for an effective civil government as the citizens of the New Haven Plantation went about their business and established the plantation and their homes. The need for civil government won out over the principle of church members only conducting civil government, but a church was gathered in New Haven on Thursday, August 22, 1639, just under three months after the civil government was established.

The third query addressed to the New Haven assembly was addressed to those who were not yet officially free planters of the community but who wished to be received into the community. The New Haven authorities did not offer the possibility of membership in the community to any and all that asked. Rather, one had to give some evidence that he was seeking to become a full member of the church in order to be admitted as a free planter. The New Haven Puritans, of course, knew that the individual process of becoming a communicant member of the gathered church might take years, even decades, but they wanted to see at least some semblance of godliness and religiosity in a candidate before he was admitted as an inhabitant. The third query reads as follows:

> QUÆR. 3. Those who have desired to be receiued as free planters, and are settled in the plantation wᵗh a purp[ose,] resolution and desire thatt they may be admitted into chur. fellowᴾ according to Christ as soone [as] God shall fitt them therevnto: were desired to espress itt by holdeing vp of hands: . . .[60]

According to the record, "a[ll] did espresse this to be their desire and purpose by holdeing vp their hands twice. . . ."[61] It is not clear whether the "all" included every male member of the gathered assembly, or every male member who wanted to become a planter but who had not yet done so, but it is evident that at least in public no one wanted to be known as a planter who was not pursuing church membership.

The fourth query articulates the purpose of civil government. Rather than simply the prevention of evil or the advancement of the social well-being of society, the express purpose of civil government in the New Haven Plantation was the establishment and maintenance of the church of Jesus Christ:

> QUÆR. 4. All the free planters were called vpon to expresse whether they held themselues bound to esta[blish] such ciuill order as might best conduce to the secureing of the purity and peace of the ordina[nces] to themselues and their posterity according to God. In answ. herevnto they expressed by hold[ing] vp their hands twice as before, thatt they held them selues bound to establish such [civil order] as might best conduce to the ends aforesaid.[62]

The word "ordinances" has several connotations in both the Bible and the history of Christian theology, and here it is not precisely clear what the writer means. In the scripture, ordinances can refer to the law of God or man, the given "order of things," or a specific religious rite or cultic practice.[63] In the latter part of the early modern period and during the modern period, the Baptists used the word "ordinance" instead of "sacrament" to refer to baptism and communion — thus utilizing the third biblical meaning of the word. The fact that the writer speaks of "the purity and peace" of the ordinances leads us to conclude that the New Haven query is referring to the religious rite as well. At a time when Archbishop Laud had been attacking the Puritan wing of the Church of England with ferocity, so much so that Davenport had to flee, the peace of the church and the purity of ecclesiastical ordinances were certainly on the minds of the New Haven Colony. Particularly odious to the Puritans, as we have pointed out earlier, were the elaborate ceremonies that the High Anglican Laudians imposed upon the celebration of the weekly worship service, a service that usually included communion and often the baptism of a child. In response to Laudianism, the New Haven Puritans desired that the church and its ordinances be pure. Thus, the preaching of the word of God, the celebration of the Lord's Supper, baptism, the government of the church, the discipline of the church, and the doctrine of the church were all ordinances that were to be purged of manmade tradition and custom that was not scriptural. They were to be reformed in such a way that they reflected the life of the New Testament church as the Puritans understood that life. As far as the New Haven Puritans were concerned, it was the chief purpose of civil government to protect the purified church that was to be established in the plantations.

The fifth query was a query that distinguished the New Haven Colony from the Connecticut Colony. It was also the query that drew a certain amount of discussion — some might even call it dissent — from the assembled planters. Davenport was aware that this query might be a stumbling block, and so he was careful to give the assembly time to let them feel and think that they had entered into this term of the covenant freely:

> Then Mr. Davenport declared vnto them by the scripture whatt kinde of persons might best be trusted w^{t}h matters of gouerm^t, and by sundry argum^{ts} from scripture proued thatt such men as were describ[ed] in Exod. 18.2. Deut. 1.13, w^{t}h Deut. 17.15, and 1. Cor. 6:1 to 7, ought to be intrusted by them, seeing [they] were free to cast themselues into thatt mould and forme of comon wealth w^{c}h appeareth bewt for them in referrence to the secureing of the pure and peacable injoym^t of all Christ his ordinances [in] the church according to God, wherevnto they have bound themselues as hath beene acknowledged. Having thus said he satt downe, praying the company freely to consider whether they would haue [it]voted att this time or nott: After some space of si-

lence Mr. Theophilus Eaton answered itt mi[ght] be voted, and some others allso spake to the same purpose, none att all opposeing itt. Then itt was propounded to vote.

QUÆR. 5. Whether Free Burgesses shalbe chosen out of chur. members they thatt are in the foundat[ion] worke of the church being actually free burgesses, and to chuse to themselues out of the li[ke] estate of church fellowp and the power of chuseing magistrates and officers from among themselues and the power of makeing and repealing lawes according to the worde, and the devideing of inheritances and decideing of differences thatt may arise, and all the buisnesses of like nature are to be transacted by those free burgesses. . . . This was putt to vote and agreed vnto by the lifting vp of hands twice as in the former itt was done.[64]

Some commentators have viewed this move as a Protestant form of ecclesiastical domination of the state such as was seen in the early medieval period. However, while the civil government of the New Haven Plantation and later the New Haven Colony was in the hands of the church members at the time of the inception of the New Haven civil government, the civil government of both colony and plantation was not a function (or ordinance) of the church as an institution. Civil affairs were not decided during church meetings. Civil affairs were decided upon at town meetings, but the people who spoke in the town meetings were church members.[65] Notice also that our earlier inclination to interpret ordinances as referring to the religious rites of the church is confirmed in this passage.

The scriptural justifications that Davenport used for this policy came from several periods of Old Testament history. Exodus 18:2 came from the account of Jethro advising an overworked and overburdened Moses to appoint rulers under him who could take care of minor problems and disputes, leaving the major disputes for Moses to settle as a court of appeal.[66] The qualifications for leadership in the Israelite camp were that they be able, that they fear God, that they be trustworthy, and that they hate dishonest gain.

The Deuteronomy passages came from a period forty years later in Israel's history, when Moses was delivering his final sermon to the assembled tribes of Israel on the Plains of Moab. In the first passage we find Moses recapitulating the Jethro account in Exodus.[67] From the first Deuteronomy passage two more traits of leadership were enunciated — the possession of wisdom and a good reputation. The Deuteronomy 17:15 reference is to a section of the Mosaic sermon that spoke of qualifications for the king of Israel that Moses predicted the Israelites would want in the future.[68] In the Mosaic legislation, the king was to be one from the community of Israel rather than an alien or sojourner. The New Haven community therefore concluded that their leaders should be part of "Israel." This did not necessarily mean that they had to be English; rather, they had to be part of the gathered church that saw itself as the inheritors of the title "Israel" through their union with Jesus Christ, the son of Abraham, Isaac, and Jacob. The Deuteronomy 17:15 passage goes on in future verses to mandate that the king should be a student of the law of God:

> And it shall be when he sitteth vpon the Throne of his kingdome, that he shall write him a copy of this Law in a booke, out of that which is before the Priests the Leuites. And it shall be with him, and hee shall reade therein all the dayes of his life, that hee may learne to feare the LORD his God, to keep all the words of this Law, and these Statutes, to do them: That his heart bee not lifted vp aboue his brethren, and that hee turne not aside from the Commandement, to the right hand, or to the left: to the end that hee may prolong his dayes in his kingdome, hee, and his children in the midst of Israel. (Deuteronomy 17:18-20)

In the same way, New Haven civil magistrates, acting as kings in God's kingdom, were to study the scriptures for guidance in the conduct of civil, ecclesiastical, and personal life.

The final passage came from the New Testament. 1 Corinthians 6:1-8 addressed a different group from ancient Israel. In this passage the Corinthian church consisted of both Jewish converts and Gentile believers, and Paul was addressing the problem of lawsuits in the Christian community between various church members. Paul was disheartened that this problem was happening:

> Dare any of you, hauing a matter against another, goe to law before the vniust, and not before the Saints? Do ye not know that the Saints shall iudge the world? And if the world shalbe judged by you, are ye vnworthy to iudge the smallest matters? Know ye not that we shall iudge Angels? How much more things that perteine to this life? If then yee haue iudgements of things perteining to this life, set them to iudge who are least esteemed in the Church. I speake to your shame. Is it so,

that there is not a wise man amongst you? no not one that shall bee able to iudge betweene his brethren? But brother goeth to law with brother, & that before the vnbeleeuers? (1 Corinthians 6:1-6)

Most commentators have interpreted this passage as saying that church members should try to settle their disputes within the church and not in front of the civil magistrate, who may or may not be a church member. But the New Haven community concluded that its civil magistrates and judges should all be church members, so that the saints (and non-saints) could settle disputes both at the civil and at the ecclesiastical level.[69]

At this juncture in the meeting there was some dissent, but it is significant that the challenge came after the vote had occurred. An unidentified individual in the meeting registered his dissent after the fact because "he would nott hinder whatt they agreed upon."[70] The essence of his argument was that all of the free planters should vote for the candidates for magistrate, but that those candidates should be church members:

> Then one man stood vp after the vote was past, and expressing his dissenting from the rest in p^t yett grantinge 1. That magistrates should be men fearing God. 2. Thatt the church is the company whence ordenaryly such men may be expected. 3. Thatt they that chuse them ought to be men fearing God: onely att this he stuck, That free planters ought nott to giue this power out of their hands: Another stoo vp and answered that in this case nothing was done but w^{t}h their consent. The former answered thatt all the free planters ought to resume this power into their owne hands againe if things were nott orderly carryed.[71]

The dissent did not come as a total surprise, because Davenport then admitted that he and the individual in question had had some discussion about this matter in earlier days. Evidently the individual did not want to directly challenge the pastoral authority of Davenport, but he wanted at least to leave the door a little bit ajar for reform if matters did not work out as expected. He realized that to formally and legitimately challenge the tide of public opinion and the pastoral authority behind it was a less effective strategy than to discreetly plant seeds of doubt in people's minds. Again Davenport asked for a show of hands, and the motion was unanimously carried.

But then several more people contributed to the discussion, this time in favor of the motion. Significantly, those who spoke indicated their doubts even of that very day:

. . . And some of them professed thatt whereas they did wauer before they came to the assembly they were now fully convinced thatt itt is the minde of God. One of them said that in the morning, before he came, reading Deut. 17.15. he was convinced att home, another said thatt he came doubting to the assembly butt he blessed God by whatt had beene said he was now fully satisfied thatt the choyce of burgesses out of chur. members, and to intrust those w^{t}h the power before spoken off is according to the minde of God reuealed in the scriptures. All haveing spoken their apprehensions, itt was agreed vpon, and Mr. Robt Newman was desired to write itt as an order wherevnto euery one thatt hereafter should be admitted here as planters should submitt and testefie the same by subscribeing their names to the order, namely, that church members onely shall be free burgesses, and thatt they onely shall chuse magistrates & officers among themselues to haue the power of transacting all the publique ciuill affayres of this Plantation. . . .[72]

Once again the contributions to the discussion were expressed after the second round of voting, indicating a lack of desire to challenge the leadership directly. This last excerpt also indicates that the platform laid out by Davenport in the six queries had been publicized well in advance of the meeting, and that it had been debated and discussed informally before its formal presentation at the June 4 meeting.

That church members only should hold civil office and exercise the privilege of the franchise was the distinctive principle of the New Haven Colony. The New Haven leaders also realized that it was the principle that would consistently be challenged by newcomers and by the next generation. Therefore, of all of the commitments that the New Haven men made in June 1639, this was the one that was written out and that newcomers to the community had to sign and submit to in order to become a new citizen of New Haven. Immediately after the account of the events of June 4 was a paragraph that expounded this policy:

Whereas there was a foundamentall agreem^t made in a generall meeting of all the free planters of this towne, on the 4th of the fowerth moneth called June, namely thatt church members onely shall be free burgesses, and they onely shall chuse among them selues magistrates and officers to ha[ve] the power of transacting all publique ciuill affayres of this plantation, of makeing and repeali[ng] lawes, devideing inherritances, decideing of differences thatt may arise, and doeing all things and businesses of like nature. Itt was therefore ordered by all the said free planters thatt all those thatt hereafter should be receiued as planters into this plantation should allso submitt to the said foundamentall agreem[t], and testifie the same by subscribeing their names vnder the names of the aforesaid planters as followeth.[73]

A list of sixty-three names of male planters followed, written by Thomas Fugill; these were not signatures. After the list of sixty-three names came the signatures of forty-eight males, ending with Theophilus Higginson, David Atwater, and Matthew Camfeld. These were the men who had joined the plantation after 1639. We can ascertain that Higginson arrived in New Haven in 1644, Atwater in 1638, and Camfeld in 1644, indicating that the requirement that this term of the covenant be signed ended in 1644.[74]

The final item of business that concerned the newly formed plantation of New Haven was the initiation of the process of gathering a church. This was essential to the success of the civil government because the identification of church members would automatically lead to the identification of burgesses, or local magistrates. As in the case of many early New England towns, a winnowing process inaugurated by the New Haven civil government led to the identification of the foundation stones, or founding members, of the local church. Into the hands of these founding members were placed "the keys of the kingdom," and they would then begin the cycle of admittance or non-admittance into the gathered church. The means by which these members were identified were the weekly "private meetings" devoted to the study of scripture, prayer, the exchange of testimonies concerning God's work in one's life, and the examination and evaluation of accounts of conversion. These meetings were organized on a regional basis throughout the new town. The record keeper chronicles the process in the following manner:

> Mr. Davenport proceeded to propound some things to consideracion aboute the gathering of a chur. And to prevent the blemishing of the first beginnings of the chur. worke, Mr. Davenport aduised thatt the names of such as were to be admitted might be publiquely propounded, to the end thatt they who were most approued might be chosen, for the towne being cast into seuerall pruiate meetings wherein they thatt dwelt nearest together gaue their accounts one to another of Gods gracious worke vpon them, and prayed together and conferred to their mutuall ediffication, sundry of them had knowledg one of another, and in euery meeting some one was more approued of all then any other, For this rea-

son, and to prevent scandalls, the whole company was intreated to consider whom they found fittest to nominate for this worke.

QUAE. 6. Whether are you all willing and doe agree in this thatt twelue
men be chosen thatt their fitnesse for the foundacion worke may be
tried, howeu^r there may be more named yett itt may be in the^r power
who are chosen to reduce them to twelue, and itt be in the power of
those twelue to chuse out of themselues seauen that shall be most approved of the major part to begin the church.[75]

The result of this move was to place all of the power and authority of the
plantation — both civil and ecclesiastical — into the hands of a spiritual
elite. Furthermore, this select group of twelve was to narrow itself down to
seven individuals who would be the foundation members of the New Haven
First Church. In the end, only eleven were found to be possible candidates
for the foundation membership of the church. These eleven men were subject to a review process by the whole community, and opportunity was given
in the following months for any one to raise objections to their candidacy.

We have no record of how the June 4, 1639, meeting concluded, and
it is especially regrettable that no record of the founding of the New Haven
First Church and its church covenant survived. All we know is that the
New Haven First Church was founded on Thursday, August 22, 1639
(Wednesday, August 21, 1639, or Friday, August 23, 1639, are also possibilities), in tandem with the Milford, Independent Colony First Church.[76] We
do, however, know who ultimately did become the foundation members in
New Haven, because at the inauguration of the New Haven general court
the list is given, along with the charter members of the first general court of
the New Haven Plantation.

The first action of the New Haven general court on Friday, October
25, 1639, was to require of all freemen assent to a loyalty oath that was
called the "Free Man's Charge."[77] This oath first of all required no treasonous action by any freeman, and dictated that any freeman who knew of
such activity was to reveal it to the magistrate. It next required the promo-
tion of the well-being of the plantation and submissive obedience to its
magistrates and laws — both current magistrates and laws and future magistrates and laws. Finally, there was a command to vote not according to
personal advantage but according to what one in his conscience thought
was best for the plantation. The oath is written upon the early New Haven
records in the handwriting of Francis Newman, not Thomas Fugill:

Free Man's Charge. Yow shall neither plott, practise nor consent to any evill or hurt against this Jurisdiction, or any {pa}rte of it, or against the civill gouvernment here established. And if you shall know any p{er}son, or p{er}sons wch intend, plott, or conspire any thing wch tends to the hurt or prejudice of the same, yow shall timely discouer the same to lawfull authority here established, and yow shall assist and bee helpfull in all the affaires of the Jurisdiction, and by all meanes shall promove the publique wellfare of the same, according to yor, ability, and opp{or}tunity, yow shall give due honno^r to the lawfull magistrats, and shall be obedience and subject to all the wholesome lawes and orderes, allready made, or wch shall be hereafter made, by lawfull authority afforesaid. And that both in yor p{er}^son and estate: and when yow shall be duely called to give yor vote or suffrage in any election, or touching any other matter, wch concerneth this common wealth, yow shall give it as in yor conscience yow shall judg may conduce to the best good of the same.[78]

Following the taking of this oath, the court proceeded to the election of one governor and four deputies. As preparation for this Rev. Davenport preached a sermon, again on Deuteronomy 1:13 and Exodus 18:21, "wherein a magistrate according to Gods minde is discribed."[79] Not surprisingly, Theophilus Eaton was elected governor for a term of one year. Other officers were chosen, their terms set at one year, and the business of the day concluded with a resolution "thatt the worde of God shall be the onely rule to be attended vnto in ordering the affayres of gouerment in this plantation."[80]

The early years of the New Haven Plantation seemed prosperous, at least in political and religious terms. At virtually the same time that New Haven was established, the independent Guilford Plantation was founded, and a covenant was signed aboard ship anchored off New Haven on Saturday, June 1, 1639, four days before the New Haven meeting that ratified the civil covenant. Later on, in November 1639, a contingent that was mainly from Hertfordshire and that had joined the New Haven founders in the months before New Haven's formation cordially broke off from New Haven and founded the independent Milford Plantation. They used the same governmental model developed by New Haven, and, as noted above, their church was gathered in tandem with New Haven's church. The next year (1640) the New Haven Plantation sponsored two daughter plantations: Stamford, and Southold on Long Island. At about the same time a daughter plantation was founded in the Delaware River Valley on the coast of New Jersey. The Varkin's Kill (Salem

Creek) Plantation later became Salem, New Jersey. In October 1643, New Haven, Southold, Stamford, Guilford, and Milford united to form the New Haven Colony, and New Haven became more than simply a small plantation. The plantation of New Haven now became the town of New Haven, and it was the capital of the New Haven Colony; the general court always met there. Economically, however, the New Haven Plantation and then the New Haven Colony began to struggle, and during the latter half of the 1640s and on into the 1650s it faltered, even though it continued to add already established plantations to its roster (Greenwich) and to found other plantations that included Branford, the failed plantation of Paugaset.[81]

At the very same time that the New Haven Plantation and its civil agreement was being formed along Old Testament covenantal and theocratic lines, the Providence Plantation was emerging about 100 miles to the north with a much more secular form of government. The first combination that the founders of Providence Plantation signed represents a significant step in the secularization process of American political life. From 1637 to 1644, Providence Plantation was an independent plantation dominated by Roger Williams.[82] In 1644, it united with the Newport and Portsmouth plantations under a charter granted by Parliament. The united jurisdiction was called the Colony of Rhode Island and Providence Plantations. The story of Roger Williams's banishment from the Massachusetts Bay Colony is well known, and will not be repeated here.[83] Williams was joined, however, by other individuals in the Providence area, and sometime between 1637 and 1639 they combined to form Providence Plantation with a brief but significant civil compact that reads as follows:

> We whose names are here*under* desirous to inhabitt in ye towne *of* prouidence do promise to subiect *ourselves* in actiue or passiue obedience to all such orders or agreements as shall *be* made | for publick good of o^r body in an orderly *way* | by the maior consent of the *present* Inhabitants maisters of families *Incorporated* together into a towne fellowship *and* others whome they shall admitt *unto them* only in ciuill things.
>
> {13 signers}[84]

This brief statement essentially subjected the signers to all laws passed by the male citizens who were heads of households. For the governance of the plantation these "maisters of families" met together in a general council rather than a representative assembly. A simple majority would hold sway, and this group would admit new residents as they saw fit. The last phrase, "only in ciuill things," is what makes this civil covenant unique for seventeenth-century New England. That one clause disestablished any and all churches that would be founded in Providence, limited the power of what had been traditionally thought of as religion in the operation of the state, and restricted the power of the civil government to politics and economics. It was not the state's function to be a "nursing maid" to the church, as in the other New England colonies. There was never an established state church in Rhode Island Colony, and a perusal of its colonial records indicates that, unlike the Massachusetts Bay Colony in particular, its general court never interfered in church matters and church controversies. There was a complete separation of church and state. The Providence Plantation was the first secularized government in the Western world. Its *degree* of secularization, however, was limited. It was the hope of Roger Williams and his colleagues that Christian virtue would spill over into the conduct of government, as we have seen earlier. This did not mean, moreover, that Providence was a harmonious plantation. Along with its reputation for a more secularized state, Providence had a reputation for being one of the most argumentative plantations in New England, and within a period of ten years it signed at least five more civil covenants in an attempt to draw its various factions together.[85]

Were similar patterns of secularization emerging in the local plantations emerging in other parts of New England? Woburn, Massachusetts Bay Colony, drew up a brief covenant on Tuesday, December 18, 1640.[86] While it begins with a Preamble that calls for the preservation of "humanity, civility, and Christianity," the majority of the document is fairly mundane:

Town Orders for Woburn, Agreed Upon by the Commissioners at their First Meeting, December 18, 1640.

The full fruition of such libertys and prvileges of humanity civility and Christianity cals for as due to every man with his place and proportion without impeachment or infringing which hath euer bine and euer will bee: the tranquility and stability of Christian commonwealths and the denyall or the drprivall thereof the disturbance if not the end{?} of them both

We hold it therefore our duty and faculty{?} for the better diffusing of all laws and benefits of the Town of Woburne and for the preventing of all troublesome complaynts and the maintenance of love and Agreement

"It is required that all persons admitted to the Inhabitance in the said Towne shall by voluntary Agreement subscribe to these Orders following; upon which Condition, they are admited.

"First Order for Sixpenc an Acre." "For the caring one [carrying on] Common Charges, all such persons as shall bee thought meete to haue land and admittance for inhabitance, shall paye for every Acre of land formerly layd out by Charlestowne, but now in the limmets of Woburne, six pence; and for all hereafter layd out, twelve pence."

"Second Order: to returne their lotts, if not improved in 15 months." "Every person taking lott or land in the said Towne shall within fiueteen months after the laying out of the same, bulde [build] for dwelling therone, and improve the said land by planting ether in part or in whole; or surrender the same upp to the towne againe: also they shall not make sale of it to any person but such as the Towne shall approve of."

"Third Order: About fencing." "That all manner of persons shall fence their Catell of all sorts ether by fence or keeper: only it is Required all garden plots and orchards shall bee well inclosed ether by pale or otherwayes."

"ffourth Order about Inmats." "That Noe manner of person shall entertayne Inmate, ether married or other, for longer time than three days, without the consent of fower [four] of the Selectmen; Every person ofending in this perticqler [particular] shall paye to the use of the Towne for every day they offend herein six pence."

"fiuft Order: about Timber." "That noe person shall sell or cutt any younge Oake lyke to bee good timber, under eaight inches square, upon forfitur [forfeiture] of fiue shillings for euery such offence."

"These Persons subscribed to these Orders."
{32 signers}[87]

The price of land, and its development through housing, fencing, and timber preservation, is the focus of the Woburn civil covenant. Certainly not all of the civil combinations and compacts deal with such routine and uninspiring matters, but as the century progressed a good many of them were like the Woburn covenant, particularly the combinations emerging out of the Massachusetts Bay Colony. Mundane details tend to crowd out the theological vision.

Nine years later a group of people covenanted together to found the plantation or town that would become Medfield, Massachusetts Bay Colony.[88] The civil covenant they drew up began with echoes of the structure of the federal theology, but the document does not sustain that theme at any length:

> For as much as for the further promulgation of the Gospel and the subduing of this part of the Earth, amongst the rest given to the sons of Adam, and the enlargement of the bounds of the habitations formerly designed by God to some of his people in this wilderness, it hath pleased the Lord to move and direct as weel the much honored General Court as also the inhabitants of the Town of Dedham, each of them in part to grant such a tract of land in that place called Bogastow and the adjacent parts thereabouts, as is adjudged a meet place for the erecting and settling a Towne, we the persons whose names are here underwritten being by the inhabitants of Dedham, elected, chosen, and authorized, for the ordering and managing the said Town, or villiage, to be erected for the due settling thereof, as also for the preventing of questions, mistakes, disorders and contentions that might arise, do order, determine and resolve as followeth:
>
> 1st. That all persons whatsoever that shall receive lands by grants from the said Town now called Medfield, shall become subject to all such orders in any part of points of Town government as are at present or hereafter by the authorities of the said town shall be made and appointed for the ordering, regulating, or government thereof, provided they be not repugnant to the orders, or any order, of the General Court, from time to time, and that every such grantee shal for the firmer engagement of himself and his successors, their use, subscribe his name to our Town Book, or otherwise his grants made to him shall hereby be made void and of none effect.
>
> 2d. That if differences, questions, or contentions shall fall out or arise, any manner of ways in our society, or between any parties therein, that they shall really endeavor to resolve and issue the same in the most peacable way and manner, before it shall come to any place of public judicature, except it be in our own town.

3d. That we shall all of us in said town faithfully endeavor that only such be received to our society and township, as we may have sufficient satisfaction in; that they are honest, peaceable, and free from scandal and erroneous opinions.

4th. That none of us, the inhabitants aforesaid, or our successors at any time hereafter for the space of seven years from the date hereof, upon any pretence whatsoever, without the consent of the selectmen for the time being first had and obtained, shall alienate, assign, and set over for the space of one whole year, any part of parcel of land formerly granted to him or them by the Town, except it be to some formerly accepted of by our society; always provided, that this shall in no sort hinder any heir at common law.

{7 signers}[89]

Three only of this committee, Messrs. Wheelock, Wight, and Hinsdale, removed to Medfield. Forty-three persons subscribed to form the society for removing to Medfield.[90] The Medfield combination had much more of a religious vision to it than the Woburn combination. It opened up with an explicitly Christian commitment, and then spoke of the Medfield project being part of a much larger process, "the subduing of the earth." This theme comes directly from the first chapter of the Bible, where Adam and Eve in the Edenic state were given a command by God to reproduce and "have dominion" over the earth: "And God blessed them, and God said vnto them, Be fruitfull, and multiply, and replenish the earth, and subdue it, and haue dominion ouer the fish of the sea, and ouer the foule of the aire, and ouer euery liuing thing that mooueth vpon the earth" (Genesis 1:28). In the schema of the federal theology this theme of the cultural mandate is part of the prelapsarian covenant of works. The Medfield people therefore saw the conquest of the wilderness and its taming as part of a vast biblical project wherein God had given them the land to extend the Kingdom of God, both from the mandate for creation given to the first Adam and the mandate to spread the gospel through the second Adam.

The Medfield combination was composed by the committee of selectmen listed directly below the text of the covenant. Unlike the Woburn covenant, its focus was communal harmony: those who moved there covenanted to subject themselves to the governing authorities. Furthermore, points of difference would not be publicly carried outside the town, troublemakers in conduct or doctrine would not be admitted to the community, and in order to make those policies effective land would not be sold to outsiders unless approved by the town fathers. Interestingly enough, there is little mention of land, money, economic advancement, or loyalty to Old England.

The vast majority of the Massachusetts Bay Colony documents are similar to those of Woburn and Medfield. They were generally mundane documents that did not attempt to work out a theoretical or theological vision. They were not theocentric or christocentric, but neither were they totally secular. They assumed that the larger vision that was derived from Puritan Christianity was implicit, or that it was explicitly worked out in the documents at the colonial level.

We turn now to the only inter-colonial document generated by early New England. The document formulating the Confederation of New England, known as "The Articles of Confederation of the United Colonies of New England," was written in 1643 and is another type of grassroots compact or combination, but this time the parties entering into the agreement were colonies that were corporate entities. The formation of the Confederation of New England also represents a trend away from self-sufficiency toward interdependency among the various colonies and small independent plantations founded in early New England.[91] Over time many of the smaller independent plantations concluded that they should join themselves to the larger New England colonies.[92]

Three pressures in particular propelled both smaller plantations and larger colonies in this direction: in the 1630s and 1640s some (but certainly not all) of the Native Americans, aided by the French in the St. Lawrence Valley, were at enmity with most of the English colonies of the northeast. A second pressure that compounded the first pressure was the fact that the government of Old England was embroiled in a civil war and revolution, a fact that the New Englanders maintained the Native Americans knew.[93] The third pressure came in the 1650s, in the wake of the 1651 Navigation Act, when tensions between England and the Netherlands increased to such an extent that the first Anglo-Dutch war was fought between 1652 and 1654. Therefore, many of the independent colonies submitted themselves to a larger colony such as the Massachusetts Bay or united with other independent plantations to form a larger colony. The larger colonies formed the Confederation of New England for mutual aid and defense. The Confederation of New England is the first attempt at some sort of united colonial organization in the North American English colonies, and presents an important backdrop to the Articles of Confederation (1777) and the Constitution of the United States (1787).

A careful reading of "The Articles of Confederation of the United Colonies of New England" (hereinafter referred to as the "New England Articles of Confederation" to distinguish them from the 1777 document) reveals that it too was a reactive rather than a proactive document. That is, the New England confederation was designed to deal with one problem — military defense — but articulated in the text of its foundation document was a covenantal and Christian vision for the colonies that joined. The term "confederation" denotes a governmental situation in which the central government is limited and the individual components retain their autonomy, and that is exactly what the document articulated. The New England Articles of Confederation, however, are much more elaborate than the Mayflower Compact, speak more clearly of the public purposes of the colonies, and read much more like a constitution. The New England confederation was formed by four colonies: the Connecticut Colony, the Massachusetts Bay Colony, the New Haven Colony, and the New Plymouth Colony. Providence Plantation and the Rhode Island colonies did not participate, not even after they united and received a charter from the English Parliament in 1644. New Hampshire slowly came under the authority of the Massachusetts Bay Colony in the 1640s, while the same thing happened to Maine in the 1650s. Maine Province and New Hampshire Province therefore became part of the confederation by default, but never sent commissioners to the annual meeting.

The opening paragraph of the New England Articles of Confederation articulates a common purpose for each of its member colonies and speaks of a desire for one unified government:

> Whereas we all came into these parts of America with one and the same end and aim, namely, to advance the Kingdom of our Lord Jesus Christ and to enjoy the liberties of the Gospel in purity with peace; and whereas in our settling (by a wise providence of God) we are further dispersed upon the sea coasts and rivers than was at first intended, so that we can not according to our desire with convenience communicate in one government and jurisdiction. . . .[94]

While the colonies and plantations might be scattered, and while they might disagree about the practical outworking of principles and the establishment of institutions that they deemed to be biblical, the United Colonies of New England asserted a christocentric vision for all of New England. The New England Articles of Confederation were ratified by the central governments of the four colonies via their general courts, and as such the articles therefore represent a common denominator that the colonial charters, issued by the Crown, did not articulate as clearly. The leadership of the colonies maintained that the four colonies had much more in common than in what divided them:

> We therefore do conceive it our bounden duty, without delay to enter into a present Consociation amongst ourselves, for mutual help and strength in all our future concernments: That, as in nation and religions, so in other respects, we be and continue one according to the tenor and true meaning of the ensuing articles: Wherefore it is fully agreed and concluded by and between the parties of Jurisdictions above named, and they jointly and severally do by these presents agree and conclude that they all be and henceforth be called by the name of the United Colonies of New England.[95]

While the first reason stated for the existence of each of the colonies might be the advancement of the Kingdom of Christ and the enjoyment of the liberties of the gospel, another reason stated later for the confederation or consociation was the external threat of hostile Native American tribes to the west:

> . . . and whereas we live encompassed with people of several nations and strange languages which hereafter may prove injurious to us or our posterity. And forasmuch as the natives have formerly committed sundry insolence and outrages upon several Plantations of the English and have of late combined themselves against us: and seeing by reason of those sad distractions in England which they have heard of, and by which they know we are hindered from that humble way of seeking advice, or reaping those comfortable fruits of protection, which at other times we might well expect.[96]

The theme of defense, with certain strategies and activities with respect to religious and theological commitment that reflect a proactive stance, continues in the actual paragraph that forms the confederation:

> The said United Colonies for themselves and their posterities do jointly and severally hereby enter into a firm and perpetual league of friendship and amity for offence and defence, mutual advice and succor upon

all just occasions both for preserving and propagating the truth and liberties of the Gospel and for their own mutual safety and welfare.[97]

The rest of the document outlined the way whereby the confederation would work. In essence, it was a constitution. Ten remaining points delineated the working of the confederation. The first point (Point 3 in the document) discussed the jurisdiction of the four respective colonies and the plantations that were under their respective authority. The four colonies were not to have overlapping claims, nor were other entities (plantations, new colonies, or colonies formed from the merger of plantations) to become members of the confederation without following the procedures laid out in the New England articles. Furthermore, two colonies could not merge and overpower the confederation.

Point 4 spoke of proportionate shares in the defense budget: the proportion was to be decided by the enumeration of males aged sixteen to sixty years old in each colony. Any spoils of war were to be divided proportionately as well. Point 5 also spoke of proportional responsibility, this time in the case of surprise attacks against any one of the confederation. Troops were to be sent by the other jurisdictions proportionately. However, if, after a meeting of the commissioners of the confederation, the commissioners decide that the attacked jurisdiction was at fault in inciting the war, the jurisdiction responsible was to make restitution to the enemy and pay for the entire military project itself. Such a provision therefore discouraged precipitous action on the part of individuals, towns, and colonies and encouraged self-control on the part of magistrates and individuals.

Point 6 spoke of the representation of the confederation; two commissioners were to be chosen from each jurisdiction (even though the proportion of population was uneven). These commissioners were to meet at least once a year in September, and then at times when there were emergencies. The annual meetings were to be held in the four capitals successively. It was assumed that the commissioners would be members of the church, although technically Connecticut Colony and New Plymouth Colony did not require that their magistrates be members of the gathered church:

> two Commissioners shall be chosen by and out of each of these four Jurisdictions . . . being all in church-fellowship with us, which shall bring full power from their several General Courts respectively to hear, examine, weigh, and determine all affairs of our war, or peace, leagues,

aids, charges, and numbers of men for war, division of spoils and what-soever is gotten by conquest, receiving of more Confederates for Plantations into combination with any of the Confederates, and all things of like nature, which are the proper concomitants or consequents of such a Confederation for amity, offence, and defence: not intermeddling with the government of any of the Jurisdictions, which . . . is preserved entirely to themselves.[98]

That last phrase about "intermeddling" was critical and crucial, and defined the United Colonies as a confederation rather than a federation: the central government by definition was weaker than the individual colonial governments. Point 7 also limited the power of the president of the United Colonies: he was assigned the duty of moderating the commission and of executing its decisions, but he could not act independently apart from the commission.

While the central government was limited, the confederation did agree that it could decree for all of the colonies certain policies "in general cases of a civil nature." The reason for this was to hold the confederation together at points where there was potential conflict or already had been conflict. These points included removal of residents from one plantation to another, and then policies towards the Native Americans, runaway servants, and escaped criminals. The beginning of Article 8 stated:

It is also agreed that the Commissioners for this Confederation hereafter at their meetings, whether ordinary or extraordinary, do endeavor to frame and establish agreements and orders in general cases of a civil nature, wherein all the Plantations are interested, for preserving of peace among themselves, for preventing as much as may be all occasion of war or differences with others, as about the free and speedy passage of justice in every Jurisdiction. . . .[99]

The rest of the Articles discussed the nuts and bolts of the functioning of the confederation: Article 9 stated that no single colony can declare war on behalf of the entire confederation, while Article 10 discussed extraordinary occasions in time of war when, because of the emergency, not all of the commissioners can meet together to consult. Article 11 spoke of the serious nature of the situation should any one of the members of the confederation break the agreement, but it did not define any sanctions or consequences in that event:

11. It is further agreed that if any of the Confederates shall hereafter break any of these present articles, or be any other ways injurious to any one of the other Jurisdictions; such breach of agreement or injury shall be duly considered and ordered by the Commissioners for the other Jurisdictions, that both peace and this present Confederation may be entirely preserved without violation.[100]

The Articles of the New England Confederation were a civil covenant that was a combination, but a very specific type of combination: it was the voluntary association of four colonies for military and defense purposes. The only other things the New England Confederation was to concern itself with were migration policy, Native American policy, and policy concerning fleeing servants and criminals. All four of those essentially dealt simply with the movement of people, whether the movement be legal or illegal. While the confederation was a weak organization, it was explicit in its articulation of the purpose of the four colonies: the advancement of the Kingdom of Jesus Christ and the Christian gospel. It would go into action and be tested severely during King Philip's War, then dissolve in 1684, only to be replaced by a very different entity — the Dominion of New England — in 1686-88. By contrast, the Dominion of New England was not even a federation: it was a unitary government dominated by Edmund Andros who consolidated power in Boston.[101]

While the New England Confederation represented and articulated a creedal unity centered around the historic Christian faith, what happened when that creedal unity was strained? Were there limits to what could be included in that creedal unity? How far could that creedal unity be stretched? We get an answer in the final example of civil combination, the compact of Swansea, New Plymouth Colony, in 1663, a break-off community from Rehoboth, New Plymouth Colony.

There had been Baptist and dissenting influence in Rehoboth long before Rev. John Myles left Ilston, Glamorganshire, Wales, in 1662. But probably Myles migrated to Rehoboth (after being removed from his Baptist pulpit in the 1662 Great Ejection) because of the presence of Baptists in Rehoboth. During the fifteen years previous to Myles's arrival in 1665 there had been a major ongoing dispute between the minister of Rehoboth, Rev. Samuel Newman, and a group of dissenters that was holding services in competition with the First Church of Rehoboth.[102] The dissenters were originally led by Obadiah Holmes, well known to history for undergoing a whipping by the magistrates of the Massachusetts Bay Colony on account of the exercise and teaching of his Baptist principles within the precincts of the Bay Colony.[103] Holmes had originally settled in Salem, Massachusetts Bay Colony. In 1645 he removed to Rehoboth, New Plymouth Colony, where he joined himself to the Rehoboth First Church. Again he fell into a situation where charges were lodged against him, this time by Rev. Samuel Newman, the pastor of the Rehoboth Church. Holmes and eight others withdrew from the Rehoboth Church in 1649 and established another church within the bounds of Rehoboth. Sometime in 1649 Holmes and his church concluded that they were Baptists. They then elected Mr. Holmes pastor, and they were rebaptized by Rev. John Clark of Newport, Rhode Island Colony. A flurry of petitions were filed against Holmes and his group in the New Plymouth Colony general court, including papers from Rehoboth, Taunton, all but two of the New Plymouth Colony clergy, and the government of the Massachusetts Bay Colony. On October 29, 1649, "Obadiah Hullme" lodged a charge of slander against Rev. Newman. Newman admitted to saying that Holmes had "taken a false oath in court." Holmes won his suit, and instead of settling for the original £100 that he called for he accepted a public apology from Rev. Newman and Newman's payment of the court costs, which amounted to £1 6d.[104] This was only the beginning of the troubles, however. At the June 5, 1650, meeting of the New Plymouth Colony general court, further action was taken concerning the Rehoboth situation: meetings "from house to house" were prohibited by the civil magistrate.[105] This did not deter Holmes and his colleagues, who were presented four months later by a grand jury to the New Plymouth Colony general court for disobeying the June injunction:

> October the 2^cond, 1650. Wee, whose names are heer vnder written, being the grand inquest, doe present to this Court John Hazaell, Mr Edward Smith and his wife, Obadia Holmes, Joseph Tory and his wife, and the wife of James Man, William Deuell and his wife, of the towne of Rehoboth, for the continewintg of a meeting vppon the Lords day from house to house, contrary to the order of this Court enacted June the 12th, 1650.[106]

Shortly afterward, this group dissolved and scattered, ending up, for the most part, in Newport or Providence, Rhode Island Colony.

But that did not mean that all of the Baptists departed from Rehoboth. One John Browne remained, and two years later Mr. Browne brought a second suit for slander to the New Plymouth Colony courts. In this suit,

Browne asked for £500. The records for June 4, 1652, read that Mr. John Browne brought "an action of defamacon against Mr. Samuel Newman to the damage of fiue hundred pounds. The jury find for the plaintife, and assessed an hundred pound damage, and the charges of the Court."[107] For the second time Rev. Samuel Newman lost a suit for slander in the New Plymouth courts; and again, the monetary award was forgiven him by his opponent, save for court costs. Such activity indicates that Rev. Newman and his opponents were fighting a war of words but not of actions. Rev. Newman mounted his attack via the pulpit and the public declarations of the ministry, whereas the dissenters mounted their attack via the legal system. Even Roger Williams was not impressed with the tactics of Browne. On February 24, 1649/50, he wrote John Winthrop, Jr.:

> Mr. Browne hath often profest Libertie of Conscience, but now the way of New baptisme spreads at Secunck as well as at Providence and the Iland. I have bene so bold as to tell him that he persecutes his Son and the people and on the other side Mr. Newman also.[108]

Matters quieted down for a couple of years, but the Rehoboth situation reemerged in the central colony court in 1655. This time a petition was presented concerning compulsory tithes, or rates, within Rehoboth. The petitioners were the group in favor of compulsory tithes, who thought it unfair that some within the town (probably Baptists) were not paying. The general court record reads as follows:

> Wheras a petition was psented to the Generall Court att Plymouth, the fift of June, 1655, by seuerall inhabitants of the towne of Rehoboth, whose hands were thervnto subscribed, desiring the Court to asis them in a way according to the orders of other collonies about them, for the raising mayntaynance for the minnestrey. The some of the petition seemed to hold forth, that those how hands were not subscribed contributed nothing, or soe little as was not esteemed, of which petition occationed some desputes about a foracable way to compell all the inhabitants of that towne to pay a certaine sum euery yeare towards the mayntainance of the minnester; . . .[109]

One of the magistrates sitting on the general court that year was John Browne, who was taken by surprise by this petition. That Browne did not know about the submission of such a petition from his own town to the general court that he was sitting on indicates that beneath the surface tensions continued to simmer. Browne was a member in good standing at the paedobaptist Rehoboth First Church, but he seems to have inherited the leadership of the dissenting party from Obadiah Holmes. In order to smooth over relations within the town and the colony, he proposed a temporary solution that would last for at least seven years:

> . . . Mr John Browne, one of the majestrates then siting in Court, and being one of the inhabitants of that towne, and not being made acquainted with the said petition vntill the names of the inhabitants were subscribed, to issue the said troublesome contraversy and take of the odivm from others, did propound that, forasmuch as those who hands were to the petition desired to submitt themselues vnto a rate, that iff the Copurt would send two of the majestrates vnto Rehoboth to take notice of the estates of the petitioners, hee would engage himselfe in the behalfe of those whoe were then inhabitants of the said towne, whoe hands were not subscribed to the petition, that they should voulentarily contribute according to their estates; and if any of them fall short in this busines, hee would suply that want out of his owne estate, and this hee would make good by ingageing his land for seuen yeares in theire behalfe while they stayed, though hee himselfe should remoue from the place; which was approued of, and Capt Standish and Mr Hatherley were then made choise of by the Court to see it ordered accordingly.[110]

The fact that the New Plymouth Colony was willing to accept this solution, albeit a temporary one, to the question of compulsory tithes indicates a greater willingness to be flexible about the Baptist issue than the Massachusetts Bay Colony was. While Baptist convictions concerning the relationship of church and state were still nascent, the later history of Rehoboth and Swansea leads us to believe that the individuals not paying the compulsory tithes included among their number those who did not believe in an established state church, a classic Baptist stance.

On April 10, 1662, John Browne, Sr., died. A little over a year later his antagonist, Rev. Samuel Newman, also died, on July 5, 1663. In the interval between the two deaths, steps were taken by the proprietors of Sowams (later Swansea) to mend fences among the leaders of the community. On January 29, 1662/3, a new contract of agreement was adopted at the Rehoboth town meeting between Captain Thomas Willett and the rest of the Sowams purchasers and the town of Rehoboth "to prevent both present and future troubles."[111] The fact that Thomas Willett stood out apart from "the rest of the Sowams purchasers" indicates that his policies were the focus of some disagreement among the other authorities of Rehoboth.

After Rev. Newman's death in July 1663, Mr. Zechariah Symmes, Jr., was engaged that summer to carry on the preaching and teaching responsibilities in Rehoboth. He remained unordained, however. Two years later, in January 1664/5, Captain Thomas Willett was given authority for a second time to secure a minister to assist Mr. Symmes. It seems to have been Willett, later the first mayor of New York City after the English reconquered it from the Dutch in 1674, who was responsible for bringing Rev. John Myles to Rehoboth. Rev. John Myles was one of the small number of clergy who came to New England after the Restoration and the Great Ejection of 1662.[112] Born in 1621 in Newton, Hertfordshire, he matriculated at Brazenose College, Oxford, at the age of fifteen years. On October 1, 1649, he formed a Baptist church at Ilston, just west of Swanzey, Glamorganshire, Wales. Soon after he formed an association of Welsh Baptist churches and served as a delegate of those churches to a meeting of Baptist ministers in London in 1651. After his ejection in 1662 he and some of his church migrated to New England. He brought with him the records of the Ilston Baptist Church.[113] Later he became the pastor of the First Baptist Church of Boston.

In 1666, both Symmes and Myles were admitted to Rehoboth as inhabitants:

> 18 Apr. 1666 — Mr. Symmes was admitted by the town as an inhabitant to purchase or hire for his money. . . . Mr. Myles was voted to be a Lowed viz to preach one day a fortnight on y^t week day & one on ye Sabbath day.[114]

Two months later, three Baptists were placed into positions of authority within the town. These positions were called "Selectmen" and took the place of the plurality of freemen who were called "Townsmen" and who had conducted the business of Rehoboth in town meetings. This decision fits in with the pattern emerging in many of the New England colonies: an increasing population, a related increase of day-to-day governance work on the part of colony and town officials, and a declining membership in the gathered churches. In addition, the Restoration in Old England had stabilized the political situation in both Old and New England (not necessarily

to the liking of all in New England). Finally, many on both sides of the Atlantic were tiring of wild-eyed schemes to remake the world. Instead of inspired plenary sessions that rallied significant portions of the community
to social action and religious participation, it was simply easier to let the
town council govern and an appointed committee handle the organization
of the new town.

Rehoboth's relation with its assistant pastor did not have a long hon-
eymoon. The record of August 13, 1666, reveals that Rev. Myles was probably going to have a short tenure:

> 13 Aug. 1666 — It was voted & agreed upon by the towne that an able
> man for the work of the ministry shalbe w^{t}hall Convenient speed,
> Looked for, as an officer ofr this Church, & a minster for the towne,
> such a one as may be satisfactory to the generallity.
>
> At the same tyme it was alsoe voted & agreed upon by the towne
> that Mr. myles shall still continue a Lecture on the work day, & further
> on the Sabbath, if he be thear unto Legally Called.[115]

Neither Symmes nor Myles, it seemed, was satisfactory "to the generallity."
Myles's preaching schedule was curtailed, and both were given the hint that
they should seek greener pastures. Doubt was cast as to whether Myles was
even "legally called" to occupy the pulpit in Swansea, even on a temporary
basis.

Myles found those pastures under his very nose, among those with
Baptistic leanings who continued to live in Rehoboth. Eighteen years after
Obadiah Holmes had founded a Baptist dissenting church in Rehoboth, another was organized in 1666-67. Isaac Backus dates the founding of this
church to 1663, and because of Backus's dating the church and community
has adopted this date as its founding date, but it is evident from the records
that Myles was still serving as stated supply in the First Church of
Rehoboth in 1663.[116] We also know that on July 2, 1667, a general court
found John Myles and James Browne guilty of disturbing the public peace
in Rehoboth by starting another church:

> Mr Myles and Mr Browne, for theire breach of order in seting vp of a
> publicke meeting without the knowlidge and approbation of the Court,
> to the disturbance of the peace of the place, are fined, each of them, the
> sume of fiue pounds, and Mr Tanner the sume of twenty shillings.
>
> And wee judge, that theire continuance att Rehoboth, being very

prejudiciall to the peace of that church and that towne, may not be alowed, and doe therfore order all psons concerned therin wholly to desist from the said meeting in that place or township within this month; yett incase they shall remoue theire meeting vnto some other place, where they may not prejudice any other church, and shall giue vs any reasonable satisfaction respecting theire principles, wee know not but they may be pmitted by this goument soe to doe.[117]

The second paragraph was a historic watershed in the history of New England. It contained the first alternative proposal for a state church in the history of New England, and perhaps within the Western world. In essence, it proffered the possibility of a state church established at the local but not at the colonial level. In the colony of Massachusetts Bay and its provinces of New Hampshire and Maine, the colony of Connecticut, and the colony of New Haven, there was only one established state church for the entire colony: the paedobaptist Congregational church. The general court of the New Plymouth Colony was now willing to consider another alternative: Christianity should be the established civil religion at the colonial level, and there should be a state church, but there could be less religious uniformity at the *colonial* level and a requirement of religious uniformity at the *local* level. Not all churches in the New Plymouth Colony had to be uniform and conform to the standing order of paedobaptist Congregationalist churches. While most of the established churches in the New Plymouth Colony would be paedobaptist and congregational, the leaders of the New Plymouth Colony were willing to set aside a section of their territory for a town to be established that would have the Baptist church as the only church in town, supported by compulsory tithes. Those who joined themselves to that town voluntarily placed themselves under the authority of that religious establishment. If they disliked it, they could move to a neighboring town whose religious establishment was more to their liking.

There were hints of this arrangement in the church covenant signed by the founders of the Swansea Baptist Church. While the covenant follows many of the patterns that we will explicate in another chapter, there are certain clauses in it that give hints of the experiment that would be proposed in the new town of Swansea. A portion of the Swansea Baptist Church covenant reads as follows:

And we do humbly engage that through his strength we will henceforth endeavor: to perform all our respective duties toward God and each other; to practice all the ordinances of Christ according to what is or shall be revealed to us in our respective places; to exercise, practice and submit to the government of Christ in this His Church:

Namely — further protesting against all rending or dividing principles or practices from any of the people of God, as being most abominable and loathsome to our souls and utterly inconsistent with that Christian charity which declares men to be Christ's disciples;

Indeed further declaring that, as union in Christ is the sole ground of our communion with each other,

Seo we are ready to accept and receive too, and hold communion with all such as by a judgement of charity we conceive to be fellow members with us in our head Christ Jesus, though differing from us in such controversial points as are not absolutely and essentially necessary to salvation.[118]

The criterion for unity in the Christian faith were those essentials of the faith "necessary to salvation." Those essentials were spelled out in negotiations between the proprietors of Swansea, the new Swansea civil government, and the gathered Baptist church in the coming months.

Within three months Captain Willett and Rev. Myles had organized a petition for a new township, a move noted at the meeting of the New Plymouth Colony general court on October 30, 1667.[119] By the following spring, the town was established. The general court records read:

5 Mar. 1667/8 — The Court doe alow and approue that the township graunted vnto Captaine Willett and others, his naighbours, att Wannamoisett and places adjacent, shall hensforth be called and knowne by the name of Swansey.

The Court haue appointed Captaine Willett, Mr Paine, Seni^r, Mr Browne, John Allin, and John Butterworth to haue the trust of admittance of towne inhabitants into the said towne, and to haue the dispoall of lands thein, and ordering of other the affaires of the said towne.[120]

That very month Noah Newman was installed as pastor of the church in Rehoboth, succeeding his father Samuel; by June, the Baptists John Allin, James Browne, and Nathaniel Pecke were seated as delegates for Swansea at the New Plymouth Colony general court.[121] At the very same time the governance of Rehoboth was placed again into the hands of Congregational paedobaptists.

Willett apparently took the lead in establishing standards of admission to the new town. These standards were stated in the negative, and were probably aimed at sectaries in the Rhode Island Colony nearby. A lengthy explanatory codicil was added by the leaders of the Swansea Baptist Church, giving us insight into how this particular group of Baptists was working out their new relationship with the civil realm. What is significant about the standards and the explanatory codicil is that they are both found in the civil records, not the church records, and that they were generated by Baptists — Baptists, we should add, who were living directly next door to Providence, the plantation that had covenanted to stay together as a town "in civil things only."

> Whereas, Captain Thomas Willett shortly after the grant of this township, made the following proposals unto those who were with him, and by the Court at Plymouth empowered for the admission of inhabitants and granting of lots, viz.
>
> 1. That no erroneous person be admitted into the township either as an inhabitant or sojourner.
> 2. That no man of any evil behaviour as contentious person, &c., be admitted.
> 3. That none may be admitted that may become a charge to the place.
>
> The church of Christ here gathered and assembling, did thereupon make the following address unto the said Captain Willett and his associates the trustees aforesaid. * * * [torn off] being with you engaged, (according to our capacity,) in the carrying on of a township according to the grant given us by the honored Court, and desiring to lay such a foundation thereof as may effectually tend to God's glory, our future peace and comfort, and the real benefit of such as shall hereafter join with us herein, as also to prevent all future jealousies and causes of dissatisfaction or disturbances in so good a work, do in relation to the three proposals made by our much honored Captain Willett, humbly present to your serious consideration, (before we proceed further therein,) that the said proposals may be consented to and subscribed by all and every townsman under the following explications.

That the first proposal relating to the non-admission of erroneous persons may be only understood under the explications following, viz. of such damnable heresies inconsistent with the faith of the gospel, as to deny the Trinity or any person there; the Deity or sinless humanity of Christ, or the union of both natures in him, or his full satisfaction of divine justice by his active and passive obedience for all his elect, or his resurrection, ascension to heaven, intercession, or his second personal coming to judgement, or else to deny the truth or divine authority of any part of canonical scripture, or the resurrection of the dead, or to maintain any merit of works, consubstantiation, transubstantiation, giving divine adoration to any creature, or any other antichristian doctrine, thereby directly opposing the priestly, prophetical or kingly office of Christ or any part thereof.

Or secondly, or of such as hold such opinions as are inconsistent with the well being of the place, as to deny the magistrate's power to punish evil doers as well as to encourage those that do well, or to deny the first day of the week to be observed by divine institution as the Lord's or christian sabbath, or to deny the giving of honor to whom honor is due, or to oppose those civil respects that are usually performed according to the laudable custom of our nation each to other as bowing the knee or body, &c.

Or else, to deny the office, use, or authority of the ministry, or a comfortable maintenance to be due them from such as partake of the teaching, to speak reproachfully of any of the other churches of Christ in the country, or of any such other churches as are of the same common faith with us and them.

We desire that it be also understood and declared, that this is not understood of any holding any opinion different from others in any disputable point yet in controversy among the godly learned, the belief thereof being not essentially necessary to salvation, such as paedo-baptism, anti-paedo-baptism, church discipline, or the like, but that the minister or ministers of the said town may take their liberty to baptise infants or grown persons as the Lord shall persuade their consciences, and so also the inhabitants to take their liberty to bring their children to baptism or forbear.

That the second proposal relating to the known reception of any evil behaviour such as contentious persons, &c, may be only understood of those truly so called, and not of those who are different in judgement in the particulars last mentioned, and may not be therefore accounted contentious by some though they are in all fundamentals of faith, orthodox in judgement, and excepting common infirmities, blameless in conversation.

That the proposal relating to the non-admission of such as may become a charge to the town, be only understood so as that it may not hinder any godly man from coming among us whilst there is accomodation that may satisfy him, if some responsible townsman will be bound to save the town harmless.

These humble tenders of our desires, we hope you will without offence receive, excusing us herein, considering that God's glory, the future peace and well being, not only of us and of our posterity who shall settle here, but also of those several good and peacable minded men whom you already know are like, though with very inconsiderable outward accommodation to come amongst us, are very much concerned herein; our humble prayers both for ourselves and you is that our God would be pleased to cause us to aim more and more at his glory and less at our own earthly concernment, that so we may improve the favors that hath been handed to us by our honored, nursing fathers, to the advancement of the glory of God, the interest of our Lord Jesus Christ, and to the common benefit, both of the township and colony where he hath providentially disposed of us to serve our generation.

Your brethren to serve you in Christ.

Signed on the behalf and in the name of the church-meeting at Swansey by
JOHN MYLES, Pastor,
JOHN BUTTERWORTH.[122]

The seventeenth-century Baptist community of Swansea was very specific about who was acceptable and who was not acceptable for their town, and they were willing to allow the civil authority to enforce those standards. A long list of people holding to erroneous doctrine were excluded, and the only standards that they were willing to bend on were baptism and church governance — the very issues that divided them from the majority of orthodox New England congregationalists and Old England Anglicans.

After this document was negotiated by the Swansea Baptist Church with Willett, the town required all inhabitants to sign the civil covenant on Monday, February 22, 1668/9, and to affirm both Willett's standards and the explanatory postscript:

At a town-meeting Lawfully warned on the two and twentieth day of the twelfth moneth commonly called February, in the year of our Lord one Thousand six hundred sixty and nine, it is ordered that all persons that are or shall be admited inhabitants within this Town, shall subscribe to the three proposalls abovewriten and to the several Conditions and Explanations therein Expressed, before any Lot of Land be confirmed to them or to any of them.

[We] whose names are hereunderwritten, doe freely uppon our [admissi]on to be Inhabitants of This town of Swansey, assent to the above [writt]en agreement, made betwen the Church of Christ now meeting [here] at Swanzey, and Capt Thomas Willett and his associats, as aforewriten, with the several Conditions and Explanations [t]hereof, concerning the present and future settlement of this Township. In witness whereof, we have hereunto subscribed.

{54 signers}

> Truly drawn of out of the
> beginning of Land Book
> of Records Attest
> Joseph Mason Town
> Cle[rk][123]

Within three months, the secretary of the New Plymouth Colony could name with precision all of the nine freemen of the community of Swansea. From the record of Friday, November 18, 1670, we know that Willett and his colleagues established a three-tier class system in the town of Swansea. There were upper, middle, and lower classes that went by the titles first rank, second rank, and third rank. Francis Baylies indicates that this arrangement was the only one of its kind within New Plymouth Colony.[124] The record reads as follows:

February 7th, 1670, (1671). It was ordered that all lots and divisions of land that are or hereafter shall be granted to any particular person, shall be proportioned according to the three ranks and written so, that where those of the first rank shall have three acres, those of the second rank shall have two acres, and those of the third rank shall have one acre, and that it shall be in the power of the selectmen for the time being, or committee for admission of inhabitants, to admit of, and place such as shall be received as inhabitants into either of the said ranks as they shall judge fit, till the full number of threescore such inhabitants shall be made up, and that when the said number of threescore is accomplished.

The said first rank are only such as are in this column	The abovesaid second rank are only such as are in this column	The said third rank are only such as are in this column.
{8 names, 3 of whom were freemen}	{23 names, 3 of whom were freemen}	{15 names, of whom 1 was a freeman}[125]

While this arrangement may be unique for the New Plymouth Colony, we know that in other New England colonies land was also divided unequally. What makes this list different is the clear distinctions made in columnar form that indicate the status of the three groups. The committee for organizing the town continued to maintain this list and promoted or demoted people from the list as they saw fit. By 1681, the committee for the admission of inhabitants took the bold step of granting "the full right and interest of the highest rank" to another group of elite members of the community. This authoritarian move elicited cries of protest, and a declaration was made in the town government that the act was "utterly void and of no effect." After 1681, the system collapsed and fell into disuse.[126]

Contrary to the classic vision of a Baptist community with an egalitarian town, a secularized government, and a rigid distinction between the church and the state, the community of Swansea represents an experiment on the part of early modern and colonial American Baptists. This Baptist community did draw a distinction between the function of the church and the function of the state, but the civil authority was established to uphold not only civil righteousness but also doctrinal uniformity in essential matters that had to do with classical orthodox Christianity and the eternal salvation of individuals. The uniformity, however, was on a micro or local level rather than on a macro or colonial level. The Swansea experiment represents another Baptist alternative to the one Roger Williams and the Providence Plantation established: one in which the state might not be proactively zealous for the honor of God and of Christ but which would restrain doctrinal error and civil unrighteousness.

The examples of compact or combination that we have discussed indicate that there was a great variety of this type of document. The variety reflects an unusual situation: in a fluid governance situation European settlers had to devise makeshift governance documents whereby they could establish a civil order that reflected the reality that they had known in northern Europe. In a couple of cases, groups tried to improve upon the governance principles and structure that they had lived under in Europe: the most interesting and significant examples are the secularism of the Providence Plantation and the Old Testament theocratic commitments of the New Haven Plantation. Significantly, both of those stances were soon modified: when Providence joined the Rhode Island colonies to form the Rhode Island Colony, it became *less* secular in its civil commitments. The New Haven Plantation and Colony, on the other hand, lasted only one generation before it merged with the more liberal Connecticut Colony; it therefore lost its theocratic fervor. But many, if not most, of the early New England compacts and combinations were rather dry documents that focused on the nuts and bolts of daily governance. While not uniform, they were similar. As the century progressed, the town combinations and compacts became fewer and fewer. What took their place were the second set of documents we will consider, the legislative statutes, charters, and patents issued by the superior power of the central colonial governments. Because they came from a more central and unified source, they too reflected a high degree of uniformity.[127]

The legislative record was the first form of civil covenant established by the central colonial government. When a town was incorporated by the general court of a colony, some legislative records contained only the briefest of annotations. For instance, the record for the incorporation of Sudbury, Massachusetts Bay Colony, in 1638 reads as follows in the general court records:

> It was ordered, that the newe plantation by Concord shalbee called Sudbury.[128]

In the period after 1664 the Rhode Island Colony, on the other hand, drew up extremely detailed legislation concerning the organization of virtually all of the Rhode Island Colony towns founded after that date.[129] The legislative record for East Greenwich, Rhode Island Colony, is an example. There was not a lot of controversy in the founding and settling of East Greenwich.[130] At the conclusion of King Philip's War in 1677, the Rhode

Island Colony laid claim to the territory known as the Narragansett Territory, competing with the Connecticut Colony and the Massachusetts Bay Colony in its claim. However, Charles II had granted a charter to Roger Williams, which sealed a victory for Rhode Island Colony in its claim to the territory.[131] The territory was granted by the colony of Rhode Island to Rhode Island residents who had aided the colony during the War. One other group, led by John Fones, had purchased an overlapping land claim from the Native Americans and laid claim to what became known as the Fones Purchase. The Fones group, however, seems to have settled amicably with the legislature and with the individuals granted land to form East Greenwich, and so the development of East Greenwich continued.[132]

Passed in the general assembly of the Rhode Island Colony on Wednesday, October 31, 1677, the legislative act establishing East Greenwich reads as follows:

Act for the Incorporation of East Greenwich

In General Assembly, at Newport, October 31, 1677.
Voted, Whereas, at the General Assembly held for the Collony, at Newport, in May last, it was ordered that a certain tract of land in some convenient place in the Narragansett Country shall be laid forth into hundred acre shares with the house lots, for the accommodatinge of soe many of the inhabitants of this Collony as stand in need of land, and the General Assembly shall judge to be supplyed. In pursuance of said act of the General Assembly this present court doe enact and declare that the said tract of land be forthwith layd forth to containe five thousand acres, which shall be divided as followeth; five hundred acres shall be divided into fifty house lots, and the remainder of the said five thousand acres, being four thousand five hundred acres, shall be divided into fifty equal share or great divisions; and that each person hereafter named and admitted by this Assembly to have land in the said tract, shall have and enjoy to him and his heirs and assigns forever in manner and forme, and under the conditions and limitations hereinafter expressed, one of the said house lots and one great division, containing in the whole one hundred acres.

And further this Assembly do enact, order and declare, that the persons before named, that is to say, — {47 males}, are the persons unto whom the said tract of land is granted, and who shall possess and enjoy the same, their heirs and assigns, according to the true intent and meaninge of this present grant. And to the end that the said persons and their successors, the proprietors of the said land from time to time may be in the better capacity to manage their public affaires, this Assembly doe enact and declare that the said plantation shall be a Towne, by the name and title of East Greenwich, in His Majesty's Collony of Rhode Island and Providence Plantations, with all rights, libertys, and privileges whatsoever unto a Towne appertaininge; and that the said persons above mentioned, unto whom the said grant is made, are by this present Assembly and the authority thereof, made and admitted the freemen of the said Towne, and they, or soe many of them as shall be then present, not being fewer than twelve on the said land, are required and empowered to meet together upon the second Wednesday in April next, and constitute a Town Meeting, by electing a Moderator, a Towne Clerk, with such Constables as to them shall seem requisite; and also to choose persons their Deputies to sitt in General Assembly, and two persons, one to serve on the Grand Jury, and one on the Jury of Legalls, and soe the like number and for the said services at the said Court from time to time. And to the end that the said plantation may be speedily settled and improved according to the end of this present court in the granting thereof; be it enacted and ordained, that each person mentioned in this present grant, shall, within one year after the publication thereof make a settlement on his house lott, by building a house fit and suitable for habitation; and in case any person who hath any of the said house lotts shall neglect or refuse by himselfe or his assignee to build accordingly, he shall forfeit both the house lott and greater division, to be disposed by any succeedinge General Assembly as they see cause.

And further this Assembly doe enact and declare, that if any person unto whom the said land is granted, by this present act, shall at any time within one and twenty years after the date hereof, sell, grant, make over or otherwise dispose of any of the land or lands hereby granted unto him unto any other person interested in the said plantation, that then the said person or persons soe sellinge or disposinge of the land, shall lose all other lands whatever that he is possessed of in the said plantation, and also the lands soe disposed of to be and remaine to this Collony, anything to the contrary thereof in this present act declared notwithstanding.

And further it is enacted, and declared by this Assembly and the authority thereof, that the freeman of the said Towne shall make and lay out convenient highways from the Bay up into the country, throughout the whole Towneship, as shall be convenient for the settlement of the country above and about the said Township.[133]

This act of incorporation has as its focus land. Significantly, the land is divided equally into 50-acre lots and allotted equally to each resident. No resident received more than another, nor was there any division of land according to social stratification, size of family, or the drawing of lots. In the preliminary motion passed by the legislature in May 1677, the land was originally awarded for service in King Philip's War. In the final version, the land was granted to "soe many of the inhabitants of this Collony as stand in need of land, and the General Assembly shall judge to be supplyed"; the act then names forty-seven male grantees. As we would expect in a Rhode Island Colony charter, there is no mention of the church nor of religion in the legislative act. Freemanship was awarded simply on the basis of ownership of land and a grant from the central colony; it in no way depended on church membership. The central government provided for a town government and even specified the day that the new government should meet, and then concluded with a proviso for more effective transportation in the town via well-developed roads. The pattern of developing an extensive and lengthy legislative record and then utilizing it as an organizational instrument placed the onus of leadership on the central colonial government rather than on the individuals forming the new town. The central legislature, however, was not usually heavy-handed; once the institutions of government had been set up it left them alone to function within their bounds.

Patents also served as civil covenants and became far more common after the Restoration as a form of New England civil covenant. A patent is defined as a grant of very specific rights and privileges for a very specific purpose. Patents were usually granted by legislatures and often resembled legislative motions. In quite a few cases, however, patents self-consciously identified themselves as patents, and it is to an example of this sort of document that we want to turn. Simsbury, Connecticut Colony, received a patent from the Connecticut Colony general court in 1685.[134] The general court of Connecticut Colony began to grant patents in 1685 because it wanted to forestall trouble, particularly from the Crown. This was especially the case because Charles II and Whitehall had vacated the Charter of the Massachusetts Bay Colony in the autumn of 1684. Therefore, in May 1685 the Connecticut Colony general court passed such an act "for the prevention of future trouble, and that every township's grants of land as it hath been obteyned by gift, purchass or otherwayes, of the natives and grant of this Court, may be settled upon them, their heires, successors and assignes for ever."[135] Accordingly, the town leaders of Simsbury applied for a patent. The Simsbury Patent reads as follows:

> Whereas the Generall Court of Connecticutt have formerly Granted unto the proprietors, Inhabitants of Simsbury all those land both Meadowes and upland within these abuttments. upon Farmington Rounds, on the South and to Runne east and west Ten Miles and from the South Bound north Ten Miles and abutts on the wilderness on the north and on the Wilderness on the West and on Windsor Bounds on the east: The whole Tract being Tenn Miles square, the said lands and premises haveing ben by purchas or otherwise Lawfully obteyned of Indian Native proprietors and by the proprietors, Inhabitants of Simsbury aforesaid and whereas the Inhabitants of Simsbury, in the collony of connecticut in Newengland have made application to the Governor & Company of the said Collony of connecticutt assembled in Court the Fourteenth of May 1685 that they may have a patent for Confirmation of the aforesaide lands to them so purchased and Granted to them as aforesayd. & which they have stood seized and quietly possessed of for Som yeares past; without interruption. Now for a more full Confirmation of the aforesayd Tracte of Land as it is Butted and Bounded as aforesayd tracts of Land as it is Butted and Bounded as aforesayed unto the present proprietors of the sayd Township of Simsbury. Know ye that the sayd Governor and Company assembled: In Generall Court according to the Commission & by vertue of the power Granted to them. by our late sovereigne lord King charles the Second of blessed Memorie in his late patent Beareing Date the 23 day of Aprill in the Fourteenth year of his sayd Majisties Reigne hath given and Granted. & by these Presents do give Grant Ratifie and Confirme vnto Major John Tallcott Captain Benjamin Newbery Ensign John Terry Mr John Case Mr Joshua Holcomb Mr Samuell Willcoxsun Mr John Higley Mr Thomas Barber: and unto the rest of the present proprietors of the Township of Simsbury and their Heyrs and assigns for ever and to ech of them in such proportion as they have already agreed upon for the division of the Same: all that aforesayd Tract and percells of Land as it is butted and Bounded. together with all the woodes vplands, erable Lands Meadows pastures ponds waters rivers Islands Fishings Huntings Fowleings Mines Mineralls Quarries, & precious stones vpon or within

y^e sayd Tract of Land with all other profits and Commodities thereunto belonging or in any wise appertayning = And do also Grant unto the a Forenamed Major John Talcott Captain Benjamin Newbery Ensign John Terry Mr. John Case, Mr. John Higley Mr. Joshua Holcomb Mr. Samuell Willcoxsun Mr. Thomas Barber and the rest of the present proprietors Inhabitants of Simsbury and their Heyrs and assignes for ever. that the Foresayd Tract of Lands shall be forever hereafter deemed reputed and be an Intire Township of it selfe. to have and to hold the sayd Tracts of Land and premises. with all and singular their appurtinances together with the priviledges immunities and Franchises herein given and Granted to the Sayd . . . {see above} and other the present proprietors inhabitants of Simsbury. their Heyrs & asigns forever. and to the only proper Vse and Behoofe of the Sayd . . . {see above} & other the present proprietors Inhabitants of Simsbury; their Heyrs and assignes for ever. According to the Tenor of His Majisties Manor of East Greenwich in the County of Kent in the Kingdom of England in free and Common Soccage & not in Capitee nor by Knight service they yeilding and paying therefore to our Sovereign Lord the King his Heyers and successours only the fifth part of all the oare of gold and Silver which from time to time and at all times here after, shall be gotten there. had or obteyned in leiue of all rents, services, deuties or demands whatsoever according to the Charter:

in Witnesse whereof we have caused the Seal of the Collony to be hereunto affixed this eleventh day of Merch one thousand six hundred eighty five six and in the Second year of the reigne of our Sovereign Lord James the Second by the grace of God of England, Scotland France and Ireland, King defender of the Faith.

Robert Treat Governor

p^r Order of the Gener^{ll} Court of Conecticut signed
pr John Allyn Secretary[136]

A comparison with the previous legislative action concerning East Greenwich indicates how a patent was different from a legislative motion. The language of Simsbury's patent confirms the ownership of land, and then proceeds to describe in legal terms a series of benefits that were derived from the land. The Simsbury patent and others like it follow a legal model and were designed to stand up in a court of law as far away as London. While there is mention of royal authority there is no mention of the church, nor of the form the local government of Simsbury should take. The general court of Connecticut Colony was careful to point out that it derived its authority to grant this particular patent from the charter granted to Connecticut Colony on Thursday, April 23, 1674.[137] While a charter was more comprehensive in its granting of land and rights, a patent was a miniature charter, in that it granted specific rights and not other rights from a superior to an inferior body.

What larger patterns can we see from this examination of the grass roots civil covenants of early New England? A review of Appendix 2 reminds us of the variety of civil covenanting activity that occurred in seventeenth-century New England. What is most relevant to our discussion at present are the two columns on the right, which indicate the type of civil covenant for which evidence exists and whether the entire body politic of the town was a party to the civil covenant or whether the body politic was represented by a committee. With respect to the question of who was a party to the covenant, in some cases neither category was appropriate; this was particularly the case when charters or land grants were issued to nebulous groups of people like "the town."

What is striking as one follows the final column in Appendix 2 from beginning to end is the preponderance of documents that involved the entire body politic ("whole body") towards the beginning of our period and the increasing rate of reliance on a committee towards the middle and end of the century. Essentially, the New Englanders were becoming less intimately involved in civic formation and formulation as the century wore on and were more inclined to let someone else (usually an elite) initiate and complete the task. This trend is illustrated in Figures 1 and 2. While the practice of local combination continued at least into the early eighteenth century, we note that civil covenanting was becoming more and more of a detached and remote thing done by leaders. This trend indicates that both the leaders and the general population moved away from that sense of government as a holy function of God's anointed, and more of a routine matter that needed to be expedited. The fury and frustration with Charles I and his followers in the period 1625 to 1649 were so great that when Puritan New Englanders had an opportunity to do something completely different from the Stuart governmental agenda, they seized the opportunity. But as in the church, the next generation did not have the fervency that the first generation had, and so were willing to drift into a

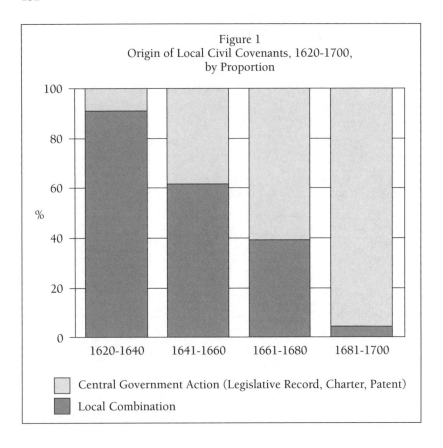

Figure 1
Origin of Local Civil Covenants, 1620-1700,
by Proportion

routine. Interestingly enough, the use of the committee began to increase rapidly just at the time of the Restoration, in 1662, and is a phenomenon that parallels the rise of the half-way covenant and the early New England jeremiad. Figures 1 and 2 illustrate that the civil covenants became more uniform as each New England colony became more and more established. During the first two decades of New England's existence, combination was the most popular method of establishing the magistracy. Citizens came together, generated a document acceptable to most male inhabitants, and signed these documents, thus instituting a local civil government. Between 1620 and 1640, more than 80 percent of the extant civil covenants for that period were combinations. By 1681 to 1700, the proportion of combinations had sunk to less than 15 percent of extant civil covenant documents. Other types of civil covenants had taken the place of the combination, most notably charters, legislative records, and patents. The ori-

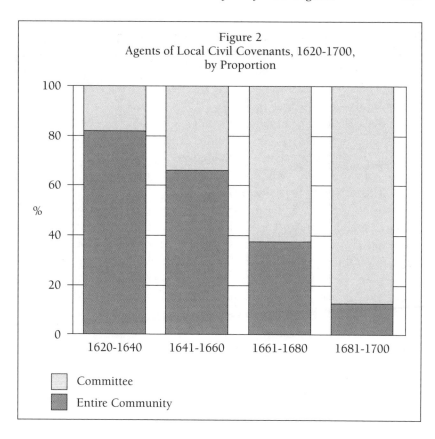

Figure 2
Agents of Local Civil Covenants, 1620-1700,
by Proportion

Committee

Entire Community

gins of these later documents came from the superior authority of the central colonial government.

Second, the agents of civil covenanting moved away from being composed of the entire community to representatives on a committee. King Philip's War and its aftermath of discouraged groups of survivors seems particularly to have been a watershed. Both trends indicate that by 1700, the civil covenants were for the most part uniform, legal documents controlled by higher powers on behalf of lower powers. This was the case on both the colonial and the local level.

There was no singular "New England Mind" concerning the civil magistracy or its specific foundational conceptualization, and the diverse types of civil covenant documents reflect the various institutional functions of the early New England magistracy. Some of the purposes of the civil magistracy were to restrain evil, sponsor and then nurture the church both spiritually and financially, divide the land according to an agreed-upon process, establish a formal social structure, resolve disputes, divide inheritances, regulate the admission, dismissal, and, if necessary, the ejection of inhabitants, establish justice at the local level of a lower court, and keep records of all of these processes.

While there may not have been unity among the early New Englanders concerning the purpose and functions of civil government, it is valid to say that as people and churches coming from the early modern Reformed world, they tended to embrace a minimalist conception of civil government. The early New Englanders did not believe that the state could be the agent to bring about significant societal change, whether it be moral reform, economic reform, social change, or religious transformation. In terms of eternity, the state was a temporary institution established after the Fall; it would disappear at the end of time. It would not be needed in the New Heavens and the New Earth where the saints would live in perfection before God: in that world, there would be no evil to restrain. The end result was that the establishment of the church was a much more important covenanting procedure in early New England than the establishment of the civil magistracy: the church would last for eternity, the state for a short time in the temporal world. We therefore see that in early New England the establishment of the state was generally a mundane affair. This is reflected in a variety of ways as we examine the evidence of early civil covenants in New England. The Mayflower Compact was a stopgap measure to deal with a crisis. The New Haven Colony's resolute strictness began to fray at the edges within a couple of years when it started to admit neighboring towns, and the colony collapsed within two decades: it could not sustain the covenantal vision it had committed itself to.

Using these dynamics as a lens, we can discern six categories that can serve as a classification system for the civil governments of the early New England colonies. While the terminology of "left" and "right" has connotations of modern ideologies, the fact that there is a definite spectrum on these matters leads us to use these terms; perhaps we can think in terms of a spectrum with a "pre-industrial right" and a "pre-industrial left." On the right would be the New Haven Colony, the strict colony that wanted to establish an explicitly theocentric state using Old Testament patterns. Next to it we can place the Massachusetts Bay Colony, with the provinces of New Hampshire and Maine. This category embodies the idea that an established state church, congregational in nature, should be the focus of a colony's attention. The presence of an established state church implied that the state was Christian — witness the statements of the Articles of Confederation of the United Colonies of New England — but there was little mention of this fact in the covenant documents at either a colonial level or a town level. The civil state existed, and it fostered many functions related to Christianity, but it had not been constituted as a holy instrument to be placed in the hands of God's elect saints. Nevertheless, the franchise and the holders of civil offices were restricted to members of the gathered church. However, the strict application of this practice was not able to be sustained, and at a local level non-members and half-way members started to participate in civil affairs, if not as office holders, then at least as voters. The Connecticut Colony comes next, in that it too ran under similar assumptions to its parent, the Massachusetts Bay Colony. From the inception of the Connecticut Colony, however, the colony allowed the franchise to be granted to non-members of the local established church. Up to the north was the small colony of Gorgeana in Maine. Its patent wished to duplicate the established arrangement in Old England, with an Anglican state church and a civil hierarchy controlled by the aristocracy.

A little farther to the left is the New Plymouth Colony. Founded as a Separatist colony, it had detached itself from the Church of England, but not from the English body politic. Thus, in the Mayflower Compact, the colony swore allegiance to James I and instituted the colony for a Christian purpose. During the second half of its existence, however, it started to adopt policies that paralleled the Clarendon codes in Old England: a town could be established with a state Baptist church at its core if the dissenting group could locate land within the colony for that purpose. Uniformity of religion could be required at a local level but not at a colonial level. Finally, on the left was the Rhode Island Colony. A harbinger of modernity, it postulated that religion should be a private affair and that the civil covenant should deal only with civil affairs. Nevertheless, the virtues of Christian citizens were to act as "salt and light" in the sphere of civil affairs.

The spectrum of covenant assumptions and documents illustrates well the heterogeneity of early New England attitudes toward civil government, and the flexibility that could be found in the arrangements of church, state, religion, and society. With the move toward centralized colonial control of the civil governments by the colonial legislature, that flexibility became more uniform and rigid during the second half of the century, while at the same time paving the way for greater flexibility in the religious and ecclesiastical realm. It is therefore to those covenantal commitments — the church covenants — that we now turn.

4

The Church Covenants
of Early New England I:
The Standing Order

O Prayse the Lord, call on his Name.
    mong people shew his facts.
Sing unto him, sing psalmes to him:
    talk of all's wondrous acts.
Let their hearts joy, that seek the Lord:
    boast in his Holy-Name.
The Lord seek, & his strength: his face
    alwayes seek yee the same.
Those admirable works that hee
    hath done remember you:
his wonders, & the judgements which
    doe from his mouth issue.
O yee his servant Abrahams seed:
    sonnes of chose Iacob yee.
He is the Lord our God: in all
    the earth his judgements bee.
His Covenant for evermore,
    and his comanded word,
a thousand generations to
    he doth in minde record,
Which he with Abraham made, and's oath
    to Isack. Made it fast,
    a law to Iacob: & Isr'ell
    a Cov'nant aye to last.

He sayd, I'le give thee Canans Land:
by lot, heirs to be there.

(Psalm 105:1-11; Bay Psalm Book)

At the heart of each early New England community was its church. While not all in New England appreciated the New England Way, the leaders of New England and a large number of its citizenry treasured their local church. For the orthodox, it was the institution that brought them closest to God, and for many it was the very reason that motivated them to leave Old England and start anew in the New World. With the exception of Rhode Island, all people were compelled by law to attend morning worship on the Sabbath in all of the seventeenth-century New England colonies. This was the case even if they were not one of the gathered saints or, later on, a half-way member.[1]

In classical early modern Protestantism, the marks of the true church were the preaching of the Word of God, the sacraments rightly administered, and the exercise of church discipline. In New England Puritanism, the marks of the true church were more numerous. The church was the group of saints redeemed by the finished work of Jesus Christ and gathered out of the world through the covenant of grace. The new covenant administration of the covenant of grace was manifest in various ways: in preaching, prayer, singing of Psalms, and particularly in the sacraments of baptism and the Lord's Supper. In New England, however, the covenant of grace was also made manifest through the ecclesiological construct of the church covenant, a document signed by the charter members of the Congregational church in a day-long ceremony that took much time, effort, and preparation. In the following weeks, months, and years the church covenant document was signed by other men and women who joined the gathered church. While earlier historians have focused on the theological statement of the covenant of grace,[2] we are turning our attention to another, almost untouched facet of New England covenant theology: the church covenants themselves.[3]

The church covenant usually appeared at the beginning of the official record book of the church and laid out the covenantal vision that the foundation members had for the congregation for future years.[4] Nevertheless, the evidence that we will examine for this study of the early New England church covenants consists of documents that have often undergone a series of convoluted redactions. In fact, we can point to at least ten different formats of the church covenant that serve as evidence of what the church covenants said on the day a congregation was gathered.

The first format, of course, is the original covenant itself, signed by the foundation members; this would take the form of a page in the new church record book or a piece of paper. The Salem Village, Massachusetts Bay Province, First Church has such a covenant at the beginning of its record book, including the original signatures of the male foundation members and a list of the female foundation members.[5] The church records of the Bradford, Massachusetts Bay Colony, First Church indicate that the Bradford church used a separate piece of paper first, and then renewed its covenant in the church book:

> At a private fast of ye Church of Christ at Bradford 20 of 4th 1683 it was judged convenient for ye brethren of this Church who did first embody themselves together in this place, to subscribe their names in this church book to that confession of faith and the Church covenant therein recorded, partly because the loose papers to which our names were formerly affixed, were in danger to be worn out and lost, and partly to renew ye covenant at least implicitly with God and with each other at this time.[6]

We know that the Bradford First Church was gathered on Wednesday, December 27, 1682; this note is dated Wednesday, June 20, 1683. That leaves a gap of six months, and so we can be certain that this covenant renewal reflects the content of the original church covenant.

Usually, however, early New England churches were not as careful to record and preserve the *autographa* of their church covenants. A second and far more common format of a surviving covenant is a copy of the autographed document, a copy that may be official or unofficial. In this case the record may be either a modern precise transcription or an edited version of older records that a pastor, local historian, or parish clerk made. The clerk's record would be a more official record of the covenant that would be written down in the legal record book of the congregation. Such a record book would be a public document that would be passed on by the clerk to the succeeding clerk. The problem with such records is that at times clerks inscribed important information in sections of the book where it was convenient or where it fit. Such records, therefore, could be non-sequential and non-chronological. At times, succeeding clerks inaugurated new record books and copied out portions of the old record book into the new book. In so doing they concluded that some information was more important than other information. They would therefore edit information from previous records and write down for future generations only "the highlights." But what the clerk thought were highlights and what modern historians think are highlights might not necessarily coincide. While such records might be useful, we must bear in mind that they can reflect the editorial mind of the transcriber or editor; furthermore, we do not necessarily know if the editor or transcriber was working from the original *autographa* or from a copy of the *autographa* or a copy of a copy. Hartford, Connecticut Colony's, Second Church has such a record. The church was gathered in 1669/70, but its original records no longer exist. Rev. Thomas Buckingham, the pastor from 1694 to 1731, did, however, gather together some of the relevant records of the years before he commenced his duties and put them together in a book. The book begins as follows:

> Some Acts Done by the Second Church in Hartford after their Settlement in a Distinct State, ffeb^{ry} 12: 1669 — [7]

Buckingham then began his record with an event that occurred in 1677. As in the Bradford case, we know the details of the original covenant document through a covenant renewal that occurred a little over fifteen years after the church was gathered:

> March 24, 1685/6, the church and children of it renewed the covenant as may be seen in the forme as it is written in a loose Sheete among the papers belonging to ye church. . . .[8]

Buckingham continues in an historical vein and asserts that he is working with the original covenant:

> Having had the consent and countenance of the General Court and the advice of an ecclesiasticall councill to incourage us in imbodying as a church by ourselves, Accordingly, upon the day of compleating our distinct state (viz. ffeb^{ry} 12, 1669), *This paper was read* before the messengers of the churches, and consented to by ourselves, viz.: . . . {the church covenant follows}.[9]

Edwin Parker then published Buckingham's record "almost in its entirety" as the third appendix of his history of the Hartford Second Church. His modern editorial comment at the beginning indicates the blessing but also the pitfalls of a "secondary source that is almost primary":

> [This appendix is a *partial* copy of the records of the Second Church of Christ in Hartford].[10]

The minister's record of what happened is another type of record and the third in our typology of formats. Such a record might not be an official public document, but might be a personal diary entry or a personal journal of what happened at the church. At times, the minister's personal journal became the official record book of the congregation after his death. The Stratford, Connecticut Colony, Second Church (now Woodbury, Connecticut, First Church), founded in 1670, has an example of such a record. Rev. Zechariah Walker was the founding pastor, and he began his narrative of the church foundation with the following words:

May, 1670.

> A record of ye proceedings, & affaires of ye 2^d chh at Stratford, from its first beginning. By me Zechariah Walker.[11]

Walker then gave a narrative of the procedures and controversies leading to the formation of the church, and then gave the text of the church covenant. The precision with which he makes his assertions leaves us little room for doubt that what he gave was the true text of the covenant, a covenant that had already been entered into before the formation of the Stratford Second Church:

> And having attained ye approbation of ye chhes of Fairfield, Killingworth, & ye new chh at Windsor, we did solemnly renew o^r said covenant the first of May, 1670. The covenant thus entered into by us, & renewed as is aboves^d was as followeth.

"The Covenant.
. . . {Text of the Covenant} . . .

> "The names of ye persons y^t subscribed this covenant, & again publickly owned it, May 5th, viz: ye day of my ordination, were as followeth . . .

"On ye 5th of May, 1670, I was ordained pasto^r of ye 2^d chh: at Stratford."[12]

A fourth type of format for the record of the covenant might be the record or the recollections of laity or of ecclesiastical tradition. The recollection might have been written down the next day, the next month, the next year, or many years later. The covenant of the Concord, Massachusetts Bay Colony, First Church, signed in 1636, is an example of such a record. While no official church records for Concord predate 1736, Lemuel Shattuck cited this covenant in his *History of the Town of Concord*.[13] Shattuck introduced the document as follows:

> Among other old family papers, transmitted from an early member of the church, is the following, endorsed "Concord Church Covenants, which was adopted by them." Though without signatures or date, it has internal evidence of authenticity, and of being the first church covenant. The orthography only is altered.[14]

Typical of nineteenth-century local historians, Shattuck did not cite the 1836 location of the document, the name of the member, or the name of his or her family, nor the nature of the "internal evidence of authenticity."

The fifth format of the original covenant text might be found in the covenant renewal that took place in succeeding years. While the church records might not have a record of the original covenantal event, it might have a record of a covenant renewal. Like the documents of the laity, the covenant documents found in such renewals could be fraught with unknown complications. The documents used in covenant renewals could take three forms: either they could purport to be exact copies of the original covenant (cf. what Zechariah Walker said concerning the Stratford Second Church covenant), or they could be admitted reconstructions of what the renewers thought the covenant had said or what they remembered it to say, or they could simply be documents drawn up from scratch. Obviously, the last category would not help us, but the first two categories do. An example of the second category can be found in the records of the Plymouth First Church, after the general court called for a fast and covenant renewal in the wake of the 1676 King Philip's War:

> The Generall Court in June, being sensible of the heavy hand of God upon the country in the continuance of war with the heathen ap-

pointed a day of Humiliation to be kept, 22 day of it & added thereto a solemne motion to all our ches to renew a covenant engagement to God for Reformation of all provoking evils. . . . After Prayer for Gods direction & blessing in soe solemne a matter, A church-covenant was read, & the chh voted that it should be left upon record as that which they did owne to be the substance of that Covenant which their Fathers entered into at the first gathering of the church, which was in these words following: . . .[15]

Note that the clerk spoke of "a covenant" and not "the covenant," and that the congregation spoke of this covenant as "the substance" of the original covenant. But they did not have the original covenant to renew fifty-six years after the famous year of 1620. And indeed, where "the first gathering of the Plymouth Church" occurred, and whether it even occurred, is not clear. Was the church gathered in Scrooby? Or Amsterdam? Or Leyden? Or New Plymouth? We have no record of a gathering of the Plymouth First Church.[16] Neither did the third generation of Separatist pilgrims, which is why they came up with "a covenant" rather than "the covenant."

The records of the Scituate, New Plymouth Colony, Second Church (now the Norwell, Massachusetts, First Church) indicate how a covenant renewal also acted as an initiatory covenant. The Scituate Second Church was formed out of a conflict with the Scituate First Church, and the details of that conflict are not relevant for our present point.[17] The papers that narrate the formation of the Scituate Second Church do, however, give us insight into how the Second Church utilized the covenant of the First Church for its formation. The italicized portions in particular reflect the situation:

Renewal of Covenant by the Church of Christ in Scituate, distinct from that of which Mr Chuancy is Pastor.
February 2d, 1642,
    Wheras in former tyme, whilst Mr. Lothrop was at Scituate Mr. William Vassall, Thomas King, Thomas Lapham, Judith Vassall, Suza King, Anna Stockbridge, together with many more, were together in Covenant in one Church, and that many of them, with Mr Lothrop our Pastor, departed and went to live at Barnstable, and did leave one part of the Church at Scituate, who by consent of all the Church, became a Church, remaining at Scituate, and admitted into their fellowship John Twisden and many more, and so continued in one Church some tyme till part of this Church called Mr Chauncy to be their Pastor, which

William Vassall, Thomas King, John Twisden, Thomas Lapham, Suza King, Judith White and Anna Stockbridge refused to do: *and that since Mr Chauncy was called to be their Pastor, the s^d Mr. Chuancy and that parte of the Church that called him, have renounced their Church standing whereon we stood a Church together, and will be a Church together by some other standing, and so refuse us to be parte of their Church, except we will enter into a new Covenant with them, which for diverse reasons we find we may not do, but remaining still together in a Church state, and knowing that being forsaken by them, we remain a Church, yet forasmuch as some are not clearly satisfied that we are a Church — therefore —*

We do here now further covenant, and renew that Covenant that we were formerly in together as a Church, . . . {text of the church covenant}.[18]

One year later, further action had to be taken in response to counsel from a source outside the New Plymouth Colony, namely, a committee from the Massachusetts Bay Colony that had been appointed to try to resolve the dispute between the two groups:

A declaration entered on the Church Records, 1643.

"Whereas, since the Covenant above written was made, we have met with many oppositions from Mr Chuancy and the rest of the Church with him, and that the last meeting of the Elders in the Bay, and this present, it was their judgements, and that from the tyme that they denied communion with us we were free from them, that *their advice to us was, to renew our former Covenant in a publicke manner, which we are contented to do in convenient tyme:* yet nevertheless we hope that all the Churches of Christ that shall take notice of our Covenant, will acknowledge us to be a true Church of Christ, and hold communions with us in the mean tyme. . . ."[19]

In looking, therefore, at the Scituate Second Church covenant we are given insight into the Scituate First Church's covenant, signed seven years earlier on Thursday, January 8, 1634/5. While we have a narration of the Scituate church gathering, we do not have a covenant document.[20]

Another method of discerning what the original covenant said is to look at the formulary used to receive new members into the congregation; while the original covenant might not exist, the formulary for the reception of new members could at times contain the text of the original covenant. The Boston First Church records give us an example of this method, which is the sixth in our list of formats. The Boston First Church was founded in 1630. The pages of its early records reflect a general state of confusion and flux that often characterized early New England church records. The records begin with two memoranda from the clergy of 1728 and 1828. Possibly they reflected preparations for centennial and bicentennial celebrations in 1730 and 1830, respectively. The notes are as follows:

> Memorandum May 1728 I had the Church book new bound; and the blank paper in the old one being very unfit for use, having been damnify'd with water some time formerly, I order'd new and good paper to be put in its room, exactly answering to the number of Pages taken out: and though some of the Leaves were necessarily torn, yet not a single Leaf or Line is left out of the Records THOMAS FOXCROFT. . . .
>
> The parchment cover enclosing these records having become much "damnify'd" by the wear of a hundred years, the volume was put into a new binding in Russian Leather, with the greatest care that nothing should be omitted or changed in the MS. by N. L. Frothingham. May, 1828.[21]

The second page is blank, while the third page is a list of ministers from 1630 to 1815. The fourth page is blank, while the fifth page has some notations from 1687. The sixth page is blank, and it is not until we get to page 7 that we find the church covenant, set up in such a way that it can be utilized for the reception of new members:

The Church Covenant

Query; Per Elder Bridgeman (in margin)
Whether you be willing to Enter into a holy Covenant with God and his people in this Church; You promise, by the grace and help of Christ. . . .[22]

A second version of that covenant is found on page 13, in the hand of James Allen, the pastor of the church from 1668 to 1710:

CHURCH COVENANT
The Member

I do promise. . . .

The Church by an officer

> We promise in the name of this church And by the help of the Lord
> Jesus. . . .[23]

One might wonder whether this is the construction of succeeding generations of clergy and lay elders. In the case of Boston First Church, however,
we can confirm that these two covenants were slightly revised forms of the
original covenant because John Cotton, the pastor of Boston's First Church,
published the covenant in 1641. The title is instructive: *A coppy of a letter of
Mr. Cotton of Boston, in New England, sent in answer of certaine objections
made against their discipline and orders there, directed to a friend. With the
questions propounded to such as are admitted to the Church-fellowship, and the
covenant it selfe.*[24] A comparison of the covenant found on pages 5 and 6 of
that short pamphlet with the records of the Boston First Church indicates
that there were only minor changes in the wording of the covenant.

In a couple of cases, most notably Salem First Church and Boston
First Church, the covenants were printed up and published, sometimes
without the authorization of the church. Such publication could occur
soon after a covenant ceremony or many years after, and provides the seventh format by which we might try to discern an original covenant text.[25]

A similar phenomenon would be the publication of church handbooks and manuals, a practice that blossomed in the nineteenth century.
This is the eighth format for the covenant. These handbooks typically had
bylaws, lists of members, descriptions of church life, and, at the end, copies of the covenants used at the time for baptism of infants or children and
the reception of new members. From time to time they would also include
the original text of the covenant, or what they maintained was the original
text. Such covenants need to be scrutinized closely, if possible in conjunc-
tion with the original records, because sometimes they were covenants
signed a century after the founding of the church that were uncritically
published as the original covenant. The "Handbook" of the Wenham, Massachusetts Bay Colony, First Church is a helpful example here. The
Wenham-1 First Church was gathered on Tuesday, October 8, 1644. Rev.
John Fiske then led a group from the Wenham-1 First Church to
Chelmsford, where the Chelmsford First Church was gathered in 1655.
But on Tuesday, December 8, 1663, the Wenham-2 First Church was gathered to replace the church gathered nineteen years earlier. We have no
covenant for 1644, but we do have some narrations of grace. The covenant

for 1663 was located in the 1840 "Handbook" because of a comment made in a published sermon of 1845. The succeeding manuals or handbooks after 1840 did not mention the original covenant, but fortunately, the 1840 "Handbook" did: "In 1663, a church was gathered, and the Rev. Antipas Newman ordained their pastor. The following is a copy of the Covenant then adopted and signed by the pastor and nine others, whose names are appended: . . ."[26]

Such variety in the form of covenant documents might lead one to conclude that while multiple covenants might exist, few can be regarded with certainty as the texts of what was signed on the foundation day of a church. Indeed, a careful, critical reading of the materials for over 250 congregations resulted in only about fifty-five texts that can be considered authentic — that is, as being the texts utilized on the day that a church was gathered and inaugurated. The evidence that we do have, however, fits together into a coherent picture that reflects a mind-set of the elect saints who founded the churches, a mind-set that also began to change subtly as the seventeenth century concluded and the eighteenth century commenced.

Analyses of the ecclesiastical covenants of early New England have been done only in a cursory manner and are quite limited in scope and methodological sophistication. At the beginning of the twentieth century, Champlin Burrage approached the topic in *The Church Covenant Idea: Its Origins and Its Development.*[27] Burrage, writing from a Baptist perspective, begins his survey with the Anabaptists on the Continent, a group that emerged in the confusion of the Reformation of the sixteenth century. Burrage points out that the phenomenon of formulating, signing, and then keeping a covenant is not a practice limited to any one group in the early modern Protestant world. His survey of the practice moves on from the Anabaptist world to the Protestant world of Scotland that emerged after 1560. In both cases, and particularly in the Scottish case, covenants were formulated and signed during periods of reformation. The Scots signed a covenant in 1581, and then renewed it in 1638 as a protest against the attempts of Charles I and William Laud to impose episcopacy and Anglican high church worship on Scotland. In 1643, as a condition for Scottish military aid against the army of Charles I, the English Parliament consented to signing the Solemn League and Covenant, a shorter document that was more positive in spirit and tone than the earlier Scottish covenants. In actuality, these covenants were more civil covenants than they were church covenants, and they were documents that articulated *re*formation rather than formation and institution. Burrage then continues his study with the

Separatist, Puritan, Independent, Dissenting, and Baptist scenes in England.

According to Burrage, the turning point in the use of covenants in the Anglo-American world is the year 1640, toward the beginning of the English Revolution and Civil War, when various groups were beginning to leave the established Church of England and forming their own church out of frustration and disgust with Archbishop Laud and King Charles I. These therefore are covenants of formation and institution. In contrast to the Scottish situation, those who were leaving the Church of England at this stage were those who had concluded that there was no hope of reforming the monolithic state church, and that in actuality the scriptures, and in particular the New Testament, taught that the congregational form of church government was the form taught by Christ and the Apostles. Therefore, the list of covenants and examples that Burrage assembled differed from one another; there was no standard, uniform covenant that all adhered to. We should add, at this point, that the Scottish world, with its presbyterian form of church government that was parochial in organization, produced only a couple of covenants. The Scottish church was smaller and as a result more cohesive; furthermore, because the king and the archbishop of Canterbury were at a more remote distance in London, the Scots had felt less pressure in the previous four decades to conform to Anglican ways. Therefore, there was not a Separatist movement in the Church of Scotland as there had been in England during the period 1560 to 1640. When the heavy-handed policies of the regime of Charles I emerged in the late 1630s, the Scots united behind the Covenant of 1638.[28] Burrage's work gives a lot of good texts, but has very little analysis and provides no interpretive framework for the documents that he uncovered. Each chapter of his work is arranged chronologically, and he draws no relationships between any of the documents. His chapter on New England focuses on the half-way covenant and some examples of the texts used in the establishment of that practice, and then he turns his attention to the Baptist covenants of early New England.

Over a decade after Burrage's work appeared, William E. Barton, a Congregationalist minister and professor of ecclesiastical law at the University of Chicago Divinity School, attempted to "assemble all the general confessions of faith of the Congregational Churches that have any present claim to authority . . . and also to gather representative covenants adopted by or employed in representative churches . . . from the beginning of modern Congregational history."[29] Barton relied heavily on Burrage's work, and the phrase "representative covenants" indicates that his work is very limited. His book has as its focus all of Congregational history, and in addition the creeds and confessions of faith developed by the Congregationalist churches. He therefore devoted only about thirty pages to early New England, and, like Burrage, did very little to elucidate what the New Englanders were saying theologically.

The work of Perry Miller, while deeply flawed, opened up the world of early New England thought to us in ways unimaginable in the period before World War I.[30] Part of Miller's central thesis was that the idea of the covenant and the early New Englanders' use of the covenant idea was the framework by which they ordered their society. In his exploration of the covenant theme, Miller quoted from dozens of Puritan writers.[31] Miller's work is problematic, however, in that in his development of his motifs he wrests quotations out of their immediate context and also fails to grasp the long-range historical context of the source that he is citing. Furthermore, the title of his work implies that he is looking at all of New England, while in reality his work focuses in on the most powerful and largest of the New England colonies, the Massachusetts Bay Colony. The nuanced differences between the Maine Province, the New Hampshire Province, the Massachusetts Bay Colony, the New Plymouth Colony, the Colony of Rhode Island and Providence Plantations, the Colony of New Haven, and the Connecticut Colony were not included within Miller's vision of a unitary New England mind. He did, however, exhibit the varied themes of early New England Puritanism, and an army of successors have explored such themes as preparationism, law, antinomianism, rhetoric, Aristotelianism, the doctrine of conversion, the sacraments, religious liberty, and the half-way covenant in seventeenth-century New England, producing a series of studies that exhibit much greater care and precision than Miller gave to his topics. These newer studies indicate that New Englanders were at times deeply divided over a host of issues.

During the 1960s and 1970s, a new generation of historians started to rewrite the history of early New England. According to these social historians, approaching the history of New England from the perspective of intellectual history generated a version of history that favored the intellectual elite of the period and took little if any notice of the plebeian classes of early New England. Furthermore, while many grand ideas were articulated by the clerical elites, historians had no idea whether what was preached was being practiced. While Perry Miller attempted to provide a discussion of the theory that the New Englanders developed, the social historians attempted to examine the praxis that they exhibited. On a whole host of topics — witchcraft, the half-way covenant, Native American missions, church membership — the social historians sorted through piles of records of events (church and town records, tax lists, land records, court and criminal records, genealogical data, wills), piecing together a story from scraps of evidence to see whether the New Englanders practiced what they preached, or what was preached to them.[32]

In the post-Miller period only one other person has broached the topic of early New England church covenants. Charles W. Deweese completed a 1973 dissertation on Baptist church covenants.[33] Like Burrage and Barton's work, Deweese's work is a survey of the use of church covenants in the Baptist tradition both in history and in contemporary life. His early chapter on the analysis of extant covenants is somewhat helpful (length, similarities in themes, terminology and phrasing, content), but he explores many themes that are particular to the Baptist world (e.g., attitudes of Baptists toward the use of covenants), and he attempts to cover the region of Old England in addition to New England. When he finally does get to New England, he gives only four pages to the subject of the church covenants of the Baptist churches of early New England.[34]

While there has been some exploration of church covenants in seventeenth-century New England, no systematic, methodical study of the extant church covenants has been attempted, because no systematic, methodical search for these covenant texts had been undertaken. Now that such a search has been completed, however, we are able to assess with confidence the evidence that has survived, and to interpret the extant covenant texts generated by the ecclesiastical institutions of seventeenth-century New England. While much has been made of the covenant idea in New England, our understanding of that idea has been derived from the trajectory of intellectual and theological history that has been gleaned from the theological discussions of the covenant in the seventeenth century. The nuances of such a complex and difficult subject have been brought to our attention through these primary and secondary sources. But are these nuances found in the actual covenants themselves? The church (and town) covenants of early New England open for us a window into a world that is located between the elite and popular cultures of that time. While the intellectual elite often composed these covenants, they did so as to make the covenant explicit and practical to the general population. Foundation members were not the only ones who needed to understand the church covenant; future members admitted to the congregation in coming years by the foundation members also needed to comprehend their covenantal commitments. We also have evidence that at times the foundation members themselves (perhaps with the assistance of the clerical leader), composed the covenantal texts. Those texts composed by the foundation members themselves allow us to understand how the laity comprehended the covenantal ideas and the federal theology that the clergy explicated in their teaching ministry. In sum, an exploration of the covenants spawned by the early New England churches offers us an uncommon opportunity to explicate a major theme of early American history.

The first question we need to address is the degree of uniformity and standardization that we find in the documents. Are these covenants essentially copies of one another? Did the early covenants essentially act as templates for the later covenants? Can we trace relationships between mother and daughter churches — that is, did the daughter churches essentially copy the covenant of the mother churches? The texts of the covenant documents reflect the New England congregational system as a whole, in that there is a unity and a diversity evident simultaneously. Each congregation independently wrote up its own covenant, a practice that led to dozens of slightly different covenant commitments. Nevertheless, the congregational documents on the whole reflect a unity of thought that was only beginning to fray in the last two decades of the century. Even the covenants of non-established dissenting churches follow a generally discernable pattern. Amidst the variations of style, phrasing, and length, certain common themes begin to emerge from all of them. Furthermore, what we might call a "covenant formulary" emerged after the mid-1630s that reflected a consistent structure and similar theology for all of the early New England covenanting churches.[35] For our purposes in this chapter we will turn our attention to several examples from the dominant congregational tradition. The examples that we will scrutinize come from the entire chronological and geographical spectrum of New England covenantal activity. We will investigate the examples in chronological sequence. We should note, however, that we have a few covenant documents from non-established churches that did not have the sanction of the state and therefore did not exercise religious hegemony in a particular community. Examples of those documents will be considered in the next chapter.

The Charlestown, Massachusetts Bay, First Church was gathered on Friday, November 2, 1632.[36] The covenant that the founding members signed is written into the first page of the church record book, along with "The Names" {N.B. not the signatures or autographs} "of those who did enter into the Covenant first."[37] The covenant text is then immediately given:

The forme of the Covenant. . . .

In the Name of oʳ Lord God, and in Obedience to his holy will and divine or {sic} ordinances. Wee whose names are heer written Beeing by his most wise and good providence brought together, and desirous to unite oʳ selus into one congregation or church, under oʳ Lord Jesus Christ our Head: In such sort as becometh all those whome he hath Redeemed and sanctified unto himselfe, Doe heer sollemnly and Religiously as in his most holy presence, Promice and bynde oʳ selus to walke in all oʳ wayes according to the Rules of the Gospell, — and in all sinceer conformity to his holy ordinances: and in mutuall Love and Respect each to other: so near as God shall give us grace.[38]

In comparison to many of the other covenants that we will examine, this is a relatively short example.[39] It begins with a preamble ("In the Name . . .") and proceeds to discuss the gathering church as a group of people. Not surprisingly, the preamble is theocentric, but it is not specifically trinitarian. The body of the covenant text, however, does have as its focus Jesus Christ, who is identified as the Lord and as "our Head"; since this is the gathering of the church, such a reference is to Christ's role as primary leader of the church. It should be noted that this acknowledgment is in contradistinction to Canterbury or the Crown being recognized as the head of the church. There is a further silent jab at the Church of England with the words "In such sort as becometh all those whome he hath Redeemed and sanctified unto himselfe" — in essence saying that in Old England people did not unite themselves "in such sort" a way. The covenant promise that the congregation made was to God, in the presence of God. God is both witness and party to the promise. This theme is a theme that will recur numerous times in the early New England covenants, and is reflective of the theological and biblical concept of the aseity of God. The aseity of God refers to the absolute "otherness" of God: God is absolutely independent of the created order that he has instituted. Therefore, the only absolutely credible witness for such a solemn covenant with God as the party would be a non-created being, and the only entity that fits such a category is God himself. The writer of the Book of Hebrews expresses the concept in this manner:

For when God made promise to Abraham, because he could swear by no greater, he sware by himself, Saying, Surely blessing I will bless thee, and multiplying I will multiply thee. And so, after he had patiently endured, he obtained the promise. For men verily swear by the greater:

and an oath for confirmation is to them an end of all strife. Wherein God, willing more abundantly to show unto the heirs of promise the immutability of his counsel, confirmed it by an oath: That by two immutable things, in which it was impossible for God to lie, we might have a strong consolation, who have fled for refuge to lay hope upon the hope set before us: Which hope we have as an anchor of the soul, both sure and steadfast, and which entereth into that within the veil. . . . (Hebrews 6:13-19)

There will be other witnesses, including angels, that will be referred to in some of the covenants, but most of the covenant texts make God both witness and party to the covenant.

The remaining sentences of this covenant deal with ethical commitment to God and to one's neighbor: the walk according to "Rules of the Gospell" and "conformity to {God's} holy ordinances" are more vague phrases that might be open to interpretation, but such ethical conformity, it was hoped, would lead to mutual love and respect within the gathered church. The final sentence reminds those who took the covenant that their ability to keep it was not based on the diligence, duty, and discipline of the church member but on the grace of God.[40]

Thirty-five people, both male and female, signed the Charlestown First Church covenant on foundation day. The covenant seems to have been signed by family units, first the husband, and then the wife, with three single males. While this was a gathered church, the gathering is not a restrictive gathering; it is only after 1636 that we see the practice of restricting the foundation members to only seven males. Interestingly enough, the structure of the covenant formulary changed at that very juncture too, so that there seems to be a relation between the restrictive policy concerning the number of foundation members and the conception of the covenant formulary that is the hallmark of most early New England covenants.

Dorchester-2, Massachusetts Bay Colony, First Church was inaugurated on Tuesday, August 23, 1636.[41] Seven males signed the covenant, led by Rev. Richard Mather. Mather was the author of *An Apologie of the Churches in New-England for Church-Covenant. Or, A Discourse touching the Covenant Between God and Men, and Especially Concerning Church-Covenant, that is to say, The Covenant Which a Company Doe Enter Into When They Become a Church; and Which a Particular Person Enters into When He Becomes a Member of a Church* . . . , a treatise written in 1639 but published in 1643.[42] We therefore have the textual evidence that serves as a precursor of what Mather spoke of in *An Apologie of the Churches in New-England for Church-Covenant*. The full text of the Dorchester-2 covenant is as follows:

Dorchester. the 23th day of the
6th moneth. Anno. 1636.

Wee whose names are subscribed being called of God to joyne o^{r}selves together in Church Comunion, from o^r hearts acknowledging o^r owne unworthines of such a priviledge or of the least of Gods mercyes, & likewise acknowledging o^r disability to keepe coven^t wth God or to p'fourme any spirituall duty wch hee calleth us unto, unlesse the Lord Jesus do enable us thereunto by his spirit dwelling in us, Doe in the name of Cht Jesus o^r Lord and in trust and confidence of his free grace assisting us freely Coven^t & bind ourselves solemnely in the

1. presence of God himselfe, his holy Angells and all his servants here present that wee will by his grace assisting us endeavour constantly to walke togeather as a right ordered Congregacon of Cht. according to all the holy rules of a church-body rightly established, so farre as wee do already know it to bee o^r duty or shall further und^{r}stand it out of Gods holy

2. word: Promising first & above all to cleave unto him as o^r chiefe and onley good, and to o^r Lord Jesus Cht as o^r onely spirituall husband and Lord, & o^r onely high priest & Prophet and

3. King. And for the furthering of us to keepe this blessed Comunion wth God and wth his sonne Jesus Cht and to grow up more fully therein, wee do likewise promise by his grace assisting us, to endevour the establishing amongst o^r selves of all his holy ordinances wch hee hath appointed for his churches here on earth, and to observe all and every of them in such sort as shall bee most agreeable to his will; opposing to the utmost of o^r power, whatsoever is contrary thereunto, & bewayling fro o^r hearts o^r owne neglect thereof in former tyme, and our polluting o^{r}selves therein wth any sinfull inventions of men.

4. And lastly wee do hereby Coven^t & p'mise to further to o^r utmost power, the best . . . spirituall good of each other, and of all and every one that may become members of this Congregacon, by mutuall Instruction reprehension, exhortacon, consolacon, and spirituall watchfulnes over one another for good; and to bee subject in and for the Lord to all the Administracons and Censures of the Congregacon, so farre as the same shall bee guided according to the rules of Gods most holy word.

Of the integrity of o^r heartes herein wee call God the searcher of all hearts to witnesse; beseeching him so to blesse us in this and all o^r Enterprises, as wee shall sincerely endevour by the assistance of his grace to observe this holy Coven^t and all the braunches of it inviolably for ever; and where wee shall fayle there to wayte upon the Lord Jesus for pardon and for acceptance and healing for his names sake.

{seven male signers}

. . . The names of such as since the constituting or gathering of the church at dorchester have been added to the church and joyned thereunto as members of the same body, by profession of faith and Repentance and taking hould of the Covent before the Congregacon; viz. . . .[43]

The Dorchester-2 First Church covenant is a classic example of the covenant formulary that marked the majority of the church covenants in early colonial New England. The essence of the covenant formulary can be outlined in the following manner:

1. Preamble
    a. Purpose
    b. Witnesses
2. Acceptance of and submission to God as God
3. Submission and cleaving to Jesus Christ, particularly in his three offices of prophet, priest, and king
4. Agreement to walk with the brethren in the church and to keep a holy watch over one another
5. Submission to the government of the church; at times the church covenanted to watch over the member
6. Conclusion

The majority of the early New England covenants follow this outline, but articulate the details of that outline in a variety of ways.[44]

An examination of the preamble of the Dorchester-2 church covenant first of all reveals a theme that is repeated throughout the entire covenant: the need for the grace and mercy of God and the enabling power of Christ. The Dorchester-2 foundation members publicly, at least, acknowledged that they were in total need of mercy: "from o^r hearts acknowledging o^r

owne unworthines of such a priviledge or of the least of Gods mercyes, &
likewise acknowledging o^r disability to keepe coven^t wth God or to
p'fourme any spirituall duty wch hee calleth us unto. . . ." Such phrasing is
echoed later on in the document: "bewayling fro o^r hearts o^r owne neglect
thereof in former tyme, and our polluting o^{r}selves therein wth any sinfull
inventions of men," and "where wee shall fayle there to wayte upon the
Lord Jesus for pardon and for acceptance and healing for his names sake."
While we can never know the secret thoughts of the heart, and while some
church members were doubtless proud of how humble they were, the pos-
ture that these foundation members took in the 1630s was definitely one of
humility and servility before God; nowhere is there even a hint that God
can be bargained with as an equal.

Indeed, it is the grace of God that lifts the Dorchester-2 covenanters
out of the pit of despair. The grace of God also enables and empowers the
gathered church to do the will of God: four times in this covenant we note
that the covenant signers embraced the grace of God to "assist" them "and
where wee shall fayle there to wayte upon the Lord Jesus for pardon and for
acceptance and healing for his names sake." The first mention of the sovereign grace of God indicates that these early New Englanders affirmed that
God's grace was dispensed by the operation of the Holy Spirit, specifically
the Spirit's indwelling in the members of the gathered church ("unlesse the
Lord Jesus do enable us thereunto by his spirit dwelling in us"). In the
mind of the early New Englander the grace of God gave confidence to those
touched by it so that they could approach God with boldness and do his
work in the world — whatever that might be. But the essence of grace is
that the priorities and prerogatives rest with God and not with humanity —
and the majority, if not all, of the covenants reflect that. The boldness was
the result of grace; and coupled with the boldness was a humility emerging
out of the fact that grace should even touch these individuals and their
church. Any bargaining with God — as Abraham did over Sodom and Go-
morrah (Genesis 18:23-33) — could only be done because God permitted
it out of his grace, and God continually reminded his creatures that in the
bargain he was the superior and they were the inferior. The Westminster
Confession of Faith, written about seven years after the Dorchester-2 covenant and utilized in both Old and New England, asserts that

> the Distance between God and the Creature is so great, that although
> reasonable Creatures do owe Obedience unto him as their Creator, yet
> they could never have any Fruition of him as their Blessedness and Re-

ward, but by some voluntary Condescension on God's Part, which he hath been pleased to express by way of Covenant.[45]

The preamble of the Dorchester-2 church covenant does, of course, give the purpose of the covenant — "to joyne . . . together in Church Comunion" — but it also gives what they considered to be the source of and authority for such action: both God in general ("being called of God") and specifically Jesus Christ ("Doe in the name of Cht Jesus o[r] Lord and in trust and confidence of his free grace assisting us freely Coven[t] & bind ourselves solemnely . . ."). No other mediating institution is mentioned as an authority for this action: there is no bishop, nor is there any mention of the monarchy, nor of Parliament. Christ as the locus of this authority will continue on in the church covenants through the rest of the century. This does not mean, however, that there were no institutions whatsoever that gave approval to the process. Instead of episcopal, monarchical, or parliamentary authority for the establishment of the church, the New Englanders had the central colonial government, the visiting clergy, and the prospective clergyman himself who could check the proceedings. In actuality, vetoes occasionally occurred, indicating that while the church felt itself "called of God" God's will was made known through other instituted authority other than the candidates for foundation members.[46]

Dorchester-2 had no such trouble gathering its church, but its preamble did call for a series of witnesses against it should it break the covenant: "Wee . . . Coven[t] & bind ourselves solemnely in the presence of God himselfe, his holy Angells and all his servants here present . . . to walke togeather as a right ordered Congregacon of Cht. according to al the holy rules of a church-body rightly established. . . ."[47] God, angels, and humans are called to witness the covenant commitments. One might be inclined to divide the witnesses up into two categories, heavenly and earthly, but such a division would deflect from the dynamic that is occurring at this point. We should note that the humans called to witness the covenant are not simply witnesses, but those already part of the gathered church — that is, the messengers and guests present from other churches ("all his servants here present"). Should the covenant takers abandon the grace of God and break the covenant, God and his creatures — including humans — will bear testimony against them. Such testimony will not necessarily be given in this world, but teleologically, on the day of judgment. The call for divine and heavenly witnesses, therefore, is an allusion to the consummation of all creation that will occur at the Second Coming. This segment of the covenant is a reflection of Paul's statement to the church in Corinth: "Do ye not know that the saints shall judge the world? . . . Know ye not that we shall judge angels? how much more things that pertain to this life?" (1 Corinthians 6:2-3).

After the preamble, the body of the covenant begins with a commitment first of all to God and his church: "wee will by his grace assisting us endeavour constantly to walke togeather as a right ordered Congregacon of Cht. according to al the holy rules of a church-body rightly established, so farre as wee do already know it to bee o^r duty or shall further und^{r}stand it out of Gods holy word: Promising first & above all to cleave unto him as o^r chiefe and onely good. . . ." The theocentric obligation that the Dorchester-2 church founders made reflects the Abrahamic covenantal account and the God-centered life that God commanded Abraham to embrace: "After these things the word of the LORD came unto Abram in a vision, saying, Fear not, Abram: I am thy shield, and thy exceeding great reward" (Genesis 15:1). That God is the chief and only good provides a foundation for the norms of the church — its leaders, members, and adherents. In contrast to the general population, the members of the gathered church are publicly committing themselves to ordering their church and their individual lives according to a standard that is encompassed in the theological and ethical principles found in scripture and in Reformed theology. One clause does allow for the imperfection of partial understanding, but then immediately provides for remediation and enlightenment: "so farre as wee do already know it to bee o^r duty or shall further und^{r}stand it out of Gods holy word."

In Christianity, however, the grace of God is manifested through the Son of God, Jesus Christ, and the Dorchester-2 church promised to cleave not only to God but also to the Son of God. Such a commitment is what makes the covenant explicitly Christian. The word "cleave" is appropriate for such a commitment, both to God and to Christ, but it is one of the few words in the English language that encompasses in its definitions two opposite meanings.[48] The earlier meaning of "cleave" — and the meaning that is used in this and other early New England covenants — is to adhere to or cling to some thing or some one. A later meaning of "cleave" is to break apart, as when a diamond is broken apart for sale. One of the famous uses of the word "cleave" occurs in the words of Adam in the Authorized Version of scripture as he meets Eve for the first time and "covenants" with her to be husband and wife: "And Adam said, this is now bone of my bones, and flesh of my flesh: she shall be called Woman, because she was taken out of man. Therefore shall a man leave his father and his mother, and shall cleave unto his wife: and they shall be one flesh" (Genesis 2:23-24).

The Dorchester-2 church covenant identifies Christ as a "spiritual husband," thus classifying the church and its members as being feminine in nature. This is not surprising, in that Christ is identified in the New Testament as the husband and the church as the "bride of Christ" (Revelation 21:1-6; Ephesians 5:22-33). The imagery found in scripture was amplified and embellished over the centuries to such an extent that in the Western Christian tradition the human souls of both males and females were also identified as being feminine, ready to receive either Christ or Satan as a husband.[49] The reference to Christ as spiritual husband of both the church and each of the individuals within the church matches the larger framework of medieval and early modern Christian theology.

That Jesus Christ is identified as "onely high priest & Prophet and King" is also another theme of classical Christian theology. Since the imagery that relates to Jesus Christ in the scripture alone is vast and multifarious, we might ask why it is that in this and in other covenants the imagery of the *"munus triplex"* in particular was chosen. The reason is that in Reformed theology Christ fulfilled in his work the three anointed offices of the old covenant. In the Old Testament and the old covenant, the various holders of these three offices were always anointed with oil before they commenced their work. Therefore, these three offices stood out among all of the old covenant imagery relating to the messiah (e.g., redeemer, shepherd, warrior, etc.), in that they encompassed the work of Old Testament and old covenant political and religious leadership.[50] Thus Christ as covenant head of his people leads his people, who have been called out of the world into the gathered church, through the trials and joys of this world and on into the next world — the *eschaton*. Jesus Christ, as covenant leader who is both divine and human, therefore fulfills perfectly the Old Testament offices in a way that mere humanity cannot, and offers that grace of perfect fulfillment to his imperfect people. God, and angelic and human witnesses, bear testimony to their degree of faithfulness, not so much to the stipulations of the covenant but to the degree to which the gathered church embraced the grace of God in Jesus Christ.[51]

It is significant, however, that only a few of the civil covenants of early New England identify Christ as king and leader of the civil realm. In their civil polity and political theory the New Englanders were not willing to articulate a christocentric vision for the state as they did for the church. There were at least two reasons for not articulating a christocentric state. First, in the subconscious thinking of clergy, laity, and magistrates the New England colonies were already implicitly Christian states. This is reflected in the legislative records of the central colonies, where towns are granted permission to establish themselves and to gather a church as soon as possible. The town of Chelmsford, for instance, was formed after a petition from the towns of Concord and Woburn to the Massachusetts Bay general court was granted in 1653. The granting of the petition, however, was on condition "that if the peticoners of Concord and Woobourne shall not, wth two yeares, setle a competent noumber of familjes there . . . so as they may be in capacitje of injoying all the ordjances of God there, then the graunt to be vojd."[52]

Second, the civil realm, because it exercised the power of the sword, was the subject of greater scrutiny by both Crown and Parliament. Identification of Christ as the *only* king and lawgiver would have inflamed an already tense relationship with the monarchy in Old England.

Jesus as perfect prophet, priest, and king stood in contrast not only to the New Englanders who failed but also to the Anglicans of Old England. In 1636, Puritans in both Old England and New England were furious with clergy who called themselves priests and who embraced Laudian ceremonies and doctrine but who were not, as far as the Puritans were concerned, effective and true prophets during the sermon time each Sunday morning. Furthermore, the Puritans' antipathy to Charles I later sent some of them searching for a better king. The fact that "onely" could be applied to either the "high priest" or to the "high priest, prophet and king" was perhaps an ambiguous reference to the substitution of Jesus Christ as prophet, priest, and king for the Laudian and monarchical establishment of Old England. It is significant, however, that if such was the thinking of Richard Mather and the Dorchester-2 founders, no such ambiguous (or explicit) phrasing was found in any of the civil covenants of the seventeenth century.

The means by which such a relationship with God and with Christ was sustained was in the church, particularly in its ordinances. The ordinances established in the Dorchester-2 First Church were considered holy and had their origins in God rather than in human tradition or custom:

> wee do likewise promise by his grace assistaing us, to endevour the establishing amongst o^r selves of all his holy ordinances wch hee hath appointed for his churches here on earth, and to observe all and every of them in such sort as shall bee most agreeable to his will; opposing to the utmost of o^r power, whatsoever is contrary thereunto, & bewayling fro o^r hearts o^r owne neglect thereof in former tyme, and our polluting o^rselves therein wth any sinfull inventions of men.

Unlike the Anglicans, the Puritans maintained that whatever was not explicitly commanded in scripture was not acceptable for worship, while the Anglicans said that whatever was not forbidden in scripture was acceptable if it edified the church. The ordinances of the Puritans were extemporaneous prayer, scripture reading, preaching, the two sacraments of baptism and the Lord's Supper, singing of Psalms, taking up of the offering, the church covenant itself, reception of new members by church covenant, examination of candidates for membership by the entire gathered church, catechizing, covenant renewal, church discipline, and congregational government.

The Anglicans shared some of those ordinances — prayer, scripture reading, preaching, the two sacraments of baptism and the Lord's Supper, singing of Psalms, taking up of the offering, church discipline, and catechizing. But many of the prayers were read rather than extemporaneous. And the scripture reading was set according to the cycle of the lectionary found in the *Book of Common Prayer* rather than a methodical, continuous reading and exposition of the Bible. The sermon topics were generated by the major feasts of the Anglican church calendar (Advent, Christmas, Epiphany, Lent, Holy Week, Easter, Ascension, Pentecost, and Trinity Sunday). Vestments were used in worship, and local customs of individual parishes were incorporated into the worship service. The sacraments in particular were administered in the form of a simplified medieval worship service, with overtones of baptismal regeneration lurking in the one ceremony and hints of transubstantiation and the sacrifice of the body and blood of the Lord Jesus Christ in the other. The Anglicans catechized, but they had their own catechism based on the Thirty-nine Articles of the Church of England. The Puritans were committed to opposing Anglican innovations "to the utmost of o[r] power" and "bewayling fro o[r] hearts . . . our polluting o[r]selves therein w[th] any sinfull inventions of men."[53]

The fourth part of the covenant formulary that we see here is the "holy watch" or the guarding of souls, an activity that the whole congregation engaged in rather than simply the elders or the clergy. This section of the covenant established, at least in theory, a foundation for mutual exhortation and admonition of one another. Whereas in the episcopal system the laity might simply allow the clergy to be responsible for such activity and in the presbyterian system such tasks would be left to the teaching elders (clergy) and ruling elders (lay elders), in the system of gathered Congregationalism church discipline was the responsibility of the entire gathered church. The Dorchester-2 covenant delineates the responsibilities of each member of the congregation in the following manner:

> And lastly wee do hereby Coven^t & p'mise to further to o^r utmost ppower, the best . . . spirituall good of each other, and of all and every one that may become members of this Congregacon, by mutuall Instruction reprehension, exhortacon, consolacon, and spirituall watchfulnes over one another for good. . . .

We are familiar with most of the terms listed except, perhaps, with the word "reprehension," which means rebuke or reprimand. The Dorchester-2 covenant set up a dynamic within the church that characterized much of early New England Puritanism — a communal commitment to holiness that did not allow for individual privacy or secret sin. Nevertheless, those who did place themselves under the "holy watch" did so voluntarily. Once they volunteered, however, it was very hard to get out from under these covenant obligations without some form of ecclesiastical censure and communal pressure.[54]

Submission to the governance structure of the gathered church was the fifth part of the covenant formulary. In the Dorchester-2 covenant, these words place the church member under the authority of the gathered church for disciplinary purposes:

> And lastly wee do hereby Coven^t & p'mise . . . to bee subject in and for the Lord to all the Administracons and Censures of the Congregacon, so farre as the same shall bee guided according to the rules of Gods most holy word.

The last clause provided something of an escape for creative thinkers, for who decided whether the administrations and censures of the congregation were "guided according to the rules of God's most holy word" is never stated; those flogged and fined for rebelling against the Standing Order discovered that the hegemonic rule of the congregationalists in New England was not to be challenged, at least in the first half of the century. We should note too, that the discipline was to be administered by the whole congregation, not by the professional clergy or the ordained lay elders. Whether the whole congregation voted on matters of discipline (and therefore could thwart its application) or whether they simply carried out the wishes of the leaders of the congregation varied from congregation to congregation, and is not delineated here.

The final section of the covenant formulary is the conclusion, usually asking God again to be the witness, to bless their endeavors, and to ask for pardon when those who took the covenant fail:

Of the integrity of o^r heartes herein wee call God the searcher of all hearts to witnesse; beseeching him so to blesse us in this and all o^r Enterprises, as wee shall sincerely endevour by the assistance of his grace to observe this holy Coven^t and all the braunches of it inviolably for ever; and where wee shall fayle there to wayte upon the Lord Jesus for pardon and for acceptance and healing for his names sake.

It is significant that the Dorchester-2 foundation members should call on God out "Of the integrity of o^r heartes herein wee call God the searcher of all hearts to witnesse" the covenant. Such a phrase places this text in the category of covenant rather than contract. In a contract, one can sign outwardly and not really mean it inwardly. One might fulfill the conditions of a contract, grudgingly, but in a covenant one had to fulfill the covenant with one's whole heart. Hypocrisy, therefore, the complaint of so many people about the church through the ages and the complaint of the Puritans about the parish churches of Old England, was formally forbidden in the gathered church (but still present in reality).

During the turmoil of the 1640s, two individuals published works describing and defending the New England Way and the methods it used to establish Congregational churches in the New World. Both John Cotton and Thomas Welde published their narrations of the New England Way in 1645, as the Westminster Assembly was concluding its debates concerning the mode of church government the assembly should recommend to the Parliament. Cotton's work in particular discusses the content of the church covenant in some detail. The very first chapter of *The Way of the Churches of Christ in New-England* . . . delineates the process of gathering the church. The third proposition gives essentially the covenant formulary that we have discerned emerging in the church covenants of early New England:

PROPOS. 3.

For the joyning of faithfull Christians into the fellowship and estate of a Church, we finde not in Scripture that God had done it any other way then by entering all of them together, (as one man) into an holy Covenant with himselfe, To take the Lord (as the head of his Church) for their God, and to give up themselves to him, to be his Church and people; which implyeth their submitting of themselves to him, and one to another in his feare; and their walking in professed subjection to all his holy Ordinances: their cleaving one to another, as fellow-members of the same body, in brotherly love and holy watchfulnesse unto mutuall edification in Christ Jesus: . . .[55]

The key elements of submission to God, observance of the ordinances, and submission to one another in the "holy watch" are mentioned by Cotton. Cotton went on to expand on what was in the covenant when he pursued in detail the exposition of Proposition 3:

> . . . with the silent approbation of the whole Assembly, he propoundeth the Covenant of promise, Eph. 2.12. denying also any sufficiency in themselves to keepe Covenant with God, (as having been transgressors from their youth up) they professe in the name of Christ their acceptance of the Lord for their God, and the Lord Jesus (the head and Saviour of his Church) to be their King, Priest, and Prophet; and give up themselves in professed subjection unto all his holy Ordinances, according to the Rule of the Gospel; withall they professe, their full purpose of heart, to cleave one to another in Brotherly love, and mutual subjection, according to God; nor forsaking their Assembly, (but as the Lord shall call) and ministring one to another (as becometh good Stewards of the manifold graces of God) till they all grow up to a perfect man in Christ Jesus.
>
> Having thus, or to the like purpose propounded the Covenant him-selfe, with the rest of the Brethren, who are to joyn in church-estate, they all declare their joynt consent in this Covenant, either by silence, or word of mouth, or writing.[56]

Added here are the elements of the unworthiness of those covenanting, their need for God's grace, the *"munus triplex"* or the three offices of Christ as prophet, priest, and king, and finally their resolution that they are doing this with "their full purpose of heart" and not with hypocritical intentions. While each of the early New England covenants is different, the formulary was becoming crystallized, and with the publication of Cotton's book the formulary was solidified in people's minds and available for study and future reference.

Does this formulary change over time and from colony to colony? An examination of the church covenants listed in Appendix 1 indicates that the pattern initiated in the 1630s in the Massachusetts Bay Colony did not change substantially from decade to decade or from colony to colony.

An examination of the Salem Village First Church covenant, signed in 1689, confirms this conclusion.[57] Salem Village First Church (now Danvers,

Massachusetts, First Church) was gathered on Tuesday, November 19, 1689, a little over two years before the Salem witch trials erupted in March 1691/2. One of the theses of the seminal work of Paul Boyer and Stephen Nissenbaum is that the community of Salem Village was rent by disputes and quarrels for thirty years before the witchcraft trials that occurred from March 1691/2 through September 1692. Indeed, the gathering of the church under the direction of Samuel Parris was an attempt to bridge the chasm between the side of Salem Village that was oriented toward the mercantile community of the Atlantic Ocean and the side of the village that was oriented toward inland agriculture.[58] The text of the covenant reads as follows:

> We whose names (tho unworthy of a name in this church) are hereunto subscribed, Lamenting our own great unfitness for such an Awful and solemn approach unto the Holy God and deploring all the miscarriages committed by us, either in the Days of our unregeneracy or since we have been brought into acquaintence with God, in the communion of his churches which we have heretofore been related unto: And yet apprehending ourselves called by the Most High to Embody ourselves into a different society, with a sacred covenant to serve the Lord Jesus Christ and Edifie one another according to the Rules of his holy word, Being persuaded in matters of Faith according to the Confession of Faith owned and consented unto by the Elders and Messingers of the churches assembled at Boston in New-England. May — 12 — 1680 which for the substance of it, we now own and profess
>
> We, do, in some measure of sinceritie, this day give up ourselves unto God in Christ, to be for him and for another, at the same time renouncing all the vanities and Idols of this present evil world.
>
> We give up ourselves, and offspring, unto the Lord Jehovah, the one true and living God, in three Persons, Father, Son, and Holy Ghost. To God the Father of our Lord Jesus Christ, as to our Reconciled God and Father in Christ Jesus; and unto Christ Jesus as our King, Priest and Prophet, and only Mediator: And unto the Holy Ghost as our only Sanctifyer and Comforter: As to our Best good and Last End: promising, (with divine help) to live unto, and upon, this one God in three Persons: hoping at length to live forever with him.
>
> We do likewise give up ourselves one unto another in the Lord, engaging, (with divine aid) as a church of God to submit to the order, Discipline and Government of Christ in this his church, and to the Ministerial teaching, guidance, and oversight of the Elder (or Elders)

thereof, as to such as watch for our Souls; And also to a mutuall brotherly watchfulness according to Gospel rules, so long as by such Rules we shall continue in this Relation to each other: And promise also to walk with all regular and due communion with other churches of our Lord Jesus, and in all cheerful endeavor to support and observe the pure Gospel institutions of our Lord Redeemer so far as He shall graciously reveal unto us his will concerning them.

In order hereunto:

We resolve uprightly to study what is our duty, & make it our greif, & reckon it our shame, whereinsoever we find our selves to come short in the discharge of it, & for pardon thereof humbly to betake ourselves to the Blood of the Everlasting Covenant.

And that we keep this Covenant, & all the branches of it inviolable for ever, being sensible that we can do nothing of our selves,

We humbly implore the help & grace of our Mediator may be sufficient for us: Beseeching that whilst we are working out our own Salvation, with fear & trembling, He would gratiously work in us both to will, & to do. And that he being the Great Shepherd of our Souls would lead us into the paths of Righteousness, for his own Names sake. And at length receive us all into the Inheritance of the Saints in Light.

{17 male signers}   The women which embodyed with us by
                           their severall Names as followeth Viz.
                           {10 female signers}[59]

The Salem Village First Church covenant, while retaining turns of phrase that are peculiar to itself, does not differ significantly from the covenant formulary that we have outlined earlier in this chapter. However, the phrases that distinguish it from other covenants of the same period communicate a mentalité of anxiety. The Salem Village First Church covenant is one of the few church covenants that we have from the Dominion of New England. Even so, it is not from the period of governance of Edmund Andros, but during the period that the Committee of Public Safety was ruling as the civil authority in the Massachusetts Bay.[60] The very first sentence of the covenant indicates a diffidence on the part of the author or authors (we have no evidence as to whether the author is exclusively Rev. Parris or whether the authors are the covenanting group directed by Rev. Parris): "We whose names (tho unworthy of a name in this church) . . ." is a self-

deprecating phrase that reveals an insecurity not found in the other church
covenants. The foundation members go on to "lament" their unworthiness
to gather a church and to worry about the sins that they committed both
before they were regenerated and not members of a church and then after
they were regenerated and were members of a gathered church. The evident
lack of confidence continues a couple of sentences later when room is left
for their very profession of faith to be hypocritical: "We, do, *in some measure of sinceritie,* this day give up ourselves unto God in Christ . . ." (italics
mine). The sincerity is there, but it is measured, and it may not be completely pure. The result is that while there may be hope of eternal life for
some, it may not be a reality for all who sign the covenant: "promising,
(with divine help) to live unto, and upon, this one God in three Persons:
hoping at length to live forever with him" (emphasis mine) is a clause that indicates tentativeness on the part of the author or authors that some of them
may not be in the presence of God for eternity at the end of their lives, but
under his wrath and curse in hell. When they fail to keep the covenant,
there was to be extensive sackcloth and mourning:

> We resolve uprightly to study what is our duty, & make it our greif, &
> reckon it our shame, whereinsoever we find our selves to come short in
> the discharge of it, & for pardon thereof humbly to betake ourselves to
> the Blood of the Everlasting Covenant.

Other covenants talk about failure, but the words used here ("grief,"
"shame," "coming short") indicate a more intense sense of failure than is
revealed in the other covenants of the same period. Even down to the last
paragraph, the sense of working one's salvation out before God in "fear and
trembling" is prevalent. Salem Village First Church began with the idea
that there was most likely a Judas or Judases among them. The sense of failure built into the church from the very beginning contributed to the hostil-
ities, accusations, and counter-accusations that emerged only two years
later. While none of the foundation members were executed for witchcraft,
a significant number of them, particularly Rev. Parris, the Wilkins family,
and the Putnam family, were accusers.[61]

There is one more sentence in the Salem Village First Church covenant that can be related to the context of the Salem witch trials. In the same
breath that the foundation members offer doubts about how sincere they
are, they speak of abandoning "this present evil world": "We, do, in some
measure of sinceritie, this day give up ourselves unto God in Christ, to be

for him and for another, at the same time renouncing all the vanities and Idols of this present eveil world." That the world is evil and not good indicates that this particular gathered church looked upon the world as a place of sin, where demons and witches held sway rather than the rule of Christ. It was a place to be escaped from, rather than to conquer. Indeed, when the saints of Salem Village First Church were to leave this world, they clearly thought of the future world as a much better place: "And at length receive us all into the Inheritance of the Saints in Light." Boyer and Nissenbaum maintain that economic gain was one of the major issues of contention that tore at the heart of the Salem Village community; and it is significant that here the church members are exhorted to "renounc{e} all the vanities and Idols of this present evil world."

After 1692, the Massachusetts Bay Province began to function once again with a new (but different) charter and the other New England colonies continued under the charters that had already been granted them. The boundaries of New England continued to expand, and churches were founded in far-flung areas of the region. Wells, Maine Province, gathered its church in October 1701.[62] Maine Province had originally been founded as a separate entity from the Massachusetts Bay, but during the 1650s the Bay Colony swallowed up the region without objection from the interregnum Parliament. Maine Province did, however, retain some of its own autonomy in certain civil functions.[63] The Wells First Church covenant is a fairly brief document in comparison to some of the covenants that were produced in the latter half of the seventeenth century:

> "Copy of the Covenant Engagements of the Brethren att Wells assented to and subscribed by them, October 29.1701"

> We whose names are underwritten sensibly acknowledging our own unworthiness to be in and innability to keep covenant with God as we ought, yet apprehending the Call of God unto us, to put ourselves into a relation of church communion, and to seek the settlement of the Ordinances of Christ according to gospel Institution among us: Do (abjuring all confidence in our selves and relying on Jesus Christ for Help) declare as followeth
>
> I. That we professedly acknowledge ourselves engaged to the fear and service of the only true God (Father, Son and Holy Ghost) and to the Lord Jesus Christ (The high Priest, Prophet and King of this Church) under whose conduct we submit ourselves, and on whom alone we

wait for grace and glory, to whom we declare ourselves bound in an everlasting covenant never to be broken.

II. That we are obliged to give up our selves to one another in the Lord
and to cleave one to another, as fellow members of one Body, for mutual edification, and to submit ourselves to all the holy administrations
appointed by him who is the Head and Lawgiver of His church, dispensed according to the Rules of the gospel and to give our attendance
(as God shall enable us) on all the Publick Ordinances of Christ's Institution, walking orderly as becometh saints

III. That we are under covenant engagements also to bring up our children
in the Nurture and admonition of the Lord, acknowledging our Infants
to be included with us in the gospel covenant, and to stand in covenant
relation according to gospel rules, Blessing God for such a Privilege.
Furthermore, That we are under indispensable obligations att all times
to be careful to procure the Settlement and continuence of church officers among us according to the appointment of Jesus Christ the chief
shepherd of the Flock, for the perfecting of the Saints, for the Work of
the Ministry, for the edifying of the Body of Christ, and That we are
equally oblig'd to be careful and faithfull for their maintenance,
Incouragement and Comfort, and to carry it towards as becometh
saints.

IV. Finally, solemnly and seriously professing ourselves to be a Church of
the Lord Jesus Christ, doe promise by the Help of grace to walk together as persons under such vows of God ought to doe, according to
all those Rules in the gospel prescrib'd to such a Society, so far as God
hath revealed, or shall reveal His mind to us in this Respect.

Now the Good Lord be merciful to us, and as He hath put it into our
Hearts thus to devote ourselves to Him, Let Him pity and pardon us
our frailtys, humble us out of all our carnal conferences, and keep it
forever upon our Hearts, to be faithfull to Himself and one another, for
His Praise and our eternal Comfort.

{12 male signers}[64]

What marks the Wells, Maine, covenant is the concern for the next generation — not only are the foundation members covenanting for themselves,
they are covenanting for their children. The covenant, furthermore, is "an
everlasting covenant, never to be broken." The paragraph concerning covenant children needs to be examined with greater care:

III. That we are under covenant engagements also to bring up our children
in the Nurture and admonition of the Lord, acknowledging our Infants
to be included with us in the gospel covenant, and to stand in covenant
relation according to gospel rules, Blessing God for such a Privilege. . . .

It is well known that the "rising generation" had been a matter of great concern to the New Englanders of the second half of the seventeenth century.[65]
The system of the gathered church within the parochial church had been
instituted for only one generation when cracks began to develop in its
structure. By 1655 the infants of 1635 were not professing faith and becoming communicant members at the same rate as their parents were; they
were content simply to attend church. They did not feel the need to make a
profession of faith by being examined and cross-examined by the gathered
church, and therefore they did not come to the Lord's Supper. However,
their urge to marry and have children was just as strong as that of their parents, and the question began to emerge of how their children should be
treated. Should baptized but non-communicant children of communicant
members be allowed to have their children (the grandchildren of communicant members) baptized? The Half-Way Synod of 1662 concluded that
they should have their children baptized, defending it via the concept of
the covenant; the clergy's positive response to this question, however, led to
much resistance on the part of the laity of the gathered church.[66] Amidst
this discussion, the Baptists began to emerge as a dissenting force within
both Old and New England, and while the Baptists signed covenants they
consistently denied the theology behind the practice of church covenanting. For these reasons, the covenants of the second half of the seventeenth
century pay more attention to the question of children and their covenant
obligations.

The Wells example points out the obligation particularly of the parents: since the "promise is unto you and to your children" (Acts 2:39), parents were to take special care that their children not end up in perdition as
a result of the carelessness of the parents. The Old Testament was replete
with negligent parents who let their children break the covenant. It is especially noteworthy that the covenant states that the *infants* of church members are part of the covenant; implied but not explicitly stated in that
phrase is the message that older children and adult children are to obey the
covenant of their own accord and not try to coast into heaven on their parents' profession of faith. Once you were no longer an infant, the obligations
of God descended upon you, and a more terrible judgment in hell awaited

those who had heard the gospel over and over but who refused to respond
to it. Both communicant and Half-Way parents were to raise the future generation in the "nurture and admonition of the Lord."

The church covenants of early New England offer us an opportunity
to see how a major theme of New England theological discourse was
worked out in a practical manner in the life of the individual congregations
that the New Englanders founded. Church covenants were brief and pithy
documents that emerged from an elaborate theological schema that encompassed all of biblical history. We can discern the content of the early church
covenants from careful analysis of the various forms that they took, forms
which emerged in a variety of venues, from official church records to private clerical journals to published accounts.

The independent congregational churches managed to produce individual covenants that followed a similar outline but were indigenous to the
local church. While there was a lack of uniformity — the covenants did not
use the exact same words — there was a unity of thought in all of the surviving seventeenth-century documents. This unity of thought is reflected
in the covenant formulary that the documents follow: the documents usually begin with a preamble that articulated the purpose of the church being
instituted and the witnesses, both heavenly and earthly, to the event. The
covenants usually went on to consummate a relationship with God: he was
accepted into the life of the congregation both corporately and individually,
and a hierarchical relationship of submission was inaugurated. Working
within the framework of Christian theology, specifically classical Reformed
theology, the congregation that was being inaugurated further entered into
a covenant relation with Jesus Christ the Son of God, and recognized his
work as prophet who reveals God to them, as priest who makes atonement
for them, and as king who rules over them. Having established the divine-
human vertical relationship, the horizontal relationship between fellow
church members was then established, first by establishing the mutual relationship of pastorally keeping a "holy watch" over one another, and then
by acknowledging the governance structure of the church, a structure that
was usually hierarchical and involved lay elders and professional clergy.
The covenant then concluded with a plea to God for his blessing. Two authors published accounts of how New England covenanted, John Cotton
and Thomas Welde. These publications crystallized the form of the covenants for future generations of New Englanders. In the seventeenth century
the church covenants did not change that much over time, nor did they
vary that significantly from colony to colony. At times they reflected the

personality of a congregation, as exemplified in the 1689 Salem Village (Danvers) covenant.

The early church covenants were covenants and not contracts: they reflected a relationship of grace with God and not a contractual arrangement whereby human beings could bargain with God. The content of the church covenants bestowed dignity to, yet remembered the fallibility of, human beings. Within a divine-human relationship that was hierarchical and not egalitarian the church covenants spoke of a God who reaches down to human beings in their lostness and bondage to sin. The covenant was made not only with the founding generation, but the covenant obligations and responsibilities were passed on to descending generations. Thus, the concern for the "rising generation" that is found in the sermonic literature of mid-seventeenth-century New England was also found in the covenant documents produced by the congregations themselves.

The practice of church covenanting in early New England continued on into the eighteenth and nineteenth centuries in Congregational and Baptist churches in New England and their migrational extensions further west. The documents that emerged from the practice were attempts to articulate an ecclesiology and a theology that were different from the doctrine and formulation of the church found in Old England and Europe: a theology and ecclesiology that were supposed to be more Reformed, more Protestant, more Puritan, and more biblical. The general uniformity of the seventeenth-century covenants that survive indicates that the standing order of New England Congregationalism managed to keep a coherent unity among its constituents over time and in different colonies. But ultimately, the practice of each individual Congregational church drawing up its own covenant set a precedent for the emergence of dissenting groups in the New England colonies. It is to the non-conformist covenants, particularly the covenants of the Baptist dissenters, that we now turn.

5

The Church Covenants
of Early New England II:
The Dissenters

O God, thou hast rejected us,
and scattered us abroad:
thou hast displeased been with us,
returne to us o God.
The land to tremble thou has caus'd,
thou it asunder brake:
doe thou the breaches of it heale,
for it doth moveing shake.
Thou hast unto thy people shew'd
things that are hard, thou hast
also the cup of trembleing
given to them to tast.
But unto them that doe thee feare,
a Banner to display
thou given hast to be lift up
for thy truths sake. Selah.

(Psalm 60:1-4; Bay Psalm Book)

During the first forty years of their existence, the parochial systems established by the New England colonies provided for little tolerance of dissent,
Rhode Island Colony excepted. Consequently, when conflict emerged, the
hegemonic powers at the center of the colonial governments usually acted
quickly to squelch and punish any deviation from the norm. The dissenters

had several options: submit, teach their dissenting doctrines quietly and subversively, continue their dissent vociferously, or depart either voluntarily or involuntarily. The second and third options could lead to banishment and/or corporal punishment, especially when church services were purposely disrupted. Those who dissented loudly were banished, and some formed their own churches and towns elsewhere. Those who dissented quietly often simply moved on. Rhode Island, of course, was the most famous and most obvious place to go. But Long Island was also a possibility; Lady Deborah Moody, for instance, became convinced of Baptist doctrine and practice in Lynn, Massachusetts Bay Colony, and therefore departed for Gravesend in western Long Island, an area next door to what is now Coney Island.[1] All of these dissenting communities formed towns and churches styled according to their perception of what was true.[2]

During the period 1620 to 1660 the leaders of the New England congregational standing order developed a common covenantal vision for their religious life that was articulated in the individual church covenants that were signed as they gathered their churches. This was the case no matter what colony generated a church and a church covenant. By contrast, the political vision of New England during the early part of the century was much more fragmented, as indicated in the variations among the civil covenants signed before the Restoration of 1660-62. After the Restoration, however, this fragmented political vision became more united as central colonial governments started to control the formation of towns and local civil authority. The emergence of charters and patents granted by the colonial central government was in direct response to changed political circumstances in Old England. London and Whitehall began the building of an empire, an empire that had a cohesive political vision based on legal precedent in the mother country. However, the emergence of the Clarendon Code and its modification into a policy of grudging toleration of Dissenters was a new stage in the history of both Old England and New England. Old England expected New England to follow suit.[3] Little by little, New England slowly did. With the Restoration policy of limited religious toleration of Protestant sects in Old England, all of the colonies of New England were confronted with dissenters to their own standing order. Banishment of dissenters to Rhode Island and other shores was no longer a viable option, especially after the Massachusetts Bay Colony executed four Quakers for disturbance of the public peace between 1659 and 1661.[4] In the wake of those events, Charles II and Parliament started to keep a much more careful watch over what was happening in New England.

Three varieties of Protestant dissent emerged most prominently in Restoration New England: Baptist, Quaker, and Anglican. This chapter seeks to address three questions. First, did any of these groups sign covenants in the same way that the Congregationalists signed covenants? If so, did these dissenting groups share any of the vision that the congregationalist standing order articulated in the church covenants examined in the previous chapter? And if they did not sign covenants, how did these dissenting groups establish their religious institutions? We will first look at the Anglicans, then the Quakers, and then finally the Baptists.

There were three stages to seventeenth-century Anglican development in New England. By 1708 nine Anglican churches had been formed in New England.[5] The first stage was in what is present-day Maine and New Hampshire and lasted from 1633 to 1640. During this first stage three Anglican congregations were formed.[6] However, as the Massachusetts Bay Colony took over the region of New Hampshire in the 1640s and the region of Maine in the 1650s, these churches became congregationalist in governance and worship. The second stage was the bitter dispute in 1686 in Boston, Dominion of New England, as Edmund Andros seized the building of Boston's Third Church and turned it into an Anglican chapel, thus beginning King's Chapel, Boston. The third stage began in 1698, when five Anglican churches were peacefully founded in Rhode Island, Connecticut, and Massachusetts over a ten-year period.

The example we have chosen for our purposes is Trinity Church, Newport, Rhode Island.[7] Anglican services in Newport began in 1694, and by 1701 Rev. John Lockyear was conducting services after graduating from Trinity College, Cambridge, and being ordained in London in October 1701. Sir Francis Nicholson, who had been in earlier days an assistant to Edmund Andros, was an active patron of the new Anglican group.[8] Nicholson later became governor of Virginia and Maryland and then was appointed the Crown agent charged with the task of leading the attempt to wrest Canada from the French. In late spring 1699, Richard, Earl of Bellomont, made a trip from New York to Newport. That trip resulted in contact with the Anglican community at Newport, who then drew up a petition dated September 26, 1699. The petition read as follows:

> To his Excellency, Richard, Earl of Bellomont, Captain-General and Governor-in-Chief in and over the province of the Massachusetts Bay, New York, New Hampshire and the territories thereon depending in America, and Vice-Admiral of the same:

The humble Petition of the people of the Church of England now residing in Rhode Island:

Sheweth,

That your Petitioners and other inhabitants within the Island, having agreed and concluded to erect a church for the worship of God according to the discipline of the Church of England, and tho we are disposed and ready to give all the encouragement we possibly can to a pious and learned Minister, to settle and abide amongst us, yet by reason we are not in a capacity to contribute to such an Honble maintenance as may be requisite and expedient:

Your Petitioners, therefore, humbly pray your Lordship will be pleased so far to favor our undertakings as to intercede with his Majesty for his gracious letters to this Government, on our behalf, to protect and encourage us, and that assistance towards the present maintenance of a Minister among us may be granted, as your Excellency will also be pleased to write in our behalf and favor, to the Lords of the Council of Trade and Plantations, or to such Ministers of State as your Excellency shall judge convenient in and about the premises.

And your Petitioners, as in duty bound will ever pray, &c.

{16 male signers}[9]

In this petition there is no appeal to any official of the Church of England, nor indeed to any of the three leading prelates in Canterbury, York, or London. The chief concerns are financial and legal, and the legal concern is an indirect request to the Crown to warn the government of Rhode Island that they should leave the nascent Anglican church alone.[10] The monetary concern is the adequate maintenance of a minister/missionary, and is directed to the Board of Trade and whatever "minister of state" the earl thinks would be helpful. Legal and financial officials were of greater importance than ecclesiastical officials in this endeavor. Even if there were some sort of petition or correspondence with the authorities of the Church of England that has not survived, it is significant that such documents are not mentioned in this petition, nor is there any reference to official approval from the Church of England.

The endorsement by Lord Bellomont reflects the attitude of an establishmentarian who took a very dim view of a state with no established church:

I send your Lordships the petition of several persons in Rhode Island for a Church of England Minister, and a yearly maintenance for him. I hope your Lordships will please to patronize so good a design, and will obtain his Majesty's allowance of a competent maintenance for such a minister. It will be the means I hope to reform the lives of the people in that Island, and make good Christians of 'em, who are at present all in darkness.[11]

The darkness that Lord Bellomont perceived was dispelled, because four years later Trinity Church sent a report, dated September 29, 1702, to the Society for the Propagation of the Gospel (SPG), the newly formed Anglican missionary society. In that letter, the Anglicans describe themselves as a church, even though they did not have an ordained clergyman: "Our Church is but young: it not being four years yet compleat since we began to assemble ourselves together on that occasion. . . ."[12] In that same year they finally approached the bishop of London and the SPG for a clergyman. After the death of Rev. Lockyer in April 1704, the SPG sent Rev. James Honyman to Newport, who ministered in the congregation until 1708.[13]

The establishment of Anglican churches in New England was not accomplished by covenanting. One searches in vain in all of the accounts of early New England Anglicanism for any document that has the characteristics of a New England covenant. The polity, worship, governance, and systematic doctrine of the Church of England was so different from classical New England Congregationalism that the doctrine of the covenant was not an organizing principle for the Anglican world, nor was the practice of covenanting a feature that marked the life of the established Church of England. Indeed, the Anglican establishment, both civil and ecclesiastical, had waged a fierce battle against the Covenanters of Scotland during the years 1660 to 1688, a conflict that was bitter on both sides. For Anglicans, "covenant" and "covenanting" were among the marks of dissent in both England and Scotland.

Quakers, or members of the Society of Friends, were dissenters both in Old England and New England. Was covenanting, particularly religious covenanting, one of their distinguishing marks? A vast body of literature has arisen about the community of Quakers that emerged in England during the English Revolution and its aftermath.[14] The original movement in England formed a diaspora that later founded Pennsylvania and the city of Philadelphia.[15] What is often forgotten is that New England's Quaker community predated the Pennsylvania community by twenty-five years, and that a significant Quaker presence remains in New England to this day.[16] Our purpose is not to explore the interaction of the Congregational standing order and New England civil authorities with the Quakers; that has been done extensively.[17] Rather, we want briefly to explore how a Quaker meeting was formed and compare with the Congregational Way the commitments that individual members made.

There were two stages to the early history of the Quakers. The period 1667 to 1672 marks a watershed in the history of Quakerism, for it was in those years that "the Discipline" was imposed by George Fox upon what had been a fairly rambunctious sect. Fox visited New England in 1672 and brought with him the organizational structure that is one of its distinguishing features. Quakerism was organized into the system of meetings that gave coherence and order to the movement.[18] In their organization and government the Quakers did not strive to re-enact New Testament primitivism; rather, the system of yearly meetings, half-yearly meetings, quarterly meetings, monthly meetings, and meetings for worship emerged from the mind of George Fox. Generally, yearly meetings were synonymous with a national assembly or convention, while quarterly meetings were the locus of regional authority. Monthly meetings were the local authority, and monthly meetings were formed by and reported to the quarterly meetings. Monthly meetings then sponsored preparative meetings, which prepared business for the monthly meeting. Monthly meetings and preparative meetings together sponsored meetings for worship, which could be held in localities in the neighborhood of the monthly meeting. The title of the meetings indicated how often they met: once a year, once every three months, and once a month. Meetings for worship met at least weekly, and often at other times during the week, especially on the "Fifth Day" of the week, or Thursday. It was the monthly meeting, the preparative meeting, and the meeting for worship that most Quakers interacted with; the monthly meetings sent representatives to the quarterly meetings, and the quarterly meetings sent representatives to the yearly meeting. The four strata of meetings were divided into a men's meeting and a women's meeting. In the early days of Quakerism the men's meeting made the decisions concerning policy, finance, and discipline. Women began to participate more fully in the decision making of Quaker meetings in the nineteenth century. When the men held their monthly meeting for business, the women held their monthly meeting at the same time.

An examination of the early New England Quaker meeting records reveals an important difference from the records of the Congregationalist and Baptist churches: the Quaker meeting records separated the business of the preparative, monthly, quarterly, and yearly meetings from the religious and theological context in which they were found. Monthly meetings took note of births, marriages, deaths, memberships, and transfers of "memberships" within the Quaker community. Quarterly meetings authorized the formation of monthly meetings and took note of "sufferings," or fines incurred by Quakers for refusing to pay the compulsory tithe. The quarterly and yearly meetings settled disputes and set policy for their subordinate meetings. The records are clear and orderly, but reveal little theological or religious content. In some sense, the Quakers conducted the business of running a religious organization in a secular way. The religious content of Quakerism was articulated in the meetings for worship, but no minutes were kept of meetings for worship. We therefore have to rely on the published works of Quakerism for a glimpse of their spirituality and the outworking of their theological stances.[19]

In the period before 1708 there were approximately thirteen monthly meetings in the New England Yearly Meeting and its offspring, the New York Yearly Meeting. The number of meetings for worship, on the other hand, cannot be enumerated with any certainty. Like home Bible studies in the modern church, they seemed to come and go and were ephemeral in nature. In New England the meetings for worship met mainly in homes. A monthly meeting and a preparative meeting might sponsor several meetings for worship, all of which reported each month to the monthly meeting and were supposed to be in subjection to it. An examination of the records for the monthly meetings of New England indicates that no covenantal vows were taken binding Quakers to their monthly meetings. Therefore, Quakers technically had no formal membership. And yet there was a "membership," and after 1672 there was "The Discipline," which could be imposed on members of a monthly meeting. And in difficult disputes appeals could be made to the quarterly and yearly meetings. Members could be transferred from one monthly meeting to another, but it was never quite clear how one became a "member." Evidently, one simply came to meetings for worship and then attached oneself to a monthly meeting. Nevertheless, as the years passed one could be disciplined for marrying outside the Quaker world. Such an action would be deemed an abandonment of one's "birthright" as a Quaker for those born within the Quaker world. The Quakers did not practice baptism or communion, and therefore did not join the debate in the Christian world concerning who could partake of the sacraments and what membership requirements should be imposed on candidates for either sacrament. This vagueness concerning membership was paralleled in the Quaker method of conducting business, which involved developing a consensus rather than calling for a formal vote.

The formation of the monthly meeting was controlled by the yearly or quarterly meeting, and the records of the superior meetings indicate that these formations were done in an almost perfunctory way. The formation and establishment of the Dartmouth monthly meeting is an instructive example. The New England yearly meeting met on Friday, June 9, 1699, in a private residence. The action was taken by the men's meeting:

> At a generall yearely Mens Meetinge at the house of Lathem Clarke in Newport on Rhode Island ye 9th day of ye 4th month beinge ye sixth day of ye weeke in ye yeare 1699 before ye publicke meetinge of worship began: The severall meetings were called over:
> Rhode Island Meetinge: Dartmouth friends desier to be a monthly meetinge apart from Rhode Island and to have one day more added to their yearely meetinge.[20]

The clerk then proceeded to enumerate items of business concerning other subordinate meetings before recording a minute concerning the authorization of the Dartmouth monthly meeting:

> The desier of frinds of Dartmouth to be a monthly meetinge apart from Rhode island and to have one day more added to theire yearely meetinge is granted and approved by this meetinge.
> It is the desier of this meetinge that frinds of Dartmouth and Narragansit doe consider of and approve days and times for keepinge of monthly meetings for buisnes in order to compose and make one quarterly meetinge . . . and bringe in theire result to this meeting.[21]

The New England yearly meeting did not meet for business over the weekend, and so Saturday and Sunday, June 10 and 11, 1699, were free. On Monday, June 12, 1699, the final piece of business concerning the Dartmouth monthly meeting was taken up and finalized:

> Second Day beinge ye 12th day of the month ye meeting mett accordinge to adjournment and proceeded as followeth viz
> The frinds of Dartmouth hath agreed yt theire monthly men and womens meetinge of buisnes shall be ye next second day after the

> monthly meetinge of worship at ye house of Peleg Slocumb to which
> this meetinge doth unanimously consent and aggree.[22]

It should be noted that those deciding the issues that the yearly meeting
was interested in were "the friends of Dartmouth," that is, the members of
the Dartmouth monthly meeting. The corporate body of the laity and not
just the leadership was responsible for the decisions made. While there
were elders in the monthly meeting of the Society of Friends, there is no evidence from the records that the elders had a dominant role in the proceedings during the seventeenth century, at least in the yearly and subordinate
meetings of New England and New York.

Like the Anglicans, the Society of Friends in early New England did
not covenant in the way that the New England Congregationalists did.
There was no formal mechanism for admitting people to membership, and
when they formed their local meetings, whether for worship or business,
there was no founding covenant that bound the meeting members to God
or to one another. But after intense persecution in some of the New England colonies, the Quakers multiplied and organized themselves in that
region, and along with the Anglicans posed a sharp contrast to the New England Congregationalists. After the Restoration, New England was forced
to tolerate them, although grudgingly, and this policy added to the increasing religious diversity that could be found in the various New England colonies.

Along with the Quakers and Anglicans, the Baptists also added to the
expanding religious diversity of New England. But unlike the Quakers and
Anglicans, Baptists practiced covenanting in their churches.[23] And as we
have seen earlier, we know that a number of Baptists participated in civil
covenanting. It is therefore to the Baptist church covenants that we now
turn. How much did the Baptist church covenants depart from the covenants signed by Congregational paedobaptist churches? As with the
Quakers and Anglicans, our purpose is not to review the complex history
of Baptists in the old world and the new, but to focus on their thought patterns as revealed in the covenants they signed as they gathered their
churches.[24]

There were approximately twenty-one Baptist churches formed in
New England before 1708. The full texts of only two covenants have survived from the Baptist churches that were founded in the seventeenth century: that of the First Baptist Church of Swansea, New Plymouth Colony,
and that of the Kittery Baptist Church in Kittery, Maine Province. The nar-

ration of the founding of the First Baptist Church of Charlestown/Boston includes, for all practical purposes, the bulk of the text of the covenant. Records of covenanting activity have survived for some of the other churches, but the full text of their covenants is lacking.

Baptists, or Anabaptists as they were called by the Congregationalists, had been meeting off and on secretly during the period before the Restoration. And of course, Rhode Island, contiguous to the Massachusetts Bay, New Plymouth, and Connecticut colonies, had several Baptist churches. Henry Dunster had had to resign the presidency of Harvard College because he developed Baptist convictions. And in 1651, three Baptists from Rhode Island visited a friend in the Massachusetts Bay Colony and were immediately arrested. They were tried for promoting Anabaptism, fined, and banished from the colony. Obadiah Holmes, however, refused to comply, and therefore he was publicly whipped for disturbing the peace of the colony.

The First Baptist Church of Charlestown (later Boston), Massachusetts Bay Colony, gathered on Sunday, May 28, 1665, had a difficult beginning.[25] The leader of the Baptists in Charlestown was Thomas Goold. He was a paedobaptist in 1641, but sometime between 1641 and 1655 he rejected infant baptism. When his child was born in 1655, he refused to have it baptized, and that was the beginning of his troubles. Goold was a prominent and wealthy man, and so the Charlestown church was slow to deal with him, but patiently exhorted him for ten years until his excommunication in the summer of 1665. Those ten years did witness, however, a long-range debate between Goold and the local officials of both church and state.

The First Baptist Church emerged when Goold and the Baptist followers that he had gathered around him finally came to the conclusion that they should gather a church among themselves. It was this offense, and not the question about baptism, that ultimately led to Goold's excommunication. Goold narrated the foundation of the church in this way:

> Now after this, considering with myself what the Lord would have me to do; not likely to join with any of the churches of New England any more, and so to be without the ordinances of Christ; in the meantime God sent out of Old England some who were Baptists; we, consulting together what to do, sought the Lord to direct us, and taking counsel of other friends who dwelt among us, who were able and godly, they gave us counsel to congregate ourselves together; and so we did, being nine of us, to walk in the order of the gospel according to the rule of Christ,

yet knowing that it was a breach of the law of this country; that we had not the approbation of magistrates and ministers, for that we suffered the penalty of that law, when we were called before them.[26]

The record book of the First Baptist Church opens up with an account of the gathering of this Baptist church on Sunday, May 28, 1665:

> The 28 of the 3[d] mo. 1665 in Charlestowne, Massachusetts, the Churche of Christ, commonly (though falsely) called Anabaptiste were gathered togather And entered into fellowship & communion each with other, Ingaigeing to walke togather in all the appointments of there Lord & Master the Lord Jesus Christ as farre as hee should bee pleased to make known his mind & will unto them by his word & Spirit, and then were Baptized
>
> {4 males}
> And joyned with
> {3 males and 2 females}
> who had walked in that
> order in old England
> to whom god hath added
> since. . . .[27]

We can supplement this narration with the narration of John Russell, who wrote an account of the formation of the church and published it in 1680, fifteen years after the church was gathered. Russell states that:

> It pleased God to move the Hearts of some of his dear and precious servants in this Wilderness, who he had by his good Word and Spirit taught, and instructed in the Way and Order of the Gospel, to agree together to enter into Fellowship as a particular body, or Church, engaging one to another in a solemn Covenant, in the name of the Lord Jesus Christ, to walk in fellowship and communion together, in the practice of all the Holy Appointments of Christ, which he had, or should further make known unto them. And thus they became a visible Church of Christ, Walking in the Practice, and performance of the holy Ordinances of Christ, according to Divine Institution.[28]

A cursory examination of the remains of this covenant would seem to at first indicate that what the Baptists were doing was not that much different from the paedobaptist Congregationalists of the standing order. The covenant seems to have been a short document that founded a church. There were many familiar themes that we have already encountered: the resolve to walk together in brotherly love, the following of Christ's appointments or ordinances, and so on. But there is a substantial difference when you compare this narration with the documents produced by the paedobaptist standing order. The Baptist covenant was an acknowledgment of what had already been done in the soul. This particular covenant, therefore, is not an instrument to establish a relationship with God, but an instrument to establish a public horizontal relationship with people on the basis of a private spiritual commitment in the soul. The public vehicle whereby one committed oneself to God was the ordinance of baptism. The baptism of a new believer might precede or follow the act of covenanting, but in this case the covenant itself was not a communal act of dedication to God.

The standing order Congregationalists, with their paedobaptist stance, followed a different line of thinking. The covenant theology embraced by paedobaptists counted baptized individuals, whether children or adults, as members of the church; one could be a baptized member but not a communicant member. One's relationship with Christ was finalized by entering into the congregational covenant, an action taken usually by individuals who had been baptized as infants. Thus, covenanting with God via the church covenant, especially as a church was founded, marked the end of a long process that began in infancy and included in-depth teaching and preparation. Conversion was something done in the heart of the individual by God, but it was also a communal activity, whereby those already members of the gathered church judged whether the conversion was truly a conversion or not. As we well know, the early New England Puritans were famous for their narrations of conversion and cross-examinations of those narrations. The early New England Baptist records do not reveal any narrations of conversion or evaluations of those narratives by those already in the church. It is significant that three to four months later the First Baptist Church of Charlestown/Boston submitted a Confession of Faith to the civil authorities to prove their orthodoxy. In Article (1) they made the following statement: "And those that gladly received the word & are baptised are saints by calling & fitt matter for a visible church."[29] For the Baptists, "closing with Christ" was finalized in the depths of the soul and was expressed via adult baptism. Baptism marked one's very first entrance into the church as a member. And church membership was not dependent on the cross-examination of the gathered saints.

The gathering of the First Baptist Church of Charlestown/Boston was the last straw for the First Church of Charlestown. Messengers were sent back and forth between Goold and the church, and in the end Goold refused to answer the Charlestown First Church because, he explained, he had joined another church. The records for July 1665 for the First Church read as follows:

> July 30, 1665
> Nothing of repentance intervening, Bro. Thomas Gool, Bro. Thomas Osborn, and his wife our sister Osborn, were (with the consent of the brethren) excommunicated for their impenitency in their schismatical withdrawing from the church and neglecting to hear the church.[30]

Despite his excommunication, Goold remained a resident of the Massachusetts Bay Colony and died, it is thought, in 1674.

The second Baptist covenant that survived from the seventeenth century is that of Swansea, New Plymouth Colony, now Swansea, Massachusetts.[31] It was signed sometime before July 2, 1667. The events leading to the establishment of Swansea as a town have been discussed in Chapter 3 and need not detain us here. The church covenant reads as follows:

> A true coppy of the Holy Covenant the first founders of Swanzey entered into at the first beginning and all the members thereof for Divers years.
>
> Whereas we Poor Creatures, through the exceeding Riches of Gods Infinite Grace and Mercifully Snatched out of the Kingdom of darkness — and by his Infinite Power translated into the Kingdom of his dear Son there to be partakers with all Saints of all those Privileges which Christ by the shedding of his Precious Blood, hath purchased for us and that we do find our souls in some good measure wrought on by Divine Grace to desire to be found conformable to Christ in all things being also constrained by the matchless love and wonderful Distinguishing mercies that we Abundantly Injoy from his most free grace to serve him according to our utmost capasities and that we also know that it is our most bounden Duty to walk in visible communion with Christ and each other, according to the Prescript Rule of his most holy word and also that it is our Undoubted Right through Christ to Injoy all the Privileges of God's House which our souls have for a long time panted after And finding no other way at present by the allworking

Providence of our only wise God & gracious Father to us for the enjoyment of the same We do therefore after often & solemn seeking to the
Lord for help and Direction in the fear of his holy Name, and with
hands lifted up to him the most high God Humbly and freely offer ourselves this day a Living sacrifice unto him who is our God in Covenant
through Christ our Lord and only Saviour to walk together according
to his revealed word in visible Gospel Relation, both to Christ our only
head and to each other as fellow members and Brethren and of the
same Household of faith And we do Humbly Ingage that through his
strength, we will henceforth Indeavour to Perform all our Respective
Duties toward God and each other and to practice all the ordinances of
Christ, according to what is or shall be revealed to us In our Respective
Places to Exercise Practice and Submit to the Government of Christ in
this His Church: viz: furder Protesting against all Rending or Dividing
Principles or Practices from any of the People of God, as being most
abomidable and loathsome to our souls & utterly Inconsistent with
that Christian Charity which declares men to be Christs Disciples Indeed further declaring that as Union in Christ is the sole ground of our
Communion with each other so we are Ready to accept of Receive too
& hold Communion with all such as by a judgement of Charity we
conceive to be fellow members with us in our head Christ Jesus tho differing from us in such Controversial Points as are not absolutely and
essencially Necessary to Salvation we also hope that though of ourselves we are altogether unworthy and unfit thus to offer up ourselves
to God or to do him *** or to expect any favor with or mercy from him,
[He] will Graciously accept of this our free will offering in and through
the merit and mediation of our Dear Redeemer And that he will Imploy
and Improve us in his service to his Praise to whom be all Glory &
Hon^r now and for ever Amen. . . .

The Names of the Parsons that first Joyned themselves in the Covenant aforesaid as a Church of Christ.

{7 male signers}[32]

The Swansea Baptist covenant does not follow the template or pattern
that the paedobaptist standing order churches had developed. And it is very
different from the remains of the covenant of the First Baptist Church of
Charlestown/Boston. And yet this covenant shares some of the themes we

have encountered already. There is the usual promise to pursue a holy walk before God and the congregation, as well as a recognition that duty to God and the congregation must be fulfilled. Those taking the covenant in Swansea's Baptist church promised to submit to the government of the church and to avoid division. And they wanted to be used by God for God.

Nevertheless, as in the case of the covenant of First Baptist of Charlestown/Boston, subtle differences do emerge, even in the familiar themes. The congregation was required to observe the ordinances (but not the sacraments!) that had been revealed. And the door was left open for "further ordinances" that could be revealed. This clause was probably a reference to divisions in the Baptist world that led to the emergence of Six-Principle Baptists, who maintained that the laying on of hands was also an ordinance in the same way that adult baptism was.[33] During the decade of the 1660s the discussion had not been concluded, and so this congregation left open the possibility that they might commit themselves to other "ordinances" that they might conclude were taught in Scripture.

Another subtle difference was the commitment on the part of those taking the covenant to participate in the governance of the church. While the laity of the New England paedobaptist congregations participated in the governance of their churches, the covenants that they signed reflected a concern that they submit to the government of the congregation, not that they exercise its functions; Swansea Baptists, on the other hand, were to exercise governance. This subtle difference indicates a much more proactive vision for the laity, while the Congregational standing order's attitude to church governance tended to be reactive — that is, when a problem emerged the whole congregation, under the guidance of the elders, dealt with the problem.

Swansea's Baptist covenant opens up with a statement of fact rather than a statement of commitment. Those who took the covenant had already been "snatched out" of the darkness; they already desired to be conformed to Christ and to walk with him; and they already desired to exercise the privileges of the house of God. As in the Charlestown/Boston Baptist covenant, the rhetorical stance of the Swansea covenant is that salvation has already occurred in the individual's personal relationship with Christ, a relationship that was ultimately hidden in the depths of his or her heart and expressed publicly by way of adult immersion baptism.

The Swansea Baptist covenant speaks of the vertical relationship with God. Nevertheless, it is important to note that the relationship established was not salvific, but sacrificial:

> We do therefore after often & solemn seeking to the Lord for help
> and Direction in the fear of his holy Name, and with hands lifted up to
> him the most high God Humbly and freely offer ourselves this day a
> Living sacrifice unto him who is our God in Covenant through Christ
> our Lord and only Saviour . . . we also hope that though of ourselves we
> are altogether unworthy and unfit thus to offer up ourselves to God or
> to do him *** or to expect any favor with or mercy from him, [He] will
> Graciously accept of this our free will offering in and through the merit
> and mediation of our Dear Redeemer.

The covenant was seen as the next step in one's relationship with God, not the initial step. The establishment of and membership in God's church was a "second blessing," so to speak, that followed the initial blessing of salvation.

There was an unfamiliar theme in the Swansea covenant as well. The "judgement of charity" was extended to other Christians who differ in areas not essential or necessary for salvation. The breadth of this offer is notable, in that no boundaries were given: the covenant could have in mind other Baptists, Congregationalists, Presbyterians, even Quakers. The established New England Congregationalists would never have allowed such a clause in their church covenants at this stage in their history. We have seen, however, in the Swansea civil covenant discussed earlier that while the seventeenth-century Baptist community of Swansea was willing to give the "judgement of charity" in areas "non-essential for salvation," this gathered Baptist church was very specific about who was acceptable and who was not acceptable for their town, and they were willing to allow the civil authority to enforce those standards. A long list of people holding to erroneous doctrine was drawn up, and it turned out that the only standards that they were willing to bend on were baptism and church governance — the very issues that divided them from the majority of orthodox Congregationalists and Anglicans. Congregationalists and Anglicans were in the fold; Quakers were not.

The second Baptist covenant that fully survives from seventeenth-century New England is that of the short-lived church at Kittery, Maine.[34] The First Baptist Church of Kittery, Maine Province, was gathered on Monday, September 25, 1682. It was gathered after its members had been persecuted for at least two years by the authorities of Maine Province. As part of a plea bargain, its leader, William Screven, and his Baptist followers were to remove themselves from the province and so save themselves from further prosecution. Two years later, in 1684, Screven and his group removed to

Somerset, South Carolina, near Charleston. In 1693 the church removed to Charleston itself and formed the First Baptist Church of Charleston, South Carolina — the first Baptist church in the South. The church was gathered under the guidance and authority of the First Baptist Church of Boston/ Charlestown, and the record of its covenant appears in the Boston church records. The covenant reads as follows:

A Coppy of There Said Covenant

Wee whose names are here und^e written doe solemnly & on good Consideration, god Assisting us by his grace give up our selves to ye lord & to one another in Solemn Covenant, wherein wee doe Covenant & promise to walk with god & one another In A dew and faithfull observance of all his most holy and blessed Commandm.^{tts}, Ordinances, Institutions or Appointments, Revealed to us in his sacred word of ye ould & new Testament and according to ye grace of god & light att present through his grace given us, or here after he shall please to discover & make knowne to us thro his holy Spiritt according to ye same blessed word all ye Dayes of our lives and this will wee doe, If ye lord graciously please to Assist us by his grace & Spiritt & to give us Divine wisdome, strength, knowledg, & understanding from Above to pforme ye same without which we cann doe nothing
John 15:4
2 Corinthians 3:5.

> Signed by
> {10 male signers}
> This is A true Coppy comnpared with ye origenall &
> owned by all our Brethren and seven sisters as Attest
> Wm Screeven in
> behalf of ye rest.[35]

This covenant echoes the themes of the covenants of the standing order and the Swansea Baptist covenant. It is different from the other two Baptist covenants in that a dual relationship with the community of saints and God was established. Like virtually all of the other covenants that we have considered, there is a strong emphasis on assisting grace: there is no hint that humans can bargain with God or answer back to him. The scripture verses chosen by the author(s) reflect a dependence on God:

Abide in me, and I in you. As the branch cannot bear fruit of itself, except it abide in the vine; no more can ye, except ye abide in me. (John 15:4)

Not that we are sufficient of ourselves to think any thing as of ourselves; but our sufficiency is of God. (2 Corinthians 3:5)

There is also a strong emphasis on obedience, but that obedience depends on the inward work of God, and not on the decision of the one who is taking the covenant. Finally, the door is left open for "further light" on the Scriptures that could be made known by the Spirit.

This covenant leaves out some of the elements found in the standing order covenants. The "holy watch" is absent, and so is the promise to submit to the governance of that particular congregation. Finally, while there is a closing with God, the christological formula of Jesus Christ as prophet, priest, and king is absent. This is a covenant that was composed without a model or template in mind, and it reflects the independence of the writer and the church from other covenanted churches and from the models, published and unpublished, put forth by the standing order.

The ideal of one church for one town in New England came under severe strain beginning in the 1660s, after the 1660 Restoration of Charles II. The Crown demanded greater religious toleration in the New England colonies for not only Anglicans but also Baptists and Quakers. The conclusions of the Half-Way Synod of 1662 led to splits in several parochial churches in New England, ultimately leading to the establishment of "Second Churches," particularly in the larger towns. The chaos of the English Revolution had allowed various underground groups to come above ground, or simply to come together: Quakers, Baptists, Family of Love, and various forms of antinomianism all emerged in the 1640s and 1650s and then started to make their way across the ocean to New England. The New Englanders, particularly in the Massachusetts Bay Colony and the Connecticut Colony, were exasperated by the Quakers and the Baptists. Later, when James II sent Edmund Andros over in 1686, the Massachusetts Bay Colony was furious that Governor Andros seized the meeting house of the Boston Third Congregational Church and established an Anglican chapel there. New Plymouth Colony, on the other hand, was more accepting of dissent; so was, of course, Rhode Island. After 1689 and the accession of William and Mary the Anglicans began to actively make inroads into New England, particularly in Connecticut.

As in Old England, little by little dissent to the established state church — in this case Congregational rather than Anglican — was grudgingly tolerated. An examination of the way the three main dissenting groups in seventeenth-century New England established their local assemblies indicates a broad spectrum of doctrinal understanding and commitment and different understandings of the *loci* of authority in the church. Anglicans did not covenant; the foundation of their authority for forming a new church lay theoretically with the episcopate but in actuality with the Board of Trade and the SPG. The Quakers, with their doctrine of the inner light, started to move beyond the pale of Christian orthodoxy. The formation of their meetings was placed under a mechanism that was devised by George Fox to tame the rather colorful histrionics that some Quakers were involved in during and after the English Revolution; they too did not covenant. But the Baptists, with their congregational form of church government and church covenants, had the closest affinities with the paedobaptist Congregational standing order. However, their church covenants reveal an understanding of conversion that is more individualistic than the more communally minded Congregationalists. The covenants we have examined in this chapter, all of them Baptist, along with the general phenomenon of heterogeneous groups challenging the standing order, reenforce the theme of counterpoint in seventeenth-century New England. As the century progressed, New England moved from a greater — but not uniform — state of religious unity to a state of much greater religious disunity; the political disunity of the early decades, on the other hand, moved to greater uniformity and cohesiveness.

A close examination of the covenant documents of the Congregationalists and Baptists, however, reveals an important phenomenon that until this time has been overlooked by historians. In the period after 1647, as sects and groups not authorized by the Congregational standing order established themselves in New England, Baptists and Congregationalists began to draw up confessions of faith as a prelude to their covenant. The Baptists drew up these confessional documents to prove their orthodoxy; they may also have been hammering out some of the "further light" that the Spirit was revealing to them. The Congregationalists drew up their confessions of faith as a means to resist heterodoxy, to define and defend orthodoxy, and to articulate their distinctive principles over and against the Presbyterians. Ironically, this practice, occurring within the context of Congregationalism, opened up the door to heterodoxy in the New England standing order during the final third of the seventeenth century. It is to these confessional documents that we now turn.

6

The Covenantal Confessions of
Early New England: The Seeds of Diversity

The mercyes of Iehovah sing
for evermore will I:
I'le with my mouth thy truth make known
to all posterity.
For I have sayd that mercy shall
for ever be up built;
establish in the very heav'ns
thy faithfullnes thou wilt.
With him that is my chosen one
I made a covenant:
& by an oath have sworne unto
David mine owne servant.
To perpetuity thy seed
establish-sure I will:
also to generations all
they throne I'le build up still.   Selah.
Also the heav'ns thy wonders Lord,
they shall with prayse confess;
in the assemblie of the Saints
also thy faithfullnes.

(Psalm 89:1-5; Bay Psalm Book)

The church covenants of early New England were written statements whereby the New England Congregationalists desired to establish a direct relationship with God, and both Congregationalists and Baptists desired to establish a direct relationship with the church. We have seen that the Congregational covenants, and to a large degree the Baptist covenants, did not vary significantly as the seventeenth century progressed. However, the decades between 1620 and 1708 witnessed extensive political and religious change in all of the colonies. While the church covenants themselves did not change substantially, a careful examination of the covenants, and/or the narrations describing their composition and signing, reveals that confessional statements of doctrine began to appear as prologues or epilogues to the church covenants themselves as the century progressed. Examination of church records also reveals that confessional statements appeared at the time the half-way covenant was instituted or at the time of the renewal of the church covenant.[1]

A definition of the term "confessional statement" is in order here. A confessional document is a comprehensive statement of Christian belief that is usually more detailed than a creed. It treats the main topics of systematic theology, and usually includes such topics as God, Creation, Fall, Grace, Revelation and Scripture, Jesus Christ, the Old and New Covenants, Salvation, the Christian Life, the Church, the Sacraments, Civil Government, Death, Final Judgment, and Eschatology, or the Last Things. Most, but not all, confessional documents in the Protestant tradition were authored by groups of church leaders in synods, councils, and assemblies, rather than simply coming from the hand of one person.[2] Besides being a systematic statement of Christian belief, a confession of faith in the early modern period also delineated the distinctive beliefs of a particular branch of the Christian church. In the later denominational system of the modern world, various denominations adopted "testimonies" that expanded upon points within the confessional documents in order to delineate how they were different from another denomination within the same branch of Christianity. A study of the New England church records indicates that in some cases individual congregations relied upon the standard ecclesiastical confessions drawn up by these assemblies of clergy. In other cases, the early New England congregations composed their own confessional statements, sometimes as a supplement to the standard ecclesiastical confessions. We will call those confessions originating in the localities of New England "local confessions." What is striking about these early New England local confessions is their brevity in comparison to more traditional confessional statements. With one or two exceptions, the local confessional statements of early New England are brief documents of three to five pages that summarize the beliefs of the new congregation. But they are too long to be called "creeds" — unlike creeds, the average person would have a difficult time memorizing these local confessions and reciting them in a service of worship. And only a couple were printed up in the seventeenth century.[3] Like the covenant, they simply stayed in the official handwritten record book of the church and became part of the local tradition for an individual church. Sometimes they appeared in the handbooks that many congregations published in the nineteenth century. In the battle between Trinitarian and Unitarian congregationalists, the Trinitarian congregationalists utilized them to establish the original beliefs of the early congregation. We will examine first the standard ecclesiastical confessions of faith that the early New England Congregationalists used, and then turn our attention to the local confessions that the individual congregations produced.

What traditional confessional statements served as guides and benchmarks for early New England and its churches? The collections of William E. Barton and especially Williston Walker shed light on this question, and indicate that the New Englanders were well aware of the confessional literature that had developed or was developing in the Reformed churches in Europe. Between 1536 and 1708 a series of confessions and doctrinal formulae emerged in the northern European and Anglo-American world that influenced New England and its churches and clergy. The confessions of sixteenth-century Protestantism at times responded scattershot to a whole range of issues involving late medieval and early modern Catholicism and Protestantism. The later Protestant confessional statements were much more logical and ordered, and reflect a maturity of theological thought emerging in the Protestant world.

The first document, of course, is the Thirty-nine Articles of the Church of England and its antecedents.[4] While Puritans are generally thought to have been people not generally in sympathy with the confessional stance of the Church of England, the non-separating Puritans of New England were technically bound by the Thirty-nine Articles until 1648, when the Cambridge Synod of 1648 adopted the "congregational version" of the Westminster Confession of Faith. Even the Separatists acknowledged the validity of the Thirty-nine Articles, albeit at a time when they were trying to extract permission to form a colony from the Crown. The "Seven Artikes which ye Church of Leyden sent to ye Counsell of England to bee considered of in respeckt of their judgements occasioned about theer going to Virginia Anno 1618" opens with the following words:

> 1. To ye confession of fayth published in ye name of ye Church of England & to every artikell theerof wee do wth ye reformed churches wheer wee live & also els where assent wholy.[5]

Nevertheless, other Separatists were drawing up alternative statements to the Thirty-nine Articles. The most noteworthy is that of the London-Amsterdam Separatist Church in the 1590s and published in 1596.[6] The 1596 confession is the first systematic public statement of Separatist Congregational belief. It begins with the doctrine of God and ends with the doctrine of prayer, and covers many of the "Heads of Divinity" that make up the classical topics of systematic theology.

The most comprehensive statement of Reformed theology is, of course, the Westminster Confession of Faith, along with the Larger and Shorter Catechisms, developed during the period 1643 to 1648 by the Westminster Assembly of Divines.[7] Because a large assembly of professional clergy worked on the Westminster Confession over a number of years, the finished product was a polished document that was comprehensive in scope. It began with the doctrine of Scripture and then covered the nature of God before the foundations of the world, spoke of the redemption of Christ in the fallen world, and concluded with the Final Estate after the Second Coming of Jesus Christ. The Westminster Standards articulated the federal version of covenant theology and a Presbyterian doctrine of the church, both in its nature and its governance. The governance of the church was articulated by *The Forme of Church Government* (1645), which recommended to Parliament that Presbyterianism be established as the form of church government for the Church of England. Parliament never acted on the recommendation.[8] Technically, the Westminster documents were "Humble Advice" to the Long Parliament, and only some of the documents were adopted by Parliament.[9] The General Assembly of the Church of Scotland, on the other hand, did adopt all of the documents. The Confession of Faith and catechisms were therefore set up as a standard for the British and American Presbyterian world and continue as such to the present day.

New Englanders read the documents coming from the Westminster Assembly and became concerned that should Parliament adopt them, Parliament would force the New England colonies to abandon the congregational form of church government in favor of Presbyterianism. The general court of the Massachusetts Bay Colony, therefore, called a synod that met in several sessions over the two-year period between 1646 and 1648. Because it met in Cambridge, Massachusetts Bay Colony, the synod came to be known as the Cambridge Synod. The 1646 session produced a document entitled *The Result of a Synod at Cambridge in New-England, Anno. 1646. Concerning the Power of Magistrates in matters of the First Table. Nature and Power of Synods; and other matters thereunto belonging,* which was not published until 1654.[10] In 1648 the Cambridge Synod published *A Platform of Church Discipline. . . .*[11] While the Cambridge Synod addressed itself to specific concerns that need not concern us here, the preface to *A Platform of Church Discipline* reported that the synod had committed itself to most of the Westminster standards. The preface makes the following statement:

> The more wee discern, (that which wee doe, & have cause to doe with incessant mourning & trembling) the unkind, & unbrotherly, & unchristian contentions of our godly brethren, & countrymen, in matters of church-government: the more ernestly doe wee desire to see them joyned together in one common faith, & our selves with them. For this end, having perused the publick confession of faith, agreed upon by the Reverend assembly of Divines at Westminster, & finding the summ & substance therof (in matters of doctrine) to express not their own judgements only, but ours also: and being likewise called upon by our godly Magistrates, to draw up a publick confession of that faith, which is constantly taught, & generaly professed amongst us, wee thought good to present unto them, & with them to our churches, & with them to all the churches of Christ abroad, our professed & hearty assent & attestation to the whole confession of faith (for substance of doctrine) which the Reverend assembly presented to the Religious & Hononable Parlamet of England: Excepting only some sections in the 25 30 & 31. Chapters of their confession, which concern points of controversie in church-discipline; Touching which wee refer our selves to the draught of church discipline in the ensueing treatise.[12]

It remained for the general courts and individual churches of the Massachusetts Bay, New Plymouth, Connecticut, and New Haven colonies to commit themselves to the Cambridge Platform and thus to the essence of the Westminster standards. Rhode Island, of course, did not participate in any of the proceedings.

As the assembly brought its main work to a conclusion, the Presbyterian movement in Old England was eclipsed by the rise of Independency and radical sectarianism, the execution of Charles I, and the disturbances of the Interregnum. Independents ruled England from 1649 to 1658, with a lot of input and pressure from radical sectarians. In 1658, in the very last weeks of Oliver Cromwell's life, the Independents gathered a synod together at the Savoy Palace in London and adopted a revised form of the Westminster standards.[13] The revisions included an amplification of the federal theology found in the Westminster documents, along with the addition of the Trinitarian covenant of redemption, a covenant made before the foundations of the world. The Savoy Declaration described the work of Christ as being both "active" and "passive," and not surprisingly left out two entire chapters of the Westminster Confession of Faith: "Chapter 30: Of Church Censures" and "Chapter 31: Of Synods and Councils."

But there was another revision of critical importance: the Savoy Declaration completely rewrote the paragraphs on the civil magistracy that dealt with the relationship of the state and the church. Because the death of Cromwell and the Restoration moved the Independents of Old England into a minority — and indeed, powerless — position, this section was moot for Independents in Old England. But for the New England Puritan Congregationalists, who remained in power through the end of the seventeenth century, the rewritten paragraphs were very important. And this was especially the case when the Reforming Synod of 1679-80 adopted the Savoy Declaration for the Massachusetts Bay Colony, a colony that would soon merge with the New Plymouth Colony. That importance would be magnified when the Saybrook Platform adopted the Savoy Declaration in 1708 for the Connecticut Colony, a colony that included the communities of the New Haven Colony. The New England Reforming Synod rewrote the church-state paragraphs of the Savoy Declaration in 1680, and the Saybrook Synod adopted that rewritten paragraph in 1708. A closer look at these changes is therefore necessary.

Table 2 gives the texts of the rewritten church-state paragraphs from the chapters that deal with the civil magistrate in the Westminster Confession of Faith (1647-48), the Cambridge Platform (1648),[14] the Savoy Declaration (1658), and the revision of the Savoy Declaration's paragraph that was adopted by the Massachusetts Bay Colony's Reforming Synod (1679-80) and Connecticut's Saybrook Synod (1708).[15] For comparison the parallel section on the civil magistrate is added from the Baptist Confession of 1688; like the Savoy Declaration, the Baptist Confession of 1688 is a modified version of the Westminster Confession of Faith.[16] It is important to remember that the paragraphs cited here are in the larger context of entire chapters. These chapters are usually entitled "Of the Civil Magistrate." Furthermore, these excerpts are limited to the interaction of the civil magistracy and the church.

Table 2
Texts of the Church-State Paragraphs found in the Civil Magistrate Chapters of the Anglo-American Reformed Confessions, 1647-1708

Westminster Confession of Faith, 1647
Chapter XXIII: Of the Civil Magistrate, Paragraph III

The civil magistrate may not assume to himself the administration of the Word and Sacraments, or the power of the keys of the kingdom of heaven: yet he hath authority, and it is his duty to take order, that unity and peace be preserved in the Church, that the truth of God be kept pure and entire, that all blasphemies and heresies be suppressed, all corruptions and abuses in worship and discipline prevented or reformed, and all the ordinances of God duly settled, administered, and observed. For the better effecting whereof he hath power to call synods, to be present at them, and to provide that whatsoever is transacted in them be according to the mind of God.

Source: Schaff, *Creeds,* 3.652-55.

The Cambridge Platform, 1648
Chapter XVII: Of the Civil Magistrates powr in Matters Ecclesiastical

It is lawfull, profitable. & necessary for christians to gather themselves into Church estate, and therin to exercise all the ordinaces of christ according unto the word, although the consent of the Magistrate could not be had thereunto, because the Apostles & christians in their time did frequently thus practice, when the magistrates being all of them Jewish or pagan, & mostly persecuting enemies, would give no countenance or consent to such matters. 2. Church-government stands in no opposition to civil government of comon-welths, nor any intrencheth upon the authority of Civil Magistrates in their jurisdictions; nor any whit weakneth their hands in governing; but rather strengthneth them, & furthereth the people in yielding more hearty & conscionable obedience unto them. . . . [3]. The powr & authority of Magistrates is not for the restraining of churches, or any other good workes, but for helping in & furthering thereof; & therfore the consent & countenance of Magistrates when it may be had, is not to be sleighted, or lightly esteemed; but on the contrary; it is part of that honour due to christian Magistrates to desire & crave their consent & approbation therin: which being obtayned, the churches may then proceed in their way with much more encouragement, & comfort. 4. It is not in the powr of the Magistrates to compell their subjects to become church-members. . . . 5. As it is unlawfull for church-officers to meddle with the sword of the Magistrate, so it is unlawfull for the Magistrate to meddle with the work proper to church-officers. . . . 6. It is the duty of the Magistrate, to take care of matters of religion, & to improve his civil authority for the observing of the duties commanded in the first, as well as for observing of the duties commanded in the second table. . . . 7. The object of the powr of the Magistrate, are not things meerly inward, & so not subject to his cognisance & view, as unbeleife hardness of heart, erronious opinions not vented; but only such things as are acted by the outward man; . . . 8. Idolatry, Blasphemy, Heresy, venting corrupt & pernicious opinions, that destroy the foundation, open contempt of the word preached, prophanation of the Lords day, disturbing the peaceable administration & exercise of the worship & holy things of God, & the like, are to be restrayned, & punished by civil authority. 9. If any church one or more shall grow schismaticall, rending it self from the communion of other churches, or shall walke incorrigibly or obstinately in any corrupt way of their own, contrary to the rule of the word; in such case, the Magistrate is to put forth his coercive powr, as the matter shall require.

Source: Walker, *Creeds and Platforms*, 234-37.

Savoy Declaration, 1658
Chapter XXXIV: Of the Civil Magistrate, Paragraph III

Although the Magistrate is bound to incourage, promote, and protect the professor and profession of the Gospel, and to manage and order civil administrations in a due subserviency to the interest of Christ in the world, and to that end to take care that men of corrupt mindes and conversations do not licentiously publish and divulge Blasphemy and Errors in their own nature, subverting the faith, and inevitably destroying the souls of them that receive them: Yet in such differences about the Doctrines of the Gospel, or ways of the worship of God, as may befall men exercising a good conscience, manifesting it in their conversation, and holding the foundation, not disturbing others in their ways or worship that differ from them; there is no warrant for the Magistrate under the Gospel to abridge them of their liberty.

Source: Walker, *Creeds and Platforms*, 393-94.

Reforming Synod, 1679-80
Saybrook Platform, 1708
Chapter XXXIV: Of the Civil Magistrate, Paragraph III

They who upon pretense of Christian liberty shall oppose any lawful power, or the lawful exercises of it, resist the Ordinance of God, and for their publishing of such opinions, or maintaining of such practices as are contrary to the Light of Nature, or to the known Principles of Christianity, whether concerning faith, worship, or conversation, or to the power of godliness, or such erronious opinions or practices, as either in their own nature, or in the manner of publishing or maintaining them, are destructive to the external peace and order which Christ hath established in the Church, they may lawfully be called to account, and proceeded against by the censures of the Church, and by the power of the civil Magistrate; yet in such differences about the Doctrines of the Gospel, or wayes of the worship of God, as may befal men exercising a good conscience, manifesting it in their conversation, and holding the foundation, and duely observing the Rules of peace and order, there is no warrant for the Magistrate to abridge them of their liberty.

Source: Walker, *Creeds and Platforms,* 393-94, n. 5.

The Baptist Confession of 1688 (The Philadelphia Confession)
Chapter XXXIV: Of the Civil Magistrate

Civil Magistrates being set up by God for the ends aforesaid, subjection in all lawful things commanded by them ought to be yielded by us in the Lord, not only for wrath, but for conscience' sake; and we ought to make supplications and prayers for kings and all that are in authority, that under them we may live a quiet and peaceable life, in all godliness and honesty.

Source: Schaff, *Creeds,* 3.738.

The chronological progression of thought in these paragraphs is striking. The Westminster standards (1646-47) give the magistracy the power to intrude upon church affairs to ensure that church decisions be "according to the mind of God." The Westminster paragraph starts out in the negative by defining what the civil magistrate cannot do (preaching; sacraments; church discipline), but then moves to the positive by defining what it can do: protect the church, the truth, and the ordinances. Finally, the civil magistracy can put "pressure" on church government.

The Cambridge Platform of 1648 has the most developed vision of the relationship between church and state. In large part it endorses the Westminster position, but it becomes very specific. The power of the civil magistrate should be applied not only to individuals who are dissenting to the established state church, but also to corporate bodies, or dissenting churches, that are refusing to conform to the established state church. Schism and corruption were valid reasons for the magistrate to enter into the situation and restrain those groups. There is no provision, however, for who decides when this is necessary, or when the matter shall require such action. Does the magistrate or do the elders of the church decide when an individual or group has overstepped the boundaries?

The Savoy Declaration of 1658 states what the civil magistrate can do: it can protect and promote the gospel and suppress blasphemy and error. Unlike the Westminster standards and the Cambridge Platform, it gives a reason for such suppression: blasphemy and error lead to the eternal destruction of body and soul in hell. But the Savoy Declaration allows for compromise in areas not foundational to the gospel. This reflects a critical shift in the thinking of Reformed confessional literature concerning the magistracy and the established state church. The Congregationalist Savoy Declaration allows for a scenario in which there could be two or more churches within a particular locale. If the non-established church holds to the foundations of the gospel but disagrees with other churches on less foundational matters, the civil magistracy is to let that church be. We therefore see articulated in a confessional document the beginning of the end of the state church system in the Anglo-American world, and the seeds of the voluntary denominational system of modern times.

The New England Reforming Synod of 1679-80, composed of clergy from the Massachusetts Bay Colony and New Plymouth Colony, adopted the Savoy Declaration. The Massachusetts Bay Colony and the New Plymouth Colony, therefore, vacated the Westminster Confession, but held on to the Cambridge Platform.[17] Later on, in 1708, the Saybrook Synod adopted the Saybrook Platform and vacated the Westminster Confession, but adopted the Congregational-Presbyterian Heads of Unity instead of the Cambridge Platform.[18] But the Reforming Synod of 1679-80 and the Saybrook Synod of 1708 did not adopt the Savoy Declaration's statement concerning the civil magistracy. Instead, the Reforming Synod of 1679-80 adopted a revision of Chapter XX, Paragraph 4, of the Westminster Confession of Faith; the title of that chapter was "Of Christian Liberty, and Liberty of Conscience," and it had little to say concerning the civil magistrate.[19] That revision in turn was included in the Saybrook Platform of 1708.[20] The resulting statement had much more to say about dissenters. What is significant is that the New England statements of 1679-80 and 1708 focus not upon the destructive force of heresy upon the souls of the population, but upon the disturbance that dissent causes on the external peace and order of the churches, particularly the New England churches. A people noted for their concern with the inner soul and psyche of the individual became confessionally committed to the preservation of external peace and quiet.

At least theoretical allowance was made for Baptists, Presbyterians, Anglicans, and even "Second Churches" to exist in the towns of New England unmolested; the Reforming Synod and the Saybrook Synod copied the Savoy Declaration's statement of toleration in cases where dissenters held to the core of orthodoxy but differed in the peripheral details. Quakers were still outside the pale of orthodoxy, but the door was opened in New England for grudging toleration of a variety of forms of historic Christianity. The seeds of the destruction of the standing order and its congregational state church had been sown by the Independents and Congregationalists themselves.

Given this backdrop of a softening of confessional orthodoxy concerning dissenters over the century in both New England and Old England, we can now turn our attention to the "local confessional statements," the confessional documents drawn up for a local congregation in early New England. In a couple of cases we have "confessional statements" that deal with only one or two issues, most commonly the half-way covenant. Technically, these documents are not confessional statements, because they do not deal with the full scope of classical Christian doctrine but are limited to a specific question or questions. Indeed, a systematic reading of church and civil records, along with published and unpublished writings of clergy and laity, reveals that a whole series of problems agitated the various congregations of New England over the entire century: the form of church government, infant baptism versus paedobaptism, the practice of church covenanting, the legitimacy of the gathered church, the fact that the proportion of the gathered church was getting smaller in relation to the expanding general population, the children of the covenant and their perceived lack of spirituality, church discipline, the franchise, issues of church and state, antinomianism, and simply quarrels and dissensions over doctrine, polity, and practice. Each of these issues gave rise, at times silently, to new churches and to migrations of groups of people in different directions (usually westward). And at times, these issues are referenced in the documentation surrounding the emergence of a new church. Those writings, however, cannot really be considered confessional statements; some of them might be called, as Williston Walker styled them, "platforms."

Table 3 lists the local confessional statements or references to local confessional statements that emerged from the record of New England covenanting activity in the seventeenth century. Several caveats ought to be sounded concerning this table. First, this table lists both confessional documents and references to confessional documents, even if the confessional

Table 3
Early New England Confessions of Faith
Associated with Covenanting, Arranged Chronologically

Year	Town Name	Church Name	Colony	Type/Reference
1618	Leyden/New Plymouth	First Church	NPC	Local*: reference† to Thirty-nine Articles
1629	Salem	First Church	MBC	Local: reference only. "Substance" published in 1665.
1638	Dedham	First Church	MBC	Local: reference only
1647	Windsor	First Church	CTC	Local
1660	Natick	Indian Church	MBC	Local: composed by John Eliot
1661	Northampton	First Church	MBC	Local: composed by Eleazer Mather
1663	Swansea	First Baptist Church	NPC	Local: anathemas against error presented to civil authorities
1665	Boston	First Baptist Church	MBC	Local
1667	Killingworth	First Church	CTC	Local
1667	Beverly	First Church	MBC	Local
1668	Middletown	First Church	CTC	Local
1669/70	Hartford	Second Church	CTC	Local
1670	Stratford	Second Church	CTC	Westminster Confession of Faith: reference only
1674	Woodbury	First Church	CTC	Westminster Confession of Faith: reference only

*Local indicates that the Confession was generated by church leaders from the local area.

†Reference indicates that the records contain a reference to a confession but that the confession itself is not written out in the records.

Year	Town Name	Church Name	Colony	Type/Reference
1674	Stonington	First Church	CTC	Local
1678	Milton	First Church	MBC	Local: reference only
1679	Westfield	First Church	MBC	Local
1682	Kittery-5	First Baptist Church	MeP	London Confession "of 1682" (1677?): reference only
1682	Bradford	First Church	MBC	Local: reference only
1684	Marblehead	First Church	MBC	Local
1689	Salem Village	First Church	DNE	1680 New England Confession: reference only
1694	Middle-borough-2	First Church	MBP	Local
1695	Stratfield	First Church	CTC	Local: reference only
1696	Lexington/ Cambridge Farms	First Church	MBP	1680 New England Confession: reference only
1698	Preston	First Church	CTC	Local: copy of Stonington, CT, First Church Confession
1698	Exeter-2	First Church	NHP	Local
1699	Boston	Fourth Church: Brattle Street	MBP	Local: with reference to Westminster Confession of Faith
1700	Harwich	First Church	MBP	Westminster Shorter Catechism: reference
1700	Lebanon	First Church	CTC	Local
1702	Kittery-2 (Berwick)	First Church	MBP	Local
1704	East Haddam	First Church	CTC	Local
1704	Little Compton	First Congregational Church	MBP	Local

documents are unavailable in modern times. Second, in some cases we have a covenant from a church but the church is not listed in this table because no evidence of any confessional statement can be found.[21] That does not mean, however, that no confessional document existed with that covenant. The absence simply means that the evidence does not exist. Finally, in a couple of cases we have a confessional statement or a reference to a confessional statement but no covenant.

Table 3 indicates that, except for the examples of Salem, Massachusetts Bay Colony, and Dedham, Massachusetts Bay Colony, the confessional documents start to appear in 1647 and became more numerous after the Restoration of 1660-62. The confessions from both Salem and Dedham have been lost, but reference is made to them in contemporary documents. In the case of Salem, the documentation is somewhat confusing, in that we have church records, two publications from the church and its clergy, and the narrative of Nathaniel Morton, a New England historian, writing forty years later. All of these narrative documents date from the period 1660 and after. The original records of the Salem, Massachusetts Bay Colony First Church from 1629 to 1660 are lost. A new church book was started in 1660, and many but perhaps not all of the records from the previous thirty-one years were then copied into the church book. The covenant opens up the 1660 book, but no mention is made of any confession of faith. The covenant of 1629 is enfolded in the larger covenant of 1636, and the 1636 covenant is rightly recognized as a covenant renewal.[22] The anti-Quaker article mentioned earlier was added to a renewal of the 1636 covenant in 1660.[23] Then, in 1665, John Higginson, son of Rev. Francis Higginson, one of the founding ministers of the Salem First Church and a fourteen-year-old eyewitness of the gathering of the church in 1629, published *The Direction of 1665,* which contained another covenant in the form of a reception covenant for new members, along with a confession of faith and a baptismal formula for covenant children.[24] Finally, in 1680, a fourth covenant was published as a covenant renewal in response to the request of the Reforming Synod of 1679-80.[25] Salem First Church therefore had four versions of a covenant, articulated in the years 1629, 1636, 1665, and 1680.

The Salem, Massachusetts Bay Colony First Church also had two confessions of faith in the seventeenth century. Nathaniel Morton, basing his account on the memories of Rev. John Higginson, who was a teenager in 1629, indicates that a confession of faith was very much a part of the covenanting process in 1629:

When the sixth of August came it was kept as a day of Fasting and Prayer, in which after Sermons and Prayers of the two Ministers, in the end of the day, the . . . Confession of Faith and Covenant being solemnly read, the forenamed persons did solemnly profess their Consent thereunto. . . . The Confession of Faith and Covenant . . . was acknowledged onely as a Direction pointing unto that Faith and Covenant contained in the holy Scripture, and therefore no man was confined unto that form of words, but onely to the Substance, End and Scope of the matter contained therein: And for the Circumstantial manner of joyning to the Church, it was ordered according to the wisdome and faithfulness of the Elders, together with the liberty and ability of any person. Hence it was, that some were admitted by expressing their Consent to that written Confession of Faith and Covenant; others did answer to questions about the Principles of Religion that were publickly propounded to them; some did present their Confessions in writing, which was read for them, and some that were able and willing did make their Confession in their own words and way.[26]

Morton makes reference to thirty copies of the confession of faith, which were written out and delivered to the thirty foundation members for their subscription. No copy of this 1629 confession exists, but John Higginson maintains that "the substance of it" was published in *The Direction of 1665.*[27]

The evidence of the Dedham, Massachusetts Bay Colony First Church's confession is easier to analyze. The narrative of the gathering is at the opening of the church book, and refers to a day when the prospective foundation members examined each other on the "heads of Christian religion":

> . . . we sett apart one day in speciall manner to declare all our judgem[te] upon all y[e] heads of Christian religion, & to declare & testifie how we found our harts inclined by y[e] lord to y[e] loue of one an other. wherin one begining to speake of one point of religion ev'ry one in order spake ther thoughts of y[e] same. . . .[28]

The prospective foundation members then appointed Rev. John Allin as the spokesperson for their confession. On the day of the gathering of the Dedham First Church he was to propound the confession of faith first, and then give his testimony of saving grace. The others were to follow, "testify-

ing ther consent to ye D' of faith before p'fessed and declaring ye workings
of gods grace in ther harts. wch was accordingly p'formed."[29] Neither the
words nor the "substance" of this doctrinal commitment remains for our
examination:

> [John Allin] . . . made a large p'fession of D' & of ye worke of grace: w^ch
> is too long to insert ye substance of y^earticles of faith remaine in private
> notes wch were further inlarged in ye p'fession. . . .[30]

More than twenty years later, in 1659, the Dedham First Church committed itself to the Westminster Confession of Faith with the modifications of
the Cambridge Synod of 1648.[31]

Why did the New Englanders produce these local confessional statements, especially after 1647? There were several reasons. The first and
most important reason has already been referred to: the Westminster Assembly was actively producing a confessional statement, two catechisms, a
directory for worship and a directory of church government that was designed for Old England, and, presumably, for New England. The church
government platform, sent to Parliament on December 11, 1644, was Presbyterian in orientation despite the attempts of Independents in Old England to sway the assembly toward Independency. The first edition of the
Westminster Confession that was presented to the English Parliament was
printed December 5, 1646. New Englanders were quietly alarmed by the
Presbyterian church government platform, but they came to appreciate the
doctrinal portions of the Westminster Confession so much that the Cambridge Synod adopted it in a "congregational form" in 1648.

Nevertheless, the New Englanders were not interested in uniform
confessionalism. As Congregationalists, they wanted each congregation to
work out its own confession so that the local body of believers could "own"
it. Relying on what the Presbyterians had done, even in a revised congregational form, seemed too much like lazy conformity rather than rigorous
grappling with doctrinal issues. This explains the title of the Salem Covenant and Confession in 1665, which states that:

> The Genuine use of a Confession of Faith is, that under the same Form
> of Words they express the substance of the same common Salvation or
> unity of their Faith. Accordingly it is to be looked upon as a fit meanes,
> whereby to expres that their Common Faith and Salvation, and not to
> be made use of as an imposition upon any.[32]

A "genuine use" of a confession existed when a people had studied and internalized what they believed. Edward Taylor found this out the night before his church was to be gathered in 1679. Much to his shock, Solomon Stoddard and the visiting messengers did not feel that simple adherence to the Westminster standards was adequate as a confessional foundation for the Westfield, Massachusetts Bay Colony First Church. Taylor relates in his "Church Records," that

> The Elders, & Messengers comings all over night, except such as came from Sp[ringfield] Church, consulted our preparation; which in some things they did not well approove of, [as we] had not drawn up a profession of our Faith . . . as [to our Pro]fession of Faith, Temptations had so often encountered, in our proceeding formerl[y as] I could not tell how to go about that labour, as thinking it might be in vain, unt[ill we] wrote unto the Churches, & then finding our worke so much that I could not well [get through] it, concluding to do it by a professing the Doctrine laid down in the Catichisme of the Assemblies of Divin[es at West]menster so far as it goes, & where it is deficient, to acknowledge the Platform of C[hurch disci]pline put forth by the Rev. Elders & Messengers in a Synode held at Cambridge in [Anno Domi 1647], if this would not be acceptible, then to give an account of our profession, the which I did at last, they not accepting of the former; & indeed did stickle more [than] was meet, till Cousin Glover came.[33]

There were, of course, other reasons for the generation of local confessions in early New England. Baptists, Quakers, and other sectarians were emerging from the chaos of the English Revolution and were washing up on the shores of New England. The Salem, Massachusetts Bay Colony Covenant, printed in 1680, records the concerns of 1660:

> This forementioned Covenant was often read and Renewed by the Church at the end of dayes of Humiliation, especially in the year 1660, on the sixth of the first moneth; when also considering the hour of Temptation amongst us by reason of the Quakers Doctrine, to the levening of some in the place where we are, and endangering of others, we doe see cause to remember the admonition of our Saviour Christ unto his Disciples, Math. 16. Take heed and beware of the leven of the doctrine of the Pharisees. And doe judge (so far as we understand it) that the Quakers doctrine is as bad or worse then that of the Pharisees.

> Therefore, We doe Covenant by the help of Jesus Christ, to take heed
> and beware of the leven of the doctrine of the Quakers.[34]

As we have seen in earlier parts of this study, both Baptists and Quakers
were a cause of great alarm to the standing order of New England. A clear
delineation of confessional orthodoxy was needed, lest "the Pharisees" infiltrate the emerging New England community. While the Quakers were
heterodox enough in worship and doctrine to be very different from the established order, the Baptists were much closer to New England Congregationalism's standards for doctrine, worship, and governance.[35] And the
Baptists were putting forth their own confessional statements to prove their
brand of orthodoxy.[36] The standing order of New England wanted to make
sure that the paedobaptist congregational brand of orthodoxy was not confused with the Baptist brand of orthodoxy.

The Restoration of 1660-62 also made the matter of confessional articulation urgent, in that the Church of England ultimately decided to return
to the Elizabethan Thirty-nine Articles as the confessional standard for Anglicans. Both Baptists and Congregationalists wanted to prove to "the
world" — specifically the Anglican world and the world of the other Reformed European churches — that they were orthodox. The development of
confessional statements was part of the apologetical stance that each church
was taking either toward other churches or to a "standing order" to which
they were dissenting. An example of this can be found in the beginning of
the 1665 Confession of Faith put forward by the First Baptist Church of
Charlestown/Boston:

> The church being gathered mett with great opposition from the govern-
> ment of the place, upon which they drew up and delivered to the Court
> {the general court of the Massachusetts Bay Colony} this confession as
> followeth to let the world know there faith & order proved from the
> word of God.[37]

Concern for the world was matched by concern for their own. Besides
confessional camps that were now clearly defined, the second generation of
New England leaders sensed that there was greater heterogeneity in their
own ranks. Some of that diversity was seen from the very beginning, in the
quarrels that marked the first generation, but the concern for the rising generation and the perceived declension that was marked by the half-way covenant are signals that New England was changing. No longer could the church

be gathered around simply a covenant, a relation with God and Christ. The church had to be gathered around both a divine covenantal relationship and around doctrinal uniformity that gave consistency and content to that relationship. Covenant and confession were therefore inextricably linked.

A reading of the New England local confessions indicates that these confessional documents were to be used to teach two groups of young people. The first group was the children of the covenant, who in turn were now falling out into two subgroups: those who became full communicant members and those who became half-way members. The second group was the young people who were not children of the covenant; their parents had never become full communicant members, or their origins were veiled in obscurity because they had arrived in New England as indentured servants, seamen, or youthful "adventurers." The records of the Northampton, Massachusetts Bay Colony First Church give us an example of this use of the local confession:

> In order to the more comfortable progress in the work of religious reformation, amongst us, respecting particularly the children of the Covenant: It is voted and agreed by this Church that a System, or short sum of the Principal or choice Heads of the Reformed Christian Religion, be compiled from God's Holy Word; this to be owned as the Profession of Faith of this Church, and to be consented unto, by all adult persons that shall be acknowledged regular and approved members thereof.[38]

Besides the covenant children, these confessions were used for adult members studying for church membership (some of which may have been covenant "children" in the minds of the elders and pastor). Buried in the Plymouth, New Plymouth Colony, First Church records is a section on the questions that the elders and gathered congregation would ask its prospective members. We will quote just the beginning portion of that section:

> The Elders allowed & encouraged any person to declare his confession of faith in his owne way & method, but if any persons through bashfullnesse or defect of memory chose to be asked, such questions as these were usually put to them.

> Q. what doe you beleve concerning God? unity of Essence & Trinity of Persons & some of his Attributes were usually given in answer, as also his workes of Creation & Providence in both Parts of it, preservation & gubernation.

Q. what . . . concerning man? The state in which He was created, & his Apostacy & the Tempter to it, & the sin itselfe & the Effects of it in the curse on himselfe & posterity, inward & outward, here & for ever, were here spoken to.

Q. what . . . concerning mans Recovery? by whom & how? Here the two Natures of christ were asserted, & the reason, why God & why man? Also his three offices & the worke of each office.[39]

The questions continue on in the area of christology, the *ordo salutis,* or order of salvation, the church, the sacraments, Christian conduct, and eschatology. Those answering such ambitious questions needed instruction and preparation, and the local confessions were pedagogical tools for preparation of adults for communicant membership. The clerk of Plymouth First Church indicated those applying for full communicant membership in Plymouth's First Church were up to the task:

I know not in these 30 yeares, that any person examined in private by the Elders but they did in some degree give some satisfying answer to these things though some much more fully then others, & though some did not presently give a direct & proper answer to the Question, yet in further discourse about it, it usually appeared, they competently understood the thing.[40]

But the degree of latitude indicates that, at least for most laity, heart knowledge was more important than head knowledge.

That was not the case, however, for foundation members who were involved in the gathering of the church. Their role as charter members and as inaugurators of the process of examination for church membership required that these foundation members have a more thorough head knowledge of doctrine in addition to their heart knowledge of the Lord. Such training was usually done by the founding pastor, and required a substantial amount of time. In some cases the need for further preparation of foundation members probably delayed the gathering of a church for years, perhaps even decades. Edward Taylor makes the following comment in his detailed record of the gathering of the Westfield, Massachusetts Bay Colony First Church in 1679:

I being now brought amongst them, did not determine any Settlement [*at once*] but when I had served some two years here, we set up Conference me[eting in] in which I went over all the Heads of Divinity unto the means of the Application [of Re]demption, in order to prepare them for a Church State before we did [*enter.*][41]

Clearly, then, there were manifold uses of these local confessions. Within the congregational framework of church governance, the "ownership" of the confession of faith was placed in the congregation and its pastor and foundation members. But in the long term the placement of the formulation of doctrine into the hands of individual pastors and their congregations opened up the door for heterogeneity rather than homogeneity.

What can we say about these confessional documents as a group? Do they express a belief system that is within the mainstream of Christian theology and in particular early modern Protestant theology? What deviations from the norm, either classically Protestant or classically congregational, can be found in these statements? A careful reading of all of these documents indicates that all were orthodox; that is, they fell within the pale of the Christian church. They were not, however, uniform. Because their composition was in the hands of each local congregation and its pastor, there was a large degree of variation with respect to topics covered. There was also variation in the ordering of these topics. Generally, however, one can find a progression from the doctrine of God, to the doctrine of creation and its human inhabitants, to the doctrine of the fall and its effects, to the doctrine of redemption in Jesus Christ, to the doctrine of the church and the Christian life that the members of the church were to live, to the doctrine of the last things.

What is not covered in these documents is of interest as well: there is some mention of covenant doctrine and covenant theology, but covenant theology in general and the federal theology in particular are not the controlling templates for most of these local confessions. At times, the theme of the First Adam and the Second Adam emerges, but the contrast and relationship between them is not a consistent topic.[42] There is little consideration given to the doctrine and practice of worship,[43] and the theme of the millennium is hardly even touched.[44] Finally, the threat of Arminianism is not mentioned, even though the Arminian controversy was a major issue in Protestant Europe during the entire seventeenth century. We will, however, return to Arminianism before we are finished. Some of the clusters of ideas not mentioned are reputed to have been the linchpin around which New England was built, but none of them come through as a dominant theme in any of the local confessions.

There were also variations of depth and authorship: Edward Taylor's "Profession of Faith" represents the outline of an unfinished individual systematic theology authored by Taylor himself, while John Eliot's *A Christian Covenanting Confession* is a brief one-page document designed for Native Americans in the non-Western tradition.[45] Generally, however, the local confessional statements were usually documents of three or four pages and designed to be digestible for the average lay person. A close reading of the church records and local confessions indicates that the founding pastors had a large hand in the authorship of these documents, but that the foundation members — more often than not lay leaders already — also participated in their composition. The visiting "messengers" who came for the gathering of a church did have final veto power over the confession before and even during the gathering of the church, and at times they exercised that authority. But on the whole these are not highly polished documents that encapsulate and respond to hundreds of years of theological discussion or the latest theological controversy. Rather, they represent standard Christian orthodoxy.

But with so many authors over half a century in various colonies, can we find deviations of doctrine among these documents? Three confessional documents in particular stand out as being either somewhat different or very different from all of the others. The first two have subtle variations in their doctrine of fallen humanity, while the third strikes out in new directions, a move made in the last two years of the seventeenth century.

The first document is the confession of faith of Killingworth, Connecticut Colony, where a church was gathered in 1667. In the Killingworth confession there is one phrase that is worth mentioning that deals with fallen humanity. In speaking of the state of humanity after the fall, the Killingworth confession uses the following words:

> . . . man being created after his Image, in a state of Integrity & Blessedness hath now suffered the Loss of both, by his disobedience to, and his disunion from God, and is by nature in a state of spiritual weakness, enmity, pollution, guilt unrighteousness & wrath.[46]

The key phrase in the above paragraph is "spiritual weakness." Such a phrase implies that human beings can do something for their own salvation. Classical Reformed theology consistently speaks of fallen humanity as being in a state of spiritual *death,* unable to do anything to effect their salvation unless made alive by the Spirit of God and regenerated by the grace of Christ. The theme of a weak but not dead humanity continues a little further on, when the remedy for sin and the fall is discussed. When the fullness of time had come God sent the "holy spirit to inlighten, convince, call and sanctify all those that are given unto him, who, being enabled to believe in his name . . . shall be adjudged to eternal life. . . ."[47] That the sinner needs "enlightenment" and "enablement" rather than quickening and resurrection indicates a state of sin wherein one has ability to do something once the light has penetrated. With only a couple of phrases, one congregation had started to drift towards the Arminian doctrine that human beings could initiate the process of salvation, a thing Reformed theologians said was impossible for spiritually dead people to do.

That theme was continued seventeen years later in Marblehead, Massachusetts. The Marblehead, Massachusetts Bay Colony, First Church was gathered on Wednesday, August 13, 1684. Like the Salem Village (Danvers) First Church gathered in 1689, it was an offshoot of the First Church of Salem. However, the community of Marblehead was oriented toward the world of Atlantic trade, and was not split between the maritime and agricultural focal points that characterized Salem Village and contributed to the tensions that led to the witch trials.[48] The Marblehead confession has two sections dealing with fallen humanity. The first is found in the second paragraph of the confession:

> The Lord made man at first in his own image, in knowledge, righteousness and holiness; from which state man failing by transgressing the law of his creation, all his posterity are corrupted in their whole nature, — averse to all good and strongly inclined to all evil, from whence do proceed all actual transgressions which bind men over to death temporal, spiritual and eternal.[49]

"And strongly inclined to evil" reveals a subtle slippage in the direction of human ability. Fallen human beings are not dead in their sin, they are simply "inclined" to sin, an inclination that they can perhaps battle with their own ability. That pattern of thought is repeated in the "Condensed Confession of Faith . . . used in receiving persons into the Communion of the Church":

> Art. 3. You believe that by nature man is destitute of holiness and inclined to sin, so that without a change of heart he cannot enter the kingdom of God.[50]

While fallen human beings are "destitute of holiness" in this sentence, they are not totally depraved in the sight of God. There is almost an unspoken implication that there is some sort of neutral estate for fallen human beings, and that they can then choose to be inclined to sin, or choose to have a change of heart that will lead to entrance into the kingdom of God. Such slippage will multiply and accelerate in the eighteenth century.

The final document that we will consider is the famous *Manifesto* of the Brattle Street Congregational Church, founded in Boston in 1699-1700. The Brattle Street Church was the fourth Congregational church founded in Boston, Massachusetts Bay Province, but it was never called the "Fourth Congregational Church of Boston." Rather, it was known more popularly as "The Manifesto Church," and was gathered on Tuesday, December 12, 1699.[51] No covenant document exists for the Brattle Street Church, but in the last months of 1699 the congregation, under the leadership of its new pastor, Benjamin Colman, published a document that they called a "Manifesto." Its purpose was to assure the rest of New England that while they were founding a church that was going to be purposefully "countercultural," they were still orthodox in doctrine. The opening statement reads as follows:

> We think it Convenient, for preventing all Misapprehensions and Jealousies, to publish our Aims and Designs herein, together with those Principles and Rules we intend by GODS Grace to adhere unto. We do therefore as in the Presence of GOD our Judge, and with all the Sincereity and Seriousness, which the nature of our present Engagement Commands from us, Profess and Declare both to one another, and to all the World, as follows.[52]

Technically, the *Manifesto* is not a confession of faith at all. But because it makes a reference to a confession of faith, and because it is so very different from anything that has appeared in the foundational records of New England up to this point, it is important to examine the *Manifesto* with care. Almost everything about the Brattle Street Church went against the normative patterns developed in New England over the previous eighty years. They adopted the Westminster Confession of Faith when the rest of New England was abandoning it for the Savoy Declaration. The Brattle Street Church did not apply for or receive recognition from the civil government, and the other three Congregational churches in Boston gave the new congregation only lukewarm endorsements.[53] Even the title of the

Manifesto reveals a group of people determined not to follow the norm: *A Manifesto or Declaration, Set forth by the Undertakers of the New Church Now Erected in Boston in New-England, November 17th. 1699.*[54] The foundation members of the church do not refer to themselves as "foundation stones" but as "undertakers," connoting an independence of action and liberty of spirit that reflects the mercantile backgrounds of many of them. These were not people who were going to be subservient to the hoary orthodoxy of the elders of the First, Second, and Third Churches of Boston; rather, they were engaged in an adventurous project.

That sense of adventure was reflected in the life of Benjamin Colman. A native of Boston and a graduate of Harvard College, Colman wrote a sketch of his life at the beginning of the "Church Book." For four years he had lived in England, where he had been a candidate for the "Evangelical Ministry" — a phrase not used by seventeenth-century New Englanders. Colman had had the experience of preaching in London, at Cambridge University, at Ipswich, Suffolk, and then, for two years, at Bath, Somersetshire. He had been ordained by the Presbyterian Board at London for the Bath ministry. Unlike most of the rising generation of clergy at the turn of the century, Colman had had a breadth of international experience akin to the first generation of New Englanders. He brought back with him a sense of where the "Dissenters" of Old England were situating themselves with respect to the established Church of England, and, while consenting to pastor a Congregational church, probably was the one who urged the "undertakers" to adopt the Presbyterian Westminster Confession without reference to the 1648 Cambridge Platform.[55] The commitment to the Westminster Confession is put forth in the first article of the *Manifesto*: "First of all, We approve and subscribe the Confession of Faith put forth by the Assembly of Divines at Westminster."[56]

The model of the church put forth by Colman and his undertakers is deliberately based on the pattern that had emerged since 1662 among the Dissenters of Old England rather than on the pattern developed in New England. In the second section, the section that deals with worship, the undertakers explicitly state that they were conforming to the "known practice of many of the Churches of the UNITED BRETHREN in London, and throughout all England."[57] Clearly, the undertakers were taking as their benchmark for orthodoxy an entirely different standard. They were building a new church in the new world using the standards of an old church in the old world. In so doing they were becoming avant-garde, knowing full well that any from New England who attacked them as "unorthodox" ran the risk of sundering fellowship with the Congregationalists of Old England and inviting attack from the national government that had come to a settlement about these matters in the decade after 1689. Significantly, the new way of gathering a church was coming from the old world.

The remaining part of the *Manifesto* discusses issues of worship, relations with other congregations, church government, baptism, communion, the process of becoming a member of the church, church discipline, the church itself, and the question of the participation of women in the affairs of the church. In all of these areas, the Brattle Street undertakers ran contrary to the accepted standards that had developed in seventeenth-century New England. In the issue of worship, for instance, Colman and the undertakers felt that the Scripture could be read independent of preaching, a custom that the New England Puritans had identified with High Church Anglicanism. With respect to baptism, the *Manifesto* rejects the half-way covenant, affirming that baptism of children should be administered only to children of communicant members. However, they significantly loosened the requirements for communicant membership by not requiring that a public relation of grace be presented before the gathered church: "But we assume not to our selves to impose upon any a Publick Relation of their Experiences; however, if any one thinking himself bound in Conscience to make such a Relation, let him do it."[58] The Church would baptize any child who was offered by any professed Christian, provided the parents "engaged" to see it "Educated . . . in the Christian Religion."[59] That last phrase is significant. Children are to be "educated." The word reflects some of the tenor of the next century, with its focus on "enlightenment." The phrase "Christian Religion" also reflects a differing emphasis from the seventeenth century: a child was to be educated in a body of doctrine rather than be "raised in the nurture and admonition of the Lord." The Brattle Street congregation therefore moved in the direction of accepting what the earlier Puritans called "historical faith" rather than "saving faith" as a criterion for communicant membership.

The shifting foundations of the Brattle Street Church are also illustrated in another phrase further on in the *Manifesto*. In Sections XIII and XIV there is a discussion of the ecclesiastical commitments that the members of the congregation were making. The section reads as follows:

> XIII. We apprehend that a particular Church, as such, is a Society of Christians by mutual agreement, usually meeting together for Publick Worship in the same place, and under the same Ministry, attending on

the Ordinances of God there. XIV. In every such Society, the Law of nature dictates to us, that there is implied a mutual promise and engagement of being faithful to the Relations they bear to each other, whither as private Christians, or as Pastor and Flock, so long as the Providence of God continues them in those Relations.[60]

Note that the framework for commitment to the pastor and each other is "the Law of nature." Natural law has now replaced the covenantal stipulations of Scripture as the foundation for ethical commitment. The secularization of the covenant in the colonial world had roots not only in the state but also in the church.

The final facet of the Brattle Street confession that we want to look at is the expansion of participation in church affairs, particularly in the election of the pastor. The last section of the Brattle Street *Manifesto* concludes with these words:

> XVI. Finally, We cannot confine the right of chusing a Minister to the Male Communicants alone, but we think that every Baptized Adult Person who contributes to the Maintenance, should have a Vote in Electing.[61]

Significant is the fact that more than communicant members have a voice in such an important vote: the criteria instead are twofold: baptism, and voluntary financial contributions. Often in seventeenth-century New England towns the parish and the town voted for and called a minister rather than the gathered church, so this is perhaps not that different a policy. But what is different is the practice of financial contributions for the support of the church: since Brattle Street Church did not have the sanction of the state, it did not benefit from the compulsory tithe system ("the rates") that the other churches of the Massachusetts Bay Province benefited from. The fact that financial contributions came in voluntarily surely changed the dynamics of the congregation: one would feel that a compulsory tithe was a "tax" to be endured, whereas a nonmember or baptized member of a congregation might take a greater interest in an organization that his voluntary contributions were helping to support, even if he were not a full communicant member. But such interest at times could be unhealthy, since some might view the organization as a "religious club" rather than an established church.

The explicit expansion of voting membership to females was also a harbinger of a new era in New England. In our conclusion we will note a parallel movement in terms of the composition of foundation members: during the period 1684 to 1708 New England moved away from patriarchal foundation cohorts to a pattern of mixed cohorts of men and women.[62] The Brattle Street *Manifesto* is the first explicit written evidence from this period that reflects what was largely a silent shift toward the greater and more active participation of women in the affairs of the New England churches.

The Brattle Street *Manifesto* is an anomaly in seventeenth-century confessional statements. Its appearance in November 1699, just as New England was moving into the eighteenth century, marks an end to the confessional congruence and uniformity that was the hallmark of virtually all of the colonies except Rhode Island. The increase in population, along with changed political and ecclesiastical circumstances in Old England, led to a widening of parameters for confession and practice in the eighteenth century, all of which is a topic for another time and place. However, Brattle Street Church's reliance on the standards and benchmarks of Old England fit in with the pattern of other groups receiving their norms from England and from Europe — Anglicans in Boston and Connecticut who looked to the bishop of London, Quakers who looked for guidance to the London yearly meeting, Baptists who kept up relations with the brethren in Old England, and French Huguenots who kept in contact with the French Reformed Church. In 1620, the Mayflower Separatists had come to New England to be left alone; by 1700, their grandchildren were surrounded by thousands of neighbors representing a much higher degree of heterogeneity with respect to religious belief. And with the emergence of the Brattle Street Church, that heterogeneity was invading the standing order of Congregationalism itself.

Confessions of faith in the Congregationalist tradition were meant to bind only the local body that accepted that particular confession. John Higginson established this principle in the first published confession of faith generated by a local New England congregation, where he speaks of the Salem confession as a document "not to be made use of as an imposition upon any."[63] The nonbinding nature of these confessions stands in marked contrast to the subscriptionism and doctrinal uniformity of Scottish Presbyterianism. The New England confessions emerged in the wake of the Westminster Assembly and later the Restoration, and were used to prove to the rest of the Protestant world that New England was in the mainstream of early modern confessional thought. The confessional statements were also used to teach young and old in preparation for communicant membership and foundation membership and to rebut sectaries, especially

Quakers. Church members — baptized, half-way, and communicant — were thereby instructed in orthodoxy as they faced heterodoxy in the outside world.

New Englanders utilized two types of confessions as they founded their churches. The first type was the confessional statements that emerged out of the synods and assemblies of clergy that met in the early modern period. These statements carried great weight, in that they were formulated by professional theologians and clergy and carried the stamp of approval of a large body of clergy. These ecclesiastical confessions were printed up and utilized by many churches. At times one group of divines disagreed with what another group had declared, and this led to the modification, usually slight but sometimes substantial, of a standardized confessional statement. The changing conception of the relationship of church and state in these major ecclesiastical documents, along with the increasing allowance for dissent, allowed for a significant transformation of religious commitment in early New England. The Savoy Declaration of 1658, along with the Declaration of the Reforming Synod of 1679-80 and the Saybrook Platform of 1708, paved the way for New England to conform to Old England by the eighteenth century. Like Old England, New England began to tolerate dissent, at least dissent within the boundaries of historic Trinitarian Christianity. Reluctantly, the elders of the standing order of New England allowed Baptists, Anglicans, and French Huguenots to find a place in the New England world beside the Congregational churches. When the Quakers formed the New England yearly meeting in 1672, the standing order did little to stop it.

The second type of confessional document was local, and was usually composed by the founding clergyman and his foundation members. These documents were attempts to establish the individual congregation as a part of orthodox Christianity. Ironically, a peculiar dialectic became apparent. Dissenters such as Baptists wrote up confessions to show to the standing congregational order that the Baptists were not as far from the norms of orthodoxy as the paedobaptist Congregationalists thought. In response, the Congregationalists of the standing order wrote up confessional statements to distinguish themselves from the unorthodox and to teach the local church — and especially the young in that church — the straight and narrow way. Save for Rhode Island, which has given us no confessions from any religious group, the confessions of the standing order of seventeenth-century New England reflected a fairly unified mind on the part of the religious elite. But placing the composition of doctrinal statements in the hands of clergy and laity, unaided by other clergy except on the day of the church gathering, opened up the door for slippage of doctrine in the standing order, a slippage that we begin to see at the end of the century. The slippage was made possible by the nature of Congregationalism itself, with its series of independent congregations and its policy of non-subscription.

The seeds of religious diversity in New England came from three sources. The confessional literature of Independents and Dissenters in Old England gave official sanction to the toleration of orthodox dissent. This way of thinking emerged just as the Independents were losing power in 1658. Puritans in New England could now accept religious nonconformity because a well-known doctrinal statement that the New England clergy adopted in 1680 and 1708 permitted nonconformity and dissent to exist. Whether this policy was actually followed varied from year to year, from colony to colony, and from locality to locality. Second, the post-Restoration political policy of Old England also adopted the stance of grudging toleration. In Old England, Anglicans grudgingly tolerated Independents, Baptists, and Presbyterians, restricting them through the Clarendon Code. In New England, Puritans learned to grudgingly tolerate Anglicans, Quakers, and Baptists. They knew that they had better, or dire consequences from Old England would follow. Finally, the local confessional literature of New England emerged in individual congregations as a response to that dissent, and allowed nascent congregations the opportunity to stray from the strait and narrow path of orthodoxy. Most did not in the seventeenth century, but as the process of gathering congregations by covenant and confession proceeded, the beginnings of heterogeneity began to appear.

Conclusion

> *The earth Iehovahs is,*
> *and the fulnesse of it:*
> *the habitable world, & they*
> *that there upon doe sit.*
> *Because upon the seas,*
> *hee hath it firmly layd:*
> *and it upon the water-floods*
> *most sollidly hath stayed.*

> (Psalm 24:1-2; Bay Psalm Book)

The theme of covenant is found throughout the Old and New Testaments of the Bible, and it is well established that the covenant was a motif that provided cohesion to the nascent New England communities of the seventeenth century.[1] While there is still much discussion and debate as to the nature of the New England covenant theology, there is a general consensus that the early New Englanders — including those in Rhode Island — worked to some degree within a covenantal vision that had as its source the Bible and Reformed Protestant theology. The covenant gave boundaries to the Puritan's vertical relationship with God and his horizontal relationship with his neighbor and fellow church member. In Europe, where Christianity had been the established state religion for centuries, the covenant was utilized as an instrument of reformation. In the New World, the covenant was an instrument of formation; the foundational covenants of the civil realm and the church laid the basis for the community. Nevertheless, by the latter part of the seventeenth century New Englanders were also speaking of using the covenant as an instrument of reformation, as they saw their own generation and the rising generation stray from the original covenantal vision of the founders.

The fact that the covenant motif could be used as both an instrument of formation and reformation in both church and state perhaps belies a more profound reality about its nature: the covenant idea is a flexible concept that can be used for what are often conflicting uses and in a variety of human situations. In the Bible there is political flexibility, as the covenanted nation of Israel functioned first as a family, then as Egyptian slaves, then as a confederation of desert tribes freed from slavery, then as a government of settled tribes under Joshua, then as a confederated tribal federation under the judges, then as a federal state under Samuel and Saul, then as a federal monarchy under David, Solomon, and their successors, then as Babylonian exiles, then as returned exiles subject to the Persians and later the Macedonian Greeks, then as independent Maccabeans, and finally as residents subject to the Romans. Beginning in 600 B.C., even in 721 B.C., the Israelites sustained a diaspora community that continues to the present. But while there is flexibility, there is also form as well. Daniel Elazar comments on the flexibility of the Sinaitic covenant in particular:

> This makes it possible for the Bible to chronicle later changes in the political constitution of the Jewish people without raising covenantal problems involving the changes per se. The only test imposed by the Bible is whether or not the changes were such that the covenantal relationship and its obligations are maintained. . . . These changes of regime were possible because no single political structure is imposed by the covenant. On the contrary, the Bible makes it clear that there are options. But each structure, each form of government, is measured against the covenantal model to see whether the relationships are appropriate, whether they fit the model of theo-political relationships established by the covenant.[2]

Besides the biblical tradition, the covenant idea was utilized since the close of the biblical canon by many groups of people in many historical contexts, specifically both church and state. That therefore leads to a variety of influences on the motif, influences that are of particular interest to American constitutional historians who are seeking to delve into the sources of the Constitution and their historical development.[3] Historians have documented and explored reciprocal influences on the themes of covenant, contract, and constitution in a variety of historical phases in the Western world. That is, the historical milieu of major historical periods has influenced the cluster of ideas associated with covenant, contract, and constitution. But the reverse is also true: the ideas of covenant, contract, and, in modern times, constitution have also profoundly influenced the culture around them. Those historical periods, cultures, traditions, and historical figures have included the world of the Bible, ancient Greece, ancient Rome, the medieval world, English common law, the English Parliamentary tradition, the Renaissance, the Reformation, the Lutheran tradition, the Calvinist tradition, the Mennonite and Radical Reformation tradition, Puritanism, English Separatism, the commercial revolution fostered by mercantilism, Thomas Hobbes, John Locke, the English Whig tradition, the scientific revolution, the Enlightenment, the American colonial constitutions, the American founding fathers, the United States Constitution, "modernity," and the "Western secular tradition."[4]

The flexibility of covenant theory and practice can explain, therefore, the various highways and byways that the covenant concept and the various forms of Puritanism took in both Old and New England.[5] The covenant was used by Puritans in both Englands to espouse individualism and individual freedom over community goals and values.[6] But Puritans also used the covenant concept to articulate and defend communal values and authority over individual liberties.[7] The covenant was utilized to express Puritan conceptualizations of marriage,[8] but was also used to describe a relationship with Satan.[9] Yet another Puritan use of the covenant concept was millenarian, wherein the future held a restoration for either the church, the state, or both spheres to some biblical pattern from the past. That pattern might be characterized as the Adamic administration in Eden, the Noachic covenant of primeval times, the Abrahamic or Mosaic covenants of the ancient world, or the new covenant of the New Testament church.[10] On the other hand, the covenant could be used as a foundation for modernization — as a tool or instrument from the ancient past that laid out a vision for the future. The future, after all, was the focus of the ancient biblical covenants, as these covenants articulated what God was going to do with and for numerous biblical characters in the future, a future that was worked out in later biblical history.[11] The covenant was utilized to develop a variety of conceptualizations of the relationship between church, state, and religion in early New England and early modern England, and was integral in laying out a greater separation between the two spheres of church and state, yet it could also be used to sustain a religious vision of the state as found in the New Haven Colony.[12] The covenant could be used to advance the cause of democracy and freedom, as it laid out, in a written document that could be constantly referenced, fundamental principles of political governance in church and state.[13] On the other hand, recent historians have maintained that the doctrines of historic Christianity, including the covenant, have led to oppression and despotism, both religious and political.[14] Nevertheless, it is undeniable that the ideas of toleration and then, later, positive religious freedom and right, were forged in the crucible of early modern Western Christianity, particularly the Anglo-American world that included New England.[15] And many have commented over the years that the church covenant, its practice, and its outworking influenced the emergence of the civil covenant and the voluntary form of representative government that marks the modern American world.[16]

The covenant was the initial means by which the leaders of New England, both civil and ecclesiastical, established hegemony over the varied constituencies that made up early New England. While articulating a vertical relationship between God, humanity, and the institution of church and state, the civil and ecclesiastical covenants laid the foundation for the norms of New England society, norms that would be articulated in various ways as the years passed. In the dialogue between theory and practice, the civil and ecclesiastical covenants were the theory — popularized theory, but theory nevertheless. The degree to which the New Englanders practiced their theory and lived up to their ideals varied from colony to colony and from generation to generation.

Some major patterns do emerge from our study of early New England civil and church covenants, patterns that do have to be seen in transatlantic perspective.[17] During the period 1620 to 1660, the civil covenants that set out the vision of the political realm were mainly grassroots combinations and exhibited a diversity of thought concerning the nature of that realm, its relation to classical Christianity, and the institutional church that gave embodiment to that faith. The church covenants were much more standard and uniform, because they emerged from the context of Separatist and non-Separatist Puritanism in Old England. In that world, church covenanting was a common practice, while civil covenanting was not. To separate from the established church and to form a new church by covenant, or to form a conventicle by covenant within the established state church, was a practice that many Puritans engaged in during the sixteenth and seventeenth centuries in England. But to separate from the established government of England and form a covenanted state within the realm was a project no one undertook, for such action would result in a trial for treason and the penalty of death. Thus, as the early New Englanders reached the shores of the New World, they proposed a variety of visions for the civil realm and a much more uniform vision for the church.

The transition period was the years 1660-62, when many New Englanders abandoned the original Puritan vision of New England's established leaders for a more general English Reformed Protestant vision. In 1660 the Restoration of Charles II was secured and the failure of the Cromwellian Protectorate became obvious; the Puritan and Independent failure in Old England was made even more evident by the Great Ejection of 1662. And it was in 1662 that the half-way covenant was adopted by the New England synod, allowing the modified parochial system of New England to resemble more closely the parochial system that was still in existence in Old England. In both Old and New England, the parochial system began to develop in such a way that dissenting Protestant groups were allowed to coexist with established parish churches, but not on an equal level.[18]

The period 1662 to 1708 saw the fracturing of the New England ecclesiastical vision as set forth by John Cotton, John Winthrop, John Davenport, and others.[19] New England, like Old England, slowly learned to live with an established state church and dissenting Christian groups functioning alongside of the parochial church. But the vision of the New Englanders for the civic realm became much more uniform: more and more, the local and colonial civic arena was built on the foundation of the patents and charters found in the English common law tradition, and the combinations that articulated local and colonial covenantal visions for the state were abandoned for the uniformity and standardization of legal documents that were developed by lawyers who were for the most part Royalist and Anglican. This counterpoint between visions of church and state led to what some have called the "Anglicization" of New England, and is one of the factors that accounts for the transition "from Puritan to Yankee." New England was becoming more English as the century passed, and took its political and many of its ecclesiastical cues from Old England after the Restoration of 1662 and the Glorious Revolution of 1688-89.[20]

A second broader pattern that we should note is that the variety of civil covenants reveal a number of differing foci for the civil and church covenants. Some civil covenants were focused around the God of the Old Testament, a deity that many monotheists might, in future generations, give some degree of assent to. Such a deity would serve as a lowest common denominator for civic religion, justice, and virtue. Some civil covenants were specifically Christian, focused around the God of the Old Testament who continues to reveal himself in the New Testament and the new covenant. The more specifically Christian civil covenants were concerned with the kingdom of Christ or the church of Christ, but only a few were focused on the person and work of Christ or intent on dedicating the state to Christ as king. Some of the other foci of the civil covenants included land and its division, wealth, governance authority, governance structure, ecclesiastical establishment, assertions of allegiance to the English crown, the maintenance of the common good over the assertion of individual rights, and the exclusion of heretics and sectarians from the local community. The net result was that the civil covenants became more generic, secularized, and English as the century proceeded. The church covenants could subtly change their focus as well. While members of the Congregational standing order felt that they were establishing a relationship with God and Christ in the church covenants, Baptists tended to look at the church covenant as a means of establishing horizontal relationships with the church and its members.

A third pattern to consider is the nature of the civil and ecclesiastical covenants. Were they covenants, or were they in actuality contracts? And do we see any transition from covenant to contract during the seventeenth century? A brief exploration of the differences between covenant and contract is necessary before we answer that question. In the biblical record, the covenant theme harks back to the ancient Near Eastern suzerainty treaty in which a covenant is articulated by a superior party (a "lord") with a lesser party (a "vassal"). Even in biblical covenants between human beings of equal social status (for example, between kings), God (the superior) was invoked as a party to the covenant and therefore there was a superior party in the arrangement. That tradition continued on in the Christian church, and the 1646-47 Westminster Confession of Faith reaffirms the hierarchical nature of the covenant:

Chap. VII.
Of God's Covenant with Man.

1. The Distance between God and the Creature is so great, that although reasonable Creatures do owe Obedience unto him as their Creator, yet they could never have any Fruition of him as their Blessedness and Reward, but by some voluntary Condescension on God's Part, which he hath been pleased to express by way of Covenant.

2. The first covenant made with Man, was a Covenant of Works, wherein Life was promised to Adam, and in him to his Posterity; upon Condition of perfect and personal Obedience. . . .

Chap. XIX
Of the Law of God.

1. God gave to Adam a Law as a Covenant of Works, by which he bound him and all his Posterity to personal, entire, exact and perpetual Obedience; promised Life upon the fulfilling, and threatened Death upon the Breach of it; and indued him with Power and Ability to keep it.
2. This Law after his Fall, continued to be a perfect Rule of righteousness, and [as such] was delivered by God upon Mount Sinai. . . .
5. The Moral Law doth for ever bind all, as well justified Persons as others, to the Obedience thereof; and that not only in regard of the Matter contained in it, but also in respect of the Authority of God the Creator who gave it. Neither doth Christ in the Gospel any way dissolve, but much strengthen this Obligation.[21]

A contract, on the other hand, implied that the parties could, but might not necessarily be, equal, and that if one of the parties broke the contract the other party had the right to discontinue the relationship and not be bound to the obligations of the contract. Part of the burden of Perry Miller's *New England Mind* is that the New Englanders made a transition from covenant to contract during the late seventeenth and early eighteenth century. Some have also seen the alleged transition from covenant to contract as the prelude to the movement from hierarchical monarchicalism to egalitarian democracy. And as one looks at the five major colonial powers in the western hemisphere (England, the Netherlands, Spain, France, and Portugal), England, and later Great Britain, stood out as a Protestant nation that had moved away from the hierarchicalism of the Roman Catholic world, with its various strata of society: pope, king, nobility, gentry, peasantry, and so on. The dynamic of the Spanish mission and the French trading post was different from the New England town.[22] However, a careful examination of both church and civil covenants indicates that seventeenth-century New England continued to have a deep sense of hierarchy, and that none of the civil or church covenants are cast as contracts. God, Christ, king, the central colonial government, and the local town council were superiors in the civil covenants, and God, Christ, clergy, and elders were the superiors in the church covenants. Seventeenth-century New England did not generate modern contracts. The inferior, or vassal parties, submitted themselves to their covenantal superiors.

A fourth pattern to consider is the question of covenant remembrance and renewal. While New Englanders often spoke of the covenantal structure of the society that they were forming, the question needs to be asked whether the signers and their successors were kept aware of and reminded of their covenant obligations. Or were the church and civil covenants simply documents gathering dust in the first town book and/or first church book? And do we get any sense that there was a descending obligation on succeeding generations to keep the covenant? Such questions are hard to answer, but a general reading of the evidence indicates that the original civil covenants were relegated more often to obscurity, while the church covenants and their obligations were more readily embraced over and over again. Sustaining a covenantal vision in the civil realm was much harder to do than in the ecclesiastical realm. We have no record of any civil covenant renewals, but we have many church covenant renewals in the records of the early New England churches. In some sense the church renewed its covenant every Sabbath Day, and some of those Sabbaths were days on which the sacraments of the new covenant, baptism and communion, were observed. And special days were set aside to renew the church covenant, in a couple of cases at the instigation of the central colonial governments.

A fifth pattern to keep in mind is that there was indeed a separation of church and state in seventeenth-century New England: each institution had its sphere of responsibility. An examination of the written records from the towns and churches indicates that the New Englanders consistently had two sets of records: the town records and the church records. Each recorded a different series of meetings, actions, and functions. The church was viewed as an advisor to the state, but the church did not get involved in the multitude of activities that the state got involved in: land division, tax assessment, criminal prosecution, estate settlement, and so on. Often the personnel overlapped, and this was especially true in the colonies where only the members of the gathered church could exercise the functions of civil government, but the two institutions were distinct and separate. In actuality, an oligarchy of the same personnel governed both the church and the state. Furthermore, New England was not a world in which the clergy acted as civil governors. While clergy were often influential in the early New England colonies, one does not find dozens of clergy exercising civil office in early New England. Their focus was the church.

A final general pattern that we should note is that the church and civil covenants were vehicles by which a civil and ecclesiastical community could balance the tension between the past, the present, and the future. New Englanders could look at biblical and secular history as God's gracious dealings with his people through time, and see themselves as part of a larger picture of world history. The gospel and its fruits had gone forth, and the New England story was one subsection of a vast cosmic plan on God's part to redeem the world and the universe. While at times New Englanders succumbed to the temptation to see New England as the penultimate culmination of that plan, the larger framework of history gave them a sobering perspective that they were just one little corner in one short time period of a much larger frame of reference. In terms of the present, the covenant gave them a rudder by which they could conduct their daily lives, a means by which they could articulate their individual, ecclesiastical, and societal purposes in a "mission statement" — much like contemporary companies and organizations develop mission statements to remind employees of the larger goals that should transcend the daily routine. Finally, in terms of the future, the covenants gave a series of long-range goals for institutions and people, goals toward which to work and which emerged out of the past and present circumstances that each town, plantation, and colony found itself in. Significantly enough, no millennial vision could be found in either the civil or ecclesiastical covenants. Such a vision would have been temporary any way, lasting only a period of a thousand years. But the final goal of the eternal new heavens and new earth was clearly articulated, particularly in the church covenants.

While we began this volume with the covenants that affected the many (the civil covenants) and then examined the covenants that affected the few (the church covenants), we will reverse that order and draw out some broader themes that emerge from the covenants for the few (the church covenants) and then conclude with some thoughts about the covenants for the many (the civil covenants).

The first thing to be said about the church covenants is how simple, yet how profound, they were. Written by both clergy and laity, the church covenants were documents located between the high cultural and theological tradition of the New England clergy and the more simple tradition of lay piety. They were unconditional covenants of grace, and not conditional covenants of works nor conditional contracts between equals. One looks in vain for the complexities of covenant theology described in Perry Miller's *New England Mind,* and there is little said about the relationships among predestination, foreknowledge, freedom or bondage of the will, preparationism, repentance, justification, obedience, sanctification, assurance of salvation, false assurance of salvation and hypocrisy, and the relationship between grace and works. The standing order of New England Congregationalism developed a "covenant formulary" that was fairly consistent and did not vary significantly over the entire century — a significant feat for a group of people committed to Congregationalism and the independence of churches from one another. The covenant formulary began with a preamble, outlining the purpose of the covenant and naming the earthly and heavenly witnesses to the covenant. It then usually moved to an acceptance of God as God, and then to an acceptance of the work of Christ, particularly in his office as prophet, priest, and king. The next step in the church covenant formulary was the submission of the members one to another in the "holy watch," and then finally a promise to submit to the governance of the church. The church covenant usually concluded with a final commitment to the terms of the covenant and a reminder to the reader of the document that this was being done in the presence of God, his holy angels, and the congregation.

There was, however, significant change in the religious life of New England after the Restoration of Charles II in 1660. The emergence, and then reluctant toleration on the part of the Congregational standing order, of Baptists, Anglicans, and Quakers signaled a shattering of any consensus that the New Englanders had with respect to church, state, and religion. The very fact that several colonies rather than one single colony had emerged between 1620 and 1660 indicates that the consensus of 1620-60 was fragile, if not nonexistent, and any hope of religious unity disappeared after 1660 with the emergence of dissenting groups.[23] The Baptist church covenants followed many of the same lines of thought as the Congregational covenants, but they looked at the covenant as a confirmation of what had happened in the inner heart and in the public ordinance of adult baptism. They therefore tended to view the covenant as a means of establishing a visible church on earth and of allowing people to submit themselves to that visible church, rather than as a means to establish a relationship with God. Quakers and Anglicans did not covenant, but pursued other mechanisms to found their religious institutions.

This shattering of religious unity was made more apparent by another significant development related to the church covenants: after 1647, the church covenants began appearing with short confessions of faith attached to them, confessions that were utilized to demonstrate to the standing order a dissenting congregation's orthodoxy. Confessions also began to be utilized by the orthodox standing order to demonstrate to other related churches in the standing order that a newly gathered church was committed to orthodoxy. Some churches adhered to standard statements developed by early modern Protestants in Europe, particularly the Westminster standards developed by the Presbyterians, the Savoy Declaration developed by the Independents, and the London Baptist Confession of 1689. The Cambridge Platform of 1646-48, the Reforming Synod of 1680, and the Saybrook Synod of 1708, while addressing questions peculiar to New England, adopted confessional statements from Old England. Significantly, however, these New England synods adjusted the sections on church and state to their particular situation and time. Religious toleration within the bounds of Trinitarian Christianity did not, therefore, simply emerge from Old England and the religious policies of the Restoration. The section on church and state in the Savoy Declaration of 1658 opened the door within Independency and Congregationalism for religious dissent within Trinitarian Christianity. The New England Reforming Synod of 1680 modified this stance even more, and that stance was adopted by the Saybrook Synod of 1708.

But a significant number of New England churches developed their own local confessional statements. While intended to force independent congregations to grapple with doctrinal issues, and while generally uniform in the seventeenth century, this practice, especially in light of emerging dissent in New England after 1660, opened the door for slippage in the seventeenth century and heterodoxy in the eighteenth century. The newer churches of the standing order were trying to guard against the influence of Baptist, Quaker, and Anglican doctrine, and teach its rising generation, now drifting in the direction of half-way covenantal commitment, the basic outlines of Reformed Christian doctrine, the congregational form of church government, and the New England Way of the gathered church. But the net result of local confessionalism, along with the modification of European confessional statements by the official New England synods, was that there was no semblance of a New England mind by 1700 in the sphere of religious commitment.[24] Perhaps one way of understanding the Salem trials of 1692 was that they were an attempt to draw a line in the sand: the New England Congregational standing order and the colonial governments had found themselves tolerating Baptists, Anglicans, and even Quakers, but it drew the line at witchcraft.

A pattern that we have not discussed earlier in this volume but that paralleled this movement was the breakdown of the use of selectively small, male, groups as foundation members. Increasingly, as the seventeenth century progressed, the groups diversified by becoming larger and by including more women. Many congregations required a minimum number of charter members to found a church — a sort of "minyan" that was usually set at seven. These seven essentially formed a "spiritual elite" — the "elect of the elect," one might say, because they inaugurated the process of admitting new members to the gathered church. Communities might go for years without gathering a church because they could find only five or six — but not seven — individuals who could convince themselves, the resident clergyman, the community at large, and the visiting clergy on Foundation Day not only that they were truly saved but that they were fit candidates for charter membership in the church. The scriptural justification for the number seven was a text from the book of Proverbs, in which Wisdom is personified and invites all to come into her house:

> Wisedome hath builded he house: she hath hewen out her seuen pillars. She hath killed her beastes; she hath mingled her wine: she hath also furnished her table. She hath sent forth her maidens; she cryeth vpon the highest places of the citie. Who so is simple, let him turne in hither: as for him that wanteth vnderstanding, she sayth to him: Come, eate of my bread, and drinke of the wine, which I haue mingled. Forsake the foolish, and liue; and goe in the way of vnderstanding. (Proverbs 9:1-6)

At what point did the number of seven men become standard practice in New England, and was it uniformly practiced in each colony (apart, of course, from Rhode Island)? One possible answer to this question may be found in Winthrop's *Journal*. Winthrop gave an account of the gathering of the Cambridge-2, Massachusetts Bay Colony, First Church on Monday, February 1, 1635/6:

> then the Elder desired to knowe of the Churches Assembled, what <number> . . . were needfull to make a Churche: & how they ought to proceed in this Action: wherevpon some of the Auncient ministers conferringe shortly togither, gave answeare: that the Scripture did not sett downe any certaine rule for the number: 3: (they thought) were too fewe because by math: 18: an appeale was allowed from 3: . . . but that 7: might be a fitt number. & for their proceedinge, they advised, that suche as were to ioyne should make confession of their Faithe. . . .[25]

Table 4 (on pp. 234-35) indicates that prior to 1636 larger numbers of both males and females inaugurated the church, but that from 1636 to 1667, small numbers of males served as foundation members. After 1667, the pattern broke down and we see both male and female cohorts gathering the church in either small or large numbers and also smaller, exclusively male cohorts gathering the church. But it is evident that the consensus on how to gather a church in New England broke down after the 1660s.[26]

The covenants that affected virtually all citizens of seventeenth-century New England were the civil covenants. Because they affected "the many" of the general citizenry rather than "the few" of the gathered church, the civil covenants are of critical importance in our understanding of the "mission statement" of early New England. While the sphere of New England religion was shattered by 1700, as evidenced by its ecclesiastical diversity, its civil covenants indicate that a much larger degree of civil and political uniformity had emerged by 1700, a uniformity that was based on the traditions of post-Restoration England. This is evidenced not only by the colonial charters handed down by the superior power of the government of Old England all through the century but also by the abandonment of compacts and combinations in favor of patents and charters designed by the central colonial governments during the period after the Restoration. It was in the civil covenants for the many that the interplay between the state, the institutional church, and religion was played out.

Objections to nonsecular states have been numerous over the centuries. Many have said that only the few (the godly) willingly subject themselves to the state, and that these few usually imposed their will upon the larger majority of the population, and that this imposition was done in the name of God, and in Christendom, in the name of Christ, with the aid of the sword. Others have objected that, in parts of the world where Christianity is dominant, God, Christ, and the world of the sacred are often dragged through the mud of political struggle. Yet another objection was that even when citizens and politicians submit themselves as dissenters to a state that has foundations in the realm of the sacred, they are simply paying lip service in order to strive for political power and are therefore speaking and acting hypocritically. Finally, some have often complained that the written statement bears little resemblance to the daily reality, and that therefore the world of the sacred is being used to uphold and maintain a form of civil hypocrisy.

Despite these objections, the written civil covenants of New England provided a normative public theology for future generations of colonial

Table 4
Number and Gender of Foundation Members in New England Congregational and Baptist Churches, 1620-1708[27]

Year*	Total Number of Foundation Members	Male	Female
1630	4	4	0
1632	35	20	15
1634	7	7	0
1634/5	13	9	4
1636	7	7	0
1638	8	8	0
1639	7	7	0
1639	8	8	0
1639	7	7	0
1640/41	7	7	0
1641/2 (2nd)	7	4	3
1642	7	7	0
1643	7	7	0
1644?	7	7	0
1645	10	10	0
1650 (2nd)	7	7	0
1652	7	7	0
1655	14	14	0
1660	8	8	0
1661	8	8	0
1663	10	10	0
1665 (Baptist)	9	7	2
1667	5	5	0
1667	51	24	27
1668	10	10	0
1669 (3rd)	28	28	0
1669/70 (2nd)	33	15	18
1670 (2nd)	20	20	0

*Parenthetical notations following the year indicate the following:
2nd, 3rd, 4th = the number of a congregation of that type found in a specific town
Baptist = Baptist Church
RI = a Rhode Island church

Year	Total Number of Foundation Members	Male	Female
1671	9	9	0
1671 (Baptist/RI)	7	4	3
1674	9	9	0
1678	12	12	0
1679	7	7	0
1682	18	18	0
1684	54	14	40
1685	7	7	0
1687 (RI)	8	8	0
1687/8	7	7	0
1689	27	17	10
1691	7	7	0
1692	10	10	0
1694	20	11	9
1695	10	10	0
1696	9	9	0
1696	12	12	0
1696	14	14	0
1697	42	25	17
1698	13	13	0
1698	26	17	9
1698	18	7	11
1699 (4th)	14	14	0
1700	8	8	0
1700	10	10	0
1700	15	15	0
1701	19	19	0
1701	13	13	0
1702	11	11	0
1702	18	18	0
1703	8	8	0
1704	8	8	0
1704 (RI)	11	11	0
1706	29	10	19
1707	13	13	0
1707/8	4	4	0

New Englanders. And there were nuanced differences among these documents. These differences provided a choice of alternatives for those unhappy in a particular colony. And the written word therefore affected where people settled and lived. When those written documents became more standardized and were patterned after the tradition of English common law during the second half of the century, the New England colonies changed, albeit often grudgingly, with what was written and printed. As stated at the beginning of our study, covenants were documents that were effectual in establishing a civil government or church in a particular region. Given that the civil covenants did what they were intended to do, that is, deliver the power of government and the sword into the hands of various parties, the changes that appeared in the civil covenants and charters over the decades of the seventeenth century did have a long-term effect on the general culture and thought patterns of colonial New England.

In 1653, Thomas Mayhew gave a narration of a civil covenanting ceremony that occurred on Martha's Vineyard the previous year:

> This last spring, the Indians of their own accord made a motion to me they might have some way ordered amongst them, as a means whereby they might Walk in good subjection to the Law of God, wherunto they desired to enter into Covenant; they told me that they were very desirous to have their sins suppressed which God did forbid, and the duties performed, which he hath Commanded in his Word; and thereunto they desired me to inform them, what punishment the Lord did appoint to be inflicted on those which did break any part of his Law, for they were very willing to submit themselves to what the will of the Lord is in this kind. I was not willing on the sudden to draw forth in writing an Answer to their desire, but rather chose to take a longer time of Consideration in a Work of so great Concernment, and refer them to the Word of God, shewing them many places for their information, most whereof they had heard of formerly: They also further desired, That they might have some men Chosen amongst them with my Father and my self, to see that the Indians did walk orderly, and that such might be incouraged, but that those which did not, might be dealt with according to the word of the Lord; I could not but approve and incourage the motion, seeing they spake not as those in Psal. 2.3. "Let us break their bands asunder and cast away their cord from us," but sought totall subjection and strict obedience to God: yet I told them that it was a matter of great weight, shewing them many things which I

thought necessary for them to know, but needless now to relate. A Day of fasting and prayer to repent of our sins, and seek the gracious help of our God for Christ Jesus sake, we appointed; and another shortly after to finish the work in: Some of the Indians spake something for their benefit; and about ten or twelve of them prayed, not with any set Form like Children, but like Men indued with a good measure of the knowledge of God, their own wants and the wants of others, with much affection, and many Spiritual Petitions, savoring of a Heavenly mind; and so are they streitned in respect of help from man, that it appears the more plainly to be the Dictates of Gods Spirit. A Platform of the Covenant in Answer to their desires, I drew forth the same morning in the Indian Language, which I have here sent in English.

> Wee the distressed Indians of the Vineyard (Or Nope the Indian name of the Island) That beyond all memory have been without the True God, without a Teacher, and without a Law, the very Servants of sin and Satan, and without Peace, for God did justly vex us for our sins; having lately through his mercy heard of the Name of the True God, the Name of his Son Christ Jesus, with the Holy Ghost the Comforter, three persons, but one most Glorious God, whose Name is JEHOVAH: We do praise His Glorious Greatness, and in the sorrow of our hearts, and shame of our faces, we do acknowledg and renounce our great and many sins, that we and our Fathers have lived in, do run unto him for mercy, and pardon for Christ Jesus sake; and we do this day through the blessing of God upon us, and trusting to his gracious help, give up our selves in this Covenant, Wee, our Wives, and Children, to serve JEHOVAH: And we do this day chuse JEHOVAH to be our God in Christ Jesus, our Teacher, our Law-Giver in his Word, our King, our Judg, our Ruler by his Magistrates and Ministers; to fear God Himself, and to trust in Him alone for Salvation, both of Soul and Body, in this present Life, and the Everlasting Life to come, through his mercy in Christ Jesus our Savior, and Redeemer, and by the might of his Holy Spirit; to whom with the Father and Son, be all Glory everlasting. Amen.

After I had often read this Covenant and expounded it unto them, they all with free Consent willingly and thankfully joyned therein, and desired Jehovah his blessing for Jesus Christ his sake, the Lord be gracious to our beginnings. . . .[28]

Whether or not all the Native Americans were as enthusiastic as Mayhew made them out to be about this matter, and whether they understood all that was in the civil covenant that they signed that day, we cannot discern. What we can discern, however, is the explicit way in which Mayhew drew these Martha's Vineyard Indians into the orbit of Christendom. As far as Mayhew was concerned, these Native Americans were without law and were the servants of sin and Satan. They were now abandoning their old animistic ways and were adopting Jehovah, or YHWH, the God of the Scripture, to be their God. Furthermore, they were acknowledging the kingship of Jesus Christ, along with his legal, magisterial, judicial, and educative roles. Finally, Mayhew had his Native Americans acknowledge the transcendent importance of not just this life, but of the life to come.

By contrast, the majority of civil covenants generated by seventeenth-century New Englanders were considerably more mundane. Their commitment to Christianity was much more implicit than it was explicit. The fact that many of the civil covenants made provision for ecclesiastical ordinances such as a "godly, orthodox minister," set off land for his support, and spoke of rate lists for compulsory tithes, indicates that, save for the residents of Rhode Island Colony, the New Englanders considered themselves to be within the bounds of Christendom. It is this very reason, it seems, that led to their lack of a grand vision for the establishment of Christianity and the church in New England. The church was already established, and the Christian commitments of the dominant Puritan majority was assumed rather than asserted. While it was felt that Native Americans needed an explicit civil covenant asserting that they were now following Christ as king and acknowledging him as the source of law and authority, the civil covenants designed for the New England towns and plantations have few references to such themes in their texts. As far as the New England leaders were concerned, they were already Christianized, despite the fact that several colonies reserved the gathered church for the "true" Christians.

The civil covenants were less articulate than we might have imagined for New England Puritans, and some of them, such as the Mayflower Compact, were stopgap measures to contain a crisis. Others did reflect a much greater degree of thoughtfulness, but even then they tended to be reactive responses to emergencies, problems (what to do, for example, about the policies of Charles II or James II), or needs. Generally, they were not proactive articulations of a covenantal vision that was theocentric or christocentric. For a series of colonies that took covenant theology and its specific subdivision, the federal theology, seriously, we find very little biblical covenantal thinking in the civil covenants of early New England. Furthermore, the references to God were much more theocentric than christocentric. There was little reference to law — divine, natural, or statutory. The lack of a developed theology and christology in the civil covenants later ultimately paved the way for a more secularized New England.[29] This transformation was legally articulated by the Rhode Island Colony, which disestablished both the church and what has been traditionally termed "religion" in its civil covenants.

For the most part groups of New England citizens, and later committees, treated the responsibility of establishing the civil magistracy as a mundane affair. The gathered church was considered a much more important institution than the civil magistracy. New Englanders found that they could sustain a radical and transforming covenantal vision in their churches for much longer periods of time than in their civil governments and political relationships. To a certain degree, this phenomenon emerged as a result of a great deal of classical Reformed thinking concerning civil authority. Many in the Reformed camp taught that civil authority was a temporary institution that emerged as a result of the Fall. Unlike the family and the procreation of children, the Sabbath, the moral law, and one's vocation, all of which were creation ordinances established under the covenant of works in Eden, civil government came about as a result of sin and was designed to restrain sin. It was therefore not a tool that God and humanity could use as a creation ordinance to build the kingdom of God, of Christ, or of humanity. Rather, it was a temporary but necessary evil that needed to be restrained. And civil government was an entity that Satan could certainly use for evil purposes if left unchecked.

In speaking of the civil covenants, we usually frame the discussion in terms of church and state, the institutions generated by the process of covenanting. However, a third aspect of the process is the religious impulses that stood behind the church and town covenants, that informed these documents as they were being articulated, and that sustained the institutions that were created. Unlike the institutional state church, religious impulses can at times be more ephemeral, but a careful reading of the records of covenanting and of the central colonial governments that authorized the process reveals seven possible stances that New Englanders could adopt concerning the relationship between the state and religion. The first possibility was that the state could be explicitly Christian, covenantally dedicated to Jesus Christ as king and Lord. Besides the Native American tribes discipled by John Eliot in Natick and the Mayhews in Martha's Vineyard, only one other plantation articulated this type of civil covenant. On Wednesday, March 7, 1638, the Portsmouth Plantation signed this civil covenant under the leadership of William Coddington:

> We whose names are underwritten do here solemnly in the presence of Jehovah incorporate ourselves into a Bodie Politick and as he shall help, will submit our persons, lives and estates unto our Lord Jesus Christ, the King of Kings and Lord of Lords and to all those perfect and most absolute lawes of his given us in his holy word of truth, to be guided and judged thereby.
>
> Exodus 24.3, 4.
2 {sic 1} Cron. 11.3.
2 Kings. 11.17.
>
> {19 male signers}[30]

At the same time, only a few miles away, the Providence Plantation was covenanting to establish a government concerned "with civil things only." In 1644 both plantations gave up their original commitments and joined the effort to maintain a neutral state, a neutral state that in 1663 was to be influenced by the salt and light of confessing Christians. And both Natick and the Martha's Vineyard communities lost their independence in King Philip's War, with the result that a civil state explicitly dedicated to Christ the king faded out in seventeenth-century New England.

Another possibility was that the state could be implicitly Christian and utilize the covenantal procedures outlined in the Old Testament to establish itself. The Old Testament references, particularly to the Sinaitic period of the Mosaic epoch, moved the community in the direction of being a theocracy with a view of civil government rooted in the Pentateuch and the Mosaic law. The New Haven Plantation is the most famous example of this type of community, and the narration of its founding indicates that there were some references to the church and the Christian faith, but little if any mention of Christ as king of both church and state.

A third possibility was that the state could be implicitly Christian but lack a covenantal vision of the relationship between the state and God. Such a situation might result in the formation, protection, and maintenance of the church as an institution, but the civil covenants would not explicitly say that the state was dedicated to God. In this case, various groups, of course, could argue over which was the true church. One of the functions of the state was to protect the church and the faith, but most of the civil covenants have no theological vision for the state imbedded in their texts. This arrangement was the most common in seventeenth-century New England. The small number of Anglicans in Maine and New Hampshire, and later Connecticut, would fit into this category as well.

A fourth possibility was to attempt to create a state neutral to religion, with the hope that a majority of Christians would so conduct themselves within the civil realm that the culture and the state would be influenced and informed by biblical and Christian principles. The Providence Plantation and its civil covenant of 1637-39, along with the charters issued in 1644 and 1663 to the Colony of Rhode Island and Providence Plantations, reflect this arrangement. It is this arrangement that in many respects won the day as the United States of America emerged in the late eighteenth century. A fifth possibility was to attempt a neutral state, with the state neither favoring or disfavoring a religion and the citizenry compartmentalizing their private religious convictions from their participation in the public realm. Such a stance was proposed in the eighteenth century by various proponents of the Enlightenment. But such a stance would have been a theological and philosophical impossibility for a seventeenth-century Puritan, who would certainly remember the words of Jesus: "He that is not with me, is against me . . ." (Matthew 12:30).

A sixth possibility was for another religion to serve as the foundation for the state. New Englanders would have had some inkling of this in their encounters with the Native American world, but for any of the colonies to even consider such a possibility was unthinkable. A final seventh possibility was for a secular state to be hostile toward Christianity and the institutional church. No New England civil jurisdiction adopted this last option. One is therefore left with the first four possibilities serving as options for the early New England world.

We should note that these seven theoretical arrangements might involve differing arrangements with respect to a state church or religious establishment, the exercise or nonexercise of the franchise by non-church members, and the ability or inability of nonmembers of the gathered church to hold civil office. In actuality, who got to exercise the franchise and who was allowed to hold civil office in New England varied from colony to colony, from town to town, over time, and whether the office was local, regional, or colony-wide. And the changing policies were not necessarily direct results of their civil covenant commitments.[31]

New England was only able to sustain its experiments for two genera-

tions, from 1620 to 1660. The failure of the Cromwellian regime in England and the Restoration of Charles II to the throne in 1660, followed by
the Great Ejection of Puritan pastors from their parish charges in 1662, was
the critical transition period in New England. New England and New Englanders began to realize that they had crossed the rubicon of the Atlantic
Ocean and there was no turning back: there would be no return to Old England to claim the victory after the defeat of Antichrist, nor was Old England going to imitate their "city set upon a hill," nor were they going to
show England how to set up a gathered church within a parochial system
and structure. The children and grandchildren of those born in Old England were in New England now. For the rising generation, Old England
was simply a remote childhood memory, or the "old country" of their parents, a country these offspring had never seen. The old leaders were dead
or dying, and the next generation was in New England to stay. But amaz-
ingly, even with the system of gathered churches that had been set up, sin
and sinners seemed to spring forth from the covenant people of God, and
the vision of a cohesively sacred people in holy New England was threatened. Therefore, the middle generation of leaders set up the half-way covenant system in order to bring more inhabitants under clerical and ecclesiastical authority, to allow larger groups of people to form churches, and to
turn their attention away from Old England to the rising generation. Nevertheless, the unregenerate seemed to multiply, and covenant renewal became the watchword as the second generation began to die off.[32] By 1700,
third and fourth generation New Englanders were much less concerned
with the fate of Old England. But Old England was much more concerned
with the fate of New England. And ironically, the civil and ecclesiastical
covenants of late seventeenth-century New England reveal that Old England and its emerging First British Empire was far more influential on the
civil and religious life of New England than New England actually realized.
The New England Puritans had now become Anglicized Yankees.

Appendix 1

A Listing of Seventeenth-Century Towns, Churches, and Native American Praying Places in or Related to New England, Including a Checklist of Covenant and Foundational Activity, 1620-1708

Appendix 1 presents in tabular form a summary of all incorporated localities, legally recognized regions, and all established religious institutions in New England and related regions from 1620 to 1708. Listed also is all known foundational covenantal activity during that time, both civil and ecclesiastical. Since the listing is foundational, i.e. having to do with the initial establishment of civil and religious institutions, subsequent covenant activity (half-way covenanting and covenant renewals) is excluded. The list was compiled from the references in the Bibliographical Essay, especially "Section III. Geographical Locations and Religious Institutions in New England: Bibliographies and Finding Aids" and "Section IV. Bibliographies and Finding Aids for Unpublished Town and Church Records." Also important are the works by Frederick L. Weis, *The Colonial Clergy and the Colonial Churches of New England* (Lancaster, MA, 1936); *The Colonial Clergy of the Middle Colonies: New York, New Jersey, and Pennsylvania, 1628-1776* (Worcester, MA, 1957); *The Colonial Churches and the Colonial Clergy of the Middle and Southern Colonies, 1607-1776* (Lancaster, MA, 1938).

The towns and churches are arranged alphabetically in the Appendix because this seemed to be the least awkward way. They could have been arranged by colony, and then within the colony either alphabetically or by year of founding, but many towns were located in two or more colonies over the years, and it would be difficult to list them under either one or the other. If they were arranged by state, the same problem would exist. They could be arranged by year of founding, but then which founding? — town (i.e. date of incorporation by the central government)? Or church? Some towns and some churches had two "incarnations" (e.g. Dorchester, Massachusetts Bay Colony). Arranging them by the name of the church would have resulted in a multitude of "First Church" entries. It seemed therefore that the alphabetical method was the best. If a church or town had two incarnations, the first incarnation is referred to as "Dorchester-1" and the second "Dorchester-2." A further point should be pursued here; some towns had as many as five "incarnations" (e.g. Kittery, now in Maine). This is not always because of successive migrations. The numerous listings connected with a town could be due to many reasons: subdivisions, attacks by Native Americans that resulted in the need to reorganize a town and church, and submission to a colony that resulted in a new state church (Exeter, now in New Hampshire, originally had an Anglican church; it later formed a Puritan Congregational church).

The second sort of category in the list is the name of the religious organization (Column 4), which resulted in multiple listings for a town but prevented duplicate listings for a religious organization. Some towns had several churches or religious organizations: Boston is a notable example. There are therefore several entries for Boston, each for a different church. This arrangement also allows us to see where there was variegated religious activity, rather than simply a single established church in a locality. The listing stops in 1708, but in some cases there are either civil or ecclesiastical institutions that have listings beyond 1708 because the parallel institution of either church or state had some sort of foundational activity in 1708 or before.

Explanatory notes for some of the columns and categories of the list follow. Abbreviations used in Appendix 1 then follow.

Column 1: Name of Town/Region

Towns and regions had multiple names in the seventeenth century. The name listed here is the most common for the seventeenth century. Therefore, current-day Danvers, Massachusetts, is listed as Salem Village, Massachusetts Bay Province. Discussions of colonial and township boundaries are endless in both the local and the colony records; I have not entered into that quagmire, but boundaries were constantly shifting as disputes were settled in various executive, judicial, and legislative deliberations. The later subdivisions of New England towns into others that had a separate legal existence, or the development of parishes within those towns, particularly after 1692, along with expansion, annexation, and even some failed towns divided among neighboring towns, have led to certain messy and confusing distinctions. In some cases towns disappeared altogether: e.g. the town of

Westchester, New York Colony, straddled the current Bronx-Westchester County border and included the southern part of Westchester County. The area now is subdivided into Bronx County, New York City, and a variety of Westchester County towns, none of which are named Westchester — although the county now bears that name. And one of those Westchester towns is now called Eastchester.

Columns 2-3: Colony, State

Some towns moved back and forth between colonies. That fact is reflected in the multiple listings of colonies for some of the towns. The precise dates for the colonial central government's jurisdiction over a town are usually discernable by consulting the local histories of a town and the legislative records of the colonial legislature. The state listing indicates the modern state or province designation for the location of the colony.

Column 5: Church Covenant Exist? and
Column 9: Civil Covenant Exist?

The complexity of ecclesiastical and civil activity in some cases led to multiple covenants in either church or state. That phenomenon is annotated by multiple appearances of the letter "y" (for "yes"): "y, y." "y*" appears only in "Column 9: Civil Covenant Exist?" and indicates that there is one civil covenant for several places (the towns of Martha's Vineyard are a case in point) or for several religious institutions (Boston). In the latter case, multiple ecclesiastical listings for a particular place led to several lines for one civil jurisdiction; e.g. Boston. Therefore, the "y's" in the final column are not an exact enumeration of the civil covenants; but the "y's" in "Column 5: Church Covenant Exist?" are a fairly exact enumeration. Note that incorporation or recognition by a central colonial government was not necessarily the same as the practice of civil covenanting; however, central government recognition or incorporation led to a listing in this appendix.

Column 7: Day, Month, Date, and Year of Church Gathering

Because we are dealing with events on specific days, particularly in the case of church gatherings, and because the British did not adopt the new Gregorian calendar developed by the Vatican and Pope Gregory XIII in 1582, all dates in this Appendix and in the body of the book are given in Old Style.

The new Gregorian calendar was adopted by most Roman Catholic countries in 1582; the British finally followed suit in 1752. Seventeenth-century New England, therefore, followed the older Julian calendar. Followers of both the original Julian and the later Gregorian calendar all agreed on the name of a particular day; however, they numbered that day differently. Consequently, with respect to a date between 1582 and 1752 in a British document, the Old Style and New Style information for that date can be identified via the tables in C. R. Cheney (ed.), *Handbook of Dates for Students of English History* (Cambridge, 1945; rpt. 1996), 83-161; cf. also the fuller explanatory note in David A. Weir, "Church Covenanting in Seventeenth-Century New England," 293-94.

Abbreviations Used in Appendix 1

B	Baptist	NC	North Carolina (State)
C	Congregational	NH	New Hampshire (State)
Ch.	Church	NHC	New Haven Colony
Cov.	Covenant	NHP	New Hampshire Province
CS	Confessional Statement	NJ	New Jersey (State)
CT	Connecticut (State)	NNC	New Netherland Colony
CTC	Connecticut Colony	NPC	New Plymouth Colony
DNE	Dominion of New England	NS	Nova Scotia
E	Episcopal	NY	New York (State)
ENJ	East New Jersey	NYCol.	New York Colony
(F)	Failed	NH	New Hampshire (State)
I	Indian	PA	Pennsylvania
IB	Indian Baptist	Q	Quaker
IND	Independent (Town or Colony)	QMM	Quaker Monthly Meeting
Ind.	Independent (Church)	r	reference only (to a confession of faith)
IPT	Indian Praying Town	RI	Rhode Island (State)
MA	Massachusetts (State)	RIC	Rhode Island Colony
MBC	Massachusetts Bay Colony	s	signers
MBP	Massachusetts Bay Province	SC	South Carolina (State)
		SCC	South Carolina (Colony)
MD	Maryland (State)	SDB	Seventh-Day Baptist
MDC	Maryland Colony	VA	Virginia (State)
ME	Maine	VAC	Virginia Colony
NB	New Brunswick	WNJ	West New Jersey

1 Town/Region	2 Colony	3 State	4 Religious Organization	5 Church Covenant	6 CS	7 Date of Church Gathering	8 Foundation Members Total	Male	Female	9 Civil Covenant
Acoaxet IPT	NPC	MA								
Acushnet IPT	NPC	MA								
Amesbury	MBC	MA	1st			1672?				y, y
Andover	MBC	MA	1st	s		Friday, 10/24/1645	10	10	0	
Annapolis	MD/IND/MD	MD	1st							
Appledore	MBC	NH	1st			Wed., 7/26/1732				
Aquidneck/Rhode Island	IND	RI								
Arcadia	IND	ME								
Assawompsett IPT	MBC	MA	1							
Attleboro (North Attleboro)	MBP	MA	1st			Wed., 11/12/1712				y
Bahamas	IND									
Barnstable	NPC	MA	1st			11/1639				
Barnstable	NPC	MA	2nd (F)			9/1661				
Bedford	CTC/NY Col.	NY	1st			1680				y, y
Bermuda	IND									
Beverly	MBC	MA	1st	y	y	Friday, 9/20/1667	51	24	27	
Billerica	MBC	MA	1st			Wed., 11/11/1663				
Bloody Point	NHP	NH								
Boston	MBC	MA	1st	y		Friday, 7/30/1630	4	4	0	
Boston	MBC	MA	2nd	y		Wed., 7/5/1650	7	7	0	
Boston	MBC	MA	1st B	y	y	Sunday, 5/28/1665	9	7	2	
Boston	MBC	MA	3rd	y		Wed., 5/12/1669	28	28	0	
Boston	MBP	MA	French Huguenot							

1 Town/Region	2 Colony	3 State	4 Religious Organization	5 Church Covenant	6 CS	7 Date of Church Gathering	8 Foundation Members Total	Male	Female	9 Civil Covenant
Boston	DNE	MA	King's Chapel			Tuesday, 7/15/1686				
Boston	MBP	MA	4th (Brattle Street)		y	Tuesday, 12/12/1699	14	14	0	
Boston	MBC	MA	QMM			1700				
Boxford	MBP	MA	1st	s		Wed., 12/30/1702	11	11	0	
Bradford	MA	MA	1st	y	r	Wed., 12/27/1682	18	18	0	
Braintree	MBC	MA	1st	y		Monday, 9/16/1639	8	8	0	
Braintree	MBP	MA	2nd	y		Wed., 9/10/1707				
Branford-1	NHC	CT	1st	n		1647				
Branford-2 (1 Mission)	NHC	CT								
Branford-3	DNE	CT	1st	y		Wed., 3/7/1687/8	7	7	0	y
Bridgehampton	CTC/NYCol.	NY	1st							
Bridgewater	NPC	MA	1st			Thursday, 2/18/1664				
Bristol	DNE	RI	1st	s		Tuesday, 5/3/1687	8	8	0	y
Brookhaven	IND/CTC/NYCol.	NY								y, y
Brookline	MBP	MA	1st			Saturday, 10/26/1717	17	22	39	y
Byfield	MBP	MA	1st			1704/6				y
Cambridge-1	MA	MA	1st			Friday, 10/11/1633				
Cambridge-2	MBC	MA	1st			Monday, 2/1/1635/6				
Canaumet IPT	NPC	MA								
Canterbury	CTC	CT	1st			Wed., 7/13/1711	7	7	0	
Cape Fear	IND	NC								
Cape Porpus	IND/MBC	ME								
Cape Sable	MBP	NS								

1 Town/Region	2 Colony	3 State	4 Religious Organization	5 Church Covenant	6 CS	7 Date of Church Gathering	8 Foundation Members Total	Male	Female	9 Civil Covenant
Casco Bay (Spurwink)	IND/MBC	ME	E							
Cataumet IPT	NPC	MA								
Chappaquiddick	MBC	MA	I			1659				y*
Charleston	SCC	SC								
Charlestown	MBC	MA	1st	y		Friday, 11/2/1632	35	20	15	y
Charlestown	RIC	RI	I			1702				y*
Charlestown	RIC	RI	SDB							y*
Chaubunagungamaug IPT	MBC	MA								
Chelmsford	MBC	MA	1st	s		Thursday, 11/15/1655	14	14	0	
Chequaquet IPT	NPC	MA								
Chilmark	MBP	MA	1st			1715?				
Christiantown IPT	MBC	MA	I			1680				y*
Cocheco	NHP	NH								
Cohanzy (Fairfield Ch.)	WNJ	NJ								
Cohanzy	WNJ	NJ	1st B							
Colchester	CTC	CT	1st			Monday, 12/20/1703				y, y, y
Concord	MBC	MA	1st	y		Tuesday, 7/5/1636				
Connecticut	CTC	CT								
Cooxisset IPT	NPC	MA								
Cotuit IPT	NPC	MA								y, y
Cromwell	CTC	CT				Tuesday, 1/5/1714/15	24	10	14	

1 Town/Region	2 Colony	3 State	4 Religious Organization	5 Church Covenant	6 CS	7 Date of Church Gathering	8 Foundation Members Total	Male	Female	9 Civil Covenant
Danbury	CTC	CT	1st			1696				y
Dartmouth (Apponegansett)	NPC	MA	QMM			Saturday, 6/10/1699				y*
Dartmouth	NPC	MA	B			1686				y*
Dartmouth	NPC	MA	1st			1716?				y*
Dedham	MBC	MA	1st	y	r	Tuesday, 11/13/1638	8	8	0	y*
Deerfield-1	MBC	MA	1st							
Deerfield-2	DNE	MA	1st			Wed., 10/17/1688				
Derby	CTC	CT	1st			1678				
Dominion of New England	DNE									y
Dorchester	SCC	SC	1st	s		Tuesday, 10/22/1695	9	9	0	
Dorchester-1	MBC	MA	1st			January?, 1629/30				
Dorchester-2	MBC	MA	1st	y		Tuesday, 8/23/1636	7	7	0	
Dover-1	IND/MBC/NHP/	NH	E						y*	
Dover-2	IND/MBC/NHP/	NH	1st			Sunday? 1/13?/1638/9				y*
Dover-3	MBC/NHP	NH	QMM			1672				
Dover Neck		NHP	NH							
Dracut	MPB	MA	1st			Monday, 3/20/1720/1				
Dunstable	MBC	NH	1st			Wed., 12/16/1685				
Durham	CTC	CT	1st			Saturday, 2/11/1711				
Duxbury	NPC	MA	1st							
East Greenwich	RIC	RI	B			1700				y, y
East Haddam	CTC	CT	1st	y	y	Wed., 5/3/1704	8	8	0	
East Haven	CTC	CT	1st			Monday, 10/8/1711				

1 Town/Region	2 Colony	3 State	4 Religious Organization	5 Church Covenant	6 CS	7 Date of Church Gathering	8 Foundation Members Total	Male	Female	9 Civil Covenant
East New Jersey	ENJ	NJ								y, y, y
East Windsor	CTC	CT	1st							
Eastchester	NYCol.	NY								y
Eastham	NPC	MA	1st			1646?				
Easthampton	IND/CTC/NYCol.	NY	1st							y*
Easthampton Indian Mission	IND/CTC/NYCol.	MA	I							y*
Edgartown	IND/MBC	MA	1st			1642?				
Elizabeth	ENJ	NJ	1st							y, y, y
Elizabeth Islands IPT	MBC	MA								
Enfield	MBC	CT	1st			1699?				y
Essex	MBC	MA	1st	y		Sunday, 8/12/1683				
Exeter-1	IND/MBC/NHP	NH	1st			1638				y*, y*
Exeter-2	IND/MBC/NHP	NH	1st	y	y	Wed., 9/7/1698	26	17	9	y*, y*
Fairfield	CTC	CT	1st			1650				
Falmouth	IND/MBC	ME	(F)							
Farmington	CTC	CT	1st	s		Wed., 10/13/1652	7	7	0	
Flushing	NNC	NY	QMM			Tuesday, 5/23/1671				
Framingham	MBP	MA	1st	y		Wed., 10/8/1701	19	19	0	y, y, y
Freetown	NPC	MA	1st			1747				y
Gay Head IPT	MBP	MA	IB							y*
Gay Head IPT	MBC	MA	IC			1663				y*
Gay Head IPT	MBC	MA	I							y*

1 Town/Region	2 Colony	3 State	4 Religious Organization	5 Church Covenant	6 CS	7 Date of Church Gathering	8 Foundation Members			9 Civil Covenant
							Total	Male	Female	
Glastonbury	CTC	CT	1st			Thursday, 7/28/1692				y
Glocester	RIC	RI	1st B			1700				y
Gloucester	MBC	MA	1st			1642				
Gravesend	NNC/NYCol	NY								y
Greenland	MBP	NH	1st	s		7/1706	29	10	19	y
Greenwich	CTC	CT	E							
Greenwich	NHC/NNC/IND/NHC/CTC	CT	1st			Wed., 2/2/1669/70				
Groton	CTC	CT	1st B	s		1704				y
Groton	CTC	CT	1st			1705				y
Groton	MBC	MA	1st			Wed., 7/13/1664				y
Guilford	IND/NHC	CT	1st	s		Monday, 7/19/1643	7	7	0	y, y
Haddam	CTC	CT	1st	s		1696	14	14	0	
Hadley	MBC	MA	1st			Sunday, 10/14/1638?				y
Hampton	MBC/NHP	NH	1st			Monday, 6/16/1701				
Hampton	NHP	NH	QMM			Friday, 10/11/1633				
Hartford	IND/CTC	CT	1st		y	Saturday, 2/12/1669/70	33	15	18	
Hartford	CTC	CT	2nd	y		1701/2				
Hartford	CTC	CT	3rd							
Harwich	MBP	MA	1st	y	r	Wed., 10/16/1700	8	8	0	y
Hassanamesit IPT	MBC	MA	1			Saturday, 9/23/1671				
Hatfield	MBC	MA	1st			1670/1				y
Haverhill	MBC	MA	1st			Friday, 10/24/1645				
Hempstead	NNC	NY	1st							y, y, y

1 Town/Region	2 Colony	3 State	4 Religious Organization	5 Church Covenant	6 CS	7 Date of Church Gathering	8 Foundation Members Total	Male	Female	9 Civil Covenant
Herring Ponds IPT	NPC	MA	I							
Hingham	MBC	MA	1st			Friday, 9/18/1635	11			
Hull	MBC	MA	1st			Tuesday, 9/13/1670				y, y, y
Huntington	IND/CTC	NY	1st							
Ipswich	MBC	MA	1st	s		7/1634	7	7	0	
Jamaica	NNC/NYCol.	NY	1st							
Jamestown	RIC	RI								
Jemseg	MBP	NB								
Kekamoochuck IPT	MBP	MA								
Killingworth	CTC	CT	1st	y	y	1667	5	5	0	y
Kingston	RIC	RI	1st B			1666				
Kingston (St. Paul's)	RIC	RI	E			1707				
Kittery-1 (Kittery Point)	IND/MBC	ME								y*, y*
Kittery-2 (Berwick)	IND/MBC	ME		y	y	Thurs., 7/4/1702	18	18	0	y*, y*
Kittery-3 (Eliot)	IND/MBC	ME								y*, y*
Kittery-4 (Lower Kittery)	IND/MBC	ME								y*, y*
Kittery-5	IND/MBC	ME	1st B			Monday, 9/25/1682	?	10	?	y*, y*
Lancaster-1	MBC	MA	(F)							y*
Lancaster-2	MBC	MA	1st			9/1660				y*
Lebanon	CTC	CT	1st	y	y	Wed., 11/27/1700	10	10	0	y, y
Lewisboro	NYCol.	NY								
Lexington	MBC	MA	1st	y	r	Wed., 10/21/1696	12	12	0	
Little Compton	NPC/MBP/RIC	RI	1st	y	y	Wed., 11/1/1704	11	11	0	y, y

1 Town/Region	2 Colony	3 State	4 Religious Organization	5 Church Covenant	6 CS	7 Date of Church Gathering	8 Foundation Members Total	Male	Female	9 Civil Covenant
Long Island (Western)	various	NY								y
Louisbourg	MBP	NS								
Lyme (Old Lyme)	CTC	CT	1st			1693				y
Lynn-1	MBC	MA	1st			1632				
Lynn-2	MBC	MA	1st			Tuesday, 11/8/1636				
Madison (Guilford 2nd)	CTC	CT	1st	s?		Tuesday, 11/25/1707	13	13	0	
Magunkog IPT	MBC	MA								
Maine Province	MeP	ME								y, y, y, y
Malden	MBC	MA	1st			1649				
Manchaug IPT	MBC	MA								
Manchester	MBC	MA	1st			Wed., 11/7/1716				
Manexit IPT	CTC	CT								
Mannamit IPT	NPC	MA								
Manomet Ponds IPT	NPC	MA								
Mansfield	CTC	CT	1st			Wed., 10/18/1710				y
Marblehead	MBC	MA	1st	y	y	Wed., 8/13/1684	54	14	40	
Marlborough	MBC	MA	1st			1666				
Marshfield	NPC	MA	1st			1632				
Martha's Vineyard	IND/NY/MBP	MA								y*
Maryland	MDC	MD								y
Mashpee IPT	NPC	MA	IC			Wed., 8/17/1674				y
Maspeth (Newtown-1)	NNC	NY								

1 Town/Region	2 Colony	3 State	4 Religious Organization	5 Church Covenant	6 CS	7 Date of Church Gathering	8 Foundation Members Total	Male	Female	9 Civil Covenant
Massachusetts Bay Colony	MBC	MA								y
Massachusetts Bay Province	MBP	MA								y
Matakees IPT	NPC	MA								
Matakesit IPT	NPC	MA								
Medfield	MBC	MA	1st			12/1651				y
Medford	MBC	MA				Tuesday, 2/11/1712/13	15	15	0	
Mendon	MBC	MA	1st			Wed, 12/1/1669				y
Meshawn IPT	NPC	MA								y
Middleborough-1	NPC	MA								
Middleborough-2	NPC	MA	1st	y	y	Wed, 12/26/1694	20	11	9	y
Middleburgh (Newtown-2)	NNC	NY	(F)							
Middletown	CTC	CT	1st	y	y	Wed, 11/4/1668	10	10	0	
Milford	IND/NHC/CTC	CT	1st	y		Thursday, 8/22/1639	7	7	0	
Milton	MBC	MA	1st	y	r	Wed, 4/24/1678	12	12	0	
Mohegan I Mission	CTC	CT								
Monomoy IPT	NPC	MA								
Mortlake	CTC	CT	(F)							
Muckuckhonnike IPT	MBC	MA								y*
Musketaquid IPT	MBC	MA								
Mystic I Mission	CTC	CT								

1 Town/Region	2 Colony	3 State	4 Religious Organization	5 Church Covenant	6 CS	7 Date of Church Gathering	8 Foundation Members Total	Male	Female	9 Civil Covenant
Nansemond	VAC	VA	Ind.			1642				
Narragansett Country										
Narragansett	RIC	RI	Huguenot Ch							
Narragansett	RIC	RI	QMM			Monday, 6/12/1699				y*
Nashamoiess IPT	MBC	MA								
Nashaway IPT	MBC	MA								
Nashnakemmuck IPT	MBC	MA	I/IB?			1674				y*
Nashobah IPT	MBC	MA								
Natick IPT	MBC	MA	I	y	y	1660	8	8	0	y
Nauset IPT	NPC	MA								
Nemasket IPT	NPC	MA	I							
Neponset IPT	MBC	MA								
New England Yearly Meeting	n/a	n/a	Q			1600				y, y, y, y, y
New Hampshire Province	NHP	NH/MA								
New Haven	IND/NHC	CT	1st			Thurs., 8/22/1639	7	7	0	y, y
New Haven Colony	NHC	CT/NY								
New Jersey Colony	NJC	NJ								y, y, y
New London	MBC/CTC	CT	1st			1642				
New London	CTC	CT	Rogerene (B/Q)			1677				
New London Mission	CTC	CT								

1 Town/Region	2 Colony	3 State	4 Religious Organization	5 Church Covenant	6 CS	7 Date of Church Gathering	8 Foundation Members Total	Male	Female	9 Civil Covenant
New Netherland Colony	NHC	NY								
New Oxford-1	MBC	MA	Huguenot (F)			1686?				
New Oxford-2	MBP	MA	Huguenot							
New Oxford-3	MBP	MA	1st			Wed., 1/18/1720/1				
New Plymouth Colony	NPC	MA								y
New Shoreham	RIC	RI				1772				
New York Colony	NYCol.	NY								
Newark	ENJ	NJ	1st							y, y, y
Newbury	MBC	MA	B			1682				
Newbury	MBC	MA	1st			1635				
Newbury	MBP	MA	2nd	y		Wed., 10/26/1698				
Newcastle (Great Island)	NHP	NH	1st			Wed., 11/8/1704				y
Newport	RIC	RI	1st B			1644				y*, y*
Newport	RIC	RI	2nd B			1656				y*, y*
Newport	RIC	RI	3rd B (SDB)	s		Saturday, 12/23/1671	7			y*, y*
Newport Touro	RIC	RI	Synagogue			1658		4		y*, y*
Newport Trinity	RIC	RI	E			1698			3	y*, y*
Newton	MBC	MA	1st			Wed., 7/20/1664				y*, y*
Newtown-3 (Hastings)	NYCol./CTC	NY								y
Nipmuck Country/ Scottish Town	MBC	MA	(F)							

1 Town/Region	2 Colony	3 State	4 Religious Organization	5 Church Covenant	6 CS	7 Date of Church Gathering	8 Foundation Members Total	Male	Female	9 Civil Covenant
Nobscusset IPT	NPC	MA								
Nonantum IPT	MBC	MA								
North Yarmouth	MBC	ME	(G)							
Northampton	MBC	MA	1st	y	y	Wed., 11/18/1730	8	8	0	
Northfield	MBP	MA	(F)							
Norwalk	CTC	CT	1st			1652?				
Norwich	CTC	CT	1st			1660				
Nukkehkummees	NPC	MA	1			1690				
Numepoag IPT	MBC	MA								y*
Occawan	MBC	MA	1							
Occawan IPT	NYCol./MBC	MA	1st I							
Okkokonimesit IPT	MBC	MA								
Oyster Bay	IND/CTC/IND/NYCol.	NY	1st							y
Pakachoog IPT	MBC	MA								
Passyunk	NHC	PA	(F)							
Paugaset	NHC	CT	(F)							
Pawpoesit IPT	NPC	MA								
Penobscot	MBC	ME								
Piscataqua (Portsmouth)	IND/NHP	NH	Piscataqua QMM			1672				
Piscataway	ENJ	NJ	1st							
Pisspogutt IPT	NPC	MA								
Plainfield	CTC	CT	1st			Wed., 1/3/1704/5	10	?	?	y
Plymouth	IND/NPC	MA	1st	y		1606/7				y
Plympton	MBP	MA	1st	s		Thurs., 10/27/1698	18	7	11	

1 Town/Region	2 Colony	3 State	4 Religious Organization	5 Church Covenant	6 CS	7 Date of Church Gathering	8 Foundation Members Total	Male	Female	9 Civil Covenant
Pocasset IPT	NPC	RI								
Pompesspisset IPT	NPC	MA								
Port Royal	MBP	NS								
Portsmouth	IND/MBC/NHP	NH	E							y*
Portsmouth	IND/MBC/NHP	NH	1st	y		Wed., 7/12/1671	9	9	0	y*
Portsmouth	IND/RIC	RI								y
Portsmouth Village	MBC/NHP	NH	1st			Wed., June 18, 1755				
Portsmouth Village	MBC/NHP	NH								
Potanumaquut IPT	NPC	MA	I							
Pound Ridge	CT/NYCol.	NY								
Preston	CTC	CT	1st	y	y	Wed., 11/16/1698	13	13	0	y
Providence	IND/RIC	RI	1st B			1639				y*, y*, y*, y*, y*, y*
Providence	RIC	RI	2nd B			1654				y*, y*, y*, y*, y*, y*
Punkapoag IPT	MBC	MA								
Punonakanit IPT	NPC	MA								
Quabaug IPT	MBC	MA								
Quantisset IPT	CTC	CT								
Quincy (Christ)	MBP	MA	E			1704				
Quinshepauge IPT	MBC	MA								
Quittacus IPT	NPC	MA								
Reading	MBC	MA	1st	y		Wed., 11/5/1645				
Rhode Island	RIC	RI	QMM			6/1658				

1 Town/Region	2 Colony	3 State	4 Religious Organization	5 Church Covenant	6 CS	7 Date of Church Gathering	8 Foundation Members Total	Male	Female	9 Civil Covenant
Rhode Island+ Providence Plantations	RIC	RI								y, y
Rehoboth	IND/NPC/MBP	MA	1st			1643				y
River St. John	MBP	NB								
Rochester	NPC	MA	1st	y		Wed., 10/13/1703	8	8	0	
Rowley	MBC	MA	1st			Tuesday, 12/3/1639				
Roxbury	MBC	MA	1st			7/1632				
Rye	NNC/CTC/NYCol./NY CTC/NYCol.									y, y
Saco	IND/MBC/ Gorgeana/MBC	ME	1st	s		Thursday, 4/30/1730	13	13	0	
Sagadahoc	IND	ME								
Sakonnet IPT	NPC	RI								
Salem	MBC	MA	1st	y	r	Thursday, 8/6/1629	30	?	?	
Salem	MBC	MA	QMM			1672				
Salem Village	MBC	MA	1st	y	r	Tuesday, 11/19/1689	27	17	10	
Salisbury	MBC	MA	1st			1638				
Saltwater Pond IPT	NPC	MA								
Sanchacantacket IPT	MBC	MA	1			1670				y*
Sandwich	NPC	MA	1st			1638				
Sandwich	MBP	MA	QMM			1672				
Santuit IPT	NPC	MA								
Satucket IPT	NPC	MA								

1 Town/Region	2 Colony	3 State	4 Religious Organization	5 Church Covenant	6 CS	7 Date of Church Gathering	8 Foundation Members Total	Male	Female	9 Civil Covenant
Saybrook	IND/CTC	CT	1st			1646				
Scarborough	IND/MBC	ME	1st			9/1727				
Scituate	NPC	MA	1st	s		Thursday, 1/8/1634/5	13	9	4	
Scituate	NPC	MA	2nd	y		Wed., 2/2/1642/3	7	4	3	
Scituate (Pembroke)	NPC	MA	QMM			Monday, 6/15/1702				
Seconchgut IPT	MBC	MA	(F)							y*
Seppekann	NPC	MA								
Sherborn	MBC	MA	1st	s		Thursday, 3/26/1685	7	7	0	y
Sherburne (Nantucket)	NYCol./MBC	MA	QMM			Sunday, 6/13/1708				
Sherburne (Nantucket)	NYCol./MBC	MA	2nd I							
Sherburne (Nantucket)	NYCol./MBC	MA	3rd I (B)							
Sherburne (Nantucket) (Wammasquid IPT)	NYCol./MBC	MA								
Sherburne (Nantucket) (Squatesit IPT)	NYCol./MBC	MA								
Sherburne (Fifth IPT)	NYCol./MBC	MA								
Shumuit IPT	NPC	MA								
Simsbury	CTC	CT	1st	y		Wed., 11/10/1697	42	25	17	y
Skauton IPT	NPC	MA								

1 Town/Region	2 Colony	3 State	4 Religious Organization	5 Church Covenant	6 CS	7 Date of Church Gathering	8 Foundation Members Total	Male	Female	9 Civil Covenant
Smithfield	RIC	RI	1st B			1706				y
Smithtown	NYCol.	NY	1st			1675				y, y
South Carolina Colony	SCC	SC								
Southampton	IND/CTC/NYCol.	NY	1st			11?/1640?				y, y
Southold	NHC/CTC/NYCol. NNC/NYCol.	NY	1st			Wed., 10/21/1640				y
Springfield	MBC	MA	1st			1637?				y*
Springfield	MBP	MA	2nd			Thursday, 7/16/1698				y*
Squatesit IPT	MBC	MA								
Stamford	NHC	CT	1st			1635				y
Stonington	CTC	CT	1st	y	y	Wed., 7/3/1674	9	9	0	y
Stow	MBC	MA	1st			1699-1701				
Stratfield	CTC	CT	1st/Society	s	r	Thursday, 7/13/1695	10	10	0	
Stratford (Christ)	CTC	CT	E			1707				y*
Stratford	CTC	CT	1st			1639?				y*
Stratford	CTC	CT	2nd	y	r	Sunday, 5/1/1670	20	20	0	y*
Succonesit IPT	NPC	MA	1st							
Sudbury	MBC	MA	1st	y?		8/1640				
Suffield	MBC	CT	1st			Tuesday, 4/26/1698				y, y
Swansea	NPC	MA	1st B	y	y	1663				y*, y*, y*
Swansea	MBP	MA	[2nd] [B]	y		1693				y*, y*, y*
Takeme IPT	MBC	MA								y*
Talhanio IPT	MBC	MA								y*

1 Town/Region	2 Colony	3 State	4 Religious Organization	5 Church Covenant	6 CS	7 Date of Church Gathering	8 Foundation Members Total	Male	Female	9 Civil Covenant
Taunton	NPC	MA	1st			1637?				
Tisbury	IND/MBC/NYCol./MBP	MA	1st							y
Titicut IPT	NPC	MA	I			1674				
Tiverton	MBP	RI	1st			Wed., 8/20/1746				y*, y
Tolland	CTC	CT	1st			1723?				
Topsfield	MBC	MA	1st			Wed., 11/4/1663				
Truro	MBP	MA	1st			Thursday, 11/1/1711				y
United Colonies of New England										
Varkin's Kill	NHC	NJ								
Virginia Colony	VAC	VA								y, y, y, y
Wabaquasset Country	CTC	CT	(F)							
Wabquissit IPT	MBC	CT								
Waeunttug IPT	MBC	MA								
Wallingford	CTC	CT	1st			1675				y, y
Wamesit IPT	MBC	MA								
Wammasquid IPT	MBC	MA								
Wappetaw	SC	SC	Ind./C							
Waquoit IPT	NPC	MA								
Warwick	RIC	RI	Gortonist			1641				y
Waterbury	CTC	CT	1st	s		Wed., 8/26/1691	7	7	0	y
Watertown	MBC	MA	1st	y		Friday, 7/30/1630				y

1 Town/Region	2 Colony	3 State	4 Religious Organization	5 Church Covenant	6 CS	7 Date of Church Gathering	8 Foundation Members Total	Male	Female	9 Civil Covenant
Watertown Middle Precinct (Waltham)	MBP	MA	1st			Tuesday, 2/4/1696/7				
Watertown West Precinct (Weston)	MBP	MA	1st	y		Wed., 10/12/1709	19	19	0	y
Weesquobs IPT	NPC	MA								
Wells	IND/MBC	ME	1st	y		Wed., 10/29/1701	13	13	0	
Wenham-1	MBC	MA	1st	s		Tuesday, 10/8/1644	8?			
Wenham-2	MBC	MA	1st	y		Tuesday, 12/8/1663	10	10	0	
West Greenwich	CTC	CT	2nd C			1716?				y
West New Jersey	WNJ	NJ								
West Springfield	MBP	MA								y
Westbury	NYCol.	NY	QMM							y; y, y
Westchester	NNC/CTC/NYCol.	NY								y, y
Westerly	RIC	RI	SDB	y		Tuesday, 9/28/1708				
Westfield	MBC	MA	1st			Wed., 8/27/1679	7	7	0	
Wethersfield-1	MBC	MA	1st			1636?				
Wethersfield-2	MBC/CTC	CT	1st	s		Sunday, 2/28/1640/41	7	7	0	
Weweantic IPT	NPC	MA								
Weymouth-1	MBC	MA	1st			Wed., 1/30/1638/9				
Weymouth-2	MBC	MA	1st	s		Tuesday, 12/10/1700	15	15	0	
Windham	CTC	CT	1st	y						
Windsor	IND/CTC	CT	1st	y	y	January?, 1629/30				y
Windsor	CTC	CT	2nd			1669				y
Windsor Farms	CTC	CT	1st							
Woburn	MBC	MA	1st	y		Sunday, 8/14/1642	7	7	0	y

1 Town/Region	2 Colony	3 State	4 Religious Organization	5 Church Covenant	6 CS	7 Date of Church Gathering	8 Foundation Members			9 Civil Covenant
							Total	Male	Female	
Woodbridge	ENJ	NJ	1st	s		Thursday, 1/29/1707/8	4	4	0	y
Woodbury	CTC	CT	1st	y	r	Sunday, 5/1/1670	20	20	0	y
Woodstock	MBP/CTC	CT	1st			1686				
Worcester	MBC	MA	1st			1719				
Wrentham	MBC	MA	1st	y		Wed., 4/13/1692	10	10	0	y
Yarmouth-1	NPC	MA	(F)			1638				
Yarmouth-2	NPC	MA	1st			Sunday, 11/3/1639				
York	IND/MBC	ME	1st			Wed., 12/3/1673				y, y

Sources: The church and town covenants of early New England, along with related narratives and data, have been published multiple times in different publications. In this appendix, primary sources and citations were always preferred over secondary sources, but at times I had to rely on a reliable secondary source (e.g., the 1843 citation of the Wenham-1 First Church covenant in the 1843 *Wenham First Church Manual*). Frequently multiple sources were used because one source often filled in details that another source did not include. At times there were conflicting accounts and ambiguities, especially with respect to dates. No distinction has been made between citation of sources for church covenants or civil covenants, but usually the civil covenant source comes first. Distinctions were made for different religious institutions within the same town or region. Because some failed towns, plantations, and regions emerged with different modern names that do not appear in the bibliographies of the CNEB, I have included documentation for those towns legally recognized by a central colonial government but which function in modern times under a different name or series of names. Where there were two towns with the same name, I gave the modern state after the name of the town (e.g., Groton, MA and Groton, CT). For further information about each listing, consult the CNEB or the listing for the non-New England towns and churches in the Bibliographical Essay.

Abbreviations and Short Titles for this Source Note

Backus, *History,* ed. Weston	Isaac Backus, *A History of New England with Special Reference to the Denomination of Christians Called Baptists,* 2nd edn. ed. by David Weston, 2 vols. (1871; rpt. Paris, AR, n.d., The Baptist History Series, #s 3-4)
CHS, *List*	Connecticut Historical Society, *List of Congregational Ecclesiastical Societies Established in Connecticut before October 1818 with Their Changes* (Hartford, CT, 1913)
Contributions . . . Connecticut	*Contributions to the Ecclesiastical History of Connecticut; Prepared under the Direction of the General Association . . .* (New Haven, CT, 1861)
Hill, *Monthly Meetings*	Thomas C. Hill, *Monthly Meetings in North America: A Quaker Index,* 4th edn. (Cincinnati, OH, 1997)
Thorpe, *Federal and State Constitutions*	Francis N. Thorpe, *The Federal and State Constitutions, Colonial Charters and Other Organic Laws of the States,* 7 vols. (Washington, DC, 1909)
Weis, *Colonial Clergy and . . . Churches of New England*	Frederick L. Weis, *The Colonial Clergy and the Colonial Churches of New England* (Lancaster, MA, 1936)
Weis, "New England Company"	Frederick L. Weis, "The New England Company of 1649 and Its Missionary Enterprises," *CSMP,* 38 (1947-51), 158.
Winthrop, *Journal*	John Winthrop, *The Journal of John Winthrop, 1630-1649,* ed. Richard S. Dunn, James Savage, and Laetitia Yeandle (Cambridge, MA, 1996)

Acoaxet IPT: now in Westport, MA; Weis, "New England Company," 191.

Acushnet IPT: now in New Bedford, MA; Weis, "New England Company," 181.

Amesbury: Joseph Merrill, *History of Amesbury, Including the First Seventeen Years of Salisbury, to the Separation in 1654* . . . (Haverhill, MA, 1880), 50-53 and 53-54.

Andover: Abiel Abbot, *History of Andover from Its First Settlement to 1829* (Andover, MA, 1829), 73-74.

Annapolis: came from Nansemond, VA.

Appledore, ME (MBC)/Isles of Shoals/Gosport, NH/now Rye, NH: Weis, *Colonial Clergy and . . . Churches of New England,* 239 and 251 (under Gosport, NH).

Aquidneck (the actual island of Rhode Island, where a colonial government comprised of Portsmouth and Newport was formed, 1641-44): Thorpe, *Federal and State Constitutions,* 6.3207-9.

Assawompsett IPT: now in Lakeville, MA: Weis, "New England Company," 169.

Attleboro (now North Attleboro): Weis, *Colonial Clergy and . . . Churches of New England,* 263 (under North Attleboro); Worthley, *Inventory,* 436-37; John Daggett, *A Sketch of the History of Attleborough, from its Settlement to the Division,* ed. Amelia Daggett Sheffield (Boston, 1894), 20-21, 226-30.

Barnstable: "Scituate and Barnstable Church Records," ed. Amos Otis, *NEHGR,* 10 (1856), 37 and 39, which are days of humiliation and thanksgiving, and not, contra Worthley, *Inventory,* 25-26, references to the actual gathering; for Barnstable Second Church, see Worthley, *Inventory,* 28.

Bedford: Robert Bolton, *The History of the Several Towns, Manors, and Patents of the County of Westchester, from Its First Settlement to the Present Time,* 1 (New York, 1881), 24-25, 34.

Beverly: Beverly, MA, First Church, "Beverly First Church Records," ed. William P. Upham, *EIHC,* 35 (1899), 180-82; these records were also published as a single volume in 1905.

Billerica: Henry A. Hazen, *History of Billerica, Massachusetts* . . . (Boston, 1883), 160.

Bloody Point: NHP, *Documents and Records Relating to the Province of New-Hampshire, from the Earliest Period of Its Settlement: 1623-1686,* *NHHSP,* 1 (1867), 427; see listing for Dover.

Boston: First Church: Boston, MA, First Church, *The Records of the First*

Church in Boston, 1630-1868, ed. Richard D. Pierce, *CSMP,* 39 (Boston, 1961), 12-15; pp. 4-5 and 10 are slightly later covenants; Second Church: Chandler Robbins, *A History of the Second Church, or Old North, in Boston* (Boston, 1852), 209-10; First Baptist: Rollin H. Neale, *An Address Delivered on the Two Hundredth Anniversary of the Organiza-tion of the First Baptist Church, Boston . . .* (Boston, 1865), 9-10, 72-73, 70-72; Nathan E. Wood, *The History of the First Baptist Church of Boston (1665-1899)* (Philadelphia, 1899), 56-57, 64-66; Third Church: Hamil-ton A. Hill, *History of the Old South Church (Third Church) Boston, 1669-1884,* 1 (Boston, 1890), 126-28; King's Chapel: Henry W. Foote, *Annals of King's Chapel from the Puritan Age to the Present Day,* 1 (Boston, 1882), 44-45; Brattle Street/Fourth Church: Samuel K. Lothrop, *A His-tory of the Church in Brattle Street, Boston* (Boston, 1851), 55; cf. also Boston, Brattle Street Church, *The Manifesto Church: Records of the Church in Brattle Square, Boston . . . 1699-1872* (Boston, 1902), 3-4; Quaker Monthly Meeting: George A. Selleck, *Quakers in Boston, 1656-1964 . . .* (Cambridge, MA, 1976), 42-43; Boston was part of Salem Monthly Meeting; Hill, *Monthly Meetings,* 37, does not recognize this meeting, although when Salem Monthly Meeting met in Boston it was called "Boston Monthly Meeting."

Boxford: Sidney Perley, *The History of Boxford . . .* (Boxford, MA, 1880), 83-84; Boxford, MA, First Parish Church, "Church Records, 1702- . . . ," FHLCTHM #: 0877752, vol. 1, p. 10; also transcription in vol. 3; Winnifrid C. Parkhurst, *History of the First Congregational Church, Boxford, Massachusetts, 1702-1952* (Topsfield, MA, 1952), 12.

Bradford: John D. Kingsbury, *Memorial History of Bradford, Massachusetts* (Haverhill, MA, 1883), 26-35.

Braintree: First Church: William S. Pattee, *A History of Old Braintree and Quincy, with a Sketch of Randolph and Holbrook* (Quincy, MA, 1878), 194-95; Second Church: Braintree, MA, Second Church, *A Church Manual; with Brief Historical Notices . . .* (Boston, 1860), 5-6 and 9.

Branford: Elijah P. Baldwin, "Branford Annals," *NHCHSP,* 3 (1882), 249-70; 4 (1888), 262-63; Timothy P. Gillett, *The Past and the Present, in the Secular and Religious History of the Congregational Church and Society of Branford* (New Haven, CT, 1858), 10-11; Jesse Rupert Simonds, *A History of the First Church and Society of Branford, Connecticut, 1644-1919* (New Haven, CT, [1919]), 46-47; *Contributions . . . Connecticut,* 354, along with Weis, *Colonial Clergy and . . . Churches of New En-gland,* 243, give the date of 1647; CHS, *List,* 6, gives the date of 1644;

Branford-2: Rev. Abraham Pierson's Mission to the Indians: Weis, "New England Company," 156.

Bridgewater: "A Description of Bridgewater, 1818," *MHSC*, ser. 2, 7 (1818), 161-62.

Bristol: Wilfred H. Munro, *The History of Bristol, Rhode Island: The Story of the Mount Hope Lands . . .* (Providence, RI, 1880), 60-64.

Brookhaven: Frederick Van Wyck, ed., *Select Patents of Towns and Manors* (Boston, 1938), 3-20.

Brookline: John Pierce, "Historical Sketch of Brookline," *MHSC*, ser. 2, 2 (1814), 146-47; Weis, *Colonial Clergy and . . . Churches of New England*, 243.

Byfield Parish: Thomas Gage, *The History of Rowley, Anciently Including Bradford, Boxford, and Georgetown, from the Year 1639 to the Present Time* (Boston, 1840), 97.

Cambridge: Worthley, *Inventory*, 135-39; Winthrop, *Journal*, 101, 168-71.

Canaumet IPT: now in Mashpee, MA; Weis, "New England Company," 174.

Canterbury: Canterbury, CT, First Church, *Records of the Congregational Church in Canterbury, Connecticut, 1711-1844*, ed. Albert C. Bates (Hartford, CT, 1932), 1-4.

Cape Porpus (briefly part of Saco; formerly known as Arundel; now known as Kennebunkport): *RM*, 4-1.164-65.

Casco Bay: Spurwink Episcopal Church: Weis, *Colonial Clergy and . . . Churches of New England*, 244.

Cataumet IPT: now in Bourne, MA; Weis, "New England Company," 154.

Chappaquidick: Corporation for Propagating the Gospel [in New England], *Tears of Repentance, MHSC*, ser. 3, 4 (1834), 206-7; now located in Edgartown, MA; Weis, "New England Company," 162, 198.

Charlestown (Boston), MA: Henry H. Sprague, *The Founding of Charlestown by the Spragues: A Glimpse of the Beginning of the Massachusetts Bay Settlement* (Boston, 1910), 38-39; Charlestown (Boston), MA, First Church, *Records of the First Church in Charlestown, Massachusetts, 1632-1789*, ed. James F. Hunnewell (Boston, 1880), 7-8.

Charlestown, RI: Charlestown, RI, *Vital Record of Rhode Island*, ed. James N. Arnold, vol. 5, pt. v: *Charlestown* (Providence, RI, 1892), iii-iv; Weis, "New England Company," 158; Charleston I Church: Weis, "New England Company," 158.

Chaubunagungamaug IPT: now in Webster, MA; Weis, "New England Company," 190.

Chelmsford: Wilson Waters, *History of Chelmsford, Massachusetts* (Lowell,

MA, 1917), 2-3; John Fiske, *The Notebook of the Reverend John Fiske, 1644-1675*, ed. Robert G. Pope, *CSMP,* 47 (1974), 105.

Chequaquet IPT: now in Barnstable, MA; Weis, "New England Company," 154.

Chilmark: Charles E. Banks, *The History of Martha's Vineyard . . . ,* vol. 2: *Town Annals* (Edgartown, MA, 1966), 49; Nashnakemmuck: Weis, "New England Company," 159; First Church now extinct, and records lost: Worthley, *Inventory,* 158-60, 198.

Christiantown IPT: now in West Tisbury, MA; see Chappaquidick for civil covenant; Weis, "New England Company," 191-92, 198.

Cocheco: see listing for Dover; also NHP, *Documents and Records Relating to the Province of New-Hampshire, from the Earliest Period of Its Settlement: 1623-1686,* NHHSP, 1 (1867), 427.

Colchester: Colchester, CT, *Extracts from the Records of Colchester, with Some Transcripts from the Recording of Michaell Taintor, of "Brainford," Connecticut,* ed. Charles M. Taintor (Hartford, CT, 1864), 5-6; Edward M. Day, *An Historical Address Delivered at the . . . First Church of Christ, in Colchester, Connnecticut . . .* (Hartford, CT, 1903), 8; CHS, *List,* 8; *Contributions . . . Connecticut,* 364.

Concord: Lemuel Shattuck, *A History of the Town of Concord . . .* (Boston, 1835), 150-51; Worthley, *Inventory,* 165-66.

Connecticut Colony: "Fundamental Orders of Connecticut — 1638-39," Thorpe, *Federal and State Constitutions,* 1.519-23; "Charter of Connecticut," *ibid.,* 1.529-36.

Cooxisset IPT: now in Rochester?, MA; Weis, "New England Company," 186.

Cotuit IPT: now in Mashpee, MA; Weis, "New England Company," 174-75.

Cromwell: Homer W. Hildreth (ed.), *History of the First Church in Cromwell, 1715-1915* (Middletown, CT, 1915), 28; Weis, *Colonial Clergy and . . . Churches of New England,* 246; *Contributions . . . Connecticut,* 368; CHS, *List,* 9.

Danbury: James M. Bailey and Susan B. Hill, *History of Danbury, Connecticut, 1664-1896* (New York, 1896), 42-44; Joel J. Hough, *The First Congregational Church of Danbury, Connecticut: Historical Sketch* (Danbury, CT, 1876), 8; CHS, *List,* 9; *Contributions . . . Connecticut,* 369.

Dartmouth: Leonard B. Ellis, *History of New Bedford and Its Vicinity, 1602-1892* (Syracuse, NY, 1892), 20; Quaker Monthly Meeting: Hill, *Monthly Meetings,* 89; Daniel J. Ricketson, *The History of New Bed-*

ford . . . (New Bedford, MA, 1853), 37-43; First Church: Jesse Fillmore Kelley and Adam McKie, *History of the Churches of New Bedford* (New Bedford, MA, 1869), 5; Baptist Church: Weis, *Colonial Clergy and . . . Churches of New England,* 274, which gives a date of 1684 and identifies it as the "Baptist Church of Dartmouth, Tiverton and Little Compton."

Dedham: Dedham, MA, *The Early Records of the Town of Dedham, Massachusetts, 1636-1659,* Dedham Historical Records, 3 (Dedham, MA, 1888), 1-3; Dedham, MA, First Church, *The Record of Baptisms, Marriages and Deaths, and Admissions to the Church and Dismissals Therefrom, Transcribed from the Church Records in the Town of Dedham, Massachusetts, 1639-1845,* ed. Don G. Hill, Dedham Historical Records, 2 (Dedham, MA, 1888), 1-13, esp. 12-13.

Deerfield: Worthley, *Inventory,* 179-80.

Derby: Samuel Orcutt and Ambrose Beardsley, *The History of the Old Town of Derby, Connecticut, 1642-1880* . . . (Springfield, MA, 1880), 64-65; CHS, *List,* 9; *Contributions . . . Connecticut,* 372, gives the year 1677, but Orcutt and Beardsley, along with *PRCC,* say 1678.

Dominion of New England: RCRI, 312-18; "Commission of Sir Edmund Andros for the Dominion of New England, April 7, 1688," Thorpe, *Federal and State Constitutions,* 3.1863-69.

Dorchester, SC: Henry A. M. Smith, "The Town of Dorchester, in South Carolina — A Sketch of Its History," *The South Carolina Historical and Genealogical Magazine,* 6 (1905), 65.

Dorchester, MA: Dorchester, MA, First Church, *Records of the First Church at Dorchester in New England, 1636-1734* (Boston, 1891), iii, 1-3; Noah Clap, "A Letter from the Town Clerk of Dorchester to the {Massachusetts} Historical Society," *MHSC,* ser. 1, 1 (1792), 98; majority of the church migrated to Windsor, CTC; see listing for Windsor, below.

Dover: John Scales, *Historical Memoranda concerning Persons and Places in Old Dover, N.H.* . . . . (Dover, NH, 1900), 20-21; David Root, *A Bi-Centennial Sermon . . . First Congregational Church in Dover, New Hampshire* . . . (Dover, NH, 1839), 5; George B. Spalding, *A Discourse Delivered in the First Church of Dover* . . . (Dover, NH, 1873), 11 n*; John Scales, *History of Dover, New Hampshire,* 1 (Manchester, NH, 1923), 145-48, esp. 145; rpt. as *Colonial Era History of Dover, New Hampshire* (Bowie, MD, 1977); Quaker Monthly Meeting: Hill, *Monthly Meetings,* 97.

Dover Neck: see listing for Dover; also NHP, *Documents and Records Re-*

lating to the Province of New-Hampshire, from the Earliest Period of Its Settlement: 1623-1686, NHHSP, 1 (1867), 427.

Dracut: Silas R. Coburn, *History of Dracut, Massachusetts* . . . (Lowell, MA, 1922), 182-202, which deals with the history of the First Church but says little about its gathering or covenant; Worthley, *Inventory,* 187-89.

Dunstable: John W. Churchill, *History of the First Church in Dunstable-Nashua, New Hampshire* . . . (Boston, 1918), 11.

Durham: *PRCC,* 5.49; *Contributions . . . Connecticut,* 372.

East Greenwich: D. H. Greene, *History of the Town of East Greenwich and Adjacent Territory, from 1677 to 1877* (Providence, RI, 1877), 9-11; East Greenwich, RI, *Vital Record of Rhode Island,* ed. James N. Arnold, vol. 1, pt. 2: *East Greenwich* (Providence, RI, 1891), iii-iv.

East Haddam: East Haddam, CT, First Church, First Congregational Church and Ecclesiastical Society, "Church Records, 1702-1837," FHLC™M #: 0004112, vol. 1, pp. 1-4; *id.,* "Record of the First Congregational Church at East Haddam, Connecticut," ed. Gertrude A. Barber, FHLC™M #: 0547537, pp. 5-8; Isaac Parsons, *A Retrospect . . . First Congregational Church of Christ in East Haddam, Conn.* (Hartford, CT, 1841), 9-11.

East Hartford: *Contributions . . . Connecticut,* 378.

East Haven: *PRCC,* 3.57-58 and 5.24; Sarah E. Hughes, *History of East Haven* (New Haven, CT, 1908), 76-77; D. William Havens, *Historical Discourse* . . . (New Haven, CT, 1876), 24; Harry Kelso Eversull, *The Evolution of an Old New England Church* . . . (East Haven, CT, 1924), 43.

East New Jersey (see also listings for New Jersey and West New Jersey): "Duke of York's Confirmation to the 24 Proprietors . . . 1682," Thorpe, *Federal and State Constitutions,* 5.2567-73; "The Fundamental Constitutions for the Province of East New Jersey . . . 1683," *ibid.,* 5.2574-82; "The King's Letter Recognizing the Proprietors' Right to the Soil and Government — 1683," *ibid.,* 5.2582-83.

Eastchester: Eastchester, NY, *Eastchester, NY, Records* . . . , ed. Eastchester Historical Society, 1 (New York, 1964), 74-75.

Eastham: Worthley, *Inventory,* 198-99.

Easthampton: David Gardiner, *Chronicles of the Town of Easthampton, County of Suffolk, New York* (New York, 1871), 43; Frederick Van Wyck, *Long Island Colonial Patents* (Boston, 1935), 113-30; Easthampton I Mission: Weis, "New England Company," 162.

Edgartown: Worthley, *Inventory,* 204-6; Edgartown, MA, First Church,

"Edgartown, Mass., Church Record," *NEHGR,* 60 (1906), 159; Winthrop, *Journal,* 492; Charles E. Banks, *The History of Martha's Vineyard . . . ,* 2 (Edgartown, MA, 1966), 142-43.

Elizabeth: Edwin F. Hatfield, *History of Elizabeth, New Jersey, Including the Early History of Union County* (New York, 1868), 29-30; Harry C. Ellison, *Church of the Founding Fathers of New Jersey: A History* (Cornish, ME, 1964), 2-3, 7-10, 32-33.

Elizabeth Islands IPT: now in Gosnold, MA; Weis, "New England Company," 166-67.

Enfield: Francis O. Allen, *The History of Enfield, Connecticut,* 1 (Lancaster, PA, 1900), 60-65; Enfield, CT, First Church, *Historical Notice of the Congregational Church, in Enfield, Connecticut* (Hartford, CT, 1845), 4; CHS, *List,* 11; *Contributions . . . Connecticut,* 383, says that church was organized in 1683, but all others say 1699.

Essex: Robert Crowell, *History of the Town of Essex, from 1634 to 1868 . . .* (Essex, MA, 1868), 92; E. P. Crowell, "Historical Discourse," in *Essex, MA, First Church, Two Centuries of Church History . . .* (Salem, MA, 1884), 36; Weis, *Colonial Clergy and . . . Churches of New England,* 249, gives the earlier date of September 9, 1681.

Exeter: Charles H. Bell, *The History of Exeter* (Exeter, NH, 1888); rpt. as: *History of the Town of Exeter, New Hampshire* (Exeter, NH, 1979), 15, 18-19, 17-18; Exeter, NH, First Church, *The Confession of Faith and the Covenant of the First Congregational Church in Exeter, N.H.* (Exeter, NH, 1832), 9-11, 13; id., *Manual of the First Church in Exeter . . .* (Exeter, NH, 1888), 3, 6-8; John Taylor Perry, "The Church's History," in Exeter, NH, First Church, *The First Church in Exeter, New Hampshire, 1638-1888 — 1698-1888* (Exeter, NH, 1898), 41-42, 53-54.

Fairfield: *Contributions . . . Connecticut,* 385; Weis, *Colonial Clergy and . . . Churches of New England,* 249, says 1643.

Falmouth, MA: Charles H. Washburn, "Historical Address Covering the 200 Years' History of the First Congregational Church in Falmouth, Mass.," in Falmouth, MA, First Church, *Two Hundredth Anniversary, First Congregational Church, Falmouth, Massachusetts* (Falmouth, MA, 1908), 18-19; Worthley, *Inventory,* 214-16, describes October 10, 1708, as a gathering, but the event of that day was really a dismissal from the Barnstable First Church; Quaker Monthly Meeting: Hill, *Monthly Meetings,* 336 (Sandwich/Pembroke).

Falmouth, ME: Edwin Arnold Churchill, "Too Great the Challenge: The Birth and Death of Falmouth, Maine, 1624-1676" (diss. Maine, 1979).

Farmington: Mabel S. Hurlburt, *Farmington: Church and Town* (Stonington, CT, 1967), 3; Farmington, CT, First Church, "Church Records, Vols. 1-5, 1652-1938," FHLC™M #: 0004241, vol. 1, p. 15.

Flushing: G. Henry Mandeville, *Flushing, Past and Present: A Historical Sketch* (Flushing, NY, 1860), 13-23; Frederick Van Wyck, *Select Patents of New York Towns* (Boston, 1938), 3-80; Quaker Monthly Meeting: Hill, *Monthly Meetings*, 130, 125, 251; Flushing QMM also known as New York QMM.

Framingham: William Barry, *A History of Framingham, Massachusetts . . . with an Appendix, Containing a Notice of Sudbury and Its First Proprietors . . .* (Boston, 1847), 472-74; Framingham, MA, *Memorial of the Bi-Centennial Celebration of the Incorporation of the Town of Framingham, Massachusetts* (South Framingham, MA, 1900), 204; William Barry, *A History of Framingham, Massachusetts . . .* (Boston, 1847), 106-7; J. H. Temple, *History of Framingham, Massachusetts, Early Known as Danforth's Farms, 1640-1880 . . .* (Framingham, MA, 1887), 150-51; John Marshall, "John Marshall's Diary," ed. Charles F. Adams, Jr., *MHSP*, ser. 2, 14 (1900-1901), 32.

Freetown: Worthley, *Inventory*, 225-26; Weis, *Colonial Clergy and . . . Churches of New England*, 250; John M. Bumsted, "Orthodoxy in Massachusetts: The Ecclesiastical History of Freetown, 1683-1776," *NEQ*, 43 (1970), 274-84.

Gay Head: see Chappaquidick for civil covenant; Weis, "New England Company," 164-66, 198.

Glastonbury: *Wethersfield and Her Daughters: Glastonbury, Rocky Hill, Newington, from 1634 to 1934* (Hartford, CT, n.d.), 45; Glastonbury, CT, First Church, *Catalogue of the First Church of Christ in Glastonbury; Together with a Brief Outline of Its History . . .* (Hartford, 1859), 3; Weis, *Colonial Clergy and . . . Churches of New England*, 251; *Contributions . . . Connecticut*, 389; CHS, *List*, 13.

Glocester, RI: Glocester, RI, *Vital Records of Rhode Island*, ed. James N. Arnold, vol. 3, pt. i: *Glocester* (Providence, RI, 1892), iii-iv; Weis, *Colonial Clergy and . . . Churches of New England*, 251.

Gloucester, MA: John J. Babson, *History of the Town of Gloucester, Cape Ann . . .* (Gloucester, MA, 1860), 189; id., *Notes and Additions to the History of Gloucester; Part Second: Early Records* (Salem, MA, 1891), 3; Worthley, *Inventory*, 233-35; Alfred Mansfield Brooks, "The First Parish in Gloucester, 1642-1942," *UHSP*, 8 (1947-50), #1, 37-41.

Grafton: Weis, "New England Company," 167.

Gravesend: Peter Ross, *A History of Long Island* . . . , 1 (New York, 1905), 357-59; *The Documentary History of the State of New York* . . . , ed. Edmund B. O'Callaghan, 1 (Albany, NY, 1850), 411-12.

Greenland: M. O. Hall, *Rambles about Greenland* . . . (Boston, 1900), 92-93; Francis Dion, *Upon This Rock: A History of the Community Congregational Church, Greenland, New Hampshire* (Portsmouth, NH, 1956), p. 3 of text (no pagination).

Greenwich, CT: First Church: CHS, *List*, 13; *Contributions . . . Connecticut*, 395; Weis, *Colonial Clergy and . . . Churches of New England*, 252.

Groton, CT: Charles R. Stark, *Groton, Connecticut, 1705-1905* (Stonington, CT, 1922), 74-76; J. A. Woodhull, *A Review of the Congregational Church of Groton, Connecticut* . . . (New London, CT, 1877), 5; Simeon Gallup, *Historical Sketch of the First Baptist Church of Groton, at Old Mystic, Conn., from Its Organization in 1705* . . . (New London, CT, 1901), 2-4; Charles R. Stark, *Groton, Connecticut, 1705-1905* (Stonington, CT, 1922), 126-27; Carol W. Kimball, *The Groton Story*, Pequot Town Histories, ser. 1 (Stonington, CT, 1965), 45; CHS, *List*, 14; *Contributions . . . Connecticut*, 398.

Groton, MA: Samuel A. Green, *Two Chapters in the Early History of Groton* (Boston, 1882), 6-9; rpt. in *Groton Historical Series*, 20 (1887); Caleb Butler, *History of the Town of Groton* . . . (Boston, 1848), 156.

Guilford: Ralph D. Smith, *The History of Guilford, Connecticut, from Its First Settlement in 1639, from the Manuscripts of Honorable Ralph D. Smith* (Albany, NY, 1877), 11-14; Bernard C. Steiner and Ralph D. Smyth, *A History of the Plantation of Menunkatuck, and of the Original Town of Guilford, Connecticut* . . . (Baltimore, 1897), 35-37; Thomas Ruggles, "Extracts from Ruggles's MS. History," *MHSC*, ser. 1, 10 (1809), 92; CHS, *List*, 14; *Contributions . . . Connecticut*, 398.

Haddam: Haddam, CT, First Church, *The Two Hundredth Anniversary of the First Congregational Church of Haddam, Connecticut* (Haddam, CT, 1902), 2-9; *Contributions . . . Connecticut*, 400, says 1700.

Hadley: Sylvester Judd and Lucius M. Boltwood, *History of Hadley, Including the Early History of Hatfield, South Hadley, Amherst and Granby, Massachusetts* . . . *with Family Genealogies* (Northampton, MA, 1863; rpt. Springfield, MA, 1905), 11-12.

Hampton: Quaker Monthly Meeting (also known as Seabrook Monthly Meeting or Amesbury Monthly Meeting), Hill, *Monthly Meetings*, 158, 10.

Hartford: First Church (gathered in Cambridge, MA; same as Cambridge-1

First Church): Worthley, *Inventory,* 135-39; Winthrop, *Journal,* 115, 118, 121, 125-28, 158; *Contributions . . . Connecticut,* 404; Second Church: Edwin P. Parker, *History of the Second Church of Christ in Hartford, 1670-1892* (Hartford, CT, 1892), 46-48, 287-91; Third Church (now known as East Hartford First Church): East Hartford, CT, First Church, *The First Congregational Church, East Hartford, Connecticut, 1702-1902* (Hartford, CT, 1902), 40.

Harwich (Brewster): Josiah Paine, *A History of Harwich, Barnstable County, Massachusetts, 1620-1800, Including the Early History of the Part Now Brewster* (Rutland, VT, 1937), 94-95; Harwich, MA, *275th Anniversary, Harwich, Massachusetts: A Sketch of the Years 1694-1969, in Text and Pictures* (Harwich, MA, 1969), 3; Brewster, MA, First Church, *Records of the Brewster Congregational Church, Brewster, Massachusetts, 1700-1792* (Boston, 1911), 1-6.

Hassanamesit IPT: now in Grafton, MA; Weis, "New England Company," 167, 198.

Hatfield: Daniel W. Wells and Reuben F. Wells, *1660 — A History of Hatfield, Massachusetts . . . — 1910* (Springfield, MA, 1910), 51-52, 55-56, and 62-64.

Haverhill: "An Historical Sketch of Haverhill . . . Massachusetts . . . ," *MHSC,* ser. 2, 4 (1816), 138; Benjamin L. Mirick, *The History of Haverhill, Massachusetts* (Haverhill, MA, 1832), 26.

Hempstead: Frederick Van Wyck, *Long Island Colonial Patents* (Boston, 1935), 145-61.

Herring Ponds IPT: now in Bourne, MA and Plymouth, MA; Weis, "New England Company," 154-55.

Hingham: Hingham, MA, *History of the Town of Hingham,* vol. 1, pt. 2 (Cambridge, MA, 1893), 1; Worthley, *Inventory,* 286-91.

Hull: Worthley, *Inventory,* 300-301; [Lincoln Solomon], *Sketch of Nantasket (Now Called Hull) . . .* (Hingham, MA, 1830), 10.

Huntington: Frederick Van Wyck, ed., *Select Patents of Towns and Manors* (Boston, 1938), 21-62.

Ipswich: Worthley, *Inventory,* 303-5; Thomas F. Waters, *Ipswich in the Massachusetts Bay Colony,* 1 (Ipswich, MA, 1905), 56.

Kekamoochuck IPT: now in Oxford, MA; Weis, "New England Company," 185.

Killingworth: Killingworth, CT, "Town Records (Land), Vols. 1-3, 1664-1738," FHLC™M #: 0004621, p. 5; Clinton, CT, First Church, *Two*

Hundredth Anniversary of the Clinton Congregational Church . . . (New Haven, 1868), 12, 44-45; *PRCC*, 1.414.

Kingston: Weis, *Colonial Clergy and . . . Churches of New England,* 264; Herbert Richard Cross, "The Church of Saint Paul in Narragansett," in n.a., *Facts and Fancies concerning North Kingstown, Rhode Island* (North Kingston, RI, 1941), 6; Quaker Monthly Meeting: see Narragansett Monthly Meeting.

Kittery: Everett S. Stackpole, *Old Kittery and Her Families* (Lewiston, ME, 1903), 142-46; Kittery-2: Berwick (South Berwick), ME, "Records of the First Church of Berwick (South Berwick), ME," ed. John Clark Scates, *NEHGR,* 82 (1928), 71-74 (18 foundation members: 17 brethren with Rev. John Wade the 18th); Kittery-5: Henry S. Burrage, "Rev. William Screven," *MeHSC,* ser. 2, 1 (1890), 51; *id.,* "The Baptist Church in Kittery," *MeHSC,* ser. 2, 9 (1898), 382-91, esp. 388-89; cf. Schaff, *Creeds,* 3.738, preface which refers to the London Confession published in 1677; Backus, *History,* ed. Weston, 1.404-5 and 2.479-80; Nathan E. Wood, *The History of the First Baptist Church of Boston (1665-1899)* (Philadelphia, 1899), 179-83.

Lancaster: Lancaster, MA, *The Early Records of Lancaster, Massachusetts, 1643-1725,* ed. Henry S. Nourse (Lancaster, MA, 1884), 27-31 and 37-38; Worthley, *Inventory,* 315-16, gives the date of September, 1660 for First Church, while Weis, *Colonial Clergy and . . . Churches of New England,* 256 gives the earlier date of 1653.

Lebanon: Lebanon, CT, First Church, "Church Records, 1700-1883," FHLC™M #: 1010739, vol. IV, pp. 1-4, 22, 120, and vol. V, pp. 1-5; Lebanon, CT, "Land Records, vol. 1: 1695-1730," FHLC™M #: 0004707, Item #2, p. 1; *PRCC,* 4.334-35.

Lexington (Cambridge Farms): Lucius R. Paige, *History of Cambridge, Massachusetts; 1630-1877; with a Genealogical Register* (Boston, 1877), 119-21; Charles Hudson, *History of the Town of Lexington . . . ,* 2nd edn. (Boston, 1913), 306-7, 316-18; Cambridge, MA, First Church, *Records of the Church of Christ at Cambridge in New England, 1632-1830 . . . ,* ed. Stephen P. Sharples (Boston, 1906), 76-78.

Little Compton: Benjamin F. Wilbour and Carlton C. Brownell, *Notes on Little Compton* (Little Compton, RI, 1970), 17; Little Compton, RI, *Vital Record of Rhode Island,,* ed. James N. Arnold, vol. 4, pt. vi: *Little Compton* (Providence, RI, 1893), iii-iv; Robert L. Eddy, *The United Congregational Church of Little Compton, Rhode Island, 1704-1954: An*

Historical Essay (Little Compton, RI, 1954), ii-iv, 2-8; see also Dartmouth and Tiverton.

Long Island (combination of Captain John Scott and the English towns of Long Island): Martha Bockeé Flint, *Early Long Island: A Colonial Study* (New York, 1896), 285-87.

Louisbourg: also known as Port aux Baleines.

Lyme (Old Lyme): Barbara Dietrick (ed.), *The Ancient Town of Lyme* (n.p., 1965), 2-3; Arthur Shirley, *Discourse Delivered on the Two Hundredth Anniversary of the Organization of the Old Lyme Congregational Church, 1693-1893* (Lyme, CT, 1893), 11; *Contributions . . . Connecticut*, 461.

Lynn: Winthrop, *Journal*, 143, 197-99.

Madison: Bernard C. Steiner and Ralph D. Smyth, *A History of the Plantation of Menunkatuck, and of the Original Town of Guilford, Connecticut . . .* (Baltimore, 1897), 352.

Magunkog IPT: now in Ashland, MA; Weis, "New England Company," 153.

Maine: "A Grant of the Province of Maine to Sir Ferdinando Gorges and John Mason . . . 1622," Thorpe, *Federal and State Constitutions*, 2.1621-25; "Grant of the Province of Maine — 1639," *ibid.*, 2.1625-37; "Grant of the Province of Maine — 1664," *ibid.*, 2.1637-40; "Grant of the Province of Maine — 1674," *ibid.*, 2.1641-44.

Malden: Deloraine P. Corey, *The History of Malden, Massachusetts, 1633-1785* (Malden, MA, 1899), 104, 107-8.

Manchaug IPT: now in Sutton, MA; Weis, "New England Company," 189.

Manchester: Darius F. Lamsoln, *History of the Town of Manchester . . . Massachusetts, 1645-1895* ([Manchester, MA, 1895]), 225.

Manexit IPT: now in Thompson, CT; Weis, "New England Company," 189.

Mannamit IPT: now in Bourne, MA; Weis, "New England Company," 155-56.

Manomet Ponds IPT: now in Plymouth, MA; Weis, "New England Company," 185.

Mansfield: Mansfield, CT, "Proprietors' Records, 1702-1730," FHLC[TM]M #: 0004865, pp. 5-6; Mansfield Historical Society, History Workshop, *Chronology of Mansfield, Connecticut, 1702-1972* (Mansfield, CT, 1974), 18.

Marblehead: Marblehead, MA, First Church, *The Bi-Centennial of the First Congregational Church, Marblehead, Mass. . . .* (Marblehead, MA, 1884), 81-85; id., *Under the Golden Cod: A Shared History of the Old North Church and the Town of Marblehead, Massachusetts, 1635-1985* (Canaan, NH, 1984), 18-20.

Marlborough: Levi A. Field, *An Historical Sketch of the First Congregational Church in Marlborough, Mass.* . . . (Worcester, MA, 1859), 5.

Marshfield: Worthley, *Inventory*, 353-55; Ebenezer Alden, *Document of the Pilgrim Conference of Churches, Containing an Historical Sketch of the First Church in Marshfield* (Boston, 1854), listing for 1632; Joseph C. Hagar et al., *Marshfield* . . . *The Autobiography of a Pilgrim Town* (Marshfield, MA, 1940), 5-6.

Martha's Vineyard: Corporation for Propagating the Gospel [in New England], *Tears of Repentance, MHSC*, ser. 3, 4 (1834), 206-7.

Maryland: "The Charter of Maryland — 1632," Thorpe, *Federal and State Constitutions,* 2.1669-86.

Mashpee IPT: Weis, "New England Company," 172-75; Worthley, *Inventory*, 356-58; John Eliot, *A Brief Narrative of the Progress of the Gospel amongst the Indians in New England, in the Year 1670* . . . (London, 1671), rpt. as "Eliot's Brief Narrative," *Old South Leaflets*, General Series, 21, p. 17; Weis, "New England Company," 172-74 and 198, which give a date of 1670 for the church gathering.

Maspeth (Newtown): James Riker, Jr., *The Annals of Newtown in Queens County, New York* . . . (New York, 1852), 17-19.

Massachusetts Bay Colony/Province: "The Charter of New England — 1620," Thorpe, *Federal and State Constitutions,* 3.1827-40; "The Charter of Massachusetts Bay — 1629," *ibid.,* 3.1846-60; "The Charter of Massachusetts Bay {Province} — 1691," *ibid.,* 3.1870-86.

Matakees IPT: now in Yarmouth, MA; Weis, "New England Company," 193.

Matakesit IPT: now in Pembroke, MA; Weis, "New England Company," 185.

Medfield: Herman Mann, *Historical Annals of Dedham* (Dedham, MA, 1847), 98-99; Worthley, *Inventory*, 359-61.

Medford: Medford, MA, First Church, "Church Records, 1712-1823," FHLC[TM]M #: 0886764, pp. 1-9; Charles Brooks and James M. Usher, *History of the Town of Medford* . . . *Massachusetts* . . . (Boston, 1886), 226-27.

Mendon: John G. Metcalf (ed.), *Annals of the Town of Mendon, from 1659 to 1880* (Providence, RI, 1880), 3-4; Worthley, *Inventory*, 364-66.

Meshawn IPT: now in Truro, MA; Weis, "New England Company," 189.

Middleborough: Middleborough, MA, *Celebration of the Two-Hundredth Anniversary of the Incorporation of Middleborough, Massachusetts* . . . (Middleborough, MA, 1870), Appendix; Middleborough, MA, "Town Records, 1658-1705, 1746-1802," FHLC[TM]M #: 0945011, pp. 10-11;

RCNP, 5.19-20, 5.177, and 6.48; Weis, "New England Company," 175-76; Middleborough, MA, First Church, *Book of the First Church of Christ, in Middleborough . . . Massachusetts . . .* (Boston, 1852), 13-19.

Middleburgh, NNC (Newtown-2, NY): James Riker, Jr., *The Annals of Newtown . . .* (New York, 1852), 26-61.

Middletown: Azel W. Hazen, *A Brief History of the First Church of Christ in Middletown, Connecticut . . .* (Middletown, CT, 1918), 149-51; Middletown, CT, First Church, "Church Records, 1668-1871," FHLC^{TM}M #: 0004848, first pages (no pagination).

Milford: Milford, CT, First Church, *Manual of the Church of Christ, Congregational, Milford, Connecticut* (Milford, CT, 1935), 7, 9-10; id., "Church Records, 1639-1964," FHLC^{TM}M #: 1012263, opening pages (no pagination) and 1-4.

Milton: Albert K. Teele (ed.), *The History of Milton, Massachusetts, 1640 to 1887* (Boston, 1887), 275-76.

Mohegan Indian Mission: now in Norwich, CT; Weis, "New England Company," 182-83.

Monomoy IPT: now in Chatham, MA; Weis, "New England Company," 158-59.

Mortlake, CTC: *PRCC,* 3.246-47; in Wabaquassett Country; now Pomfret and Brooklyn, CT; Ellen D. Larned, *History of Windham County, Connecticut,* 2 vols. (Worcester, MA, 1874-80); Richard Mather Bayles, *History of Windham County, Connecticut* (New York, 1889); Allen B. Lincoln (ed.), *A Modern History of Windham County, Connecticut . . . ,* 2 vols. (Chicago, 1920).

Muckuckhonnike IPT: now in Chilmark, MA; Weis, "New England Company," 159.

Musketaquid IPT: now in Concord, MA; Weis, "New England Company," 160.

Mystic Indian Mission: Weis, "New England Company," 176.

Nansemond: Joseph B. Dunn, *The History of Nansemond County, Virginia* (Suffolk, VA, 1907?), 19; "Two 1642 Letters from Virginia Puritans," ed. Jon Butler, *MHSP,* 84 (1973), 99-109; some went to Annapolis, MD.

Narragansett Country: *RCRI,* 3.197-98; Elisha R. Potter, Jr., *The Early History of Narragansett . . . , RIHSC,* 3 (Providence, RI, 1835); Francis Brinley, "A Briefe Narrative of That Part of New England Called the Nanhiganset Country," Rhode Island Historical Society, *Publications,* 8 (1900), 69-96; a version is also in *MHSC,* ser. 3, 1 (1825), 209-19;

Richard S. Dunn, "John Winthrop, Jr., and the Narragansett Country," *WMQ,* ser. 3, 13 (1956), 68-86; now Washington County and parts of Kent County, RI; Huguenot Church: "Records of the French Church at Narragansett, 1686-1691," *New York Genealogical and Biographical Review,* 70 (1939), 236-41, 359-65 and 71 (1940), 56-61; Jon Butler, *The Huguenots in America: A Refugee People in New World Society* (Cambridge, MA, 1983), 48, 60-63; Narragansett Quaker Monthly Meeting: also known as Greenwich, RI, QMM or Kingston, RI, QMM (now at East Greenwich, RI); Hill, *Monthly Meetings,* 242, 153, 315.

Nashamoiess IPT: now in Edgartown, MA; Weis, "New England Company," 162-63.

Nashaway IPT: now in Lancaster, MA; Weis, "New England Company," 169-70.

Nashnakemmuck IPT: now in Chilmark, MA; Weis, "New England Company," 159.

Nashobah IPT: now in Littleton, MA; Weis, "New England Company," 170-71.

Natick: John Eliot, *Strength Out of Weakness* (London, 1652), in *MHSC,* ser. 3, 4 (1834), 172-73; id., *A Further Account of the Progress of the Gospel amongst the Indians in New England: Being a Relation of the Confessions Made by Several Indians . . . in Order to Their Admission into Church-Fellowship* (London, 1660); id., *Christianae Oonoowae sampoowaonk: A Christian Covenanting Canfession [sic]* (Cambridge, MA, 1660); David A. Weir, "*Church Covenanting in Seventeenth-Century New England*" (diss. Princeton University, 1992), "Chapter 4: The Pattern of Native America," 68-134, esp. 127-32, 315-36; Weis, "New England Company," 179-81, 198.

Nauset IPT: now in Eastham, MA and Orleans, MA; Weis, "New England Company," 184.

Nemasket IPT: now in Lakeville, MA; Weis, "New England Company," 168-69.

Neponset IPT: now in Dorchester, MA; Weis, "New England Company," 161.

New Castle: John Albee, *New Castle . . .* (Boston, 1884), 130-32.

New England Yearly Meeting: Hill, *Monthly Meetings,* x-xi.

New Hampshire Province: "Grant of New Hampshire to Capt. John Mason . . . 1629," Thorpe, *Federal and State Constitutions,* 3.2433-36; "Grant of the Province of New Hampshire to John Wollaston, Esq. . . . 1635," *ibid.,* 3.2437-38; "Grant of the Province of New Hampshire from Mr.

Wollaston to Mr. Mason . . . 1635," *ibid.*, 3.2439-40; "Grant of the
Province of New Hampshire to Mr. Mason . . . 1635, by the Name of
Masonia," *ibid.*, 3.2441-43; "Grant of the Province of New Hampshire
to Mr. Mason . . . by the Name of New Hampshire," *ibid.*, 3.2443-44;
[Commission of John Cutt, 1680]," *ibid.*, 3.2446-51.

New Haven (Plantation): *RCPNH*, 11-15, 17; John Cotton, *A Copy of a Letter of Mr. Cotton of Boston, in New England* . . . ([London], 1641), 5-6
(this is the church covenant, acc. to Rev. Peter Ives, Senior Minister in
1986); Oscar E. Maurer, *A Puritan Church and Its Relation to Community, State and Nation* (New Haven, CT, 1938), 23-24; Leonard Bacon,
Thirteen Historical Discourses . . . *of the First Church in New Haven* . . .
(New Haven, CT, 1839), 24.

New Haven (Colony): "Government of New Haven Colony," Thorpe, *Federal and State Constitutions*, 1.526-29.

New Jersey (see also listings for East New Jersey and West New Jersey): "The
Duke of York's Release to Lord John Berkeley, and Sir George Carteret
. . . 1664," Thorpe, *Federal and State Constitutions*, 5.2533-35; "The
Concession and Agreement of the Lords Proprietors of the Province of
. . . New Jersey . . . 1664," *ibid.*, 5.2535-44; "A Declaration of the True
Intent and Meaning of Us the Lords Proprietors, and Explanation of
Their Concessions . . . 1672," *ibid.*, 5.2544-46; "His Royal Highness's
Grant to the Lords Proprietors, Sir George Carteret . . . 1674," *ibid.*,
5.2546-48; "The Charter or Fundamental Laws, of West New Jersey,
Agreed Upon — 1676," *ibid.*, 5.2548-51; "Quintipartite Deed of Revi-
sion, between E. and W. Jersey . . . 1676," *ibid.*, 5.2551-60.

New London: First Church: S. Leroy Blake, *The Early History of the First
Church of Christ, New London, Conn.* (New London, CT, 1897), 49;
S. Leroy Blake, *The Early History of the First Church of Christ, New
London, Conn.*, 178; the church was organized in Gloucester, MA, and
then relocated to New London; CHS, *List*, 21; *Contributions* . . . *Con-
necticut*, 442; Rogerene Baptist/Quaker Church: Francis M. Caulkins,
History of New London, Connecticut (New London, CT, 1852), 206;
New London I Mission: Weis, "New England Company," 181-82.

New Netherland Colony: "Gov. Colves' Charter to the Several Towns on
Long Island. Anno. 1673," *The Documentary History of the State of
New-York* . . . , 1 (Albany, NY, 1850), 426-27.

New Oxford: New Oxford-1 French Huguenot Church: George F. Daniels,
History of the Town of Oxford, Massachusetts . . . (Oxford, MA, 1892),
10; New Oxford-3 First Church: Worthley, *Inventory*, 466-68; Jon But-

ler, *The Huguenots in America: A Refugee People in New World Society* (Cambridge, MA, 1983), 48, 63-64.

New Plymouth Colony: Thorpe, *Federal and State Constitutions*, 3.1841-46.

New Shoreham: Weis, *Colonial Clergy and . . . Churches of New England*, 263; Samuel T. Livermore, *A History of Block Island . . .* (Hartford, CT, 1877; rpt. Forge Village, MA, 1961), 249-50.

New York Yearly Meeting: Hill, *Monthly Meetings*, xi.

Newark: New Jersey Historical Society, *Proceedings Commemorative of the Settlement of Newark, New Jersey, on Its Two Hundredth Anniversary . . . , NJHSC*, 6-Supplement (Newark, NJ, 1866), 159-66; Newark, NJ, *Records of the Town of Newark, New Jersey, from its Settlement in 1666, to Its Incorporation as a City in 1836, NJHSC*, 6 (Newark, NJ, 1864), 1-2, 283-86.

Newbury: Joshua Coffin, *A Sketch of the History of Newbury, Newburyport, and West Newbury, from 1635 to 1845* (Boston, 1845), 16-17; Eliza J. Little and Lucretia J. Ilsley, *The First Parish, Newbury, Massachusetts, 1635-1935* (Newburyport, MA, 1935), 11-12; Second Church (now West Newbury First Church): Eliza J. Little and Lucretia J. Ilsley, *The First Parish, Newbury, Massachusetts, 1635-1935*, 31; John J. Currier, *History of Newbury, Mass. . . . 1635-1902* (Boston, 1902), 347-48, 352; Baptist Church: Joshua Coffin, *A Sketch of the History of Newbury, Newburyport, and West Newbury, from 1635 to 1845*, 135; Backus, *History*, ed. Weston, 1.405.

Newcastle: Weis, *Colonial Clergy and . . . Churches of New England*, 261.

Newport: *RCRI*, 1.86 and 1.93; First Baptist Church: Backus, *History*, ed. Weston, 1.395; Second Baptist Church (Six Principles Baptist Church): Susan B. Franklin, *Historical Sketch of Second Baptist Church, Newport, Rhode Island, 1656-1936* ([Newport, 1936]), 3; Third Baptist (Seventh-Day Baptist): William L. Burdick, "Historical Address," in *Bi-Centennial Celebration of the First Seventh-Day Baptist Church of Hopkinton, Located at Ashaway, R.I.* (Ashaway, RI, 1908), 28; Touro Synagogue: Morris A. Gutstein, *The Story of the Jews in Newport: Two and a Half Centuries of Judaism, 1658-1908* (New York, 1936); *id., To Bigotry No Sanction: A Jewish Shrine in America, 1658-1958* (New York, 1958); Max Kohler, "The Jews in Newport," American Jewish Historical Society, *Publications*, 6 (1897), 61-80; Samuel Oppenheim, "The First Settlement of the Jews in Newport: Some New Matter on the Subject," *ibid.*, 34 (1937), 1-10; Trinity Episcopal Church: Newport, RI, Trinity Church (Episcopal), *Annals of Trinity*

Church, Newport, Rhode Island, 1698-1821, ed. George C. Mason (Newport, RI, 1890), 9-11.

Newton: Jonathan Homer, "Description and History of Newton, in the County of Middlesex," *MHSC,* ser. 1, 5 (1796), 266; Worthley, *Inventory,* 426.

Nipmuck Country: *RM,* 5.263; see also listing for Quinshepauge IPT and Mendon.

Nobscusset IPT: now in Dennis, MA; Weis, "New England Company," 161.

Nonantum IPT: now in Newton, MA; Weis, "New England Company," 182.

North Yarmouth, ME: *RM,* 5-273; destroyed by Native Americans, 1688; Weis, *Colonial Clergy and . . . Churches of New England,* 264; William Hutchinson Rowe, *Ancient North Yarmouth and Yarmouth, Maine, 1636-1936* (1937; Somersworth, NH, 1980), 32-116, 121-23.

Northampton: James R. Trumbull, *History of Northampton, Massachusetts, from Its Settlement in 1654,* vol. 1 (Northampton, MA, 1898), 105-9. Northampton, MA, First Church, "Old Covenant and Confession of the Northampton Church," ed. Zachary Eddy, *CQ,* 3 (1861), 168-79.

Northfield (also known as Squakeage): *RM,* 4–2.528-29, 542; 5.360 and 5.482.

Norwalk: *Contributions . . . Connecticut,* 457-58; CHS, *List,* 23.

Norwich: CHS, *List,* 24; *Contributions . . . Connecticut,* 458.

Nukkehkummees: now in Dartmouth, MA; Weis, "New England Company," 160-61, 198.

Nunnepoag IPT: now in Edgartown, MA; Weis, "New England Company," 163.

Occawan: now in Nantucket, known as "Sherburne" in the seventeenth century; Weis, "New England Company," 176-78; see also listings for Sherburne, Squatesit, and Wammesquid.

Okkokonimesit IPT: now in Marlborough, MA; Weis, "New England Company," 172.

Oyster Bay: Oyster Bay, NY, *Oyster Bay Town Records,* vol. 1: *1653-1690* (New York, 1916), 307-10.

Pakachoog IPT: now in Auburn, MA and Worcester, MA; Weis, "New England Company," 154.

Passyunk (at mouth of Schuylkill River in what is now Philadelphia; begun 1641, destroyed by Dutch and Swedes, 1642); George Morgan, *The City of Firsts . . .* (Philadelphia: 1926), 33, 39, and 331; J. Thomas Scharf and Thompson Westcott, *History of Philadelphia, 1609-1884,* vol. 1 (Philadelphia, 1984), 67-70.

Paugaset (later Derby, CT): *RCPNH,* 77, 148, 232, 376, 410, 478, 490; *RCJNH,* 156-57, 221-22, 298, 361.

Pawpoesit IPT: now in Mashpee, MA; Weis, "New England Company," 175.

Piscataqua Monthly Meeting: Hill, *Monthly Meetings,* 288, 97.

Pisspogutt IPT: now in Bourne, MA; Weis, "New England Company," 156.

Plainfield: Henry T. Arnold, "The Churches of Plainfield," in Plainfield, CT, *Plainfield Bicentennial* (Norwich, CT, 1899), 99-100 for the civil covenant and 99 for the record of the church gathering.

Plymouth: *[Mourt's Relation]: A Relation or Journal of the Beginning and Proceedings of the English Plantation Settled at Plymouth in New England . . .* (London, 1622); edited, critical edition: *A Journal of the Pilgrims at Plymouth: Mourt's Relation: A Relation or Journal of the English Plantation Settled at Plymouth in New England . . . ,* ed. Dwight B. Heath (New York, 1963), 17-18; Nathaniel Morton, *New England's Memorial . . . ,* 6th edn. (Boston, 1855), 24-27; William Bradford, *Of Plymouth Plantation, 1620-1647,* ed. Samuel Eliot Morison (New York, 1952), 75-76; "Charter of the Colony of New Plymouth Granted to William Bradford and His Associates — 1629," Thorpe, *Federal and State Constitutions,* 3.1841-46; Douglas Horton, "The Scrooby Covenant," *UHSP,* 11 (1956-57), #2, 1-13, esp. 1-2.

Plympton: Plymouth, MA, First Church, *Plymouth Church Records, CSMP,* 22 (Boston, 1920), 185-86.

Pocasset IPT: now in Bourne, MA, and Tiverton, RI; Weis, "New England Company," 156, 194.

Pompesspisset IPT: now in Bourne, MA; Weis, "New England Company," 156.

Port Royal: also known as Annapolis Royal or Lower Granville.

Portsmouth, NH: George M. Adams, *An Historical Discourse, Delivered at the . . . Anniversary of the Formation of the North Church, Portsmouth, New Hampshire . . .* (Portsmouth, NH, 1871), 29-34.

Portsmouth, RI: Ralph May, *Early Portsmouth History* (Boston, 1926), 131-32; *RCRI,* 1.52-53; *The Early Records of the Town of Portsmouth,* ed. Clarence S. Brigham (Providence, RI, 1901), 1-3.

Portsmouth Village, NH: *RM,* 4-2.546-47; became Barrington, NH; Weis, *Colonial Clergy and . . . Churches of New England,* 240 (under Barrington, NH).

Potanumaquut IPT: now in Orleans, MA, and Harwich, MA; Weis, "New England Company," 184-85.

Pound Ridge: Robert Bolton, *The History of the Several Towns, Manors, and*

Patents of the County of Westchester, from Its First Settlement to the Present Time, 2 (New York, 1881), 107.

Preston: Preston, CT, First Church, *The Bi-Centennial Celebration: First Congregational Church of Preston, Connecticut, 1698-1898* (Preston, CT, 1900), 19-20, 129, 200-201.

Providence: Providence, RI, *The Early Records of the Town of Providence,* 1 (Providence, RI, 1892), 1; William R. Staples, *Annals of the Town of Providence, from Its First Settlement* (Providence, RI, 1843), 40-43, 60-63, 68-70, and 73-74; First Baptist Church: Winthrop, *Journal,* 286, 300; William B. Hague, *An Historical Discourse Delivered at the Celebration of the . . . Anniversary of the First Baptist Church, in Providence . . .* (Providence, RI, 1839), 32; Samuel L. Caldwell, *The Two Hundred and Fiftieth Anniversary of the Formation of the First Baptist Church in Providence, Rhode Island* (Providence, RI, 1889), 13-14; Henry M. King, *Historical Catalogue of the Members of the First Baptist Church in Providence . . .* (Providence, RI, 1908), 1-2; Backus, *History,* ed. Weston, 1.87, 2.285, and 2.490; Second Baptist Church: *ibid.,* 1.405 and 2.490-91.

Punkapoag IPT: now in Canton, MA; Weis, "New England Company," 157-58.

Punonakanit IPT: now in Wellfleet, MA; Weis, "New England Company," 190.

Quabaug IPT: now in Brookfield, MA; Weis, "New England Company," 156-57.

Quantisset IPT: now in Pomfret, CT; Weis, "New England Company," 186.

Quincy: William Grainger, *The Oldest Parish in Massachusetts: Christ Church, Quincy* (Quincy, MA, 1915), 4-5.

Quinshepauge IPT: now in Mendon, MA; Weis, "New England Company," 175.

Quittacus IPT: now in Lakeville, MA; Weis, "New England Company," 169.

Reading: Winthrop, *Journal,* 615, 764; James Flint, *Historical Address . . . Delivered at the Bi-Centennial Celebration of the Incorporation of the Old Town of Reading . . .* (Boston, 1844), 7-8; Charles R. Bliss, *Wakefield Congregational Church: A Commemorative Sketch, 1644-1877* (Wakefield, MA, 1877), 8-9, n*.

Rehoboth (East Providence, RI): Sylvanus C. Newman, *Rehoboth in the Past . . .* (Pawtucket, RI, 1860), 50-51; Leonard Bliss, Jr., *The History of Rehoboth . . .* (Boston, 1836), 28; Weis, *Colonial Clergy and . . . Churches of New England,* 249 (under East Providence).

Rhode Island: Quaker Monthly Meeting: Hill, *Monthly Meetings*, 315; see also Aquidneck.

Rhode Island and Providence Plantations: "Patent for Providence Plantations — 1643," Thorpe, *Federal and State Constitutions*, 6.3209-11, also in *RCRI*, 1.143-46; "Charter of Rhode Island and Providence Plantations — 1663," *ibid.*, 6.3211-22.

Rochester: Rochester (Marion), MA, *Rochester's Official Bi-Centennial Record* (New Bedford, MA, 1879), 104; *Mattapoisett and Old Rochester, Massachusetts . . .* , 2nd edn. (Mattapoisett, MA, 1932), 73; Leander Cobb, *Historical Sketch of the Congregational Church in Marion, Mass. . . .* (New Bedford, MA, 1862).

Rowley: Thomas Gage, *The History of Rowley . . .* (Boston, 1840), 11; Winthrop, *Journal*, 270-71, 286-87, 316; Worthley, *Inventory*, 527-29.

Roxbury: Walter E. Thwing, *History of the First Church in Roxbury, Massachusetts, 1630-1904* (Boston, 1908), v-vi.

Rye: Robert Bolton, *The History of the Several Towns, Manors, and Patents of the County of Westchester, from Its First Settlement to the Present Time*, 2 (New York, 1881), 141-42.

Saco: Daniel E. Owen, *Old Times in Saco . . .* (Saco, ME, 1891), 65.

Sagadahoc: also known as The Popham Colony, Fort St. George, or Fort Popham; existed 1607-08; now in Phippsburg, ME.

Sakonnet IPT: now in Little Compton, RI; Weis, "New England Company," 170.

Salem: Salem, MA, First Church, *The Records of the First Church in Salem, Massachusetts, 1629-1736*, ed. Richard D. Pierce (Salem, MA, 1974), xi-xviii, 3-6; [John Higginson], *A Direction for a Publick Profession in the Church Assembly, after Private Examination by the Elders . . .* ([Cambridge, MA, 1665]); Salem, MA, First Church, *A Copy of the Church-Covenants Which Have Been Used in the Church of Salem . . .* (Boston, 1680); C. H. Webber and W. S. Nevins, *Old Naumkeag: An Historical Sketch of the City of Salem . . .* (Salem, MA, 1877), 12-16; Sidney Perley, *The History of Salem, Massachusetts*, 1 (Salem, MA, 1924), 162-64; Quaker Monthly Meeting: Hill, *Monthly Meetings*, 331.

Salem Village: Sidney Perley, *The History of Salem, Massachusetts*, 2 (Salem, MA, 1926), 436-38, 444-45; Paul Boyer and Stephen Nissenbaum, *Salem Possessed: The Social Origins of Witchcraft* (Cambridge, MA, 1974), frontispiece; Salem, MA, First Church, *Confession of Faith and Covenant of the First Church in Danvers . . .* (Boston, 1864), 13 (the confession and covenant are more modern, but this is an historical note).

Salisbury: Worthley, *Inventory*, 554-56.

Saltwater Pond IPT: now in Plymouth, MA; Weis, "New England Company," 185.

Sanchacantacket IPT: now in Oak Bluffs, MA; Weis, "New England Company," 183, 198.

Sandwich: First Church: Weis, *Colonial Clergy and . . . Churches of New England*, 270; Worthley, *Inventory*, 558-60; Quaker Monthly Meeting: Hill, *Monthly Meetings*, 336; John H. Dillingham, *The Society of Friends in Barnstable County, Massachusetts . . .* (New York, 1891).

Santuit IPT: now in Mashpee, MA; Weis, "New England Company," 175.

Satucket IPT: now in Harwich, MA; Weis, "New England Company," 168.

Saybrook (now Old Saybrook): Old Saybrook, CT, First Church, *Manual of the Congregational Church, in Old Saybrook, Conn.* (New London, 1859), 3; *Contributions . . . Connecticut*, 461-62.

Scarborough: *RM*, 4-1.359-61.

Scituate: First Church: Scituate, MA, First Church, "Scituate and Barnstable Church Records," *NEHGR*, 9 (1855), 279; Samuel Deane, *History of Scituate, Massachusetts, from Its Settlement to 1831* (Boston, 1831), 59; Second Church (Norwell, MA, First Church): *ibid.*, 60-62; Quaker Monthly Meeting: Hill, *Monthly Meetings*, 342, 277.

Seconchgut IPT: now in Chilmark, MA; Weis, "New England Company," 159.

Seppekann: *RCNP*, 1.108 and 2.170; later became Rochester, MA, and Marion, MA; D. Hamilton Hurd, *History of Plymouth County, Massachusetts . . .* (Philadelphia, 1884), 321-39.

Sherborn: Abner Morse, *A Genealogical Register of the Descendents of the Early Planters of Sherborn, Holliston and Medway, Massachusetts* (Boston, 1855), 275-76; William Biglow, *History of Sherburne, Massachusetts* (Milford, MA, 1830), 25-26; Abner Morse, *A Genealogical Register of the Descendants of the Early Planters of Sherborn, Holliston and Medway, Massachusetts*, 289-90; Sherborn Historical Society, *Sherborn, Past and Present: 1674-1924* (Sherborn, MA, 1924), 6.

Sherburne (Nantucket): Quaker Monthly Meeting: Hill, *Monthly Meetings*, 241; Weis, "New England Company," 176-78; Weis does not speak of a 4th IPT; see also listings for Occawan, Wammasquid, and Squatesit;

Shumuit IPT: now in Mashpee, MA; Weis, "New England Company," 175.

Simsbury: Lucius I. Barber, *A Record and Documentary History of Simsbury*

(1931; rpt. Simsbury, CT, 1974), 107-9, 175-76; Noah A. Phelps, *History of Simsbury, Granby and Canton, from 1642 to 1845* (Hartford, CT, 1845), 52-55; Dudley Woodbridge, *Rev. Dudley Woodbridge, His Church Record at Simsbury in Conn., 1697-1710,* ed. Albert C. Bates (Hartford, CT, 1894), 13-14; *Contributions . . . Connecticut,* 476, along with CHS, *List,* 27, give the date of 1682, but that is only the permission from the General Court.

Skauton IPT: now in Sandwich, MA; Weis, "New England Company," 186.

Smithfield: Smithfield, RI, *Vital Records of Rhode Island,* ed. James N. Arnold, vol. 3, pt. vi: *Smithfield* (Providence, RI, 1892), iii-iv; Backus, *History,* ed. Weston, 2.395.

Smithtown: Frederick Van Wyck, *Long Island Colonial Patents* (Boston, 1935), 162-67; J. Richard Mehalick, *Church and Community, 1675-1975: The Story of the First Presbyterian Church of Smithtown, New York* (Hicksville, NY, 1976); Richard Smythe lived in Southampton from 1643 to 1656, but was then banished; he then moved to Setauket, where he lived from 1656 to 1665; in 1663 he began developing the manor that became Smithtown, after receiving the property from Lion Gardiner; Robert B. MacKay, Geoffrey L. Rossano, and Carol A. Traynor, *Between Ocean and Empire: An Illustrated History of Long Island* (Northridge, CA, 1985), 42-43.

South Carolina: "Charter of Carolina — 1663," Thorpe, *Federal and State Constitutions,* 5.2743-53; "A Declaration and Proposals of the Lord Proprietor of Carolina . . . 1663," *ibid.,* 5.2753-55; "Concessions and Agreements of the Lords Proprietors of the Province of Carolina, 1665," *ibid.,* 5.2756-61; "Charter of Carolina — 1665," *ibid.,* 5.2761-71; "The Fundamental Constitutions of Carolina — 1669," *ibid.,* 5.2772-86.

Southampton: Southampton, NY, . . . *Records of the Town of Southampton,* vol. 1: *The First Book of Records of the Town of Southampton, with Other Ancient Documents of Historic Value . . .* (Sag Harbor, NY, 1874), 1-7; George R. Howell, *The Early History of Southampton, Long Island, New York . . . ,* 2nd edn. (Albany, NY, 1887), 21-23, 99-100, which indicates that both church and town were organized in Boston; Frederick Van Wyck, ed., *Select Patents of Towns and Manors* (Boston, 1938), 83-100.

Southold: Frederick Van Wyck, *Long Island Colonial Patents* (Boston, 1935), 168-71; Epher Whitaker, "The Early History of Southold, Long Island," *NHCHSP,* 2 (1877), 3-4.

Springfield: Henry M. Burt, *The First Century of the History of Springfield: The Official Records from 1636 to 1736; with an Historical Review and Biographical Mention of the Founders,* 1 (Springfield, MA, 1898), 156-58; Beatrice B. Littlefield, *History of the First Parish and the First Congregational Church of West Springfield, Massachusetts* (n.p., 1948), 2-3; First Church: Worthley, *Inventory,* 587-89; Second Church (West Windsor First Church): William B. Sprague, *An Historical Discourse Delivered at West Springfield . . .* (Hartford, CT, 1825), 26.

Squatesit IPT: now in Nantucket, called "Sherburne" in the seventeenth century; Weis, "New England Company," 178; see also listings for Occawan, Sherburne, and Wammesit.

Stamford: Elijah B. Huntington, *History of Stamford, Connecticut, from Its Settlement in 1641, to the Present Time . . .,* 2nd edn., ed. Ronald Marcus and Grace H. Walmsley (Harrison, NY, 1979), 15-18; First Church organized in Wethersfield, CT, and the majority took the church and records to Stamford in Spring 1641: Samuel Scoville, "Historical Address," in Stamford, CT, First Church, *250th Anniversary of the [Stamford] Congregational Church . . . 1885* (Stamford, CT, 1885), 4; *Contributions . . . Connecticut,* 483-84.

Stonington: Richard A. Wheeler, *History of the Town of Stonington, County of New London, Connecticut, from Its First Settlement in 1649 to 1900, with a Genealogical Register of Stonington Families* (1900; rpt. Baltimore, 1977), 6-10, 43-44; *Contributions . . . Connecticut,* 486, says 1640.

Stow: J. Sidney Moulton, "[Historical] Sermon," in Stow, MA, First Church, *1702-1902: The Two Hundredth Anniversary of the First Parish Church of Stow, Massachusetts,* ed. J. Sidney Moulton and Samuel C. Beane ([Stow, MA], 1902), 7-8; Worthley, *Inventory,* 599-600; Preston R. Crowell and Olivia Crowell, *Stow, Massachusetts: 1683-1933* (Stow, MA, 1933), 33.

Stratfield (Bridgeport/Fairfield): United Congregational Church, Bridgeport, CT, "Church Records, 1695-1911," FHLC™M #: 0003830; Bridgeport, CT, First Church, *Manual of the First Congregational Church of Bridgeport, Connecticut* (New Haven, CT, 1901), 5; George C. Waldo, *History of Bridgeport and Vicinity,* 1 (New York, 1917), 18-19.

Stratford: "The Patent or Charter of the Town of Stratford, 1686," Fairfield County Historical Society, *Annual Report, 1891-92,* pp. 95-97; Christ Church, Episcopal: Kenneth Walter Cameron, *The Genesis of Christ*

Church, Stratford, Connecticut . . . (Hartford, CT [1957]), 22; First Church: Samuel Orcutt, *A History of the Old Town of Stratford and the City of Bridgeport, Connecticut,* 1 (New Haven, CT, 1886), 164; Second Church: *ibid.,* 180; William H. Wilcoxson, *History of Stratford, Connecticut, 1639-1939* (Stratford, CT, 1939), 166; William Cothren, *History of Ancient Woodbury, Connecticut* . . . , 1 (Waterbury, CT, 1852), 131-33; see listing for Woodbury, CT.

Succonesit IPT: now in Falmouth, MA; Weis, "New England Company," 163-64.

Sudbury: First Church: Alfred S. Hudson, *The History of Sudbury, Massachusetts, 1638-1889* (Boston, 1889; rpt. Sudbury, MA, 1968), who says (p. 98) that the church covenant "is still preserved" but does not give its text, signers, or location.

Sudbury East (now Wayland): Weis, *Colonial Clergy and* . . . *Churches of New England,* 276 (under Wayland); Alfred S. Hudson, *The History of Sudbury, Massachusetts, 1638-1889,* 283-94.

Suffield: Hezekiah Sheldon, *Documentary History of Suffield in the Colony and Province of the Massachusetts Bay, in New England, 1660-1749* (Springfield, MA, 1879; Hartford, CT, 1882-88), 46-49 and 53-57; CHS, *List,* 30, along with *Contributions* . . . *Connecticut,* 486-87, says that the church was gathered on Tuesday, April 26, 1698, which is certainly when Benjamin Ruggles was ordained; however, the church records give the date of Tuesday, March 20, 1693/94, as the year of the gathering; cf. Suffield, CT, First Church, "Church Records, 1741-1917," FHLC™M #: 1014184, p. 4: "This Church was organized and established 20th March, 1693/4"; but that is a retrospective comment from 1741 or later.

Swansea: Otis O. Wright, *History of Swansea, Massachusetts, 1667-1917* (Fall River, MA, 1917), 47-49, 73-75, 101-3; First Baptist Church: Swansea, MA, First Baptist Church, *1663-1963: 300th Anniversary Year Book of the First Baptist Church, Swansea, Mass.* ([Swansea, MA, 1963?]), opening page (no pagination); *id.,* "Parish Register (Transcription)," FHLC™M #: 0104833, pp. 122, 203-4b; Thomas W. Bicknell, "John Myles: Religious Tolerance in Massachusetts," *Magazine of New England History,* 2 (1892), 213-42, esp. 225-27; [Second Baptist] Church of Christ (now First Christian Congregational Church): Otis O. Wright, *History of Swansea, Massachusetts, 1667-1917* (Swansea, MA, 1917), 108.

Takeme IPT: now in West Tisbury, MA; Weis, "New England Company," 192.

Talhanio IPT: now in Chilmark, MA; Weis, "New England Company," 160.

Taunton: Samuel H. Emery, *The Ministry of Taunton*, 2 (Boston, 1853), 40-41; Taunton, MA, First Church, *325th Anniversary of the First Parish Church of Taunton, Massachusetts* (Taunton, MA, 1962), 11.

Tisbury: Tisbury, MA, *Records of the Town of Tisbury, Mass., Beginning June 29, 1669, and Ending May 16, 1864* (Boston, 1903), v-vi.

Titicut IPT: now in Middleborough, MA; Weis, "New England Company," 175-76, 198.

Tiverton: Tiverton, RI, *Vital Record of Rhode Island*, ed. James N. Arnold, vol. 4, pt. vii; *Tiverton* (Providence, RI, 1893), iii-iv; *ARPMB*, 7.174; see also Dartmouth and Little Compton; Tiverton Indian Church: see listing for Pocasset IPT.

Tolland: Harold Weigold, *Tolland: The History of an Old Connecticut . . . Town* (Chester, CT, 1971), 53.

Topsfield: George F. Dow, *History of Topsfield, Massachusetts* (Topsfield, MA, 1940), 271.

Truro: Worthley, *Inventory*, 625-26.

United Colonies of New England (also known as The New England Confederation) "The Articles of Confederation of the United Colonies of New England — 1643-1684," Thorpe, *Federal and State Constitutions*, 1.77-81.

Virginia: "The First Charter of Virginia — 1606," Thorpe, *Federal and State Constitutions*, 7.3783-89; "The Second Charter of Virginia — 1609," *ibid.*, 7.3790-3802; "The Third Charter of Virginia — 1611-12," *ibid.*, 7.3802-10; "Ordinances for Virginia . . . 1621," *ibid.*, 7.3810-12.

Wabaquassett Country: *PRCC*, 3.202-3; 4.453; Wabquissit IPT: now in Woodstock, CT; Weis, "New England Company," 192-93; Woodstock, CT, called New Roxbury and settled by people from the Massachusetts Bay.

Waeuntug IPT: now in Uxbridge, MA; Weis, "New England Company," 189-90.

Wallingford: Charles H. S. Davis, *History of Wallingford, Conn., from Its Settlement in 1670 to the Present Time . . .* (Meriden, CT, 1870), 76-78; *Contributions . . . Connecticut*, 493; CHS, *List*, 31.

Wamesit IPT: now in Lowell, MA; Weis, "New England Company," 171-72;

Wammasquid IPT: now in Nantucket, called Sherburne in the seventeenth century; see also listings for Occawan, Sherburne, and Squatesit.

Waquoit IPT: now in Falmouth, MA; Weis, "New England Company," 164;

Warwick: Oliver P. Fuller, *The History of Warwick, Rhode Island . . .* (Providence, RI, 1875), 32-33; Weis, *Colonial Clergy and . . . Churches of New England,* 276.

Waterbury: Henry Bronson, *The History of Waterbury, Connecticut . . .* (Waterbury, CT, 1858), 8-10, 206-7; Joseph Anderson, *The Town and City of Waterbury, Connecticut,* 1 (New Haven, CT, 1896), 229; *Contributions . . . Connecticut,* 496, gives a date of 1683, but CHS, *List,* 31, and others correct that with a date of 1691.

Watertown: Convers Francis, *An Historical Sketch of Watertown, in Massachusetts, from the First Settlement of the Town to the Close of Its Second Century* (Cambridge, MA, 1830), 12-13, 132-35; Henry L. Bond, *Family Memorials: Genealogies of . . . Watertown, Massachusetts . . . to Which Is Appended the Early History of the Town,* 2nd edn. (Boston, 1860), 980-82; Henry D. Locke, *An Ancient Parish: An Historical Summary of the First Parish, Watertown . . .* (Boston, 1930), i-iii.

Watertown Middle Precinct: there was a dispute with the Watertown First Church over the status of this church; according to Worthley, *Inventory,* 636-38, and Weis, *Colonial Clergy and . . . Churches of New England,* 275, the church was gathered on Tuesday, February 4, 1695/96, and Rev. Samuel Angier was installed on May 25, 1697; while many clergy were invited for Angier's installation, few came, indicating disapproval of the proceedings; Convers Francis, *An Historical Sketch of Watertown, in Massachusetts, from the First Settlement of the Town to the Close of Its Second Century,* 62-64; Henry L. Bond, *Family Memorials: Genealogies of . . . Watertown, Massachusetts . . . to Which Is Appended the Early History of the Town,* 2nd edn., 1053; Charles A. Nelson, *Waltham, Past and Present . . .* (Cambridge, MA, 1879), 54.

Watertown West Precinct (also known as Watertown Farms or Watertown Farmers' Precinct; now Weston, MA): ARPMB, 21.686-87; Henry L. Bond, *Family Memorials: Genealogies of . . . Watertown, Massachusetts . . . to Which Is Appended the Early History of the Town,* 2nd edn., 1054-55; Daniel S. Lamson, *History of the Town of Weston, Massachusetts, 1630-1890* (Boston, 1913), 1-9, 210-11.

Weesquobs IPT: now in Mashpee, MA; Weis, "New England Company," 175.

Wells: James R. Cushing, *Historical Discourse; Delivered at the . . . Anniversary of the Organization of the First Congregational Church . . . Wells, Maine* (Portland, ME, 1851), 13; Wells, ME, First Church, "Records of the First Church of Wells, ME," ed. George S. Stewart, *NEHGR,* 75 (1921), 42-43; Esselyn Gilman Perkins, *Wells: The Frontier Town of Maine,* 2 (Ogunquit, ME, 1971), 16-17.

Wenham: Adeline P. Cole (comp. and ed.), *Notes on Wenham History, 1643-1943* (Salem, MA, [1943]), 23; Wenham, MA, First Church, *Confession of Faith, and Covenant of the Congregational Church in Wenham* . . . (Boston, 1840), 3-4; this 1840 pamphlet is extremely rare and is the only publication that contains the Wenham-2 Covenant of 1663; the only copy I could locate was in the New England Historic Genealogical Society, Boston; cf. Daniel Mansfield, *Two Sermons, Delivered on the* . . . *Anniversary of the Organization of the First Church* . . . *in Wenham* (Andover, MA, 1845), 10; cf. also Worthley, *Inventory,* 654-57.

Westbury: Quaker Monthly Meeting: Hill, *Monthly Meetings,* 408-9.

West Greenwich: Spencer P. Mead, *Ye Historie of Ye Town of Greenwich, County of Fairfield, and State of Connecticut* . . . (New York, 1911), 43-44; 1705 is the traditional date for the gathering of the church, but cf. *PRCC,* 5.581, which calls for a date of 1716 or after, and Oliver Huckel, *The Old Church Tells Her Story* (Greenwich, CT, 1930), 129, which quotes a 1728 reference to "The Church of Christ in the West Society of Greenwich"; Huckel discusses the evidence (pp. 125-30) and goes with the 1705 date; I am convinced of the 1716-28 date; cf. also CHS, *List,* 13, and *Contributions* . . . *Connecticut,* 396, both of which call for a 1705 date.

West New Jersey (see also listings for New Jersey and East New Jersey): "Duke of York's Second Grant . . . for the Soil and Government of West New Jersey . . . 1680," Thorpe, *Federal and State Constitutions,* 5.2560-65; "Province of West New-Jersey . . . 1681," *ibid.,* 5.2565-67;

Westchester: Frederick Van Wyck, *Select Patents of New York Towns* (Boston, 1938), 94-144; *PRCC,* 1.411.

Westerly: Westerly, RI, *Vital Record of Rhode Island,* ed. James N. Arnold, vol. 5, pt. iv: *Westerly* (Providence, RI, 1894), iii-iv; SDB Church is now located in Hopkinton: S. S. Griswold, *An Historical Sketch of the Town of Hopkinton, from 1757 to 1876* . . . (Hope Valley, RI, 1877), 13; William L. Burdick, "Historical Address," in *Bi-Centennial Celebration of the First Seventh-Day Baptist Church of Hopkinton, Located at Ashaway, R.I.* (Ashaway, RI, 1908); Backus, *History,* ed. Weston, 2.396.

Westfield: Edward Taylor {and Westfield, MA, First Church}, *Edward Taylor's*

"Church Records" and Related Sermons, vol. 1 of *The Unpublished Writings of Edward Taylor,* ed. Thomas M. and Virginia L. Davis (Boston, 1981), 5, 160-61; John H. Lockwood, *Westfield and Its Historic Influences, 1669-1919,* 1 (Westfield, MA, 1922), 102-25, esp. 117-19.

Wethersfield: Sherman W. Adams and Henry R. Stiles, *The History of Ancient Wethersfield, Connecticut . . . ,* 1 (New York, 1904), 135-36; cf. also Winthrop, *Journal,* 158; Wethersfield, CT, First Church, *Manual of the Congregational Church, Wethersfield, Conn.* (Hartford, CT, 1860), 6.

Weweantic IPT: now in Wareham, MA; Weis, "New England Company," 190.

Weymouth: Winthrop, *Journal,* 281-82; Clarence W. Fearing, "Ecclesiastical History of Weymouth," in Weymouth Historical Society, *History of Weymouth, Massachusetts,* 1 (Weymouth, MA, 1923), 218.

Windham: Windham, CT, First Church, *Records of the Congregational Church in Windham, Connecticut (Except Church Votes) 1700-1851* (Hartford, CT, 1943), 3-4; J. E. Tyler, *Historical Discourse . . . First Church and Society of Windham, Connecticut* (Hartford, CT, 1851), 4-6; *Contributions . . . Connecticut,* 509-10.

Windsor: Henry R. Stiles, *The History of Ancient Windsor, Connecticut . . .* (New York, 1859), 866-67; First Church: church gathered in Plymouth, England, and then migrated to Dorchester, MBC; see listing for Dorchester, MA; David M'Clure, "Settlement and Antiquities of the Town of Windsor, in Connecticut," *MHSC,* ser. 1, 5 (1798), 166; Florence B. Mills, *Highlights of History of the First Church in Windsor,* 2nd edn. ([Windsor, CT], privately mimeographed, 1972), 25-27; CHS, *List,* 34; *Contributions . . . Connecticut,* 510-511; Second Church: Henry Stiles, *ibid.,* 179; church organized 1669 and dissolved by 1684, having reunited with First Church; *Contributions . . . Connecticut,* 513; Windsor Farms: became South Windsor; Weis, "Colonial Clergy and . . . Churches of New England," 272, gives the 1698 date, while *Contributions . . . Connecticut,* 480-81, gives a date of 1690; CHS, *List,* p. 28, identifies this group as the "Second Society in Windsor," but also lists the "Windsor Second Society" (1669-80), a church that did not continue, on p. 34.

Woburn: Samuel Sewall, *The History of Woburn . . .* (Boston, 1868), 20-23, 539-40; Woburn, MA, First Church, *Manual of the First Congregational Church, Woburn, Mass.* (Woburn, MA, 1871), 36-38; Worthley, *Inventory,* 702-4.

Woodbridge: Joseph W. Dally, *Woodbridge and Vicinity: The Story of a New Jersey Township* (New Brunswick, NJ, 1873), 298-302; Woodbridge, NJ, First Presbyterian Church, History (Carteret, NJ, 1975), 8-9.

Woodbury: William Cothren, *History of Ancient Woodbury, Connecticut, from 1659 to 1854 . . .*, 1 (Waterbury, CT, 1854), 131-33; founded as Stratford, CT, Second Church, the majority left Stratford in 1672 and brought with them the church records, retaining their embodiment as a church; see listing for Stratford, CT, Second Church.

Woodstock: *PRCC*, 3.202; *RN*, 5.426, 468; *CSMP*, 62.226; *ARPMB*, 21.670; *Contributions . . . Connecticut,* 516, gives the date of 1686, while CHS, *List,* 35 gives the date of 1690; founded as New Roxbury in 1686 by Massachusetts Bay people from Roxbury; Ellen D. Larned, *History of Windham County, Connecticut,* 1 (Worcester, MA, 1874), 22; see Wabaquasset County.

Worcester: Timothy Paine et al., ". . . Particulars Relating to Worcester . . . ," *MHSC*, ser. 1,1 (1792), 112-16; town laid out in 1668, but conflicts with Native Americans prevented its settlement; settled 1685; further conflicts with Native Americans in 1701 disbanded the community; resettled in 1713.

Wrentham: Samuel J. Warner, "Historical Sketch of Wrentham," in Wrentham, MA, *History and Directory of Wrentham and Norfolk, Massachusetts for 1890* (Boston, 1890), 17-19 and 23-24; Wrentham, MA, Original Congregational Church, *The Covenants and Sketch of the History of the Original Congregational Church of Christ, in Wrentham . . .* (Dedham, MA, 1818), 3-7; *id., Historical Sketch, Articles of Faith, and Covenants, of the Original Congregational Church, in Wrentham, Massachusetts . . .* (Boston, 1845), 3-5, 12-20, some of which may be more modern.

Yarmouth: Winthrop, *Journal,* 252-53, 283, 299; Worthley, *Inventory,* 712-14; John W. Dodge, *A History of the First Congregational Church, Yarmouth, Mass. . . .* (Yarmouth Port, MA, 1873), 4-5.

York: York, ME, "York Records," FHLC™M #: 0012837; Charles E. Banks and Angevine W. Gower, *History of York, Maine . . .*, 2 (Boston, 1950), 126-27; also known as Agamenticus (1632-38), Bristol (1638-41), and Gorgeana (1641-52); First Church: Weis, *Colonial Clergy and . . . Churches of New England,* 280.

Appendix 2

Typology of Early New England Local Civil Covenants, Arranged Chronologically, Excluding Colony Charters from the English Government

Abbreviations Used in Appendix 2

CTC   Connecticut Colony
ENJ   East New Jersey
IND   Independent (Town or Colony)
IPT   Indian Praying Town
MBC   Massachusetts Bay Colony
MBP   Massachusetts Bay Province
NA   Not Applicable
NH   New Hampshire (State)
NHC   New Haven Colony
NHP   New Hampshire Province
NNC   New Netherland Colony
NPC   New Plymouth Colony
NYCol.   New York Colony
RI   Rhode Island (State)
RIC   Rhode Island Colony
u   unknown

Name of Town/Colony/Plantation	Colony	Year	Type of Civil Covenant	Parties
Plymouth	NPC	1620	Combination	Whole Body
Charlestown	MBC	1634	Combination	Whole Body
Springfield	MBC	1636	Combination	Whole Body
Dedham	MBC	1636	Combination	Whole Body
Providence, Civil Covenant-1	IND	u	Combination	Whole Body
Portsmouth, Civil Covenant-1 (RI)	IND	1638	Combination	Whole Body
Southampton, Civil Covenant-1	IND	1638	Combination	Committee
Newport, Civil Covenant-1	IND	1639	Combination	Whole Body
Portsmouth, Civil Covenant-2 (RI)	IND	1639	Combination	Whole Body
Guilford, Civil Covenant-1	IND	1639	Combination	Whole Body
New Haven, Civil Covenant-1	NHC	1639	Combination	Whole Body
Exeter, Civil Covenant-1	IND	1639	Combination	u
Newport, Civil Covenant-2	IND	1639	Legislative Record	Committee (Legislature)
New Haven, Civil Covenant-2	NHC	1639	Combination	Whole Body
Exeter, Civil Covenant-2	IND	1640	Combination	Whole Body
Portsmouth (NH)	IND	1640	Combination	Whole Body
Providence, Civil Covenant-2	IND	1640	Combination	Whole Body (Prepared by Committee)
Dover	IND	1640	Combination	Whole Body
Stamford, Civil Covenant-1	NHC	1640	Legislative Record	Committee
Woburn	MBC	1640	Combination	Whole Body (Prepared by Committee)
Southampton, Civil Covenant-2	IND	1640	Combination	Whole Body
Rhode Island	RIC	1640	Combination	Committee
York, Civil Covenant-1	IND	1641	Charter	NA
York, Civil Covenant-2	IND	1641	Charter	NA
Maspeth (Newtown), Civil Covenant-1	NNC	1641	Charter	NA
United Colonies of New England-1	NA	1643	Combination	Committee

Name of Town/Colony/Plantation	Colony	Year	Type of Civil Covenant	Parties
Guilford, Civil Covenant-2	NHC	1643	Combination/Town Record	Whole Body
Seekonk/Rehoboth (East Providence, RI)	IND	1643	Combination	Whole Body
United Colonies of New England-2	NA	1643	Combination	Committee
New Haven Colony	NHC	1643	Combination	Committee
Hempstead Civil Colony-1	NNC	1644	Patent	Committee
Flushing, Civil Covenant-1	NNC	1645	Patent	Whole Body
Gravesend	NNC	1645	Patent	Committee
Providence, Civil Covenant-3	RIC	1645	Combination	Whole Body
Warwick	RIC	1647	Charter	NA
Providence, Civil Covenant-4	RIC	1647	Combination	Committee
Providence, Civil Covenant-5	RIC	1647	Combination	Committee
Providence, Civil Covenant-6	RIC	1648	Charter	NA
Medfield	MBC	1649	Combination	Committee/Whole Body
Natick IPT	MBC	1651	Combination	Whole Body
Kittery, Civil Covenant-1	IND	1652	Combination	Whole Body
Kittery, Civil Covenant-2	MBC	1652	Charter	NA
Martha's Vineyard IPT	IND	1652	Combination	Whole Body
Dartmouth	NPC	1652	Patent	Whole Body
Lancaster, Civil Covenant-1	MBC	1653	Combination	Whole Body
Amesbury, Civil Covenant-1	MBC	1653	Combination	Whole Body
Amesbury, Civil Covenant-2	MBC	1654	Combination	Whole Body
Easthampton	IND	1655	Combination	Whole Body
Stonington, Civil Covenant-2	MBC	1658	Combination	Whole Body
Hadley	MBC	1659	Combination	Whole Body
Suffield, Civil Covenant-1	MBC	1660	Legislative Record	Whole Body
Newark, Civil Covenant-2	ENJ	1661	Charter	Committee

Name of Town/Colony/Plantation	Colony	Year	Type of Civil Covenant	Parties
Mendon	MBC	1662	Patent	Committee
Newark, Civil Covenant-3	ENJ	1662	Charter	NA
Newark, Civil Covenant-4	ENJ	1663	Charter	Committee
Killingworth	CTC	1663	Charter	Committee
Elizabeth, Civil Covenant-2	ENJ	1664	Charter/Patent	Committee
Lyme	CTC	1664	Combination	Committee
Eastchester	NYCol.	1665	Combination	Whole Body
Elizabeth, Civil Covenant-3	ENJ	u	Charter	NA
Elizabeth, Civil Covenant-4	ENJ	1665	Combination	Whole Body
Smithtown, Civil Covenant-1	NYCol.	1665/6	Patent	"Committee of One"
Brookhaven, Civil Covenant-1	NYCol.	1666	Patent	Committee
Huntington, Civil Covenant-1	NYCol.	1666	Patent	Committee
Newark, Civil Covenant-6/1	ENJ	1666	Combination	Whole Body
Flushing, Civil Covenant-2	NYCol.	1666/7	Patent	Committee
Hempstead, Civil Covenant-2	NYCol.	1666/7	Patent	Committee
Westchester, Civil Covenant-1	NYCol.	1666/7	Patent	Committee
East Greenwich, Civil Covenant-1	RIC	1667	Legislative Record	Whole Body
Newark, Civil Covenant-6/2	ENJ	1667	Combination	Whole Body
Swansea, Civil Covenant-1	NPC	1667	Legislative Record	Committee
Swansea, Civil Covenant-2	NPC	1667	Legislative Record	Committee
Woodbridge	ENJ	1669	Charter	NA
Hatfield, Civil Covenant-2	CTC	1669	Combination	Committee
Wrentham, Civil Covenant-1	MBC	1669	Combination	NA
Westerly	RIC	1669	Legislative Record	Committee
Tisbury	IND	1671	Charter	NA
Wallingford, Civil Covenant-1	CTC	1669	Combination	Committee

Name of Town/Colony/Plantation	Colony	Year	Type of Civil Covenant	Parties
Swansea, Civil Covenant-3	NPC	1669	Combination	Whole Body
Wallingford, Civil Covenant-2	CTC	u	Combination	Whole Body
Suffield, Civil Covenant-4	MBC	1670	Combination	Committee
Woodbury	CTC	1672	Combination	Committee
Little Compton, Civil Covenant-1	NPC	1673	Combination	Whole Body
Waterbury	CTC	1674	Combination	Whole Body
Southold	NYCol.	1676	Patent	Committee
Smithtown, Civil Covenant-2	NYCol.	1676/7	Patent	"Committee of One"
Branford-2	CTC	1677	Combination	Whole Body
Middleborough-2	NPC	1677	Combination/Town Record	NA
East Greenwich, Civil Covenant-2	RIC	1677	Legislative Record	Whole Body
Enfield	MBC	1679	Patent	Whole Body
Sherborn, Civil Covenant-2	MBC	1679	Combination	Whole Body
Middleborough-2, Civil Covenant-2	NPC	1680	Combination	Whole Body
Bristol	NPC	1680	Patent	Whole Body
Rye, Civil Covenant-1	CTC	1685	Legislative Record	Committee
Hempstead, Civil Covenant-3	NYCol.	1685	Patent	Committee
Simsbury	CTC	1685	Patent/Legislative Record	Committee
Windsor	CTC	1685	Patent	Committee
Flushing, Civil Covenant-3	NYCol.	1685/6	Patent	Whole Body
Westchester, Civil Covenant-2	NYCol.	1685/6	Patent	Committee
Brookhaven, Civil Covenant-2	NYCol.	1686	Patent	Committee
Stratford	CTC	1686	Patent/Legislative Record	Committee
Huntington, Civil Covenant-2	NYCol.	1688	Patent	Committee
Glastonbury	CTC	1690	Legislative Record	NA
New Castle	NHP	1693	Charter	NA
Attleboro/North Attleboro	MBP	1694	Legislative Record	NA

Name of Town/Colony/Plantation	Colony	Year	Type of Civil Covenant	Parties
Harwich (Brewster), Civil Covenant-2	MBP	1694	Legislative Record	NA
Huntington, Civil Covenant-3	NYCol.	1694	Patent	Committee
Rye, Civil Covenant-2	CTC	1696	Patent	Committee
West Springfield (Precinct)	MBP	1696	Legislative Record	NA
Bedford, Civil Covenant-1	CTC	1697	Patent/Legislative Record	Committee
Westchester, Civil Covenant-3	NYCol.	1697	Patent	Committee
Colchester, Civil Covenant-1	CTC	1698	Legislative Record	Committee
Watertown West/Weston	MBP	1698	Legislative Record	NA
Colchester, Civil Covenant-2	CTC	1699	Legislative Record	NA
Plainfield	CTC	1699	Combination	Whole Body
Colchester, Civil Covenant-3	CTC	1699	Legislative Record	Committee
Framingham, Civil Covenant-2	MBP	1700	Legislative Record	NA
Lebanon	CTC	1700	Legislative Record	NA
Danbury	CTC	1702	Patent/Legislative Record	Committee
Mansfield	CTC	1703	Patent	Committee
Bedford, Civil Covenant-2	NYCol.	1704	Patent	Whole Body
West Greenwich	CTC	1705	Combination	Committee
Groton	CTC	1705	Legislative Record/Patent	NA
Byfield Parish	MBP	1706	Combination	Whole Body
Newark, Civil Covenant-7	ENJ	1713	Charter	Committee
Charlestown	RIC	1730	Patent/Legislative Record	NA
Gloucester	RIC	1730	Patent/Legislative Record	NA
Smithfield	RIC	1730	Patent/Legislative Record	NA
Westerly	RIC	1730	Patent/Legislative Record	NA
Little Compton, Civil Covenant-2	RIC	1746	Patent/Legislative Record	NA
Tiverton	RIC	1746	Patent/Legislative Record	NA
Hopkinton	RIC	1757	Patent/Legislative Record	NA

Bibliographical Essay

The study of colonial New England has produced a vast body of primary and secondary sources. The sources consulted for this study would be too numerous to list in a formal bibliography, but I have endeavored to cite critically all important bibliographical information in the notes. Fortunately, there are tools that can be used to locate primary and secondary sources about early New England and its larger context of colonial America, and this essay is therefore a guide to the tools which I used to construct this study. It is divided into nine sections:

    I. Bibliographies of States, Colonies, and Regions
   II. A Bibliography of Towns, Churches, and Regions Not Included in the Work of the Committee for a New England Bibliography (CNEB)
  III. Geographical Locations and Religious Institutions in New England: Bibliographies and Finding Aids
  IV. Bibliographies and Finding Aids for Unpublished Town and Church Records
   V. Unpublished Town and Church Records Available via The Family History Library System of The Church of Jesus Christ of Latter-day Saints
  VI. Colony Records
 VII. Puritanism and Congregationalism
VIII. Reference Works
  IX. General Bibliographies

Since this study began, many major research libraries have developed websites on the World-Wide Web. Their catalogs are either partially or wholly electronic. The retrospective nature of these libraries, along with the vast size of some of them, have allowed them to electronically catalog only recent works. In many cases the old paper card catalogs took over a century to develop. To electronically catalog these records is a project that will take decades for many libraries. Princeton University developed one solution to this probem by scanning its entire paper card catalog onto the Web. This makes the older, nonelectronic catalog available, but the bibliographical data on those millions of cards is not in database form. Many, if not most, of the libraries listed in my Acknowledgements have webpages and electronic catalogs; however, I found that I was visiting certain electronic catalogs more often than others. Because the addresses of electronic catalog websites often become outdated, I will not list those websites. However, the electronic catalogs of the following libraries are particularly helpful in locating bibliographical information concerning colonial New England history: the American Antiquarian Society Library; the Columbia University Library; the Family History Library of the Church of Jesus Christ of Latter-day Saints; the Harvard University Library; the Haverford College Library; the Library of Congress; the New England Historic Genealogical Society; the New York Public Library; the Newberry Library of Chicago; the Princeton Theological Seminary Library; the Princeton University Library; and the Yale University Library.

I. Bibliographies of States, Colonies, and Regions

The Thirteen Colonies

Milton M. Klein and Jacob E. Cooke have edited the series *A History of the American Colonies in Thirteen Volumes*. Each one of the volumes in this series has a magisterial bibliography, and in some cases the only comprehensive bibliography for that particular colony. Nine volumes were relevant for my purposes. For **New Hampshire**, Jere R. Daniell, *Colonial New Hampshire: A History* (Millwood, NY, 1981). For **Massachusetts**, Benjamin W. Labaree, *Colonial Massachusetts: A History* (Millwood, NY, 1979). For **Rhode Island**, Sydney V. James, *Colonial Rhode Island: A History* (New York, 1975). For **Connecticut**, Robert J. Taylor, *Colonial Connecticut: A History* (Millwood, NY, 1979). For **New York**, Michael Kammen, *Colonial New York: A History* (New York, 1975). For **New Jersey**, John E. Pomfret, *Colonial New Jersey: A History* (New York, 1973). For **Maryland**, Aubrey C.

Land, *Colonial Maryland: A History* (Millwood, NY, 1981). For **Virginia**, Warren M. Billings, John E. Selby, and Thad W. Tate, *Colonial Virginia: A History* (White Plains, NY, 1986). For **South Carolina**, Robert M. Weir, *Colonial South Carolina: A History* (Millwood, NY, 1983).

New England

There are dozens of bibliographies of various aspects of New England colonial history and New England history in general. My work was greatly enhanced by the labors of the Committee for a New England Bibliography (CNEB). The CNEB cites almost every published secondary source and many published primary sources for New England history. All periods are covered, from pre-Columbian times to the present. There is a volume for each state, a volume for New England in general, and 1989 and 1994 updates for the entire region. Each volume cites works dealing with the state, then with each county, and then with each locality. The bibliographic details for the CNEB are as follows: Committee for a New England Bibliography, ed. John B. Armstrong, 9 vols. (Boston, Hanover, NH, and London, 1976-94); Vol. 1: *Massachusetts: A Bibliography of Its History*, ed. John D. Haskell, Jr. (Boston, 1976); Vol. 2: *Maine: A Bibliography of Its History*, ed. *id.* (Boston, 1977); Vol. 3: *New Hampshire: A Bibliography of Its History*, ed. *id.* and T. D. Seymour Bassett (Boston, 1979); Vol. 5: *Rhode Island: A Bibliography of Its History*, ed. Roger Parks (Hanover, NH, 1983); Vol. 6: *Connecticut: A Bibliography of Its History*, ed. Roger Parks (Hanover, NH, 1986); Vol. 7: *New England: A Bibliography of Its History*, ed. Roger Parks (Hanover, NH, 1989); Vol. 8: *New England: Additions to the Six State Bibliographies*, ed. Roger Parks et al. (Hanover, NH, 1989); Vol. 9: *Further Additions, to 1994*, ed. Roger Parks (Hanover, NH, 1994). Needless to say, I did not utilize Vol. 4, which deals with Vermont.

The CNEB was designed to be comprehensive, and therefore its listings contain a mixture of professional, semiprofessional, and amateur historical writing. Furthermore, it covers the period from before 1492 to the late twentieth century. One therefore has to sort through each local, county, state, and regional listing to find what one really needs. In the case of less critical historical works, it should be noted that in some cases that is all we have about the founding of a particular town and church. Furthermore, I must emphasize that without the amateur and semiprofessional work of thousands of local historians and genealogists over the centuries we would know little about church and town foundings in colonial New England and the covenant documents they generated. Besides the CNEB, the following list of bibliographical items are helpful for identifying primary and secondary sources. They are listed geographically from north to south.

For **the Atlantic Provinces of Canada** in general, cf. William F. E. Morley, *The Atlantic Provinces: Newfoundland, Nova Scotia, New Brunswick, Prince Edward Island,* Vol. 1 of *Canadian Local History to 1950: A Bibliography* (Toronto, 1967); Alice R. Stewart, *The Atlantic Provinces of Canada: Union Lists of Materials in the Larger Libraries of Maine,* University of Maine Studies, ser. 2 (Orono, ME, 1965).

For **New Brunswick** specifically, cf. Hugh A. Taylor (ed.), *New Brunswick History: A Checklist of Secondary Sources . . .* (Fredericton, NB, 1971).

For **Newfoundland** specifically, cf. Agnes C. O'Dea and Anne Alexander (eds.), *Bibliography of Newfoundland,* 2 vols. (Toronto, 1986).

For **Maine,** cf. Bangor, ME, Public Library, *Bibliography of the State of Maine* (Boston, 1962); "Bibliography of Eastern Maine," *Bangor Historical Magazine,* 5 (1889-90), 221-25; H. W. Bryant, Booksellers, Portland, ME, *A Check List of Maine Town Histories . . . (1902)* [Portland, ME, 1904]; Charles E. Clark, *Maine during the Colonial Period: A Bibliographical Guide* (Portland, ME, 1974); John E. Frost, *Maine Genealogy: A Bibliographical Guide* (Portland, ME, 1977); Drew B. Hall, "Reference List on Maine Local History," New York State Library, *Bibliography Bulletin,* 28 (1901), 775-917, rpt. under the same title (Albany, NY, 1901); Stanley Howe, "Select List of Maine History Theses," *Maine History News,* 21 (1985), January, p. 7, April, p. 10, July, pp. 9, 14; A. J. Huston, Bookseller, Portland, ME, *A Check List of Maine Local Histories . . .* [Portland, ME], 1915; William B. Jordan, Jr. (ed.), *A Bibliography of Maine Bibliography* (n.p., 1952); Maine, State Library, *Bibliography on Maine History* [Augusta, ME, 1931]; Reginald W. Noyes, *A Guide to the Study of Maine Local History* ([Ann Arbor?, MI], 1936); Elizabeth Ring, *Maine Bibliographies: A Bibliographical Guide* (Portland, ME, 1973); "Select List of Unpublished Master's Theses from the University of Maine," *Maine Historical Society News,* 8 (1969), 8-15; 9 (1969-70), 17-19; Edward O. Schriver, "Maine: A Bibliographical Review," *Acadiensis,* 5 (1976), 154-62; William Willis, "A Descriptive Catalogue of Books and Pamphlets Relating to the History and Statistics of Maine, or Portions of It," *Historical Magazine,* 7 (1870), 145-82; Joseph Williamson, *A Bibliography of the State of Maine . . . to 1891,* 2 vols. (Portland, ME, 1896); Robert M. York, "Suggested Reading in Maine History: A Bibliography of Religious History," *Maine Historical Society News,* 4 (1965), 7-10.

For **New Hampshire,** cf. George L. Balcom, *Catalogue of the . . . Library, of the Late George L. Balcom . . . Comprising an Extensive Collection of*

Historical Books Relating to New Hampshire, Including [a] Nearly Complete Set of New Hampshire Town, County, and Regimental Histories, Genealogies . . . (Boston, 1901); William Copely, "Doctoral Dissertations in New Hampshire History," *HNH,* 31 (1976), 44-51; Samuel C. Eastman, "A Descriptive Catalogue of Books and Pamphlets Relating to the History and Statistics of New Hampshire or Portions of It," New Hampshire State Librarian, *Report,* 22 (1891), 181-273; Otis Grant Hammond, *Checklist of New Hampshire History,* ed. E. J. Hanrahan (Somersworth, NH, 1971); John N. McClintock, "Bibliography of New Hampshire," *Granite Monthly,* 4 (1880-81), 286-91; Richard Sliwoski, "Additional Doctoral Dissertations in New Hampshire History," *HNH,* 33 (1978), 334-45; *id.,* "History from the Masters: Theses on New Hampshire History from New Hampshire Colleges and Universities," *HNH,* 35 (1980), 66-74; James D. Squires, *New Hampshire: A Student's Guide to Localized History* (New York, 1966); [Bryant F. Tolles, Jr.], *Bibliography on New Hampshire History* [Concord, NH, 1972?].

For **Massachusetts Bay**, cf. Jeremiah Colburn, *Bibliography of the Local History of Massachusetts* (Boston, 1871); Charles A. Flagg, *A Guide to Massachusetts Local History* (Salem, MA, 1907); Martin Kaufman, John F. Ifkovic, and Joseph Carvalho (eds.), *A Guide to the History of Massachusetts* (New York, 1988); William J. Reid, *Massachusetts: A Students' Guide to Localized History* (New York, 1965).

For **New Plymouth**, cf. George D. Langdon, Jr., "Bibliographic Essay [on Published and Manuscript Sources for the Study of Plymouth Colony in the Seventeenth Century]," *Occasional Papers in Old Colony Studies,* 1 (1969), 41-50; W. Pierce, "Select Bibliography of the Pilgrim Fathers of New England," *TCHS,* 8 (1920-23), 16-23, 59-68; Edwin G. Sanford, *The Pilgrim Fathers and Plymouth Colony: A Bibliographical Survey of Books and Articles Published During the Past Fifty Years* (Boston, 1970).

For **Rhode Island**, cf. John Russell Bartlett (ed.), *Bibliography of Rhode Island* . . . (Providence, RI, 1864); Clarence S. Brigham (ed.), *Bibliography of Rhode Island History* (n.p., 1902); rpt. from Edward Field (ed.), *State of Rhode Island and Providence Plantations at the End of the Century: A History,* 3 vols. (Boston, 1902); *id., List of Books Upon Rhode Island History* ([Providence, RI], 1908); Howard M. Chapin, *Bibliography of Rhode Island Bibliography* . . . (Providence, RI, 1914); Morgan Edwards, "Materials for a History of the Baptists in Rhode Island," *RIHSC,* 6 (1867), 301-70; Hope F. Kane, "Doctoral and Master's Theses Relating to Rhode Island," *RIHSC,* 34 (1941), 128-29; Clifford P. Monahan, *Rhode Island: A Student's Guide to Localized History* (New York, 1965).

For **Connecticut**, see Elizabeth Abbe, "Connecticut Genealogical Research: Sources and Suggestions," *NEHGR*, 134 (1980), 3-26; Rheta A. Clark, David M. Roth, and Arthur E. Soderlind (eds.), *Connecticut Yesterday and Today: A Selected Bibliography* . . . (Hartford, CT, 1974); Christopher B. Collier (ed.), "Doctoral Dissertations of Interest to Connecticut Historians, 1882-1984: Analysis and Compilation," Association for the Study of Connecticut History, *Newsletter* (Fall, 1985), 3-12; Christopher B. Collier and Bonnie B. Collier, *The Literature of Connecticut History,* The Connecticut Scholar: Occasional Papers of the Connecticut Humanities Council, 6 (Middletown, CT, 1983); "Current Research in Connecticut History . . . Completed Projects . . . ," *Connecticut History Newsletter,* 8 (1971), 26-40; 10 (1972), 25-45; 12 (1973), 27-51; Bruce C. Daniels, "Antiquarians and Professionals: The Historians of Colonial Connecticut," *Connecticut History,* 23 (1982), 81-97; Charles A. Flagg (ed.), *Reference List on Connecticut Local History* (Albany, NY, 1900); Sophie A. Frankel (ed.), *Connecticut Town and County Histories: A Bibliography* (Hartford, CT, 1944); Thomas Jay Kemp, *Connecticut Researcher's Handbook,* Gale Genealogy and Local History Series, 12 (Detroit, MI, 1981); John Magnesi, "Masters' Theses on Connecticut: A Bibliography," *CHSB,* 42 (1977), 40-61, 76-94; David M. Roth, *Connecticut History and Culture: An Historical Review and Resource Guide* . . . (Hartford, CT, 1985); Robert E. Schnare, *Local Historical Resources in Connecticut: A Guide to Their Use* (Darien, CT, 1975); Bruce P. Stark (ed.), "Checklist of Recent Dissertations on Connecticut History," Association for the Study of Connecticut History, *Newsletter* (Spring, 1979), 2-5; *id.,* "A Guide to Connecticut History Bibliography," *Connecticut History,* 20 (1979), 27-36; Albert P. Van Dusen (ed.), "Connecticut History to 1763: A Selective Bibliography," *Connecticut History,* 15 (1975), 49-55; Linda S. Winters (ed.), "Ph.D. Dissertations Related to Connecticut on Microfilm in Connecticut State Library," Association for the Study of Connecticut History, *Newsletter,* 13 (January 1974), 16-21.

II. A Bibliography of Towns, Churches, and Regions Not Included in the Work of the Committee for a New England Bibliography (CNEB)

One of the challenges scholars of early colonial American history face is the fact that the boundaries of colonies shifted and overlapped as colonies merged or divided. Thus, since Maine and New Hampshire were under the rule, both directly and indirectly, of the Massachusetts Bay Colony during the seventeenth century, some of the sources for those colonies/provinces, both primary and secondary, are found in the studies and bibliographies for modern-day Massachusetts. The Connecticut CNEB volume has all of the citations for the study of the New Haven Colony, and the *Documentary History of the State of New York,* ed. Christopher Morgan and Edmund B. O'Callahan, 4 vols. (New York, 1849-51), contains references to the New Haven Colony's settlement in the Delaware Valley in what is now New Jersey; the reason for the latter fact is that during the 1640s and 1650s, before there was an East New Jersey and a West New Jersey, the entire region of New Jersey was under the hegemony first of the Colony of New Sweden and then of the Colony of New Netherland, which, of course, was subsumed into the State of New York. There are, however, some excellent bibliographies for each state, and through them we can find the references to the earlier colonies and their local towns and churches. What follows, therefore, are citations of critical works that deal with the institution of civil government and the founding of a religious institution related to New England but not *in* New England in the period 1620-1708.

Generally, the word "state" in our context denotes the territory which a colony ruled over at the time of the American Revolution and the adoption of the American Constitution (1776-89); while there have been some adjustments in boundaries and territories since then (e.g., Maine gained its statehood in 1820 and emerged from Massachusetts) the changes after 1789 have not been of great consequence.

While each New England town has, in almost every case, extensive documentation on the local level, information about communities outside of New England is often found in the county histories. Therefore, the modern county of each town is cited at the end of a town listing. Included in this listing are New England communities which failed during the seventeenth or early eighteenth centuries, i.e. a church and/or a town were established but for one reason or another the venture was not successful, and these communities are therefore not listed in the CNEB under their original names. In these instances, I point out the current towns that cover these areas, along with the county or counties that they are found in. New England Native American communities and churches listed in Appendix 1 also largely fall into the category of failed communities, but since written records of their activities are largely missing, they are not included in this bibliographical list, which is intended as an aid for further research and not a comprehensive census. Furthermore, many of the Native American communities dissolved in the eighteenth and nineteenth centuries, and not in the seventeenth century.

Annapolis, Maryland: Clayton C. Hall, *Narratives of Early Maryland, 1633-1684* (New York, 1910); Elmer Martin Jackson, Jr., *Annapolis* (Annapolis, MD?, 1936-37); Babette M. Levy, "Early Puritanism in the Southern and Island Colonies," *AASP,* 70 (1960), 69-348; Maryland, General Assembly, *Proceedings and Acts of the General Assembly of Maryland, January, 1637/8–September, 1664,* ed. William Hand Browne, Archives of Maryland (Baltimore, 1883); George Petrie, *Church and State in Early Maryland, JHUSHPS,* ser. 10, #IV (Baltimore, MD, 1892), 5-49; Daniel R. Randall, "The Puritan Colony at Annapolis, Maryland" (diss. Johns Hopkins, 1887); partially republished as: *A Puritan Colony in Maryland, JHUSHPS,* ser. 4, #VI (Baltimore, MD, 1886), 5-47 [215-57]; David Ridgely (ed.), *Annals of Annapolis . . .* (Baltimore, MD, 1841); Elihu S. Riley, *"The Ancient City": A History of Annapolis, in Maryland, 1649-1887* (Annapolis, MD, 1887); Owen M. Taylor, *The History of Annapolis . . .* (Baltimore, MD, 1872); Lewis W. Wilhelm, *Local Institutions of Maryland, JHUSHPS,* ser. 3, #V-VI-VII (Baltimore, MD, 1885). Anne Arundel County, Maryland.

Annapolis Royal, Massachusetts Bay Province. Same as **Port Royal, Nova Scotia**. Annapolis County, Nova Scotia.

Bahama Islands: Paul Albury, *The Story of the Bahamas* (New York, 1975); Paul B. Boultbee (ed.), *The Bahamas,* World Bibliographical Series, #108 (Santa Barbara, CA, 1989); Michael Craton, *A History of the Bahamas,* 3rd edn. (Waterloo, ON, 1986); Michael Craton and Gail Sanchez, *Islanders in the Stream: A History of the Bahamian People,* Vol. 1: *From Aboriginal Times to the End of Slavery [1834]* (Athens, GA, 1992); John T. Hassam, "The Bahama Islands: Notes on an Early Attempt at Colonization," *MHSP,* ser. 2, 13 (1899-1900), 2-58; Sandra Riley, *Homeward Bound: A History of the Bahama Islands to 1850 . . .* (Miami, FL, 1983); Gregory Edwin Shipley, "Turbulent Times, Troubled Isles: The Rise and Development of Puritanism in Bermuda and the Bahamas, 1609-1684" (diss. Westminster Theological Seminary, 1989).

Bedford, New York: Charles W. Baird, *History of Bedford [N.Y.] Church . . .* (New York, 1882); Joseph Barrett, "Bedford," in J. Thomas Scharf (ed.), *History of Westchester County, New York . . . ,* 2 (Philadelphia, 1886), 574-605; Robertson T. Barrett, "Bits of Bedford History," *Westchester County Historical Bulletin,* 27 (1951), 1-23; Robertson T. Barrett, *The Town of Bedford: A Commemorative History, 1680-1955* (Bedford, NY, 1955); Bedford, NY, *Historical Records,* 9 vols. (Bedford, NY, 1966-78); Robert Bolton,

"The Town of Bedford," in Robert Bolton, *The History of the Several Towns, Manors, and Patents of the County of Westchester, From its First Settlement . . .* , ed. C. W. Bolton, 1 (New York, 1881), 3-69; P. B. Heroy, *A Brief History of the Presbyterian Church at Bedford, N.Y., from the Year 1680 . . .* (New York, 1874); Donald W. Marshall, *Bedford Tricentennial, 1680-1980 . . .* (Bedford Hills, NY, 1980). Westchester County, New York.

Bermuda: W. Robson Notman, "The Early Bermuda Church," *The Presbyterian and Reformed Review*, 7 (1896), 630-47; Gregory Edwin Shipley, "Turbulent Times, Troubled Isles: The Rise and Development of Puritanism in Bermuda and the Bahamas, 1609-1684"; Louise Marie Timko, "Puritans in Bermuda, 1612-1650" (diss. Drew, 1996).

Bridgehampton, New York: Paul H. Curtis, *Bridgehampton's Three Hundred Years* (Bridgehampton, NY, 1957); Henry P. Hedges, *A Centennial and Historical Address, Delivered at Bridge-Hampton, L.I.* (Sag Harbor, NY, 1876). Suffolk County, New York.

Bronx County, New York: Janet Butler (ed.), *Bibliography of the Bronx . . .* (Bronx, NY, 1974); Randall Comfort, *History of Bronx Borough, City of New York* (New York, 1906); Otto Hufeland, *A Check List of Books, Maps, Pictures and Other Printed Matter Relating to the Counties of Westchester and Bronx*, Westchester County Historical Society, *Publications*, 6 (New York, 1929); Lloyd Ultan, *The Bronx in the Frontier Era: From the Beginning to 1696* (Dubuque, IA, 1993); Stephen Jenkins, *The Story of the Bronx . . .* (New York, 1912); Narcisco Rodriguez, *The Bronx in Print: An Annotated Catalogue of Books and Pamphlets about the Bronx,* ed. Candace Kuhta (Bronx, NY, 1981). Cf. items in Westchester County, New York, listing.

Brookhaven, New York: Edwin P. Adkins, *Setauket: The First Three Hundred Years, 1655-1955* (New York, 1955); Brookhaven, NY, *Records, Town of Brookhaven, up to 1800 . . .* , ed. Benjamin T. Hutchinson and Cynthia Hutchinson (Patchogue, NY, 1880) (extracts, not a comprehensive edition); Brookhaven, NY, *Brookhaven Town Records*, Vol. I: *1662-1679,* ed. Archibald C. Weeks (New York, 1924); Brookhaven, NY, *Records of the Town of Brookhaven,* ed. William J. Weeks, 3 vols. (New York, 1930-32); Mildred H. Gillie et al., *Historical Sketches of Settlements and Villages of North Brookhaven Town . . . 1655-1955* (Bellport, NY, 1955); John H. Innes, "The Earliest Records of Brookhaven (Setauket) on Long Island," *NYSHAP,* 16 (1935), 436-48; Edward P. Rindler, "The Migration from the New Haven Colony to Newark, East New Jersey: A Study of Puritan Values and Behavior, 1630-1720" (diss. University of Pennsylvania, 1977); Egbert T. Smith, *Brookhaven, 1665-1876* (n.p., 1876); Kate W. Strong (ed.), *First Presbyte-*

rian Church in Brookhaven, at Setauket (Setauket, NY, 1942). Suffolk County, New York.

Cape Fear, North Carolina: Louise Hall, "New Englanders at Sea: Cape Fear before the Royal Charter of 24 March 1662/3," *NEHGR*, 124 (1970), 88-108. Failed.

Cape Sable, Massachusetts Bay Province: Same as **Clark's Harbor, Nova Scotia**. See entries for **Nova Scotia**, especially William F. E. Morley, *Canadian Local Histories to 1950: A Bibliography*, Vol. 1: *The Atlantic Provinces: Newfoundland, Nova Scotia, New Brunswick, Prince Edward Island* (Toronto, 1967). Shelburne County, Nova Scotia.

Charleston, South Carolina: Babette M. Levy, "Early Puritanism in the Southern and Island Colonies," *AASP*, 70 (1960), 69-348; Charleston, SC, City Council, *Church Histories: Republished from the Yearbook of the City of Charleston, South Carolina, 1882* (Charleston, SC, 1883); David Ramsay, *The History of the Independent or Congregational Church in Charleston, South Carolina from Its Origins Till the Year 1814* (Philadelphia, 1815); George Sheldon, *The Hand of God Recognized* . . . (Charleston, SC, 1846). Charleston County, South Carolina.

Clark's Harbor, Massachusetts Bay Province: Same as **Cape Sable, Nova Scotia**. Shelburne County, Nova Scotia.

Cohanzy, New Jersey (Fairton, New Jersey): Frank D. Andrews, *Inscriptions on the Grave Stones in the Old "New England Town" Burying Ground, Fairton, Fairfield Township, Cumberland County, New Jersey* . . . (Vineland, NJ, 1909); rpt. in *Genealogy: A Weekly Journal of American Ancestry*, 1 (1912), #9, 67-68 and #12, 92-93; Frank D. Andrews (ed.), *Residents of Greenwich, New Jersey Who Paid Taxes in the Year 1843: With Notes on the First Settlers* (Vineland, NJ, 1916); Rebecca A. Andrews, *Historical Sketches of Greenwich in Old Cohansey* (Vineland, NJ, 1905); Allen H. Brown, *An Outline History of the Presbyterian Church in West or South Jersey* (Philadelphia, 1869); H. Stanley Craig (ed.), *Cumberland County, New Jersey Genealogical Data* . . . *Prior to 1800* (Merchantville, NJ, n.d.); Thomas Cushing and Charles E. Sheppard, *History of the Counties of Gloucester, Salem and Cumberland, New Jersey* . . . (Philadelphia, 1883), 666-68, 682-84, 695-97; Index: *An Index to the Cushing and Sheppard History of Gloucester, Salem, and Cumberland Counties, New Jersey*, ed. Donald A. Sinclair ([New Orleans, LA], 1975); Lucius Q. C. Elmer, *History of the Early Settlement and Progress of Cumberland County, New Jersey* . . . (Bridgeton, NJ, 1869), 90, 102-5; Fairfield, NJ, First Presbyterian Church, *Bi-Centennial Celebration of the Old Stone Church* . . . (Bridgeton, NJ, 1881); Sarah S. Hancock, *Story of*

Greenwich (n.p., n.d.); David C. Laubach, *Three Hundred Years of Baptist Witness: A History of Cohansey Baptist Church [of Roadstown, New Jersey]* (Roadstown, NJ, 1983); William McMahon, *Historic South Jersey Towns* (Atlantic City, NJ, 1964); Lawrence C. Roff, *The Fairfield Presbyterians: Puritanism in West Jersey from 1680* (Bridgeton, NJ, 1980); Joseph S. Sickler, *Tea Burning Town: Being the Story of Ancient Greenwich on the Cohansey in West Jersey* (New York, 1950). Cumberland County, New Jersey.

Dorchester, South Carolina: This community and its church was continued in the eighteenth century by the Midway Presbyterian Church, Liberty County, Georgia. Francis J. Bremer, "'A New Errand': Massachusetts Puritans and the Founding of Dorchester, South Carolina," *BCL*, 28 (1976-77), #2, 4-10; "Instructions for Emigrants from Essex County, Mass. to South Carolina 1697," in Charleston, SC, City Council, *Yearbook of the City of Charleston for 1899* (Charleston, SC, 1899), 149-54; Babette M. Levy, "Early Puritanism in the Southern and Island Colonies," *AASP*, 70 (1960), 69-348; Liberty County, GA, Midway Congregational Church, *History and Published Records of the Midway Congregational Church, Liberty County, Georgia . . . with Addenda by Elizabeth C. Quarterman*, ed. James Stacy (Spartanburg, SC, 1979); "Joseph Lord," in John L. Sibley and Clifford K. Shipton, eds., *Biographical Sketches of Graduates of Those Who Attended Harvard College*, 4 (Cambridge, MA, 1933), 101-6; Paul M. McIlvaine, *The Dead Towns of Sunbury, GA., and Dorchester, S.C.*, 3rd edn. (Hendersonville, NC, 1976); William Pratt, "Journal of Elder William Pratt, 1695-1701," in *Narratives of Early Carolina, 1650-1708*, ed. Alexander S. Salley (New York, 1911), 191-200; Henry A. Middleton Smith, "The Town of Dorchester, in South Carolina — A Sketch of Its History," *The South Carolina Historical and Genealogical Magazine*, 6 (1905), 62-95, 127-30; Henry A. Middleton Smith, *The Town of Dorchester in South Carolina* (Charleston, SC, 1905); *id.*, "The Upper Ashley; and the Mutations of Families," *The South Carolina Historical and Genealogical Magazine*, 20 (1919), 151-98, esp. 157-58; James Stacy, *A History of the Presbyterian Church in Georgia* (Newnan, GA, 1912). Dorchester County, South Carolina.

Eastchester, New York: Robert Bolton, "The Town of East Chester," in Robert Bolton, *The History of the Several Towns, Manors, and Patents of the County of Westchester, From its First Settlement . . .*, ed. C. W. Bolton, 1 (New York, 1881), 201-43; William S. Coffey, "East Chester," in J. Thomas Scharf (ed.), *History of Westchester County, New York . . .*, 2 (Philadelphia, 1886), 720-46; Eastchester, NY, *Records . . .*, ed. Eastchester Historical So-

ciety, 9 vols. (Eastchester, NY, 1964); Stephen L. Schechter, "The Founding
of American Local Communities: A Study of Covenantal and Other Forms
of Association," *Publius*, 10 (1980), 165-85; *The Story of a Living Shrine: St.
Paul's Church, Eastchester, [New York], 1693-1765* (Mount Vernon, NY,
1927); *Village Green Fair Commemorating the 275th Anniversary of the
Founding of Historic St Paul's Church Eastchester, 1665-1940* (Mount Vernon,
NY, 1940). Westchester County, New York.

Easthampton, New York: Timothy H. Breen, *Imagining the Past: East
Hampton Histories* (Reading, MA, 1989); David Gardiner, *Chronicles of the
Town of Easthampton, County of Suffolk, New York* (New York, 1871);
Henry P. Hedges, *An Address, Delivered on . . . the Celebration of the Two Hun-
dredth Anniversary of the Settlement of the Town of East-Hampton, Together
with an Appendix, Containing a General History of the Town from its First Set-
tlement to the Year 1800* (Sag Harbor, NY, 1850); id., *A History of the Town of
East-Hampton, New York . . .* (Sag Harbor, NY, 1897); Jeannette Edwards
Rattray, *East Hampton History, Including Genealogies of Early Families* (East
Hampton, NY, 1953). Suffolk County, New York.

Elizabeth, New Jersey: Mary E. Alward, "Early History of the First
Presbyterian Church of Elizabeth, N.J.," Union County Historical Society,
Proceedings, 2 (1923-34), 147-72; Elizabeth, NJ, First Presbyterian Church,
*Church Manual, for the Members of the First Presbyterian Church, Elizabeth-
Town, N.J.*, ed. John M'Dowell (Elizabeth-Town [Elizabeth], NJ, 1824);
Elizabeth, NJ, First Presbyterian Church, *Manual . . .* (New York, 1858);
Harry C. Ellison, *Church of the Founding Fathers of New Jersey: A History*
(Cornish, ME, 1964); Edwin F. Hatfield, *History of Elizabeth, New Jersey, In-
cluding the Early History of Union County* (New York, 1868); A. V. D.
Honeyman et al., *History of Union County, N.J., 1664-1923*, 3 vols. (New
York, 1923); Frank B. Kelley and Warren R. Dix (eds.), *Historic Elizabeth,
1664-1914* (Elizabeth, NJ, 1914); Nicholas Murray, *Notes Historical and
Biographical Concerning Elizabeth-Town . . .* (1844) (rpt. New York, 1941);
F. W. Ricord, *History of Union County, New Jersey . . .* (Newark, NJ, 1897);
William B. Sprague, *A Discourse, Addressed to the First Presbyterian Congre-
gation of Elizabeth . . . On Occasion of the Completion of Its Second Century*
(Albany, NY, 1867); Theodore Thayer, *As We Were: The Story of Old
Elizabethtown*, *NJHSC*, 13 (1964); William A. Whitehead, "A Review of
Some of the Circumstances Connected with the Settlement of Elizabeth,
New Jersey," *NJHSP*, ser. 2, 1 (1867-69), 153-76; Clayton W. Woodford, *His-
tory of Union and Middlesex Counties, New Jersey . . .* (Philadelphia, 1882).
Union County, New Jersey.

Fairton, New Jersey: See **Cohanzy, New Jersey**. Cumberland County, New Jersey.

Flushing, Queens, New York: Martha Bockée Flint, *Early Long Island: A Colonial Study* (New York, 1896), 173-88; Trébor Haynes, *Colonial Flushing: A Brief History of the Town of Flushing . . .* (Flushing, NY, 1945); *id., The Flushing Remonstrance* (Flushing, NY, n.d.); G. Henry Mandeville, *Flushing, Past and Present: A Historical Sketch* (Flushing, NY, 1860); Henry D. Waller, *History of the Town of Flushing, Long Island, New York* (Flushing, NY, 1899). Queens County, New York.

Gravesend, Brooklyn, New York: A. P. Stockwell and William H. Stillwell, "A History of the Town of Gravesend . . . and of Coney Island . . . ," in Henry R. Stiles et al. (eds.), *The Civil, Political, Professional and Ecclesiastical History . . . of the County of Kings and The City of Brooklyn, N.Y. from 1683 to 1884* (New York, 1884), rpt. under the title of the chapter (Brooklyn, NY, 1884); Martha Bockée Flint, *Early Long Island: A Colonial Study* (New York, 1896), 104-15. Kings County, New York.

Hempstead, New York: George D. Combes, "The Fifty Original Proprietors of Hempstead," *Nassau County Historical Journal*, 18 (1967), 1-16; Courtney R. Hall, "Early Days in Hempstead, Long Island," *NYH*, 24 (1943), 534-47; Edward P. Rindler, "The Migration from the New Haven Colony to Newark, East New Jersey: A Study of Puritan Values and Behavior, 1630-1720" (diss. University of Pennsylvania, 1977); Hempstead, NY (North Hempstead, NY and South Hempstead, NY), *Records of the Towns of North and South Hempstead, Long Island, N.Y.*, 8 vols. (Jamaica, NY, 1896); Henry Onderdonk, Jr., *The Annals of Hempstead; 1643 to 1832 . . .* (Hempstead, NY, 1878); *id., Antiquities of the Parish Church, Hempstead, Including Oyster Bay and the Churches in Suffolk County* (Hempstead, NY, 1880); Bernice Schultz, *Colonial Hempstead* (Lynbrook, NY, 1937). Nassau County, New York.

Huntington, New York: Robert Davidson, *Historical Discourse, on the Bi-Centennial Commemoration of the Founding of the First Christian Church in the Town of Huntington, L.I.* (Huntington, NY, 1866); Huntington, NY, *Huntington Town Records, Including Babylon, L.I., N.Y.*, Vol. I: *1653-1688*, ed. Charles R. Street (Huntington, NY, 1887); Huntington, NY, First Presbyterian Church, *Records of the First Church in Huntington, Long Island, 1723-1779* (Huntington, NY, 1899); Edward P. Rindler, "The Migration from the New Haven Colony to Newark, East New Jersey: A Study of Puritan Values and Behavior, 1630-1720" (diss. University of Pennsylvania, 1977); Romanah Sammis, *The Records of Huntington, Suffolk County* (Albany, NY, 1921). Suffolk County, New York.

Jamaica, Queens, New York: Anna E. Foote, "The First Presbyterian Church in Jamaica," *NYH*, 22 (1941), 342-43; Jamaica, NY, *Records of the Town of Jamaica, Long Island, New York, 1656-1751*, ed. Josephine B. Frost, 3 vols. (Brooklyn, NY, 1914); Margaret M. Kennedy, "Jamaica, Long Island, during the Colonial and Revolutionary Eras, 1655-1789" (M.A. thesis, Columbia, 1934); James M. MacDonald, *A Sketch of the History of the Presbyterian Church in Jamaica, L.I.* (New York, 1847); *id., Two Centuries in the History of the Presbyterian Church, Jamaica, L.I.* . . . (New York, 1862); Jean B. Peyer, "Jamaica, Long Island, 1656-1776: A Study of the Roots of American Urbanism" (diss. City University of New York, 1974); George W. Winans, *Three Hundred Years of Worship and Service: The First Presbyterian Church in Jamaica, New York, 1662-1962* (Jamaica, NY, 1962); *id., First Presbyterian Church of Jamaica, New York, 1662-1942: A Narrative History of Its Two Hundred and Eighty Years of Continuous Service* (Jamaica, NY, 1943). Queens County, New York.

Jemseg, Massachusetts Bay Province: See entries for New Brunswick, especially William F. E. Morley, *Canadian Local Histories to 1950: A Bibliography,* Vol. 1: *The Atlantic Provinces: Newfoundland, Nova Scotia, New Brunswick, Prince Edward Island.* Queens County, New Brunswick.

Kings County, New York: J. T. Bailey, *An Historical Sketch of the City of Brooklyn* . . . (Brooklyn, NY, 1840); Kings County, NY, Commissioner of Records, *Report of the Commissioner of Records, Kings County* (New York, 1910); Stephen M. Ostrander, *A History of the City of Brooklyn and Kings County* . . . , ed. Alexander Black, 2 vols. (Brooklyn, NY, 1894); Henry R. Stiles et al., *The Civil, Political, Professional, and Ecclesiastical History* . . . *of the County of Kings and the City of Brooklyn, N.Y.* . . . , 2 vols. (New York, 1884).

Lewisboro, New York: J. W. Keeler, "Lewisboro," in J. Thomas Scharf (ed.), *History of Westchester County, New York* . . . , 2 (Philadelphia, 1886), 535-59.

Long Island: Eugene R. Arbruster, *History of Long Island* (Brooklyn, NY, 1914); Paul Bailey, *Long Island: A History* (New York, 1949); Fessenden S. Blanchard, *Long Island Sound* (Princeton, NJ, 1958); James E. Bunce and Richard P. Hammond (eds.), *Long Island as America: A Documentary History to 1896* (Port Washington, NY, 1977); W. Oakley Cagney and Joan D. Berbrich, *The Heritage of Long Island,* Empire State Historical Publications, 90 (Port Washington, NY, 1970); Charles E. Craven, "The Planting of the Puritans on Long Island," *NYH*, 14 (1933), 401-10; Verne Dyson, *Anecdotes and Events in Long Island History,* Empire State Historical Publications Series, 79 (Port Washington, NY, 1969); Martha Bockée Flint, *Early Long Island: A Colonial Study* (New York, 1896); Gabriel Furman, *Antiquities of Long Island* (New York, 1875); Ralph H. Gabriel, *The Evolution of Long Island: A Story of Land and Sea* (New Haven, CT, 1921), based on a 1919 Yale dissertation; Henry Hazleton, *The Boroughs of [New York City] . . . 1609-1824,* 4 vols. (New York, 1925); Long Island Historical Society, *Catalogue of the Library of the Long Island Historical Society, 1863-1893* (Brooklyn, NY, 1893); *id., Proceedings; id., Quarterly;* Sean Manley, *Long Island Discovery* (New York, 1966); Nathaniel S. Prime, *A History of Long Island . . .* (New York, 1845); Karl Proehl and Barbara A. Shupe, *Long Island Gazetteer: A Guide to Current and Historical Place Names* (New York, 1984); Everett T. Rattray, *The South Fork . . .* (New York, 1979); Peter Ross and William S. Pelletreau, *A History of Long Island from Its Earliest Settlement to the Present Time,* 3 vols. (New York, 1905); Richard B. Sealock, *Long Island Bibliography* (Baltimore, MD, 1940); Suffolk Museum of Stony Brook [New York], *Long Island's Religious History . . .* (Stony Brook, NY, 1963); Benjamin F. Thompson, *History of Long Island . . .* (New York, 1839); Charles H. Townshend, *The Early History of Long Island Sound and Its Approaches* (New Haven, CT, 1894); Frederick Van Wyck, *Long Island Colonial Patents* (Boston, 1935); Marilyn E. Weigold, *The American Mediterranean: An Environmental, Economic, and Social History of Long Island Sound* (Port Washington, NY, 1974); Rufus R. Wilson, *Historic Long Island* (New York, 1902); Silas Wood, *A Sketch of the First Settlement of the Several Towns on Long-Island . . .* (Brooklyn, NY, 1865).

Louisbourg, Massachusetts Bay Province: Same as **Port aux Baleines, Nova Scotia**. Cape Breton County, Nova Scotia.

Maspeth, New Netherland Colony: See **Newtown, Queens, New York**. Queens County, New York.

Mortlake, Connecticut Colony: *PRCC,* 3.246-47; in Wabaquassett Country; now Pomfret and Brooklyn, CT; Ellen D. Larned, *History of Windham County, Connecticut,* 2 vols. (Worcester, MA, 1874-80); Richard Mather Bayles, *History of Windham County, Connecticut* (New York, 1889); Allen B. Lincoln (ed.), *A Modern History of Windham County, Connecticut . . .,* 2 vols. (Chicago, 1920). Failed.

Middleburgh, New Netherland Colony: See **Newtown, Queens, New York**. Queens County, New York.

Nansemond, Virginia: Nansemond County, Virginia. "Two 1642 Letters from Virginia Puritans," ed. Jon Butler, *MHSP,* 84 (1973), 99-109; Evelyn Hurf Cross, *Nansemond Chronicles, 1606-1800: Virginia Colony* (n.p., 1973); Joseph B. Dunn, *The History of Nansemond County, Virginia* (Suffolk, VA, 1907?).

Nassau County, New York: Nassau County was set off in 1898 from Queens County, New York. *Nassau County Historical Journal*, 1937-62; *Nassau County Historical Society Journal*, 1962-.

New Brunswick: New Brunswick was ruled by the Massachusetts Bay Province from 1692 to 1714. New Brunswick Province was partitioned off from Nova Scotia in 1784. See also entries for Nova Scotia. Michael Collie, *New Brunswick* (Toronto, 1974); [Peter Fisher], *Sketches of New Brunswick: Containing an Account of the First Settlement of the Province . . .* (Saint John, NB, 1825); William F. Ganong, *Monographs of the Place-nomenclature, Cartography, Historic Sites, Boundaries and Settlement — Origins of the Province of New Brunswick . . .*, Contributions to the History of New Brunswick, #s 1-7, Royal Society of Canada, *Transactions*, Section 2 (1895-1906); the 7 parts are often bound into one volume; Abraham Gesner, *New Brunswick . . . Comprehending the Early History . . .* (London, 1847); James Hannay, *History of New Brunswick*, 2 vols. (St. John, NB, 1909); Calvin F. Hathaway, *The History of New Brunswick, from Its First Settlement . . .* (Fredericton, NB, 1846); William F. E. Morley, *Canadian Local Histories to 1950: A Bibliography*, Vol. 1: *The Atlantic Provinces: Newfoundland, Nova Scotia, New Brunswick, Prince Edward Island* (Toronto, 1967); New Brunswick Historical Society, *Collections*; Alice R. Stewart, *The Atlantic Provinces of Canada: Union Lists of Materials in the Larger Libraries of Maine*, University of Maine Studies, ser. 2 (Orono, ME, 1965); Hugh F. Taylor (ed.), *New Brunswick History: A Checklist of Secondary Sources* (Fredericton, NB, 1971).

New Jersey/East New Jersey/West New Jersey/New Sweden/New Haven Outpost at Varkin's Kill (Salem Creek): Nelson R. Burr, *A Narrative and Descriptive Bibliography of New Jersey*, The New Jersey Historical Series, 21 (Princeton, NJ, 1964); Historical Records Survey, New Jersey, *Inventory of the Church Archives of New Jersey: Presbyterians: Presbyterian Church in the U.S.A. [and] United Presbyterian Church of North America* (Newark, NJ, 1940); Doris M. Perry, *This Is New Jersey: A Tercentenary Bibliography* (Trenton, NJ, 1963).

New Netherland Colony: Gerald F. DeJong, "The Formative Years of the Dutch Reformed Church on Long Island," *Journal of Long Island History*, 8 (Summer-Fall, 1968), 1-16; 9 (Winter-Spring, 1969), 1-20; Albert E. McKinley, "The English and Dutch Towns of New Netherland," *AHR*, 6 (1900), 1-18; New Netherland Colony, *The Register of New Netherland, 1626 to 1674*, ed. Edmund B. O'Callaghan (Albany, NY, 1865); Edmund B.

O'Callaghan, *History of New Netherland; or, New York Under the Dutch,* 2 vols. (New York, 1846-48); Frederick J. Zwierlein, "New Netherland Intolerance," *Catholic Historical Review,* 4 (1918-19), 186-216; id., *Religion in New Netherland: A History of the Development of the Religious Conditions in the Province of New Netherland, 1623-1664* (Rochester, NY, 1910; rpt. New York, 1971), a 1910 University of Louvain dissertation.

New York Colony/New Netherland Colony/Long Island (New Haven Colony and Connecticut Colony): Charles A. Flagg and Judson T. Jennings, *Bibliography of New York State History,* New York State Library, *Bulletin,* 56 (1901), 289-558, rpt. under the same title (Albany, NY, 1901); Historical Records Survey, New York, *Inventory of the Church Archives of New York City: Presbyterian Church in the United States of America* (New York, 1940); Long Island Historical Society, *Catalogue of the Library* (Brooklyn, NY, 1893); Manuel D. Lopez, *New York: A Guide to Information and Reference Sources* (Metuchen, NJ, 1980); Harold Nestler, *A Bibliography of New York State Communities,* Empire State Historical Publications Series, 51 (Port Washington, NY, 1968); New York Colony, *Calendar of Council Minutes, 1668-1783,* ed. A. J. F. Van Laer, New York State Library, *Bulletin, History:* 6, 58 (1902), rpt. under the same title (Albany, NY, 1902); New York Colony, *The Documentary History of the State of New York;* New York Colony, "Annotated List of Manuscripts," ed. George R. Howell and Charles A. Flagg, New York State Library, *Bulletin, History:* 3 (1899); New York Colony, "Colonial Records: General Entries," ed. George R. Howell, New York State Library, *Bulletin, History:* 2 (1899); Richard B. Sealock, *Long Island Bibliography* (Baltimore, MD, 1940).

New York Colony: John Romeyn Brodhead (ed.), *Documents Relating to the Colonial History of the State of New-York; Procured in Holland, England and France . . . ,* 20 vols. (Albany, NY, 1853-87); vols. 12-15 form a new series and are sometimes numbered "n.s., vols. 1-4"; Albert C. Darning et al., *Congregationalists in New York . . .* (New York, 1894); Frederick Van Wyck, *Select Patents of Towns and Manors* (Boston, 1938); Edgar A. Werner, *Civil List and Constitutional History of the Colony and State of New York* (Albany, NY, 1889); Langdon G. Wright, "In Search of Peace and Harmony: New York Communities in the Seventeenth Century," *NYH,* 61 (1980), 5-21.

New York Colony — Society of Friends: Hugh Barbour (ed.), *Quaker Crosscurrents: Three Hundred Years of Friends in the New York Yearly Meetings* (Syracuse, NY, 1995); John Cox, Jr., *Quakerism in the City of New York, 1657-1930* (Rahway, NJ, 1930); Mildred Murphy DeRiggi, "Quakerism on Long Island: The First Fifty Years, 1657-1707" (diss. State University of

New York at Stony Brook, 1994); Henry Onderdonk, Jr., *The Annals of Hempstead; 1643 to 1832: Also the Rise and Growth of Friends on Long Island and in New York City* (Hempstead, NY, 1878).

Newark, New Jersey: Joseph Atkinson, *The History of Newark, New Jersey* . . . (Newark, NJ, 1878); Ann H. Benson, *Newark-in-Print: References to Newark in Books . . . and in Records Which Tell the Story of the Growth of Newark from 1666 through 1930* (Newark, NJ, 1931); *Biographical and Genealogical History of the City of Newark and Essex County, New Jersey,* 2 vols. (New York, 1898); Isaac Watts Crane, *An Oration Delivered in the Presbyterian Church in Newark* . . . (Newark, NJ, 1797); Howard L. Hayes, *Home Lots of the First Settlers of Newark* (Newark, NJ, 1892); *A History of the City of Newark, New Jersey,* 3 vols. (New York, 1913); Daniel Jacobson, "Origins of the Town of Newark," *NJHSP,* 75 (1957), 158-69; Alexander MacWhorter, *A Century Sermon, Preached in Newark, New-Jersey . . . 1801, Containing a Brief History of the Presbyterian Church* . . . (Newark, NJ, 1807); T. Aird Moffat, "Newark Settled by a Congregational Church," *NJHSP,* ser. 3, 10 (1915), 13-24; Newark, NJ, *Records of the Town of Newark, New Jersey, from Its Settlement in 1666, to Its Incorporation as a City in 1836,* ed. Samuel H. Congar, *NJHSC,* 6 (1864); Newark, NJ, First Presbyterian Church, *Church Manual for the Members of the First Presbyterian Church, Newark, N.J.* . . . (Newark, NJ, 1827); Newark, NJ, First Presbyterian Church, *The Old First Presbyterian Church, Newark, N.J., the Founding Church of Newark, 1666-1966* (South Hackensack, NJ, 1966); Walter S. Nichols, "Early Newark as a Puritan Theocracy in Colonial New Jersey," *NJHSP,* ser. 4, 5 (1920), 200-224; David L. Pierson, *Narratives of Newark (in New Jersey) from the Days of Its Founding* (Newark, NJ, 1917); *Proceedings Commemorative of the Settlement of Newark, New Jersey, on Its Two Hundredth Anniversary . . . , NJHSC,* 6-Supplement; Edward S. Rankin, "The Newark-Elizabethtown-Barbadoes Neck Controversy," *NJHSP,* n.s., 11 (1926), 353-64; John L. Rankin, "Newark Town Government from 1666-1833, Part One," *NJHSP,* ser. 3, 10 (1915), 1-12; Arnold S. Rice (ed.), *Newark: A Chronological and Documentary History, 1666-1970* (Dobbs Ferry, NY, 1977); Frederick W. Ricord, *Biographical and Genealogical History of the City of Newark . . . New Jersey,* 2 vols. (New York, 1898); Edward P. Rindler, "The Migration from the New Haven Colony to Newark, East New Jersey: A Study of Puritan Values and Behavior, 1630-1720" (diss. University of Pennsylvania, 1977); Jonathan F. Stearns, *Historical Discourses, Relating to the First Presbyterian Church in Newark . . .* (Newark, NJ, 1853); Charles H. Stewart, *The Founding of Newark by the Puritans . . .* [Newark, NJ, 1916];

Frank J. Urquhart, *A Short History of Newark* (Newark, NJ, 1908); Frank J. Urquhart, *Newark: The Story of Its Early Days* (Newark, NJ, 1904); William R. Ward, "The Old First Church of Newark and Four of Its Pastors," *NJHSP,* 62 (1944), 20-24. Essex County, New Jersey.

Newtown, Queens, New York: Walter J. Hutter et al., *Our Community, It's* [sic] *History and People: Ridgewood, Glendale, Maspeth, Middle Village, Liberty Park* ([Brooklyn, NY], 1976); Jessica Kross, *The Evolution of an American Town: Newtown, New York, 1642-1775* (Philadelphia, 1983); Newtown, Queens, NY, *Town Minutes of Newtown,* 2 vols. (New York, 1940-41); James Riker, Jr., *The Annals of Newtown in Queens County, New York . . .* (New York, 1852); Edward P. Rindler, "The Migration from the New Haven Colony to Newark, East New Jersey: A Study of Puritan Values and Behavior, 1630-1720" (diss. University of Pennsylvania, 1977). Queens County, New York.

Nipmuck Country: *RM,* 5.263; now mainly Worcester County, MA.

Nova Scotia: Nova Scotia was ruled by the Massachusetts Bay Province from 1692 to 1714. New Brunswick Province was partitioned off from Nova Scotia in 1784. See also entries for New Brunswick. *Acadiensis;* John Bartlett Brebner, *New England's Outpost: Acadia before the Conquest of Canada* (New York, 1927), a 1927 Columbia dissertation; Duncan Campbell, *Nova Scotia in Its Historical, Mercantile and Industrial Relations* (Montreal, 1973); Nicolas Denys, *The Description and Natural History of the Coasts of North America (Acadia),* ed. William F. Ganong (Toronto, 1908); Bruce Fergusson and William Pope, *Glimpses into Nova Scotia History* (Windsor, NS, 1974); Charles Bruce Fergusson, *Place-Names and Places of Nova Scotia . . . ,* Publications of the Public Archives of Nova Scotia, Nova Scotia Series, III (Halifax, NS, 1967); Thomas C. Haliburton, *An Historical and Statistical Account of Nova-Scotia . . . ,* 2 vols. (Halifax, NS, 1829); James Hannay, *The History of Acadia, from Its First Discovery to Its Surrender to England by the Treaty of Paris* (St. John, NB, 1879); David Laing, *Royal Letters, Charters, and Tracts, Relating to the Colonization of New Scotland . . . 1621-1638* (Edinburgh, 1867); Peter L. McCreath and John G. Leefe, *A History of Early Nova Scotia* (Tantallon, NS, 1982); Ian F. MacKinnon, *Settlements and Churches in Nova Scotia, 1749-1776* (Montreal, 1930); William F. E. Morley, *Canadian Local Histories to 1950: A Bibliography,* Vol. 1: *The Atlantic Provinces: Newfoundland, Nova Scotia, New Brunswick, Prince Edward Island* (Toronto, 1967); William Inglis Morse (ed.), *Acadiensia Nova (1598-1779) . . . New and Unpublished Documents and Other Data Relating to Acadia (Nova Scotia, New Brunswick, Maine, etc.)* (London, 1935); Beamish Murdoch, *A History of Nova-Scotia, or Acadie,* 2 vols. (Halifax, NS, 1865); Nova Scotia

Historical Society, *Collections;* Agnes C. O'Dea and Anne Alexander (eds.), *Bibliography of Newfoundland*, 2 vols. (Toronto, 1986); George A. Rawlyk, *Nova Scotia's Massachusetts: A Study of Massachusetts–Nova Scotia Relations* (Montreal, 1973); Edith Janet Sloan, "Perilous Early Canada," in Peter Steven Gannon (ed.), *Huguenot Refugees in the Settling of Colonial America* (New York, 1985), 75-88; John G. Reid, *Acadia, Maine, and New Scotland: Marginal Colonies in the Seventeenth Century* (Toronto, 1981); Edouard Richard, *Acadia: Missing Links of a Lost Chapter in American History*, 2 vols. (New York, 1895); Philip H. Smith, *Acadia: A Lost Chapter in American History* (Pawling, NY, 1884).

Oyster Bay, New York: Martha Bockée Flint, *Early Long Island: A Colonial Study* (New York, 1896), 188-97; Van S. Merle-Smith, Jr., *The Village of Oyster Bay: Its Founding and Growth from 1653-1700* (Garden City, NY, 1953); Oyster Bay, NY, *Oyster Bay Town Records*, Vol. 1: *1653-1900*, ed. John Cox, Jr. (New York, 1916). Nassau County, New York.

Port aux Baleines, Massachusetts Bay Province: Same as **Louisbourg, Nova Scotia**. See entries for Nova Scotia, especially William F. E. Morley, *Canadian Local Histories to 1950: A Bibliography*, Vol. 1: *The Atlantic Provinces: Newfoundland, Nova Scotia, New Brunswick, Prince Edward Island* (Toronto, 1967). Cape Breton County, Nova Scotia.

Port Royal, Massachusetts Bay Province: Same as **Annapolis Royal, Nova Scotia**. See entries for Nova Scotia, especially William F. E. Morley, *Canadian Local Histories to 1950: A Bibliography*, Vol. 1: *The Atlantic Provinces: Newfoundland, Nova Scotia, New Brunswick, Prince Edward Island*. Annapolis County, Nova Scotia.

Pound Ridge, New York: Robert Bolton, "The Town of Poundridge," in Robert Bolton, *The History of the Several Towns, Manors, and Patents of the County of Westchester, from Its First Settlement . . .* , ed. C. W. Bolton, 2 (New York, 1881), 102-12; Jay Harris, *God's Country: A History of Pound Ridge, New York* (Chester, CT, 1971); George Thatcher Smith, "Poundridge," in J. Thomas Scharf (ed.), *History of Westchester County, New York . . .* , 2 (Philadelphia, 1886), 561-71. Westchester County, New York.

Providence Island, Colombia: Karen O. Kupperman, *Providence Island, 1630-1641: The Other Puritan Colony* (New York, 1993); Arthur P. Newton, *The Colonising Activities of the English Puritans: The Last Phase of the Elizabethan Struggle with Spain* (1914; new edn. Port Washington, NY, 1966); James Jerome Parsons, *San Andrés and Providencia: English-Speaking Islands in the Western Caribbean*, University of California Publications in Geography, 12, #1 (Berkeley, CA, 1956).

Queens County, New York: *History of Queens County, New York . . .* (New York, 1882).

River St. John, Massachusetts Bay Province: See entries for New Brunswick, especially William F. E. Morley, *Canadian Local Histories to 1950: A Bibliography*, Vol. 1: *The Atlantic Provinces: Newfoundland, Nova Scotia, New Brunswick, Prince Edward Island* (Toronto, 1967). St. John County, New Brunswick.

Rye, New York: Charles W. Baird, *Chronicles of a Border Town: History of Rye . . . 1660-1870 . . .* (New York, 1871); *id.,* "Rye," in J. Thomas Scharf (ed.), *History of Westchester County, New York . . . ,* 2 (Philadelphia, 1886), 643-93; Robert Bolton, "The Town of Harrison," in Robert Bolton, *The History of the Several Towns, Manors, and Patents of the County of Westchester, From its First Settlement . . . ,* ed. C. W. Bolton, 1 (New York, 1881), 361-73; *id.,* "The Town of Rye," in *ibid.,* 2 (New York, 1882), 127-85; *id.,* "The Town of White Plains," in *ibid.,* 2 (New York, 1882), 535-48; Chauncy Ives, *The "World War" History of the Village of Rye, 1917-1918, With an Appendix of a Short, Concise History of Rye . . . 1660, to . . . 1904* (New York, 1923); Louisa C. Lockwood, *The World War History of the City of White Plains, 1917-1918, Together with a Concise Historical Sketch of White Plains from the First Settlement, 1683, to the Incorporation of the City, 1916* (White Plains, NY [?], 1926); Ellen Cotton McKay, *A History of the Rye Presbyterian Church . . .* (Rye, NY, 1957); Josiah S. Mitchell, "White Plains," in J. Thomas Scharf (ed.), *History of Westchester County, New York . . . ,* 2 (Philadelphia, 1886), 714-37; Samuel K. Piercy, *The White Plains [New York] Presbyterian Church, 1722-1922,* ed. Florence Gilbert (White Plains, NY, 1921); Esmond Shaw, *Christ's Church at the Town of Rye . . . New York, 1695-1945* (Rye, NY [?], 1945). Westchester County, New York.

Seppekann, New Plymouth Colony: Now the towns of Marion, Mattapoisett, and Rochester, Massachusetts. Plymouth County, Massachusetts. Failed.

Sagadahoc (Kennebec, Maine): Failed. Alfred A. Cave, "Why Was the Sagadahoc Colony Abandoned? An Evaluation of the Evidence," *NEQ,* 68 (1995), 625-40. Now Phippsburg, ME. Sagadahoc County, Maine.

Setauket, New York: See Brookhaven, New York. Suffolk County, New York.

Smithtown, New York: J. Richard Mehalick, *Church and Community, 1675-1975: The Story of the First Presbyterian Church of Smithtown, New York* (Hicksville, NY, 1976); J. Lawrence Smith, *The History of Smithtown* (1882; Smithtown, NY, 1961), rpt. from *The History of Suffolk County, New*

York . . . (New York, 1882), [Part II] "Town and Village Histories: Smithtown," 1-42 (separate pagination); Smithtown, NY, *The Records of Smithtown,* ed. Frank E. Brush (Albany, NY, 1917).

Southampton, New York: James Trusloe Adams, *History of the Town of Southampton (East of Canoe Place)* (Bridgehampton, NY, 1918); *Addresses Delivered at the Celebration of the 250th Anniversary of the Village and Town of Southampton* . . . (Sag Harbor, NY, 1890); George R. Howell, *The Early History of Southampton, L.I., New York with Genealogies,* 2nd edn. (Albany, NY, 1887); Edward P. Rindler, "The Migration from the New Haven Colony to Newark, East New Jersey: A Study of Puritan Values and Behavior, 1630-1720" (diss. University of Pennsylvania, 1977); Southampton, NY, *Records of the Town of Southampton,* 9 vols., Vol. I: *The First Book of Records of the Town of Southampton with Other Ancient Documents of Historical Value* . . . (Sag Harbor, NY, 1874); Lizbeth H. White, "Southampton: — Her Records and Her Landmarks," *NYH,* 14 (1933), 370-81. Suffolk County, New York.

Southold, New York: Augustus Griffin, *Griffin's Journal: First Settlers of Southold* . . . (Orient, NY, 1857); Chris Hunter, "Southold, Long Island and Its Relation to the New Haven Colony," *NHCHSJ,* 17 (1968), 85-89; Wayland Jefferson, *Cutchogue: Southold's First Colony* (New York, 1940); Charles B. Moore, *Town of Southold, Long Island: Personal Index Prior to 1698, and Index of 1698* (New York, 1868); E. Hoyt Palmer and Maud H. Terry, *A History of the First Presbyterian Church of Southold, Long Island, N.Y.* ([Southold, NY], 1940); Edward P. Rindler, "The Migration from the New Haven Colony to Newark, East New Jersey: A Study of Puritan Values and Behavior, 1630-1720" (diss. University of Pennsylvania, 1977); Southold, NY, *Southold Town Records,* ed. J. Wickham Case, 2 vols. (New York, 1882-84); Epher Whitaker, "The Early History of Southold, Long Island," *NHCHSP,* 2 (1877), 1-29; *id., History of Southold, L.I.: Its First Century* (Southold, NY, 1881). Suffolk County, New York.

Suffolk County, New York: Richard M. Bayles, *Historical and Descriptive Sketches of Suffolk County* . . . (Port Jefferson, NY, 1874); Thomas R. Bayles, *The Ten Towns of Suffolk County, Long Island, New York* (Middle Island, NY, 1964); *History of Suffolk County, New York* . . . (New York, 1882); Henry Nicoll, *Early History of Suffolk County, Long Island* (Brooklyn, NY, 1866); Henry Onderdonk, Jr., *Antiquities of the Parish Church, Hempstead, Including Oyster Bay and the Churches in Suffolk County* (Hempstead, NY, 1878).

Varkin's Kill (Salem Creek), New Jersey: Now Salem, New Jersey. Edward E. Atwater, *History of the Colony of New Haven to Its Absorption into Connecticut,* ed. Robert Atwater Smith et al. (Meriden, CT, 1902), 192-205;

Charles H. Levermore, *The Republic of New Haven, JHUSHPS*, Extra Volume, I (Baltimore, 1886), 90-120; Isabel M. Calder, *The New Haven Colony* (New Haven, CT, 1934), 76-79, 166-67, 184-205; B. Fernow (ed.), *Documents Relating to the History of the Dutch and Swedish Settlements on the Delaware River . . .* , 12 (Albany, NY, 1877), iii-xvii; Albert Cook Myers (ed.), *Narratives of Early Pennsylvania, West New Jersey, and Delaware, 1630-1707*, Original Narratives of Early American History (New York, 1912); Rollin G. Osterweis, *Three Centuries of New Haven, 1638-1938* (New Haven, CT, 1953), 26-31; Epher Whitaker, "New Haven's Adventure on the Delaware Bay," *NHCHSP*, 4 (1888), 209-30. Salem County, New Jersey.

Virginia: Earl G. Swem, *A Bibliography of Virginia* (Richmond, VA, 1916-55).

Wappetaw, Wando Neck, Christ Church Parish, South Carolina: George Howe, *History of the Presbyterian Church in South Carolina*, 2 vols. (Columbia, SC, 1870-83); Mabel L. Weber, "Inscriptions from the Church Yard of the Independent or Congregational Church at Wappetaw, Christ Church Parish," *The South Carolina Historical and Genealogical Magazine* 25 (1924), 136-39. Berkeley County, South Carolina.

Westchester, New York Colony: Now dissolved; not to be confused with Westchester County, New York. Robert Bolton, "The Town of Westchester," in Robert Bolton, *The History of the Several Towns, Manors, and Patents of the County of Westchester, from Its First Settlement . . .* , ed. C. W. Bolton, 2 (New York, 1881), 263-350; Fordham Morris, "Westchester Town," in J. Thomas Scharf (ed.), *History of Westchester County, New York . . .* , 2 (Philadelphia, 1886), 768-817; Frederic Shonnard and W. W. Spooner, *History of Westchester County, New York . . .* (New York, 1900), 83-131, 226-34. Cf. items in Bronx County listing. Bronx County and Westchester County, New York.

Westchester County, New York: Robert Bolton, *A History of the County of Westchester . . .* (New York, 1848); *id., The History of the Several Towns, Manors, and Patents of the County of Westchester, from Its First Settlement . . .* , ed. C. W. Bolton, 2 vols. (New York, 1881); Alvah P. French (ed.), *History of Westchester County, New York*, 5 vols. (New York, 1925-27); Richard Lederer, Jr., *The Place Names of Westchester County, New York* (Harrison, NY, 1978); J. Thomas Scharf (ed.), *History of Westchester County, New York . . .* , 2 vols. (Philadelphia, 1886); Frederic Shonnard and W. W. Spooner, *History of Westchester County, New York . . .* (New York, 1900); Henry Townsend Smith (ed.), *Manual of Westchester County, Past and Present . . .* , 3 vols. (White Plains, NY, 1898-1913); *The Westchester Historian*, 1

(1925)-; WPA, *Historical Development of Westchester County: A Chronology . . .* , 2 vols. (White Plains, NY, 1939). Cf. items in Bronx County, New York, listing.

Woodbridge, New Jersey: W. Woodford Clayton, *History of Union and Middlesex Counties, New Jersey* . . . (Philadelphia, 1882); Joseph W. Dally, *Woodbridge and Vicinity: The Story of a New Jersey Township* (New Brunswick, NJ, 1957); Mrs. Charles W. Jorgensen, *History of the Stelton Baptist Church (Formerly the First Baptist Church of Piscataway), 1689-1964* . . . ([Piscataway, NJ, 1964]); John M. Kreger, *Township of Woodbridge, New Jersey, 1669-1781* (Colonia, NJ, 1976); Oliver B. Leonard, *Outline Sketches of the Pioneer Progenitors of the Piscataway Planters, 1666-1716* . . . (Plainfield, NJ, 1890); Walter C. Meuly, *History of Piscataway Township, 1666-1976* (Somerville, NJ, 1976); Earl S. Miers, *Where the Raritan Flows* (New Brunswick, NJ, [1964]); Orra E. Monnette, *First Settlers of Ye Plantations of Piscataway and Woodbridge, Olde East New Jersey, 1664-1714*, 7 vols. (Los Angeles, 1930-35); Donald J. Mrozek, "The Distribution of Land in Seventeenth-Century Woodbridge, New Jersey," *Journal of the Rutgers University Library*, 35 (1971), 1-14; Piscataway, NJ, "Piscataway Register of Marriages and Deaths from the Town Book (1668-1805)," *NJHSP*, n.s., 4 (1919), 33-43; Piscataway, NJ, First Baptist Church, *History of the First Baptist Church of Piscataway* . . . (Stelton, NJ, 1889); Piscataway, NJ, "Piscataway Register of Births from the Town Book (1671-1793)," ed. William A. Whitehead, *NJHSP*, ser. 3, 2 (1897-98), 73-80; 3 (1898-1900), 10-18; John P. Wall et al., *History of Middlesex County, New Jersey*, 3 vols. (New York, 1921); William A. Whitehead, *Contributions to the Early History of Perth Amboy and Adjoining Country* . . . (New York, 1856), esp. 355-414; Ruth Wolk, *History of Woodbridge* (Woodbridge, NJ, 1875); Woodbridge, NJ, First Presbyterian Church, *History* (Carteret, NJ, 1975). Middlesex County, New Jersey.

III. Geographical Locations and Religious Institutions in New England: Bibliographies and Finding Aids

Much of my work has been based on local town and church records, both published and unpublished. Before I could approach those records, however, I needed to develop a list of all civil and ecclesiastical bodies in New England that were formally instituted before 1709. That list ultimately developed into Appendix 1. However, finding places can be quite a problem in Old England and New England studies, especially in the seventeenth century when in America the boundaries of townships and colonies were fluid. The list began with Frederick L. Weis, *The Colonial Clergy and the Colonial Churches of New England* (Lancaster, MA, 1936). Weis also compiled *The Founders of the Churches of Christ in New England, 1620-1650* (Lancaster, MA, 1943) and wrote a helpful article on "The New England Company of 1649 and Its Missionary Enterprises," *CSMP,* 38 (1947-51), 153-94; this article gives a listing of Native American Praying Towns and organized churches for the entire colonial period. Weis also developed checklists for the remaining early American colonies: *The Colonial Clergy of the Middle Colonies: New York, New Jersey, and Pennsylvania, 1628-1776* (Worcester, MA, 1957); *The Colonial Churches and the Colonial Clergy of the Middle and Southern Colonies, 1607-1776* (Lancaster, MA, 1938). Weis worked from the series of articles in the *American Quarterly Register* that deal with New England history. Richard H. Taylor has also completed a listing for all of New England: *The Churches of Christ of the Congregational Way in New England* (Benton Harbor, MI, 1989); later on, he produced *Southern Congregational Churches* (Benton Harbor, MI, 1994). Another helpful work for all of New England is Peter Benes and Jane Montague Benes (eds.), *New England Prospect: Maps, Place Names, and the Historical Landscape,* 5th Dublin Seminar for New England Folklife (Boston, 1980). The work of Weis was supplemented by a variety of sources, mainly developed by genealogists for their research. The work of the professional genealogists was helpful for my purposes because it was comprehensive and also attentive to the precise local detail that I needed — e.g. which towns were daughters of mother towns, when counties were established, when borders for localities were changed. Especially helpful for all of New England was Marcia Wiswall Lindberg, *Genealogist's Handbook for New England Research* (3rd edn., Boston, 1993). Terence M. Punch's *Genealogist's Handbook for Atlantic Canada Research* (Boston, 1989) was helpful for identifying Canadian communities that were under the authority of the Massachusetts Bay Province from 1691 through 1713. Many of these resources are cataloged under the Library of Congress subject heading "(Name of State) — Administrative and Political Divisions." Other helpful works on the entire region included: John W. Barber, *The History and Antiquities of New England, New York and New Jersey . . .* (Worcester, MA, 1841) and Joseph B. Felt, *The Ecclesiastical History of New England,* 2 vols. (Boston, 1855-62). The bibliographies of church and town records listed in the next section also helped to identify geographical settlements and religious institutions.

For the **Anglicans**, it is easiest to divide the resources by state, but there are some resources for the entire region of New England that are helpful: Kenneth W. Cameron (ed.), *Ethos of Anglicanism in Colonial New England and New York: Gleanings from the S.P.G. Abstracts (1704-1785) Concerning the Church of England in the Northern Plantations and Nearby Areas* . . . (Hartford, CT, 1981); id., *The Episcopal Church in Connecticut and New England: A Bibliography* (Hartford, CT, 1981), which was preceded by *Anglicanism in Early Connecticut and New England: A Selective Bibliography* (Hartford, CT, 1977); J. P. K. Henshaw, *A Discourse Delivered in Grace Church, Providence, on the Occasion of the . . . One Hundred and Fiftieth Anniversary of the Society for the Propagation of the Gospel in Foreign Parts . . .* (Providence, RI, 1851). For Connecticut, cf. E. Edwards Beardsley, *The History of the Episcopal Church in Connecticut . . .* , 2 vols. (New York, 1865-68); Kenneth W. Cameron (ed.), *Historical Resources of the Episcopal Diocese of Connecticut* (Hartford, CT, 1966); id., *Early Anglicanism in Connecticut . . .* (Hartford, CT, 1962); Samuel Hart, *How the [Episcopal] Church Came to Connecticut* (Hartford, 1936); id., "Historical Sermon," *Connecticut Churchman*, 1 (1907), 17-26; Francis L. Hawks and William S. Perry (eds.), *Documentary History of the Protestant Episcopal Church in the United States . . . Connecticut . . .* , 2 vols. in 1 (1863-64; rpt. Hartford, CT, 1959); Lucy J. Jarvis, *Sketches of Church Life in Colonial Connecticut . . .* (New Haven, CT, 1902); Hector G. L. M. Kinloch, "Anglican Clergy in Connecticut, 1701-1785" (diss. Yale, 1960); Maud O'Neil, "A Struggle for Religious Liberty: An Analysis of the Work of the S.P.G. in Connecticut," *HMPEC*, 20 (1951), 173-89; Edgar L. Pennington, *Church of England Beginnings in Connecticut . . .* (Hartford, CT, 1938); Origen S. Seymour, *The Beginnings of the Episcopal Church in Connecticut* ([New Haven], 1934); David H. Villers, "Connecticut Anglicanism and Society to 1783: A Review of the Historians," *HMPEC*, 53 (1984), 45-59; WPA, Historical Records Survey, *Inventory of the Church Archives of Connecticut: Protestant Episcopal* (New Haven, CT, 1940). For Rhode Island, cf. Edgar L. Pennington, *The First Hundred Years of the Church of England in Rhode Island* (Hartford, CT, [1935]); Dudley Tyng, *Rhode Island Episcopalians, 1653-1953 . . .* (Providence, RI, [1954]). For Massachusetts, cf. Edward Midwinter, "The Society for the Propagation of the Gospel and the Church in the American Colonies, III: Massachusetts," *HMPEC*, 4 (1935), 100-115; Henry L. Parker, "The Anglican Church in the Colonies," Worcester Historical Society, *Proceedings*, 1887, 182-207; Edgar L. Pennington, "Anglican Beginnings in Massachusetts," *HMPEC*, 10 (1941), 242-89; William S. Perry (ed.), *Papers Relating to the History of the*

[Episcopal] Church in Massachusetts, A.D. 1676-1785 (Boston, 1873); Dudley Tyng, Massachusetts Episcopalians, 1607-1957 (Pascoag, RI, 1957). For New Hampshire, cf. Edgar L. Pennington, Story and Pageant: The Church of England in Colonial New Hampshire . . . (Hartford, CT, 1937). For Maine, cf. Edward Ballard, "The Early History of the Protestant Episcopal Church in the Diocese of Maine," MeHSC, 6 (1859), 171-202; Lawrence Crumb, "The Anglican Church in Colonial Maine," HMPEC, 33 (1964), 251-60.

For the **Baptists**, cf. Isaac Backus, A History of New England with Special Reference to the Denomination of Christians Called Baptists, 2nd edn., ed. by David Weston, 2 vols. (1871; rpt. Paris, AR, n.d., The Baptist History Series, #s 3-4); John W. Brush, Baptists in Massachusetts (Valley Forge, PA, 1970); Henry S. Burrage, History of the Baptists in Maine (Portland, ME, 1904); C. Raymond Chappell, Baptists in New Hampshire ([Manchester, NH, 1950]); John L. Denison, Some Items of Baptist History in Connecticut (Philadelphia, 1900); Morgan Edwards, "Materials for a History of the Baptists in Rhode Island," RIHSC, 6 (1867), 301-70; Robert G. Gardner, Baptists of Early America: A Statistical History, 1639-1790 (Atlanta, GA, 1983); "Historical Sketch of the Baptist Denomination in Maine," Baptist Memorial and Chronicle, 3 (1843), 353-63; Katherine W. Johnson, Rhode Island Baptists: Their Zeal, Their Times (Valley Forge, PA, 1970); Joshua Millet, A History of the Baptists in Maine . . . (Portland, ME, 1845); William H. Shailer, A Historical Discourse . . . (Portland, ME, 1874); "The Six Principle Baptists in the Narragansett Country," Narragensett Historical Register, 1 (1882-83), 203-8; WPA, Historical Records Survey, Rhode Island, Inventory of the Church Archives of Rhode Island: Baptist (Providence, RI, 1941); WPA, Historical Records Survey, New Jersey, Inventory of the Church Archives of New Jersey: Baptist Bodies, Seventh Day Baptist Supplement (Newark, NJ, 1939), which includes material on all Seventh Day Baptist churches, since the denomination's headquarters and archives were located in New Jersey at the time of publication.

For the **Huguenots**, cf. Jon Butler, The Huguenots in America : A Refugee People in New World Society (Cambridge, MA, 1983); Abraham D. Lavender, French Huguenots: From Mediterranean Catholics to White Anglo-Saxon Protestants (New York, 1990); Huguenot Society of America, Proceedings.

The Society of Friends, or Quakers, found themselves at odds with the established civil authorities of early New England and organized themselves in a manner that paid less attention to the colonial boundaries established by those authorities. The best resource for discerning where the

Quakers were in early New England can be found in Thomas C. Hill, *Monthly Meetings in North America: A Quaker Index,* 4th edn. (Cincinnati, OH, 1997). For Long Island, cf. William Wade Hinshaw, Thomas Worth Marshall, and John Cox, Jr., *Encyclopedia of American Quaker Genealogy* (Ann Arbor, MI, 1936-50), esp. Vol. III (1940), which deals with New York and Long Island (see under records, below), along with the listings under **New York Colony — Society of Friends**, above.

The various colonies/states also have helpful resources for identifying colonial New England communities and religious bodies. For **Maine**, cf. Ava H. Chadbourne, *Maine Place Names and the Peopling of Its Towns* (Portland, ME, 1955); Michael J. Denis, *Maine Towns and Counties: What Was What, Where and When* (Oakland, ME, 1981); Joel N. Eno, "The Expansion of Maine — Chronological — Based on Official Records," *Americana* 25 (1931), 380-410; Jonathan Greenleaf, *Sketches of the Ecclesiastical History of the State of Maine, from the Earliest Settlement . . .* (Portsmouth, NH, 1821); Moses Greenleaf, *A Survey of the State of Maine . . .* (Portland, ME, 1829); WPA, Historical Records Survey, Maine, *Counties, Cities, Towns and Plantations of Maine: A Handbook of Incorporations, Dissolutions, and Boundary Changes* (Portland, ME, 1940; rpt. Augusta, ME, 1980); *id., Directory of Churches and Religious Organizations in Maine* (Portland, ME, 1940); *The Maine Atlas and Gazetteer . . .* (Yarmouth, ME, 1979); Albert P. Marble, *Geography of Maine* (Cincinnati, OH, 1880); Phillip R. Rutherford, *The Dictionary of Maine Place-Names* (Freeport, ME, 1971); George J. Varnes, *A Gazetteer of the State of Maine* (Boston, 1881); Joseph Whipple, *A Geographical View of the History of Maine* (Bangor, ME, 1816).

For **New Hampshire**, cf. James G. Carter, *A Geography of New-Hampshire . . .* (Portsmouth, NH, 1831); "Churches . . . in New Hampshire," *MHSC,* ser. 3, 1 (1825), 153-55 and 2 (1830), 299-322; Michael J. Denis, *New Hampshire Towns and Counties: What was What, Where and When* (Oakland, ME, 1982); *Documents and Records Relating to Towns in New Hampshire . . . , NHSP,* 9 (1875); *Documents Relating to Towns in New Hampshire, NHSP,* 11-13 (1882-84); Joel N. Eno, "The Expansion of New Hampshire — Chronological — from Provincial, State, and Town Papers," *Americana,* 25 (1931), 83-99; John Farmer, *An Ecclesiastical Register of New-Hampshire . . . 1623 to 1822 . . .* (Concord, NH, 1821); John Farmer and Jacob B. Moore, *A Gazetteer of the State of New-Hampshire* (Concord, NH, 1823); John Farmer, "A List of the Congregational and Presbyterian Ministers in the State of New Hampshire . . . to the Year 1834 . . . ," *AQR,* 6 (1833-34), 234-49; Alonzo J. Fogg, *The Statistics and Gazetteer of New-Hampshire* (Concord, NH, 1874);

John Hayward, *A Gazetteer of New Hampshire* . . . (Boston, 1849); Henry A. Hazen, "Ministry and Churches of New Hampshire," *CQ*, 17 (1875), 545-74; 18 (1876), 283-314, 592-600; Elmer M. Hunt, *New Hampshire Town Names and Whence They Came* (Peterborough, NH, 1971); Robert F. Lawrence, *The New Hampshire Churches* . . . (Claremont, NH, 1856); Asa McFarland, "Names of Counties and Towns in New Hampshire," *Granite Monthly*, 1 (1877-78), 120-22; Eliphalet Merrill and Phineas Merrill, *Gazetteer of the State of New Hampshire* . . . (Exeter, NH, 1817); *New Hampshire Town and City Notes*, 1 (1948)-; *New Hampshire Town Charters*, ed. Albert S. Batchillor, *NHSP*, 24-29 (1894-96); Edwin D. Sanborn, *Churches of New Hampshire* . . . (Bristol, NH, 1876).

For **Massachusetts**, cf. John W. Barber, *Historical Collections of Every Town in Massachusetts* (Worcester, MA, 1839); James G. Carter, *A Geography of Massachusetts* . . . (Boston, 1830); Joseph S. Clark, *A Historical Sketch of the Congregational Churches in Massachusetts* . . . *1620-1858* (Boston, 1858); Charlotte P. Davis, *Directory of Massachusetts Place Names: Current and Obsolete Counties, Cities, Towns, Sections or Villages, Early Names* (Lexington, MA, 1987); William T. Davis, *Ancient Landmarks of Plymouth*, 2 vols. (2nd edn., Boston, 1899); Michael J. Denis, *Massachusetts Towns and Counties: What Was What, Where and When* (Oakland, ME, 1984); John Eliot, "Ecclesiastical History of Massachusetts," *MHSC*, ser. 1, 7 (1800), 262-80; 9 (1804), 1-49; 10 (1809), 1-37; ser. 2, 1 (1814), 194-210; Joel N. Eno, "The Expansion of New England as Begun in Plymouth," *Americana*, 23 (1929), 403-10; *id.*, "The Expansion of Massachusetts — Chronological — Based on the Official Records," *Americana*, 24 (1930), 28-40; Henry Gannett, *A Geographical Dictionary of Massachusetts* (Washington, D.C., 1894); [Thomas Greenleaf], *Geographical Gazetteer of the Towns in the Commonwealth of Massachusetts* (Boston, 1784-85); John Hayward, *A Gazetteer of Massachusetts* . . . , rev. edn. (Boston, 1849); Albert P. Marble, *Geography of Massachusetts* (Cincinnati, OH, 1878); Massachusetts Geodetic Survey, *Massachusetts Localities: A Finding List of Massachusetts Cities and Towns* . . . ([Boston], 1938); Massachusetts, Secretary of the Commonwealth (also identified as the Secretary of State), *Historical Data Relating to Counties, Cities and Towns in Massachusetts*, ed. William Francis Galvin (1920; 5th edn., Boston, 1997); Elias Nason, *A Gazetteer of the State of Massachusetts* . . . (Boston, 1874); Jeremiah Spofford, *A Historical and Statistical Gazetteer of Massachusetts* . . . (Haverhill, MA, 1860); WPA, Massachusetts, Writers' Project, *The Origins of Massachusetts Place Names of the State, Counties, Cities, and Towns* (New York, 1941).

For **Rhode Island**, cf. Henry Gannett, *A Geographic Dictionary of Rhode Island* (Washington, DC, 1894); Henry Jackson, *An Account of the Churches in Rhode-Island . . .* (Providence, RI, 1854); WPA, Federal Writers' Project, Rhode Island, *Rhode Island: A Guide to the Smallest State* (Boston, 1937).

For **Connecticut**, cf. John W. Barber, *Connecticut Historical Connections* (New Haven, CT, 1836); Ann P. Barry, "Connecticut Towns and Their Establishment" (Hartford, CT, 1989; leaflet of the Connecticut State Library); [Albert C. Bates], *List of Congregational Ecclesiastical Societies Established in Connecticut before October, 1818, with Their Changes* (Hartford, CT, 1913); Calvin A. Carter, "Connecticut Boroughs," *NHCHSP,* 4 (1888), 139-92; Franklin B. Dexter, "The History of Connecticut, as Illustrated by the Names of Her Towns . . . ," *AASP,* n.s., 3 (1885), 421-48; Joel N. Eno, "The Expansion of Connecticut — Chronological — Based on the Official Records," *Americana,* 24 (1930), 401-11; General Association of Connecticut, *Contributions to the Ecclesiastical History of Connecticut {Volume I}* (New Haven, CT, 1861); Connecticut Conference of the United Church of Christ (successor to the General Association of Connecticut), *Contributions to the Ecclesiastical History of Connecticut: Volume II* (n.p., 1967); Arthur H. Hughes and Morse S. Allen (eds.), *Connecticut Place Names* (Hartford, CT, 1976); A. D. Jones, *The Illustrated . . . Gazetteer . . . of Connecticut* (New Haven, CT, 1857); Benjamin Trumbull, *A Complete History of Connecticut, Civil and Ecclesiastical . . . ,* 2 vols. (1797; rpt. New London, CT, 1898); Benjamin Trumbull (ed.), "Extracts of Letters to Rev. Thomas Prince, Containing Historical Notions of Sundry Towns," *CHSC,* 3 (1895), 271-320; Silas Wood, *A Sketch of the First Settlement of the Several Towns on Long-Island . . .* (Brooklyn, NY, 1865).

For **New York**, cf. John W. Barber and Henry Howe, *Historical Collections of the State of New York . . .* (New York, 1841); Richard M. Bayles, *Historical and Descriptive Sketches of Suffolk County . . .* (Port Jefferson, NY, 1874); Albert C. Carning et al., *Congregationalists in New York . . .* (New York, 1894); J. H. French, *Gazetteer of the State of New York . . .* (Syracuse, NY, 1860); H. T. F. Gordon, *Gazetteer of the State of New York* (Philadelphia, 1836); Albert E. McKinley, "The English and Dutch Towns of New Netherland," *AHR,* 6 (1900), 1-18; Robert H. Nichols, *Presbyterianism in New York State: A History of the Synod and Its Predecessors* (Philadelphia, 1963); Nathaniel S. Prime, *A History of Long Island . . .* (New York, 1845); Karl Proehl and Barbara A. Shupe, *Long Island Gazetteer: A Guide to Current and Historical Place Names* (New York, 1984); Peter Ross and William S.

Pelletreau, *A History of Long Island from Its Earliest Settlement to the Present Time*, 3 vols. (New York, 1905); H. G. Spofford, *A Gazetteer of the State of New-York* . . . (1813; 2nd edn., Albany, NY, 1824); Silas L. Wood, *A Sketch of the First Settlement of the Several Towns on Long-Island* . . . , 1865 edn. ed. Alden J. Spooner (Brooklyn, NY, 1865).

For **New Jersey**, cf. John W. Barber and Henry Howe, *Historical Collections of New Jersey* . . . (New Haven, CT, 1868); *A Geographical Dictionary of New Jersey* (Baltimore, 1978); Thomas F. Gordon, *Gazetteer of the State of New Jersey* (Cottonwood, LA, 1973); New Jersey, State, Department of Transportation, *Local Names, Municipalities and Counties in New Jersey* (Trenton, NJ, 1995).

For **Virginia**, cf. Joseph Martin, *A New and Comprehensive Gazetteer of Virginia and the District of Columbia* . . . (Charlottesville, VA, 1836).

For the **United States**, cf. U.S. Geological Survey, *The National Gazetteer of the United States of America* (Washington, DC, 1982).

Counties have not been quite as important as administrative units in New England as towns have been. However, the following are helpful references for identifying counties: John H. Long (ed.) and Gordon Den Boer, *Atlas of Historical County Boundaries: Connecticut, Maine, Massachusetts, Rhode Island* (New York, 1994); Kathryn Ford Thorne and John H. Long, *Atlas of Historical County Boundaries: New York* (New York, 1993). P. William Filby (ed.), *A Bibliography of American County Histories* (Baltimore, 1987), is also a helpful reference work.

IV. Bibliographies and Finding Aids for Unpublished Town and Church Records

Once a baseline list of communities had been established, the search for church and town records was made easier by the following resources. The CNEB, of course, listed most, if not all, of the published records of churches and towns. However, the published records represented less than 50 percent of the total surviving records. We therefore had to turn to unpublished town and church records. Many, but certainly not all, of these unpublished records can be accessed on microfilm through The Family History Library System of The Church of Jesus Christ of Latter-day Saints, described below. However, the following reference sources made locating these records much easier.

For all of **New England**, Ann S. Lainhart, *Digging for Genealogical*

Treasure in New England Town Records (Boston, 1996) is a recent guide. The Works Project Administration (WPA) of the 1930s, led by Luther H. Evans, prepared the Historical Records Survey just before World War II. The projects relevant to New England are listed individually by state. However, readers should be aware of the following guides: WPA, *Index of Research Projects,* 1 (Washington, DC, 1938), 56-65, #s 589-796 and 3 (Washington, DC, 1939), 47, #s 4198-4206; *id., Bibliography of Research Projects Reports: Check List of Historical Records Survey Publications,* WPA Technical Series, Research and Records Projects Bibliography No. 4 (Washington, DC, 1940); *id., Bibliography of Research Projects Reports: Check List of Historical Records Survey Publications,* ed. Sargent B. Child, Dorothy P. Holmes, and Cyril E. Paquin, WPA Technical Series, Research and Records Bibliography No. 7 (Washington, DC, 1943) (this supersedes the 1940 edition). In 1980, a guide to the *unpublished* Historical Records Survey material was completed by Loretta L. Hefner: *The WPA Historical Records Survey: A Guide to the Unpublished Inventories, Indexes, and Transcripts* (Chicago, 1980). The tragedy of what happened to many of the unpublished New England WPA materials can be found in Leonard Rapport, "Dumped from a Wharf into Casco Bay: The Historical Records Survey Revisited," *American Archivist,* 37 (1974), 201-10.

For **Maine**, cf. {Joseph C. Anderson II} et al., "Early Congregational Churches in Maine: Locations of Original Records and Transcripts," *The Maine Genealogist,* 16 (1994), 47-49, 72-76; *id.,* "Saints and Sinners: Exploring Congregational Church Records," *The Maine Genealogist,* 17 (1995), 84-91; *Maine's Historical Records: A Guide to Collections of Original, Unpublished Materials* (Augusta, ME, 1992); WPA, Historical Records Survey, Maine, *Inventory of the Town and City Archives of Maine,* 7 vols. (Portland, ME, 1938-40); *id., Town Government in Maine . . .* (Portland, ME, 1940).

For **New Hampshire**, cf. WPA, Historical Records Survey, New Hampshire, *Guide to the Church Vital Statistics Records in New Hampshire,* preliminary edn. (Manchester, NH, 1942); *id., Inventory of the Town Archives of New Hampshire,* 10 vols. (Manchester, NH, 1939-42); *id., Guide to Depositories of Manuscript Collections in the United States: New Hampshire,* preliminary edn. (Manchester, NH, 1940).

For **Massachusetts**, Harold Field Worthley's *An Inventory of the Records of the Particular (Congregational) Churches of Massachusetts Gathered 1620-1805,* Harvard Theological Studies, 25/UHSP, 16, #1-2 (Cambridge, MA, 1970) is priceless and saved me vast quantities of time. Cf. also Richard Bowen, *Massachusetts Records: A Handbook . . .* (Rehoboth, MA, 1957);

John M. Bumsted, "Bibliography . . . of Church, Town and Parish Records," in *The Pilgrim's Progress: The Ecclesiastical History of the Old Colony, 1620-1775* (New York, 1989), a 1965 Brown dissertation; Mary F. Morgan, "Records of Massachusetts Congregational Churches," Massachusetts Genealogical Council, *Newsletter,* 2 (1983), #4, 2-3; reprinted and updated as Massachusetts Genealogical Council Publication, 3 (n.p., 1997); Frederick L. Weis, Christopher R. Eliot, and Robert D. Richardson, "Early Records of the Seventeenth Century Churches in Massachusetts Which Became Unitarian," *UHSP,* 7 (1940-41), #2, 11-22; Carroll D. Wright, *Report on the Custody and Condition of the Public Records of Parishes, Towns, and Counties* (Boston, 1889); WPA, Historical Records Survey, Massachusetts, *Inventory of City and Town Archives of Massachusetts,* 22 vols. (Boston, 1939-42); *id., Guide to the Public Vital Records in Massachusetts* (Boston, 1942).

For **Rhode Island**, cf. WPA, Historical Records Survey, Rhode Island, *Inventory of the Church Archives of Rhode Island: Society of Friends* (Providence, RI, 1939); *id., Inventory of the Church Archives of Rhode Island: Baptist* (Providence, RI, 1941).

In **Connecticut**, many of the town and church records were deposited in the Connecticut State Library in Hartford. Cf. State of Connecticut, Examiner of Public Records, *Report of the Examiner of Public Records* (Hartford, CT, 1913-). The Connecticut State Library's *Bulletin (CSLB)* has done an excellent job of providing guides to the local records: Connecticut State Library, *Progress of Work upon the Public Records and Archives . . . , CSLB,* 6 (1914); *id., Instructions for Care of Archives in the Connecticut State Library,* prepared by Effie M. Prickett, *CSLB,* 8 (1920) (actually a guide to the archives); *id., Select List of Manuscripts in the Connecticut State Library, CSLB,* 9 (1920); *id., History, Progress and Work of the Emery Record Preserving Co., Taunton, Mass., in Connection with the Public Records of Our Land,* prepared by Allen P. Hoard, *CSLB,* 12 (1926); *id., Connecticut Town Records, June 30, 1930,* prepared by Lucius B. Barbour, *CSLB,* 15 (1930); *id., List of Church Records on Deposit at Connecticut State Library as of March 1, 1942, CSLB,* 18 (1942); *id., List of Church Records on Deposit at Connecticut State Library as of September 1, 1951, CSLB,* 19 (1951).

The Society of Friends, or Quakers, established a New England Yearly Meeting that was connected to the New York Yearly Meeting. The Archives of the New England Yearly Meeting of the Society of Friends are located at the Rhode Island Historical Society, Providence, Rhode Island; many of the early records are on microfilm; cf. WPA, Historical Records Survey, Rhode Island, *Inventory of the Church Archives of Rhode Island: Soci-*

ety of Friends, along with Archives of the New England Yearly Meeting of
Friends at the Rhode Island Historical Society Library, *Guide to the New En-
gland Yearly Meeting of Friends (Quaker) Microfilm Collection* (TS, April
1993; located on site at the Rhode Island Historical Society Library). The
New York Yearly Meeting maintained an Archives at the Haviland Records
Room in Manhattan, New York. As of December 31, 1997, the archives of
the Haviland Records Room, formerly located at 15 Rutherford Place, New
York, New York 10003 were relocated to the Friends Historical Library at
Swarthmore College, 500 College Avenue, Swarthmore, Pennsylvania
19081. Most of the records are available via the Family History Library Sys-
tem. A useful introduction to Quaker records by non-Quakers is Ellen
Thomas Berry and David Allen Berry, *Our Quaker Ancestors: Finding Them
in Quaker Records* (Baltimore, 1987).

V. Unpublished Town and Church Records
Available via The Family History Library System
of The Church of Jesus Christ of Latter-day Saints

As part of its vast genealogical endeavors, The Family History Library System of The Church of Jesus Christ of Latter-day Saints maintains a microfilm collection of church and town records of all geographical localities in
the Western world, including seventeenth-century New England. Its resources were especially useful for locating unpublished records for this period, and at times I utilized the System to access books and pamphlets that
were difficult to find. The Family History Library Catalog™ is now available online. Library branches are called centers and are usually connected
to local congregations of The Church of Jesus Christ of Latter-day Saints.

In this monograph citations of many unpublished church and town
records utilize a Family History Library System Microfilm Number
(FHLC™M #). At times, there are cases where there is an overlap of microfilms: i.e. a microfilm may have been made in 1952, but a second microfilm-
ing team came several decades later with better equipment to make a better
copy. Furthermore, transcriptions were often made by local historians. In
order to minimize confusion, *each* relevant microfilm is listed below, even if
there is a certain amount of overlap. I should also note that at times records
from more recent periods are listed. In that case what is listed is the earliest
record that exists for a particular locality or religious institution, and these
records were explored in the hope that the clerk might have put in some

"retrospective records" from the "old book" that was decaying or was burned but no longer exists today. Finally, if there was a case in which there were little if any town records, I ordered the first volume of land records that existed in the hope that at the beginning of the voluminous land records there might be some town records that would include a civil covenant.

I would like to extend my thanks to Mr. David Bishop and the staff members of the Westchester, New York, Family History Center (located in Scarsdale, New York) and the Family History Library of Salt Lake City, Utah, for their help in securing many microfilms for me.

If a town or church is not listed here, then its records are either a.) published (and thus listed in the CNEB or in Section II of the Bibliographical Essay: "A Bibliography of Towns, Churches, and Regions Not Included in the Work of the Committee for a New England Bibliography (CNEB)" (cf. above); b) non-existent, or c) unpublished and unavailable via the Family History Library System. In this listing, the names of towns and localities are cited as found in the Family History Library Catalog™. The titles of the manuscripts, as listed in The Family History Library Catalog™ have been occasionally modified for purposes of conciseness; the titles on the title pages in the microfilms themselves are so varied and inconsistent that it is impossible to list them as in a traditional bibliography of published works. Furthermore, the records are sometimes a potpourri of miscellaneous items, some with their own title pages, some just gathered together with hardly any identification at all except that they came from the early days of the settlement of a locale. Thus, the Call Numbers (FHLC™M #) are the best way to access these records, for the Call Numbers follow a standard system. The Family History Library System maintains an Internet website and CD-ROM whereby the Family History Library Catalog™ can be searched via Call Numbers; this makes referencing the list below easier because for each community there are sometime hundreds of microfilms that cover records that stretch well into the twentieth century.

Berwick, ME. Minutes of Parish and Selectmen Meetings, [1701-1812]. . . .
    FHLC™M #: 0010552.
Berwick, ME. Town and Vital Records, 1701-1776. FHLC™M #: 0010551.
Boston, MA. Earliest Records of the Town of Boston, 1634-60. FHLC™M #:
    0477587.
Boston, MA. King's Chapel. Church Records . . . 1703- . . . FHLC™M #:
    0837128.

Boxford, MA. First Parish Church. Church Records, 1702- . . . FHLC™M #: 0877752.

Bradford, MA. Records of Town Meetings, 1668-1842. FHLC™M #: 0893123.

Branford, CT. Land Records, Vols. 1-2, 1645-1710. FHLC™M #: 0003699.

Branford, CT. First Church. Church Records, 1687-1899. FHLC™M #: 0003712.

Bridgeport, CT. United Congregational Church. Church Records, Vols. 1-3, 1695-1911. FHLC™M #: 0003830.

Bridgeport, CT. United Congregational Church. Church Records, Vol. 6. FHLC™M #: 00013832.

Dorchester, SC [Midway, GA]. Midway Congregational Church. Church Records, 1754-1867. FHLC™M #s: 0203209, 0203210, 0203211.

Dunstable, MA. [Town Records]: Births, Marriages and Deaths, 1679-1844; Proceedings. . . . FHLC™M #: 0763713.

East Haddam, CT. Land Records, Vol. 1., 1687-1725. FHLC™M #: 0004096.

East Haddam, CT. Land Records, General Index. FHLC™M #: 0004110.

East Haddam, CT. First Church. First Congregational Church and Ecclesiastical Society, Church Records, 1702-1837. FHLC™M #: 0004112.

East Haddam, CT. First Church. Record of the First Congregational Church at East Haddam, Connecticut, ed. Gertrude A. Barber. FHLC™M #: 0547537.

Eastham, MA. Town Records, 1643-1770. FHLC™M #: 0905407.

Eastham, MA. Town Records, 1654-1863 (Transcription). FHLC™M #: 0907350.

Fairton, NJ. Fairfield Presbyterian Church. Church Records, 1759-1970. FHLC™M #: 1310562.

Fairton, NJ. [Fairfield Presbyterian Church]. Presbyterian Church Records, 1759-1846 (Typescript). FHLC™M #: 0006302.

Farmington, CT. First Church. Church Records, Vols. 1-5, 1652-1938. FHLC™M #: 0004241.

Glastonbury, CT. Land Records, Vols. 1-3, 1690-1737. FHLC™M #: 0004377.

Greenwich, CT. Town Records, 1658-1848. FHLC™M #: 0185372.

Greenwich, CT. Land Records, 1640-1724. FHLC™M #: 0004313.

Greenwich, RI. Society of Friends. Monthly Meeting. Greenwich Monthly Meeting Records, 1699-1900. FHLC™M #: 0001332.

Groton, CT. Land Records, Vols. 1A-1B, 1705-1723. FHLC™M #: 0004293.

Haddam, CT. Land Records, Vols. 1-2. FHLC™M #: 0004464.

Hartford, CT. Second Church. Records, 1669-1731, transcribed by Nathaniel Goodwin. FHLC™M #: 1010728. Listed under "Goodwin" in the FHLC™.

Killingworth, CT. Town Records (Land), Vols. 1-3, 1664-1738. FHLC™M #: 0004621.

Lebanon, CT. Land Records, Vol. 1, 1695-1730. FHLC™M #: 0004707.

Lebanon, CT. Land Records, Vols. 2-3, 1706-25. FHLC™M #: 0004708.

Lebanon, CT. First Church. Church Records, 1700-1883. FHLC™M #: 1010739.

Mansfield, CT. Proprietors Records, 1702-1730. FHLC™M #: 0004865.

Marblehead, MA. Town Records, 1648-1839. FHLC™M #: 0864833.

Marblehead, MA. Town Records, 1649-1788. FHLC™M #: 0864834.

Medford, MA. Town Records, 1675-1791. FHLC™M #: 0968005.

Medford, MA. Town Records, 1673-1781 (Transcription). FHLC™M #: 0886758.

Medford, MA. First Church. Church Records, 1712-1823. FHLC™M #: 0886764.

Middleboro, MA. Town Records, 1658-1705, 1746-1802 (Transcription). FHLC™M #: 0945011.

Middleboro, MA. Proprietors Records, 1661-1887. FHLC™M #: 0945018.

Middletown, CT. Land Records, Vols. 1-2, 1654-1742. FHLC™M #: 0004792.

Middletown, CT. First Church. Church Records, 1668-1871. FHLC™M #: 0004848.

Midway, GA. See Dorchester, SC.

Milford, CT. Land Records, Vols. 1-4, 1639-1798. FHLC™M #: 0004918.

Milford, CT. First Church. Church Records, 1639-1964. FHLC™M #: 1012263.

Nantucket, MA. Society of Friends. Monthly Meeting. Nantucket Monthly Meeting Records, 1660-1899. FHLC™M #s: 0909501, 0909502, 0909503.

Nantucket, MA. Society of Friends. Monthly Meeting. Nantucket Monthly Meeting Records, 1602-1944. FHLC™M #: 0912142.

Nantucket, MA. Society of Friends. Monthly Meeting. Nantucket Monthly Meeting Records, 1708-1873. FHLC™M #: 0014776.

New Bedford, MA. Society of Friends. Monthly Meeting. New Bedford Monthly Meeting Minutes, 1698-1887. FHLC™M #: 0001337.

New York. Society of Friends. New York Yearly Meeting. Memorials . . . of Deceased Friends (Manuscript). FHLC™M #: 00017353.

New York. Society of Friends. New York Yearly Meeting. New York Yearly Meeting Friends Records, 1671-1792 (Transcription). Transcribed by John W. Cox and George W. Cox. FHLC™M #: 0017256.

Pembroke, MA. Society of Friends. Pembroke Monthly Meeting. Records, 1676-1876. FHLC™M #: 0001335.

Preston, CT. Town Records, 1706-43. FHLC™M #: 0005380.

Preston, CT. Town Records (Land), Vols. 1-3, 1687-1722. FHLC™M #: 0005381.

Preston, CT. Town Records (Land), General Index. FHLC™M #: 0005392.

Preston, CT. First Church. Church Records, 1698-1917. FHLC™M #: 1011968.

Reading, MA. Town Records, 1638-1814. FHLC™M #: 0886200.

Rochester, MA. Records, Proprietors, Vital and Town, 1673-1893. FHLC™M #: 0482220.

Rochester, MA. Town and Vital Records, 1694-1866. FHLC™M #: 0482224.

Rowley, MA. Town Meeting Records, 1648-1832. FHLC™M #: 0887752.

Rowley, MA. Early Records of the Town of Rowley . . . 1639-1672. FHLC™M #: 0887760.

Sandwich, MA. Society of Friends. Sandwich Monthly Meeting. Records, 1672-1818. FHLC™M #: 0001330.

Seabrook, NH. Society of Friends. Seabrook Monthly Meeting. Men's Minutes, 1701-1804. FHLC™M #: 0001313.

Seabrook, NH. Society of Friends. Seabrook Monthly Meeting. Women's Minutes, 1701-1888. FHLC™M #: 0001315.

Springfield, MA. Town Records, Various Civil Records, 1638-1736. FHLC™M #: 0480835.

Springfield, MA. Proceedings of Town Meetings, Vol. 3, 1664-1736. FHLSM #: 0904748.

Springfield, MA. Proceedings of Town Meetings, Vol. 3, 1664-1736 (Typescript). FHLSM #: 0886994.

Stow, MA. Town Records, 1660-1779. FHLSM #: 0815617.

Suffield, CT. First Church. Church Records, 1741-1917. FHLC™M #: 1014184.

Swansea, MA. Parish Register (Transcription). FHLC™M #: 0104833.

Tiverton, RI. Tiverton Town Meetings and Receipts from 1600s. FHLC™M #: 0802451.

Tiverton, RI. Town Meetings, 1697-1906. . . . FHLC™M #: 0913076.
Tiverton, RI. Proprietors Records, 1679-1817 (Transcription). FHLC™M
     #: 0913078.
Wallingford, CT. Deeds, Vol. 1-2, 1670-1716. FHLC™M #: 0006018.
York, ME. York Records. FHLC™M #: 0012837.

VI. Colony Records

I found that the records for the central government of each colony were
harder to trace than I had originally imagined. There were several reasons
for this problem. First, corporate bodies use different names to describe
themselves (e.g., Massachusetts has a General Court; Virginia has a House
of Burgesses). Second, the various colonies had variegated systems of uni-
cameral legislatures, bicameral legislatures, councils of safety, and autocratic regimes, systems which changed over time. Third, the functions of
the ruling bodies, particularly the legislative and judicial, were mixed.
Finally, there are some gaps, which in some cases have now been filled after
the official records had been published; usually this has been done by the
publication of missing journals and records in the serials listed in the *Abbreviations* list. The only comprehensive listing of legislative and judicial
records for all thirteen colonies is excellent but now dated: Library of Congress, *A Guide to the Microfilm Collection of Early State Records,* ed.
Lillian A. Hamrick and William S. Jenkins, 2 vols. (Washington, DC, 1950-
51). The microfilm collection itself consists both of printed and manuscript
works, and is a vast collection. Whenever I wanted to investigate a gap in
the central records of a colony the *Guide* usually had an answer. Like the
modern bibliographies, it is arranged by state, not by colony. Three other
helpful articles are David H. Flaherty, "A Select Guide to the Manuscript
Court Records of Colonial New England," *American Journal of Legal History,* 11 (1967), 107-26; William Jeffrey, "Early New England Court Records: A Bibliography of Published Materials," *ibid.,* 1 (1957), 119-47;
Herta Prager and William W. Price, "A Bibliography on the History of the
Courts of the Thirteen Original States, Maine, Ohio and Vermont," *ibid.,* 1
(1957), 336-62 and 2 (1958), 32-52, 148-54; and Richard B. Morris, *Studies
in the History of American Law with Special Reference to the Seventeenth and
Eighteenth Centuries,* 2nd edn. (New York, 1964), esp. Chapter V: "Bibliographical Essay," 259-73.
     Another complicating factor in the legislative records of the

seventeenth-century colonies is the fact that the regime of Governor Edmund Andros ruled all of the existing colonies in New England, along with the New York Colony, from December 1686–April 1689. The period after 1689 and before 1692 marks a time when the various colonies recovered from the shock of the Andros administration. Connecticut and Rhode Island returned to their original charters and conducted business as usual. Massachusetts had no charter, for its charter had been vacated in October 1684. Therefore, Governor Simon Bradstreet formed another Council of Safety and ruled not only the Massachusetts Bay Colony but also New Hampshire and Maine by this council. Herbert Parker, *Courts and Lawyers of New England* (New York, 1931), states that New Hampshire had no government except town government during the period 1689-92; cf. 2.497. For a summary of the Andros regime, see Viola F. Barnes, *The Dominion of New England: A Study in British Colonial Policy* (New Haven, CT, 1923); cf. also *Calendar of State Papers, Colonial Series: Edward Randolph,* ed. Robert Toppan, Prince Society Publications (Boston, 1898-99).

The following is as comprehensive a listing as possible of the central records for each of the colonies in this study. After the record listings relevant secondary articles are arranged alphabetically.

Connecticut

The Connecticut Colony was founded in 1639 by representatives of three towns (Wethersfield, Windsor, and Hartford) whose inhabitants had migrated three years earlier from the Massachusetts Bay Colony.

Connecticut. Colony. General Court. *The Public Records of the Colony of Connecticut . . .* , ed. J. Hammond Trumbull, Vols. 1-5 (1636-1716) (Hartford, CT, 1850-70).
Connecticut. Colony. Particular Court. *Record of the Particular Court of Connecticut, 1639-1663, CHSC,* 22 (1928).

The Dominion of New England/The Andros Regime

The Dominion of New England (DNE) included all of New England and New York and existed from January 1686/7 to April 1689. The DNE was headquartered in Boston. The legislative records of the colonies in some cases continue to record activities of the colonial governments and legislatures during that time period, and should therefore be consulted as well.

New Hampshire. Province. *Laws of New Hampshire . . .* , ed. Albert S. Batchellor, Vol. 1: *Province Period* (Manchester, NH, 1904); contains all of the Andros Regime laws for New Hampshire.

The Andros Records, ed. Robert N. Toppan, *AASP,* n.s., 13 (1899-1900), 237-68, 463-99. December 20, 1686–March 17, 1686/7 and May 4, 1687–March 27, 1689.

The Glorious Revolution in Massachusetts: Selected Documents, 1689-1692, ed. Robert E. Moody and Richard C. Simmons, *CSMP,* 64 (1988). This work includes all available legislative documents.

Calendar of State Papers, Colonial Series: Edward Randolph, ed. Robert Toppan, Prince Society Publications (Boston, 1898-99).

Randolph, Edward. *Edward Randolph: Including His Letters and Official Papers from the New England, Middle and Southern Colonies in America, With Other Documents Relating Chiefly to the Vacating of the Royal Charter of the Colony of Massachusetts Bay, 1676-1703,* ed. Robert N. Toppan and Alfred T. S. Goodrich, 7 vols. (Boston, 1898-1909).

Documents Relative to the Colonial History of New York . . . , Vol. 3, ed. Edmund B. O'Callaghan (Albany, NY, 1853).

Barnes, Viola F. *The Dominion of New England: A Study in British Colonial Policy* (New Haven, CT, 1923).

Maine

Maine was a series of independent colonies until the territory was subsumed by the Massachusetts Bay Colony in the 1650s. It was a province of Massachusetts until the Missouri Compromise in 1820, when it became a state.

Council for New England. "Records of the Council for New England," *AASP,* ser. 1, 1867, 53-131; 1875, 49-63. The Gorges group, established in 1620. The original records are in the Public Record Office, London. This company dissolved in 1635-38.

Maine. Province. *Province and Court Records of Maine,* ed. Maine Historical Society, 4 vols. (Portland, ME, 1928-58).

Maine. Province. "Extracts from the Early Records of the Province of Maine," *MeHSC,* ser. 1, 1 (1865), 363-402.

Maryland

The Colony of Maryland was founded in 1634 as a Roman Catholic colony.

Maryland. Colony and State. *Archives of Maryland*, 72 vols. (Baltimore, MD, 1883-1972).

Massachusetts

The Massachusetts Bay Colony received its charter in 1629 from the Crown. It had a continuous existence until 1686, when it was ruled by a Council of Safety from May to December. Its charter had already been vacated by order of Charles II in October 1684. In January 1686/7 Governor Edmund Andros took over and ruled all of New England and New York as the "Dominion of New England." Andros was in control until 1689, when he was overthrown and eventually sent back to England. After the capture of Andros the elected government of the Massachusetts Bay Colony was restored, but without a charter. Finally, in 1692 a new charter was granted from William and Mary. The Massachusetts Bay Colony merged with Plymouth Colony to become the Province of Massachusetts Bay.

Massachusetts Bay. Company. "Records of the Company of the Massachusetts Bay, to the Embarkation of Winthrop and His Associates for New England," *AASTC*, 3 (1857), ix-cxxxviii, 1-107.

Massachusetts Bay. Governor and Company. *Records of the Governor and Company of the Massachusetts Bay in New England . . .* , ed. Nathaniel B. Shurtleff . . . , 5 vols. (Boston, 1853-54).

Massachusetts Bay. Court of Assistants. *Records of the Court of Assistants in Massachusetts Bay, 1630-1692*, ed. John E. Noble, 3 vols. (Boston, 1901-28).

Massachusetts Bay. Colony. Council of Safety. "Dudley Records," *MHSP*, ser. 2, 13 (1899), 226-85. May 25, 1686–December 16, 1686.

The Glorious Revolution in Massachusetts: Selected Documents, 1689-1692, ed. Robert E. Moody and Richard C. Simmons, *CSMP*, 64 (1988). This work includes all available legislative documents.

Massachusetts Bay. Province. *The Acts and Resolves, Public and Private, of the Province of the Massachusetts Bay . . .* , Vols. 1-9, 21 (Boston, 1869-1922).

Black, Barbara A. "The Judicial Power and the General Court in Early Massachusetts (1634-1686)" (diss. Yale, 1975).

Pearson, George E. "The Great and General Court of Massachusetts, 1628-1691: A Study of its Early History with Special Reference to Its Organization" (diss. Tufts, 1910).

Rose-Troup, Frances. *The Massachusetts Bay Company and Its Predecessors* (New York, 1930).

New Hampshire

New Hampshire was a series of independent colonies until 1641, when they began to be slowly subsumed during the 1640s into the Massachusetts Bay Colony; in 1679 New Hampshire was chartered as a Royal Province, but Massachusetts Bay Colony still directed it.

New Hampshire. Province. *Documents and Records Relating to the Province of New-Hampshire, from the Earliest Period of Its Settlement: 1623-1686, NHHSP,* 1 (1867).

New Hampshire. Province. *Documents and Records Relating to the Province of New Hampshire, from 1686 to 1722, NHHSP,* 2 (1868).

New Hampshire. Province. *Province Records and Court Papers from 1680 to 1692 . . . , NHHSC,* 8 (1866).

New Hampshire. Province. *Laws of New Hampshire . . . ,* ed. Albert S. Batchellor, Vol. 1: *Province Period* (Manchester, NH, 1904); contains all of the Andros Regime laws for New Hampshire.

New Hampshire. Province. *Documents and Records Relating to the Province of New-Hampshire, from 1692 to 1722 . . . Containing the "Journal of the Council and General Assembly," NHHSP,* 3 (1869).

Documents and Records Relating to Towns in New Hampshire . . . , NHHSP, 9 (1875).

Documents Relating to Towns in New Hampshire, NHHSP, 11 (1882)–13 (1884).

New Hampshire Town Charters, NHHSP, 24 (1894)–29 (1896).

New Hampshire. *[Provincial and State Papers],* ed. Nathaniel Bouton, Isaac W. Hammond, Albert S. Batchellor, Henry H. Metcalf, and Otis G. Hammond, 40 vols. (Concord, NH, 1867-1943).

Batchellor, Albert S. *The Government and Laws of New Hampshire Before the Establishment of the Province, 1623-1679* (Manchester, NH, 1904).

Mevers, Frank C., and Harriet C. Lacy. "Early Historical Records (c. 1620–

c. 1817) at the New Hampshire State Archives," *HNH*, 31 (1976), 108-18.

Wallace, R. Stuart. "The *State Papers*? A Descriptive Guide," *HNH*, 31 (1976), 119-28.

New Haven Colony

New Haven Colony was founded in 1639 and merged with Connecticut Colony in December 1664.

New Haven. Colony. *Records of the Colony and Plantation of New Haven, from 1638 to 1659,* ed. Charles J. Hoadly (Hartford, CT, 1857).

New Haven. Colony. *Records of the Colony or Jurisdiction of New Haven, From May, 1653, to the Union . . .* , ed. Charles J. Hoadly (Hartford, CT, 1858).

New Jersey

New Netherland ruled the area called New Jersey until 1664. In 1676 it was divided up into the Province of East New Jersey and the Province of West New Jersey. In 1702 the Provinces were reunited under the same royal governor.

New Jersey. Colony. *Documents Relating to the Colonial History of the State of New Jersey . . .* [Archives of the State of New Jersey; also called the New Jersey Archives]; ser. 1, 1 (1880)–42 (1949); ser. 2, 1 (1901)–5 (1917); ser. 3, 1 (1974)-.

New Jersey. Governor and Council of East New Jersey. *Record of the Governor and Coun^cill in East Jersie . . . [1682-1714], New Jersey Archives,* ser. 1, 13 (1890); an earlier uncritical edition is *The Journell of the Procedure of the Governor and Councill of the Province of East New Jersey from After the First Day of December Anno Dmni 1682* (Jersey City, NJ, 1872).

New Jersey. General Board of Proprietors of the Eastern Division of New Jersey. *The Minutes of the Board of Proprietors of the Eastern Division of New Jersey . . . 1685-1764,* ed. George J. Miller, 3 vols. (Perth Amboy, NJ, 1949-85).

Lyon, Adrian. *The Records of the East Jersey Proprietors* ([Newark, NJ, 1916]).

New Jersey. Council of Proprietors of the Western Division of New Jersey [Council of Proprietors of West New Jersey]. *Records of the Proprietors of the Western Division of New Jersey.* (Microfilms on deposit at the New Jersey State Archives).

New Jersey. Province of West New Jersey. *The Concessions and Agreements of the Proprietors, Freeholders and Inhabitants of the Province of West New Jersey in America,* ed. Henry H. Bisbee (Burlington, NJ, 1951).

New Jersey Historical Commission. *The West Jersey Concessions and Agreements of 1676/77: A Round Table of Historians,* Occasional Papers, 1 (Trenton, NJ, 1979).

The Proprietors of East New Jersey functioned from 1684 to 1998. Their headquarters was the Surveyor General's Office, City Hall Square, Perth Amboy, New Jersey. The Proprietors of West New Jersey are still functioning and based in the Surveyor General's Office, West Broad Street, between High and Wood Streets, Burlington, New Jersey; cf. Austin Scott, "The Influence of the Proprietors in Founding the State of New Jersey," *JHUSHPS,* ser. 3, # VIII (Baltimore, 1885), 439-60; John M. Metzger, "The General Board of Proprietors of the Eastern Division of New Jersey, 1684-1998: Survey of a Land Company," *NJHSP,* 118 (2000), 3-33.

New Netherland Colony

New Netherland had its beginnings with the arrival of Henry Hudson in 1609. The English conquered it in 1664; the Dutch won parts of it back in 1673-74, but then lost it again.

New Netherland. Colony. *The Register of New Netherland, 1626 to 1674,* ed. Edmund B. O'Callaghan (Albany, 1865).

The Documentary History of the State of New-York . . . , ed. Edmund B. O'Callaghan, 4 vols. (Albany, NY, 1850-51); esp. Vol. 4, #s 1-6.

Documents Relative to the Colonial History of the State of New York Procured in Holland, England and France . . . , Vols. 1-11 (Albany, NY, 1856-61).

New York

New York Colony began in 1664, after the area had been dominated by New Netherland Colony since 1609. The Netherlands managed to reclaim some of its territory temporarily in 1674, but soon lost it. The records for New York Colony begin in 1686 with the Andros regime.

Documents Relative to the Colonial History of New York . . . , Vol. 3, ed. Edmund B. O'Callaghan (Albany, NY, 1853).

New York. Colony. General Assembly. *Journal of the Votes and Proceedings of the General Assembly of the Colony of New York*, Vol. 1: . . . *1691* . . . *1743*, ed. Abraham Lott, Jr. (New York, 1764).

New York. Colony. "The Missing New York Assembly Journal of April, 1692," ed. Lawrence A. Leder, *NYHSQ*, 49 (1965), 5-27.

New York. Colony. Supreme Court of Judicature. *[Minutes of the] Supreme Court of Judicature of the Province of New York, 1691-1704*, ed. Paul M. Hamlin and Charles E. Baker, *NYHSC*, 78 (1945)–80 (1947).

New York. Colony. Legislative Council. *Journal of the Legislative Council of the Colony of New York*, Vol. 1: . . . *1691 [to] 1743* (Albany, NY, 1861).

New York. Colony. "Colonial Records: General Entries," ed. George R. Howell, New York State Library, *Bulletin, History: 2* (1899).

New York. Colony. *Calendar of Council Minutes, 1668-1783*, ed. A. J. F. Van Laer (Albany, NY, 1902); rpt. from New York State Library, *Bulletin, History: 6*, 58 (1902).

The Documentary History of the State of New-York . . . , ed. Edmund B. O'Callaghan, 4 vols. (Albany, NY, 1850-51).

Documents Relative to the Colonial History of the State of New York Procured in Holland, England and France . . . , Vols. 1-11 (Albany, NY, 1856-61).

Documents Relating to the Colonial History of the State of New-York; Procured in Holland, England and France . . . , ed. B. Fernow, 4 vols. (Albany, NY, 1881-87). These volumes are connected to the earlier series of 1856-61, and can be numbered Vols. 1-15 or an 1856-87 series. Furthermore, vols. 12-15 form a new series and are sometimes numbered "n.s., vols. 1-4."

Plymouth Colony (New Plymouth Colony/"The Old Colony")

The Plymouth Colony was founded by Separatist Puritans in 1620. It merged with the Massachusetts Bay Colony in 1692 to form the Massachusetts Bay Province.

New Plymouth. Colony. *Records of the Colony of New Plymouth in New England*, ed. Nathaniel B. Shurtleff and David B. Pulsifer, 12 vols. (Boston, 1855-61).

Rhode Island

Like New Hampshire, Rhode Island was a series of independent colonies until Roger Williams secured a charter for the "Colony of Rhode Island and Providence Plantations" in 1644.

Rhode Island. Colony. *Records of the Colony of Rhode Island and Providence Plantations in New England,* ed. John R. Bartlett, Vols. 1-4, 1636-1740 (Providence, RI, 1856-59).

"Chronology and Documents of Rhode Island, 1634-1683," *MHSC,* ser. 1, 5 (1798), 216-52.

"Rhode Island State Papers," *MHSC,* ser. 2, 7 (1818), 75-113.

Virginia

The Virginia Colony was founded in 1607. In 1624 it became a royal colony.

Virginia Company of London. *The Records of the Virginia Company of London . . . [1609-1626],* ed. Susan Myra Kingsbury, 4 vols. (Washington, DC, 1906).

Brown, Alexander. *The Genesis of the United States: A Narrative of the Movement, 1605-1616, Which Resulted in the Plantation of North America by Englishmen . . . Set Forth through a Series of Historical Manuscripts . . . Tracts . . . and Brief Biographies,* 2 vols. (London, 1890).

Craven, Wesley Frank. *Dissolution of the Virginia Company: The Failure of a Colonial Experiment* (New York, 1932).

Kingsbury, Susan Myra. *An Introduction to the Records of the Virginia Company of London . . .* (Washington, DC, 1905).

Neill, Edward D. *History of the Virginia Company of London . . .* (Albany, NY, 1869).

Virginia Colony. Council. *Executive Journals of the Council of Colonial Virginia,* 6 vols. (Richmond, VA, 1925-66).

Virginia Colony. Council. *Legislative Journals of the Council of Virginia,* 3 vols. (Richmond, VA, 1918).

Virginia Colony. Council. *Minutes of the Council and General Court of Colonial Virginia,* 2nd edn. (Richmond, VA, 1979).

Virginia Colony. House of Burgesses. *Journals of the House of Burgesses of Virginia, 1619-1776,* 13 vols. (Richmond, VA, 1905-15).

Virginia Colony. *The Statutes at Large . . . ,* ed. William Waller Hening, 13 vols. (Richmond, VA, 1809-23; 2nd edn. New York, 1823).

Virginia. Colony. "Some Acts Not in Hening's *Statutes* . . .," ed. Warren M. Billings and Jon Kukla, *Virginia Magazine of History and Biography*, 83 (1975), 22-76, 77-97.

Andrews, Matthew Page. *The Soul of a Nation: The Founding of Virginia and the Projection of New England* (New York, 1943).

Brown, Alexander. *The First Republic in America* . . . (Boston, 1898).

Meyer, Virginia M., and John Frederick Dorman. *Adventurers of Purse and Person, Virginia, 1607-1624/5*, 3nd edn. (Richmond, VA, 1987).

Sam, Conway Whittle. *The Conquest of Virginia: The Second Attempt* . . . (Norfolk, VA, 1929).

VII. Puritanism and Congregationalism

It is well known that the works on New England Puritanism are legion. I am making no attempt to chonicle that vast body of literature in detail here. The following works describe the contours of the field during the twentieth century: Darrett B. Rutman, "God's Bridge Falling Down: 'Another Approach' to New England Puritanism Assayed," *WMQ*, ser. 3, 19 (1962), 408-21; Michael McGiffert, "American Puritan Studies in the 1960s," *WMQ*, ser. 3, 27 (1970), 36-67; Stanley B. Rushing, "The Recovery of New England Puritanism: A Historiographical Investigation" (diss. New Orleans Baptist Theological Seminary, 1971); Laura B. Ricard, "New England Puritan Studies in the 1970s," *F + H*, 15 (1983), #2, 6-27; David D. Hall, "On Common Ground: The Coherence of American Puritan Studies," *WMQ*, ser. 3, 44 (1987), 193-229. Michael Montgomery has compiled a very useful bibliography of dissertations on American Puritanism: Michael S. Montgomery (ed.), *American Puritan Studies: An Annotated Bibliography of Dissertations, 1882-1981* (Westport, CT, 1984).

For Congregationalism as a movement and as a form of church government, see the following: Preston Cummings, *A Dictionary of Congregational Usages and Principles According to Ancient and Modern Authors*, 8th edn. (Boston, 1856); Joseph B. Felt, *Ecclesiastical History of New England*, 2 vols. (Boston, 1855-62); Bruce L. Shelley, "Congregationalism and American Culture," *F + H*, 21 (1989), #2, 38-50; J. William T. Youngs, *The Congregationalists*, Denominations in America, 4 (New York, 1990); John von Rohr, *The Shaping of American Congregationalism, 1620-1957* (Cleveland,

OH, 1992); James F. Cooper, Jr., *Tenacious of Their Liberties: The Congrega-tionalists in Colonial Massachusetts* (New York, 1999).

VIII. Reference Works

A Dictionary of English Church History, ed. S. L. Ollard, 2nd edn. (London, 1948); *Encyclopedia of Politics and Religion,* ed. Robert Wuthnow (Wash-ington, DC, 1998); *Encyclopedia of the American Constitution,* 2nd edn., ed. Leonard W. Levy and Kenneth L. Karst, 6 vols. (New York, 2000); *The New Schaff-Herzog Encyclopedia of Religious Knowledge,* 13 vols. (New York, 1908-14); *The Oxford English Dictionary . . . ,* 12 vols. (Oxford, 1933); *Theologische Realencyklopädie* (Berlin, 1977-). For biographical informa-tion, see the following: *Dictionary of American Biography,* 29 vols. (New York, 1928-90); *Dictionary of American Religious Biography,* 2nd edn., ed. Henry W. Bowden (Westport, CT, 1993); *Dictionary of National Biography,* 32 vols. (Oxford, 1885-1990); James Savage, *A Genealogical Dictionary of the First Settlers of New England . . . ,* 4 vols. (1860-62; rpt. Baltimore, 1965); John L. Sibley and Clifford K. Shipton, eds., *Biographical Sketches of Graduates of Harvard University . . . ,* Vols. 1-5 (Cambridge, MA and Boston, MA, 1873-1937); William B. Sprague, *Annals of the American Pulpit,* 9 vols. (New York, 1857-69); Frederick L. Weis, *The Colonial Clergy and the Colo-nial Churches of New England* (Lancaster, MA, 1936); *id., The Colonial Clergy of the Middle Colonies: New York, New Jersey, and Pennsylvania, 1628-1776* (Worcester, MA, 1957); *id., The Colonial Churches and the Colonial Clergy of the Middle and Southern Colonies, 1607-1776* (Lancaster, MA, 1938).

IX. General Bibliographies

The following items, listed alphabetically, will help fill in details of biblio-graphical information: *America: History and Life,* 1- (Santa Barbara, CA, 1964-); David L. Ammerman and Philip D. Morgan, *Books about Early America: 2001 Titles* (Williamsburg, VA, 1989); T. D. Seymour Bassett, "A List of New England Bibliographies," *NEQ,* 44 (1971), 278-300; *Biblio-graphic Guide to North American History* (Boston, 1977-) (produced annu-ally); "Bibliography of Congregational Church History," *TCHS,* 2 (1905-6), 119-35, 337-38; "Bibliography of Congregationalism," *TCHS,* 9 (1924-26),

200-203; Edward H. Bloomfield, *The Opposition to the English Separatists, 1570-1625: A Survey of the Polemical Literature Written by the Opponents to Separatism* (Washington, DC, 1981); British Museum, Department of Printed Books, Thomason Collection, *Catalogue of the Pamphlets, Books, Newspapers and Manuscripts Relating to the Civil War, the Commonwealth, and Restoration, Collected by George Thomason, 1640-1661,* 2 vols. (London, 1908); Nelson R. Burr, *Critical Bibliography of Religion in America* (Princeton, NJ, 1961); *id., Religion in American Life* (New York, 1971); Congregational Library, London, *A Catalogue of the Congregational Library . . . ,* 2 vols. (London, 1895-1910); Thomas J. Davis (ed.), *The Reformed Traditions, 16th-19th Centuries: A Bibliography Selected from the ATLA Religion Database* (Chicago, 1986); Henry Martyn Dexter, *Collections Toward a Bibliography of Congregationalism* (New York, 1880); Charles Evans, *American Bibliography,* Vol. 1: *1639-1729* (New York, 1941); also Roger P. Bristol, *Supplement to Charles Evans' American Bibliography* (Charlottesville, VA, 1970); Harriette M. Forbes (ed.), *New England Diaries, 1602-1800: A Descriptive Catalogue of Diaries . . .* (Topsfield, MA, 1923); Appleton P. Griffin, "Bibliography of the Historical Publications of the New England States," *CSMP,* 3 (1895), 94-139, rpt. under the title *Bibliography of the Historical Publications Issued by the New England States . . .* (Cambridge, MA, 1895); Leonard A. Jones and Frank Ellsworth Chipman (eds.), *An Index to Legal Periodical Literature,* 6 vols. (Boston, 1888-1939), supplemented and continued by *Index to Legal Periodicals and Law Library Journal* (New York, 1908-94); Ronald D. Karr (ed.), "New England Community Studies Since 1960: A Bibliography," *NEHGR,* 138 (1984), 186-202, 290-308; Peter Milward, *Religious Controversies of the Elizabethan Age: A Survey of Printed Sources* (Lincoln, NE, 1977); *id., Religious Controversies of the Jacobean Age: A Survey of Printed Sources* (Lincoln, NE, 1978); Peter G. Mode, *Source Book and Bibliographical Guide for American Church History* (Boston, 1964), esp. Chapters 4-7; Verne D. Morey, "American Congregationalism: A Critical Bibliography, 1900-1952," *CH,* 21 (1952), 323-44; New York Public Library, *Dictionary Catalog of the History of the Americas,* 28 vols. (Boston, 1961); *id., Dictionary Catalog of the History of the Americas, Supplement,* 9 vols. (Boston, 1973); *id., Dictionary Catalog of the Research Libraries of the New York Public Library, 1911-1971,* 800 vols. (Boston, 1979); *National Union Catalogue, Pre-1956 Imprints . . . ,* 754 vols. (London, 1968-80); Corrine M. Nordquest, "Congregationalism in America: Its Origins, History and Polity: A Bibliography," *BCL,* 13 (1961-62), #2, 5-11; #3, 4-9; George Selement, "A Checklist of Manuscript Materials Relating to

Seventeenth-Century New England Printed in Historical Collections," New York Public Library, *Bulletin*, 79 (1975-76), 416-34; *A Short-Title Catalogue of Books Printed in England, Scotland and Ireland and of English Books Printed Abroad, 1475-1640*, ed. Alfred W. Pollard and Gilbert R. Redgrave (London, 1926); *Short-Title Catalogue of Books Printed in England, Scotland, Ireland, Wales and British America and of English Books Printed in Other Countries, 1641-1700*, ed. Donald Wing, John J. Morrison, Carolyn W. Nelson, and Matthew Seccombe, 2nd edn., revised and enlarged, 2 vols. (New York, 1982-94); James W. Smith and Leland Jamison (eds.), *Religion in American Life*, 3 vols. (Princeton, NJ, 1961); University Microfilms International, Ann Arbor, MI, *Accessing Early English Books, 1641-1700*, 4 vols. (Ann Arbor, MI, 1981-82); *id.*, *Early English Books, 1641-1700: A Cumulative Index to Units 1-60 of the Microfilm Collection*, 9 vols. (Ann Arbor, MI, 1990); *id.*, *The Thomason Tracts, 1640-1661: An Index to the Microfilm Edition of the Thomason Collection of the British Library*, 2 vols. (Ann Arbor, MI, 1981); H. G. Tibbutt, "Sources for Congregational Church History," *TCHS*, 19 (1960), 33-38; Alden T. Vaughan, *The American Colonies in the Seventeenth Century*, Goldentree Bibliographies in American History (New York, 1971); David A. Weir, "A Bibliography of the Federal Theology and the Covenant Idea before 1750," in *The Origins of the Federal Theology in Sixteenth-Century Reformation Thought* (Oxford, 1990), 160-95; *id.*, "Church Covenanting in Seventeenth-Century New England" (diss. Princeton University, 1992), 380-93, and notes, 293-363; John F. Wilson, *Church and State in America: A Bibliographical Guide: The Colonial and Early National Periods* (New York, 1986).

Notes

Notes to Introduction

1. *The Whole Booke of Psalmes Faithfully Translated into English Metre . . .* ([Cambridge, MA], 1640); hereinafter referred to as the Bay Psalm Book.

2. Perry Miller, *The New England Mind,* vol. 1, *The Seventeenth Century* (Cambridge, MA, 1939) and vol. 2, *From Colony to Province* (Cambridge, MA, 1953) along with James F. Hoopes, ed., *Sources for The New England Mind: The Seventeenth Century* (Williamsburg, VA, 1981); Perry Miller, "The Marrow of Puritan Divinity," *CSMP,* 32 (1935), 247-300; *id.,* "The Puritan Theory of the Sacraments in Seventeenth Century New England," *Catholic Historical Review,* 22 (1937), 409-25. For a discussion of Miller's legacy, cf. Gene Wise, "Implicit Irony in Perry Miller's *New England Mind," JHI,* 29 (1968), 579-600; George M. Marsden, "Perry Miller's Rehabilitation of the Puritans: A Critique," *CH,* 39 (1970), 91-105; Stanley B. Rushing, "The Recovery of New England Puritanism: A Historiographical Investigation" (diss. New Orleans Baptist Theological Seminary, 1971); Stanford J. Searl, Jr., "Perry Miller as Artist: Piety and Imagination in *The New England Mind: The Seventeenth Century," EAL,* 12 (1977-78), 221-33; Bruce Tucker, "Early American Intellectual History after Perry Miller," *CRevAS,* 13 (1982), 145-57; Francis T. Butts, "Norman Fiering and the Revision of Perry Miller," *CRevAS,* 17 (1986), 1-25.

3. (Chicago, 1917).

4. The colonial charters have been collected and reprinted in a superb collection edited by Francis N. Thorpe: *The Federal and State Constitutions, Colonial Charters and Other Organic Laws of the States,* 7 vols. (Washington, DC, 1909; Gross Pointe, MI, 1968 and St. Clair Shores, MI, 1977); earlier editions of this collection were edited under the title *The Federal and State Constitutions, Colonial Charters, and Other Organic Laws of the United States,* ed. Benjamin Perley Poore, 2 vols. (Washington, DC, 1877), and 2nd edn. (Washington, DC, 1878). William MacDonald compiled and edited a reader of similar documents designed for classroom use: *Select Charters and Other Documents Illustrative of American History, 1606-1775* (New York, 1899); however, MacDonald's work suffers from the abridgements and superficiality needed for the publication of such a volume. Donald Lutz completed a similar project that also featured abridgements: *Documents of*

Political Foundation Written by Colonial Americans: From Covenant to Constitution (Philadelphia, 1986). Cf. also William F. Swindler, *Sources and Documents of United States Constitutions,* 10 vols. (Dobbs Ferry, NY, 1973-79).

The most recent commentary on this topic is by Jack P. Greene, *Peripheries and Center: Constitutional Development in the Extended Polities of the British Empire and the United States, 1607-1789* (Athens, GA, 1986). Cf. also Yunlong Man, "English Colonization and the Formation of Anglo-American Polities, 1606-1664" (diss. Johns Hopkins, 1994); William Johnson Everett, *God's Federal Republic: Reconstructing Our Governing Symbol* (New York, 1988); Louise Phelps Kellogg, *The American Colonial Charter: A Study of English Administration in Relation Thereto, Chiefly after 1688* (1904; rpt. New York, 1971); Donald Lutz, *The Origins of American Constitutionalism* (Baton Rouge, LA, 1988); Charles McIlwain, *Constitutionalism Ancient and Modern,* rev. edn. (Ithaca, NY, 1947); Andrew C. McLaughlin, *The Foundations of American Constitutionalism* (New York, 1932); Breckinridge Long, *Genesis of the Constitution of the United States of America* (New York, 1926); Israel Mauduit, *A Short View of the History of the New England Colonies, With Respect to Their Charters and Constitution* (4th edn., London, 1776); Benjamin F. Wright, "The Early History of Written Constitutions in America," in *Essays in History and Political Theory* (Cambridge, MA, 1936), 344-71.

5. David A. Weir, *The Origins of the Federal Theology in Sixteenth-Century Reformation Thought* (Oxford, 1990); based on a previous dissertation: "*Foedus Naturale:* The Origins of Federal Theology in Sixteenth-Century Reformation Thought" (diss. St. Andrews, 1984).

6. Many have spoken about the relationship between church and state in both colonial America and in the United States generally. There are, nevertheless, works of critical importance both for colonial New England and for the general subject. The place to begin is the massive work by Anson Phelps Stokes, *Church and State in the United States: A Historical Survey, Source Book, and Interpretation of Documents and Events Showing the Growth of Religious Freedom under the Friendly Constitutional Separation of Church and State . . . ,* 3 vols. (New York, 1950), which was supplemented by a shorter, revised, one-volume edition (New York, 1964). Stokes's work is helpful in that he defines and analyzes certain critical words that are utilized in the entire discussion. A shorter collection with a helpful analytical essay was put together by John F. Wilson in 1965; it has now appeared in its third edition: *Church and State in American History: Key Documents, Decisions, and Commentary from the Past Three Centuries, Third Edition Expanded and Updated,* ed. John F. Wilson and Donald L. Drakeman (Boulder, CO, 2003). Wilson has also put together and edited a bibliography of materials on the subject, including a series of critical essays on the various chronological periods in American history: *Church and State in America: A Bibliographical Guide;* the relevant volume for this study is vol. 1, *The Colonial and Early National Periods* (New York, 1986). Other works that deal with the topic in a broad way are Robert D. Linder, "Church and State Relations in the United States: Sources and Scholars," *BHH,* 33 (1998), #1, 86-96; Thomas J. Curry, *The First Freedoms: Church and State in America to the Passage of the First Amendment* (New York, 1986); id., "Church and State in Seventeenth and Eighteenth Century America," *JLR,* 7 (1989), 261-73; Timothy L. Smith, "Congregation, State, and Denomination: The Forming of the American Religious Structure," *WMQ,* ser. 3, 25 (1968), 155-76; Thomas G. Sanders, *Protestant Concepts of Church and State: Historical Backgrounds and Approaches for the Fu-*

ture (New York, 1964), a work that was deeply criticized by Winthrop S. Hudson in "Protestant Concepts of Church and State: A Review Article," *CH,* 35 (1966), 227-34. For colonial New England in general, the following are helpful: Mark Allen Carden, "God's Church and a Godly Government: A Historiography of Church-State Relations in Puritan New England," *F + H,* 19 (1987), #1, 51-66; Mark Valeri, "Puritanism and the Civil Order in New England from the First Settlements to the Great Awakening," in Wilson, ed., *Church and State in America: A Bibliographical Guide,* vol. 1, *The Colonial and Early National Periods,* 43-73; Augustus F. Moulton, "Church and State in New England," *MeHSC,* ser. 3, 1 (1904), 221-51; and Paul E. Lauer, *Church and State in New England, JHUSHPS,* ser. 10, # II-III (Baltimore, 1892), 83-188; rpt. (New York, 1973). For Old England, cf. Leo F. Solt, *Church and State in Early Modern England, 1509-1640* (New York, 1990); James E. Wood, Jr., "Editorial: Church and State in England," *JCS,* 9 (1967), 305-16; and Harry F. Snapp, "Church and State Relations in Early Caroline England," *JCS,* 9 (1967), 332-48. The various colonies had different arrangements of church and state which changed over time. For Massachusetts Bay, cf. Avihu Zakai, "The Ministers' View of Church and State in Early Massachusetts," in *Studies in American Civilization,* ed. E. M. Budick et al., *Scripta Hierosolymitana: Publications of the Hebrew University, Jerusalem,* 32 (Jerusalem, 1987), 1-25; Richard J. Hoskins, "The Original Separation of Church and State in America," *JLR,* 2 (1984), 221-39; and the important article by Aaron B. Seidman, "Church and State in the Early Years of the Massachusetts Bay Colony," *NEQ,* 18 (1945), 211-33. J. M. Bumsted has covered the New Plymouth Colony in "A Well-Bounded Toleration: Church and State in the Plymouth Colony," *JCS,* 10 (1968), 265-79, while Roger Williams and the Rhode Island Colony has been covered in Mauro Calamandrei, "Theology and Political Thought of Roger Williams" (diss. Chicago, 1953) and Edmund S. Morgan, *Roger Williams: The Church and the State* (New York, 1967). The Baptist contribution to the discussion is analyzed in Slayden A. Yarbrough, "Church and State in Baptist History," *BHH,* 33 (1998), #1, 4-11; G. Hugh Wamble, "Baptist Contributions to Separation of Church and State," *BHH,* 20 (1985), #3, 3-13; and William G. McLoughlin, *New England Dissent, 1630-1833: The Baptists and the Separation of Church and State,* 2 vols. (Cambridge, MA, 1971); vol. 1, which covers the years 1630-1800, is especially relevant to this study.

7. Daniel J. Elazar is one of the few scholars who has tried to synthesize the many variegated strands of covenantal thinking into some sort of coherent framework, particularly in the realm of political theory. Working in the field of political science, Elazar's major premise was that covenant emerged from the world of theology, became a political and constitutional concept, and then was secularized into the modern idea of contract. Among his numerous works are the following: Daniel J. Elazar and John Kincaid (eds.), *The Covenant Connection: From Federal Theology to Modern Federalism* (Lanham, MD, 2000), including "Appendix: Publications of the Covenant Workshops," 305-8; "Covenant," *Encyclopedia of Politics and Religion,* ed. Robert Wuthnow (Washington, DC, 1998), 193-99; *The Covenant Tradition in Politics,* 4 vols. (New Brunswick, NJ, 1995-98); vol. 1, *Covenant and Polity in Biblical Israel: Biblical Foundations and Jewish Expressions* (1995); vol. 2, *Covenant and Commonwealth: From Christian Separation through the Protestant Reformation* (1996); vol. 3, *Covenant and Constitutionalism: The Great Frontier and the Matrix of Federal Democracy,* esp. "Introduction: The New World Experience," pp. 1-14 and "Chapter 1: Covenant and the American Founding," pp. 17-45 (1998);

Covenant and Civil Society: The Constitutional Matrix of Modern Democracy (1998); "The Almost-Covenanted Polity: [America and the Federalist Revolution]" (Israel: Bar-Ilan University, Department of Political Studies/Center for Jewish Community Studies, 1982); Daniel J. Elazar and John Kincaid (eds.), "Covenant, Polity, and Constitutionalism," *Publius*, 10 (1980), #4; rpt. under the same title (Lanham, MD, 1983); Daniel J. Elazar, "The Political Theory of Covenant: Biblical Origins and Modern Developments," *Publius*, 10 (1980), #4, 3-30; "[Editorial]: Federalism as Grand Design," *Publius*, 9 (1979), #4, 1-8; "[Editorial]: The Themes of a Journal of Federalism," *Publius*, 1 (1971), #1, 1-9.

8. Cf. Delbert R. Hillers, *Covenant: The History of a Biblical Idea* (Baltimore, 1969); George E. Mendenhall, *Law and Covenant in Israel and the Ancient Near East* (Pittsburgh, PA, 1955); id., "Covenant," in *The Interpreter's Dictionary of the Bible,* 1 (Nashville, TN, 1962), 714-23; Meredith Kline, *Treaty of the Great King: The Covenant Structure of Deuteronomy* (Grand Rapids, 1963); *"diatheke"* in *Theological Dictionary of the New Testament,* 2 (Grand Rapids, MI, 1964), 106-34; M. Weinfield, *"Berith,"* *Theological Dictionary of the Old Testament,* 2 (Grand Rapids, MI, 1975), 253-79; Joachim Guhrt and Oswald Becker, "Covenant, Guarantee, Mediator," in *The New International Dictionary of New Testament Theology,* ed. Colin Brown, 1 (Grand Rapids, MI, 1975), 365-76; Dennis J. McCarthy, *Treaty and Covenant* (Rome, 1978); Elmer B. Smick, *"(b^erit)* covenant," in *Theological Wordbook of the Old Testament,* ed. R. Laird Harris, Gleason L. Archer, Jr., and Bruce K. Waltke, 1 (Chicago, 1980), 128-30; the series of articles on covenantal themes in *ISBE,* 1.790-97; Thomas E. McComiskey, *The Covenants of Promise* (Grand Rapids, 1985); E. W. Nicholson, *God and His People: Covenant and Theology in the Old Testament* (New York, 1986); George E. Mendenhall and Gary A. Herion, "Covenant," in *The Anchor Bible Dictionary,* 1 (New York, 1992), 1179-1202; Gordon J. McConville, *"(berit),* treaty, agreement, alliance, covenant," in *The New International Dictionary of Old Testament Theology and Exegesis,* ed. Willem A. Van Gemeren et al., 1 (Grand Rapids, MI, 1997), 747-55; along with other references in David A. Weir, *The Origins of the Federal Theology,* p. 39, n. 12, and p. 60, n. 3.

9. For the texts of these two creeds and other creeds, see Philip Schaff, *Creeds of Christendom* (New York, 1877; rpt. 1977) (hereinafter referred to as "Schaff, *Creeds*"); "Symbolum Apostolicum," 2.45-55; "Symbolum Nicaeno-Constantinopolitanum," 2.57-61; cf. also John H. Leith, *Creeds of the Churches . . .* (rev. edn., Richmond, VA, 1973).

10. We need to point out that the creedal collections of both Schaff and Leith include many confessions of faith.

11. Cf. Exodus 24:7-8; 25:16; 31:18; 32:15; 34:10, 27-29; Leviticus 26:15; Deuteronomy 4:13; 5:2-3; 9:9-19; 29:1-29.

12. Cf. P. D. L. Avis, "Moses and the Magistrate: A Study in the Rise of Protestant Legalism," *JEH,* 26 (1975), 149-72; George A. Billias, *Law and Authority in Colonial America: Selected Essays* (Barre, MA, 1965); Stephen Botein, *Early American Law and Society* (New York, 1983); Daniel R. Coquillette (ed.), *Law in Colonial Massachusetts, 1630-1800, CSMP,* 62 (Charlottesville, VA, 1984); Eugene R. Fingerhut, "Were the Massachusetts Puritans Hebraic?" *NEQ,* 40 (1967), 521-31; David H. Flaherty (ed.), *Essays in the History of Early American Law* (Chapel Hill, NC, 1969); F. C. Gray, "Remarks on the Early Laws of the Massachusetts Bay," *MHSC,* ser. 3, 8 (1843), 191-215; George Lee Haskins, *Law and Authority in Early Massachusetts: A Study in Tradition and Design* (New

York, 1960); *id.,* "Ecclesiastical Antecedents of Criminal Punishment in Early Massachusetts," *MHSP,* 71 (1957-60), 21-35; *id.,* "The Legal Heritage of Plymouth Colony," in David H. Flaherty (ed.), *Essays in the History of Early American Law,* 121-34; Charles J. Hilkey, "Legal Development in Colonial Massachusetts, 1630-1686" (diss. Columbia, 1910); Abraham Katsh, "The Impact of the Bible on American Legislation," in Joseph Armenti (ed.), *Transcendence and Immanence: Reconstruction in the Light of Process Thinking: Festschrift in Honour of Joseph Papin,* 2 (St. Meinrad, IN, 1976), 386-98; James B. Jordan, "Calvinism and the Judicial Law of Moses," *JCR,* 5 (1978-79), #2, 17-48; "Symposium on Puritanism and Law," *JCR,* 5 (1978-79), #2, pp. 1-193; Eldon Ray Turner, "Law and Political Culture: A Functional Study of the Relation of Theology to Jurisprudence, Political Values and Legal Activity in Colonial Suffolk County, Massachusetts 1671-1680" (diss. Kansas, 1973); Richard B. Morris, *Studies in the History of American Law with Special Reference to the Seventeenth and Eighteenth Centuries,* 2nd edn. (New York, 1964); Katherine A. Hermes, "Religion and Law in Colonial New England, 1620-1730" (diss. Yale, 1995); Charles Edward Smith, "Massachusetts' *Laws and Liberties* and the Revolutionary Idea That Law Should Serve the Public Good" (diss. Chicago, 1998).

13. David A. Weir, "Church Covenanting in Seventeenth-Century New England" (diss. Princeton University, 1992). Horton Davies discusses the founding of two Massachusetts Bay congregations in the 1630s and the 1640s: those of Dedham First Church and Woburn First Church. The narratives of both foundings and Davies' discussion of them give a good general sense of what happens on a Foundation Day in a seventeenth-century church, but Davies' concerns are with the broader context of early New England worship and not the specifics of early New England church formation; *The Worship of the American Puritans, 1629-1750* (New York, 1990), 213-17.

Town formation in seventeenth-century New England, on the other hand, has been a topic of intense modern historical research, primarily because it has involved the formation of the modern American political process. Most of the discussion has involved arguments over political theory, but very recently a more encyclopedic survey has emerged from the work of John F. Martin; cf. *Profits in the Wilderness: Entrepreneurship and the Founding of New England Towns in the Seventeenth Century* (Chapel Hill, NC, 1991), based on a more comprehensive dissertation completed at Harvard in 1985. Martin has in many ways restated and elaborated upon the thesis of James T. Adams, who maintained that the New England Puritans came to the new world primarily for profit; *The Founding of New England* (Boston, 1920).

14. Cf. David A. Weir, "Church Covenanting in Seventeenth-Century New England."

15. Viewing New England as part of a larger English — and after 1707 — (First) British Empire (1607-1783) was an approach championed by historians of the earlier period of the twentieth century. Both James Truslow Adams, in *The Founding of New England* and Charles M. Andrews, in *The Colonial Period of American History,* 4 vols. (New Haven, CT, 1934) concluded that an imperial and international frame of reference was most helpful in viewing the British, and specifically New England, colonies. During the middle of the twentieth century, only a few joined Lawrence H. Gipson to push that stance, as New England studies broke down into small particular analyses that were responses to the work of Perry Miller; cf. Lawrence H. Gipson, *The British Empire before the American Revolution: Provincial Tendencies in the Era preceding the American Crisis,* 15

vols. (Caldwell, ID and New York, 1936-70) and "The Imperial Approach to Early Amer-
ican History," in *The Reinterpretation of Early American History: Essays in Honor of John
Edwin Pomfret*, ed. Ray Allen Billington (San Marino, CA, 1966), 185-200; also Max
Savelle, "The International Approach to Early Anglo-American History, 1492-1763," in
The Reinterpretation of Early American History, ed. Billington, 201-31; and Alison G.
Olson and Richard Maxwell Brown, *Anglo-American Political Relations, 1675-1775* (New
Brunswick, NJ, 1970). However, the last thirty years of the twentieth century has seen a
reawakening of the need to see a larger international context for colonial New England
and for other North American colonies. Ian K. Steele recounts some of that literature in
"The Empire and Provincial Elites: An Interpretation of Some Recent Writings on the
English Atlantic, 1675-1740," *Journal of Imperial and Commonwealth History*, 8 (1979-
80), #2, 2-32, a discussion which is amplified in *The English Atlantic, 1675-1740* (New
York, 1986). Richard R. Johnson focused in on the New England world soon after Steele's
article appeared, with his *Adjustment to Empire: The New England Colonies, 1675-1715*
(New Brunswick, NJ, 1981). Johnson's focus is political and institutional history, and he
emphasizes that New England underwent a process wherein royal supervision increased
greatly and New England accommodated itself to that pattern in a process called "anglicization." Ian K. Steele and Stephen Saunders Webb agree that the framework of empire
is important, but contend that religion played as large a role as politics and economics,
and that these religious divisions led to an empire dominated by the military; cf. Ian K.
Steele, "Notes and Documents: Governors or Generals? A Note on Martial Law and the
Revolution of 1689 in English America," *WMQ*, ser. 3, 46 (1989), 304-14, and Stephen
Saunders Webb, *Lord Churchill's Coup: The Anglo-American Empire and the Glorious Revolution Reconsidered* (New York, 1995). Within the imperial thesis group, arguments have
emerged over precisely when the authorities of Old England thought in terms of an En-
glish Empire. Robert M. Bliss, in *Revolution and Empire: English Politics and the American
Colonies in the Seventeenth Century* (New York, 1990) argues that even Charles I in 1625
thought in terms of an empire, but that the turning point was the Restoration. Alison
Gilbert Olson, while focusing on the eighteenth century in her *Making the Empire Work:
London and American Interest Groups, 1690-1790* (Cambridge, MA, 1992), points out that
various interest groups in England start to emerge in the 1660s; cf. also George L. Beer,
The Old Colonial System . . . 1660-1688, 2 vols. (Gloucester, MA, 1958) and Jack M.
Sosin, *English America and the Restoration Monarchy of Charles II* (Lincoln, NE, 1980).
Webb, on the other hand, contends that 1676 and King Philip's War marked the empire's
beginnings; cf. *1676: The End of American Independence* (New York, 1984). Paul Lucas as-
serts that Charles II and his court thought in terms of an empire from 1661 to 1666, but
then they changed their focus when politics on the Continent began to heat up; cf.
Paul R. Lucas, "Colony or Commonwealth: Massachusetts Bay, 1661-1666," *WMQ*, ser.
3, 24 (1967), 88-107. The various strands of the imperial discussion can be found in
Nicholas Canny (ed.), *The Origins of Empire: British Overseas Enterprise to the Close of the
Seventeenth Century*, vol. 1 of *The Oxford History of the British Empire* (Oxford, 1998) and
Robin Winks (ed.), *Historiography*, vol. 5 of *The Oxford History of the British Empire*, esp.
P. J. Marshall, "The First British Empire," 43-53, and Stephen Foster, "British North
America in the Seventeenth and Eighteenth Centuries," 73-93. Other relevant works are:
Karen O. Kupperman, "[Review]: The American Colonies: Another British Kingdom,"
JBS, 34 (1995), 277-81; Richard R. Johnson, "The Imperial Webb: The Thesis of Garri-

son Government," *WMQ*, ser. 3, 43 (1986), 408-30; and Stephen Saunders Webb, "The Data and Theory of Restoration Empire," *WMQ*, ser. 3, 43 (1986), 431-59.

16. CNEB, *Bibliographies of New England History*, ed. John B. Armstrong, 9 vols. (Boston, Hanover, NH and London, 1976-94).

17. "The church records antedating 1756 were sequestered by Rev. Nathaniel Hancock at the time of his dismissal," Worthley, *Inventory*, 681-82. A more exciting fate befell the church records of the Charleston, South Carolina, Independent or Congregational Church (the Circular Church), which was founded by New England emigrants: "the Church records were in the possession of the rev. Mr. Livingston in 1713, who lived in a wooden house on White Point. In the fall of that year a violent hurricane beat off the weather-boards of the house, carried away the book which contained the church records, and the furniture of the rooms on the lower floor," David Ramsay, *The History of the Independent or Congregational Church in Charlestown, South Carolina, From its Origin Till the Year 1814 . . .* (Philadelphia, 1815).

18. Cf. Ann S. Lainhart, *Digging for Genealogical Treasure in New England Town Records* (Boston, 1996).

19. *The New England Mind*, vol. 1, *The Seventeenth Century* and vol. 2, *From Colony to Province*; Perry Miller, "Thomas Hooker and the Democracy of Connecticut," *NEQ*, 4 (1931), 663-712; *id.*, "The Half-Way Covenant"; *id.*, *Orthodoxy in Massachusetts, 1630-1650* (Cambridge, MA, 1933); *id.*, "The Marrow of Puritan Divinity"; *id.*, "The Puritan Theory of the Sacraments in Seventeenth Century New England."

For the discussion of the covenant theme in New England, cf. the following: Champlin Burrage, *The Church Covenant Idea: Its Origin and Development* (Philadelphia, 1904); John T. Blodgett, "The Political Theory of the Mayflower Compact," *CSMP*, 12 (1908-9), 204-13; Sandford Fleming, *Children and Puritanism: The Place of Children in the Life and Thought of New England Churches, 1620-1847* (New Haven, CT, 1933), based on a 1929 Yale dissertation; Peter Y. De Jong, *The Covenant Idea in New England Theology, 1620-1847* (Grand Rapids, MI, 1945), based on a dissertation completed in 1942; Wayne H. Christy, "John Cotton: Covenant Theologian" (M.A. thesis, Pittsburgh-Xenia Theological Seminary, 1942); (Aleck) Lewis Smith, "Changing Conceptions of God in Colonial New England" (diss. Iowa, 1953); H. Richard Niebuhr, "The Idea of Covenant and American Democracy," *CH*, 23 (1954), 126-35; Alan Simpson, "The Covenanted Community," in *Puritanism in Old and New England* (Chicago, 1955), 19-38; Edwin S. Gaustad, *The Great Awakening in New England* (New York, 1957), 7-8; Emery J. Battis, *Saints and Sectaries: Anne Hutchinson and the Antinomian Controversy in the Massachusetts Bay Colony* (Chapel Hill, NC, 1962), based on a 1958 Columbia dissertation; Daniel J. Boorstin, "The Puritan Tradition: Community Above Ideology," *Commentary*, 26 (1958), 288-99; Larzer Ziff, "The Social Bond of Church Covenant," *AQ*, 10 (1958), 454-62; William G. Wilcox, "New England Covenant Theology: Its English Precursors and Early American Exponents" (diss. Duke, 1959); James R. Fulcher, "Puritan Piety in Early New England: A Study in Spiritual Regeneration from the Antinomian Controversy to the Cambridge Synod of 1648 in the Massachusetts Bay Colony" (diss. Princeton University, 1963); Edmund S. Morgan, *Visible Saints: The History of a Puritan Idea* (New York, 1963); Norman Pettit, *The Heart Prepared: Grace and Conversion in Puritan Spiritual Life* (New Haven, CT, 1966), based on a 1963 Yale dissertation; Lewis M. Robinson, "A History of the Half-Way Covenant" (diss. Illinois, 1963); C. John Somerville, "Conversion, Sacrament and Assurance in the Puritan Covenant of Grace, to 1650" (M.A. thesis, Kansas, 1963); Loren Baritz, *City on a Hill: A History of Ideas and Myths in America* (New York, 1964); Raymond P. Stearns, "The Half-Way Covenant and New England History," *BCL,* 17 (1965-66), #3, 8-14; David L. Beebe, "The Seals of the Covenant: The Doctrine and Place of the Sacraments and Censures in the New England Puritan Theology Underlying the Cambridge Platform of 1648" (diss. Pacific School of Religion, 1966), 122-46; Mary C. Foster, "Hampshire County, Massachusetts, 1729-1754: A Covenant Society in Transition" (diss. Michigan, 1967); Edmund S. Morgan, *Roger Williams: The Church and the State* (New York, 1967); Robert G. Pope, *The Half-Way Covenant: Church Membership in Puritan New England* (Princeton, NJ, 1969), based on a 1967 Yale dissertation; Richard M. Reinitz, "Symbolism and Freedom: The Use of Biblical Typology as an Argument for Religious Toleration in Seventeenth Century England and America" (diss. Rochester, 1967); Timothy H. Breen, *The Character of the Good Ruler: A Study of Puritan Political Ideas in New England, 1630-1730* (New Haven, CT, 1970), a revision of a 1969 Yale dissertation; David D. Hall, "Understanding the Puritans," in *The State of American History,* ed. Herbert J. Bass (Chicago, 1970), 330-49; E. Brooks Holifield, *The Covenant Sealed: The Development of Puritan Sacramental Theology in Old and New England 1570-1720* (New Haven, CT, 1970) based on an earlier Yale dissertation; James T. Meigs, "The Half-Way Covenant: A Study in Religious Transition," *Foundations,* 13 (1970), 142-58; William K. B. Stoever, *"A Faire and Easie Way to Heaven": Covenant Theology and Antinomianism in Early Massachusetts* (Middletown, CT, 1978), based on a 1970 Yale dissertation; Richard P. Gildrie, *Salem, Massachusetts, 1626-1683: A Covenant Community* (Charlottesville, VA, 1975), based on a 1971 University of Virginia dissertation; T. H. Breen, "English Origins and New World Development: The Case of Covenanted Militia in Seventeenth-Century Massachusetts," *P+P,* 57 (1972), 74-96; Michael McGiffert, "Introduction," in *God's Plot: The Paradoxes of Puritan Piety: Being the Autobiography and Journal of Thomas Shepard* (Amherst, MA, 1972), 3-32; Harry M. Ward, *Statism in Plymouth Colony* (Port Washington, NY, 1972), 3-14, 52-63; James W. Jones, *The Shattered Synthesis: New England Puritanism before the Great Awakening* (New Haven, CT, 1973); Timothy H. Breen and Stephen Foster, "The Puritans' Greatest Achievement: A Study of Social Cohesion in Seventeenth-Century Massachusetts," *JAH,* 60 (1973-74), 5-22; Cushing Strout, *The New Heavens and the New Earth: Political Religion in America* (New York, 1974); William K. B. Stoever, "Nature, Grace and John Cotton: The Theological Dimension in the New England Antinomianism Controversy," *CH,* 44 (1975), 22-34; James F. Ward, "Consciousness and Community: American Idealist Social Thought from Puritanism to Social Science" (diss. Harvard, 1975); Michael McGiffert, "The Problem of the Covenant in Puritan Thought: Peter Bulkeley's *Gospel Covenant,*" *NEHGR,* 130 (1976), 107-29; Philip J. Anderson, "Presbyterianism and the Gathered Churches in Old and New England, 1640-1662: The Struggle for Church Government in Theory and Practice" (diss. Oxford, 1979); Gary North, "From Covenant to Contract: Pietism and Secularism in Puritan New England, 1691-1720," *JCR,* 6 (1979-80), #2, 155-94; Michael D. Reed, "Early American Puritanism: The Language of Its Religion," *American Imago,* 37 (1980), 278-333; Harry S. Stout, "Word and Order in Colonial New England," in *The Bible in America,* ed. Nathan O. Hatch and Mark A. Noll (New York, 1982), 19-38; Michael McGiffert, "God's Controversy with New England," *AHR,* 88 (1983), 1151-74; Philip F. Gura, *A Glimpse of Sion's Glory: Puritan Radicalism in New England, 1620-1660*

(Middletown, CT, 1984); John R. Higgins, "Aspects of the Doctrine of the Holy Spirit during the Antinomian Controversy of New England with Special Reference to John Cotton and Anne Hutchinson" (diss. Westminster Theological Seminary, 1984); Richard J. Hoskins, "The Original Separation of Church and State in America"; David M. Scobey, "Revising the Errand: New England Ways and the Puritan Sense of the Past," *WMQ,* ser. 3, 41 (1984), 3-31; Charles L. Cohen, *God's Caress: The Psychology of Puritan Religious Experience* (New York, 1986) based on a dissertation completed at the University of California, Berkeley in 1982; Michael R. McCoy, "In Defense of the Covenant: The Sacramental Debates of Eighteenth Century New England" (diss. Emory, 1986); Harry S. Stout, *The New England Soul: Preaching and Religious Culture in Colonial New England* (New York, 1986); Donald S. Lutz and Jack D. Warren, *A Covenanted People: The Religious Tradition and the Origins of American Constitutionalism* (Providence, RI, 1987); Richard T. Hughes and C. Leonard Allen, *Illusions of Innocence: Protestant Primitivism in America, 1630-1875* (Chicago, 1985); Elizabeth Reis, "Witches, Sinners, and the Underside of Covenant Theology," *EIHC,* 129 (1993), 103-18. Cf. also the bibliography of covenant theology in David A. Weir, *The Origins of the Federal Theology,* 160-95.

20. The theoretical underpinnings were set out by Conrad Arensburg, "American Communities," *American Anthropologist,* 57 (1955), 1143-62; reviews and citations of the various studies can be found in the following: J. M. Bumsted and J. T. Lemon, "New Approaches in Early American Studies: The Local Community in New England," *Histoire Sociale/Social History,* 2 (1968), 98-112; Rhys Isaac, "Order and Growth, Authority and Meaning in Colonial New England," *AHR,* 76 (1971), 728-37; John Murrin, "Review Essay [on the New England Town]," *History and Theory,* 11 (1972), 226-75; Jack P. Greene, "Autonomy and Stability: New England and the British Colonial Experience in Early Modern America," *Journal of Social History,* 7 (1974), 171-94; Richard R. Beeman, "The New Social History and the Search for 'Community' in Colonial America," *AQ,* 29 (1977), 422-43; Eric G. Nellis, "Social History, Local Studies and the Institutions of Early America," *CRevAS,* 11 (1980), 327-45.

21. One exception is the brief article by R. Tudur Jones concerning the covenants generated by the Separatists, Congregationalists, and Independents of Old England: "The Church Covenant in Classical Congregationalism," *The Presbyter: A Journal of Reformed Churchmanship,* 7 (1947), #4, 9-20.

22. See, for instance, Stephen L. Schechter (ed.), with Richard B. Bernstein and Donald S. Lutz, *Roots of the Republic: American Founding Documents Interpreted* (Madison, WI, 1990). In "The Founding of American Local Communities: A Study of Covenantal and Other Forms of Association," *Publius,* 10 (1980), #4, 165-85, Schechter analyzes one local civil covenant, that of Eastchester, New York. Other collections and analyses of political covenants include: Andrew C. McLaughlin, *The Foundations of American Constitutionalism;* Charles McIlwain, *Constitutionalism Ancient and Modern;* and Donald Lutz, *The Origins of American Constitutionalism,* along with the works cited in Chapter 2: The Colonial Charters of Early New England.

Notes to Chapter 1

1. Leviticus 27:30-33; Numbers 18:25-32; Deuteronomy 12:17-19; 14:22-29; Deuteronomy 26:1-15; cf. also 2 Chronicles 31:4-6; Amos 4:4-5; Malachi 3:8-12.

2. Richard Fletcher, *The Barbarian Conversion: From Paganism to Christianity* (Berkeley, CA, 1997); M. Deanesly, *A History of the Medieval Church, 590-1500,* 7th edn. (London, 1951).

3. A. Harnack, "Organization of the Early Church," *NSHE,* 8 (1910), 259-68; Ulrich Stutz, "Parish and Pastor," *ibid.,* 353-56; E. Sehling, "Tithes," *ibid.,* 11 (1911), 453-56; Bernhard Blumenkranz, "Tithes, Church," *Encyclopedia Judaica,* 15 (1972), 1162-63; Edward J. Kilmartin, S.J., "Offerings," in *Encyclopedia of Early Christianity,* ed. Everett Ferguson et al. (New York, 1990), 658-59; Louis J. Swift, "Almsgiving," *ibid.,* 26-27.

4. For a general survey of parochial government in England, see the article by E. W. Watson and G. Crosse in *DECH,* 453-57. The *OED* (7.P.479-80) has a useful survey of the use of the word "parish," and its examination of the word "chapel" is also helpful (2.C.274-76). *The Phillimore Atlas and Index of Parish Registers,* ed. Cecil R. Humphery-Smith (Baltimore, 1984), while intended for genealogists, is an important reference work which illustrates clearly the way every shire in England is divided into parishes. Other key critical works on the parochial system in medieval and early modern England are the following: Toulmin Smith, *The Parish: Its Powers and Obligations at Law* . . . (London, 1857); C. Arthur Lane, *Illustrated Notes on English Church History,* 1 (London, 1894), 93-94; Edward McClure, *Historical Church Atlas . . . Illustrating the History of . . . the Anglican Communion until the Present Day* (London, 1897); W. Page, H. A. Doubleday, et al. (eds.), *Victoria History of the Counties of England,* vols. 1- (London, 1900-); Sidney and Beatrice Webb, *English Local Government from the Revolution to the Municipal Corporations Act: The Parish and the County* (London, 1906); A. H. Thompson, *Parish History and Records* (London, 1926); Charles J. Cox and Charles B. Ford, *The Parish Churches of England* (1934; 5th edn. rev. London, 1946), esp. Chapter 1: "The Church, the Parish, and the People"; Peter D. Thomson, *Parish and Parish Church: Their Place and Influence in History* (London, 1948); George W. Addleshaw, *The Development of the Parochial System from Charlemagne (768-814) to Urban II (1088-99),* St. Anthony's Hall Publications, 6 (York, 1954); Charles Drew, *Early Parochial Organization in England* . . . , St. Anthony's Hall Publications, 7 (London, 1954); George W. O. Addleshaw, *The Beginnings of the Parochial System,* 2nd edn., St. Anthony's Hall Publications, #3 (York, 1959); Christopher Hill, "The Secularization of the Parish" and "Individuals and Communities," in *Society and Puritanism in Pre-Revolutionary England* (London, 1964), 420-42 and 482-500; W. E. Tate, *The Parish Chest: A Study of the Records of Parochial Administration in England* (3rd edn., London, 1969); W. O. Ault, "The Village Church and the Village Community in Mediaeval England," *Speculum,* 45 (1970), 197-215; Robert E. Rodes, Jr., *Ecclesiastical Administration in Medieval England: The Anglo-Saxons to the Reformation* (Notre Dame, IN, 1977); J. H. Bettey, *Church and Community: The Parish Church in English Life* (New York, 1979); Robert M. Kingdon, "Protestant Parishes in the Old World and the New: The Case of Geneva and Boston," *CH,* 48 (1979), 290-309; C. J. Kitching, "Church and Chapelry in Sixteenth-Century England," in Derek Baker, ed., *The Church in Town and Countryside,* SCH(L), 16 (Oxford, 1979), 279-90; J. H. Bettey, *Church and Parish: An Introduction for Local Historians* (London, 1987); Susan J. Wright, *Parish, Church, and People: Local Studies in Lay Religion, 1350-1750* (London, 1988); Katherine L. French, Gary Gibbs, and Beat A. Kümin (eds.), *The Parish in English Life, 1400-1600* (Manchester, 1997); Anthea Jones, *A Thousand Years of the English Parish: Medieval Patterns and Modern Interpretation* (Bath, 2000); N. J. G. Pounds, *A History of the English Parish: The Cul-*

ture of Religion from Augustine to Victoria (Cambridge, 2000); Katherine L. French, *The People of the Parish: Community Life in a Late Medieval English Diocese* (Philadelphia, 2001); for a discussion of the transfer of the English parochial system from England, see Edward Ingle, "The English Parish in America," in *Local Institutions of Virginia, JHUSHPS,* ser. 3, II-III (Baltimore, MD, 1885), 151-75.

5. Approximately 23 parishes were founded by Act of Parliament between the years 1509 and 1700. It should be noted that these were cases of parish formations; unification of parishes was a more common occurrence and has not been counted in this census; cf. W. J. Sheils, "Religion in Provincial Towns: Innovation and Tradition," in Felicity Heal and Rosemary O'Day (eds.), *Church and Society in England: Henry VIII to James I* (Hamden, CT, 1977), 160. It was possible for non-English groups to establish churches in England; cf. John S. Burn, *The History of the French, Walloon, Dutch, and Other Foreign Protestant Refugees Settled in England, from the Reign of Henry VIII, to the Revocation of the Edict of Nantes . . .* (London, 1846); F. De Schickler, *Les Églises du Refuge en Angleterre,* 3 vols. (Paris, 1892); Patrick Collinson, "The Elizabethan Puritans and the Foreign Reformed Churches in London," Huguenot Society of London, *Proceedings,* 20 (1964), 528-55; *id.,* "Calvinism with an Anglican Face: The Stranger Churches of Early Elizabethan London and Their Superintendent," in Derek Baker, ed., *Reform and Reformation: England and the Continent c. 1500–c. 1750,* SCH(L), subsidia, 2 (Oxford, 1979), 71-102; Peter O. Grell, *Dutch Calvinists in Early Stuart London: The Dutch Church in Austin Friars, 1603-1642* (Leiden, 1989).

6. The best standard summary of the English Reformation is A. G. Dickens, *The English Reformation* (London, 1967); for other sources, cf. David A. Weir, "Church Covenanting in Seventeenth-Century New England," 297-98.

7. There was at least one exception: Whitegate, Cheshire was a parish formed from a monastic establishment in 1541/2; cf. William Dugdale, *Monasticon Anglicanum: A History of the Abbies and Other Monasteries . . . in England and Wales . . . ,* 8 vols., 2nd edn. ed. John Caley et al. (London, 1817-30); Francis A. Hibbert, *The Dissolution of the Monasteries . . .* (London, 1910); David Knowles, *The Monastic Order in England* (Cambridge, 1940); rpt. under the title *Medieval Religious Houses: England and Wales,* ed. David Knowles and R. Neville Hadcock (London, 1953); David Knowles, *The Tudor Age,* vol. 3 of *The Religious Orders in England* (Cambridge, 1959); cf. esp. "The Disposal of the Lands," 393-401; this volume was abridged as *Bare Ruined Choirs: The Dissolution of the English Monasteries* (New York, 1976); G. W. O. Woodward, *The Dissolution of the Monasteries* (London, 1966); Joyce Youings, *The Dissolution of the Monasteries* (New York, 1971); Christopher Kitching, "The Disposal of Monastic and Chantry Lands," in Heal and O'Day (eds.), *Church and Society in England,* 119-36.

8. The Reformation on the Continent and in Scotland involved four distinct areas: worship, doctrine, governance, and discipline. The *BCP* and the Thirty-nine Articles became normative statements for the reformation of worship and doctrine in the Church of England. The reformation of governance was stalled, principally by Queen Elizabeth herself. The delay ultimately led to one of the early manifestations of Puritanism: the movement for Presbyterian reform. Earlier proposals for ecclesiastical reform utilizing a modified form of episcopacy along with parochial church government can be found in: *The Reformation of the Ecclesiastical Laws of England, 1552,* ed. James C. Spalding, *Sixteenth Century Essays and Studies,* 19 (Kirksville, MO, 1992); cf. esp. "Preface," xi-xiii;

"Editor's Introduction," 1-57; "Concerning Parish Boundaries," 152-53; "Concerning Tithes," 181-89.

9. W. H. Summers, "List of Persons Burnt for Heresy in England," *TCHS,* 2 (1905-6), 362-70; cf. also Christina Garrett, *The Marian Exiles: A Study in the Origins of Elizabethan Puritanism* (Cambridge, 1938). For an account of the more than 300 Roman Catholic martyrs in England, cf. P. Caraman et al., "England, Scotland and Wales, Martyrs of," *New Catholic Encyclopedia . . . ,* 5 (Detroit, 2003), 224-38.

10. Roland G. Usher, *The Reconstruction of the English Church . . . ,* 2 vols. (New York, 1910); Henry Gee, *The Elizabethan Clergy and the Settlement of Religion, 1558-1564* (Oxford, 1898); Norman L. Jones, *Faith by Statute: Parliament and the Settlement of Religion, 1559* (Atlantic Highlands, NJ, 1982).

11. Henry O. Wakeman, *The Church and the Puritans, 1570-1660* (London, 1887); Marshall M. Knappen, *Tudor Puritanism: A Chapter in the History of Idealism* (Chicago, 1939); Leonard J. Trinterud, "The Origins of Puritanism," *CH,* 20 (1951), 37-57; Charles H. George, "A Social Interpretation of English Puritanism," *Journal of Modern History,* 25 (1953), 327-42; Jerald C. Brauer, "Reflections on the Nature of English Puritanism: Three Interpretations," *CH,* 23 (1954), 99-108; Patrick Collinson, *The Elizabethan Puritan Movement* (Berkeley, CA, 1967) based on a 1957 dissertation completed at the University of London; William M. Dietel, "Puritanism versus Anglicanism: A Study of Theological Controversy in Elizabethan England" (diss. Yale, 1959); Charles H. George and Katherine George, *The Protestant Mind of the English Reformation, 1570-1640* (Princeton, NJ, 1961); David Little, "The Logic of Order: An Examination of the Sources of Puritan-Anglican Controversy and of Their Relation to Prevailing Legal Conceptions of Corporation in the Late 16th and Early 17th Century in England" (diss. Harvard Divinity School, 1963); revised and published as: *Religion, Order and Law: A Study in Pre-Revolutionary England* (New York, 1969); Michael Walzer, "Puritanism as a Revolutionary Ideology," *History and Theory,* 3 (1963), 59-90; John F. H. New, *Anglican and Puritan: The Basis of Their Opposition, 1558-1640* (Stanford, CA, 1964); George L. Mosse, "Puritanism Reconsidered," *ARG,* 55/1 (1964), 37-47; Christopher Hill, *Society and Puritanism in Pre-Revolutionary England* (London, 1964); Michael Walzer, *The Revolution of the Saints: A Study in the Origins of Radical Politics* (Cambridge, MA, 1965); Basil Hall, "Puritanism: The Problem of Definition," in SCH(L), ed. G. J. Cuming (London, 1965), 283-96; Charles H. George, "Puritanism as History and Historiography," *P+P,* 41 (1968), 77-104; William M. Lamont, "Puritanism as History and Historiography," *P+P,* 44 (1969), 133-46; James B. Bross, "Puritan versus Anglican: An Attempt to Define the Difference" (diss. Iowa, 1972); T. H. Clancy, "Papist-Protestant-Puritan: English Religious Taxonomy, 1565-1665," *RH,* 13 (1976), 196-211; Robert O. Stuart, "The Breaking of the Elizabethan Settlement of Religion: Puritan Spiritual Experience and the Theological Division of the English Church" (diss. Yale, 1976); J. Sears McGee, *The Godly Man in Stuart England: Anglicans, Puritans and the Two Tables, 1620-1670* (New Haven, 1976); Felicity Heal, "The Church of England and Its Opponents from Reformation to Revolution (Review Article)," *Historical Journal,* 24 (1981), 201-20; Peter Lake, "Defining Puritanism—Again?" in Francis J. Bremer (ed.), *Puritanism: Transatlantic Perspectives on a Seventeenth-Century Anglo-American Faith* (Boston, 1993), 3-29.

12. Samuel Hopkins, *The Puritans . . . During the Reign of Edward VI and Elizabeth,* 3 vols. (Boston, 1859-61); M. M. Knappen, *Tudor Puritanism;* Frederick G. Lee, *The Church Under Queen Elizabeth . . .* (London, 1896); Henry N. Birt, *The Elizabethan Religious Settle-*

ment: *A Study of Contemporary Documents* (London, 1907); Walter H. Frere, *The English Church in the Reigns of Elizabeth and James (1558-1625),* vol. 5 of *A History of the English Church* (London, 1911); J. V. P. Thompson, *Supreme Governor: A Study of Elizabethan Ecclesiastical Polity and Circumstance* (London, 1940); W. M. Dietel, "Puritanism versus Anglicanism"; Carl S. Meyer, *Elizabeth I and the Religious Settlement* (Saint Louis, MO, 1960); Irvonwy Morgan, *The Godly Preachers of the Elizabethan Church* (London, 1965); Patrick Collinson, *The Elizabethan Puritan Movement;* William P. Haugaard, *Elizabeth and the English Reformation* (London, 1968); Leonard J. Trinterud (ed.), *Elizabethan Puritanism* (New York, 1971); R. O. Stuart, "The Breaking of the Elizabethan Settlement of Religion: Puritan Spiritual Experience and the Theological Division of the English Church"; Christopher M. Dent, *Protestant Reformers in Elizabethan Oxford* (Oxford, 1983).

13. Patrick Collinson, *The Elizabethan Puritan Movement;* cf. also George Yule, "Theological Developments in Elizabethan Puritanism," *JRH,* 1 (1960), 16-25; George Yule, "Developments in English Puritanism in the Context of the Reformation," in *Studies in the Puritan Tradition: A Joint Supplement of the Congregational and Presbyterian Historical Societies* (Chelmsford, Essex, England, 1964), 8-27; Peter Lake, *Moderate Puritans and the Elizabethan Church* (Cambridge, 1982); Patrick Collinson, *Godly People: Essays on English Protestantism and Puritanism* (London, 1983); Peter Lake, *Anglicans and Puritans? Presbyterianism and English Conformist Thought from Whitgift to Hooker* (London, 1988).

14. Joshua Toulmin, *An Historical View of the State of the Protestant Dissenters in England, and of the Progress of Free Enquiry and Religious Liberty, from the Revolution to the Accession of Queen Anne* (London, 1814); Alexander Young, *Chronicles of the Pilgrim Fathers of the Colony of Plymouth, from 1602 to 1625,* 2nd edn. (Boston, 1844); Joseph Hunter (ed.), *Collections Concerning the Church or Congregation of Protestant Separatists Formed at Scrooby in North Nottinghamshire . . .* (London, 1854); John Waddington, *The Track of the Hidden Church; or, the Springs of the Pilgrim Movement* (Boston, 1863); John Waddington, *Congregational History: 1200-1567,* 2 vols. (London, 1869-80); John Brown, *History of Congregationalism* (London, 1877); Henry M. Dexter, *The Congregationalism of the Last Three Hundred Years* (New York, 1880); John A. Goodwin, *The Puritan Conspiracy Against the Pilgrim Fathers and the Congregational Church, 1624* (Boston, 1883); Alexander MacKennal, *The Story of the English Separatists* (London, 1893); id., *Sketches in the Evolution of English Congregationalism* (Boston, 1901); Frederick J. Powicke, "Lists of Early Separatists," *TCHS,* 1 (1901-4), 141-58; Edwin H. Hall, "The Origin of Congregationalism," *CSMP,* 8 (1902-4), 326-33; Champlin Burrage, *The True Story of Robert Browne (1550?-1633), Father of Congregationalism . . .* (Oxford, 1906); Robert W. Dale, *History of English Congregationalism* (London, 1907); Champlin Burrage, *The Early English Dissenters in the Light of Recent Research (1550-1641),* 2 vols. (Cambridge, 1912); Roland G. Usher, *The Pilgrims and Their History* (New York, 1918); John Brown, *The Pilgrim Fathers of New England and Their Puritan Successors,* 4th edn. (London, 1920); Albert Peel, *The First Congregational Churches: New Light on Separatist Congregations in London, 1567-1581* (Cambridge, 1920); Albert Peel, *The Brownists in Norwich and Norfolk about 1580* (Cambridge, 1920); H. F. Sanders, "Early Puritanism and Separatism in Nottingham," *TCHS,* 12 (1933-36), 100-111; Robert Harrison and Robert Browne, *The Writings of Robert Harrison and Robert Browne,* ed. Albert Peel and Leland H. Carlson (London, 1953); Barrington R. White, *The English Separatist Tradi-*

tion: From the Marian Martyrs to the Pilgrim Fathers (London, 1971), based on a 1960 Oxford dissertation; George Selement, "The Covenant Theology of English Separatism and the Separation of Church and State," *Journal of the American Academy of Religion,* 41 (1973), 66-74; C. Robert Cole and Michael E. Moody (eds.), *The Dissenting Tradition* (Athens, OH, 1975); Murray Tolmie, *The Triumph of the Saints: The Separate Churches of London, 1616-1649* (Cambridge, 1977); Michael Watts, *The Dissenters* (Oxford, 1978); Lowell H. Zuck, "Reviewing Congregational Origins among Puritans and Separatists in England," *BCL,* 29 (1977-78), #2, 4-13; Michael Moody, "Puritan versus Separatist: A New Letter," *JURCHS,* 2 (1981), #7, 243-45; J. W. Martin, "The Protestant Underground Congregations of Mary's Reign," *JEH,* 35 (1984), 519-38; William G. Chrystal, "John Robinson and William Ames: A New Look at Old Debates about Separatism," *BCL,* 36 (1984-85), #2, 4-11; J. W. Martin, "'The First That Made Separation from the Reformed Church of England,'" *ARG,* 77 (1986), 281-312; Stephen Brachlow, *The Communion of Saints: Radical Puritan and Separatist Ecclesiology, 1570-1625* (Oxford, 1988), based on a 1979 Oxford dissertation.

15. Champlin Burrage, *The Church Covenant Idea: Its Origin and Development; id., The Early English Dissenters in the Light of Recent Research;* Stephen Mayor, *The Lord's Supper in Early English Dissent* (London, 1972); Barrington R. White, *The English Separatist Tradition: From the Marian Martyrs to the Pilgrim Fathers.*

16. For the discussion of tithes in early modern England, see the following primary sources: *Tithes and Oblations. According to the Lawes Established in the Church of England* (n.p., 1595); George Carleton, *Tithes Examined and Proued to be due to the Clergie by a Diuine Right . . .* , 2nd edn. (London, 1611); John Selden, *The Historie of Tithes . . .* (London, 1618); Henry Spelman, *The Larger Treatise Concerning Tithes . . .* (London, 1647); Lancelot Andrewes, *Of the Right of Tithes . . .* (London, 1647); *Epistola Medio-Saxonica, or, Middlesex First Letter to . . . the Lord General Cromwell: Together with their Petition Concerning Tithes and Copy-Holds of Inheritance . . . to which is added . . . Tithes Totally Routed by Magna Charta* (London, 1653); William Prynne, *Ten Considerable Quaeries Concerning Tithes . . .* (London, 1659).

The following secondary works discuss the history of tithes in England during all periods: John S. Brewer, *The Endowments and Establishment of the Church of England . . .* , 3rd edn. ed. Lewis T. Dibdin (London, 1886); William Easterby, *The History of the Law of Tithes in England* (Cambridge, 1888); Henry W. Clarke, *A History of Tithes,* 2nd edn. (London, 1894); Margaret James, "The Political Importance of the Tithes Controversy in the English Revolution, 1640-60," *History,* 26 (1941), 1-18; A. G. Little, "Personal Tithes," *EHR,* 60 (1945), 67-88; Christopher Hill, *Economic Problems of the Church* (Oxford, 1956); "Tithing Customs and Disputes: The Evidence of Glebe Terriers, 1698-1850," *Agricultural History Review,* 18 (1970), 17-35; Alan Wharham, "Tithes in Country Life," *History Today,* 22 (1972), 426-33; Eric J. Evans, *The Contentious Tithe: The Tithe Problem and English Agriculture, 1750-1850* (London, 1976); Eric J. Evans and C. A. Robertson, "The Tithe Heresy of Friar William Russell," *Albion,* 8 (1976), 1-16; Eric J. Evans, "Tithes," in N. L. Matthews, *William Sheppard, Cromwell's Law Reformer,* 2 (Cambridge, 1985), 389-405; R. Kain and H. Prince, *The Tithe Surveys of England and Wales* (Cambridge, 1985); R. J. P. Kain, R. E. J. Fry, and H. M. E. Holt, *An Atlas and Index of the Tithe Files of Mid-Nineteenth Century England and Wales* (Cambridge, 1986). The Quakers in particular conscientiously objected to compulsory tithes: Nicholas J. Morgan, "Lancashire Quakers and the Tithe, 1660-1730," *JFHS*, 54 (1980), 235-54; Barry Reay, "Quaker Opposition to Tithes, 1652-1660," *P+P*, 86 (1980), 98-120; Alfred W. Braithwaite, "Early Tithe Prosecutions: Friends as Outlaws," *JFHS*, 49 (1960), 148-56; Eric J. Evans, "'Our Faithful Testimony': The Society of Friends and Tithe Payments, 1690-1730," *JFHS*, 52 (1968-71), #2 (1969), 106-21; Edward Bryan, "Irish Tithes in British Politics," *HMPEC*, 39 (1970), 295-306. For New England, cf. Samuel S. Green, "Voluntary System in the Maintenance of Ministers," *AASP*, n.s., 4 (1885-87), 86-126.

17. One aspect of early modern life that has received a lot of critical attention has been the matter of the Elizabethan poor laws. After 1601, poor relief was to be administered through the parish; this policy resulted from the demise of the old medieval system of charity, primarily centered in monasteries and manors, and from the inflationary shift in the economy which multiplied greatly the number of poor in England; cf. Richard Burn, *The History of the Poor Laws . . .* (London, 1764); James Dunston, *A Treatise of the Poor Law . . .* (London, 1850); E. M. Leonard, *The Early History of English Poor Relief . . .* (Cambridge, 1900); Sidney Webb and Beatrice Webb, *English Local Government: English Poor Law History . . .*, 2 vols. in 3 (New York, 1927-29); John J. Clarke, *Social Administration, Including the Poor Laws*, 2nd edn. (London, 1935); Dorothy Marshall, "Revisions in Economic History. VII: The Old Poor Law, 1662-1795," *Economic History Review*, 8 (1937), 38-47; Carl R. Steinbicker, *Poor Relief in the Sixteenth Century* (Washington, DC, 1937); Christopher Hill, "Puritans and the Poor," *P+P*, 2 (1952), 32-50; V. Kiernan, "Puritanism and the Poor," *P+P*, 3 (1953), 45-54; Christopher Hill, "The Poor and the Parish," in *Society and Puritanism in Pre-Revolutionary England*, 259-97; John J. Bagley and Alexander J. Bagley, *The English Poor Law* (New York, 1966); James S. Taylor, "The Mythology of the Old Poor Law," *Journal of Economic History*, 29 (1969), 292-97; Neil L. Kunze, "Origins of Modern Social Legislation: The Henrician Poor Law of 1536," *Albion*, 3 (1971), 9-20; Donald N. McCloskey, "New Perspectives on the Old Poor Law," *Explorations in Economic History*, 10 (1972-73), 419-36; Geoffrey W. Oxley, *Poor Relief in England and Wales, 1601-1834* (Newton Abbot, Devon, England, 1974); Mary MacKinnan, "English Poor Law Policy and the Crusade against Out-Relief," *Journal of Economic History*, 47 (1987), 603-25; P. Rushton, "The Poor Law, the Parish and the Community in North-East England, 1600-1800," *Northern History*, 25 (1989), 135-52.

18. Albert Peel identifies 42 individuals who died as martyrs; 34 "died in prison"; 8 were executed, usually by hanging; *The Noble Army of Congregational Martyrs* (London, 1948); Albert Peel, "Congregational Martyrs at Bury St. Edmunds: How Many?" *TCHS*, 15 (1945-48), 64-67.

19. Alexander Young, *Chronicles of the Pilgrim Fathers of the Colony of Plymouth*; "The Brownists in Amsterdam," *TCHS*, 2 (1905-6), 160-72; George Sumner, "Memoirs of the Pilgrims at Leyden," *MHSC*, ser. 3, 9 (1846), 42-74; John Waddington, *The Track of the Hidden Church; or, the Springs of the Pilgrim Movement*; John Waddington, *Congregational History, 1567-1700*; William M. Coleman, *The History of the Primitive Yankees; or, the Pilgrim Fathers in England and Holland* (Washington, DC, 1881); J. De Hoop Scheffer, *History of the Free Churchmen Called the Brownists, Pilgrim Fathers and Baptists in the Dutch Republic, 1581-1701*, trans. William E. Griffis (Ithaca, NY, 1922); William E. Griffis, *The Influence of the Netherlands in the Making of the English Commonwealth and the American Republic . . .* (Boston, [1891]); Henry M. Dexter, "English Exiles in Amster-

dam, 1597-1625," *MHSP,* ser. 2, 6 (1890-91), 41-64; Talbot W. Chambers, "Holland and Religious Freedom," ASCH, *Papers,* ser. 1, 5 (1893), 89-97; Douglas Campbell, *The Puritan in Holland, England and America . . .* , 3rd edn. (New York, 1893); Edward Arber (ed.), *The Story of the Pilgrim Fathers, 1606-1623 A.D., as Told by Themselves, Their Friends, and Their Enemies* (Boston, 1897); Morton Dexter, "The Members of the Pilgrim Company in Leyden," *MHSP,* ser. 2, 17 (1903), 167-84; Henry M. Dexter and Morton Dexter, *The England and Holland of the Pilgrims* (Boston, 1905); Worthington C. Ford (ed.), "Letters Relating to Holland and New England, 1624-1636," *MHSP,* ser. 3, 2 (1908-9), 203-34; J. C. Whitebrook, "Preachers in the Netherlands in 1634," *TCHS,* 5 (1911-12), 290-92; W. T. Whitley, "The Rise of Lay Preaching in Holland," *TCHS,* 5 (1911-12), 282-89; Winslow Warren and Henry H. Edes, "The Pilgrims in Holland and America," *CSMP,* 18 (1915-16), 130-52; R. G. Usher, *The Pilgrims and Their History;* Frederick Smithen, *Continental Protestantism and the English Reformation* (London, 1927); Raymond P. Stearns, "The New England Way in Holland," *NEQ,* 6 (1933), 747-92; *id., Congregationalism in the Dutch Netherlands: The Rise and Fall of the English Congregational Classis, 1621-1635,* SCH, 4 (Chicago, 1940); John J. Murray, "The Cultural Impact of the Flemish Low Countries on Sixteenth- and Seventeenth-Century England," *AHR,* 62 (1956-57), 837-54; R. R. Darlington et al., *The English Church and the Continent* (London, 1959); Keith L. Sprunger, *The Learned Doctor William Ames: Dutch Backgrounds of English and American Puritanism* (Urbana, IL, 1972), based on a 1963 dissertation completed at the University of Illinois; Alice C. Carter, *The English Reformed Church in Amsterdam in the Seventeenth Century* (Amsterdam, 1964); J. W. Verbugt, *Leyden and the Pilgrim Fathers* (Leyden, 1970); Derek Baker (ed.), *Reform and Reformation: England and the Continent c. 1500– c. 1750;* Keith L. Sprunger, "Other Pilgrims in Leiden: Hugh Goodyear and the English Reformed Church," *CH,* 41 (1972), 46-60; *id.,* "English Puritans and Anabaptists in Early Seventeenth-Century Amsterdam," *Mennonite Quarterly Review,* 46 (1972), 113-28; *id.,* "Archbishop Laud's Campaign against Puritanism at The Hague," *CH,* 44 (1975), 308-20; *id., Dutch Puritanism: A History of English and Scottish Churches of the Netherlands in the Sixteenth and Seventeenth Centuries* (Leiden, 1982); Patrick Collinson, "England and International Calvinism, 1558-1640," in Menna Prestwich (ed.), *International Calvinism, 1541-1715* (Oxford, 1985), 197-223.

It should be noted that fleeing to the Continent from Anglicanism is different from fleeing to the Continent from Marian Roman Catholicism; cf. Christina Garrett, *The Marian Exiles;* Patrick Collinson, "The Authorship of *A Brieff Discours off the Troubles begonne at Franckford,*" *JEH,* 9 (1958), 188-208; John M. Krumm, "Continental Protestantism and Elizabethan Anglicanism (1570-1595)," in Franklin H. Littell (ed.), *Reformation Studies: Essays in Honor of Roland Bainton* (Richmond, VA, 1962), 129-44.

20. Ian Breward, "The Life and Theology of William Perkins, 1558-1602" (diss. Manchester, 1963); Victor Lewis Priebe, "The Covenant Theology of William Perkins" (diss. Drew, 1967); William Perkins, *The Work of William Perkins,* ed. Ian Breward (Appleford, Abingdon, England, 1970); Charles Robert Munson, "William Perkins: Theologian of Transition" (diss. Case Western Reserve, 1971); Lionel Greve, "Freedom and Discipline in the Theology of John Calvin, William Perkins and John Wesley: An Examination of the Origin and Nature of Pietism" (diss. Hartford Seminary Foundation, 1975); R. T. Kendall, *Calvin and English Calvinism to 1649* (Oxford, 1979), based on a 1976 Oxford dissertation; Richard A. Muller, "Perkins' *A Golden Chaine:* Predestinarian

System or Schematized *Ordo Salutis?*" *SCJ*, 9 (1978), 68-81; Mark R. Shaw, "The Marrow of Practical Divinity: A Study in the Theology of William Perkins" (diss. Westminster Theological Seminary, 1981); Donald K. McKim, "William Perkins and the Theology of the Covenant," in Horton M. Davies (ed.), *Studies of the Church in History* (Allison Park, PA, 1983), 85-101; Mark R. Shaw, "Drama in the Meeting House: The Concept of Conversion in the Theology of William Perkins," *Westminster Theological Journal*, 45 (1983), 41-72; Richard A. Muller, *Christ and the Decree: Christology and Predestination in Reformed Theology from Calvin to Perkins* (Durham, NC, 1986); Donald K. McKim, *Ramism in William Perkins' Theology* (New York, 1987).

21. *The Thirty-Nine Articles of the Church of England* (1571) did have a statement about coming to Communion in an unsaved state: "XXIX. Of the wicked which do not eate the body of Christe in the vse of the Lordes Supper. The wicked, and suche as be voyde of a liuelye fayth, although they do carnally and visibly presse with their teeth (as Saint Augustine sayth) the Sacrament of the body and blood of Christ: yet in no wyse are they partakers of Christe, but rather to their condemnation do eate and drinke the signe or Sacrament of so great a thing," Schaff, *Creeds*, 3.506-7.

The *BCP* did have instructions to the local clerics about participation in the Lord's Supper: "So many as intend to be partakers of the holy Communion shall signify to the Curate over night, or else in the morning afore the beginning of Morning prayer, or immediately after. And if any of these be an open and notorious evil liver, so that the Congregation by him is offended, or have done any wrong to his neighbours, by word or deed; the Curate having knowledge thereof, shall call him, and advertise him in any wise not to presume to the Lord's Table, until he hath openly declared himself to have truly repented and amended his former naughty life, that the Congregation may thereby be satisfied, which before were offended; and that he hath recompensed the parties, to whom he hath done wrong, or at least declare himself to be in full purpose so to do, as soon as he conveniently may. The same order shall the Curate use with those betwixt whom he perceiveth malice and hatred to reign; not suffering them to be partakers of the Lord's Table, until he know them to be reconciled." "The Order for the Administration of the Lord's Supper, or Holy Communion," in *BCP*; quoted from *Liturgiae Britannicae, or the Several Editions of The Book of Common Prayer of the Church of England . . . Together with the Liturgy set Forth for the Use of the Church of Scotland, Arranged to shew Their Respective Variations,* ed. William Keeling (London, 1851); cf. also *The English Rite, Being a Synopsis of the Sources and Revisions of the Book of Common Prayer,* ed. F. E. Brightman (London, 1915). Included in the *Liturgiae Britannicae* are the *BCPs* for 1549, 1552/1559, and 1662, along with the Scottish Liturgy of 1604. While the above-quoted rubric sounds like a Puritan statement, the experimental Puritan would maintain that a person should prove his sainthood first and then be admitted to communion; the Anglican would maintain that a person was admitted already to communion by virtue of his baptism and childhood confirmation in the parish, and should only be excluded when there was evidence of egregious sin.

22. The two best recent surveys of Puritan evangelism and spirituality are those by Charles L. Cohen and Joel R. Beeke: Charles L. Cohen, *God's Caress: The Psychology of Puritan Religious Experience* (New York, 1986), based on a 1982 dissertation completed at the University of California at Berkeley; Joel R. Beeke, *Assurance of Faith: Calvin, English Puritanism, and the Dutch Second Reformation* (New York, 1991). Beeke's focus is

theological; Cohen's work deals with both the theoretical issues and actual case studies and accounts of conversion found in the Puritan literature. Edmund S. Morgan made a significant earlier contribution to the discussion with his *Visible Saints: The History of a Puritan Idea.*

For the English tradition cf. also Norman Pettit, *The Heart Prepared: Grace and Conversion in Puritan Spiritual Life;* also his "[Essay Review]: The Work of the Spirit in Old and New England," *NEQ,* 57 (1984), 421-27; C. J. Sommerville, "Conversion, Sacrament and Assurance in the Puritan Covenant of Grace, to 1650"; James L. Shields, "The Doctrine of Regeneration in English Puritan Theology, 1604-1689" (diss. Southwestern Baptist Theological Seminary, 1965); C. J. Sommerville, "Conversion versus the Early Puritan Covenant of Grace," *Journal of Presbyterian History,* 44 (1966), 178-97; Lynn Baird Tipson, Jr., "The Development of a Puritan Understanding of Conversion" (diss. Yale, 1972); J. Sears McGee, "Conversion and the Imitation of Christ in Anglican and Puritan Writing," *JBS,* 15 (1976), 21-39; Jerald C. Brauer, "Conversion: From Puritanism to Revivalism," *JR,* 58 (1978), 227-43; Mark R. Shaw, "Drama in the Meeting House: The Concept of Conversion in the Theology of William Perkins"; Mary C. Grimes, "Saving Grace among Puritans and Quakers: A Study of 17th and 18th Century Conversion Experiences," *QH,* 72 (1983), 3-26.

On the American Puritan side see the following: Everett H. Emerson, "Thomas Hooker and the Reformed Theology: The Relationship of Hooker's Conversion Preaching to Its Background" (diss. Louisiana State, 1955); James Rodney Fulcher, "Puritan Piety in Early New England: A Study in Spiritual Regeneration from the Antinomian Controversy to the Cambridge Synod of 1648 in the Massachusetts Bay Colony"; Richard A. Hasler, "Thomas Shepard: Pastor-Evangelist (1605-1649): A Study in the New England Puritan Ministry" (diss. Hartford Seminary Foundation, 1964); Daniel B. Shea, Jr., *Spiritual Biography in Early America* (Princeton, NJ, 1968); Michael McGiffert, "Introduction," in *God's Plot: The Paradoxes of Puritan Piety; Being the Autobiography and Journal of Thomas Shepard* (Amherst, MA, 1972), 3-32; George J. Selement, "The Means to Grace: A Study of Conversion in New England" (diss. New Hampshire, 1974); John Fiske, *The Notebook of the Reverend John Fiske, 1644-1675,* ed. Robert G. Pope, *CSMP,* 47 (1974); Patricia L. Caldwell, "A Literary Study of Puritan Testimonies of Religious Experience from the 1630s to the 1660s, Including a Critical Edition of Thomas Shepard's Manuscript, 'The Confessions of diverse propounded to be received and were entertayned as members,' from the First Church of Cambridge, Massachusetts, 1637-1645" (diss. Harvard, 1979); Murray G. Murphey, "The Psychodynamics of Puritan Conversion," *AQ,* 31 (1979), 135-47; Phyllis M. Jones, "Puritan's Progress: The Story of the Soul's Salvation in the Early New England Sermons," *EAL,* 15 (1980), 14-28; Thomas Shepard, *Thomas Shepard's Confessions,* George Selement and Bruce C. Wooley (eds.), *CSMP,* 58 (1981); Patricia Caldwell, *The Puritan Conversion Narrative: The Beginnings of American Expression* (Cambridge, 1983); and John R. Higgins, "Aspects of the Doctrine of the Holy Spirit during the Antinomian Controversy of New England with Special Reference to John Cotton and Anne Hutchinson."

23. William W. Beach, "The Meaning and Authority of Conscience in Protestant Thought of Seventeenth-Century England" (diss. Yale, 1944); C. J. Sommerville, "Conversion, Sacrament and Assurance in the Puritan Covenant of Grace"; John von Rohr, "Covenant and Assurance in Early English Puritanism," *CH,* 24 (1965), 195-203;

George H. Williams, "Called by Thy Name Leave Us Not: The Case of Mrs. Joan Drake, a Formative Episode in the Pastoral Career of Thomas Hooker in England," *Harvard Library Bulletin*, 16 (1968), 278-300; Robert W. A. Letham, "Saving Faith and Assurance in Reformed Theology: Zwingli to the Synod of Dort" (diss. Aberdeen, 1979); Murray G. Murphey, "The Psychodynamics of Puritan Conversion"; M. Charles Bell, *Calvin and Scottish Theology: The Doctrine of Assurance* (Edinburgh, 1985), based on a 1982 dissertation completed at the University of Aberdeen; John O. King, *The Iron of Melancholy: Structures of Spiritual Conversion in America from the Puritan Conscience to Victorian Neurosis* (Middletown, CT, 1983); John von Rohr, *The Covenant of Grace in Puritan Thought* (Atlanta, 1986); Charles L. Cohen, *God's Caress: The Psychology of Puritan Religious Experience;* Joel R. Beeke, *Assurance of Faith: Calvin, English Puritanism, and the Dutch Second Reformation.*

24. In early New England, the adoption of the congregational form of government combined with the requirement that a public testimony of faith be given led to the practice of the entire gathered congregation examining an applicant for full church membership. However, this practice was not always followed with rigor, particularly in the case of women; cf. Robert A. Rees, "Seeds of Enlightenment: Public Testimony in the New England Congregational Churches, 1630-1750," *EAL*, 3 (1968), 22-29; L. Baird Tipson, "Invisible Saints: The 'Judgement of Charity' in the Early New England Churches," *CH*, 44 (1975), 460-66.

25. trans. Talcott Parsons (New York, 1930).

26. Cf. also W. Lawrence Highfill, "Faith and Works in the Ethical Theory of Richard Baxter" (diss. Duke, 1954); Hideo Oki, "Ethics in Seventeenth Century English Puritanism" (diss. Union Theological Seminary, NYC, 1960); James Frank Veninga, "Covenant Theology and Ethics in the Thought of John Calvin and John Preston," 2 vols. (diss. Rice, 1974); Richard Forrer, "The Puritan Religious Dilemma: The Ethical Dimensions of God's Sovereignty," *Journal of the American Academy of Religion*, 44 (1976), 613-28; Robert S. Paul, "Social Justice and the Puritan 'Dual Ethic,'" in *Intergerini Parietis Septum (Ephesians 2:14): Essays Presented to Markus Barth on His Sixty-Fifth Birthday*, ed. Dikran Y. Hadidian (Pittsburgh, PA, 1981), 251-84.

27. The concern over works, grace, and justification emerged at the same time as the federal theology was developed with its prelapsarian "covenant of works"; cf. Albrecht B. Ritschl, *Die christliche Lehre von der Rechtfertigung und Versöhnung* (Bonn, 1870); English translation: *A Critical History of the Christian Doctrine of Justification and Reconciliation*, trans. John S. Black (Edinburgh, 1872); N. Diemer, *Het scheppingsverbond met Adam (het verbond der werken), bij de theologen der 16e, 17e, en 18e eeuw in Zwitserland, Duitschland, Nederland en Engeland*, with a Preface by F. W. Grosheide (Kampen, 1935); William K. B. Stoever, *"A Faire and Easie Way to Heaven": Covenant Theology and Antinomianism in Early Massachusetts;* Holmes Rolston III, "Responsible Man in Reformed Theology: Calvin versus the Westminster Confession," *Scottish Journal of Theology*, 23 (1970), 129-56; Holmes Rolston III, *John Calvin versus the Westminster Confession* (Richmond, VA, 1972); John S. Bray, "The Value of Works in the Theology of Calvin and Beza," *SCJ*, 4 (1973), 77-86; William K. B. Stoever, "Nature, Grace and John Cotton: The Theological Dimension in the New England Antinomianism Controversy"; R. Sherman Isbell, "The Origin of the Concept of the Covenant of Works" (Master of Theology thesis, Westminster Theological Seminary, 1976); Mark Walter Karlberg, "The

Mosaic Covenant and the Concept of Works in Reformed Hermeneutics: A Historical-Critical Analysis with Particular Attention to Early Covenant Eschatology" (diss. Westminster Theological Seminary, 1980); Michael McGiffert, "Grace and Works: The Rise and Division of Covenant Divinity in Elizabethan Puritanism," *HThR,* 75 (1982), 463-502; Robert W. A. Letham, "The *Foedus Operum:* Some Factors Accounting for Its Development," *SCJ,* 14 (1983), 457-67; Michael McGiffert, "God's Controversy with New England"; *id.,* "From Moses to Adam: The Making of the Covenant of Works," *SCJ,* 19 (1988), 131-55; David A. Weir, *The Origins of the Federal Theology in Sixteenth-Century Reformation Thought* (Oxford, 1990); Alan C. Clifford, *Atonement and Justification: English Evangelical Theology, 1640-1790: An Evaluation* (Oxford, 1990).

28. For an explanation of antinomianism, see A. H. Newman, "Antinomianism and Antinomian Controversies," *NSHE,* 1 (1908), 196-201; J. McBride Sterrett, "Antinomianism," *ERE,* 1 (1908), 581-82; Gertrude Huehns, *Antinomianism in English History, with Special Reference to the Period 1640-1660* (London, 1951); William K. B. Stoever, "The Covenant of Works in Puritan Theology: The Antinomian Crisis in New England"; revised and published as *"A Faire and Easie Way to Heaven": Covenant Theology and Antinomianism in Early Massachusetts; id.,* "Nature, Grace and John Cotton"; Norman B. Graebner, "Protestants and Dissenters: An Examination of the Seventeenth-Century Eatonist and New England Antinomian Controversies in Reformation Perspective" (diss. Duke, 1984); David A. Weir, *The Origins of the Federal Theology,* 6, 20-21, 65. Charles Cohen, *God's Caress: The Psychology of Puritan Religious Experience,* 288-89, gives a summary of the primary and secondary sources for the New England Antinomian Controversy, 1636-38.

29. Archibald W. Harrison, *The Beginnings of Arminianism to the Synod of Dort* (London, 1926); *id., Arminianism* (London, 1937); Frederick J. Pamp, Jr., "Studies in the Origins of English Arminianism" (diss. Harvard, 1951); Carl Bangs, "Arminius and the Reformation," *CH,* 30 (1961), 155-70; *id., Arminius: A Study in the Dutch Reformation* (Nashville, TN, 1971); Gerrit J. Hoenderdaal, "Arminius . . . Arminianismus," *Theologische Realencyklopädie,* 4 (1979), 63-69; Richard A. Muller, "The Federal Motif in Seventeenth Century Arminian Theology," *Nederlands Archief voor Kerkgeschiedenis,* 62 (1982), 102-22; John M. Hicks, "The Theology of Grace in the Thought of Jacobus Arminius and Philip van Limborch: A Study in the Development of Seventeenth-Century Dutch Arminianism" (diss. Westminster Theological Seminary, 1985).

30. For discussion of preparationism, see Norman Pettit, "The Image of the Heart in Early Puritanism: The Emergence in England and America of the Concept of Preparation for Grace"; later revised and published as: *The Heart Prepared: Grace and Conversion in Puritan Spiritual Life;* also Perry Miller, " 'Preparation for Salvation' in Seventeenth Century New England," *JHI,* 4 (1943), 253-86. Other works that deal with the subject are: Howard M. Feinstein, "The Prepared Heart: A Comparative Study of Puritan Theology and Psychoanalysis," *AQ,* 22 (1970), 166-76; Alfred Habegger, "Preparing the Soul for Christ: The Contrasting Sermon Forms of John Cotton and Thomas Hooker," *American Literature,* 41 (1970), 342-54; David L. Parker, "The Application of Humiliation: Ramist Logic and the Rise of Preparationism in New England" (diss. University of Pennsylvania, 1972); R. T. Kendall, *Calvin and English Calvinism to 1649.* The Westminster Assembly specifically rejected preparationism: "Man, by his fall into a state of sin, hath wholly lost all ability of will to any spiritual good accompanying salvation: so as, a natu-

ral man, being altogether averse from that good, and dead in sin, is not able, by his own strength, to convert himself, or to prepare himself thereunto"; *WCF,* Chapter 9.4; Schaff, *Creeds,* 3.623.

31. Rosemary O'Day and Felicity Heal (eds.), *Continuity and Change: Personnel and Administration of the Church of England, 1500-1642* (Leicester, 1976); Rosemary O'Day, *The English Clergy: The Emergence and Consolidation of a Profession* (Leicester, 1979); A. Tindal Hart, *Clergy and Society, 1600-1800* (London, 1968); F. Heal, "Economic Problems of the Clergy," in Heal and O'Day (eds.), *Church and Society in England,* 99-118; R. Houlbrooke, "The Protestant Episcopate, 1547-1603: The Pastoral Contribution," in Heal and O'Day (eds.), *Church and Society in England,* 78-98; R. O'Day, "Ecclesiastical Patronage: Who Controlled the Church?" in Heal and O'Day (eds.), *Church and Society in England,* 137-55.

32. Paul Seaver, *The Puritan Lectureships: The Politics of Religious Dissent, 1560-1662* (Stanford, CA, 1970); cf. also Christopher Hill, "The Ratsbane of Lecturing," in *Society and Puritanism in Pre-Revolutionary England,* 79-123; Patrick Collinson, "Lectures by Combination: Structures and Characteristics of Church Life in 17th-Century England," Institute of Historical Research, *Bulletin,* 48 (1975), 181-273.

33. This is reinforced in the *BCP,* which provides for an offering to be taken up before Holy Communion; however, the offering is for "alms for the poor," *not* tithes. At this point in time in the Anglican church the tithe was seen as a tax, not as an act of worship. It is interesting to note that most New England towns began with a system of tithing that was a tax, but John Cotton challenged the practice in Boston and started the practice of financing the maintenance for the minister and the expenses of the Boston church through weekly offerings: "After much deliberation and serious advice, the Lord directed the teacher, Mr. Cotton, to make it clear by the scripture, that the minister's maintenance, as well as all other charges of the church, should be defrayed out of a stock, or treasury, which was to be raised out of the weekly contribution; which accordingly was agreed upon" (John Winthrop, *The Journal of John Winthrop, 1630-1649,* ed. Richard S. Dunn, James Savage, and Laetitia Yeandle [Cambridge, MA, 1996], 106-7). Some New England churches followed suit, others kept the system of "rates" in which the tithe was a tax.

34. Henry B. Bell, *Archbishop Laud and Priestly Government* (London, 1905); Hugh Trevor-Roper, "Archbishop Laud," *History,* 30 (1945), 181-90; James T. Addison, "William Laud, Prelate and Champion of Order," *HMPEC,* 21 (1952), 17-61; Hugh Trevor-Roper, *Archbishop Laud, 1573-1645,* 2nd edn. (Hamden, CT, 1962); Nicholas Tyacke, *Anti-Calvinists: The Rise of English Arminianism, c. 1590-1640* (New York, 1987).

35. Henry A. Parker, "The Feoffees of Impropriations," *CSMP,* 11 (1906-7), 263-76; E. W. Kirby, "Lay Feoffees: A Study in Militant Puritanism," *Journal of Modern History,* 14 (1942), 1-25; Isabel M. Calder, "A Seventeenth-Century Attempt to Purify the Anglican Church," *AHR,* 53 (1947-48), 760-75.

36. Cf. John Winthrop's famous words: "For wee must consider that wee shall be a citty upon a hill. The eies of all people are uppon us. Soe that if wee shall deale falsely with our God in this worke we haue undertaken, and soe cause him to withdrawe his present help from us, wee shall be made a story and a by-word through the world . . ."; *A Modell of Christian Charity . . . ,* rpt. in *MHSC,* ser. 3, 7 (1838), 47.

Notes to Chapter 2

1. There is only one exception: the Parliament of England granted Rhode Island Colony its first charter on Tuesday, March 12, 1643/4; cf. Thorpe, *Federal and State Constitutions*, 6.3209-11. Even that charter acknowledges Charles as "our Sovereign Lord King Charles," cf. p. 3211.

2. Ian K. Steele, *The English Atlantic, 1675-1740: An Exploration of Communication and Community.*

3. On the First British Empire in North America, cf. n. 15 in the Introduction, above.

4. Herbert L. Osgood, "England and the Colonies," *Political Science Quarterly*, 2 (1887), 440-69; *id.*, "England and the American Colonies in the Seventeenth Century," *Political Science Quarterly*, 17 (1902), 206-22; Charles M. Andrews, *The Colonial Period of American History*; Robert M. Bliss, *Revolution and Empire: English Politics and the American Colonies in the Seventeenth Century*; Great Britain, England, Privy Council, "Orders in Council, 1660-61 to 1692 [Concerning New England]," *MHSC*, ser. 4, 2 (1854), 279-304.

5. The general overviews for New England can be found in: Jeremiah Dummer, *A Defence of the New-England Charters* (1721; London, 1765); Israel Mauduit, *A Short View of the History of the New England Colonies, With Respect to Their Charters and Constitution* (1769; 4th edn., London, 1776); Melville Egleston, "The Land System of the New England Colonies," *JHUSHPS*, ser. 4 (Baltimore, 1886), #11-12, 545-600; G. T. Curtis, *Constitutional History of the U.S.* (New York, 1889); Herbert L. Osgood, "The Corporation as a Form of Colonial Government," *Political Science Quarterly*, 11 (1896), 259-77, 502-33, 694-715; *id.*, "The Proprietary Provinces as a Form of Colonial Government," *AHR*, 2 (1896-97), 644-64; 3 (1897-98), 31-55, 244-65; Andrew C. McLaughlin, *The Foundations of American Constitutionalism*; Benjamin F. Wright, "The History of Written Constitutions in America," in *Essays in History and Political Theory* (Cambridge, MA, 1936), 344-71; Walter H. Bennett, *American Theories of Federalism* (Tuscaloosa, AL, 1964), a revision of a dissertation completed at Duke in 1940; Charles McIlwain, *Constitutionalism Ancient and Modern*; George C. Bryan, "Concepts of Leadership in American Political Thought: The Puritan Period" (diss. Harvard, 1950); Patricia M. Lines and John McClaughry, *Early American Community Development Corporations: The Trading Companies* (Cambridge, MA, 1970); David O. Damerall, "The Modernization of Massachusetts: The Transformation of Public Attitudes and Institutions, 1689 to 1715" (diss. University of Texas, Austin, 1981); Leonard W. Levy, "Social Compact Theory," *Encyclopedia of the American Constitution* 4 (1986), 1700-1702; *Encyclopedia of the American Constitution*; Jack P. Greene, *Peripheries and Center: Constitutional Development in the Extended Polities of the British Empire and the United States, 1607-1789*; Donald S. Lutz and Jack D. Warren, *A Covenanted People: The Religious Tradition and the Origins of American Constitutionalism*; Donald Lutz, *The Origins of American Constitutionalism*; William Johnson Everett, *God's Federal Republic: Reconstructing Our Governing Symbol* (New York, 1988); Donald S. Lutz, ed., *Colonial Origins of the American Constitution: A Documentary History* (Indianapolis, IN, 1998).

The English background can be found in: Philip S. Haffenden, "The Crown and the Colonial Charters, 1675-1688," *WMQ*, ser. 3, 15 (1958), 297-311, 452-66; Margaret A. Judson, *The Crisis of the Constitution: An Essay in Constitutional and Political*

Thought in England, 1603-1645 (New Brunswick, NJ, 1949); William H. Whitmore, *Increase Mather: The Agent of Massachusetts Colony in England for the Concession of a Charter* (Boston, 1869); Charles Deane, "The Forms in Issuing Letters Patent by the Crown of England," *MHSP,* 1 (1869-70), 166-96; Paul R. Hyams, "The Charter as a Source for the Early Common Law," *Journal of Legal History,* 12 (1991), 173-89; J. P. Wallis, "Early Colonial Constitutions," Royal Historical Society, *Transactions,* ser. 2, 10 (1896), 59-83; Louise Phelps Kellogg, "The Colonial Charter: A Study in English Colonial Administration" (diss. Wisconsin, 1902); rev. and published as *The American Colonial Charter: A Study of English Administration in Relation Thereto, Chiefly After 1688* in American Historical Association, *Annual Report . . . 1903,* vol. 1 (Washington, DC, 1904), 185-341; rpt. New York, 1971, based on a 1902 dissertation completed at the University of Wisconsin; Edward P. Cheyney, "The Manor of East Greenwich in the County of Kent," *AHR,* 11 (1905-6), 29-35; B. L. K. Henderson, "The Commonwealth Charters," Royal Historical Society, *Transactions,* ser. 3, 6 (1912), 129-62; Albert Mathews, "Notes on the Massachusetts Royal Commissions, 1681-1775," *CSMP,* 17 (1913-14), 293-391; Clyde M. Ferrell, "The Massachusetts Colonial Agents in England" (diss. Wisconsin, 1923); James J. Burns, "The Colonial Agents of New England" (Washington, DC, 1935; rpt. Philadelphia, 1975), a dissertation completed at the Catholic University of America that same year.

For Connecticut see: Henry Williams and Henry H. Edes, "On the Charter Oak and the Connecticut Charter," *CSMP,* 5 (1897-98), 216-20; Leonard Bacon, *A Discourse on the Early Constitutional History of Connecticut . . .* (Hartford, CT, 1843); James H. Trumbull, *Historical Notes on the Constitutions of Connecticut, 1639-1818 . . .* (1873; rpt. Hartford, CT, 1901); Henry Bronson, "Chapters on the Early Government of Connecticut: With Critical and Explanatory Remarks on the Constitution of 1639," *NHCHSP,* 3 (1882), 293-403; Alexander Johnston, *The Genesis of a New England State (Connecticut) . . .* (1883; rpt. New York, 1973); William Bliss, "The Charter of Connecticut and the Charter of Yale College," *New Englander and Yale Review,* 43 (1884), 394-423, 501-26; Simeon E. Baldwin, *The Three Constitutions of Connecticut . . . , NHCHSP,* 5 (1894), 179-245; Herbert L. Osgood, "Connecticut as a Corporate Colony," *Political Science Quarterly,* 14 (1899), 251-80; Roger Welles, "Constitutional History of Connecticut," *CM,* 5 (1899), 86-93, 159-62; Melbert B. Cary, *The Connecticut Constitution* (New Haven, CT, 1900); Charles J. Hoadly, *The Three Constitutions of Connecticut, 1638-1639, 1662, 1818* (Hartford, CT, 1901); Anna L. Wetmore Smith, "The Birth of a Commonwealth," *CM,* 7 (1901), 162-68; Charles J. Hoadly, *The Warwick Patent,* Acorn Club Publication, #7 [(Hartford, CT, 1902)]; Arlon T. Adams, "Government Founded on the Will of the People," *CM,* 8 (1903), 513-19; *id.,* "The First Written Constitution Known to History," *CM,* 8 (1903), 273-78; Epaphroditus Peck, *Thomas Hooker and His Relation to American Constitutional History . . .* (n.p., n.d. [1904]); W[illiam] H. Gocher, *Wadsworth: Or, The Charter Oak* (Hartford, CT, 1904); Lynde Harrison, "The Charter and Constitution of Connecticut," *American Historical Magazine,* 11 [1906], 261-70; Adna W. Risley, "The First Written Constitution," *Grafton Magazine of History and Genealogy,* 1 (1908), 25-35; Forrest Morgan, *Connecticut's "Warwick Patent": Solution of an Historic Mystery* (n.p., 1910) (rpt. of articles in the *Magazine of History,* 10 [1909], 1-8, 137-42, 220-30); Clarence W. Bowen, "The Charter of Connecticut," American Historical Association, *Annual Report . . . 1912* (Washington, DC, 1914), 105-11; Samuel Hart, "The Fundamental Orders and the Charter," *NHCHSP,* 8 (1914), 238-54; Lemuel A. Welles, "The Loss of the Charter Government in Connecticut," *NHCHSP,* 9 (1918), 90-128; Perry Miller, "Thomas Hooker and the Democracy of Early Connecticut," *NEQ,* 4 (1931), 663-712; Albert C. Bates, *The Charter of Connecticut: A Study* (Hartford, CT, 1932); Tercentenary Commission [of Connecticut], *Publications* (New Haven, CT, 1933-36); Roy V. Coleman, *A Note Concerning the Formulation of the Fundamental Orders Uniting the Three River Towns of Connecticut* (Westport, CT, 1934); *id., The Old Patent of Connecticut* (Westport, CT, 1936); Albert C. Bates, "Were the Fundamental Orders a Constitution?" *CBJ,* 10 (1936), 43-50; *The Tercentenary of Connecticut, 1635-1935* (n.p., 1936); Edwin S. Welles, *The Origin of the Fundamental Orders, 1639* . . . (Hartford, CT, 1936); George M. Decker (ed.), *Tercentenary of the Fundamental Orders of Connecticut* . . . (Hartford, CT, [1939]); Edward F. Humphrey, "Connecticut's First Constitution," *CBJ,* 13 (1939), 44-51; Philip McCook, "The Fundamental Orders," *CBJ,* 13 (1939), 52-65; Hubert J. Santos, "The Birth of a Liberal State: Connecticut's Fundamental Orders," *Connecticut Law Review,* 1 (1968), 386-400; Parker B. Nutting, "Charter and Crown: Relations of Connecticut with the British Government, 1662-1776" (diss. University of North Carolina, Chapel Hill, 1972); Christopher P. Bickford, "Connecticut and Its Charter," *CHSB,* 49 (1984), 111-22; Christopher Collier, "Why Connecticut Is the Constitution State," *CBJ,* 61 (1987), 210-14; Bruce P. Stark, "350 Years: Legal and Constitutional Development in Connecticut, 1638-1988: A Project Evaluation," Association for the Study of Connecticut History, *Newsletter* (Fall 1988), 3-9.

For New Plymouth Colony, see: Walter P. Behan, "The Social Ideals and Institutions of the Church-State of Plymouth Colony, 1620-1691" (diss. Chicago, 1899); Paul S. Howe, *The Religious and Legal Constitution of the Pilgrim State* . . . (Cape May, NJ, 1923); Samuel E. Morison, "The Mayflower's Destination and the Pilgrim Fathers' Patents," *CSMP,* 38 (1947-51), 387-413; Harry M. Ward, *Statism in Plymouth Colony.*

For Rhode Island, see: "Charter of Rhode Island," *RIHSC,* 20 (1927), 121-24; Charles Deane, "The So-Called 'Narragansett Patent,'" *MHSP,* 5 (1860-62), 399-406; Thomas Aspinwall, "The Narragansett Patent," *MHSP,* 6 (1862-63), 41-77; John H. Stiness, "The Return of Roger Williams with the First Charter of the Colony, in 1644," in Providence County Courthouse, Commissioners on Decorations and Improvements, *Report* . . . *1885* (Providence, RI, 1885), 13-58; "A Consideration of the Land Tenure Clauses as They Exist in the Charter of Maryland in 1632, and in the Charter of Rhode Island, 1663," *Book Notes,* 22 (1905), 25-31; [Terry Roderick], "The Commission of Governor Coddington and the Early Charters of Rhode Island," Newport Historical Society, *Bulletin,* 44 (1923), 1-22; Clifford C. Hubbard, "Constitutional Development in Rhode Island" (diss. Brown, 1926); Marguerite Appleton, "The Relations of the Corporate Colony of Rhode Island to the British Government" (diss. Brown, 1928); Edward H. West, "The Signing of the Compact and the Purchase of Aquidneck," *RIHSC,* 32 (1939), 66-78; Elmer J. Thompson, *A Study of the Constitution of Rhode Island and Providence Plantations* (n.p., 1954); Patrick T. Conley, "Rhode Island Constitutional Development, 1636-1775: A Survey," *RIH,* 27 (1968), 49-63, 74-94 (rpt. Providence, RI, 1968); *id.,* "Rhode Island Constitutional Development, 1636-1841: Prologue to the Dorr Rebellion" (diss. Notre Dame, 1970); Dennis A. O'Toole, "Exiles, Refugees and Rogues: The Quest for Civil Order in the Towns and Colonies of Providence Plantations, 1636-1654" (diss. Brown, 1972).

For New Hampshire, see: John S. Jenness, "Notes on the First Planting of New Hampshire and on the Piscataqua Patents," *NHSP,* 25 (1895), 663-739; James F. Colby, et al., *Manual of the Constitution of the State of New Hampshire . . .* (1902; rev. edn., Concord, NH, 1912); Elwin L. Page, "The Validity of John Mason's Title to New Hampshire," *HNH,* 9 (1953), 1-22.

For the Massachusetts Bay Colony and Province, see: Abel Cushing, *Historical Letters on the First Charter of Massachusetts Government* (Boston, 1839); John Q. Adams, *The Social Compact, Exemplified in the Constitution of the Commonwealth of Massachusetts . . .* (Providence, RI, 1842); Emory Washburn, "Did the Vacating of the Colony Charter Annul the Laws Made Under It?" *MHSP,* 13 (1873-75), 451-59; Abner C. Goodell, Jr., "The Title 'Colony' and 'Province' as Applied to Massachusetts," *MHSP,* ser. 2, 1 (1884-85), 192-99; Henry S. Burrage, "Charter Rights of Massachusetts in Maine in the Early Part of the Eighteenth Century," *MeHSC,* ser. 2, 6 (1895), 392-414; Abner C. Goodell, "Provincial Militia and Charter, 1685-1693," *MHSP,* ser. 2, 13 (1899-1900), 327-37; Horace E. Ware, "Was the Government of the Massachusetts Bay Colony a Theocracy?" *CSMP,* 10 (1904-6), 151-80; Henry R. Spencer, "Constitutional Conflict in Provincial Massachusetts: A Study of Some Phases of the Opposition between the Massachusetts Governor and General Court in the Early Eighteenth Century" (diss. Columbia, 1905); published under the same title (Columbus, OH, 1905); Horace E. Ware, "The Charter and the Men," Society of Colonial Wars, Massachusetts [*Yearbook*], (1906), 57-86; Louis Adams Frothingham, *A Brief History of the Constitution and Government of Massachusetts . . .* (1916; Boston, 1925); Samuel E. Morison, *A History of the Constitution of Massachusetts* (Boston, 1917); Julius H. Tuttle, "The Boston Petitions of 1664," *MHSP,* 52 (1918-19), 312-16; Julius H. Tuttle, *Massachusetts and Her Royal Charter Granted March 4, 1628-29* (Boston, 1924); Ellen M. Burrill, *A Monograph on the Charters and Constitution of Massachusetts* (Lynn, MA, 1932); George L. Haskins, "Gavelkind and the Charter of Massachusetts Bay," *CSMP,* 34 (1937-42), 483-98; Robert E. Moody, "A Re-Examination of the Antecedents of the Massachusetts Bay Company's Charter of 1629," *MHSP,* 69 (1947-50), 56-80; Massachusetts Bar Association, *Our Massachusetts Constitution: Its History and Purpose* ([n.p., 1956]); Theodore B. Lewis, "Royal Government in New Hampshire and the Revocation of the Charter of the Massachusetts Bay Colony, 1679-1683," *HNH,* 25 (1970), 3-45; David O. Damerall, "The Modernization of Massachusetts: The Transformation of Public Attitudes and Institutions, 1689 to 1715."

Concerning the New England Confederation and its place within the broader context of American history, see: John Q. Adams, *The New England Confederacy of MDCXLIII* (Boston, 1843); Robert M. Gatke, "Plans of American Colonial Union, 1643 to 1754" (diss. American University, 1925); Harold E. Kolling, "The New England Confederation of 1643: Its Origin, Nature and Foreign Relations, 1643-1652" (diss. Chicago, 1957); Harry M. Ward, *The United Colonies of New England, 1643-1690* (New York, 1961); Oline Carmical, Jr., "Plans of Union, 1634-1783: A Study and Reappraisal of Projects for Uniting the English Colonies in North America" (diss. Kentucky, 1975).

6. "1. A written document delivered by the sovereign or legislature, a. granting privileges to, or recognizing rights of, the people, or of certain classes or individuals . . . creating or incorporating a borough, university, company, or other corporation. . . . 2. A written evidence, instrument, or contract executed between man and man; [the word

can be applied] especially to the documents or deeds relating to the conveyance of landed property." *OED*, 2.C.294.

7. "1. . . . An open letter or document, . . . usually from a sovereign or person in authority, issued for various purposes, e.g. to put on record some agreement or contract, to authorize or command something to be done, to confer some right, privilege, title, property, or office. . . ." *OED*, 7.P.549-50. Cf. the end of the 1629 Charter of the Massachusetts Bay Colony: "In witnes whereof, Wee have caused theis our Letters to be made Patents," Thorpe, *Federal and State Constitutions,* 3.1860.

8. The political background to the period 1660-1700 and its implications for colonial America are covered in Michael G. Hall, Lawrence H. Leder, and Michael F. Kammen (eds.), *The Glorious Revolution in America: Documents on the Colonial Crisis of 1689* (New York, 1964); Theodore B. Lewis, "Massachusetts and the Glorious Revolution: A Political and Constitutional Study, 1660-1692" (diss. Wisconsin, 1967); Paul R. Lucas, "Colony or Commonwealth: Massachusetts Bay, 1661-1666"; Alison G. Olson and Richard Maxwell Brown, *Anglo-American Political Relations, 1675-1775;* David S. Lovejoy, *The Glorious Revolution in America* (New York, 1972); Jack M. Sosin, *English America and the Restoration Monarchy of Charles II: Transatlantic Politics, Commerce, and Kinship; id., English America and the Restoration of 1688: Royal Administration and the Structure of Provincial Government* (Lincoln, NE, 1982); *id., English America and Imperial Inconstancy: The Rise of Provincial Autonomy, 1696-1715* (Lincoln, NE, 1985); Robert M. Bliss, *Restoration England: Politics and Government, 1660-1688* (New York, 1985); Alison G. Olson, *Making the Empire Work: London and American Interest Groups, 1690-1790;* and Stephen Carl Arch, "The Glorious Revolution and the Rhetoric of Puritan History," *EAL,* 27 (1992), 61-74. Some of the religious aspects are covered in: Maurice Ashley, "King James II and the Revolution of 1688: Some Reflections on the Historiography," in H. E. Bell and R. L. Ollard (eds.), *Historical Essays, 1600-1750, Presented to David Ogg* (London, 1963), 185-202; Richard L. Greaves, "Conventicles, Sedition, and the Toleration Acts of 1689," *Eighteenth-Century Life,* n.s., 12 (1988), #3, 1-13; Geoffrey Huttall, "'The Sun-Shine of Liberty': The Toleration Act and the Ministry," *JURCHS,* 4 (1987-92), 239-55; cf. also n. 15 of the Introduction that discusses the American colonies as part of a larger First English/British Empire.

9. Cf. Thorpe, *Federal and State Constitutions,* 7 vols. The principal documents are listed in chronological order, with relevant sub-documents annexed to each listing: "The First Charter of Virginia — 1606," 7.3783-89; "The Charter of New England — 1620," 3.1827-40, along with its repeal: "The Act of Surrender of the Great Charter of New England to His Majesty — 1635," 3.1860-61; "A Grant of the Province of Maine to Sir Ferdinando Gorges and John Mason, Esq., 10th of August, 1622," 3.1621-25; "The Charter of Massachusetts Bay — 1629," 3.1846-60; "Charter of the Colony of New Plymouth Granted to William Bradford and His Associates — 1629," 3.1841-46, along with "William Bradford, etc. Surrender of the Patent of Plymouth Colony to the Freemen, March 2d, 1640," 3.1861-62; "Grant of New Hampshire to Capt. John Mason, 7th of Novemr., 1629," 4.2433-36; "Grant of the Province of New Hampshire to John Wollaston, Esq., A. 1635," 4.2437-38; "Grant of the Province of New Hampshire to Mr. Mason, 22 Apr., 1635, by the Name of New Hampshr.," 4.2443-44; "Grant of the Province of [\"]New Hampshire[\"] to Mr. Mason, 22 Aprill, 1635, By the Name of Masonia [Maine]," 4.2441-43; "Grant of the Province of New Hampshire From Mr. Wollaston to

Mr. Mason, 11th June, 1635," 4.2439-40; "Grant of the Province of Maine — 1639," 3.1625-37; "Patent for Providence Plantations — 1643," 6.3209-11; "Charter of Connecticut — 1662," 1.529-36; "Charter of Rhode Island and Providence Plantations — 1663," 6.3211-22; "Grant of the Province of Maine — 1664," 3.1637-40; "Grant of the Province of Maine — 1674," 3.1641-44; "[Commission of John Cutt]," ["The Commission Constituting a President and Council for the Province of New-Hampshire in New-England"], 4.2446-51; "Commission of Sir Edmund Andros for the Dominion of New England, April 7, 1688," 3.1863-69; "The Charter of Massachusetts Bay — 1691," 3.1870-86.

The charters, patents, and compacts of New England also appeared separately, often with commentary, in a variety of critical and popular editions. For Connecticut see State of Connecticut, Comptroller's Office, *The Three Constitutions of Connecticut, 1638-9, 1662, 1818* . . . ; also, John Winthrop, Jr., "Letter from Governor Winthrop Respecting the Charter of Connecticut, 1662," *CHSC*, 1 (1860), 52-55.

For New Plymouth Colony, see New Plymouth Colony, *The Compact with the Charter and Laws of the Colony of New Plymouth* . . . , ed. William Brigham (Boston, 1836); "The First Plymouth Patent," *MHSC*, ser. 4, 2 (1854), 156-63.

For Rhode Island, see: "The Text of the Commission Supposed to Have Been Given . . . to William Coddington in 1651," ed. Sidney S. Rider, *Book Notes*, 24 (1907), 185-89; Rhode Island and Providence Plantations, "Charter of Rhode Island," *RIHSC*, 20 (1927), 121-24; Charles Deane, "The So-Called 'Narragansett Patent,'" *MHSP*, 5 (1860-62), 399-406; Thomas Aspinwall, "The Narragansett Patent," *MHSP*, 6 (1862-63), 41-77; *Charters and Legislative Documents, Illustrative of Rhode-Island History* . . . (Providence, RI, 1844); Charles Carroll, *Constitution of the State of Rhode Island and Providence Plantations* . . . *With a* . . . *History of the Constitution* ([Providence, RI], 1924).

For New Hampshire, see: John W. Dean (ed.), *Capt. John Mason, the Founder of New Hampshire* . . . *the American Charters in Which He Was a Grantee* . . . (Boston, 1887); Albert S. Batchellor (ed.), *Documents Relating to the Masonian Patent, 1630-1846* . . . (Concord, NH, 1896).

For the Massachusetts Bay Colony and Massachusetts Bay Province, see: "Roger Williams on the King's Patent, 1631-1633," *MHSP*, 12; John W. Thornton, *The Landing at Cape Anne; or, the Charter of the First Permanent Colony on the Territory of the Massachusetts Company* . . . (Boston, 1854); "Exemplification of the Judgement for Vacating the Charter of the Massachusetts Bay in New England," *MHSC*, ser. 4, 2 (1854), 246-78; Joel Parker, *The First Charter and the Early Religious Legislation of Massachusetts* . . . (Boston, 1869); Massachusetts Bay Colony, *The Charter of Massachusetts Bay* . . . *(1629)* (Boston, 1889); Edward Randolph, *Edward Randolph: Including His Letters and Official Papers from the New England, Middle and Southern Colonies in America, With Other Documents Relating Chiefly to the Vacating of the Royal Charter of the Colony of Massachusetts Bay, 1676-1703*, ed. Robert N. Toppan and Alfred T. S. Goodrich, 7 vols. (Boston, 1898-1909); "The Massachusetts Patent [c. 1664]," *MHSP*, 46 (1912-13), 285-302; "The Royal Charter, or Patent, of the Colony of the Massachusetts Bay," *MHSP*, 62 (1928-29), 233-73.

For New Jersey, cf. New Jersey, *The Grants, Concessions, and Original Constitutions of the Province of New-Jersey*, ed. Aaron Leaming and Jacob Spicer (Philadelphia, 1758; rpt. Somerville, NJ, 1881).

    10. Thorpe, *Federal and State Constitutions*, 7.3783-89.

11. Virginia M. Meyer and John Frederick Dorman, *Adventurers of Purse and Person, Virginia, 1607-1624/5*, 3rd edn. (Richmond, VA, 1987), xiii.

12. Alternate names were the Virginia Company of London and the London Company of Virginia.

13. Cf. Warren E. Billings, John E. Selby, and Thad W. Tate, *Colonial Virginia: A History* (White Plains, NY, 1986), 12-13. The Plymouth Company existed from 1606 to 1619, when it was disorganized and replaced in November, 1620, by a body known as the Council for New England; cf. Benjamin W. Labaree, *Colonial Massachusetts: A History* (Millwood, NY, 1979), 25-26. The backdrop to the formation of the Virginia Company can be found in Alexander Brown, *The Genesis of the United States: A Narrative of the Movement, 1605-1616, Which Resulted in the Plantation of North America by Englishmen . . . Set Forth Through a Series of Historical Manuscripts . . . Tracts . . . and Brief Biographies*, 2 vols. (Boston, 1890). A useful section in Brown is "Brief Biographies of Persons Connected with the Founding of Virginia," 807-1068. Brown was concerned only with people connected with the founding of the Southern Plantation; he was not concerned with the Plymouth Company. Cf. also Brown's *The First Republic in America* . . . (Boston, 1898), a detailed narrative with Brown's definite opinions; also Matthew Page Andrews, *The Soul of a Nation: The Founding of Virginia and the Projection of New England* (New York, 1943); Wesley Frank Craven, *Dissolution of the Virginia Company: The Failure of a Colonial Experiment* (New York, 1932); Edward D. Neill, *History of the Virginia Company of London* . . . (Albany, 1869); and Conway Whittle Sam, *The Conquest of Virginia: The Second Attempt* . . . (Norfolk, VA, 1929).

14. Thorpe, 7.3784.

15. Cf., for instance, James T. Adams, *The Founding of New England* (Boston, 1921).

16. Cf. Francis Jennings, *The Invasion of America: Indians, Colonialism, and the Cant of Conquest* (Chapel Hill, NC, 1975).

17. Cf. "The Mass in Latin and English: The Roman Rite . . . [The] Order of Low Mass," in *Liturgies of the Western Church,* ed. Bard Thompson (Philadelphia, 1961), 63-64 (Nicene Creed); "The First and Second Prayer Books of King Edward VI, London: 1549 & 1552," in Thompson, *Liturgies,* 248, 272 (Nicene Creed); "The Shorter Catechism . . . ," in *The [Westminster] Confession of Faith; The Larger and Shorter Catechisms . . . With The Sum of Saving Knowledge . . . Covenants, National and Solemn League; Acknowledgement of Sins, and Engagement to Duties; Directories for Publick and Family Worship; Form of Church Government, etc.; Of Publick Authority in the Church of Scotland; With Acts of Assembly and Parliament, Relative To, and Approbative of, the Same* (Belfast, 1933), (Apostles' Creed), 249.

18. Psalm 2:12, Bay Psalm Book.

19. Thorpe, *Federal and State Constitutions,* 7.3783-84.

20. *Ibid.,* 7.3786-89, passim.

21. Meyer and Dorman, *Adventurers of Purse and Person, Virginia, 1607-1624/5,* 3rd edn., name Sir Thomas Gates, Sir George Somers, Richard Hakluyt, and Edward-Maria Wingfield as the London Group for 1606, and Thomas Hanham, Raleigh Gilbert, William Parker, and George Popham as the Bristol/Exeter/Plymouth Group. For the Second Virginia Charter of 1609, 659 Adventurers are listed, along with 56 trade guilds of London as "subscribers." The Third Virginia Charter of Thursday, March 12, 1612, lists

new adventurers added since the Second 1609 Charter. The division between the two groups in the 1606 Charter seems to be regional and have nothing to do with religious conviction.

22. Carl Bridenbaugh states: "We lack detailed records that would enable the historian to recount the story accurately and impartially of both the native Indians and the Englishmen from overseas" (*Jamestown, 1544-1699* [New York, 1980], vii).

23. "The Act of Surrender of the Great Charter of New England to His Majesty — 1635," Thorpe, *Federal and State Constitutions*, 3.1860-61.

24. *Ibid.*, 3.1828.

25. *Ibid.*, 3.1828-29. The word "wonderfull" used to describe the deathly plague should not be seen as an example of callousness on the part of the English; the word "wonderfull" in this context more closely resembles our use of the words "awesome" or "amazing." Cf. *OED*, 10.W.256.

26. Alfred W. Crosby, *Ecological Imperialism: The Biological Expansion of Europe, 900-1900* (New York, 1986), 195-216.

27. The 1606 First Charter of Virginia reads as follows: "And we do also ordain, establish, and agree, for Us, our Heirs, and Successors, that each of the said Colonies shall have a Council, which shall govern and order all Matters and Causes, which shall arise, grow, or happen, to or within the same several Colonies, according to such Laws, Ordinances, and Instructions, as shall be, in that behalf, given and signed with Our Hand or Sign Manual, and pass under the Privy Seal of our Realm of England. . . ." Thorpe, *Federal and State Constitutions*, 7.3785.

28. *Ibid.*, 3.1832-33.

29. *Ibid.*, 3.1836.

30. *Ibid.*, 3.1827.

31. *Ibid.*, 3.1839-40.

32. "Supremacy, Act of," in *The Oxford Dictionary of the Christian Church*, ed. F. L. Cross (2nd edn. rev., Oxford, 1974), 1324. The text can be found in Henry Gee and William J. Hardy (eds.), *Documents Illustrative of English Church History, Compiled from Original Sources* . . . (London, 1910; rpt. New York, 1972), #LV, pp. 243-44 and #LXXIX, pp. 442-58.

33. A. H. Drysdale, *History of the Presbyterians in England* . . . (London, 1889), 92-94. One example of the reluctance of English Presbyterians to take such an oath can be found in the discussions of the Dedham Classis; cf. Roland G. Usher (ed.), *The Presbyterian Movement in the Reign of Queen Elizabeth as Illustrated by the Minute Book of the Dedham Classis, 1582-1599, RHST*, ser. 3, 8 (London, 1905), xvii-xviii, 37, 57, and 89.

34. William Bradford, *Of Plymouth Plantation, 1620-1647* . . . , ed. Samuel Eliot Morison (New York, 1952). The Council for New England never formed its own settlements, but granted patents to various groups who wished to settle on its lands; it was led by Ferdinando Gorges; Samuel Foster Haven, "History of Grants Under the Great Council for New England," in *Lectures . . . Before the Lowell Institute . . . by Members of the Massachusetts Historical Society on Subjects Relating to the Early History of Massachusetts* (Boston, 1869), 127-62. Cf. also the "Records of the Council for New England," *AASP*, ser. 1, 1867, pp. 53-131; 1875, pp. 49-63. The remaining records are in the Public Record Office, London, but the only records that remain are for the years 1622-23 and 1631-38. The Council for New England was dissolved in 1635.

35. Cf. William S. Perry, *The Connection of the Church of England with Early American Discovery* (Portland, ME, 1863); *id., Historical Collections Relating to the American Colonial Church,* 5 vols. (Hartford, CT, 1870-78), esp. vol. III: *Massachusetts;* Robert C. Winthrop, "{Massachusetts and the Church of England}," *MHSP,* 18 (1880-81), 288-301; William S. Perry, *The Episcopate in America* (New York, 1895); Arthur L. Cross, "Schemes for Episcopal Control in the Colonies," American Historical Association, *Annual Report: 1896* (Washington, DC, 1897), 233-41; Simeon E. Baldwin, "The American Jurisdiction of the Bishop of London in Colonial Times," *AASP,* n.s., 13 (1900), 179-221; Arthur L. Cross, *The Anglican Episcopate and the American Colonies* (New York, 1902).

36. Thorpe, *Federal and State Constitutions,* 3.1621-25. For a summary of Gorges's activity with respect to Maine and New Hampshire, cf. Jere R. Daniell, *Colonial New Hampshire: A History* (Millwood, NY, 1981), 17-38. Cf. also C. M. MacInnes, *Ferdinando Gorges and New England* (Bristol, 1965); Richard A. Preston, *Gorges of Plymouth Fort* (Toronto, 1953), based on an earlier dissertation at Yale; and Henry M. Fuller, *Sir Ferdinando Gorges (1566-1647): Naval and Military Commander* (New York, 1952).

37. Cf. the "Form of an Oath Appointed to be taken{,} by Sir Ferdinando Gorges," in "Extracts from the Records of the Province of Maine," *MeHSC,* ser. 1, 1 (1865), 364; also found in *MHSC,* ser. 1, 1 (1792), 101.

38. Frank A. Gardner, "John Endicott and the Men Who Came to Salem in the 'Abigail' in 1628," *Massachusetts Magazine,* 3 (1910), 163-77; *id.,* "The Old Planters at Salem," *Genealogical Quarterly Magazine,* 3 (1902), 3-18; George D. Phippen, "The 'Old Planters' of Salem, Who Were Settled Here Before the Arrival of Governor Endicott, in 1628," *EIHC,* 1 (1859), 97-110, 145-53, 185-99; Herbert B. Adams, "Origin of Salem Plantation," *EIHC,* 19 (1882), 153-66; William Bentley, "A Description and History of Salem," *MHSC,* 6 (1799), 212-77; Joseph B. Felt, *Annals of Salem,* 2nd edn., 2 vols. (Salem, MA, 1845-49); Richard P. Gildrie, *Salem, Massachusetts, 1626-1683: A Covenant Community;* William A. Pew, *The Merchant Adventurers of England: A Narrative of Their Settlement in Salem* (Salem, MA, 1926); C. H. Webber and W. S. Nevins, *Old Naumkeag: An Historical Sketch of the City of Salem . . .* (Salem, MA, 1877); Christine A. Young, *From 'Good Order' to Glorious Revolution: Salem Massachusetts, 1628-1689* (Ann Arbor, MI, 1980), a revision of a 1978 University of Pennsylvania dissertation.

39. The six grantees were identified as "religious persons," "Prefatory Chapter," in "Records of the Company of the Massachusetts Bay, to the Embarkation of Winthrop and His Associates for New England . . . , *AASTC,* 3 (1857), xvi.

40. The official motion to move the Massachusetts Bay Charter to North America was moved and passed at a meeting of the Massachusetts Bay Company in Old England on August 29, 1629; *ibid.,* 49; cf. also *RM,* 1.49-51 and Thorpe, *Federal and State Constitutions,* 3.1846; Emory Washburn, "Transfer of the Colony Charter of 1628 from England to Massachusetts," *MHSP,* 4 (1858-60), 154-67; Mellen Chamberlain, "The Transfer of the Colony Charter," *MHSP,* ser. 2, 8 (1892-94), 108-12; Horace E. Ware, *The Transfer to Massachusetts of Its Charter Government, 1630* (Cambridge, MA, 1912); Charles H. McIlwain, "The Transfer of the Charter to New England, and Its Significance in American Constitutional History," *MHSP,* 63 (1929-30), 53-65 (rpt. Boston, 1931); Ronald Dale Karr, "Reconsiderations: The Missing Clause: Myth and the Massachusetts Bay Charter of 1629," *NEQ,* 77 (2004), 89-107.

41. "Exemplification of the Judgement for Vacating the Charter of the Massachu-

setts Bay in New England"; Edward Randolph, *Edward Randolph: Including His Letters and Official Papers from the New England, Middle and Southern Colonies in America, With Other Documents Relating Chiefly to the Vacating of the Royal Charter of the Colony of Massachusetts Bay, 1676-1703;* Emory Washburn, "Did the Vacating of the Colony Charter Annul the Laws Made Under It?"

42. While the Massachusetts Bay Colony did attempt to survey the three-mile boundary around the Merrimack River, the rapid expansion of the colony from the Great Migration led it to abandon the three-mile stricture. With Parliament not in session and Charles I consolidating his power in Old England, Whitehall ignored the situation, leaving it to the colonists to sort out boundaries. The result was that the legislative records of all of the New England colonies are replete with inter-colonial correspondence and complaints concerning boundaries; cf. the indices of *RM, PRCC, CRRI, RCNP, RCPNH, RCJNH* for references to the inter-colonial boundary disputes.

43. Thorpe, *Federal and State Constitutions,* 3.1853.

44. *Ibid.,* 3.1852.

45. *Ibid.,* 3.1853.

46. *Ibid.,* 3.1854.

47. *Ibid.,* 3.1857.

48. Cf. David A. Weir, "Church Covenanting in Seventeenth-Century New England," 74.

49. Cf. Perry Miller, *Errand into the Wilderness* (Cambridge, MA, 1956), 1-15.

50. Conrad Russell, *The Crisis of Parliaments: English History, 1509-1660* (London, 1971).

51. "Alsoe it shall be lawfull and free for the said William Bradford his associatts his heires and assignes att all tymes hereafter to incorporate by some usual fitt name and title, him or themselves or the people there inhabitinge under him or them with liberty to them and their successor from tyme to tyme to frame, and make orders ordinances and constituc~ons as well for the better governemente of their affairs here and the receavinge of admittinge any to his or their society as alsoe for the better governm[t] of his or their people and affaires in New Englande or of his and their people att sea in goeinge thither, or returninge from thence, and the same to putt in execuc~on by such officers and ministers as he and they shall authorize and depute: Provided that the said lawes and order be not repugnante to the lawes of Englande, or the frame of governmente by the said presidente and councell hereafter to be established," Thorpe, *Federal and State Constitutions,* 3.1844-45.

52. ". . . And now seeinge that by the speciall providence of God, and their extraordinary care and industry they have increased their plantac~on to neere three hundred people . . . ," *Ibid.,* 3.1842.

53. *Ibid.,* 3.1843.

54. Cf. Peter Milward, *Religious Controversies of the Elizabethan Age: A Survey of Printed Sources* (Lincoln, NE, 1977); id., *Religious Controversies of the Jacobean Age: A Survey of Printed Sources* (Lincoln, NE, 1978).

55. Cf. Thomas Madox, *Formulare Anglicanum: or, A Collection of Ancient Charters and Instruments of Divers Kinds . . .* (London, 1702) and Edward Jones, *Index to Records Called, the Originalia and Memoranda on the Lord Treasurer's Remembrancer's Side of the*

Exchequer . . . Also Inrollments of Charters, Grants, and Patents . . . 2 vols. (London, 1793-95).

56. Thorpe, *Federal and State Constitutions,* 4.2433-36.

57. The land just north of the Merrimack River later became part of Massachusetts Bay, where the towns of Salisbury, Haverhill, etc. were established. Salisbury was incorporated in 1639, while Haverhill was incorporated in 1641.

58. Thorpe, *Federal and State Constitutions,* 4.2436. Walter Neale went to Piscataqua to be governor of Portsmouth. During his time there he sought Lake Winnepissaukee and may have found it. He returned to Old England on Thursday, August 15, 1633. In 1634-38 he lived in London, and in 1639 was appointed Lieutenant Governor of Portsmouth; *DNB,* 14.149.

59. Thorpe, *Federal and State Constitutions,* 3.1625-37.

60. *Ibid.,* 3.1627.

61. "Chapel . . . from the *capella* or cloak of St. Martin, preserved by the Frankish kings as a sacred relic, which was borne before them in battle, and used to give sanctity to oaths, the name was applied to the sanctuary in which this was preserved under the care of its *cappellani* or 'chaplains', and thence generally to a sanctuary containing holy relics, attached to a palace, etc., and so to any private sanctuary or holy place, and finally to any apartment or building for orisons or worship, not being a church . . . a sanctuary or place of Christian worship, not the church of a parish or a cathedral church or a diocese; an oratory. (In earlier times always consecrated, and having an altar . . .); . . . 2. A private oratory or place of worship. a. A room or building for private worship in or attached to a palace, nobleman's house, castle, garden, embassy, prison, monastery, college, school or other institution," *OED,* 2.C.274-75.

62. It should be noted that all of the Puritan colonies with the exception of Rhode Island also utilized the Erastian model to one degree or another.

63. Thorpe, *Federal and State Constitutions,* 3.1628.

64. *Ibid.,* 3.1632.

65. *Ibid.,* 3.1631.

66. *Ibid.,* 3.1628.

67. *Ibid.*

68. *Ibid.,* 3.1629.

69. *Ibid.,* 3.1632-33.

70. *Ibid.,* 3.1628.

71. *Ibid.*

72. *Ibid.*

73. *Ibid.*

74. *Ibid.,* 3.1629-30.

75. Preston, *Gorges of Plymouth Fort,* 4, 12, 295-98. The Council for New England was dissolved in 1635 with the revocation of the 1620 Charter for New England.

76. Thorpe, *Federal and State Constitutions,* 3.1629.

77. *Ibid.,* 3.1636-37.

78. Our discussion of the charters for Rhode Island and, in the next chapter, of the Providence Civil Covenant makes the assumption that while Williams was not the author of all of the words of these documents, he was the primary leader of and negotiator for the colony. Therefore, his political and religious thought certainly influenced the

colony and is crucial in understanding Rhode Island. A vast amount has been written about Williams and his ideas. The post–World War II discussion begins with Mauro Calamandrei, "Theology and Political Thought of Roger Williams," an excellent University of Chicago dissertation that unfortunately remains unpublished. Some of Calamandrei's insights do appear in "Neglected Aspects of Roger Williams' Thought," *CH*, 21 (1952), 239-59. Cf. also Edmund S. Morgan, *Roger Williams: The Church and the State* (New York, 1967), who argues that Williams believed the introduction of God into the area of civil and political affairs was tantamount to blasphemy; Richard Reinitz, "Symbolism and Freedom: The Use of Biblical Typology as an Argument for Religious Toleration in Seventeenth Century England and America"; *id.,* "The Typological Argument for Religious Toleration: The Separatist Tradition and Roger Williams," *EAL*, 5 (1970-71), #1, 74-110; Hans R. Guggisberg, "Religious Freedom and the History of the Christian World in Roger Williams' Thought," *EAL*, 12 (1977-78), #1, 36-48; W. Clark Gilpin, *The Millenarian Piety of Roger Williams* (Chicago, 1979); Edwin S. Gaustad, *Liberty of Conscience: Roger Williams in America* (Grand Rapids, MI, 1991); Crawford Leonard Allen, "'The Restauration of Zion': Roger Williams and the Quest for the Primitive Church" (diss. Iowa, 1984); Timothy L. Hall, *Separating Church and State: Roger Williams and Religious Liberty* (Urbana, IL, 1998); James P. Byrd, Jr., *The Challenge of Roger Williams: Religious Liberty, Violent Persecution, and the Bible* (Macon, GA, 2002), based on a 1999 Vanderbilt dissertation.

79. Thorpe, *Federal and State Constitutions,* 6.3209-11; the quotation is from p. 3211.

80. For the formation of the Rhode Island Colony on March 16-19, 1640/1, see *Ibid.,* 6.3207-9.

81. "The settlers at Warwick, unlike those of Providence, Portsmouth and Newport had not, prior to the Charter to the Colony of March 14, 1644, combined together as a corporation, or assumed to exercise any of the powers of government. The reason for omitting to do so was not because they were opposed to any government, as has been charged against them, but because they held that so long as they were English subjects, they had no lawful right to erect a government, and could not without authority from the Crown or government in England. They denied that the self-constituted governments in the other towns were of any authority, because their power was not lawfully derived from the government to which they owed allegiance. They therefore never exercised any power of government, or proceeded to elect any officers until the organization of a government for the colony in May, 1647, under the charter of 1644," *RCRI,* 1.129; cf. "Samuel Gorton (c. 1592-1677)," *DNB,* 8.251-53 and *DAB,* 7.438-39.

82. Thorpe, *Federal and State Constitutions,* 6.3209; "Dudley, Sir Robert (1573-1649)," *DNB,* 6.122-24; cf. also "Ordinance for the Government of the Plantations in the West Indies, [2 November, 1643]," in Great Britain, Parliament, *Acts and Ordinances of the Interregnum, 1642-1660,* ed. C. H. Firth and R. S. Rait, 1 (London, 1911), 331-33.

83. Thorpe, *Federal and State Constitutions,* 6.3209-10.

84. *Ibid.,* 6.3210.

85. *Ibid.,* 6.3210-11.

86. It should be noted in this regard that just at this point in the English Revolution the Long Parliament had called the Westminster Assembly together and the Assembly had begun meeting on July 1, 1643. Its purpose was to *advise* the Parliament on the

reformation of religion in England, Scotland, and Ireland; cf. "An Ordinance of the Lords and Commons assembled in Parliament, for the calling of an Assembly of learned and godly Divines, and others, to be consulted with by Parliament, for the settling of the government and liturgy of the Church of England; and for vindicating and clearing of the doctrine of the said Church from false aspersions and interpretations. June 12, 1643," in *The [Westminster] Confession of Faith; The Larger and Shorter Catechisms . . . With The Sum of Saving Knowledge . . . Covenants, National and Solemn League; Acknowledgement of Sins, and Engagement to Duties; Directories for Publick and Family Worship; Form of Church Government, etc.; Of Publick Authority in the Church of Scotland; With Acts of Assembly and Parliament, Relative To, and Approbative of, the Same,* (Belfast, 1933), 10.

87. Thorpe, *Federal and State Constitutions,* 6.3211-12.

88. *Ibid.,* 6.3212.

89. The other "1%" would be members of the Touro Synagogue, Newport, RIC. Was it possible to be an atheist in this period? The general histories of atheism assert that atheism was vaguely found in the Renaissance, but that it was not until the mechanistic worldview developed in the late seventeenth century had become entrenched in the eighteenth century that we start getting full-fledged atheism; cf. James Thrower, *Western Atheism: A Short History* (1971; rpt. Amherst, NY, 2000), esp. 70-93; Michael Hunter and David Wootton, *Atheism from the Reformation to the Enlightenment* (Oxford, 1992); George T. Buckley, *Atheism in the English Renaissance* (Chicago, 1932); and David Berman, *A History of Atheism in Britain: From Hobbes to Russell* (London, 1988).

90. Thorpe, *Federal and State Constitutions,* 6.3212-13.

91. *Ibid.,* 6.3221.

92. J. P. Kenyon (ed.), *The Stuart Constitution, 1603-1688: Document and Commentary* (Cambridge, 1966), #102, 376-78. For the text of the 1643 Solemn League and Covenant, see *The [Westminster] Confession of Faith; The Larger and Shorter Catechisms . . . With The Sum of Saving Knowledge . . . Covenants, National and Solemn League; Acknowledgement of Sins, and Engagement to Duties; Directories for Publick and Family Worship; Form of Church Government, etc.; Of Publick Authority in the Church of Scotland; With Acts of Assembly and Parliament, Relative To, and Approbative of, the Same,* 273-78.

93. J. P. Kenyon (ed.), *The Stuart Constitution, 1603-1688,* #103, 378-82. The Clarendon Code can also be found in Henry Gee and William J. Hardy (eds.), *Documents Illustrative of English Church History Compiled from Original Sources . . . ,* #CXVI 595-640.

94. A. G. Matthews, *Calamy Revised : Being a Revision of Edmund Calamy's Account of the Ministers and Others Ejected and Silenced, 1660-2* (New York, 1988). About 1,760 ministers were ejected between 1660 and 1662. A general Puritan exodus to New England was proposed in 1662, but nothing came of it. Only 15 of the 11,760 crossed to New England (Mathews, xiv). Such a migration would have drastically affected the history of New England. However, the lack of uniform persecution of the ejected, and the fact that the penalties in England for transgressing the Clarendon Code were generally jail sentences (e.g., John Bunyan), rather than floggings, ear croppings, hangings, and incineration, led to decisions to stay in Old England, and thus we see the emergence of Nonconformity and Dissent in Old England (Mathews, lv-lx).

95. Great Britain, *Statutes of the Realm,* 5 (London, 1819), 516-20.

96. *The Stuart Constitution, 1603-1688,* #105, 383-86; also Gee and Hardy, *Documents,* #CXIX, 623-32.

97. Henry Bettenson (ed.), *Documents of the Christian Church* (2nd edn. London, 1963), 416-18; also Gee and Hardy, *Documents,* #CXVIII, 620-23.

98. For the formation of Connecticut and New Haven as colonies, see Chapter 3: "The Civil Covenants of Early New England," below.

99. Thorpe, *Federal and State Constitutions,* 1.529-36.

100. *Ibid.,* 1.529.

101. The New Haven Colony attempted to gain a charter from the Long Parliament beginning in 1644, but the agent entrusted with the application was lost at sea in 1646 and presumably drowned. The Colony did not pursue the matter because the Puritans were in power in Old England in the late 1640s and there was peace with the Netherlands; cf. Isabel M. Calder, *The New Haven Colony* (New Haven, CT, 1934), esp. 210-11; this volume is a revision of a 1929 Yale dissertation.

102. New Haven Colony and Connecticut Colony discussed merger as early as 1660. John Winthrop, Jr., negotiated the Connecticut Charter, and included New Haven Colony in his negotiations, but gave liberty to New Haven to remain independent; cf. Edward E. Atwater, *History of the Colony of New Haven to Its Absorption into Connecticut* (Meriden, CT, 1902), 445-528; also Robert W. Roetger, "New Haven's Charter Quest and Annexation by Connecticut," *Connecticut History,* 29 (Nov., 1988), 16-26; Thomas W. Jodziewicz, "Charters and Corporations, Independence and Loyalty," *Connecticut History,* 29 (Nov., 1988), 27-45.

103. Dean B. Lyman, Jr., "Notes on the New Haven Colonial Courts," *CBJ,* 20 (1946), 178-89; New Haven Colony, *The Earliest Laws of the New Haven and Connecticut Colonies, 1639-1673,* ed. John D. Cushing (Wilmington, DE, 1977); Floyd M. Shumway, "New Haven and Its First Settlers," *NHCHSJ,* 21 (1972), 45-67; Edward E. Atwater, *History of the Colony of New Haven to Its Absorption into Connecticut;* Ernest H. Baldwin, "How New Haven Came to Be in Connecticut," *NEM,* n.s., 27 (1902), 379-87; Ernest H. Baldwin, "Why New Haven Is Not a State of the Union," *NHCHSP,* 8 (1908), 161-87; Isabel M. Calder, *The New Haven Colony;* Everett G. Hill, *A Modern History of New Haven and Eastern New Haven County,* 2 vols. (New York, 1918); James L. Kingsley, *An Historical Summary . . . [on] the Two Hundredth Anniversary of the First Settlement of the Town and Colony* (New Haven, CT, 1838); Edward R. Lambert, *History of the Colony of New Haven, Before and After the Union with Connecticut . . .* (New Haven, CT, 1838; rpt. Milford, CT, 1976); Charles H. Levermore, *The Republic of New Haven: A History of Municipal Evolution* (Baltimore, 1886; rpt. Port Washington, NY, 1966), a dissertation completed at Johns Hopkins; Robert W. Roetger, "Order and Disorder in Early Connecticut: New Haven, 1639-1701" (diss. New Hampshire, 1982); *id.,* "The Transformation of Sexual Morality in 'Puritan' New England: Evidence from New Haven Court Records," *CRevAS,* 15 (1984), 125-47; *id.,* "Enforcing New Haven's Bylaws, 1639-1698: An Exercise in Local Social Control," *Connecticut History,* 27 (1986), 15-27; Floyd M. Shumway, "Early New Haven and Its Leadership" (diss. Columbia, 1968); Floyd M. Shumway and Richard Hegel (eds.), *New Haven: An Illustrated History,* 2nd edn. (Woodland Hills, CA, 1987); George V. Smith, "First Theocratic Government in the New World: Davenport and New Haven," *CM,* 8 (1903-4), 257-63; Charles W. Sorensen, "Response to Crisis: An Analysis of New Haven, 1638-1665" (diss. Michigan State, 1973); Bruce C. Steiner, "Dissension at Quinnipiac: The Authorship of *A Discourse About Civil Government in a New Plantation Whose Design is Religion,*" *NEQ,* 54 (1981), 14-32; Steven H. Ward, "A Nest of Vipers:

The Expansionist Policies of the New Haven Puritans from 1637 to 1667," *NHCHSJ*, 31 (1984), 3-12; Sarah D. Woodward, *Early New Haven* (New Haven, CT, 1912). For the founding of Newark, see esp. Edward P. Rindler, "The Migration from the New Haven Colony to Newark, East New Jersey: A Study of Puritan Values and Behavior, 1630-1720" (diss. University of Pennsylvania, 1977); also Newark, NJ, First Presbyterian Church, *Church Manual for the Members of the First Presbyterian Church, Newark, New Jersey . . .* , ed. William T. Hamilton (Newark, NJ, 1827); Howard L. Hayes, *Home Lots of the First Settlers of Newark* (Newark, NJ, 1892); Newark, NJ, *Records of the Town of Newark, New Jersey, from Its Settlement in 1666, to Its Incorporation as a City in 1836, NJHSC*, 6 (Newark, NJ, 1864); David L. Pierson, *Narratives of Newark (in New Jersey) from the Days of Its Founding* (Newark, NJ, 1917); Joseph Atkinson, *The History of Newark, New Jersey . . .* (Newark, NJ, 1878); *A History of the City of Newark, New Jersey*, 3 vols. (New York, 1913); New Jersey Historical Society, *Proceedings Commemorative of the Settlement of Newark, New Jersey, on its Two Hundredth Anniversary . . .* , *NJHSC*, 6-Supplement (1866); Jonathan F. Stearns, *Historical Discourses, Relating to the First Presbyterian Church in Newark . . .* (Newark, NJ, 1853); Frank J. Urquhart, *Newark: The Story of Its Early Days* (Newark, NJ, 1904); id., *A Short History of Newark* (Newark, NJ, 1908).

104. Thorpe, *Federal and State Constitutions*, 3.1637-40. The grant was renewed on Monday, June 29, 1674; cf. 3.1641-44.

105. *Ibid.*, 3.1637-38.

106. "James II of England," *DNB*, 10.618-19. James also spent substantial time in Holland.

107. Jere R. Daniell, *Colonial New Hampshire: A History*, pp. 25, 38, and 49; cf. also David E. Van Deventer, *The Emergence of Provincial New Hampshire, 1623-1741* (Baltimore, 1976), 40-61, and John W. Dean (ed.), *Capt. John Mason . . .* ; Albert S. Batchellor (ed.), *Documents Relating to the Masonian Patent, 1630-1846. . . .*

108. Thorpe, *Federal and State Constitutions*, 4.2446; cf. "The Commission Constituting a President and Council for the Province of New-Hampshire in New-England," New Hampshire, *Provincial Papers, Documents and Records Relating to the Province of New-Hampshire, from the Earliest Period of its Settlement: 1623-1686, NHHSP*, 1 (1867), 373-82.

109. Thorpe, *Federal and State Constitutions*, 3.1870, note a; "Exemplification of the Judgement for Vacating the Charter of the Massachusetts Bay in New England"; Edward Randolph, *Edward Randolph: Including His Letters and Official Papers from the New England, Middle and Southern Colonies in America, With Other Documents Relating Chiefly to the Vacating of the Royal Charter of the Colony of Massachusetts Bay, 1676-1703*; Emory Washburn, "Did the Vacating of the Colony Charter Annul the Laws Made Under It?"; Hamilton Hill, *History of the Old South Church (Third Church), Boston 1669-1884* (Boston, 1890), 1.250.

110. "Commission of Sir Edmund Andros for the Dominion of New England. April 7, 1688," in Thorpe, *Federal and State Constitutions*, 3.1863-69.

111. *Ibid.*, 3.1621-25.

112. Cf. *Ibid.*, 4.2433-36; for the 1635 grants to Mason, cf. 4.2537-44.

113. *Ibid.*, 4.2448.

114. *Ibid.*

115. Exeter, NH, First Church, *The First Church in Exeter, New Hampshire: 1638-*

1888 — 1698-1888 (Exeter, NH, 1898), 49-55; Charles H. Bell, *The History of Exeter* (Exeter, NH, 1888); rpt. as: *History of the Town of Exeter, New Hampshire* (Exeter, NH, 1979), 171-78; Exeter, NH, First Church, *The Confession of Faith and the Covenant of the First Congregational Church in Exeter, N.H.,* (Exeter, NH, 1832), 11; Exeter, NH, First Church, *Manual of the First Church in Exeter* . . . (Exeter, NH, 1888), 6-8.

   116. Thorpe, *Federal and State Constitutions,* 4.2451.

   117. Cf. *DNB,* 1.411; *DAB,* 1.300-301; Edmund Andros, *Sir Edmund Andros, 1637-1714 . . . Original Documents from His Papers . . .* (New York, 1978); Jeanne G. Bloom, "Sir Edmund Andros: A Study in Seventeenth-Century Administration" (diss. Yale, 1962); Viola F. Barnes, *The Dominion of New England: A Study in British Colonial Policy* (New Haven, CT, 1923); "Massachusetts Royal Commissions, 1681-1784," *CSMP,* 2 (1913); Albert Mathews, "Notes on the Massachusetts Royal Commissions, 1681-1725," in *Transactions, 1913-1914, CSMP,* 17 (1915), 2-111; *The Andros Records,* ed. Robert N. Toppan, *AASP,* n.s., 13 (1899-1900), 237-68, 463-99 (Monday, December 20, 1686–Thursday, March 17, 1686/87 and Wednesday, May 4, 1687–Wednesday, March 27, 1689); New Hampshire, Province, *Laws of New Hampshire . . . ,* ed. Albert S. Batchellor, vol. 1: *Province Period* (Manchester, NH, 1904), which contains all of the Andros Regime laws for New Hampshire; *Documents Relative to the Colonial History of New York . . . ,* vol. 3, ed. Edmund B. O'Callaghan (Albany, NY, 1853); *The Glorious Revolution in Massachusetts: Selected Documents, 1689-1692,* ed. Robert E. Moody and Richard C. Simmons, *CSMP,* 64 (1988); *Calendar of State Papers, Colonial Series: Edward Randolph,* ed. Robert Toppan (Boston, 1898-99).

   118. *RCRI,* 3.212-18.

   119. Thorpe, *Federal and State Constitutions,* 3.1863-69.

   120. The Dominion of New England consisted of five, and then seven, provinces: Massachusetts, Maine, the royal province of New Hampshire, New Plymouth (independent but charterless), and "King's Province" (the old Narragansett Country) formed the original core. Rhode Island and Connecticut were protected by charters, but flaws were found in their observance of the charter, and these colonies surrendered their charter rather than argue their case in court; cf. *DAB,* 1.300.

   121. Thorpe, *Federal and State Constitutions,* 3.1863.

   122. *Ibid.,* 3.1864.

   123. *Ibid.*

   124. *Ibid.*

   125. *Ibid.,* 3.1869.

   126. Viola F. Barnes, *The Dominion of New England: A Study in British Colonial Policy,* esp. "Chapter VI: Liberty of Conscience," 122-34.

   127. Hamilton A. Hill, *History of the Old South Church (Third Church) Boston 1669-1884,* 1.249-81.

   128. Samuel Sewall, *The Diary of Samuel Sewall, 1674-1729 . . . ,* ed. M. Halsey Thomas, 1 (New York, 1973), 162-63; quoted also in Hamilton A. Hill, *History of the Old South Church . . . Boston,* 1.270; the land in question belonged to the Cotton family and had been owned by John Cotton.

   129. Henry W. Foote, *Annals of King's Chapel from the Puritan Age to the Present Day,* 1 (Boston, 1882), 52. Governor Cranfield expressed the same frustration three years earlier. Speaking of Harvard College on Tuesday, June 19, 1683, Cranfield wrote:

"There can be no greater evill attend his Maj^{tie} affairs here, then those pernicious and Rebellious principles which flows from their Collige at Cambridge which they call their Uniuersity, from whence all the Townes both in this and the other Colonys are supplied with ffactions and Seditious Preachers who stirr up the people to a dislike of his Maj^{tie} and his Goum^t. and the Religion of the Church of England, terming the Liturgy of our Church a precident of Superstition and picked out of the Popish Dunghill; so that I am humbly of opinion this Country can never bee well settled or the people become good Subjects, till their Preachers bee reformed and that Colledge suppressed and the severall Churches supplyed with Learned and Orthodox Ministers from England as all other his Maj^{ties} Dominions in America are," Foote, *Annals*, 1.54-55.

130. *DNB*, 1.411; *DAB*, 1.300-301.

131. New Plymouth's 1629 charter was granted by the Council for New England; cf. Thorpe, *Federal and State Constitutions*, 3.1841-46.

132. William Henry Whitmore, *Increase Mather: The Agent of Massachusetts Colony in New England for the Concession of a Charter*; Israel Mauduit, *A Short View of the History of the New England Colonies, With Respect to Their Charters and Constitution*; Ellen M. Burrill, *A Monograph on the Charters and Constitution of Massachusetts*.

133. Thorpe, *Federal and State Constitutions*, 3.1870-86. The background to the 1691 charter is discussed in Philip S. Haffenden, "The Crown and the Colonial Charters, 1675-1688"; David S. Lovejoy, *The Glorious Revolution in America*; Richard R. Johnson, *Adjustment to Empire: The New England Colonies, 1675-1715*, especially the chapter entitled "London Interlude: The Quest for the Massachusetts Charter," 136-82; and Stephen Carl Arch, "The Glorious Revolution and the Rhetoric of Puritan History."

134. Thorpe, *Federal and State Constitutions*, 3.1870.

135. *Ibid.*, 3.1876.

136. John G. Reid, *Acadia, Maine, and New Scotland: Marginal Colonies in the Seventeenth Century* (Toronto, 1981), 188-90, based on a 1976 University of New Brunswick dissertation.

Reid also says that following the annexation of Maine by the Massachusetts Bay Colony, Agamenticus became York, while Black Point and Blue Point combined to form Scarborough, and Spurwink and Casco combined to form Falmouth; p. 193.

137. Because Appendix 1 is designed to be comprehensive, these marginal communities are listed and can be identified by their modern province.

138. *RM*, 1.79 and 1.87. The record for Wednesday, May 18, 1631, reads: " . . . to the end the body of the commons my be preserued of honest & good men, it was likewise ordered and agreed that for time to come noe man shalbe admitted to the freedome of this body polliticke, but such as are members of some of the churches within the lymitts of the same"; *RM*, 1.87.

139. Thorpe, *Federal and State Constitutions*, 3.1878-79.

140. *Ibid.*, 3.1880 and 1883.

141. *Ibid.*, 3.1881.

142. See, for example, "A Book of the Records of the Suffering of Friends . . . ," in Pembroke, MA [Scituate, MA], Society of Friends, "Minutes of the Monthly Meeting, 1676-1876," FHLC™M #0001335; cf. Jonathan M. Chu, "The Social Context of Religious Heterodoxy: The Challenge of Seventeenth-Century Quakerism to Orthodoxy in Massachusetts," *EIHC*, 118 (1982), 119-50; Carla G. Pestana, *Quakers and Baptists in Co-*

lonial Massachusetts (New York, 1991), based on her 1987 University of California at Los Angeles dissertation.

143. The text of the Toleration Act of 1689 can be found in Gee and Hardy, *Documents,* #CXXIII, 654-64.

144. Ferdinando Gorges had a council to assist him and resist him if necessary.

145. There were three stages to the claim of the Gorges family to this territory. The first stage was when Gorges was part of the 1606 Plymouth Company when it was associated with the London Company. Since attempts at colonization thus far had failed, the Plymouth Company was dissolved in 1619. The second stage was Gorges's formation of a second company, the New England Company, known more formally as "The Council Established at Plymouth . . . for the Planting, Ruling, Ordering and Governing of New England in America." The New England Company was incorporated on November 3, 1620, after the *Mayflower* had left and just as it was reaching its New Plymouth destination. The third stage was when Gorges obtained a new charter, making him "Lord Proprietary of the Province of Maine" in 1639. Gorges then died in 1647, leaving his vast grant of land to his son Robert. Robert did not pursue the claim, and "the interest of the Gorges family seems to have lapsed." *DNB,* 8.241-43; quotation from 243.

146. For the history of the First Presbyterian Church of Elizabeth, see: Harry C. Ellison, *Church of the Founding Fathers of New Jersey: A History* (Cornish, ME, 1964); William B. Sprague, *A Discourse, Addressed to the First Presbyterian Congregation of Elizabeth, New Jersey . . . on Occasion of the Completion of its Second Century* (Albany, NY, 1867). For the history of the First Presbyterian Church of Newark see: Newark, NJ, First Presbyterian Church, *Church Manual for the Members of the First Presbyterian Church, Newark, New Jersey . . .* ; Edward P. Rindler, "The Migration from the New Haven Colony to Newark, East New Jersey: A Study of Puritan Values and Behavior, 1630-1720"; Jonathan F. Stearns, *Historical Discourses, Relating to the First Presbyterian Church in Newark. . . .*

Notes to Chapter 3

1. Since we have already discussed the concept of the charter in the previous chapter, we will pass over local civil covenants that are classified as charters.

2. The primary and secondary sources for the Plymouth Plantation and New Plymouth Colony are legion. Four categories will suffice for our purposes: the background in Europe (England and the Netherlands); firsthand accounts that cover town, colony and church; secondary sources that consider the town and then the subsequent colony, and secondary sources that deal with the church/churches in both town and then colony.

For the background in England and the Netherlands, see nn. 14 and 18 in "Chapter 1: The European Background," and n. 5 in "Chapter 2: The Colonial Charters. . . ."

For primary sources concerning town, colony, and church, the place to begin is the writings of Governor William Bradford: William Bradford, "Governor [William] Bradford's Letter Book," *MHSC,* ser. 1, 3 (1794), 27-76; *id., Of Plymouth Plantation, 1620-1647,* ed. Samuel E. Morison, which will be the edition referred to hereafter. The other firsthand account is called "Mourt's Relation," author unknown, first published in 1622: "Mourt's Relation — 1622," *MHSC,* ser. 1, 8 (1802), 203-39; *[Mourt's Relation]: The Jour-*

nal of the Pilgrims at Plymouth (New York, 1848); Mourt's Relation, or Journal of the Plantation at Plymouth, ed. Henry M. Dexter (Boston, 1865); Mourt's Relation: A Journal of the Pilgrims at Plymouth . . . (1622), ed. Dwight B. Heath (New York, 1963). For other primary sources concerning the town and colony in general, see Edward Arber, ed., The Story of the Pilgrim Fathers; Champlin Burrage, "The Earliest Minor Accounts of Plymouth Plantation," HThR, 13 (1920), 315-44; Samuel D. Hannah, Plymouth Corporation, a Trading Company, Located at Plymouth, a Proprietary Plantation . . . (Yarmouthport, MA, 1928); Joseph Hunter, Collections Concerning the Early History of the Founders of New Plymouth, First Colonists of New England (London, 1849); Joseph Hunter, Collections Concerning the Church . . . Formed at Scrooby; John Masefield (ed.), Chronicles of the Pilgrim Fathers . . . ; Mayflower Quarterly; Occasional Papers in Old Colony Studies; Old Colony Historical Society, Collections; Plymouth, MA, Records of the Town of Plymouth, 3 vols. (Plymouth, MA, 1889-1903); RCNP; George F. Willison, The Pilgrim Reader . . . (Garden City, NY, 1953); Alexander Young, Chronicles of the Pilgrim Fathers of the Colony of Plymouth, from 1602 to 1625, 2nd edn. (1844; rpt. Baltimore, 1974). Unfortunately we do not have the earliest records of the Plymouth First Church; the church records for most of the seventeenth century consist of two accounts by Nathaniel Morton, written in 1680, and John Cotton, Jr., written in 1699: Plymouth, MA, First Church, Plymouth Church Records, ed. Arthur Lord, 2 vols., CSMP, 22-23 (1920-23).

For secondary sources that consider the town and/or the colony, see: Morton Dexter, "Some Differences Between Plymouth and Jamestown," CSMP, 12 (1908-9), 256-70; Massachusetts Historical Society, "Notes on Plymouth," MHSC, ser. 2, 3 (1815), 162-97; James Thacher, History of the Town of Plymouth . . . (1835), 3rd edn. (Yarmouthport, MA, 1972); William S. Russell, Guide to Plymouth, and Recollections of the Pilgrims (Boston, 1846); Joseph Banvard, Plymouth and the Pilgrims (Boston, 1851); William S. Russell, Pilgrim Memorials . . . (Boston, 1870); William T. Davis, History of the Town of Plymouth, with a Sketch of the Origin and Growth of Separatism (Philadelphia, 1885); Nina M. Tiffany, Pilgrims and Puritans: The Story of the Planting of Plymouth and Boston (Boston, 1888); Morton Dexter, "Alleged Facts as to the Pilgrims," MHSP, ser. 2, 10 (1895-96), 257-63; John Brown, The Pilgrim Fathers of New England and their Puritan Successors (New York, 1896); William T. Davis, Ancient Landmarks of Plymouth (1883); 2nd edn. (Boston, 1899); William W. Goodwin, "The Landing of the Pilgrims," MHSP, ser. 2, 17 (1903), 378-82; Lincoln N. Kinnicut, "The Plymouth Settlement and Tisquantum," MHSP, 48 (1914-15), 103-18; id., "Plymouth's Debt to the Indians," HThR, 13 (1920), 345-61; Arthur Lord, Plymouth and the Pilgrims (Boston, 1920); Francis R. Stoddard, The Truth About the Pilgrims (1952; rpt. Baltimore, 1976); Samuel E. Morison, The Story of the "Old Colony" of New Plymouth (New York, 1956); id., "New Light Wanted on the Old Colony," WMQ, ser. 3, 15 (1958), 359-64; John P. Demos, "Notes on Life in Plymouth Colony," WMQ, ser. 3, 22 (1965), 264-86; George D. Langdon, Jr., Pilgrim Colony: A History of New Plymouth, 1620-1691 (New Haven, CT, 1966), based on a 1961 Yale dissertation; Dorothy D. Merrick, "A Framework for 17th-Century Plymouth," Plymouth Society Notes, 12 (May 1963), 1-12; Darrett B. Rutman, Husbandmen of Plymouth: Farms and Villages in the Old Colony, 1620-1692 (Boston, 1967); John Demos, A Little Commonwealth: Family Life in Plymouth Colony (New York, 1970); L. D. Geller, They Knew They Were Pilgrims: Essays in Plymouth History (New York, 1971); Eugene A. Stratton, Plymouth Colony: Its History and People, 1620-1691 (Salt Lake City, UT, 1986).

The history of the church in Plymouth itself and the churches in New Plymouth Colony can be found in the following: "An Account of the Church of Christ, in Plymouth, 1620-1760," *MHSC*, ser. 1, 4 (1795), 107-41; Joshua W. Wellman, *Church Polity of the Pilgrims* . . . (Boston, 1857); Arthur Lord, "The Pilgrim's Church in Plymouth," *NEM*, n.s., 7 (1892-93), 777-88; John Cuckson, *A Brief History of the First Church in Plymouth, from 1606 to 1901* (Boston, 1902); George N. Marshall (ed.), *The Church of the Pilgrim Fathers* (Boston, 1950); John M. Bumsted, *The Pilgrim's Progress: The Ecclesiastical History of the Old Colony, 1620-1775* (New York, 1989), a 1965 Brown dissertation; Eugene A. Stratton, "The First Parish Church of Plymouth," *Mayflower Quarterly*, 47 (1981), 131-37.

3. While New Plymouth Plantation and Colony were called "new" to distinguish themselves from the old town of Plymouth, England, it was often called the "Old Colony" by members of the other New England colonies because it was the first organized colony in that region and was therefore older than the other colonies.

4. *A Journal of the Pilgrims at Plymouth: Mourt's Relation* . . . , ed. Dwight B. Heath, 17-18.

5. Nathaniel Morton, *New England's Memorial . . . Also Governor Bradford's History of Plymouth Colony; Portions of Prince's Chronology; Governor Bradford's Dialogue; Gov. Winslow's Visits to Massasoit; With Numerous Marginal Notes* . . . , 6th edn. (Boston, 1855).

6. *Of Plymouth Plantation, 1620-1647,* 75-76.

7. Cf. New Plymouth Colony, *The Compact with the Charter and Laws of the Colony of New Plymouth* . . . ; George E. Bowman, *The Mayflower Compact and Its Signers* (Boston, 1920); Lois K. Mathews, "The Mayflower Compact and its Descendants," Mississippi Valley Historical Association, *Proceedings*, 6 (1912-13), 79-106; Arthur Lord, "The Mayflower Compact," *AASP*, n.s., 30 (1920), 278-94; Mark L. Sargent, "The Conservative Covenant: The Rise of the Mayflower Compact in American Myth," *NEQ*, 61 (1988), 233-51.

8. *DAB*, 13.261-62; N. Morton, *New England's Memorial* . . . , 6th edn. (Boston, 1855), vi.

9. Bradford, *Of Plymouth Plantation, 1620-1647,* 28-29.

10. *Ibid.,* 29-30.

11. "John Carver (1575?-1621)," *DNB*, 3.1145-46 and *DAB*, 3.551-52; "Robert Cushman (c. 1579-1625)," *DAB*, 5.5.

12. Bradford, *Of Plymouth Plantation, 1620-1647,* 31. Bradford intimates that "other" messengers were sent, but the letter of Edwin Sandys to John Robinson and William Brewster indicate that Cushman and Carver were again sent; cf. 31-32. Bradford is therefore mistaken in his recollection.

13. The seven articles were not included in Bradford's history, but can be found in Williston Walker, *The Creeds and Platforms of Congregationalism* (New York, 1893; rpt. Boston, 1960), 87-91. The original document is in the Public Records Office, London; cf. Bradford, *Of Plymouth Plantation, 1620-1647,* 31n.

14. Walker, *Creeds and Platforms,* 89-90.

15. Cf. Horton Davies, *The Worship of the English Puritans* . . . (London, 1948); *id., Worship and Theology in England,* vol. 1, *From Cranmer to Hooker, 1534-1603* (Princeton, NJ, 1970) and vol. 2, *From Andrewes to Baxter and Fox, 1603-1690* (Princeton, NJ, 1975);

these two vols. were rpt. as *Book I: From Cranmer to Baxter and Fox, 1534-1690* (Grand Rapids, MI, 1996); *id.*, "The Worship of the First American Congregationalists," *BCL*, 9 (1957-58), #2, 5-15; and *id.*, *The Worship of the American Puritans.*

16. Over thirty years later, in 1646, Bradford appended a comment to his *History* that was composed in the wake of the English Revolution and that revealed his own assessment of the episcopal domination of the Church of England: "A Late Observation as it Were, by the Way, Worthy to be Noted. Full little did I think that the downfall of the Bishops, with their courts, canons and ceremonies, etc. had been so near, when I first began these scribbled writings (which was about the year 1630 and so pieced up at times of leisure afterward) or that I should have lived to have seen or heard of the same. . . . The Tyrannous Bishops are ejected, their courts dissolved, their canons forceless, their service cashiered, their ceremonies useless and despised, their plots for popery prevented, and all their superstitions discarded and returned to Rome from whence they came, and the monuments of idolatry rooted out of the land. And the proud and profane supporters and cruel defenders of these, as bloody papists and wicked atheists, and their malignant consorts, marvelously overthrown. And are not these great things? Who can deny it? But who hath done it? Who, even He that sitteth on the white horse, who is 'called Faithful and true, and judgeth and fighteth righteously,' Revelation xix.11 . . . ," Bradford, *Of Plymouth Plantation, 1620-1647*, Appendix I, 351-52.

17. Walker, *Creeds and Platforms, 90.*

18. Stephen J. Brachlow, "John Robinson and the Lure of Separatism in Pre-Revolutionary England"; M. Dorothea Jordan, "The Early Independents and the Visible Church"; Verne D. Morey, "The Brownist Churches: A Study in English Separatism, 1553-1630"; Donald Ashmall, "John Smyth, John Robinson, and the Church"; George Selement, "The Covenant Theology of English Separatism and the Separation of Church and State"; Timothy F. George, *John Robinson and the English Separatist Tradition;* William G. Chrystal, "John Robinson and William Ames: A New Look at Old Debates about Separatism"; Stephen J. Brachlow, *The Communion of Saints: Radical Puritan and Separatist Ecclesiology, 1570-1625.*

19. Bradford, *Of Plymouth Plantation, 1620-1647*, 31-32.

20. *Ibid.*, 33.

21. *Ibid.*, 36.

22. *Ibid.*, 354.

23. *Ibid.*, 354-55.

24. Letter of Robert Cushman to the Leyden Congregation, May 8, 1619, in *Ibid.*, 355-58.

25. *Ibid.*, 47.

26. With respect to the captain and the sailors, see *Ibid.*, 54.

27. *Ibid.*, 51; for the text of the letter, see 367-71.

28. *Ibid.*, 368.

29. *Ibid.*, 369-70.

30. *Ibid.*, 75.

31. *Ibid.*

32. Thorpe, *Federal and State Constitutions,* "Charter of the Colony of New Plymouth Granted to William Bradford and His Associates — 1629," 3.1841-46, along with

"William Bradford, etc. Surrender of the Patent of Plymouth Colony to the Freemen, March 2d, 1640," 3.1861-62.

33. See n. 15 concerning the First British Empire in the Introduction and then n. 8 in Chapter 2: The Colonial Charters of Early New England, above.

34. Cf. Appendix 1. For the 1630s, Scituate, Duxbury, Yarmouth-1 (failed), Taunton, Seppekann (failed), Yarmouth-2, Sandwich, Barnstable; for the 1640s, Marshfield and Eastham; for the 1650s, Bridgewater; for the 1660s, Dartmouth, Swansea, and Middleborough-1, and for the 1680s, Bristol, Freetown, Rochester, Falmouth, and Little Compton. Cf. George D. Langdon, Jr., *Pilgrim Colony: A History of New Plymouth, 1620-1691;* Horace C. Weston, "The Expansion of Plymouth," in L. D. Geller, *They Knew They Were Pilgrims: Essays in Plymouth History,* 67-76; W. T. Davis, *History of the Town of Plymouth;* Joel N. Eno, "The Expansion of New England as Begun in Plymouth," *Americana,* 23 (1929), 403-10.

35. The *RCNP* begin in 1633; the town records begin in 1636: Plymouth, MA, *Records of the Town of Plymouth,* vol. I: *1636 to 1705* (Plymouth, MA, 1889).

36. Thorpe, *Federal and State Constitutions,* 1.519, note a.

37. *DAB,* 11.493-94; *DNB,* 12.262-63.

38. Thorpe, *Federal and State Constitutions,* 1.519-23; also *PRCC,* 1.20-26.

39. Thorpe, *Federal and State Constitutions,* 1.519.

40. *Ibid.,* 1.523; italics are in the source cited.

41. *Ibid.,* 1.519.

42. For the general history of New Haven as a town, see "Chapter 2: The Colonial Charters of Early New England," n. 103, along with New Haven, CT, *New Haven Town Records,* ed. Franklin B. Dexter and Zara James Powers, 3 vols., New Haven Colony Historical Society, *Ancient Town Records,* vols. 1-3 (New Haven, CT, 1917-19). Cf. also John Archer, "Puritan Town Planning in New Haven," Society of Architectural Historians, *Journal,* 34 (1975), 140-49; Edward E. Atwater (ed.), *History of the City of New Haven to the Present Time* (New York, 1887); Henry T. Blake, *Chronicles of New Haven Green, from 1638 to 1862* (New Haven, CT, 1898); Isabel M. Calder, *The New Haven Colony* (New Haven, CT, 1934); Lilian Handlin, "Dissent in a Small Community," *NEQ,* 58 (1985), 193-220; Everett G. Hill, *A Modern History of New Haven and Eastern New Haven County,* 2 vols. (New York, 1918); James L. Kingsley, *An Historical Summary . . . [on] the Two Hundredth Anniversary of the First Settlement of the Town and Colony* (New Haven, CT, 1838); Edward R. Lambert, *History of the Colony of New Haven, Before and After the Union with Connecticut . . .* (New Haven, CT, 1838; rpt. Milford, CT, 1976); Charles H. Levermore, *The Republic of New Haven: A History of Municipal Evolution* (Baltimore, 1886; rpt. Port Washington, NY, 1966); New Haven, CT, *Proceedings in Commemoration of the Settlement of the Town of New Haven* ([New Haven, CT], 1888); *NHCHSJ; NHCHSP; New Haven Genealogical Magazine;* Rollin G. Osterweis, *Three Centuries of New Haven, 1638-1938* (New Haven, CT, 1953); Robert W. Roetger, "Order and Disorder in Early Connecticut: New Haven, 1639-1701" (diss. New Hampshire, 1982); id., "Enforcing New Haven's Bylaws, 1639-1698: An Exercise in Local Social Control," *Connecticut History,* 27 (1986), 15-27; Floyd M. Shumway, "Early New Haven and Its Leadership" (diss. Columbia, 1968); id., "New Haven and its First Settlers," *NHCHSJ,* 21 (1972), 45-67; Floyd M. Shumway and Richard Hegel (eds.), *New Haven: An Illustrated History,* 2nd edn. (Woodland Hills, CA, 1987); Charles W. Sorensen, "Response to Crisis: An Analysis of New Haven, 1638-

1665" (diss. Michigan State, 1973); Bruce C. Steiner, "Dissension at Quinnipiac: The Authorship of *A Discourse About Civil Government in a New Plantation Whose Design is Religion*," *NEQ*, 54 (1981), 14-32; Sarah D. Woodward, *Early New Haven* (New Haven, CT, 1912).

For New Haven as a colony, see *RCPNH; RCJNH;* New Haven Colony, *The Earliest Laws of the New Haven and Connecticut Colonies, 1639-1673,* ed. John D. Cushing (Wilmington, DE, 1977); Edward E. Atwater, *History of the Colony of New Haven to Its Absorption into Connecticut* (Meriden, CT, 1902); Edward R. Lambert, *History of the Colony of New Haven, Before and After the Union with Connecticut . . .* ; Edward P. Rindler, "The Migration from the New Haven Colony to Newark, East New Jersey: A Study of Puritan Values and Behavior, 1630-1720"; Elizabeth Tucker Van Beek, "Piety and Profit: English Puritans and the Shaping of a Godly Marketplace in the New Haven Colony" (diss. Virginia, 1993).

43. *RCPNH,* 9-21. The records of the town, edited by Franklin B. Dexter and Zara James Powers and cited above, begin in 1649.

44. *RCPNH,* 9-10.

45. C. H. Levermore, *The Republic of New Haven: A History of Municipal Evolution,* 17.

46. For Davenport, see *DNB,* 5.560-61; *DAB,* 5.85-87; William B. Sprague, *Annals of the American Pulpit,* 1 (New York, 1857), 93; *DARB,* 140-41; John Davenport, *Letters of John Davenport, Puritan Divine,* ed. Isabel M. Calder (New Haven, CT, 1937); George V. Smith, "First Theocratic Government in the New World: Davenport and New Haven," *CM,* 8 (1903-4), 257-63; Charles W. Sorensen, "John Davenport's 'Errands into the Wilderness,'" *BCL,* 29 (1977-8), #3, 4-15; John B. Davenport, "'Yours Unfeignedly in the Lord': The Theology of John Davenport (1597-1670)" (diss. Minnesota, 1994).

47. Davenport and his followers arrived in Boston on June 26, 1637, and left the next year, in 1638; cf. Edward E. Atwater, *History of the Colony of New Haven . . . ,* Chapter 4, 58-68.

48. (Cambridge, MA, 1663).

49. C. W. Sorensen, "Response to Crisis: An Analysis of New Haven, 1638-1665."

50. *RCPNH,* 11.

51. *Ibid.*

52. *Ibid.*

53. *Ibid.,* 12.

54. *Ibid.*

55. Cf. David A. Weir, *The Origins of the Federal Theology,* 3-9, and 42, n. 20.

56. Cf. NHC, *The Earliest Laws of the New Haven and Connecticut Colonies, 1639-1673;* also Isabel M. Calder, "The Laws of the New Haven Colony," New Haven County Bar Association, *Bulletin,* 21 (1938), 6-10.

57. Cf. [John Cotton and William Aspinwall], "An Abstract of the Laws of New-England," *MHSC,* ser. 1, 5 (1798), 171-92. For Connecticut Colony, see CTC, *The Connecticut Code of 1650* (Hartford, CT, 1825); id., *Blue Laws of Connecticut: A Collection of the Earliest Statutes and Judicial Proceedings of That Colony . . . ,* ed. Samuel M. Smucker (Philadelphia, 1861); CTC, *The Earliest Laws of the New Haven and Connecticut Colonies, 1639-1673.* For the Province of Maine, see Josiah H. Drummond, "Bibliographic Memorandum of the Laws of Maine," *MeHSC,* ser. 2, 2 (1891), 391-402. For the Massachusetts Bay Colony and

Province, see Isabel M. Calder, "John Cotton's *Moses His Judicials*," *CSMP,* 29 (1935), 86-94; Henry H. Edes et al., "Extracts Relating to the Body of Liberties of 1641," *CSMP,* 7 (1900-1902), 22-26; F. C. Gray, "Remarks on the Early Laws of Massachusetts Bay; With the Code Adopted in 1641, and Called *The Body of Liberties,* Now First Printed," *MHSC,* ser. 3, 8 (1843), 191-237; Joel Parker, *The First Charter and the Early Religious Legislation of Massachusetts . . .* ; MBC, *The Colonial Laws of Massachusetts,* ed. William H. Whitmore (Boston, 1887); William H. Whitmore, *A Bibliographical Sketch of the Laws of the Massachusetts Colony from 1630 to 1686 . . .* (Boston, 1890); id., "Index to Early {Massachusetts Bay} Colony Laws," *MHSP,* ser. 2, 11 (1896-97), 8-18; Worthington C. Ford, "Cotton's 'Moses His Judicials,' 1636-1641," *MHSP,* ser. 2, 16 (1902), 274-84; id., "Bibliography of the Laws of Massachusetts Bay, 1641-1776," *CSMP,* 4 (1910), 291-480; MBC, *The Laws and Liberties of Massachusetts . . . ,* ed. Max Farrend (Cambridge, MA, 1929); Thorp L. Wolford, "The Laws and Liberties of 1648: The First Code of Laws Enacted and Printed in English America," *Boston University Law Review,* 28 (1948), 426-63; MBC, *The Book of the General Lawes and Libertyes Concerning the Inhabitants of Massachusetts . . . ,* ed. G. Barnes (San Marino, CA, 1975); MBC, *The Laws and Liberties of Massachusetts, 1641-1691,* ed. John D. Cushing (Wilmington, DE, 1976); MBP, *The Massachusetts Province Laws, 1692-1699,* ed. John D. Cushing (Wilmington, DE, 1978); John D. Cushing, *A Bibliography of the Laws and Resolves of the Massachusetts Bay, 1642-1780* (Wilmington, DE, 1984). For the Province of New Hampshire, see Albert H. Hoyt, "Historical and Bibliographical Notes on the Laws of New Hampshire," *AASP,* 66 (1876), 89-104; NHP, *Index to the Laws of New Hampshire, Recorded in the Office of the Secretary of State, 1679-1883* (Manchester, NH, 1886); New Hampshire, *The Government and Laws of New Hampshire Before the Establishment of the Province, 1623-1679,* ed. Albert S. Batchellor (Manchester, NH, 1904); NHP, *Acts and Laws of New Hampshire, 1680-1726* (Wilmington, DE, 1978). For the New Plymouth Colony, see NPC, *The Compact with the Charter and Laws of the Colony of New Plymouth . . . ;* id., *The Laws of the Pilgrims: A Facsimile Edition of the Book of the General Laws of the Inhabitants of the Jurisdiction of New-Plimoth, 1672 and 1685* (Wilmington, DE, 1977). For Rhode Island, see RIC, *Charters and Legislative Documents, Illustrative of Rhode-Island History . . .* (Providence, RI, 1844); id., *The Earliest Acts and Laws of the Colony of Rhode Island and Providence Plantations, 1647-1719* (Wilmington, DE, 1977).

58. *RCPNH,* 12.

59. *Ibid.*

60. *Ibid.,* 13.

61. *Ibid.*

62. *Ibid.*

63. *ISBE,* 3.613-14.

64. *RCPNH,* 13-14.

65. New Haven, CT, First Church, "Church Records, 1639-1926," FHLC™M #: 0005343; New Haven, CT, *New Haven Town Records.*

66. The full account can be found in Exodus 18:13-27. "Exodus 18:2" is an error for "Exodus 18:21."

67. Deuteronomy 1:9-18.

68. The entire passage is Deuteronomy 17:14-21.

69. An interesting exploration in early New England social history would be to discern who initiated lawsuits against whom in each of the early New England colonies,

and whether some colonies and local communities were more successful at keeping civil lawsuits between church members to a minimum. Furthermore, the question should be asked whether lawsuits between church members and non-members, and between church members and half-way covenant members, were allowed to proceed. Who initiated lawsuits at a greater rate, church members or non-members? Finally, in cases where litigants who were not church members initiated lawsuits against church members, were the non-members given equal justice?

70. *RCPNH*, 14.

71. *Ibid.*

72. *Ibid.*, 15.

73. *Ibid.*, 17-18.

74. James Savage, *A Genealogical Dictionary of the First Settlers of New England . . .* (1860-62; rpt. Baltimore, 1965), 1.75 (Atwater), 1.332 (Camfield), and 2.44 (Higginson).

75. *Ibid.*, 15-16.

76. Milford joined itself to New Haven to form the New Haven Colony in 1643. According to Cotton Mather the churches were founded on two successive days ("Prudentius: The Life of Mr. Peter Prudden . . . ," in *Magnalia Christi Americana,* 1 [Hartford, CT, 1853], 395). The church records of Milford testify explicitly that Milford First Church was founded on Thursday, August 22, 1639; Milford, CT, First Church, *Tercentenary, Church of Christ, Congregational, Milford, Connecticut, 1639-1939* ([Milford, CT, 1940]), 7-8.

77. *RCPNH*, 20.

78. *Ibid.*, 19.

79. *Ibid.*, 21.

80. *Ibid.*

81. Cf. Steven H. Ward, "A Nest of Vipers: The Expansionist Policies of the New Haven Puritans from 1637 to 1667," *NHCHSJ,* 31 (1984), 3-12. For accounts of Varkin's Kill (Salem Creek), see C. H. Levermore, *The Republic of New Haven: A History of Municipal Evolution,* 90-99; I. M. Calder, *The New Haven Colony,* Chapter V. Paugaset later became Derby, CTC.

82. For the history of Providence, see John H. Cady, "The Divisions of the Home Lots of Providence," *RIHSC,* 31 (1938), 101-7; Howard M. Chapin, "The Lands and Houses of the First Settlers of Providence," *RIHSC,* 12 (1919), 1-8; Charles W. Hopkins, *The Home Lots of the Early Settlers of the Providence Plantations . . .* (Providence, RI, 1886); A. B. Patton, "The Early Land Titles of Providence," *Narragansett Historical Register,* 8 (1890), 156-75; Providence, RI, *The Early Records of the Town of Providence,* 21 vols. (Providence, RI, 1892-1915); Howard M. Chapin (ed.), *Documentary History of Rhode Island . . . ,* 2 vols. (Providence, RI, 1916-19); Roger Williams, *The Correspondence of Roger Williams,* ed. Glenn W. La Fantasie, 2 vols. (Hanover, NH, 1987); Samuel G. Arnold, *The Progress of Providence . . .* (Providence, RI, 1876); Henry C. Dorr, *The Planting and Growth of Providence . . .* (Providence, RI, 1882); Thomas Durfee, *A Historical Discourse Delivered on the Two Hundred and Fiftieth Anniversary of the Planting of Providence* (Providence, RI, 1887); William A. Greene et al., *The Providence Plantations for Two Hundred and Fifty Years* (Providence, RI, 1886); [Stephen Hopkins?], "An Historical Account of the Planting and Growth of Providence," *MHSC,* ser. 2, 9 (1822), 167-203; Gertrude S.

Kimball, *Providence in Colonial Times* (Boston, 1912); Dennis A. O'Toole, "Exiles, Refugees and Rogues: The Quest for Civil Order in the Towns and Colony of Providence Plantations, 1636-1654" (diss. Brown, 1973); John Pitman, *A Discourse, Delivered at Providence . . . in Commemoration of the First Settlement of Rhode-Island and Providence Plantations* (Providence, RI, 1836); Providence, RI, *Annals of the Town of Providence, from its First Settlement,* ed. William R. Staples (Providence, RI, 1843) and *RIHSC,* 5 (1843); Rhode Island Historical Society, *Providence: From Provincial Village to Prosperous Port,* ed. Linda L. Levin (Providence, RI, 1978); Bradford F. Swan, *The Rev. Thomas James, the Civil Compact and the Town Evidence* (Providence, RI, 1963); George F. Wilson, *Town and City Government in Providence* (Providence, RI, 1889).

83. *DAB,* 20.286-89 and *DNB,* 21.445-50. For other references to Williams, cf. n. 78 in Chapter 2: "The Colonial Charters of Early New England," above.

84. Providence, RI, *Early Records of the Town of Providence,* ed. Horatio Rogers et al., 1 (Providence, RI, 1892), 1; cf. also Providence, RI, *Annals of the Town of Providence . . . ,* 39.

85. Cf. esp. Dennis A. O'Toole, "Exiles, Refugees and Rogues: The Quest for Civil Order in the Towns and Colony of Providence Plantations." Some of the disputes seem to have emerged over land. In 1640, the town drew up a long document concerning land division (cf. Providence, RI, *Annals of the Town of Providence,* 40-43). In 1645/6, another group of signers accepted free land grants (*ibid.,* 60). By 1647 they covenanted to appoint individuals to organize the Colony of Rhode Island and Providence Plantations as authorized by the 1644 charter, laying out in specific detail what their expectations of their representatives were (*ibid.,* 61-63). But disputes must have been continuing, for in December of that year they had to draw up a compact that expounded the virtues of love, union, and order, along with peace and liberty (*ibid.,* 68-70). Finally, in 1648, after the central government was organized, the colonial government handed down a charter to Providence (*ibid.,* 73-74).

86. For the history of Woburn, see [Edward Johnson], *Wonder-Working Providence of Sion's Saviour in New England . . . [By Captain Edward Johnson],* ed. William F. Poole (Andover, MA, 1867) (Johnson was a resident of Woburn); *id., A History of New England . . . [Johnson's Wonder-Working Providence, 1628-1651],* ed. J. Franklin Jameson, Original Narratives of Early American History (New York, 1910); George H. Evans, *The Seven against the Wilderness: A Brief Account of the Settlement of Woburn, Massachusetts . . .* ([Somerville, MA, 1920]); Samuel Sewall, *The History of Woburn . . .* (Boston, 1868); Woburn, MA, *Proceedings . . . at the Two Hundred and Fiftieth Anniversary of the Incorporation of the Town of Woburn, Massachusetts* (Woburn, MA, 1893). The history of the established First Church can be found in Woburn, MA, First Church, *The Rules and Regulations and Confession of Faith and Covenant of the First Congregational Church in Woburn, with Lists of the Founders, Pastors, and Deacons; Together with a Catalogue of the Existing Members* (Somerville, MA, 1844); rpt. as *Manual of the First Congregational Church* (Woburn, MA, 1852); "First Congregational Church in Woburn, Ms.," *CQ,* 4 (1862), 298-300; Woburn, MA, First Church, *Commemoration of the Two Hundred and Fiftieth Anniversary of the Founding of the First Church at Woburn, Massachusetts (Congregational) Held . . . in Connection with the Civic Celebration* (n.p., 1893); Woburn, MA, First Church, *1642-1942. First Congregational Church, Woburn, Massachusetts. The Tercentenary Program . . .* (Woburn, MA, 1942).

87. Woburn, MA, "Town Records and Miscellaneous Papers: Reel 5: Town Meet-

ings, Taxes, 1640-1766," FHLC™M#: 0893363, Vol. 1, p. 2, for the Preamble; Samuel Sewall, *The History of Woburn . . .* , 529-30.

88. For the history of Medfield, MBC, see Medfield, MA, "Town and Meeting Records, 1649-1788: vol. 1-3, 1649-1788," FHLC™M #: 0832316; *id.*, "Town and Meeting Records, 1652-1742," FHLC™M #: 0836217; Medfield, MA, *Exercises at the Bi-Centennial Commemoration of the Burning of Medfield . . .* (Medfield, MA, 1876); *id.*, *Proceedings at the Celebration of the Two Hundred and Fiftieth Anniversary of the Incorporation of the Town . . .* (Boston, 1902); Daniel Clarke Sanders, *A Sermon . . .* (Dedham, MA, 1817). Medfield emerged out of Dedham, MBC. For the history of Dedham, see Dedham, MA, *The Early Records of the Town of Dedham, Massachusetts, 1636-1659,* Dedham Historical Records, 3 (Dedham, MA, 1888); Dedham Historical Records; *Dedham Historical Register;* B. Katherine Brown, "Puritan Democracy in Dedham, Massachusetts: Another Case Study," *WMQ,* ser. 3, 24 (1967), 378-96; Mark Allen Carden, "The Ministry and the Word: The Clergy, the Bible, and Biblical Themes in Five Massachusetts Towns, 1630-1700" (diss. University of California, Irvine, 1977); Robert B. Hanson, *Dedham, Massachusetts, 1635-1890* ([Dedham, MA, 1976]); Kenneth A. Lockridge, *A New England Town: The First Hundred Years: Dedham, Massachusetts, 1636-1736* (New York, 1970), based on a 1965 Princeton dissertation; *id.*, "The Population of Dedham, Massachusetts, 1636-1737," *Economic History Review,* 19 (1966), 318-44; Kenneth A. Lockridge and Alan Kreider, "The Evolution of Massachusetts Town Government, 1640-1740," *WMQ,* ser. 3, 23 (1966), 549-74; W. R. Prest, "Stability and Change in Old and New England: Clayworth and Dedham," *Journal of Interdisciplinary History,* 6 (1975-76), 359-74; Frank Smith, *A History of Dedham, Massachusetts* (Dedham, MA, 1936); Erasmus Worthington, *The History of Dedham from the Beginning of its Settlement . . .* (Boston, 1827).

89. Herman Mann, *Historical Annals of Dedham, From its Settlement in 1635, to 1847* (Dedham, MA, 1847), 98-99, which is part of a section on Medfield.

90. *Ibid.*

91. For a discussion of the Confederation of New England, cf. John Q. Adams, "The New England Confederacy of MDCXLIII"; Harold Kolling, "The New England Confederation of 1643: Its Origin, Nature, and Foreign Relations, 1643-1652"; Harry M. Ward, *The United Colonies of New England, 1643-90;* also Robert M. Gatke, "Plans of American Colonial Union, 1643 to 1754" and Oline Carmical, Jr., "Plans of Union, 1634-1783: A Study and Reappraisal of Projects for Uniting the English Colonies in North America." The records of the Confederation can be found in *RCNP,* 9 (1859) (*Acts of the Commissioners of the United Colonies of New England,* vol. I, *1643-1651*) and 10 (1859) (*Acts of the Commissioners of the United Colonies of New England,* vol. II, 1653-1679) — a very unlikely place for any one to look. Cf. also "Extracts from the Records of the Commissioners of the United Colonies," *PRCC,* 3.471-514; United Colonies of New England, Commissioners, *Extracts from the Records of the United Colonies of New England: Comprising Such Portions of the Records as are not Published in the Second Volume of Hazard's State Papers . . .* (Hartford, CT, 1859).

92. See Appendix 1, Column 2 for a listing of independent plantations and where they ultimately ended up.

93. In the Prologue of "The Articles of Confederation of the United Colonies of New England," composed in 1643, we find the following statement: "And forasmuch as the natives have formerly committed sundry insolence and outrages upon several Planta-

tions of the English and have of late combined themselves against us: *and seeing by reason of those sad distractions in England which they have heard of, and by which they know we are hindered from that humble way of seeking advice, or reaping those comfortable fruits of protection, which at other times we might well expect.* We therefore do conceive it our bounden duty, without delay to enter into a present Consociation amongst ourselves, for mutual help and strength in all our future concernments . . . ," Thorpe, *Federal and State Constitutions,* 1.77 (italics mine). Cf. Ronald D. Cohen, "Colonial Leviathan: New England Foreign Affairs in the Seventeenth-Century" (diss. Minnesota, 1967); *id.,* "New England and New France, 1632-1651: External Relations and Internal Disagreements Among the Puritans," *EIHC,* 108 (1972), 252-71; James Douglas, *New England and New France: Contrasts and Parallels in Colonial History* (New York, 1913); John Fiske, *New France and New England* (Boston, 1902); Allan Forbes, *France and New England,* 3 vols., ([Boston], 1925-29); Gabriel Druillettes, "Journal of an Embassy from Canada to the United Colonies of New England, in 1650," trans. John G. Shea, *NYSHSC,* ser. 2, 3 (1857), 303-28; Mary Ann La Fleur, "Seventeenth Century New England and New France in Comparative Perspective: Notre Dame des Anges, a Case Study" (diss. New Hampshire, 1987).

94. Thorpe, *Federal and State Constitutions,* 1.77.

95. *Ibid.*

96. *Ibid.*

97. *Ibid.*

98. *Ibid.,* 1.79.

99. *Ibid.,* 1.80.

100. *Ibid.,* 1.81.

101. "Commission of Sir Edmund Andros for the Dominion of New England. April 7, 1688," in *ibid.,* 2.1863-69. Cf. also Andros's June 3, 1686 Commission, *RCRI,* 3.212-18.

102. The First Congregational Church of Rehoboth was gathered in 1643. It later became the First Congregational Church of Seekonk, Massachusetts; it is presently the First Congregational Church of East Providence, Rhode Island.

103. Leonard Bliss, Jr., *The History of Rehoboth, Bristol County, Massachusetts: Comprising a History of the Present Towns of Rehoboth, Seekonk, and Pawtucket . . . Together with Sketches of Attleborough, Cumberland, and a Part of Swansea and Barrington . . .* (Boston, 1836), 205-8; Richard L. Bowen, *Early Rehoboth: Documented Historical Studies of Families and Events . . .,* 4 vols. (Rehoboth, MA, 1945-50); this reference is from 1.29.

104. *RCNP,* 2.147, 150-51.

105. *RCNP,* 2.156. The actual date was Wednesday, June 5, 1650, but the erroneous date of Wednesday, June 12, was given at the meeting of Wednesday, October 2, 1650, in the indictment presented against Holmes and others.

106. *RCNP,* 2.162; cf. Richard L. Bowen, *Early Rehoboth,* 1.29.

107. *RCNP,* 7.58; cf. Richard L. Bowen, *Early Rehoboth,* 1.29.

108. Roger Williams, *The Correspondence of Roger Williams,* ed. Glen W. LaFantasie et al., 1 (Hanover, NH, 1988), 310-311; "Roger Williams to John Winthrop, Jr., . . . 24th February, 1649-50," *Narragansett Club Publications,* 6.192; cf. Richard L. Bowen, *Early Rehoboth,* 1.29.

109. *RCNP,* 3.81.

110. *Ibid.*

111. Rehoboth, MA, *Rehoboth Town Meetings,* Book 1, p. 148; *Sowams Records,* 111-12; cited in Richard L. Bowen, *Early Rehoboth,* 1.32.

112. For details concerning Myles's life, cf. Weis, *The Colonial Clergy and the Colonial Churches of New England* (Lancaster, MA, 1936), 148; Isaac Backus, *A History of New England, with Particular Reference to the Denomination of Christians Called Baptists . . . Second Edition, with Notes,* [ed.] David Weston, 2 vols. (Newton, MA, 1871; rpt. Paris, AK, n.d., The Baptist History Series, #s 3-4), 1.282-86, 1.406, and 2.433; Thomas W. Bicknell, *John Myles and Religious Toleration in Massachusetts* (Boston, 1892); rpt. from *Magazine of New England History,* n.s., 2 (1892), 213-42.

113. Now deposited in the Brown University Library; cf. Swansea, MA, "Parish Register (Transcription)," FHLC™M #: 0104833.

114. Rehoboth, MA, *Rehoboth Town Meetings,* Book 1, p. 169; cited in Richard L. Bowen, *Early Rehoboth,* 1.33.

115. Rehoboth, MA, *Rehoboth Town Meetings,* Book I, p. 169; cited in Richard L. Bowen, *Early Rehoboth,* 1.33.

116. Cf. Isaac Backus, *A History of New England With Particular Reference to the Denomination of Christians Called Baptists,* [ed.] David Weston, 1.284 and 2.433; cf. also First Baptist Church, Swansea, MA, *300th Anniversary Year Book of the First Baptist Church, Swansea, Mass.* (n.p., 1963); Thomas W. Bicknell, "John Myles and Religious Toleration in Massachusetts," *Magazine of New England History,* n.s., 2 (1892), 213-42; the church covenant is found on pp. 225-27. This serial was also variously known as: *Putnam's Monthly Historical Magazine, Salem Press Historical and Genealogical Record/ Magazine of New England History,* and *The Genealogical Magazine.*

117. *RCNP,* 4.162; cf. Richard L. Bowen, *Early Rehoboth,* 1.34.

118. "The Covenant of the Founders of the First Baptist Church of Swansea," Swansea, MA, First Baptist Church, *300th Anniversary Year Book,* no pagination.

119. *RCNP,* 4.169; cf. Richard L. Bowen, *Early Rehoboth,* 1.34.

120. *RCNP,* 4.175; cf. Richard L. Bowen, *Early Rehoboth,* 1.35.

121. *RCNP,* 4.180-81; cf. Richard L. Bowen, *Early Rehoboth,* 1.35.

122. Francis C. Baylies, *An Historical Memoir of the Colony of New Plymouth, from . . . 1608, to . . . 1692,* ed. Samuel G. Drake, 2 vols. (Boston, 1866); cf. 1.236-39.

123. Richard L. Bowen, *Early Rehoboth,* 1.36; cited in Swansea, MA, *Swansea Town Meetings,* 18.

124. Francis C. Baylies, *An Historical Memoir of the Colony of New Plymouth,* ed. Samuel G. Drake, 1.245.

125. Richard L. Bowen, *Early Rehoboth,* 1.38; cf. Swansea, MA, *Swansea Proprietors' Grants and Meetings (1668-1769),* 5.

126. Francis C. Baylies, *An Historical Memoir of the Colony of New Plymouth,* ed. Samuel G. Drake, 1.246.

127. Charters and their legal characteristics have already been discussed in the previous chapter.

128. *RM,* 1.271.

129. Cf. records for New Shoreham (1664), Westerly (1669), Kingston (1674), and Tiverton (1701/2).

130. For the history of East Greenwich see William D. Miller, *Notes and Queries Concerning the Early Bounds and Divisions of the Township of East Greenwich, as Set Forth*

in William Hall's Plot of 1716 (Providence, RI, 1937); D. H. Greene, *History of the Town of East Greenwich and Adjacent Territory, from 1677 to 1877* (Providence, RI, 1877); Martha G. McPartland, *The History of East Greenwich, Rhode Island, 1677-1960, with Related Genealogy* (East Greenwich, RI, 1960); Elisha R. Potter, *The Early History of Narragansett . . . , RIHSC,* 3 (1835).

131. M. G. McPartland, *The History of East Greenwich, Rhode Island,* 14-15.

132. *Ibid.,* 17-18.

133. *RCRI,* 2.587-90; East Greenwich, RI, *Vital Record of Rhode Island,* vol. 1, part 2: *East Greenwich,* ed. James N. Arnold (Providence, RI, 1891), iii-iv. An organizational motion appears in the colonial legislative records six months earlier, with very similar wording; cf. *RCRI,* 2.574 along with D. H. Greene, *History of the Town of East Greenwich and Adjacent Territory,* 9-11.

134. For the history of the town of Simsbury, see Lucius I. Barber, *The Burning of Simsbury* (Hartford, CT, 1876); *id., A Record and Documentary History of Simsbury* (1931; rpt. Simsbury, CT, 1974); John E. Ellsworth, *Simsbury: Being a Brief Historical Sketch of Ancient and Modern Simsbury, 1642-1935* (Simsbury, CT, 1935); Noah A. Phelps, *History of Simsbury, Granby and Canton, from 1642 to 1845* (Hartford, CT, 1845); William M. Vibert, *Three Centuries of Simsbury* ([Simsbury, CT?], 1970); Evan W. Woolacott, *The Gavel and the Book: The Simsbury Town Meeting, 1670-1986* (Canaan, NH, 1987).

135. *PRCC,* 3.177.

136. L. I. Barber, *A Record and Documentary History of Simsbury,* 107-9.

137. *PRCC,* 2.3-11.

Notes to Chapter 4

1. Sabbath laws and laws requiring attendance at public worship are scattered throughout all of the legislative records of seventeenth-century New England. For New Plymouth Colony, cf. *RCNP,* vol. 1, pp. 44, 75, 80, 106, 118, and 128; vol. 2, pp. 4, 140, 156, 165, 239; vol. 3, pp. 5, 10, 47, 52, 74, 124, 150, 186, and 224; vol. 4, pp. 5, 28, 29, 42, 43, and 50; vol. 5, pp. 17, 26, 47, 51, 61, 87, 99, 118, 152, 157, 169, 234, and 254; vol. 6, pp. 16, 82, 105, 172, and 178. For the Massachusetts Bay Colony, cf. John Cotton, "Abstract of the Laws . . . [1641]" (London, 1641), VII.11, and then *RM,* vol. 1, pp. 140 and 395; vol. 2, pp. 177-78; vol. 3, pp. 99, 160, 316, and 317; vol. 4-1, pp. 150, 200, and 347; vol. 4-2, pp. 276, 395, 562; vol. 5, pp. 133, 155, 239, 243. For the Connecticut Colony, cf. *PRCC,* vol. 2, pp. 61, 88, and 280; vol. 3, pp. 148 and 203; vol. 5, pp. 130, 317, and 525. For the New Haven Colony, cf. *RCPNH,* 337 and 358; *RCJNH,* p. 605. For the United Colonies, or the New England Confederation, cf. *RCNP,* vol. 10, p. 142; vol. 11, pp. 57, 58, 64, 99, 100, 122, 176, 217, 218, 228, and 269, col. 1: "Lord's Day." For the Province of Maine, cf. *PCRM,* vol. 1, p. 348, col. 3: "Sabbath Breaking" and "Neglect of Public Worship"; vol. 2, p. 555, col. 2: "Crimes and Torts: Sabbath Breaking . . . Neglecting Public Worship"; vol. 3, p. 317, col. 1: "Crimes, Breach of Sabbath"; vol. 4, p. 422, col. 1: "Sabbath, Offenses Connected with." For New Hampshire, cf. *NHSP,* 1.387-88; 3.187; 8.15, 66, 67, and 91; also, New Hampshire, Province, *Laws of New Hampshire,* vol. 1, pp. 17, 62, 68, 564, 672, 791, and 798. For a recent discussion of the importance of the church in early New England, see Mark Allen Peterson, *The Price of Redemption: The Spiritual Economy of Puritan New England* (Stanford, CA, 1997), based on a 1993 Harvard dissertation.

2. For the discussion of the theme of the covenant of grace in New England, cf. the following (for full publication information, see p. 361, n. 19): Champlin Burrage, *The Church Covenant Idea: Its Origin and Development;* Sandford Fleming, *Children and Puritanism: The Place of Children in the Life and Thought of New England Churches, 1620-1847;* Perry Miller, *The New England Mind,* vol. 1, *The Seventeenth Century,* and vol. 2, *From Colony to Province; id.,* "The Marrow of Puritan Divinity"; *id.,* "The Puritan Theory of the Sacraments in Seventeenth Century New England"; Peter Y. De Jong, *The Covenant Idea in New England Theology, 1620-1847;* Wayne H. Christy, "John Cotton: Covenant Theologian"; Alan Simpson, "The Covenanted Community," in *Puritanism in Old and New England;* Larzer Ziff, "The Social Bond of Church Covenant"; William G. Wilcox, "New England Covenant Theology: Its English Precursors and Early American Exponents"; James R. Fulcher, "Puritan Piety in Early New England: A Study in Spiritual Regeneration from the Antinomian Controversy to the Cambridge Synod of 1648 in the Massachusetts Bay Colony"; Edmund S. Morgan, *Visible Saints: The History of a Puritan Idea;* Norman Pettit, *The Heart Prepared: Grace and Conversion in Puritan Spiritual Life;* Lewis M. Robinson, "A History of the Half-Way Covenant"; C. John Somerville, "Conversion, Sacrament and Assurance in the Puritan Covenant of Grace, to 1650"; Raymond P. Stearns, "The Half-Way Covenant and New England History"; David L. Beebe, "The Seals of the Covenant: The Doctrine and Place of the Sacraments and Censures in the New England Puritan Theology Underlying the Cambridge Platform of 1648"; Robert G. Pope, *The Half-Way Covenant: Church Membership in Puritan New England;* E. Brooks Holifield, *The Covenant Sealed: The Development of Puritan Sacramental Theology in Old and New England, 1570-1720;* James T. Meigs, "The Half-Way Covenant: A Study in Religious Transition"; William K. B. Stoever, *'A Faire and Easie Way to Heaven': Covenant Theology and Antinomianism in Early Massachusetts; id.,* "Nature, Grace and John Cotton: The Theological Dimension in the New England Antinomianism Controversy"; Michael McGiffert, "The Problem of the Covenant in Puritan Thought: Peter Bulkeley's *Gospel Covenant*"; Harry S. Stout, "Word and Order in Colonial New England," in *The Bible in America;* Michael McGiffert, "God's Controversy with New England"; Philip F. Gura, *A Glimpse of Sion's Glory: Puritan Radicalism in New England, 1620-1660;* John R. Higgins, "Aspects of the Doctrine of the Holy Spirit during the Antinomian Controversy of New England with Special Reference to John Cotton and Anne Hutchinson"; Charles L. Cohen, *God's Caress: The Psychology of Puritan Religious Experience;* Harry S. Stout, *The New England Soul: Preaching and Religious Culture in Colonial New England.* Cf. also the bibliography of covenant theology in David A. Weir, *The Origins of the Federal Theology in Sixteenth-Century Reformation Thought* (Oxford, 1990), 160-95.

3. R. Tudur Jones covers the covenants generated by the Separatists, Congregationalists, and Independents of Old England: "The Church Covenant in Classical Congregationalism."

4. A fascinating mirror image of signing the covenant in the church record book is the alleged signing of the covenant with Satan by witches and wizards. In early New England popular culture, Elizabeth S. Reis points out that the supposed signing of an explicit covenant with Satan was what defined a witch; usually, the depictions of such actions were described as signing a black book proferred by Satan; cf. "Satan's Familiars: Sinners, Witches and Conflicting Covenants in Early New England" (diss. University of

California, Berkeley, 1991); this work was revised and published as *Damned Women: Sinners and Witches in Puritan New England* (Ithaca, NY, 1997).

5. Paul Boyer and Stephen Nissenbaum, *Salem Possessed: The Social Origins of Witchcraft* (Cambridge, MA, 1974), frontispiece.

6. Bradford, MA, First Church, *Articles of Faith* (Haverhill, MA, 1886), 9.

7. Edwin P. Parker, *History of the Second Church of Christ in Hartford, 1670-1892* (Hartford, CT, 1892), 288.

8. *Ibid.*

9. *Ibid.*; italics mine.

10. *Ibid.*, 287; italics mine.

11. William Cothren, *History of Ancient Woodbury, Connecticut, from 1659 to 1854 . . .* , 1 (Waterbury, CT, 1854), 131.

12. *Ibid.*, 132-33.

13. (Boston, 1835).

14. *Ibid.*, 150. Cf. the note to the purported Essex, MBC, First Church's covenant: "Mr. Pickering, successor to Mr. Wise, says in his Record, that Mr. Wise's son, Rev. Jeremiah Wise of Berwick, Me., handed him this covenant, as the original covenant of this church"; Robert Crowell, *History of the Town of Essex, From 1634 to 1868 . . .* (Essex, MA, 1868), 92.

15. Plymouth, MA, First Church, *Plymouth Church Records, CSMP,* 22 (1920), 148; cf. p. xxxi.

16. Harold Field Worthley comments: "As far as can be determined, no new act of covenanting was undertaken after the Pilgrims' arrival at New Plymouth," Worthley, *Inventory,* 487. Cf. Douglas Horton, "The Scrooby Covenant," *UHSP,* 11 (1957), #2, 1-13.

17. Cf. Norwell, MA, First Church, [Scituate, MA, Second Church], *Scituate, Massachusetts, Second Church Records (in Abstract), 1645-1850,* ed. Wilford J. Litchfield (Boston, 1909); rpt. from the following: "Records of the Second Church of Scituate, Now the First Unitarian Church of Norwell, Massachusetts," ed. George C. Turner, Sarah Damon, Ella Bates, and Wilford J. Litchfield, *NEHGR,* 57 (1903); 58 (1904), 59 (1905), 60 (1906), passim; Samuel Deane, *History of Scituate, Massachusetts, from its Settlement to 1831* (Boston, 1831); Harvey H. Pratt, *The Early Planters of Scituate: A History of the Town of Scituate, Massachusetts from Its Establishment to the End of the Revolutionary War* ([Scituate, MA], 1929), 63-73.

18. Samuel Deane, *History of Scituate, Massachusetts,* 60-61; italics mine.

19. *Ibid.*, 61.

20. Scituate, MA, First Church and Barnstable, MA, First Church, "Scituate and Barnstable Church Records," ed. Amos Otis, *NEHGR,* 9 (1855), 279-87; 10 (1856), 37-43.

21. Boston, MA, First Church, *The Records of the First Church in Boston, 1630-1868,* ed. Richard D. Pierce, *CSMP,* 39 (Boston, 1961), 3.

22. *Ibid.*, 4-5.

23. *Ibid.*, 10.

24. ([London], 1641).

25. *A Direction for a Publick Profession in the Church Assembly, after Private Examination by the Elders . . . Being the Same for Substance which was Propounded to, and Agreed Upon by the Church of Salem, at their Beginning, the Sixte of the Sixth Moneth, 1629* ([Cam-

bridge, 1665]); rpt. in Walker, *Creeds and Platforms*, 119-22; *A Copy of The Church-Covenants which have been used in the Church of Salem . . .* (Boston, 1680); W.{illiam} R.{athband}, *A Briefe Narration of Some Church Courses Held in Opinion and Practise in the Churches Lately Erect in New England. Collect out of Sundry of Their Own Printed Papers and Manuscripts With Other Good Intelligences* (London, 1644), 16-19, which gives the Rotterdam, Netherlands, English Church covenant and the Salem First Church covenant.

26. Wenham, MA, First Church, *Confession of Faith, and Covenant of the Congregational Church in Wenham, with the Names of Surviving Members* (Boston, 1840), 3-4; the original citation is by Daniel Mansfield, in *Two Sermons, Delivered on the Second Centennial Anniversary of the Organization of the First Church, and the Settlement of the First Minister in Wenham* (Andover, MA, 1845), 10.

27. The European, and particularly English, backdrop to church covenanting was examined in a later work by Burrage: *The Early English Dissenters in the Light of Recent Research (1550-1641)*.

28. Cf. Wayne R. Spear, "Covenanted Uniformity in Religion: The Influence of the Scottish Commissioners upon the Ecclesiology of the Westminster Assembly" (diss. Pittsburgh, 1976).

29. *Congregational Creeds and Covenants*, 74.

30. "The Marrow of Puritan Divinity," published in 1937, served as a prelude to Miller's major discussion in *The New England Mind*, vol. 1, *The Seventeenth Century* (1939). In *The Seventeenth Century* Miller devotes a full quarter of his massive work to the explication of the covenant theology: cf. the Table of Contents: "Book IV. Sociology. Chapter XIII. The Covenant of Grace; Chapter XIV. The Social Covenant; Chapter XV. The Church Covenant; Chapter XVI: God's Controversy with New England; Appendix B. The Federal School of Theology" (p. xiii). After World War II, Miller came out with the second volume of *The New England Mind*, vol. 2, *From Colony to Province* (1953); in the Table of Contents, under "Book I: Declension" we find chapters on "I. The Wrath of Jehovah; II. The Jeremiad; VI. Children of the Covenant; VII. Half-Way Measures." Under "Book II, Confusion," we find chapters on "XII. Salvaging the Covenant" and "XIV. The Dilemma of the Sacraments."

In the period between the publication of the two volumes of *The New England Mind* (1939-1953) Peter Y. De Jong completed a dissertation at the Hartford Theological Seminary (1942) that was published as a book in 1945 (*The Covenant Idea in New England Theology, 1620-1847*). Unlike Miller, who limited his focus to the seventeenth and early eighteenth centuries, De Jong tried to do a comprehensive survey that covered Jonathan Edwards, the New Divinity, and the early nineteenth century. The result was a somewhat helpful work that did not deal in any depth with any single issue. The exploration of the covenant in the Puritan tradition of Old and New England continued after the publication of Miller's second volume with two dissertations completed at Yale and Duke, respectively (William Wakefield McKee, "The Idea of the Covenant in Early English Puritanism, [1580-1643]" [diss. Yale, 1948] and William G. Wilcox, "New England Covenant Theology: Its English Precursors and Early American Exponents" [diss. Duke, 1959]). While there have been hundreds of articles and book chapters written on the history of early modern and colonial American covenant theology and quite a few dissertations on the covenant theology of one or two theologians such as William Perkins (see

David A. Weir, compiler, "A Bibliography of the Federal Theology and the Covenant Idea before 1750," in *The Origins of the Federal Theology,* 160-95), only two book-length studies have emerged that deal with the history of covenant theology in any sort of comprehensive way. The first is E. Brooks Holifield, *The Covenant Sealed: The Development of Puritan Sacramental Theology in Old and New England,* a work that has as its focus one particular aspect of covenant theology. The second is John von Rohr, *The Covenant of Grace in Puritan Thought,* an excellent study that explores the various themes found in covenant theology that were developed by Puritans who were primarily in Old England and not in New England.

31. "Because the pages are loaded with quotations, the problem of annotation has proved exceedingly difficult. The number of titles by New England writers, or by English Puritans whose works need to be considered along with them, are legion; were I to supply a footnote indicating the exact source of every direct quotation or the inspiration for many remarks which are not literal citation, I should republish the complete bibliography of early New England, with various additions, not merely once but many times over, and the documentation would run to as many pages as the text. In most instances, it is a matter of complete indifference or chance that a quotation comes from Cotton instead of Hooker, from Winthrop instead of Willard; all writers were in substantial agreement upon all the propositions which I am discussing in this book, even though they differed among themselves upon some of the issues I shall take up in the sequel, and only an occasional student actively engaged in research would profit from knowing the sources for particular passages. . . . Meanwhile, an annotated copy of this volume has been filed in the Harvard College Library along with a bound set of complete notes, in which references are given to the provenience of each quotation . . ." (*The Seventeenth Century,* ix). For the sources of the quotations for *The Seventeenth Century,* see James F. Hoopes, ed., *Sources for "The New England Mind: The Seventeenth Century."* It should be noted that Hoopes's volume is only about one-fifth the size of *The Seventeenth Century.*

32. Cf. Darrett B. Rutman, "God's Bridge Falling Down: 'Another Approach' to New England Puritanism Assayed," *WMQ,* ser. 3, 19 (1962), 408-21; Michael McGiffert, "American Puritan Studies in the 1960's," *WMQ,* ser. 3, 27 (1970), 36-67; Laura B. Ricard, "New England Puritan Studies in the 1970's," *F+H,* 15 (1983), #2, 6-27; David D. Hall, "On Common Ground: The Coherence of American Puritan Studies," *WMQ,* ser. 3, 44 (1987), 193-229. It should be noted that "what occurred" is not necessarily reflected even in the case of the official records. However, collections of records penned by hundreds of individuals over many decades are less likely to mislead and distort than a carefully crafted discourse constructed by one primary source author who wishes to push an argument.

33. "The Origin, Development, and Use of Church Covenants in Baptist History" (diss. Southern Baptist Theological Seminary, 1973).

34. *Ibid.,* 74-77.

35. The concept of the covenant formulary is not original to me, but is borrowed from the fields of biblical studies and ancient Near Eastern studies. In the covenants found in both biblical and non-biblical sources, scholars have noted consistent patterns of structure and phrasing in the covenant documents themselves; cf. Klaus Baltzer, *The Covenant Formulary in Old Testament, Jewish, and Early Christian Writings;* Meredith Kline, *Treaty of the Great King: The Covenant Structure of Deuteronomy;* Dennis J. McCar-

thy, *Treaty and Covenant: A Study in Form in the Ancient Oriental Documents in the Old Testament*.

36. While Charlestown was an independent entity in the seventeenth century, it is today part of Boston, and therefore many of the Boston historical records and histories include sections on Charlestown as a subdivision of Boston. For the history of Charlestown and its First Church, see: Josiah Bartlett, "A Historical Sketch of Charlestown . . . ," *MHSC*, ser. 2, 2 (1814), 163-84; William I. Budington, *The History of the First Church, Charlestown, in Nine Lectures, with Notes* (Boston, 1845); Charlestown, MA, *Charlestown Land Records, 1638-1802*, Report of the Record Commissioners (City of Boston — Registry Department), #3 (2nd edn., Boston, 1883); Charlestown (Boston), MA, First Church, *Records of the First Church in Charlestown, Massachusetts, 1632-1789*, ed. James F. Hunnewell (Boston, 1880); Index: *Index to Records, First Church, Charlestown, 1632-1789* (Boston, 1880); these were also reprinted in *NEHGR*, 23 (1869)–33 (1879), passim; Charlestown, MA, First Church, *The Commemoration of the Two Hundred and Fiftieth Anniversary of the First Church, Charlestown, Mass.* ([Charlestown, MA?], 1882); Ralph J. Crandall, "New England's Haven Port and Charlestown and Her Restless People: A Study of Colonial Migration, 1629-1776" (diss. University of Southern California, 1975); Richard Frothingham, Jr., *The History of Charlestown, Massachusetts* (Boston, 1845); Mary McManus Ramsbottom, "Religious Society and the Family in Charlestown, Massachusetts, 1630 to 1740" (diss. Yale, 1987); Henry H. Sprague, *The Founding of Charlestown by the Spragues: A Glimpse of the Beginning of the Massachusetts Bay Settlement* (Boston, 1910); Justin Winsor, *The Memorial History of Boston . . . 1630-1880*, 4 vols. (Boston, 1880-81); T. B. Wyman, *The Genealogies and Estates of Charlestown, Massachusetts, 1629-1818*, 2 vols. (n.p., 1879).

37. Charlestown (Boston), MA, First Church, *Records of the First Church in Charlestown, Massachusetts*, 7.

38. *Ibid*.

39. The Salem, Massachusetts Bay, First Church's 1629 covenant is even shorter and more famous: "We covenant with the Lord and one with an other; and doe bynde ourselves in the presence of God, to walke together in all his waies, according as he is pleased to reveale himself unto us in his blessed word of truth," C. H. Webber and W. S. Nevins, *Old Naumkeag: An Historical Sketch of the City of Salem . . .* (Salem, MA, 1877), 14.

40. Cf. Mary McManus Ramsbottom, "Religious Society and the Family in Charlestown, Massachusetts, 1630 to 1740" for a discussion of how well the Charlestown First Church fared.

41. For the early history of Dorchester and the Dorchester-2, MBC First Church, see Dorchester, MA, First Church, *Records of the First Church at Dorchester in New England, 1636-1734* (Boston, 1891); Samuel G. Drake, *Recovery of Some Materials for the Early History of Dorchester, General and Particular* (Boston, 1851); James Blake, *Annals of the Town of Dorchester, 1750*, Dorchester Antiquarian and Historical Society, *Collections*, 2 (Boston, 1846); Barry R. Burg, "Richard Mather (1596-1669): The Life and Work of a Puritan Cleric in New England" (diss. Colorado, 1967); substantially revised and published as: *Richard Mather* (Boston, 1982); Mark Allen Carden, "The Ministry and the Word: The Clergy, the Bible, and Biblical Themes in Five Massachusetts Towns, 1630-1700"; Dorchester Antiquarian and Historical Society, *History of the Town of Dorchester,*

Massachusetts, Dorchester Antiquarian and Historical Society, *Proceedings,* 1-3 (Boston, 1851-55); Ann N. Hansen, *The Dorchester Group: Puritanism and Revolution* (Columbus, OH, 1987); Thaddeus M. Harris, *Memorials of the First Church in Dorchester* (Boston, 1830); *id.,* "Chronological and Topographical Account of Dorchester," *MHSC,* 9 (1804), 147-99; Anne B. MacLear, "Early New England Towns: A Comparative Study of their Development" (diss. Columbia, 1908); New England Historic Genealogical Society, "Old Dorchester: Recovery of Some Materials for its History, General and Particular," *NEHGR,* 40 (1886), 253-61; William D. Orcutt, *Good Old Dorchester: A Narrative History of the Town, 1630-1893* (Cambridge, MA, 1893); Gary L. Rosenberg, "Family and Society in the Early Seventeenth-Century Massachusetts Bay Area" (diss. State University of New York, Buffalo, 1980); William B. Trask, "Early Matters Relating to the Town and First Church of Dorchester," *NEHGR,* 40 (1886), 253-61; Justin Winsor, *The Memorial History of Boston,* 1.423-38.

42. (London, 1643).

43. Dorchester, MA, First Church, *Records of the First Church at Dorchester in New England, 1636-1734,* 1-2.

44. Mark Allen Carden has pointed out that the themes of the church covenant formulary appear in the preaching and teaching of the early ministers of the Massachusetts Bay Colony; cf. "The Ministry and the Word: The Clergy, the Bible, and Biblical Themes in Five Massachusetts Towns, 1630-1700."

45. *WCF,* 7; Schaff, *Creeds,* 3.616.

46. We have at least two instances in which there were blunders in the gathering of a church: Lynn and Weymouth, both in the Massachusetts Bay Colony, had to regather their churches because the validity of their first gathering was challenged; this challenge resulted in tremendous bitterness in the community; cf. John Winthrop, *The Journal of John Winthrop, 1630-1649,* ed. Richard S. Dunn, James Savage, and Laetitia Yeandle (Cambridge, MA, 1996), 143, 164-65, 171, 197-99, 281-82.

47. Dorchester, MA, First Church, *Records of the First Church at Dorchester,* 1.

48. *OED,* 2.485-86.

49. Cf. Elizabeth S. Reis, "Satan's Familiars: Sinners, Witches and Conflicting Covenants in Early New England," Chapter 3, 108-49.

50. Richard Muller, in his *Dictionary of Latin and Greek Theological Terms Drawn Principally from Protestant Scholastic Theology* (Grand Rapids, MI, 1985), elaborates: "munus triplex: *threefold office;* a christological term referring to the threefold work of Christ as prophet, priest, and king. The doctrine of a *munus triplex,* as opposed to a *munus duplex* (priest and king), was taught by Calvin and became standard among the Reformed in the sixteenth century. . . . The doctrine assumes that Christ fulfilled in his work all the anointed offices of the old covenant. Although the scholastics will speak of a *munus propheticum, munus sacerdotale, and munus regium,* a prophetic, priestly, and kingly office, there is but one office *(munus),* just as there is but one work *(officium)* of Christ. The office is a single threefold function of the Mediator. It is also an eternal office that belongs to the preexistent Word in his mediatorial work during the Old Testament dispensation and to the Word incarnate during both his earthly work and his eternal reign from the resurrection to the *eschaton* . . . and beyond. Thus, the *munus regium,* or kingly office, does not begin at the resurrection or ascension, but has always belonged to Christ as Logos, and even to the incarnate Word according to his human nature, which

exercised the *munus regium,* albeit in a hidden form, even during the *status humiliationis.* . . . Similar statements can be made of the prophetic and priestly offices. The orthodox also recognize that an office is not something which belongs to a person by nature but is something conferred upon a person. Thus, the baptism of Christ can be viewed as the temporal designation of Christ to his office and as the beginning of his official ministry. The Reformed go further than the Lutherans in elaborating this point and, early on in the era of orthodoxy, speak of the designation or self-designation of the Word to the office of Mediator; a concept that leads ultimately to the doctrine of the *pactum salutis* . . ."; Muller, pp. 197-98. The *pactum salutis* refers to the inter-Trinitarian covenant made between the Father, the Son, and the Holy Spirit to create and redeem the world, a concept developed by Johannes Cocceius during the middle part of the seventeenth century, just when the Dorchester-2 covenant was being signed; cf. Charles Sherwood McCoy, "The Covenant Theology of Johannes Cocceius" (diss. Yale, 1957); id., "Johannes Cocceius: Federal Theologian," *Scottish Journal of Theology,* 16 (1963), 352-70; id., *History, Humanity, and Federalism in the Theology and Ethics of Johannes Cocceius* (Workshop on Covenant and Politics, Center for the Study of Federalism, Temple University, Publication A-19, Philadelphia, 1980). "The Second Confession of the London-Amsterdam Church, 1596" articulated the threefold office of Christ; cf. #s 9-17; Walker, *Creeds and Platforms,* 61-64.

51. In a dissertation on the Antinomian Controversy of the late 1630s, James William Jones III discusses the degree of christocentricity of various New England theologians of the time, asserting that the Antinomians were much more radically christocentric in their thinking, placing a high value on the notion of the union of the believer with Christ, while the elders of the Massachusetts Bay were less christocentric. Four theologians were caught in the middle between the two groups, with John Cotton and Thomas Hooker leaning more towards the Antinomian side and Thomas Shepard and Peter Bulkley leaning more towards the side of the elders; cf. "The Beginnings of American Theology: John Cotton, Thomas Hooker, Thomas Shepard, and Peter Bulkley" (diss. Brown, 1970); cf. Jonathan Jong-Chun Won, "Communion with Christ: An Exposition and Comparison of the Doctrine of Union and Communion with Christ in Calvin and the English Puritans" (diss. Westminster Theological Seminary, 1989).

52. *RM,* 4-1.137. Cf., among several hundred citations of church and town formations in the early New England legislative records, the case of Killingworth (now Clinton), CTC, where the general court encouraged the gathering of a church: "This Court, upon the petition of the inhabitants of Kenilworth, doe hereby declare and give them theire approbation and encouragem^t to gather themselues into church order, according to the order of the gospell," *PRCC,* 2.71.

53. Horton Davies, *Worship and Theology in England,* vol. 1, *From Cranmer to Hooker, 1534-1603* and vol. 2, *From Andrewes to Baxter and Fox, 1603-1690.*

54. For a discussion of church discipline in early New England, cf. Emil Oberholzer, Jr., "Saints in Sin: A Study of the Disciplinary Action of the Congregational Churches of Massachusetts in the Colonial and Early National Periods" (diss. Columbia, 1954); revised and published as *Delinquent Saints: Disciplinary Action in the Early Congregational Churches of Massachusetts* (New York, 1956); Charles E. Park, "Excommunication in Colonial Churches," *CSMP,* 12 (1908-9), 321-32; Roger Thompson, "'Holy Watchfulness' and Communal Conformism: The Functions of Defamation in Early New

England Communities," *NEQ,* 56 (1983), 504-22. Cf. also James F. Cooper, Jr., "'A Mixed Form': Church Government in Massachusetts Bay, 1629-1645" (M.A. thesis, University of Connecticut, 1983), revised and published as "'A Mixed Form': The Establishment of Church Government in Massachusetts Bay, 1629-1645," *EIHC,* 123 (1987), 233-59; *id.,* "A Participatory Theocracy: Church Government in Colonial Massachusetts, 1629-1760" (diss. Connecticut, 1987); *id., Tenacious of Their Liberties: The Congregationalists in Colonial Massachusetts* (New York, 1999); Charles F. Adams, "Some Phases of Sexual Morality and Church Discipline in Colonial New England," *MHSP,* ser. 2, 6 (1890-91), 477-516.

55. John Cotton, *The Way of the Churches of Christ in New-England . . .* (London, 1645), 2.

56. *Ibid.,* 8.

57. The history of Salem, MBC, and Salem Village (now Danvers), DNE, has been written up in an overwhelming array of publications. The best modern study is Paul Boyer and Stephen Nissenbaum, *Salem Possessed: The Social Origins of Witchcraft.* But Boyer and Nissenbaum base their work on a host of historical writing that preceded them. The most important works for the history of both towns and their churches are: Danvers, MA, First Church, "Danvers Church Records," ed. William T. Harris, *NEHGR,* 11 (1857), 131-35, 316-25; 12 (1858), 245-48; 13 (1859), 55-56 (unfortunately, the Salem Village/Danvers First Church Records have not been published in comprehensive form, nor are they available on microfilm in The Family History Library System of The Church of Jesus Christ of Latter-day Saints; the first eight years (1689-97) have been published in Paul Boyer and Stephen Nissenbaum (eds.), *Salem-Village Witchcraft: A Documentary Record of Local Conflict in Colonial New England* (Belmont, CA, 1972), 268-312); John Fiske, *The Notebook of the Reverend John Fiske, 1644-1675;* Salem, MA, First Church, *Copy of Church Covenants Which Have Been Used in Salem* (Boston, 1680); Joseph B. Felt, *Did the First Church of Salem Originally have a Confession of Faith Distinct from Their Covenant?* (Boston, 1856); "The First Church," *EIHC,* 27 (1890), 183-86; Salem, MA, First Church, "Notes and Extracts from the 'Records of the First Church of Salem, 1629 to 1736,'" *EIHC,* 15 (1878), 70-85; 16 (1879), 8-18; Salem, MA, First Church, *The Records of the First Church in Salem, Massachusetts, 1629-1736,* ed. Richard D. Pierce (Salem, MA, 1974); Joseph B. Felt (ed.), "Salem Witchcraft," *MHSC,* ser. 3, 3 (1833), 169-80; Danvers, MA, "A Book of Records of the Severall Publique Transa[c]tions of the Inhabitants of Sale[m] Village Vulgarly Called the Farme[s]," *Danvers Historical Collections,* 13 (1925), 91-122; 14 (1926), 65-99; 16 (1928), 60-80; 17 (1929), 74-103; 18 (1930), 65-96; 19 (1931), 65-96; 20 (1932), 65-96; 22 (1934), 65-99; 23 (1935), 65-97; 24 (1936), 65-100; 25 (1937), 49-82; 26 (1938), 65-91; "Petition of Salem Farmers, 1667," *Danvers Historical Collections,* 9 (1921), 116-19; Paul Boyer and Stephen Nissenbaum (eds.), *Salem-Village Witchcraft: A Documentary Record of Local Conflict in Colonial New England* (Belmont, CA, 1972); *id., The Salem Witchcraft Papers: Verbatim Transcriptions of the Salem Witchcraft Outbreak of 1692,* 3 vols. (New York, 1977); Danvers, MA, First Church, *Confession of Faith and Covenant of the First Church in Danvers . . .* (Boston, 1864); *Records of Salem Witchcraft . . . ,* 2 vols. (Roxbury, MA, 1864); *id., Proceedings at the Celebration of the Two Hundredth Anniversary of the First Parish at Salem Village, now Danvers . . .* (Boston, 1874); *id., Exercises in Celebration of the Two Hundred and Fiftieth Anniversary of the First Church, Congregational, Danvers, Massa-*

chusetts (Salem, MA, 1922); Herbert B. Adams, "Origin of Salem Plantation," *EIHC,* 19 (1882), 153-66; William Bentley, "A Description and History of Salem," Naumkeag Historical Society, *Collections,* 6 (1799), 212-77; George F. Chever, "Some Remarks on the Commerce of Salem from 1626 to 1740 . . . ," *EIHC,* 1 (1859), 67-91, 117-43; Joseph B. Felt, *Annals of Salem,* 2nd edn., 2 vols. (Salem, MA, 1845-49); Richard P. Gildrie, *Salem, Massachusetts, 1626-1683: A Covenant Community; id.,* "Contentions in Salem: The Higginson-Nicholet Controversy, 1672-1676," *EIHC,* 113 (1977), 117-39; *id.,* "Salem Society and Politics in the 1680s," *EIHC,* 114 (1978), 185-206; John W. Hanson, *History of the Town of Danvers . . .* (Danvers, MA, 1848); David W. Koch, "Income Distribution and Political Structure in Seventeenth-Century Salem, Massachusetts," *EIHC,* 105 (1969), 50-71; Anne B. MacLear, "Early New England Towns: A Comparative Study of Their Development"; Sidney Perley, *The History of Salem, Massachusetts,* 3 vols. (Salem, MA, 1924-28); *id.,* "Evidence Relative to the Authenticity of the 'First Church' (so-called) in Salem," *EIHC,* 39 (1903), 229-93; James D. Phillips, *Salem in the Seventeenth Century* (Boston, 1933); Harold A. Pinkham, Jr., "The Transplantation and Transformation of the English Shire in America: Essex County, Massachusetts, 1630-1768" (diss. New Hampshire, 1980); Harriet S. Tapley, *Chronicles of Danvers (Old Salem Village) Massachusetts, 1632-1923* (Danvers, MA, 1923); C. H. Webber and W. S. Nevins, *Old Naumkeag: An Historical Sketch of . . . Salem;* Daniel A. White, *New England Congregationalism in its Origin and Purity; Illustrated by the Foundation and Early Records of the First Church in Salem, and Various Discussions Pertaining to the Subject* (Salem, MA, 1861); Christine A. Young, *From "Good Order" to Glorious Revolution: Salem Massachusetts, 1628-1689* (Ann Arbor, MI, 1981), based on a 1978 dissertation at the University of Pennsylvania.

58. *Salem Possessed.*

59. Sidney Perley, *The History of Salem, Massachusetts,* 2.444-45; cf. also the frontispiece of Stephen Boyer and Paul Nissenbaum, *Salem Possessed.*

60. Only three Congregational churches were formed during the Andros regime. This makes perfect sense in that the New Englanders, save for the Rhode Islanders, looked upon the civil authority as the "nursing mother" of the church. The Andros regime did not qualify for this function in the eyes of the New Englanders; cf. David A. Weir, "Church Covenanting in Seventeenth-Century New England," 217-20, esp. 219-20.

61. Paul Boyer and Stephen Nissenbaum (eds.), *Salem-Village Witchcraft: A Documentary Record of Local Conflict in Colonial New England,* xvii-xviii.

62. For the history of Wells, Maine Province, and its First Church, cf. Wells, ME, First Congregational Church, "Wells Church Records, 1701-1811" (unpublished; photostat on deposit at American Antiquarian Society, Worcester, MA); Edward E. Bourne, *The History of Wells and Kennebunk* (Portland, ME, 1875); James R. Cushing, *Historical Discourse, Delivered . . . at the One Hundred and Fiftieth Anniversary of the Organization of the First Congregational Church (The Second in the State), in Wells, Maine* (Portland, ME, 1851); "The First Congregational Church of Wells," *Congregationalism in Maine,* 13 (1926), 29-30; Jeremiah Hubbard and Jonathan Greenleaf, "An Account of Wells," *MeHSC,* 1 (1831), 255-68; Esselyn G. Perkins, *History of Ogunquit Village . . .* (Portland, ME, 1951); *id., Wells: The Frontier Town of Maine,* 2 vols. (Ogunquit, ME, 1970-71); *id., A New History of Ogunquit, Maine* (n.p., 1974).

63. Cf. Council for New England, "Records of the Council for New England"; these are records of the Gorges group, established in 1620; the original records are in the

Public Record Office, London; this company dissolved in 1635-38; *PCRM;* Maine Province, "Extracts from the Early Records of the Province of Maine," *MeHSC,* ser. 1, 1 (1865), 363-402. For the general history of Maine Province in the seventeenth century, see: John S. C. Abbott and Edward H. Elwell, *The History of Maine . . . ,* 2nd edn. (Portland, ME, 1892); Peleg E. Aldrich, "Massachusetts and Maine: Their Union and Separation," *AASP,* 71 (1878), 43-64; Ronald F. Banks, ed., *A History of Maine . . . ,* 4th edn. (Dubuque, IA, 1976); James P. Baxter, ed., *The Baxter Manuscripts,* 19 vols. (Portland, ME, 1889-1916); Henry S. Burrage, *The Beginnings of Colonial Maine, 1602-1658* (Portland, ME, 1914); *id., George Folsom, John A. Poor, and a Century of Historical Research with Reference to Early Colonial Maine . . .* (n.p., 1926); Charles E. Clark, *Maine: A Bicentennial History* (New York, 1977); Jonathan Greenleaf, *Sketches of the Ecclesiastical History of the State of Maine, from the Earliest Settlement . . .* (Portsmouth, NH, 1821); Robert E. Moody, "The Maine Frontier, 1607 to 1763" (diss. Yale, 1933); Elizabeth C. Nordbeck, "The New England Diaspora: A Study of the Religious Culture of Maine and New Hampshire, 1613-1763" (diss. Harvard, 1978); John G. Reid, *Maine, Charles II, and Massachusetts: Governmental Relationships in Early Northern New England* (Portland, ME, 1977); *id.,* John G. Reid, *Acadia, Maine and New Scotland: Marginal Colonies in the Seventeenth Century* (Toronto, 1981).

64. Wells, ME, First Church, "Records of the First Church of Wells, ME," *NEHGR,* 75 (1921), 42-43; *id.,* "Wells Church Records, 1701-1811," FHLC™M # 00441450, Item #1, opening pages.

65. Cf. Perry Miller, *From Colony to Province,* vol. 2 of *The New England Mind;* also, Sandford Fleming, *Children and Puritanism: The Place of Children in the Life and Thought of New England Churches, 1620-1847;* Edmund S. Morgan, *The Puritan Family* (Boston, 1944), based on a 1942 Harvard dissertation; Gerald F. Moran and Maris Vinovskis, "The Puritan Family and Religion: A Critical Reappraisal," *WMQ,* ser. 3, 39 (1982), 26-63; James B. McSwain, "The Controversy over Infant Baptism in England, 1640-1700" (diss. Memphis State, 1986); Agnes Rose Howard, "'The blessed echoes of truth': Catechisms and Confirmation in Puritan New England" (diss. Virginia, 1999).

66. Cf. Robert G. Pope, *The Half-Way Covenant: Church Membership in Puritan New England; id.,* "New England versus the New England Mind: The Myth of Declension."

Notes to Chapter 5

1. A. P. Stockwell, "History of the Town of Gravesend," in *The Civil, Political, Professional and Ecclesiastical History . . . of the County of Kings and the City of Brooklyn, N.Y. from 1683 to 1884,* ed. Henry R. Stiles (New York, [1884]), 156-88; Martha B. Flint, *Early Long Island: A Colonial Study* (New York, 1896), 104-15.

2. The study of marginal and dissenting groups in early modern Europe and colonial America has been greatly enhanced in the past three decades; one should begin with Christopher Hill, *The World Turned Upside Down: Radical Ideas during the English Revolution* (London, 1972); cf. also Philip Gura, *A Glimpse of Sion's Glory: Puritan Radicalism in Seventeenth-Century New England, 1620-1660;* Christopher Hill, *The Collected Essays of Christopher Hill,* 3 vols. (Amherst, MA, 1985-86); Barbara R. Dailey, "Root and Branch: New England's Religious Radicals and Their Transatlantic Community, 1600-1660"

(diss. Boston University, 1984); William R. Estep, "New England Dissent, 1620-1833: A Review Article," *CH,* 41 (1972), 246-52; Richard L. Greaves, *Deliver Us from Evil: The Radical Underground in Britain, 1660-1663* (Oxford, 1986); William G. McLoughlin, *New England Dissent, 1630-1833: The Baptists and the Separation of Church and State;* Bartholomew P. Schiavo, "The Dissenter Connection: English Dissenters and Massachusetts Political Culture, 1630-1774" (diss. Brandeis, 1976).

3. Cf. Wilbur Kitchener Jordan, *The Development of Religious Toleration in England . . . ,* 4 vols. (Cambridge, MA, 1932-40); Ole Peter Grell, Jonathan I. Israel, and Nicholas Tyacke, *From Persecution to Toleration: The Glorious Revolution and Religion in England* (Oxford, 1991).

4. Three men and one woman were executed. Mary Dyer, the one woman, was executed Friday, June 1, 1660, and became the most famous; cf. *DAB,* 5.584. William Robinson and Marmaduke Stephenson were executed Thursday, October 27, 1659; William Leddra was executed Thursday, March 14, 1660/1; Rufus Jones, Isaac Sharpless, and Amelia M. Gummere, *The Quakers in the American Colonies* (London, 1911), 81-89.

5. The general history of the Episcopal Church in the United States is covered in James T. Addison, *The Episcopal Church in the United States . . .* (New York, 1951). For the colonial period, see John F. Woolverton, *Colonial Anglicanism in North America* (Detroit, MI, 1984); Kenneth W. Cameron (ed.), *Anglicanism in Early Connecticut and New England: A Selective Bibliography* (Hartford, CT, 1977); *id., The Episcopal Church in Connecticut and New England: A Bibliography* (Hartford, CT, 1981); *id., Ethos of Anglicanism in Colonial New England and New York: Gleanings from the S.P.G. Abstracts (1704-1785) Concerning the Church of England in the Northern Plantations and Nearby Areas . . .* (Hartford, CT, 1981); George Hodges, "The Episcopalians," in *The Religious History of New England: King's Chapel Lectures* (Cambridge, MA, 1917), 203-47; Arthur L. Cross, *The Anglican Episcopate and the American Colonies* (New York, 1902).

For Maine, see Lawrence N. Crumb, "The Anglican Church in Colonial Maine," *HMPEC,* 33 (1964), 251-60; Edward Ballard, "The Early History of the Protestant Episcopal Church in the Diocese of Maine," *MeHSC,* 6 (1859), 171-202. For New Hampshire, see: Edgar L. Pennington, *The Church of England in Early Colonial New Hampshire . . .* (Hartford, CT, 1937). For Massachusetts, see Dudley Tyng, *Massachusetts Episcopalians, 1607-1957* (Pascong, RI, 1957); Edgar L. Pennington, "Anglican Beginnings in Massachusetts," *HMPEC,* 10 (1941), 242-89; Edward Midwinter, "The Society for the Propagation of the Gospel and the Church in the American Colonies, III: Massachusetts," *HMPEC,* 4 (1935), 100-15; Henry L. Parker, "The Anglican Church in the Colonies," Worcester Historical Society, *Proceedings,* (1887), 182-207, which, despite its title, limits itself to Massachusetts; William S. Perry (ed.), *Papers Relating to the History of the Episcopal Church in Massachusetts, A.D. 1676-1785* (Boston, 1873). For Rhode Island, see Dudley Tyng, *Rhode Island Episcopalians, 1653-1953 . . .* (Providence, RI, [1954]); Edgar L. Pennington, *The First Hundred Years of the Church of England in Rhode Island* (Hartford, CT, 1935).

Because of significant Anglican activity in Connecticut in the colonial period, the history of Anglicanism in that state has received extensive attention. Besides the works by Kenneth Cameron already cited, see his *Historical Resources of the Episcopal Diocese of Connecticut* (Hartford, CT, 1966) and *Early Anglicanism in Connecticut* (Hartford, CT, 1962). Other useful works are David H. Villers, "Connecticut Anglicanism and Society to 1783: A Review of the Historians," *HMPEC*, 53 (1984), 45-59; Hector G. L. M. Kinloch, "Anglican Clergy in Connecticut, 1701-1785" (diss. Yale, 1960); Francis L. Hawks and William S. Perry (eds.), *Documentary History of the Protestant Episcopal Church in the United States . . . Connecticut . . .* (1863-64), (rpt. 2 vols. in 1, Hartford, CT, 1959); Maud O'Neil, "A Struggle for Religious Liberty: An Analysis of the Work of the S.P.G. in Connecticut," *HMPEC*, 20 (1951), 173-89; WPA, Historical Records Survey, *Inventory of the Church Archives of Connecticut: Protestant Episcopal* (New Haven, CT, 1940); Edgar L. Pennington, *Church of England Beginnings in Connecticut . . .* (Hartford, CT, 1938); Samuel Hart, *How the [Episcopal] Church Came to Connecticut* (Hartford, CT, 1936); Origen S. Seymour, *The Beginnings of the Episcopal Church in Connecticut* ([New Haven, CT], 1934); James Shepard, *The Episcopal Church and the Early Ecclesiastical Laws of Connecticut . . .* (New Britain, CT, 1908); Lucy J. Jarvis, *Sketches of Church Life in Colonial Connecticut . . .* (New Haven, CT, 1902); E. Edwards Beardsley, *The History of the Episcopal Church in Connecticut . . .* 2 vols. (New York, 1865-68).

6. Casco Bay, MEP; Dover, NHP (Dover-1); and Portsmouth, NHP (Portsmouth-1).

7. Newport, RI, Trinity Church (Episcopal), *Annals of Trinity Church, Newport, Rhode Island, 1698-1821*, ed. George C. Mason (Newport, RI, 1890); William F. Gardner, "Robert Gardner and the Founding of Trinity Church, Newport, Rhode Island," *Newport Historical Magazine*, 7 (1887), 197-200; Daniel Goodwin, *The Making of Trinity Church, Newport* (Providence, RI, 1898); Stanley C. Hughes, "Early Days of Trinity Church," Newport Historical Society, *Bulletin*, 101 (1940), 31-41.

8. Frederick Lewis Weis, *The Colonial Clergy and the Colonial Churches of New England* (Lancaster, MA, 1936), 128.

9. Newport, RI, Trinity Church (Episcopal), *Annals*, 10-11.

10. This is a curious request, given Rhode Island's public commitment to freedom of religion and conscience. The Anglicans of Rhode Island seemed to have been quite suspicious of the Quakers and Baptists of Rhode Island. Four years later the leaders of Trinity Church, Newport, made the following comments concerning the Quakers in a letter to the SPG: "The place wherein we live is one of the Chief Nurseries of Quakerism in all America. . . . Their behaviour to us outwardly is almost as civil as is consistent with their religion. Although slily and underhand, we are sensible they would pinch us in the bud. But thanks be to God who hath put it past their power . . . ," Newport, RI, Trinity Church (Episcopal), *Annals*, 14-15.

11. *Ibid.*, 13.

12. *Ibid.*

13. *Ibid.*, 16.

14. The history of Quakers in seventeenth-century England has been ably covered in Hugh Barbour, *The Quakers in Puritan England* (New York, 1964); cf. also Richard T. Vann, *The Social Development of English Quakerism, 1655-1755* (Cambridge, 1969); Arnold Lloyd, *Quaker Social History: 1669-1738* (New York, 1950); William C. Braithwaite, *The Beginnings of Quakerism* (London, 1923); id., *The Second Period of Quakerism* (London, 1919).

15. For the history of Quakerism in general, see Howard Brinton, *Friends for 300 Years: The History and Beliefs of the Society of Friends Since George Fox Started the Quaker Movement* (New York, 1952); Elbert Russell, *The History of Quakerism* (New York, 1942);

William Sewel, *The History of the Rise, Increase and Progress of the Christian People Called Quakers,* 2 vols. (Philadelphia, 1856). For America, Hugh Barbour and J. William Frost, *The Quakers* (New York, 1988) is a good introduction to the movement. For the colonial period, see Rufus Jones, Isaac Sharpless, and Amelia M. Gummere, *The Quakers in the American Colonies* (London, 1911), which contains an excellent map of meetings, and James Bowden, *History of the Society of Friends in America,* 2 vols. (London, 1850-54).

16. The most recent coverage of the early history of the Society of Friends in New England is found in Arthur J. Worrall, *Quakers in the Colonial Northeast* (Hanover, NH, 1980) which is based on his 1969 dissertation at Indiana University ("New England Quakerism, 1656-1830"). The period in New England before 1672 is covered in Mary Hoxie Jones, *The Standard of the Lord Lifted Up: A History of Friends in New England, 1656-1700* (n.p., 1961). Cf. also *A Brief Account of the Yearly Meeting of Friends for New England* (Providence, RI, 1836).

While Quakerism was a movement that transcended colonial New England boundaries, each colony and province reacted differently to the movement. Therefore, studies of colonial New England Quakerism tend to be organized along colonial and state lines. For Massachusetts, see Carla G. Pestana, *Quakers and Baptists in Colonial Massachusetts; id.,* "The City upon a Hill under Siege: The Puritan Perception of the Quaker Threat to Massachusetts Bay, 1656-1661," *NEQ,* 56 (1983), 323-53. The other major recent contributor to the history of Quakerism in the Massachusetts region is Jonathan Chu's *Neighbors, Friends, or Madmen: The Puritan Adjustment to Quakerism in Seventeenth-Century Massachusetts Bay* (Westport, CT, 1985), based on his 1978 dissertation at the University of Washington. Chu has also written "The Social Context of Religious Heterodoxy: The Challenge of Seventeenth-Century Quakerism to Orthodoxy in Massachusetts," *EIHC,* 118 (1982), 119-50. An older treatment of Massachusetts can be found in Richard P. Hallowell, *The Quaker Invasion of Massachusetts* (Boston, 1887); cf. also Alfred R. Atwood, *Quakerism on Cape Cod* (East Denis, MA, 1936); John Hoag Dillingham, *The Society of Friends in Barnstable County, Massachusetts* (New York, 1891), which was also part of a general history of Barnstable County. For Connecticut, see Nelson R. Burr, "The Quakers in Connecticut: A Neglected Phase of History," Friends Historical Association, *Bulletin,* 31 (1942), 11-26. For Rhode Island, the "Nursery of Quakerism," see Caroline Hazard, *The Narragansett Friends Meeting in the XVIII Century, with a Chapter on Quaker Beginnnings in Rhode Island* (Boston, 1899). Quakers had extensive contact with Connecticut and New Haven Puritans on Long Island. For colonial Quakerism in New York State, see: Henry Onderdonk, Jr., *The Annals of Hempstead: also, The Rise and Growth of the Society of Friends on Long Island and in New York, 1657 to 1826* (Hempstead, NY, 1878); William Wade Hinshaw, Thomas Worth Marshall, and John Cox, Jr., *Encyclopedia of American Quaker Genealogy,* vol. 3, . . . *New York Yearly Meeting of the Society of Friends* . . . (Ann Arbor, MI, 1940); Mildred Murphy DeRiggi, "Quakerism on Long Island: The First Fifty Years, 1657-1707" (diss. State University of New York, Stony Brook, 1994); Hugh Barbour et al. (eds.), *Quaker Crosscurrents: Three Hundred Years of Friends in the New York Yearly Meetings* (Syracuse, NY, 1995).

17. Besides the works cited in the previous notes, see Charles E. Park, "Puritans and Quakers," *NEQ,* 27 (1954), 53-74; Walter H. Southwick, *Early History of the Puritans, Quakers, and Indians* . . . ([Lynn, MA, 1931]); Caleb A. Wall, *Puritans Versus Quakers: A Review of the Persecutions of the Early Quakers and Baptists in Massachusetts, with*

Notices of Those Persecuted . . . (Worcester, MA, 1888); Henry L. Southwick, *The Policy of the Early Colonists of Massachusetts Towards Quakers and Others Whom They Regarded as Intruders* (Boston, 1885); *id.,* "Puritans vs. Quakers," *The Friend,* 55 (1882), 210-11, 220, 228-29; Henry M. Dexter, *As to Roger Williams, and His "Banishment" from the Massachusetts Plantation: With a Few Further Words Concerning the Baptists, the Quakers, and Religious Liberty* (Boston, 1870).

18. Cf. William C. Braithwaite, *The Beginnings of Quakerism* and *The Second Period of Quakerism;* also Arthur J. Worrall, "Chapter III: Church Government," in "New England Quakerism, 1656-1830," esp. 36-55. Keeping track of Quaker meetings, especially in New England, is a challenge. The following were helpful in tracking the Quaker presence in New England: Rhode Island Historical Society Library, "Guide to the New England Yearly Meeting of Friends (Quaker) Microfilm Collection" (TS, RIHS; Providence, 1993); Thomas C. Hill, *Monthly Meetings in North America: A Quaker Index,* 4th edn. (Cincinnati, OH, 1997); Henry J. Cadbury, "A Map of 1782 Showing Friends Meetings in New England . . . ," *QH,* 52 (1963), 3-5; WPA, Historical Records Survey, Rhode Island, *Inventory of the Church Archives of Rhode Island: Society of Friends* (Providence, RI, 1939); Society of Friends, New York Yearly Meeting, *Directory, 1993 . . . [Including] Historical Sketches* (New York, 1993); Ellen Thomas Berry, *Our Quaker Ancestors: Finding Them in Quaker Records* (Baltimore, 1987). Jack Eckert, *Guide to the Records of Philadelphia Yearly Meeting* ([Haverford, PA, 1989]) contains an excellent introduction to how the Quaker world is organized, especially with respect to governance. It includes a glossary, and a list of all significant Quaker archives in North America. Most of the original Quaker records for the New England monthly meeting are kept in a separate collection at the Rhode Island Historical Society, Providence, RI. The records for the New York Yearly Meeting and its constituent meetings are kept at the Friends Historical Library, Swarthmore College, Swarthmore, PA.

19. See Joseph Smith, *A Descriptive Catalogue of Friends' Books . . . ,* 2 vols. (London, 1867-93). Joseph Smith has also compiled *Bibliotheca Quakeristica . . .* (London, 1883) which are observations of Quakerism by sympathetic outsiders, and *Bibliotheca Anti-Quakeriana . . .* (London, 1873) which is a collection of hostile observations.

20. New England Yearly Meeting of Friends, *Minutes of Men Friends, 1683-1787,* p. 11 (ms. held by Archives and Historical Records Committee of New England Yearly Meeting, Rhode Island Historical Society, Providence, RI; Microfilm #1). The New England Yearly Meeting was also known as the "Yearly Meeting of Rhode Island." But in 1699 the Rhode Island Quarterly Meeting was also formed.

21. *Ibid.*

22. *Ibid.,* 12.

23. Cf. Paul S. Fiddes et al., *Bound to Love: The Covenant Basis of Baptist Life and Mission* (London, 1985). The two most important works on the early Baptist practice of covenanting are: Charles William Deweese, "The Origin, Development, and Use of Church Covenants in Baptist History" (diss. The Southern Baptist Theological Seminary, 1973) and Champlin Burrage, *The Church Covenant Idea: Its Origin and Its Development.* Cf. also W. T. Whitley, "Church Covenants," *Baptist Quarterly,* n.s., 7 (1934-35), 227-34; James D. Smith III, "'To Walk with God and One Another,'" in *The Standard* 75 (1985), #2, 34-36; #3, 34-37; C. D. DeWeese, "Covenants, Baptist Church," in *Dictionary of Baptists in America,* ed. Bill J. Leonard (Downers Grove, IL, 1994), 95; "Covenants," in Wil-

liam H. Brackney, *Historical Dictionary of the Baptists* (Lanham, MD, 1999), 120-21; Paul S. Fiddes, "'Walking Together': The Place of Covenant Theology in Baptist Life Yesterday and Today," in *Pilgrim Pathways: Essays in Baptist History in Honour of B. R. White,* ed. William H. Brackney, Paul Fiddes, and John H. Y. Briggs (Macon, GA, 1999), 47-74.

24. Primary and secondary sources for the Baptist world are of course legion. Certain critical works, however, will help with the study of Baptist history in New England. The place to start is Old England, where critical consideration of the Baptist heritage began in the middle of the nineteenth century with Edward Bean Underhill, *Confessions of Faith, and Other Public Documents, Illustrative of the History of the Baptist Churches of England in the 17th Century* (London, 1854). See also: R. Evans, *The Early English Baptists,* 2 vols. (London, 1862-64); *Minutes of the General Assembly of the General Baptist Churches in England, with Kindred Records,* vol. 1: *1654-1728,* ed. W. T. Whitley (London, 1908); W. T. Whitley, *A Baptist Bibliography,* vol. 1, *1526-1776* (London, 1916); *id., A History of British Baptists* (London, 1923); A. C. Underwood, *A History of the English Baptists* (London, 1947); D. Mervyn Himbury, *British Baptists: A Short History* (London, 1962); *Association Records of the Particular Baptists of England, Wales and Ireland to 1660,* ed. Barrington R. White (London, [1971]-1977); H. Leon McBeth, *English Baptist Literature on Religious Liberty to 1689* (New York, 1980); based on a dissertation completed at Southwestern Baptist Theological Seminary in 1961. Two periodicals are also helpful with respect to Baptist history in Old England: Baptist Historical Society, *Transactions,* and *The Baptist Quarterly (BQ),* 1 (1922)-.

For the general background to Baptists in the United States, see Francis Wayland, *Notes on the Principles and Practices of Baptist Churches* (New York, 1857); *The Baptist Encyclopaedia: A Dictionary* . . . rev. edn. ed. William Cathcart, 2 vols. (Philadelphia, 1883); Thomas Armitage, *A History of the Baptists* . . . (New York, 1887); Henry C. Vedder, *A Short History of the Baptists (New . . . Edition)* (Philadelphia, 1907); William Joseph McGlothlin (ed.), *Baptist Confessions of Faith* (Philadelphia, 1911); Albert H. Newman, *A History of Baptist Churches in the United States,* 6th edn. rev. and enl. (New York, 1915); Robert B. Torbet, *A History of the Baptists,* 3rd edn. (Philadelphia, 1950); Jessie L. Boyd (ed.), *A History of Baptists in America Prior to 1845* (New York, 1957); William L. Lumpkin, *Baptist Confessions of Faith* (Chicago, 1959); Robert Baker, *A Baptist Source Book* . . . (Nashville, TN, 1966); Robert G. Gardner, *Baptists of Early America: A Statistical History, 1639-1790* (Atlanta, GA, 1983); H. Leon McBeth, *The Baptist Heritage* (Nashville, TN, 1987); William Henry Brackney, *The Baptists* (New York, 1988); *Dictionary of Baptists in America.* Two helpful serials are the *American Baptist Quarterly (ABQ),* 1 (1982) — and *Baptist History and Heritage (BHH)* 1 (1965)-.

For New England, the work of Isaac Backus is the place to begin. During the American Revolution Backus published: *A History of New-England, With Particular Reference to the Denomination of Christians Called Baptists* . . . *Collected from Most Authentic Records and Writings, both Ancient and Modern,* 3 vols. (Boston, 1777-96); a modern critical edition was published as *A History of New England, With Particular Reference to the Denomination of Christians Called Baptists* . . . *Second Edition, With Notes,* [ed.] David Weston, 2 vols. (Newton, MA, 1871; rpt. Paris, AR, n.d., The Baptist History Series, #s 3-4). See also Henry S. Burrage, *A History of the Baptists in New England* (Philadelphia, 1894); George E. Horr, "The Baptists," in *The Religious History of New England: King's Chapel Lectures* (Cambridge, MA, 1917), 135-76; Joseph Brewer, "The Relations of the

English Baptists with New England in the Seventeenth Century" (diss. Leeds, 1953); William G. McLoughlin, *New England Dissent, 1630-1833: The Baptists and the Separation of Church and State;* Edwin S. Gaustad, "The Public Role of Baptists in Colonial America," *Review and Expositor,* 97 (2000), #1, 11-20.

Besides local histories of individual Baptist churches in separate towns, many historical works concerning New England Baptists were written with colonial and state boundaries in mind. For Rhode Island, see Morgan Edwards, "Materials for a History of the Baptists in Rhode Island," *RIHSC,* 6 (1867), 301-70; Comfort E. Barrows, *The Development of Baptist Principles in Rhode Island . . .* (Providence, RI, 1875); "The Six-Principle Baptists in the Narragansett Country," *Narragansett Historical Register,* 1 (1882-83), 203-8; WPA, Historical Records Survey: Rhode Island, *Inventory of the Church Archives of Rhode Island: Baptist* (Providence, RI, 1941); Katherine W. Johnson, *Rhode Island Baptists . . .* (Valley Forge, PA, 1970). For Massachusetts, see Carla G. Pestana, *Quakers and Baptists in Colonial Massachusetts;* John W. Brush, *Baptists in Massachusetts* (Valley Forge, PA, 1970) and Francis J. Bremer, "When? Who? Why? Re-evaluating a 17th-Century Source," *MHSP,* 99 (1987), 63-75. For Maine, see "Historical Sketch of the Baptist Denomination in Maine," *Baptist Memorial and Chronicle,* 3 (1843), 353-63; Joshua Millet, *A History of the Baptists in Maine . . .* (Portland, ME, 1845); William H. Shailer, *A Historical Discourse . . .* (Portland, ME, 1874); Henry S. Burrage, *History of the Baptists in Maine* (Portland, ME, 1904). For New Hampshire, see Ebenezer E. Cummings, *Annals of the Baptist Churches in New-Hampshire . . .* (Concord, NH, 1836); Edmund Worth, *Annals of the Past . . .* (Concord, NH, 1852); William Hurlin, Orison C. Sargent, and William W. Wakeman, *The Baptists of New Hampshire* (Manchester, NH, 1902); William Hurlin, "The Baptists of New Hampshire," *Granite State Magazine,* 2 (1906), 127-35; C. Raymond Chappell, *Baptists in New Hampshire* (Manchester, NH, 1950). Finally, for Connecticut, see John L. Denison, *Some Items of Baptist History in Connecticut* (Philadelphia, 1900) and George W. Grisevich, "The Baptist-Puritan Encounter and Connecticut Religious Liberty," *Foundations,* 15 (1972), 266-72.

25. The church is now called the First Baptist Church of Boston. See Nathan Wood, *The History of the First Baptist Church of Boston (1665-1899)* (Philadelphia, 1899). The process by which the church was gathered is narrated by David A. Weir, "Church Covenanting in Seventeenth-Century New England," 175-85.

26. Nathan Wood, *The History of the First Baptist Church of Boston (1665-1899),* 50.

27. *Ibid.,* 56.

28. John Russel, *A Brief Narrative of Some Considerable Passages Concerning the First Gathering and further Progress of a Church of Christ, in Gospel Order, in Boston . . . in New . . . England . . .* (London, 1680); quoted in Nathan Wood, *The History of the First Baptist Church of Boston (1665-1899),* 152.

29. Nathan Wood, *The History of the First Baptist Church of Boston (1665-1899),* 65.

30. *Ibid.,* 42.

31. The history of Swansea, NPC, and its First Baptist Church can be found in: Swansea, MA, First Baptist Church, "Swansea, Massachusetts, Baptist Church Records," ed. Robert C. Anderson, *NEHGR,* 139 (1985), 21-49; Swansea, Wales and Swansea, MA, "Swansea Parish Register Copy," FHLC™M #: 0104833; Swansea, MA, *Book A: Records of*

the Town of Swansea, 1662 to 1705, ed. Alverdo H. Mason (East Braintree, MA, 1900); Swansea, MA, *Sowams: With Ancient Records of Sowams and Parts Adjacent — Illustrated,* ed. Thomas W. Bicknell (New Haven, 1908); Swansea, MA, "Swansea Town and Proprietors' Records (1670-1718)," FHLC™M #: 0903396; Swansea, MA, "Swansea Proprietors' Grants & Meetings (1668-1769)," *ibid.;* Swansea, MA, "Proprietors' Records, 1667-1725," *ibid.;* Isaac Backus, *A History of New England, With Particular Reference to the Denomination of Christians Called Baptists . . . Second Edition, With Notes;* Francis C. Baylies, *An Historical Memoir of the Colony of New Plymouth, From . . . 1608, to . . . 1692,* ed. Samuel G. Drake, 1 (Boston, 1866), 231-50 and 2 (Boston, 1866), 93-96; "The Early History of Swansea Church," in Ilsley Boone, ed., *Elements in Baptist Development* (Boston, 1913); John R. Hall, *In a Place Called Swansea* (Baltimore, 1987); *id.,* "The Three Rank System of Land Distribution in Colonial Swansea, Massachusetts," *RIH,* 43 (1984), 3-17; D. Hamilton Hurd (ed.), *History of Bristol County, Massachusetts . . .* (Philadelphia, 1883), 463-94, 652-78; Swansea, MA, First Baptist Church, *1663-1963: 300th Anniversary Year Book of the First Baptist Church, Swansea, Mass.;* J. J. Thatcher, *Historical Sketch of the First Baptist Church, Swansea, Mass., from Its Organization in 1663 to 1863 . . .* (Fall River, MA, 1863); Otis O. Wright, *History of Swansea, Massachusetts, 1667-1917* (Fall River, MA, 1917). The Welsh background to the Swansea church can be found in T. M. Bassett, *The Welsh Baptists* (Swansea, Wales, 1977) and B. G. Owens (ed.), *The Ilston Book: Earliest Register of Welsh Baptists* (Aberystwyth, Wales, 1996).

For Rehoboth, see: Leslie C. Abernathy III, "Landscape, Communities, and the 'Community at Palmers River': Settling a River System, 1665-1737, Rehoboth, Massachusetts" (diss. Brown, 1981); George N. Bliss, *An Historical Sketch of the Town of East Providence . . .* (Providence, RI, 1876); Leonard Bliss, Jr., *The History of Rehoboth, Bristol County, Massachusetts: Comprising a History of the Present Towns of Rehoboth, Seekonk, and Pawtucket . . . Together with Sketches of Attleborough, Cumberland, and a Part of Swansea and Barrington . . .* (Boston, 1836); Richard L. Bowen, *Early Rehoboth: Documented Historical Studies of Families and Events . . .* 4 vols. (Rehoboth, MA, 1945-50); *Historical Address . . . Delivered in the Newman Congregational Church in East Providence . . . in Commemoration of the 250th Anniversary of the Founding of the Newman Congregational Church and Ancient Town of Rehoboth* ([Pawtucket, RI, 1893?]); Sylvanus Chace Newman, *Rehoboth in the Past . . .* (Pawtucket, RI, 1860); George H. Tilton, *A History of Rehoboth, Massachusetts* (Boston, 1918).

32. Champlin Burrage, *The Church Covenant Idea: Its Origin and Its Development,* 173-76.

33. Richard Knight, *History of the General or Six Principle Baptists in Europe and America . . .* (Providence, RI, 1827; rpt. New York, 1980); "Six-Principle Baptists," in *The Baptist Encyclopaedia: A Dictionary . . . ,* 2nd edn., 2 (Philadelphia, 1883), 1060; J. T. Spivey, "Six-Principle Baptists," in *Dictionary of Baptists in America,* ed. Bill J. Leonard, 249-50; "Six Principle Calvinistic Baptists," in William H. Brackney, *Historical Dictionary of the Baptists* (Lanham, MD, 1999), 382-83.

34. See Henry S. Burrage, "The Baptist Church in Kittery," *MeHSC,* ser. 2, 9 (1898), 382-91 and Champlin Burrage, *The Church Covenant Idea: Its Origin and Its Development,* 181-86. Cf. also Everett S. Stackpole, *Old Kittery and Her Families* (Lewiston, ME, 1903); *Old Eliot: A Monthly Magazine of the History and Biography of the Upper Parish of Kittery, Now Eliot;* Ralph S. Bartlett, *The History of York County, Maine, and a . . .*

Narrative about the Town of Eliot and Its Mother-town Old Kittery . . . (Boston, 1938); John E. Frost, *The Kittery Record Book* (n.p., 1978); *Kittery: Ancient and Modern* (Kittery, ME, 1931); Kittery, ME, First Baptist Church, *The First Baptist Church of Kittery Point, Maine* (South Berwick, ME, 1973); Harry E. Mitchell et al., *The Town Register: York and Kittery, 1906* (Brunswick, ME, 1906); Charles Penrose, *Old Kittery* . . . (New York, 1947); "A Sketch of Kittery," *Maine Historical and Genealogical Recorder,* 9 (1898), 252-56; Ralph E. Thompson and Matthew R. Thompson, *Pascataway: De Facto Capital of New England, 1623-1630* (Monmouth, OR, 1973). There was also a Quaker presence in Kittery; see Jonathan M. Chu, "The Social and Political Contexts of Heterodoxy: Quakerism in Seventeenth-Century Kittery," *NEQ,* 54 (1981), 365-84.

35. Champlin Burrage, *The Church Covenant Idea: Its Origin and Its Development,* 181-82.

Notes to Chapter 6

1. For an example of a statement at the institution of the half-way covenant, see the example of Hartford, CTC, Second Church: Edwin P. Parker, *History of the Second Church of Christ in Hartford, 1670-1892* (Hartford, CT, 1892), 287-91. Northampton, MBC, First Church is an example of a confessional statement adopted at the time of covenant renewal: "Old Covenant and Confession of the Northampton Church," *CQ,* 4 (1861), 168-79.

2. For collections of confessional documents in the Reformed or Calvinistic tradition from this time period, cf. Williston Walker, *The Creeds and Platforms of Congregationalism* (New York, 1893; rpt. Boston, 1960); William E. Barton, *Congregational Creeds and Covenants* (Chicago, 1917); Philip Schaff, *Creeds of Christendom* (New York, 1877; rpt. 1977); John H. Leith, *Creeds of the Churches,* rev. edn. (Richmond, VA, 1973); E. F. K. Müller, *Die Bekenntnisschriften der reformierten Kirche (BSRK),* ed. E. F. K. Müller (Leipzig, 1903). For a discussion of Congregationalism and creeds, cf. "Creeds" in Preston Cummings, *A Dictionary of Congregational Usages and Principles* . . . (Boston, 1855), 131-39; Edward W. Gilman, "Confessions of Faith," *CQ,* 4 (1862), 179-91; Edward A. Lawrence, "Our Declaration of Faith and the Confession," *CQ,* 8 (1866), 173-90; Alonzo H. Quint, "The Savoy Declaration: Reprinted from the Edition of 1659. With Its Variations from the Westminster Confession, and from the Declaration of 1680," *CQ,* 8 (1866), 241-61, 341-44; Wolcott Calkins, "Creeds as Tests of Church Membership," *The Andover Review,* 13 (1890), 237-55; Henry Martyn Dexter, "Did the Early Churches of New England Require Assent to a Creed?" *Magazine of Christian Literature,* 2 (1890), 129-38.

3. *A Direction for a Publick Profession in the Church Assembly, after Private Examination by the Elders.* . .; rpt. in Walker, *Creeds and Platforms,* 119-22; [Brattle Street Church], *A Manifesto or Declaration, Set Forth by the Undertakers of the New Church Now Erected in Boston in New-England, November 17th. 1699.* (Boston, n.d.); rpt. in Samuel K. Lothrop, *A History of the Church in Brattle Street, Boston* (Boston, 1851).

4. Schaff, *Creeds,* 3.486-516.

5. "The Seven Articles of 1617 . . . ," in Walker, *Creeds and Platforms,* 89; cf. Chapter 3: "The Civil Covenants of Early New England," above.

6. "The Second Confession of the London-Amsterdam Church," in Walker, *Creeds and Platforms,* 41-74.

7. The Westminster Confession, and its Larger and Shorter Catechisms, can be found in *BSRK*, which contains: (a) the Latin and English texts of the *Confession*, pp. 542-612; (b) the Latin text of the *Larger Catechism*, pp. 612-43; and (c) the English text of the *Shorter Catechism*, pp. 643-52. The Latin and English texts of the *Confession*, along with the Latin and English texts of the *Shorter Catechism*, can be found in Schaff, *Creeds*, 3.598-704. Schaff does not include the *Larger Catechism*. Also relevant is Schaff, *Creeds*, 1. The *WCF* also often appears with other important documents, viz. *The {Westminster} Confession of Faith; The Larger and Shorter Catechisms . . . With the Sum of Saving Knowledge . . . Covenants, National and Solemn League; Acknowledgement of Sins, and Engagement to Duties; Directories for Publick and Family Worship; Form of Church Government, etc.; Of Publick Authority in the Church of Scotland; With Acts of Assembly and Parliament, Relative To, and Approbative of, the Same*. For the history of the Westminster Assembly, cf. Charles A. Briggs, "The Documentary History of the Westminster Assembly," *The Presbyterian Review*, 1 (1880), 12-63; Samuel William Carruthers, *The Everyday Work of the Westminster Assembly* (Philadelphia, 1943); Weldon S. Crowley, "Erastianism in the Westminster Assembly," *JCS*, 15 (1973), 49-64; *id.*, "Erastianism in the Long Parliament," *JCS*, 21 (1979), 451-67; William Maxwell Hetherington, *History of the Westminster Assembly of Divines*, 4th edn., ed. Robert Williamson (Edinburgh, 1878); Wayne R. Spear, "Covenanted Uniformity in Religion: The Influence of the Scottish Commissioners upon the Ecclesiology of the Westminster Assembly" (diss. University of Pittsburgh, 1976); Larry J. Holley, "The Divines of the Westminster Assembly: A Study of Puritanism and Parliament" (diss. Yale, 1979); John H. Leith, *Assembly at Westminster: Reformed Theology in the Making* (Richmond, VA, 1973); Alexander Mitchell, *The Westminster Assembly: Its History and Standards* (Philadelphia, 1884); Robert S. Paul, *The Assembly of the Lord: Politics and Religion in the Westminster Assembly and the "Grand Debate"* (Edinburgh, 1985); James Reid, *Memoirs of the Westminster Divines* (1811; rpt. Carlisle, PA, 1982); Benjamin Breckinridge Warfield, *The Westminster Assembly and Its Work* (New York, 1931); John L. Carson and David W. Hall (eds.), *To Glorify and Enjoy God: A Commemoration of the 350th Anniversary of the Westminster Assembly* (Edinburgh, 1994).

8. See John R. de Witt, *"Jus Divinum": The Westminster Assembly and the Divine Right of Church Government* (Kampen, 1969); *id.*, "The Form of Church Government," in John L. Carson and David W. Hall, eds., *To Glorify and Enjoy God: A Commemoration of the 350th Anniversary of the Westminster Assembly*, 143-68.

9. Schaff, *Creeds*, 3.598 and 674.

10. (London, 1654), Paper 5; excerpts in Walker, *Creeds and Platforms*, 189-93.

11. (Cambridge, MA, 1649), Paper 3; cf. "The Cambridge Synod and Platform, 1646-1648," in Walker, *Creeds and Platforms*, 157-237.

12. Walker, *Creeds and Platforms*, 194-95.

13. "The Savoy Declaration, 1658," in Walker, *Creeds and Platforms*, 340-408; cf. "The Savoy Declaration of the Congregational Churches, A.D. 1658," in Schaff, *Creeds*, 3.707-29. A discussion of the Westminster standards vis-à-vis the Savoy Declaration can be found in Peter Toon, "The Westminster and Savoy Confessions: A Brief Comparison," *Journal of the Evangelical Theological Society*, 15 (1972), 153-60; cf. also A. G. Mathews, "Introduction," in *The Savoy Declaration of Faith and Order, 1658* (London, 1959), 9-47 and Alonzo H. Quint, "The Savoy Declaration, 1658."

14. The Cambridge Platform is not a confessional statement, but it endorses a

modified form of the Westminster standards, and its last chapter has some critical points to examine concerning the relation of the civil magistrate to the church.

15. Quint, in "The Savoy Declaration, 1658," gives a full list of variants between the Westminster Confession, the Savoy Declaration, and the Massachusetts Confession of 1680.

16. Walker, *Creeds and Platforms,* 393-94; cf. "The Baptist Confession of 1688," in Schaff, *Creeds,* 3.738-41; cf. Barry Hamlin Howson, "A Historical and Comparative Study of the First and Second London Baptist Confessions of Faith with Reference to the Westminster and Savoy Confessions" (M.A. thesis, McGill, 1996).

17. Walker, *Creeds and Platforms,* 420-21, 425.

18. *Ibid.,* 422, 500-501.

19. Schaff, *Creeds,* 3.645.

20. Walker, *Creeds and Platforms,* 393-94.

21. Cf. Appendix 1.

22. Salem, MA, First Church, *The Records of the First Church in Salem, Massachusetts, 1629-1736,* ed. Richard D. Pierce (Salem, MA, 1974), 3-5; cf. also "The Development of Covenant and Creed in the Salem Church, 1629-1665," in Walker, *Creeds and Platforms,* 93-122.

23. Salem, MA, First Church, *Records of the First Church in Salem, Massachusetts,* 5; cf. also Walker, *Creeds and Platforms,* 118.

24. *A Direction for a Publick Profession in the Church Assembly, after Private Examination by the Elders . . .* ; rpt. in Walker, *Creeds and Platforms,* 119-22.

25. *A Copy of The Church-Covenants which have been used in the Church of Salem . . .* (Boston, 1680).

26. Nathaniel Morton, *New-England's Memorial . . .* (Cambridge, MA), 75-76; cf. also 6th edn. (Boston, 1855), 99-100; quoted in Salem, MA, First Church, *Records of the First Church in Salem, Massachusetts,* xiv-xv.

27. A related question is the degree to which the Separatist influence of the New Plymouth Colony affected Salem First Church's decision to adopt a covenanted congregational polity. For the issues in this discussion, see Slayden Yarbrough, "The Influence of Plymouth Colony Separatism on Salem: An Interpretation of John Cotton's Letter of 1630 to Samuel Skelton," *CH,* 51 (1982), 290-303 and Lewis J. Robinson, "The Formative Influence of Plymouth Church on American Congregationalism," *Bibliotheca Sacra,* 127 (1970), 232-40.

28. Dedham, MA, First Church, *The Record of Baptisms, Marriages and Deaths, and Admissions to the Church and Dismissals Therefrom, Transcribed from the Church Records in the Town of Dedham, Massachusetts, 1639-1845,* ed. Don G. Hill, *Dedham Historical Review,* 2 (Dedham, MA, 1888), 9.

29. *Ibid.,* 10.

30. *Ibid.,* 11.

31. *Ibid.,* 35.

32. *A Direction for a Publick Profession in the Church Assembly . . . ,* tp; Walker, *Creeds and Platforms,* 119; Walker also discusses the Congregational relationship to confessions and creeds on p. xv.

33. Edward Taylor, *Edward Taylor's Church Records and Related Sermons,* vol. 1 of

The Unpublished Writings of Edward Taylor, ed. Thomas M. Davis and Virginia L. Davis (Boston, 1981), 7-8.

34. *A Copy of The Church-Covenants which have been used in the Church of Salem . . .* , 4.

35. For a confessional summary of seventeenth-century Quaker doctrine, see: "*Theses Theologicae* of Robert Barclay," in John H. Leith, *Creeds of the Churches,* 323-33.

36. Cf. Edward Bean Underhill, *Confessions of Faith, and Other Public Documents, Illustrative of the History of the Baptist Churches of England in the 17th Century;* William Joseph McGlothlin (ed.), *Baptist Confessions of Faith;* William L. Lumpkin, *Baptist Confessions of Faith;* Joseph Brewer, "The Relations of the English Baptists with New England in the Seventeenth Century"; Gilbert R. Englerth, "American Baptists: A Confessional People?" *ABQ,* 4 (1985), 131-45.

37. Nathan Wood, *The History of the First Baptist Church of Boston (1665-1899)* (Philadelphia, 1899), 65.

38. Northampton, MA, First Church, "Old Covenant and Confession of the Northampton Church," 169-70.

39. Plymouth, MA, First Church, *Records,* 181; the entire section is found on pp. 181-82.

40. *Ibid.,* 181; the entire section is found on p. 182.

41. Edward Taylor, *Edward Taylor's Church Records and Related Sermons,* 4.

42. For covenant theology and the federal theology, along with a discussion of Arminianism, cf. Perry Miller, *The New England Mind;* David A. Weir, *The Origins of the Federal Theology;* and Richard A. Muller, "The Federal Motif in Seventeenth-Century Arminian Theology," *Nederlands Archief voor Kerkgeschiedenis,* 62 (1982), 102-22.

43. Cf. Horton Davies, *The Worship of the American Puritans, 1629-1730.*

44. The theme of millenarianism has generated a substantial literature during the last fifty years. The English background in the seventeenth century can be found in John F. Wilson, "Studies in Puritan Millenarianism under the Stuarts" (diss. Union Theological Seminary in New York, 1962); Peter Toon (ed.), *Puritans, the Millennium, and the Future of Israel: Puritan Eschatology, 1600 to 1660: A Collection of Essays . . .* (Cambridge, 1970); Katherine R. Firth, *The Apocalyptic Tradition in Reformation Britain, 1530-1645* (Oxford, 1979), a work based on a 1971 Oxford University dissertation; Bryan W. Ball, *A Great Expectation: Eschatological Thought in English Protestantism to 1660* (Leiden, 1975); and Paul Christianson, *Reformers and Babylon: English Apocalyptic Visions from the Reformation to the Eve of the Civil War* (Toronto, 1977), based on a 1971 University of Minnesota dissertation. The broader picture of America and millennial themes is discussed in Ernest Lee Tuveson, *Redeemer Nation: The Idea of America's Millennial Role* (Chicago, 1968). The idea that the New Englanders — or at least the Massachusetts Bay colonists — came to the New World to fulfill a millennial vision is put forth most vigorously by Avihu Zakai: cf. his *Theocracy in Massachusetts: Reformation and Separation in Early Puritan New England* (Lewiston, NY, 1994), based on a 1983 Johns Hopkins dissertation; *id.,* "Theocracy in New England: The Nature and the Meaning of the Holy Experiment in the Wilderness," *JRH,* 14 (1986-87), 133-51; *id.,* "Puritan Millennialism and Theocracy in Early Massachusetts," *History of European Ideas,* 8 (1987), 309-18; *id., Exile and Kingdom: History and Apocalypse in the Puritan Migration to America* (New York, 1992). T. Dwight Bozeman, *To Live Ancient Lives: The Primitivist Dimension in Puritanism* (Chap-

el Hill, NC, 1988) argues along the same lines, relating the millennial focus of the future to a return to the past, especially to the ideals and practices of the New Testament church. Rosemary K. Twomey argues that the Puritans came over to develop a pure church (albeit perhaps within an apocalyptic framework), but then adopted a millennial vision that sought not just perfection for the church but also for the entire "nation" of the Massachusetts Bay. The Massachusetts Bay Colony therefore moved from seeing itself as a group seeking to have a pure church in a sanctified state to seeing itself as a chosen nation in covenant with God that was to perform God's work through a "new kingdom" in a "new world." That process of national transformation would prefigure the new kingdom in the eschaton; cf. "From Pure Church to Pure Nation: Massachusetts Bay, 1630-1692" (diss. Rochester, 1971). Andrew Delbanco, on the other hand, concludes that the Puritans were less millennial than Zakai and others think. Instead, what millennialists there were in early New England went home at the time of the English Revolution in the 1640s: cf. "The Puritan Errand Reviewed," *JAS*, 18 (1984), 343-60. The question is how central the millennial vision was to the New Englander's normative vision and to the majority of the settlers. For discussions of early New England eschatology in general, cf. Joy Gilsdorf, *The Puritan Apocalypse: New England Eschatology in the Seventeenth Century* (New York, 1989) which appeared earlier as a Yale dissertation under the same title in 1965; W. Clark Gilpin, *The Millenarian Piety of Roger Williams* (Chicago, 1979); Michael Mooney, "Millennialism and Antichrist in New England, 1630-1760" (diss. Syracuse, 1982); and Deok Kyo Oh, "The Church's Resurrection: John Cotton's Eschatological Understanding of the Ecclesiastical Reformation" (diss. Westminster Theological Seminary, 1987).

45. Edward Taylor, *Edward Taylor's Church Records and Related Sermons*, 10-96; John Eliot, *Christianae Oonoowae sampoowaonk: A Christian Covenanting Canfession* [*sic*] (Cambridge, MA, 1660).

46. Clinton, CT, First Church, *Two Hundredth Anniversary of the Clinton Congregational Church* (New Haven, CT, 1868), 44.

47. *Ibid.*, 44-45.

48. Cf. the following for the history of Marblehead: Thomas E. Gray, *The Founding of Marblehead* (Baltimore, 1984); Marblehead, MA, First Church, *The Bi-Centennial of the First Congregational Church, Marblehead, Mass. . . .* (Marblehead, MA, 1884); Marblehead, MA, First Church, *Under the Golden Cod: A Shared History of the Old North Church and the Town of Marblehead, Massachusetts, 1635-1985* (Canaan, NH, 1984); Massachusetts Historical Society, "A Topographical and Historical Account of Marblehead," *MHSC*, ser. 1, 8 (1802), 54-78; Samuel Roads, Jr., *The History and Traditions of Marblehead*, 2nd edn. (Boston, 1881); Joseph S. Robinson, *The Story of Marblehead* (Marblehead, MA, 1936); Marblehead, MA, First Church, "First Book Containing the Records of the First Congregational Church in Marblehead Commencing 1684 and Terminating 1800" (ms. owned and held by the church), FHLC™M #: 877751; Marblehead, MA, "Town Records, 1648-1839," FHLC™M #: 0864833; Marblehead, MA, "Town Records, 1649-1788," FHLC™M #: 0864834.

49. Marblehead, MA, First Church, *Bi-Centennial*, 81.

50. *Ibid.*, 82.

51. For the history of Boston's Brattle Street Church, cf. Boston, Battle Street Church, *The Manifesto Church: Records of the Church in Brattle Square, Boston . . . 1699-*

1872 (Boston, 1902); Samuel K. Lothrop, *Memorial of the Church in Brattle Square* . . . (Boston, 1871); *id., A History of the Church in Brattle Street, Boston;* John G. Palfrey, *A Sermon Preached to the Church in Brattle Square* . . . (Boston, 1825); Caleb H. Snow, *History of Boston* . . . , 2nd edn. (Boston, 1828); Rick Alan Kennedy, "Thy Patriarchs' Desire: Thomas and William Brattle in Puritan Massachusetts" (diss. University of California, Santa Barbara, 1987).

52. Samuel K. Lothrop, *A History of the Church in Brattle Street, Boston,* 20.

53. Walker, *Creeds and Platforms,* 472-83.

54. Samuel K. Lothrop, *A History of the Church in Brattle Street, Boston,* 20.

55. Boston, Brattle Street Church, *The Manifesto Church: Records of the Church in Brattle Square, Boston,* 3.

56. Samuel K. Lothrop, *A History of the Church in Brattle Street, Boston,* 21.

57. *Ibid.,* 21. For the platform of the United Brethren, see "The Heads of Agreement of 1691," in Walker, *Creeds and Platforms,* 440-62.

58. Samuel K. Lothrop, *A History of the Church in Brattle Street, Boston,* 23.

59. *Ibid.,* 22.

60. *Ibid.,* 25.

61. *Ibid.*

62. Cf. David A. Weir, "Church Covenanting in Seventeenth-Century New England," 255-71.

63. *A Direction for a Publick Profession in the Church Assembly* . . . , tp; Walker, *Creeds and Platforms,* 119; Walker also discusses the Congregational relationship to confessions and creeds on p. xv.

Notes to the Conclusion

1. Cf., in particular, Perry Miller, "The Theory of the State and of Society," in Perry Miller and Thomas H. Johnson, *The Puritans* (New York, 1928), 181-94; *id., The New England Mind,* vol. 1, *The Seventeenth Century;* Larzer Ziff, "The Social Bond of Church Covenant"; Edmund S. Morgan (ed.), *Puritan Political Ideas, 1558-1794* (Indianapolis, IN, 1965); Timothy H. Breen, *The Character of the Good Ruler: A Study of Puritan Political Ideas in New England, 1630-1730* (New Haven, CT, 1970), based on a dissertation at Yale University completed in 1969; Stephen Foster, *Their Solitary Way: The Puritan Social Ethic in the First Century of Settlement in New England* (New Haven, CT, 1971), based on a dissertation completed at Yale University in 1966; Timothy H. Breen and Stephen Foster, "The Puritans' Greatest Achievement: A Study of Social Cohesion in Seventeenth-Century Massachusetts," *JAH,* 60 (1973-74), 5-22; Daniel J. Elazar, "The Political Theory of Covenant: Biblical Origins and Modern Developments"; Mark Allen Carden, "The Communal Ideal in Puritan New England, 1630-1700," *F+H,* 17 (1984), 25-38; John H. Peacock, Jr., "Liberty and Discipline in Covenant Theology," *CRevAS,* 15 (1984), 1-16; Virginia DeJohn Anderson, "Migrants and Motives: Religion and the Settlement of New England, 1630-1640," *NEQ,* 58 (1985), 339-83; Kathleen Kook, "Volatile Legacy: The Meaning of Community in Early New Hampshire" (diss. University of California, Berkeley, 1985); John Witte, Jr., "Blest Be the Ties That Bind: Covenant and Community in Puritan Thought," *ELJ,* 36 (1987), 579-601; *id.,* "How to Govern a City on a Hill: The Early Puritan Contribution to American Constitutionalism," *ELJ,* 39

(1990), 41-64; Augusta Pipkin Heywood, "Walking 'Fruitfully with God in the Covenant': The Origins of Justified Disobedience within the American Social Contract" (diss. Fletcher School of Law and Diplomacy, Tufts University, 1992); and cf. nn. 2, 5, and 19 in the Introduction, above.

2. "The Political Theory of Covenant: Biblical Origins and Modern Developments," *Publius*, 10 (1980), 17.

3. Cf., for instance, the 1990 "Symposium: Religious Dimensions of American Constitutionalism," *ELJ*, 39 (1990), #1, 1-266, which focuses on one dimension of the history and sources of the United States Constitution. Besides the "Introduction" by Frank S. Alexander (pp. 1-8), both Donald S. Lutz, in "Religious Dimensions in the Development of American Constitutionalism" (pp. 21-40) and John Witte, Jr., in "How to Govern a City on a Hill: The Early Puritan Contribution to American Constitutionalism" (pp. 41-64) discuss the importance of the covenant theology and covenant practice as a source for the American Constitution. Cf. also Lutz's earlier work on this topic: *The Origins of American Constitutionalism; Documents of Political Foundation Written by Colonial Americans: From Covenant to Constitution; Colonial Origins of the American Constitution: A Documentary History*; and "From Covenant to Constitution in American Political Thought," *Publius*, 10 (1980), #4, 101-33. Jack P. Greene discusses the development of constitutionalism in the American colonial world, but primarily focuses on the eighteenth century; cf. *Peripheries and Center: Constitutional Development in the Extended Polities of the British Empire and the United States, 1607-1788*. Finally the works of Daniel Elazar, cited below, are seminal in pulling together the importance of the covenant theme as a prelude to constitutionalism.

4. Cf. the bibliography of covenant theology in David A. Weir, *The Origins of the Federal Theology in Sixteenth-Century Reformation Thought*, 160-95, a bibliography which is arranged chronologically, not topically. A variety of scholars have contributed to surveys of various segments of this historical discussion. Harro Höpfl and Martyn P. Thompson made an important contribution with their article on "The History of Contract as a Motif in Political Thought," *AHR*, 84 (1979), 919-45. The work of Daniel Elazar is encyclopedic in this regard. Elazar, a political scientist, sought to trace the influence of the covenant idea throughout all of Western tradition and political theory. Cf., in particular, *The Covenant Tradition in Politics*, 4 vols. (1995-98). Vol. 1, *Covenant and Polity in Biblical Israel: Biblical Foundations and Jewish Expressions* gives a broad introduction to the theme, while vol. 2, *Covenant and Commonwealth: From Christian Separation through the Protestant Reformation* discusses the development of the theme in the medieval and early modern world. Vol. 3, *Covenant and Constitutionalism: The Great Frontier and the Matrix of Federal Democracy* has an especially important article on "Covenant and the American Founding" (pp. 17-45), while vol. 4, *Covenant and Civil Society: The Constitutional Matrix of Modern Democracy* discusses the importance of the covenant theme for modernity. Elazar also completed some shorter works, such as the article on "Covenant" in the *Encyclopedia of Politics and Religion* (1998), 193-99; and a series of articles that were gathered together in 2000: Daniel J. Elazar and John Kincaid (eds.), *The Covenant Connection: From Federal Theology to Modern Federalism* (2000). Elazar and Kincaid also edited a 1980 edition of *Publius* that was reprinted as *Covenant, Polity, and Constitutionalism* (1983). Finally, cf. these earlier, shorter works by Elazar: "The Almost-Covenanted Polity: [America and the Federalist Revolution]" (1982); "[Editorial]: Federalism as Grand Design,"

Publius, 9 (1979), #4, 1-8; and "[Editorial]: The Themes of a Journal of Federalism," *Publius,* 1 (1971), 1-9. Cf. also the work of the following: J. Wayne Baker, "Faces of Federalism: From Bullinger to Jefferson," *Publius,* 30 (2000), #4, 25-41; Joseph Martin Dawson, "Roger Williams or John Locke?" *BHH,* 1 (1966), #3, 11-14; Thomas O. Hueglin, *Early Modern Concepts for a Late Modern World: Althusius on Community and Federalism* (Waterloo, ON, 1999); Sanford Kessler, "Tocqueville's Puritans: Christianity and the American Founding," *Journal of Politics,* 54 (1992), 776-92; Martin E. Marty, "On Medieval Moraine: Religious Dimensions of American Constitutionalism," *ELJ,* 39 (1990), 9-20; Lois Kimball Mathews, "The Mayflower Compact and Its Descendants"; Perry Miller, "The Theory of the State and of Society"; George L. Mosse, "Puritanism and Reason of State in Old and New England," *WMQ,* ser. 3, 9 (1952), 67-80; *id., The Holy Pretence: A Study in Christianity and Reason of State from William Perkins to John Winthrop* (Oxford, 1957); Vincent Ostrom, "Hobbes, Covenant, and Constitution," *Publius,* 10 (1980), #4, 83-100; Ellis Sandoz, *A Government of Laws: Political Theory, Religion, and the American Founding* (Baton Rouge, LA, 1990); and Stephen L. Schechter, "[Editorial]: Federalism and Community in Historical Perspective," *Publius,* 5 (1975), #2, 1-14.

5. In the foreword to Edmund Morgan's *Puritan Political Ideas, 1558-1794,* Leonard W. Levy and Alfred Young contrast two visions of Puritanism in American history. The first school, emerging in the late nineteenth century, associates Puritanism with words such as "joyless," "dark-minded," "petty," "firm believers in human depravity," "tyranny," "witch hunters," and "theocrats." The second school, emerging out of the mid-twentieth century, emphasizes that Puritanism is a complex system of beliefs and institutions that exhibits variety and "as much diversity, creativity, and vitality as the Enlightenment" (p. v).

6. Cf. Darryl Baskin, "The Congregationalist Origins of American Pluralism," *JCS,* 11 (1969), 277-93; John A. Guegen, "Political Order and Religious Liberty: A Puritan Controversy" (diss. Chicago, 1970), which discusses the debate between John Cotton and Roger Williams; John Hunt Peacock, Jr., "The Breach of Such a Covenant: Individualism and American Community, 1630-1891" (diss. Columbia, 1980); *id.,* "Liberty and Discipline in Covenant Theology"; and Augusta Pipkin Heywood, "Walking 'Fruitfully with God in the Covenant': The Origins of Justified Disobedience within the American Social Contract."

7. Timothy H. Breen and Stephen Foster, "The Puritans' Greatest Achievement: A Study of Social Cohesion in Seventeenth-Century Massachusetts"; Mark Allen Carden, "The Communal Ideal in Puritan New England, 1630-1700"; John Witte, Jr., "Blest Be the Ties That Bind: Covenant and Community in Puritan Thought"; E. Clinton Gardner, "Justice in the Puritan Covenantal Tradition," *JLR,* 6 (1988), 39-60.

8. Cf. James T. Johnson, *A Society Ordained by God: English Puritan Marriage Doctrine in the First Half of the Seventeenth Century* (Nashville, TN, 1970), based on a 1968 dissertation; and *id.,* "The Covenant Idea and the Puritan View of Marriage," *JHI,* 32 (1971), 107-18.

9. Elizabeth S. Reis, "Satan's Familiars: Sinners, Witches and Conflicting Covenants in Early New England" (diss. University of California, Berkeley, 1991); revised and published as *Damned Women: Sinners and Witches in Puritan New England* (Ithaca, NY, 1997).

10. Concerning millenarianism, cf. n. 44 in Chapter 6: "The Covenantal Confes-

sions of Early New England: The Seeds of Diversity." For the typology of ideals for what the millennium should be like, cf. esp. T. Dwight Bozeman, *To Live Ancient Lives: The Primitivist Dimension in Puritanism* and Crawford Leonard Allen, "'The Restauration of Zion': Roger Williams and the Quest for the Primitive Church." Allen sees three types of primitivism: theocratic primitivism, in which Old Testament Israel was normative; New Testament primitivism, which rejected the Old Testament model of a godly commonwealth and magisterial reform and focused on the reformation of the church; and eschatological primitivism, which taught that there would be a restoration to New Testament models not by human reformation but by a direct action of God, who would start the new age with, as it were, a bolt of lightning from the sky. A different version of the future that incorporates a general Protestant vision can be found in Michael Robert Cavey, "'When all the world shall be combined': English Protestantism and Universal Commonwealth, 1530-1720" (diss. Rutgers, 1997); cf. also James Holstun: *A Rational Millennium: Puritan Utopias of Seventeenth-Century England and America* (New York, 1987).

11. For theories of modernization in New England, cf. Ronald P. Dufour, "Modernization in Colonial Massachusetts, 1630-1763" (diss. William and Mary, 1982) and David O. Damerall, "The Modernization of Massachusetts: The Transformation of Public Attitudes and Institutions, 1689 to 1715." For Old England, cf. Michael Walzer, *The Revolution of the Saints: A Study in the Origins of Radical Politics* (Cambridge, MA, 1965). For discussions of modernization and the theme of covenant, the following are relevant: William Johnson Everett, "Contract and Covenant in Human Community," *ELJ*, 36 (1987), 557-68; *id., God's Federal Republic: Reconstructing Our Governing Symbol;* David Zaret, *The Heavenly Contract: Ideology and Organization in Pre-Revolutionary Puritanism* (Chicago, 1985), based on a 1977 Oxford dissertation; and John Kincaid, "Influential Models of Political Association in the Western Tradition," *Publius*, 10 (1980), #4, 31-58.

12. Richard J. Hoskins, "The Original Separation of Church and State in America"; Aaron B. Seidman, "Church and State in the Early Years of the Massachusetts Bay Colony"; G. Hugh Wamble, "Baptist Contributions to Separation of Church and State"; and William G. McLoughlin, *New England Dissent, 1630-1833: The Baptists and the Separation of Church and State.*

13. Cf. Barbara Allen, "Alexis de Tocqueville and the Covenantal Tradition of American Federal Democracy," *Publius*, 28 (1998), #2, 1-23; James F. Cooper, Jr., "Higher Law, Free Consent, Limited Authority: Church Government and Political Culture in Seventeenth-Century Massachusetts," *NEQ*, 69 (1996), 201-22; Sidney E. Ahlstrom, "Thomas Hooker, Puritanism and Democratic Citizenship: A Preliminary Inquiry into Some of the Relationships of Religion and American Civic Responsibility," *CH*, 32 (1963), 415-31; Richard Niebuhr, "The Idea of Covenant and American Democracy," *CH*, 23 (1954), 126-35; Clifford K. Shipton, "Puritanism and Modern Democracy," *NEHGR*, 101 (1947), 181-98; Winthrop S. Hudson, "Democratic Freedom and Religious Faith in the Reformed Tradition," *CH*, 15 (1946), 177-94; Charles Borgeaud, *The Rise of Modern Democracy in Old and New England* (New York, 1894).

14. Cf. Forrest G. Wood, *The Arrogance of Faith: Christianity and Race in America from the Colonial Era to the Twentieth Century* (New York, 1990) and Jon Butler, *Awash in a Sea of Faith: Christianizing the American People* (Cambridge, MA, 1990).

15. The critical difference between "religious toleration" and "religious liberty" should be highlighted. "Tolerance" implies that there is a hegemony, and that those in

power are permitting deviation from the norm. "Religious liberty" implies a specific positive legal right, not just the good will of a dominant power; cf. Anson Phelps Stokes,
Church and State in the United States, vol. 1.i-49. A vast amount has been written over the
last one hundred years on the topics of religious toleration and religious liberty. Some of
the works that should be highlighted for our purposes are: James P. Byrd, Jr., *The Challenge of Roger Williams: Religious Liberty, Violent Persecution, and the Bible*; Scott
Mandelbrote, "Religious Belief and the Politics of Toleration in the Late Seventeenth
Century," *Nederlands Archief voor Kerkegeschiedenis*, 81 (2001), 93-114; Andrew R.
Murphy, *Conscience and Community: Revisiting Toleration and Religious Dissent in Early
Modern England and America* (University Park, PA, 2001), based on a 1996 dissertation
at the University of Wisconsin, Madison; Cary J. Nederman, *Worlds of Difference: European Discourses of Toleration, c. 1100-1550* (State College, PA, 2000); John Coffey, *Persecution and Toleration in Protestant England, 1558-1689* (New York, 2000); Charles J. Butler, "Covenant Theology and the Development of Religious Liberty," in Daniel Elazar
and John Kincaid (eds.), *The Covenant Connection: From Federal Theology to Modern Federalism*, 101-17; Timothy L. Hall, *Separating Church and State; Roger Williams and Religious Liberty;* John Christian Laursen and Cary J. Nederman, eds., *Beyond the Persecuting
Society: Religious Toleration before the Enlightenment* (Philadelphia, 1998); C. Berkvens-
Stevelink, J. Israel, and G. H. M. Posthumus Meyjes (eds.), *The Emergence of Tolerance in
the Dutch Republic* (Leiden, 1997); Cary J. Nederman and John Christian Laursen (eds.),
Difference and Dissent: Theories of Toleration in Medieval and Early Modern Europe
(Lanham, MD, 1996); Noel B. Reynolds and W. Cole Durham, Jr. (eds.), *Religious Liberty
in Western Thought* (Atlanta, 1996); David L. Wykes, "Friends, Parliament and the Toleration Act," *JEH*, 45 (1994), 42-63; Yuming J.B. Hu, "Colonial Origins of the United
States Government's Enforcement of Political Conformity and Ideological Exclusions"
(diss. University of North Carolina at Chapel Hill, 1994); Linda Kirk, "Toleration Post-
poned: Attacks on Religious Freedom in Late Seventeenth-Century Europe," *JURCHS*, 4
(1987-92), 265-79; K. H. D. Haley, "The Dutch Influence on English Toleration,"
JURCHS, 4 (1987-92), 255-65; Avihu Zakai, "Orthodoxy in England and New England:
Puritans and the Issue of Religious Toleration, 1640-1650," American Philosophical So-
ciety, *Proceedings*, 135 (1991), 401-41; Edwin S. Gaustad, *Liberty of Conscience: Roger
Williams in America;* William G. McLoughlin, *Soul Liberty: The Baptists' Struggle in New
England, 1630-1833* (Hanover, NH, 1991); Carla G. Pestana, *Quakers and Baptists in Co-
lonial Massachusetts;* Ole Peter Grell, Jonathan Israel, and Nicholas Tyacke (eds.), *From
Persecution to Toleration: The Glorious Revolution and Religion in England;* J. F. Maclear,
"Restoration Puritanism and the Idea of Liberty: The Case of Edward Bagshaw," *JRH*, 16
(1990-91), 1-17; John Spurr, "The Church of England, Comprehension, and the Tolera-
tion Act of 1689," *English Historical Review*, 104 (1989), 927-46; Barrington R. White,
"Early Baptist Arguments for Religious Freedom: Their Overlooked Agenda," *BHH*, 24
(1989), #4, 3-10; Avihu Zakai, "Religious Toleration and Its Enemies: The Independent
Divines and the Issue of Toleration during the English Civil War," *Albion*, 21 (1989), 1-
33; Helena Rodriguez Costa, *Liberty of Conscience and the Growth of Religious Diversity in
Early America, 1636-1786: Bibliographical Supplement* (Providence, RI, 1986); Donald S.
Lutz and Jack D. Warren, *A Covenanted People: The Religious Tradition and the Origins of
American Constitutionalism;* Ole Peter Grell, "From Uniformity to Tolerance: The Effects
on the Dutch Church in London of Reverse Patterns in English Church Policy from 1634

to 1647," *Nederlands Archief voor Kerkgeschiedenis,* n.s, 66 (1986), 17-40; Timothy J. Sehr, "Defending Orthodoxy in Massachusetts, 1650-1652," *Historical Journal of Massachusetts,* 9 (1981), #1, 30-40; Daniel P. Elazar, "The Political Theory of Covenant: Biblical Origins and Modern Developments"; Charles J. Butler, "Religious Liberty and Covenant Theology"; Hans R. Guggisberg, "Religious Freedom and the History of the Christian World in Roger Williams' Thought"; Herbert Butterfield, "Toleration in Early Modern Times," *JHI,* 38 (1977), 573-84; L. John Van Til, *Liberty of Conscience: The History of a Puritan Idea* (Nutley, NJ, 1972); T. Dwight Bozeman, "Religious Liberty and the Problem of Order in Early Rhode Island," *NEQ,* 45 (1972), 44-64; Richard Reinitz, "The Typological Argument for Religious Toleration: The Separatist Tradition and Roger Williams"; E. Brooks Holifield, "On Toleration in Massachusetts," *CH,* 38 (1969), 188-200; Henry Kamen, *The Rise of Toleration* (New York, 1967); Johannes Jacobus Laubser, "Puritanism and Religious Liberty: A Study of Normative Change in Massachusetts, 1630-1850" (diss. Harvard, 1963); Raymond Phineas Stearns, "Toleration as a Congregational Tactic in the English Civil Wars," *BCL,* 7 (1955-56), #2, 5-15; Joseph Lecler, *Historie de la Tolérance au Siècle de la Réforme,* 2 vols. (Paris, 1954); English translation: *Toleration and the Reformation,* trans. T. L. Westow, 2 vols. (New York, 1960); Mauro Calamandrei, "Neglected Aspects of Roger Willliams' Thought"; Elizabeth Hirsch, "John Cotton and Roger Williams: Their Controversy Concerning Religious Liberty," *CH,* 10 (1941), 38-51; Wilbur Kitchener Jordan, *The Development of Religious Toleration in England;* Thomas Lyon, *The Theory of Religious Liberty in England, 1603-39* (Cambridge, 1937); Perry Miller, "The Contribution of the Protestant Churches to Religious Liberty in Colonial America," *CH,* 4 (1935), 57-66; *id., Orthodoxy in Massachusetts, 1630-1650* (Cambridge, MA, 1933), esp. Chapter 8: "Tolerating Times"; Henry B. Parkes, "John Cotton and Roger Williams Debate Toleration, 1644-1652," *NEQ,* 4 (1931), 735-56; John A. Faulkner, "The Reformers and Toleration," ASCH, *Papers,* ser. 2, 5 (1917), 1-22; *id.,* "Luther and Toleration," ASCH, *Papers,* ser. 2, 4 (1914), 129-53; A. A. Seaton, *The Theory of Toleration under the Late Stuarts* (Cambridge, 1911); Hugh F. Russell-Smith, *The Theory of Religious Liberty in the Reign of Charles II and James II* (Cambridge, 1911); Henry S. Burrage, "The Contest for Religious Liberty in Massachusetts," ASCH, *Papers,* ser. 1, 6 (1894), 149-68; Talbot Wilson Chambers, "Holland and Religious Freedom," ASCH, *Papers,* ser. 1, 5 (1893), 89-97; and Philip Schaff, "The Progress of Religious Freedom as Shown in the History of the Toleration Acts," ASCH, *Papers,* ser. 1, 1 (1889), 1-126, which was revised and published that same year (New York, 1889).

16. Cf., for instance, Augusta Pipkin Heywood, "Walking 'Fruitfully with God in the Covenant': The Origins of Justified Disobedience within the American Social Contract"; Charles Borgeaud, *The Rise of Modern Democracy in Old and New England;* and Anson Phelps Stokes, *Church and State in the United States.*

17. During the last thirty years a growing scholarly consensus has emerged that asserts that New England and other English colonies cannot be considered in isolation from Old England and the larger framework of the European world. Broader perspectives can be found in the imperial literature cited in n. 15 of the Introduction and in the literature on the Restoration and Glorious Revolution found in n. 8 of Chapter 2: "The Colonial Charters of Early New England." In addition, cf. David Armitage et al., "*AHR Forum:* The New British History in Atlantic Perspective," *AHR,* 104 (1999), 426-500; Raymond Dye Irwin, "Saints, Sinners, and Subjects: Rhode Island and Providence Plan-

tations in Transatlantic Perspective, 1636-1665" (diss. Ohio State, 1996); Francis J. Bremer (ed.), *Puritanism: Transatlantic Perspectives on a Seventeenth-Century Anglo-American Faith* (Boston, 1993); Stephen Foster, *The Long Argument: English Puritanism and the Shaping of New England Culture, 1570-1700* (Chapel Hill, NC, 1991); Francis Bremer, "Communication: The English Context of New England's Seventeenth-Century History," *NEQ*, 60 (1987), 323-35; David Grayson Allen, "Both Englands," in *Seventeenth-Century New England*, ed. David D. Hall and David Grayson Allen, *CSMP*, 63 (Boston, 1984), 55-82; Jack P. Greene and Jack Pole (eds.), *Colonial British America: Essays in the New History of the Early Modern Era* (Baltimore, 1984), particularly David D. Hall, "Religion and Society: Problems and Reconsiderations," 317-44; W. A. Spech, "The International and Imperial Context," 384-407; John M. Murrin, "Political Development," 408-56; and Stanley N. Katz, "The Problem of Colonial Legal History," 457-89; Harold A. Pinkham, Jr., "The Transplantation and Transformation of the English Shire in America: Essex County, Massachusetts, 1630-1768"; John G. Reid, *Maine, Charles II, and Massachusetts: Governmental Relationships in Early Northern New England*; James M. O'Toole, "New England's Reactions to the English Civil Wars," *NEHGR*, 129 (1975), 3-17, 238-49; Francis J. Bremer, "Puritan Crisis: New England and the English Civil Wars, 1630-1670" (diss. Columbia, 1972); Parker B. Nutting, "Charter and Crown: Relations of Connecticut with the British Government, 1662-1776"; David H. Corkran, "The New England Colonists' English Image, 1550-1714" (diss. University of California, Berkeley, 1970); and Marguerite Appleton, "The Relations of the Corporate Colony of Rhode Island to the British Government."

Clusters of articles have emerged in various historical disciplines that attempt to see New England within a transatlantic context. For economic perspectives, cf. Phyllis Whitman Hunter, "Ship of Wealth: Massachusetts Merchants, Foreign Goods, and the Transformation of Anglo-America, 1670-1760" (diss. William and Mary, 1996); Ian K. Steele, *The English Atlantic, 1675-1740: An Exploration of Communication and Community*; Bernard Bailyn, "Communications and Trade: The Atlantic in the Seventeenth Century," *Journal of Economic History*, 13 (1953), 378-87; *id., The New England Merchants in the Seventeenth Century* (Cambridge, MA, 1979). Scholars of religion have long known that a transatlantic vision is important for the religious history of early New England; cf. Francis Bremer, *Shaping New Englands: Puritan Clergymen in 17th Century England and New England* (New York, 1994); *id., Congregational Communion: Clerical Friendship in the Anglo-American Puritan Community, 1610-1692* (Boston, 1992); Jon Butler, "[Review]: Transatlantic Pieties: Connections and Disconnections," *JBS*, 28 (1989), 411-18; Francis J. Bremer, "Notes and Documents: When? Who? Why? Re-evaluating a 17th-Century Source"; *id.,* "Increase Mather's Friends: The Transatlantic Congregational Network of the Seventeenth Century," *AASP*, 94 (1984), 59-96; Norman B. Graebner, "Protestants and Dissenters: An Examination of the Seventeenth-Century Eatonist and New England Antinomian Controversies in Reformation Perspective" (diss. Duke, 1984); Barbara R. Dailey, "Root and Branch: New England's Religious Radicals and Their Transatlantic Community, 1600-1660"; Stephen Foster, "New England and the Challenge of Heresy: The Puritan Crisis in Transatlantic Perspective," *WMQ*, ser. 3, 38 (1981), 624-60; Ralph F. Young, "Good News from New England: The Influence of the New England Way of Church Polity on Old England, 1635-1660" (diss. Michigan State, 1971); E. Brooks Holifield, *The Covenant Sealed: The Development of Puritan Sacramental Theol-*

ogy in Old and New England, 1570-1720; Michael G. Finlayson, "Independency in Old and New England, 1630-1660: An Historiographical and Historical Study" (diss. Toronto, 1968); Leon B. Howard, "The Puritans in Old and New England," in *Anglo-American Cultural Relations in the Seventeenth and Eighteenth Centuries . . . Fourth Clark Library Seminar, 31 May, 1958* (Los Angeles, 1958), 1-25; Alan Simpson, *Puritanism in Old and New England;* Joseph Brewer, "The Relations of the English Baptists with New England in the Seventeenth Century"; Frederick B. Tolles, "The Transatlantic Quaker Community in the Seventeenth Century," *Huntington Library Quarterly,* 14 (1950-51), 239-58; Arthur Lyon Cross, *The Anglican Episcopate and the American Colonies.* For social and cultural history, cf. Jack P. Greene, *Pursuits of Happiness: The Social Development of Early Modern British Colonies and the Formation of American Culture* (Chapel Hill, NC, 1988); David Cressy, *Coming Over: Migration and Communication between England and New England in the Seventeenth Century* (New York, 1987); Cole Harris, "European Beginnings in the Northwest Atlantic: A Comparative View," in Hall and Allen, *Seventeenth-Century New England,* 119-52; David Grayson Allen, *In English Ways: The Movement of Societies and the Transferal of English Local Law and Custom to Massachusetts Bay in the Seventeenth Century* (Chapel Hill, NC, 1981), based on a dissertation completed in 1974 at the University of Wisconsin; Timothy H. Breen, "Transfer of Culture: Chance and Design in Shaping Massachusetts Bay, 1630-1660," *NEHGR,* 132 (1978), 3-17; W. R. Prest, "Stability and Change in Old and New England: Clayworth and Dedham," *Journal of Interdisciplinary History,* 6 (1976), 359-74; Timothy H. Breen, "Persistent Localism: English Social Change and the Shaping of New England Institutions," *WMQ,* ser. 3, 32 (1975), 3-28; Jack P. Greene, "Autonomy and Stability: New England and the British Colonial Experience in Early Modern America," *Journal of Social History,* 7 (1973-74), 171-94. For legal history, cf. Mary Sarah Bilder, "Salamanders and Sons of God: Transatlantic Legal Culture and Colonial Rhode Island" (diss. Harvard, 2000).

18. Cf. the observations of J. M. Bumsted for New Plymouth Colony: "A Well-Bounded Toleration: Church and State in the Plymouth Colony," *JCS,* 10 (1968), 265-79. Both James F. Cooper, Jr., and Virginia D. Anderson in recent works also conclude that the 1660s, with its "middle generation" of Puritans, was the critical transitional decade in New England Puritanism: James F. Cooper, Jr., "A Participatory Theocracy: Church Government in Colonial Massachusetts, 1629-1760" (diss. University of Connecticut, 1987); and id., *Tenacious of Their Liberties: The Congregationalists in Colonial Massachusetts* (New York, 1999); Virginia D. Anderson, *New England's Generation: The Great Migration and the Formation of Society and Culture in the Seventeenth Century* (New York, 1991).

19. For the broader importance of the second half of the seventeenth century, see Wesley F. Craven, *The Colonies in Transition, 1660-1713* (New York, 1968); Thomas Saunders Kidd, "From Puritan to Evangelical: Changing Culture in New England, 1689-1740" (diss. Notre Dame, 2001).

20. "Anglicization" is, of course, tied up with the larger concepts of the First British Empire, the Restoration, the Glorious Revolution, and New England's role in an emerging English transatlantic world, themes that have been covered in this book. But besides politics, economics, and religion, it also involves a more ephemeral cultural dimension that is hard to measure. This dimension could best be described as "the way people think," or at least, the way the majority of a certain group thinks. Tied to this concept is the emergence of a distinctively American identity, framed by the question of

how dependent on, or independent of, Old England the New England colonies were in all of the varied aspects of life. Many in the Anglicization school hold that New England was more independent of Old England before a certain time period (usually the Restoration, but sometimes King Philip's War in 1676, or even the Dominion of New England in 1685-88), but that after that point the New Englanders themselves thought of themselves as part of Old England, and later, Great Britain. The fury exhibited by the colonists in 1763-83, therefore, was a protest over the rights of English people and British citizens, rather than an exhibit of American independence. By 1775 that battle had largely been lost, and it is only then, in 1776-89, that a truly American identity emerges. The Anglicization school is articulated in the following works, a list which is by no means exhaustive: Phyllis Whitman Hunter, "Ship of Wealth: Massachusetts Merchants, Foreign Goods, and the Transformation of Anglo-America, 1670-1760" (diss. William and Mary, 1996); Yuming J.B. Hu, "Colonial Origins of the United States Government's Enforcement of Political Conformity and Ideological Exclusions"; Timothy H. Breen, "An Empire of Goods: The Anglicization of Colonial America, 1690-1776," *JBS*, 25 (1986), 467-99; Richard R. Johnson, *Adjustment to Empire: The New England Colonies, 1675-1715*; Paul R. Lucas, "Colony or Commonwealth: Massachusetts Bay, 1661-1666"; John M. Murrin, "Anglicizing an American Colony: The Transformation of Provincial Massachusetts" (diss. Yale, 1966); Norman Pettit, "God's Englishman in New England: His Enduring Ties to the Motherland," *MHSP,* 101 (1989), 56-70; Clifford K. Shipton, "The Shaping of Revolutionary New England, 1680-1740," *Political Science Quarterly,* 50 (1935), 584-97; Alan Taylor, "[Review]: An Atlantic People," *JBS*, 29 (1990), 402-7. The stance that there was a major discontinuity between the Old World and the New World that led immediately to a distinctively American identity is articulated in the following: Sacvan Bercovitch, *The Puritan Origins of the American Self* (New Haven, CT, 1975); id., "Colonial Puritan Rhetoric and the Discovery of American Identity," *CRevAS,* 6 (1975), 131-50; J. M. Bumsted, "'Things in the Womb of Time': Ideas of American Independence, 1633 to 1763," *WMQ,* ser. 3, 31 (1974), 533-64; Michael Zuckerman, "Identity in British America: Unease in Eden," in *Colonial Identity in the Atlantic World, 1500-1800,* ed. Nicholas Canny and Anthony Pagden (Princeton, NJ, 1987); Jon Butler, *Becoming America: The Revolution before 1776* (Cambridge, MA, 2000).

21. *WCF,* 7 and 19; *BSRK,* 558-60, 581-84; Schaff, *Creeds,* 3.616-18, 640-43. The Larger Catechism covers the prelapsarian covenant in Questions 20 and 97 (*BSRK,* 614 and 625).

22. Mary Ann La Fleur, "Seventeenth Century New England and New France in Comparative Perspective: Notre Dame Des Anges: A Case Study."

23. That there was a consensus even among the standing order has been recently challenged; cf. Janice Knight, *Orthodoxies in Massachusetts: Rereading American Puritanism* (Cambridge, MA, 1994) and Louise A. Breen, *Transgressing the Bounds: Subversive Enterprises among the Puritan Elite in Massachusetts, 1630-1692* (New York, 2001) both of whom speak of disunity in the standing order. Paul Lucas and Theodore B. Lewis both point out that during the period 1660-1700 political disunity emerges as well in response to the emergence of imperial aspirations. Lucas maintains that three parties emerged in Massachusetts Bay after the Restoration: the Puritans, the moderates, and the royalists, while Lewis speaks of two parties, the moderates and the established Puritans; cf. Paul R. Lucas, "Colony or Commonwealth: Massachusetts Bay, 1661-1666"; Theo-

dore B. Lewis, "Massachusetts and the Glorious Revolution: A Political and Constitutional Study, 1660-1692"; cf. also Alan J. Silva, "Rituals of Empowerment: Politics and Rhetoric in the Puritan Election Sermon" (diss. University of California, Davis, 1993); Robert A. East, "Puritanism and New Settlement," *NEQ,* 17 (1944), 255-64.

24. Cf. Raymond P. Stearns, "Assessing the New England Mind," *CH,* 10 (1941), 246-62.

25. Winthrop, *Journal,* 169.

26. For a more in-depth discussion of this phenomenon, along with an exploration of gender differentiation in the process of gathering a church, cf. David A. Weir, "Church Covenanting in Seventeenth-Century New England," 231-32, 255-71.

27. This table is based on statistical data for the following congregations: 1630: Boston, MBC, First Church; 1632: Charlestown, MBC, First Church; 1634: Ipswich, MBC, First Church; 1636: Dorchester-2, MBC, First Church; 1638: Dedham, MBC, First Church; 1639: Braintree, MBC, First Church; 1639: New Haven, NHC, First Church; 1639: Milford, NHC, First Church; 1640/41: Wethersfield-2, CTC, First Church; 1641/2: Scituate, NPC, First Church; 1642: Woburn, MBC, First Church; 1643: Guilford, NHC, First Church; 1645: Andover, MBC, First Church; 1650: Boston, MBC, Second Church; 1652: Farmington, CTC, First Church; 1655: Chelmsford, MBC, First Church; 1660: Natick IPT, MBC, Indian Church; 1661: Northampton, MBC, First Church; 1663: Wenham-2, MBC, First Church; 1665: Charlestown (Boston), MBC, First Baptist Church; 1667: Beverly, MBC, First Church; 1667: Killingworth, CTC, First Church; 1668: Middletown, CTC, First Church; 1669: Boston, MBC, Third Church; 1669/70: Hartford, CTC, Second Church; 1670: Stratford, CTC, Second Church; 1671: Newport, RIC, Third Baptist Church (Seventh-Day Baptist Church); 1671: Portsmouth, NHP, First Church; 1674: Stonington, CTC, First Church; 1678: Milton, MBC, First Church; 1679: Westfield, MBC, First Church; 1682: Bradford, MBC, First Church; 1684: Marblehead, MBC, First Church; 1685: Sherborn, MBC, First Church; 1687: Bristol, DNE, First Church; 1687/8: Branford-3, DNE, First Church; 1689: Salem Village, MBC, First Church; 1691: Waterbury, CTC, First Church; 1692: Wrentham, MBP, First Church; 1694: Middleborough-2, MBP, First Church; 1695: Stratfield, CTC, First Church/Society; 1696: Haddam, CTC, First Church; 1696: Dorchester, SC, First Church; 1696: Lexington, MBP, First Church; 1697: Simsbury, CTC, First Church; 1698: Exeter-2, NHP, First Church; 1698: Plympton, MBP, First Church; 1698: Preston, CTC, First Church; 1699: Boston, MBP, Fourth Church (Brattle Street); 1699: Newport, RIC, Trinity Church (Episcopal); 1700: Harwich, MBP, First Church; 1700: Lebanon, CTC, First Church; 1700: Windham, CTC, First Church; 1701: Framingham, MBP, First Church; 1701: Wells, MeP, First Church; 1702: Boxford, MBP, First Church; 1702: Kittery-2 (Berwicks), MBT, First Church; 1703: Rochester, MBP, First Church; 1704: East Haddam, CTC, First Church; 1704: Little Compton, RIC, First Congregational Church; 1706: Greenland, NHP, First Church; 1707: Madison, CTC, First Church (Guilford 2nd Church); 1707/8: Woodbridge, ENJ, First Church.

28. Corporation for Propagating the Gospel [in New England], *Tears of Repentance, MHSC,* ser. 3, 4 (1834), 206-7. For Mayhew's mission on Martha's Vineyard cf. Margery Ruth Johnson, "The Mayhew Mission to the Indians, 1643-1806" (diss. Clark, 1966); also James P. Ronda, "Generations of Faith: The Christian Indians of Martha's Vineyard," *WMQ,* ser. 3, 38 (1981), 369-94; William S. Simmons, "Conversion from Indian to Puritan," *NEQ,* 52 (1979), 197-218; Charles Edward Banks, *The History of Martha's Vineyard,*

Dukes County, Massachusetts . . . , 3 vols. (Boston, 1911-25); William A. Hallock, *The Venerable Mayhews* . . . (New York, 1874); *Dukes County Intelligencer,* passim.

29. *From Puritan to Yankee: Character and the Social Order in Connecticut, 1690-1765* (Cambridge, MA, 1967).

30. *RCRI,* 1.52.

31. Discussion and debate over the franchise in early New England peaked from the 1950s to the 1970s, a phenomenon that reflected the time of the civil rights movement in modern America. Among the most important contributions are the following: Robert E. Brown, "Democracy in Colonial Massachusetts," *NEQ,* 25 (1952), 291-313; B. Katherine Brown, "Freemanship in Puritan Massachusetts," *AHR,* 59 (1953-54), 865-83; Robert E. Brown, "Restriction of Representation in Colonial Massachusetts," *Mississippi Valley Historical Review,* 40 (1953-54), 463-76; Alan Simpson, "How Democratic Was Roger Williams?" *WMQ,* ser. 3, 13 (1956), 53-67; Richard C. Simmons, "Freemanship in Early Massachusetts: Some Suggestions and a Case Study," *WMQ,* ser. 3, 19 (1962), 422-28; Walter Franklin Terris, "The Right to Speak: Massachusetts, 1628-1685" (diss. Northwestern, 1962); George D. Langdon, Jr., "The Franchise and Political Democracy in Plymouth Colony," *WMQ,* ser. 3, 20 (1963), 513-26; Richard Clive Simmons, "Studies in the Massachusetts Franchise, 1631-1691" (diss. University of California at Berkeley, 1965); B. Katherine Brown, "Puritan Democracy: A Case Study," *Mississippi Valley Historical Review,* 50 (1963-64), 377-96; *id.,* "Puritan Democracy in Dedham, Massachusetts: Another Case Study," *WMQ,* ser. 3, 24 (1967), 378-96; Stephen Foster, "Notes and Documents: The Massachusetts Franchise in the Seventeenth Century," *WMQ,* ser. 3, 24 (1967), 613-23; Richard C. Simmons, "Godliness, Property, and the Franchise in Puritan Massachusetts: An Interpretation," *Journal of American History,* 55 (1968-69), 495-511; James A. Thorpe, "Colonial Suffrage in Massachusetts: An Essay Review," *EIHC,* 106 (1970), 169-81; Robert Emmet Wall, Jr., "The Massachusetts Bay Colony Franchise in 1647," *WMQ,* ser. 3, 27 (1970), 136-44; Timothy H. Breen, "Notes and Documents: Who Governs: The Town Franchise in Seventeenth-Century Massachusetts," *WMQ,* ser. 3, 27 (1970), 460-74; Robert Emmet Wall, Jr., "The Decline of the Massachusetts Franchise: 1647-1666," *Journal of American History,* 59 (1972-73), 303-10; Theodore B. Lewis and Linda M. Webb, "Notes and Documents: Voting for the Massachusetts Council of Assistants, 1674-1686: A Statistical Note," *WMQ,* ser. 3, 30 (1973), 625-34; B. Katherine Brown, "The Controversy over the Franchise in Puritan Massachusetts, 1954 to 1974," *WMQ,* ser. 3, 33 (1976), 212-41; Robert E. Wall, "The Franchise in Seventeenth-Century Massachusetts: Dedham and Cambridge," *WMQ,* ser. 3, 34 (1977), 453-58; Richard S. Sliwoski, "The Franchise and the Election of Representatives from Colonial Western Massachusetts: A Case Study," *Historical Journal of Western Massachusetts,"* 7 (1979), 22-45.

32. Wilford O. Cross, "The Role and Status of the Unregenerate in the Massachusetts Bay Colony, 1629-1729" (diss. Columbia, 1957).

Index

Abraham, 157
Abrahamic covenant, 223
Acadia, 65
Acts (of Parliament): Conventicle Act (1664), 56; Corporation Act (1661), 56; Five-Mile Act (1665), 56; Navigation Acts (1651), 107; Toleration Act (1689), 67; of Uniformity (1662), 56
Adam, 157; and Eve, 106; First, 211; Second (Jesus Christ), 211
Adamic administration, 223
admission: of inhabitants and Swansea, New Plymouth Colony, 120-22; to church membership, 145; to towns, 124
advisor to the state, church as, 228
Allegiance, Oath of, 33
Allen, Rev. James, 144-45
Allin, Rev. John, and Dedham, Massachusetts Bay Colony First Church, 205
altar, Anglican conception of, 43
Amsterdam, 88; London-Amsterdam Separatist Church, confession of faith, 194
Anabaptists, 4. *See also* Baptists.
Andros, Sir Edmund, 7, 58; Commission to, for Dominion of New England, 61-65. *See also* Dominion of New England.
Anglicans, Anglicanism, 29, 11, 329-

30; baptism, cross in, 64; and church calendar, 160; emergence of, in New England, 174-76; High Church, 45; and holy days, 64; in Newport, Rhode Island Colony, 174; and vestments in worship, 160. *See also Book of Common Prayer;* Church of England; Laudianism; Thirty-nine Articles.
Anglicization (of New England); 225, 242, 435n.20
Anglo-Dutch War, First (1652-54), 107
animism, of Native Americans, 238
Anne, 19, 61
Antichrist, 242
Antinomian Controversy, Antinomians, 67, 412n.51. *See also* antinomianism.
antinomianism, 21, 189
anxiety, in Salem Village, Massachusetts Bay Colony, First Church covenant, 165-66
Apologie of the Churches in New-England for Church-Covenant (1643), by Rev. Richard Mather, 152-53
apostasy, 21
Apostles' Creed, 6
apostolic church, 39-40
apostolic succession, 38
Arminianism, 211

Church Covenant Idea (Champlin Burrage), 146

church covenant(s), 2, 136-90; acceptance of God and submission to God, 154; *autographa*, 138-39; Charlestown, Massachusetts Bay Colony, 150-52; Charlestown (Boston), Massachusetts Bay Colony First Baptist Church, 181-84; children in, Wells, Maine Province, First Church, 167-69; children, responsibility of, in Wells, Maine Province, First Church, 169-70; and confessions of faith as preludes, 190-220; as covenants of grace, 229; descending generations, obligations, in church covenants, 171; diversity and unity, 170; Dorchester, Massachusetts Bay Colony First Church, 150-52; Dorchester-2, Massachusetts Bay Colony First Church, 152-62; failure of church covenanters, Wells, Maine Province, First Church, 166; failure to keep, 161; formats and redactions, 138-46; formulary, 150, 154; and God as superior party, 155; horizontal relationships, 170; and humanity as inferior party, 155; humility in, 155; not covenants of works, 229; Kittery, Maine Province, Baptist Church, 187-89; obligations, to descending generations, 171; as an ordinance of the church, 160; parents, responsibility of (Wells, Maine Province, First Church), 169; preamble, 154; rejection of pride, 155; Salem Village, Massachusetts Bay Colony, First Church, 163-67; salvific nature, 171; and sovereign grace of God, 155; Swansea, New Plymouth Colony, First Baptist Church, 184-87; uniformity of, 150-71, 181-89, 229-30; unity and diversity, 170; unity of thought, 170; and use of word "cleave," 157; vertical relationship, 170; walking with brethren in, 154;

Wells, Maine Province, First Church, 167-70; witnesses, 151-52

church covenanting, 3-4, 137. *See also* church covenant(s).

church discipline, as an ordinance of the church, 160, 161

church establishment, and priority of formation of civil government, 92

church foundation members, cohort size, 231-36

church gathering or formation, 162-63, 192, 232, 359n.13; narratives of, 192. *See also* church covenanting.

Church Government, Forme of (1645) (Westminster Assembly), 194

church government: congregational, 20, 147; episcopal, 16, 17, 18, 23, 146, 147, 160; presbyterian, 147, 194, 206; submission to, in church covenant, 154

church membership, admission to, 145

church ordinance(s) (baptism; catechizing; church covenant; church covenant renewal; Communion/Lord's Supper; congregational government; discipline; offering; prayer; preaching; psalmody; reception of new members; relations of faith; sacraments; scripture reading), 93-94, 159-61. *See also* church covenants *and* church covenanting.

church records, 2-3, 9, 12-13, 137-46, 192, 193, 201; and format of church covenants, 138-46

church and state, 124; covenants as theory for, 224; in early New England, 228; in Reformed confessions, 196-201

church and state, separation of, 228. *See also* church and civil government *and* church, state, and religion.

church, state, and religion, 24-72, esp. 69-72; 73-135, esp. 131-35; 196-201; 236-42